Processing Inaccurate Information

Processing Inaccurate Information

Theoretical and Applied Perspectives from Cognitive Science
and the Educational Sciences

edited by David N. Rapp and Jason L. G. Braasch

The MIT Press
Cambridge, Massachusetts
London, England

This book was set in Stone Serif Std by Toppan Best-set Premedia Limited, Hong Kong.

Library of Congress Cataloging-in-Publication Data

Processing inaccurate information : theoretical and applied perspectives from cognitive science and the educational sciences / edited by David N. Rapp and Jason L.G. Braasch.
    pages cm
Includes bibliographical references and index.
ISBN 978-0-262-54768-0 (paperback)
ISBN 978-0-262-02758-8 (hardcover : alk. paper)   1. Errors, Scientific.   2. Common fallacies.
3. Cognitive science.   I. Rapp, David N., 1972– editor of compilation.   II. Braasch, Jason L. G., editor of compilation.
Q172.5.E77P76 2014
001—dc23
2013050251

Contents

Acknowledgments

Our interest in producing a volume on the effects of inaccurate information was initially inspired by conversations about the current state of work on language comprehension, memory processes, and educational experiences. Across these areas, we often reflected on how research and theory has considered the ways in which people might develop accurate, underinformed, and/or flawed understandings, but with most investigations focused solely on the consequences of reliable and valid presentations of materials. This struck us as surprising given that flawed news reports, biased sources, and fabricated data and arguments are regular occurrences, drawing the ire of researchers, publishers, and the general public.

During one of our conversations concerning this lack of attention, we identified researchers who have begun considering these oft-ignored issues and who have attempted to incorporate their findings and arguments into contemporary accounts of learning and comprehension. Their work was core to two particular areas of research, the educational sciences and the cognitive sciences, and exemplified by the diverse approaches, both methodological and theoretical, that these groups adopt in their investigations. Despite the innovations and important claims being derived from the emerging work, we were disappointed to find that, in many cases, there was precious little cross talk among the groups and, more broadly, across the interdisciplinary scientific fields to which members of those groups were affiliated. This offered an exciting opportunity to present the accumulating findings from those groups in a single volume that would provide a survey of relevant work and that we hoped would encourage more cross talk and more investigation on the influence of inaccurate information. The volume you are now reading is the result of these considerations.

We wish to thank each of the authors for their informative chapters and for agreeing to the process, submitting manuscripts that went through multiple iterations of evaluation and revision, with the goal of producing chapters relevant to multiple fields of inquiry. Thanks also go to Northwestern University and the University of Oslo for affording the time and resources for developing and producing the current volume. We are grateful to many individuals for discussing ideas presented in the volume, including but not limited to members of the Reading Comprehension Laboratory at Northwestern University (Jessica Andrews, Dr. Scott Hinze, Dr. Matthew Jacovina, Ryan Jenkins, and Kristine Kohlhepp) and to the members of the TextDIM group (Text Comprehension: Development, Instruction, and Multiple Texts) at the University of Oslo. Special thanks go to Philip Laughlin and the folks at MIT Press for their guidance and enthusiasm for the project. We also thank Claire Gaynor for her rousing creativity and design suggestions. And finally, special thanks to Ricky Downtown and Mr. M.

Contributors

Peter Afflerbach

University of Maryland

Patricia A. Alexander

University of Maryland

Jessica J. Andrews

Northwestern University

Peter Baggetta

University of Maryland

Jason L. G. Braasch

University of Memphis

Ivar Bråten

University of Oslo

M. Anne Britt

Northern Illinois
University

Rainer Bromme

University of Muenster

Luke A. Buckland

Rutgers University

Clark A. Chinn

Rutgers University

Byeong-Young Cho

Iowa State University

Andrea A. diSessa

University of California at
Berkeley

Sidney K. D'Mello

University of Notre Dame

Ullrich K. H. Ecker

University of Western Australia

Arthur C. Graesser

University of Memphis

Douglas J. Hacker

University of Utah

Brenda Hannon

Texas A&M University

Xiangen Hu

University of Memphis

Maj-Britt Isberner

University of Kassel

Koto Ishiwa

Universidad de Alcalá

Matthew E. Jacovina

Northwestern University

Panayiota Kendeou

University of Minnesota

Jong-Yun Kim

University of Maryland

Stephan Lewandowsky

University of Western Australia

Elizabeth J. Marsh

Duke University

Ruth Mayo

The Hebrew University of Jerusalem

Keith K. Millis

Northern Illinois University

Edward J. O'Brien

University of New Hampshire

Herre van Oostendorp

Utrecht University

José Otero

Universidad de Alcalá

David N. Rapp

Northwestern University

Tobias Richter

University of Kassel

Ronald W. Rinehart

Rutgers University

Yaacov Schul

The Hebrew University of Jerusalem

Colleen M. Seifert

University of Michigan

Marc Stadtler

University of Muenster

Brent Steffens

University of Oslo

Helge I. Strømsø

University of Oslo

Briony Swire

University of Western Australia

Sharda Umanath

Duke University

1 Accurate and Inaccurate Knowledge Acquisition

David N. Rapp and Jason L. G. Braasch

Our lives revolve around the acquisition of information. We go to work or school and immerse ourselves in topics that demand our attention, requiring us to develop our expertise through practice and study with relevant concepts and ideas. Even leisure and less career-oriented pursuits involve similar focus: Before we rest at the end of the day, we might peruse a novel or a magazine to enjoy some frivolous bit of entertainment; when we wake up, we reach for the remote or laptop to learn about what happened while we were sleeping; and we seek out information that informs our hobbies and personal interests. Throughout the day we turn on our computers and televisions and radios and are offered coverage of a near-infinite number of topics, all with varying importance. When we're done, we tell others about what we've learned and find out what they've learned too. We continuously seek out information that we hope might make us smarter, more effective, more aware, and happier than we were before encountering it. And the ready access of information through the Internet, through 24-hour news sites, through easily accessible novels and books, through video games, e-mail, and text messages, through formal and informal educational experiences, and through routine conversations with others, means there is an incredible amount of data available for our consumption and contemplation.

Understanding the ways in which we build knowledge from these various sources has led to an incredibly informative, classically studied body of work on knowledge acquisition. This work has provided both valuable theoretical articulations and important applied considerations. For example, determining the ways in which people navigate information spaces, and the knowledge-based resources they recruit to do so, proves crucial for identifying the cognitive activities that drive learning. Evaluations of how these activities can be supported and enhanced have direct consequences for the design of effective educational experiences. These theoretical and applied concerns, while often categorized separately, actually prove mutually informative, as evidenced by the kinds of work currently conducted by cognitive and educational scientists.

Consider that cognitive scientists have examined issues of learning by developing and testing theoretical models through philosophical argumentation, empirical analyses, and computational simulations. The goal with this work has been to build accounts that can describe and explain the mental processes that underlie successful and unsuccessful attempts at learning. Educational scientists are similarly interested in these issues, identifying activities, tools, and behaviors that serve to support learning. This has involved evaluations of the concomitants involved in everyday knowledge acquisition, including the characteristics of classrooms, curricula, and learning contexts, as well as attributes of the learners themselves. Careful work in both cognitive science and the education sciences, in combination, is necessary for building valid models of learning that have relevance in real-world settings, as well as for identifying practices that best support learning in the diverse settings within which it occurs.

And to date, work from these areas has provided enlightening accounts of how individuals acquire knowledge from others, from books, and from multimedia presentations, as well as how to potentially improve these interactions and experiences to help ensure long-term retention of the presented information. However, this work has mostly involved examinations of how people learn valid, accurate information that we hope they will encode into their knowledge base. Obviously people are not always presented with accurate information; they often encounter ideas and concepts that are instead inaccurate and invalid, representing misinformation (interchangeably referred to in this volume as misinformation, inaccuracies, and incorrect information). Consider that hastily updated news reports might leave out relevant details that intentionally or unintentionally distort the reality of situations, authors and speakers might twist the truth to enhance interest in the information they provide or to silence opposing points of view, and casual mistakes can be repeated by multiple sources until they gain an air of validity. Misinformation can be presented strategically and insidiously, with individuals seeking to misstate the truth for their own goals and purposes. And it can be presented accidentally and without malice, slipping into discourse for which it was not intended or based on the information provider's naïveté. Given an unbridled access to information, people regularly encounter inaccurate information from potentially questionable or unreliable sources, as well as from sources usually deemed trustworthy and diligent.

Across all of these cases, the hope is that people will resist engaging in the kinds of processes that serve to integrate misinformation into prior knowledge, in contrast to the integration we hope to see following the presentation of accurate information. The problem is that people readily encode and rely upon the inaccurate information presented in discourse (e.g., Ecker, Lewandowsky, & Tang, 2010; Johnson & Seifert, 1994; Schul & Burnstein, 1985; van Oostendorp & Bonebakker, 1999; Wilkes & Leatherbarrow, 1988). Specifically, when people read inaccurate statements about the world, they often exhibit less difficulty than they should with respect to comprehending the information (Rapp, 2008), as well as with respect to using that information later (Marsh, Meade, & Roediger, 2003). For example, consider that in the aftermath of Hurricane

Sandy in 2012, a large number of users of the popular social networking service Twitter panicked that the New York Stock Exchange had flooded and that power would go out in Manhattan based on false claims made by one malicious user (Gross, 2012). And even groups whose reputations hinge upon fact-checking are similarly corrupted by what seems to be simple cases of inaccuracies: In the wake of Osama bin Laden's assassination in 2011, several news sources proclaimed "Obama is dead" rather than referring to Osama, unintentionally mixing up two similar sounding names (Bates, 2011). Rather than carefully evaluating information, people seem to reproduce and rely on the content of what they read and hear without careful consideration of whether it is relevant and valid.

This may in many cases seem unsurprising. If readers have little familiarity with or relevant knowledge about a particular topic, and they encounter information that is false, we might not expect them to easily determine that what they are reading should be discounted. For example, textbooks that describe complex scientific topics might label components of a causal model using misspelled or inaccurate jargon; in an even more disconcerting example, a textbook might represent incorrect relationships between concepts. In either case, novices *should* fail to notice such inaccuracies given that they lack the knowledge necessary to monitor for related discrepancies. And people might expect certain sources like textbooks to be reliable and hence unlikely to contain inaccurate information, further compounding the possibility they will encode what was presented. Similar situations can occur when instructors teach students about new topics or when individuals receive breaking news about unfamiliar people and events from their favored sources.

But what is much more surprising is that people sometimes demonstrate the use of information that is *obviously* inaccurate. Despite having adequate prior knowledge and even an awareness that what they are learning about is wrong, individuals have been shown to rely on patently incorrect information (e.g., Fazio, Barber, Rajaram, Ornstein, & Marsh, 2013; Fazio & Marsh, 2008; Marsh & Fazio, 2006). Thus, the problem is not just that people rely on inaccurate information but that they rely on it *when they seemingly should know better.* This reliance has been demonstrated with information including well-known facts (e.g., the capitals of states and the contributions of famous inventors), commonplace assertions and beliefs (e.g., statements describing healthy and unhealthy behaviors), and personally experienced events (e.g., information viewed in a recently presented picture or film). And this reliance emerges following experiences with false information presented in a wide variety of materials including in word lists, in extended texts, in photographs and videos, from popular movies, and from group members working on collaborative tasks. Reliance seems to appear regardless of whether the source of some information is conveying an expository account of scientific procedures or historical occurrences, a descriptive retelling of a newsworthy event, or a fictional account of some narrative world. It can occur despite warnings about the content of what will be presented, despite instructions to carefully evaluate that content, and despite measures intended to make the presentation of the material more clear and processing of the content easier. Reliance occurs even when explicit markers highlight potential inaccuracies, and despite multiple experiences and reminders intended to raise attention to and awareness of impending inaccuracies. (See the chapters in this volume for in-depth discussions and examples of all of the above cases.)

These problematic consequences have been demonstrated with a variety of measures and assessments. First, people do not seem to exhibit the difficulty we might normally expect would be associated with processing patently false information; the lack of such difficulty suggests that inaccuracies are considered in a manner no different from accurate information rather than incurring evaluative processing, rejection of the false material, or even a modest noticing of discrepancies. For example, readers do not exhibit processing slowdowns while encountering patently false information that they regularly demonstrate with information containing syntactic discrepancies or incoherent segments of text (e.g., Rapp, 2008). Second, people exhibit clear use of false information after encountering it. This includes recall of the misinformation on memory tasks (even with instructions to avoid its use) and applications of the misinformation on subsequent problem-solving activities (e.g., Johnson & Seifert, 1994). Third, this use emerges not just immediately after presentation of the inaccurate information but also after more substantial delays between initial presentations and potential test points (e.g., Appel & Richter, 2007). And fourth, people seem to not only rely on the misinformation but also report having learned it previously, despite such learning being highly unlikely or even entirely implausible (e.g., Marsh et al., 2003).

All told, the above findings indicate that investigations of learning that focus specifically on accurate, valid information fail to take into account the types of problematic materials that people routinely experience and that have important consequences for behavior, decisions, knowledge, and comprehension. Any account, philosophical or empirical, theoretical or applied, that seeks to describe knowledge acquisition needs to carefully consider these experiences to accurately capture the nature of human learning (see table 1.1). The current volume seeks to bring together multidisciplinary research intended to inform such accounts. Specifically, the goals are twofold: (1) to provide a survey of when, how, and why individuals rely on inaccurate information, as identified by theoretical and empirical investigations from the cognitive and educational sciences, and (2) to employ those understandings in the service of combating the problematic consequences of any such reliance.

Each of these goals motivates a variety of research questions that target specific aspects of our everyday experiences with inaccurate information. We outline three core questions here as a means of summarizing the current state of the field. First, how and when do people realize they are encountering misinformation? As figure 1.1 illustrates, various factors likely influence monitoring, evaluation, and discounting

Table 1.1

Simplified problem space for research on learning

Person holds:	The information a person receives is:		
Accurate prior knowledge	Accurate	Inaccurate	Neutral/uninformative
Inaccurate prior knowledge	Accurate	Inaccurate	Neutral/uninformative
Little to no relevant knowledge	Accurate	Inaccurate	Neutral/uninformative

Note. Learning experiences can, in a greatly simplified way, be broken down into a matrix as depicted in this table, indicating the kind of information presented to a learner, and the knowledge a learner holds prior to receiving the information. To date, most research on learning has focused largely on people's acquisition of accurate information (as identified in the circled region above). Nonetheless, other cells of the problem space represent regularly occurring experiences that prove necessary for understanding and describing the processes and products of everyday learning.

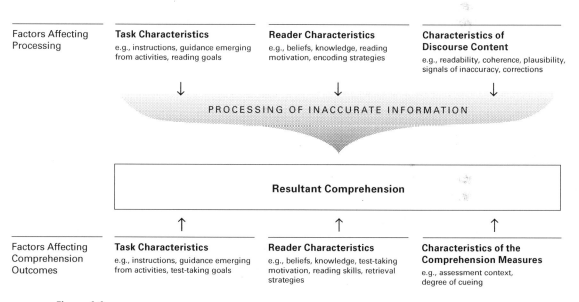

Figure 1.1

Factors influencing the detection and consequences for comprehension of inaccurate information.

processes. They include the nature of the inaccuracy (e.g., whether or not it includes explicit markings of inaccuracies and corrections; the plausibility of an inaccuracy vs. surrounding information; the popularity of the related topic) and the kind of processing engaged in when the inaccuracy is encountered (e.g., reading for study vs. for pleasure; perusing a list versus proofreading it; carefully viewing a video as part of a criminal case vs. casually watching it at home). The characteristics of the learner are also crucially important, including but not limited to reading skill, prior beliefs, knowledge and expertise with respect to the information, motivation, and strategies used to engage in the evaluation of content.

Contemporary investigations have begun outlining these factors, successfully describing a variety of circumstances that are associated with and might even drive the use of inaccurate information (Blanc, Stiegler-Balfour, & O'Brien, 2011; Hinze, Slaten, Horton, Jenkins, & Rapp, 2014; Sparks & Rapp, 2011; van Oostendorp, 1996). A second question emerges directly from the descriptions: Why do these comprehension difficulties occur? Explanatory investigations have attempted to identify the epistemological underpinnings of knowledge activation, application, and updating as a means of determining why difficulties occur (Kendeou & van den Broek, 2007; O'Brien, Rizzella, Albrecht, & Halleran, 1998; Schwarz, Sanna, Skurnik, & Yoon, 2007). Other investigations have empirically tested the ways in which higher-order cognitive functions such as memory, decision making, inferencing behavior, and discourse comprehension are linked to the learning of accurate and inaccurate information (Lewandowsky, Ecker, Seifert, Schwarz, & Cook, 2012). These investigations inform the development of explanatory accounts as to why people fall victim to inaccurate information.

A third question that is constrained by answers to the previous two is whether particular designs can be developed that support people's processing of information so they successfully discount and ignore misinformation (Ecker et al., 2010; Rapp, Hinze, Kohlhepp, & Ryskin, 2014; Schul & Manzury, 1990; Umanath, Butler, & Marsh, 2012). This specifically entails enhancing people's noticing and rejection of inaccuracies, as well as encouraging and ensuring the likelihood that people utilize accurate prior knowledge when it is appropriate to do so. The particular designs that might be supportive can be derived from the theoretical and empirical work previously described. The designs require particularly challenging development decisions and evaluative methods, given the need for their testing and implementation in real-world situations including classroom settings and the like.

The Organization and Contents of the Current Volume

The questions we have identified above undergird the central themes of identifying, understanding, and remediating people's reliance on inaccurate information that they should know to be wrong. In this book we have assembled an international group of scholars, all of whom have been interested in these themes and have addressed them using their own particular sets of expertise, methodologies, and theoretical orientations. They were specifically selected from the fields of cognitive science and education science, with their work directly focused on the role and results of experiences with inaccuracies. Their work represents diversity in the nature of the inaccuracies to be studied, including misinformation appearing in a variety of genres (e.g., narrative and expository) that potentially contradicts prior knowledge or information previously encountered in the same or across different sources and that includes inaccuracies that individuals may or may not be readily prepared for. The end result is a volume that explores in substantial depth issues related to noticing inaccuracies in texts, the processes that drive or result from noticing and failing to notice, and the ultimate representations that readers construct based on their reading experiences.

The book is divided into four parts with the chapters in each part including work from both the cognitive and education sciences. Indeed, the contents even *within* each of the contributors' chapters exhibits interdisciplinary investigations that will prove necessary to fully understand and combat the challenges that result from encountering inaccurate information. Many of the chapters provide content relevant to the topics contained within other parts, offering meaningful informative overlap and conceptual relevance to the topic, regardless of the particular experiences with misinformation one might be inclined to investigate or read about.

Part I, entitled *Detecting and Dealing with Inaccuracies*, exemplifies problems associated with encountering misinformation. The chapters in this part describe the range of behavioral challenges that result from experiences with inaccuracies, as well as possibilities for remediating any such influence. Part II, entitled *Mechanisms of Inaccurate Knowledge Acquisition*, focuses specifically on the cognitive activities that underlie the processes and products of experiences with inaccuracies. The goal here is to empirically evaluate specific mental representations and functions in a way that offers explanatory insight into why reliance on inaccurate information seems to so readily occur. Part III, entitled *Epistemological Groundings*, provides theoretical and philosophical considerations with respect to the nature of inaccuracies. Each of the contributions here offers conceptual discussion as to why information might be considered inaccurate or not, as well as how or why people might become aware of what they do or do not know. Finally, part IV, entitled *Emerging Models and Frameworks*, offers formalized, elaborated accounts intended to provide direction and organization to the array of research exemplified in this book. These chapters provide empirically derived perspectives and models that detail when and how inaccuracies will lead to potential comprehension difficulties.

As information becomes ever more accessible, the need for careful evaluation and informed skepticism becomes more crucial for everyday learning. The current volume represents a body of work that, we believe, will usefully inform theoretical understandings of knowledge acquisition when such acquisition might be problematic, as well as practical approaches intended to help learners reckon with the problem of inaccurate information.

References

Appel, M., & Richter, T. (2007). Persuasive effects of fictional narratives increase over time. *Media Psychology, 10*, 113–134.

Bates, D. (2011, May 2). *"Obama is dead": BBC and U.S. networks make embarrassing error reporting Bin Laden's death*. Retrieved from http://www.dailymail.co.uk/news/article-1382778/Obama-dead -BBC-said-basic-error-reporting-bin-Ladens-death.html.

Blanc, N., Stiegler-Balfour, J. J., & O'Brien, E. J. (2011). Does the certainty of information influence the updating process? Evidence from the reading of news articles. *Discourse Processes, 48*, 387–403.

Ecker, U. K. H., Lewandowsky, S., & Tang, D. T. W. (2010). Explicit warnings reduce but do not eliminate the continued influence of misinformation. *Memory & Cognition, 38*, 1087–1100.

Fazio, L. K., Barber, S. J., Rajaram, S., Ornstein, P. A., & Marsh, E. J. (2013). Creating illusions of knowledge: Learning errors that contradict prior knowledge. *Journal of Experimental Psychology. General, 142*, 1–5.

Fazio, L. K., & Marsh, E. J. (2008). Slowing presentation speed increases illusions of knowledge. *Psychonomic Bulletin & Review, 15*, 180–185.

Gross, D. (2012, October 31). *Man faces fallout for spreading false Sandy reports on Twitter*. Retrieved from http://www.cnn.com/2012/10/31/tech/social-media/sandy-twitter-hoax.

Hinze, S. R., Slaten, D. G., Horton, W. S., Jenkins, R., & Rapp, D. N. (2014). Pilgrims sailing the Titanic: Plausibility effects on memory for facts and errors. *Memory & Cognition, 42*, 305–324.

Johnson, H. M., & Seifert, C. M. (1994). Sources of the continued influence effect: When misinformation in memory affects later inferences. *Journal of Experimental Psychology. Learning, Memory, and Cognition, 20*, 1420–1436.

Kendeou, P., & van den Broek, P. (2007). The effects of prior knowledge and text structure on comprehension processes during reading of scientific texts. *Memory & Cognition, 35*, 1567–1577.

Lewandowsky, S., Ecker, U. K. H., Seifert, C. M., Schwarz, N., & Cook, J. (2012). Misinformation and its correction: Continued influence and successful debiasing. *Psychological Science in the Public Interest, 13*, 106–131.

Marsh, E. J., & Fazio, L. K. (2006). Learning errors from fiction: Difficulties in reducing reliance on fictional stories. *Memory & Cognition, 34*, 1140–1149.

Marsh, E. G., Meade, M. L., & Roediger, H. L., III. (2003). Learning facts from fiction. *Journal of Memory and Language, 49*, 519–536.

O'Brien, E. J., Rizzella, M. L., Albrecht, J. E., & Halleran, J. G. (1998). Updating a situation model: A memory-based text processing view. *Journal of Experimental Psychology. Learning, Memory, and Cognition, 24*, 1200–1210.

Rapp, D. N. (2008). How do readers handle incorrect information during reading? *Memory & Cognition, 36*, 688–701.

Rapp, D. N., Hinze, S. R., Kohlhepp, K., & Ryskin, R. A. (2014). Reducing reliance on inaccurate information. *Memory & Cognition, 42*, 11–26.

Schul, Y., & Burnstein, E. (1985). When discounting fails: Conditions under which individuals use discredited information in making a judgment. *Journal of Personality and Social Psychology, 49*, 894–903.

Schul, Y., & Manzury, F. (1990). The effect of type of encoding and strength of discounting appeal on the success of ignoring an invalid testimony. *European Journal of Social Psychology, 20*, 337–349.

Schwarz, N., Sanna, L. J., Skurnik, I., & Yoon, C. (2007). Metacognitive experiences and the intricacies of setting people straight: Implications for debiasing and public information campaigns. *Advances in Experimental Social Psychology, 39*, 127–161.

Sparks, J. R., & Rapp, D. N. (2011). Readers' reliance on source credibility in the service of inference generation. *Journal of Experimental Psychology. Learning, Memory, and Cognition, 37*, 230–247.

Umanath, S., Butler, A. C., & Marsh, E. J. (2012). Using popular films to enhance classroom learning: Mnemonic effects of monitoring misinformation. *Applied Cognitive Psychology, 26*, 556–567.

van Oostendorp, H. (1996). Updating situation models derived from newspaper articles. *Medienpsychologie, 8*, 22–33.

van Oostendorp, H., & Bonebakker, C. (1999). Difficulties in updating mental representations during reading news reports. In H. van Oostendorp & S. R. Goldman (Eds.), *The construction of mental representations during reading* (pp. 319–339). Mahwah, NJ: Lawrence Erlbaum Associates.

Wilkes, A. L., & Leatherbarrow, M. (1988). Editing episodic memory following the identification of error. *Quarterly Journal of Experimental Psychology, 40A*, 361–387.

I Detecting and Dealing with Inaccuracies

2 Correcting Misinformation—A Challenge for Education and Cognitive Science

Ullrich K. H. Ecker, Briony Swire, and Stephan Lewandowsky

Words have weight; something once said cannot be unsaid. Meaning is like a stone dropped into a pool; the ripples will spread and you cannot know what back they wash against.
—Philippa Gregory

Jenny McCarthy is a popular and successful U.S. TV show host, actress, and author. She is also the mother of a child diagnosed with autism, which has inspired her to become an activist and serve on the board of directors of *Generation Rescue*, an organization dedicated to informing the public about the recovery of children with autism spectrum disorders and the presumed risks of vaccinations.

In March 2012, she wrote: "MMR [i.e., the common measles–mumps–rubella vaccine], by far, has been the vaccine most commonly cited by parents as a trigger for a regression into autism" (McCarthy, 2012). This argument concerning the cause of autism originates from a 1998 publication in the medical journal *The Lancet* which suggested a relationship between the MMR vaccine and the onset of autism (Wakefield et al., 1998).

Celebrities commonly use their popularity to rally for worthy causes. Angelina Jolie raises awareness of humanitarian crises and refugee issues; Oprah Winfrey promotes education for disadvantaged girls in Africa and in the United States; Salma Hayek condemns violence against women and promotes UNICEF vaccination programs. So why did we choose McCarthy's example to open a chapter on misinformation? What's wrong with McCarthy's activism?

As it turns out, quite a few things. First and foremost, there is a strong consensus in the medical science community that there is no causal link between the MMR vaccine (or any other vaccine) and autism. This consensus is based on exhaustive and widely published global research efforts to replicate the Wakefield et al. (1998) findings. For example, a retrospective cohort study by Madsen et al. (2002) reviewed all children born in Denmark between January 1991 and December 1998 and concluded that there was no increase in the incidence of autism for vaccinated as opposed to unvaccinated children. In a review paper, DeStefano and Thompson (2004) concluded that "evidence now is convincing that the measles–mumps–rubella vaccine does not cause autism or any particular subtypes of autistic spectrum disorder" (p. 19). In fact, it has become clear that the Wakefield et al. (1998) study was a fraud. *The Lancet* officially retracted the article in 2010 (Editors of the Lancet, 2010), and the United Kingdom's General Medical Council found the lead author guilty of professional misconduct and removed him from the medical register. Hence, McCarthy's public claims represent misinformation.

The second issue regards the use of one's celebrity status to comment on scientific controversies without being an expert on those issues. This is relevant because the public is demonstrably receptive to nonexpert opinions. For example, roughly a quarter of survey respondents in the United States placed "some" (24%) or even "a lot" (2%) of trust in the opinions of celebrities on vaccine safety (Freed, Clark, Butchart, Singer, & Davis, 2011). In the present context, this affirms the likelihood that McCarthy's claims will affect people despite the plethora of evidence that shows those claims to be wrong.

The fact that people receive much of their information from potentially unreliable sources such as celebrities, popular "infotainment" TV shows, and nonexpert Web sites poses a problem in particular because it is known that misinformation continues to exert an influence on people's opinions even after it has been retracted. To illustrate, in 2002, when it had become clear and widely publicized that the Wakefield et al. (1998) findings had no scientific value, 24% of mothers in the United Kingdom still erroneously considered the vaccine a greater risk than the disease it was preventing (Smith & Yarwood, 2007). Even after a decade of public corrections—efforts by doctors, scientists, health agencies, and some media outlets to correct the misconceptions—as well as events such as the vaccine-preventable mumps epidemic in the United Kingdom in 2005, rates of immunization in the United Kingdom still had not returned to the level of 1996–1997 (Health Protection Agency, 2011). Clearly, erroneous information can have adverse consequences for public health and society at large, despite subsequent corrections and widespread efforts to disseminate the correct information.

In this chapter, we outline how retracted misinformation still influences people's reasoning, and why misinformation can persist in society, being surprisingly difficult to eradicate. We discuss how attempts to correct misinformation can under some circumstances even *worsen* the problem, but we will also explore ways in which misinformation can be useful for educational purposes. We use the term "misinformation" for any information that is (or might reasonably be) believed to be valid when first acquired, but which is subsequently shown to be incorrect or superseded by updated information.

Misinformation Effects and Individual-Level Cognition

In contemporary information-driven societies we are confronted with a myriad of information sources, and it can be difficult to distinguish fact from fiction. Considering how much information we process and how quickly the world can change, people actually do a remarkable job at updating their knowledge and mental models of the world—hardly anyone would think George W. Bush was still the U.S. president, and we can generally keep track of the things we have done versus those that are still on our to-do list. However, human memory is faced with the conundrum of maintaining stable memory representations (which is the whole point of having a memory in the first place) while also allowing for flexible modulation of memory representations to keep up-to-date with reality. Memory has evolved to achieve both of these aims, and hence it does not work like a blackboard: Outdated things are rarely actually wiped out and overwritten; instead, they tend to linger in the background, and access to them is only gradually lost (De Beni & Palladino, 2004; Oberauer & Vockenberg, 2009).

Retractions and the Provision of Alternatives—The Continued Influence Effect
The degree to which outdated information lingers depends on the likelihood that it will become relevant again in the future. Hence, when people are provided with a plausible alternative to replace the original misinformation, memory updating is often successful and people no longer rely on the initial, later retracted, information (H. Johnson & Seifert, 1994; Ecker, Lewandowsky, & Tang, 2010). Once you understand that your parents sneakily exchanged the baby teeth under your pillow for money, you no longer have a reason to believe in the tooth fairy.

However, if the valid alternative is unknown, or difficult to understand, misinformation will prevail. In the case of autism, the retraction of Wakefield et al.'s (1998) claims might have been more successful had the actual causes of autism been better understood and offered to the general public as an alternative account. A retraction creates a gap in a person's mental model of the world, and without a plausible alternative account, people may continue to make use of retracted misinformation, preferring an outdated, possibly incorrect model of the world to an *incomplete* model of the world. Hence, plain retractions—simply stating that something is incorrect—are usually rather ineffective in correcting misinformation (Ecker, Lewandowsky, Swire, & Chang, 2011; Ecker et al., 2010; H. Johnson & Seifert, 1994; van Oostendorp & Bonebakker, 1999; cf. also Rapp & Kendeou, 2007, 2009). People's ongoing reliance on corrected misinformation is known in the literature as the "continued influence effect" (H. Johnson & Seifert, 1994; see Lewandowsky, Ecker, Seifert, Schwarz, & Cook, 2012, for a review).

Classic laboratory studies by Wilkes and Leatherbarrow (1988) and H. Johnson and Seifert (1994) have demonstrated that people rely on information after it is no longer relevant (see also Ecker, Lewandowsky, & Apai, 2011b; Ecker et al., 2010). In these studies, participants were given a transcript of a fictitious event, such as a warehouse fire. As the story is being told, negligent storage of volatile materials (oil paint and pressurized gas cylinders) is originally imputed as a likely cause of the fire. Similar to a news story changing as new information comes to light, some participants were then told that actually no such materials had been found. When participants were asked about the presence of corrections in the report, they acknowledged the absence of oil paint and gas cylinders. However, when the same participants were making inferences to more indirect questions such as "What was the cause of the explosions?" people seemed to fall back on the only explanation they knew, namely the pressurized gas cylinders. Explicit knowledge of a correction is therefore no barrier to people's using the outdated information during their reasoning. In these studies, reliance on outdated misinformation was eliminated only if people were given an alternative account of the fire (i.e., evidence for arson, such as petrol-soaked rags, was found at the scene). Access to this alternative explanation enabled people to (largely) discount the volatile materials as the cause of the fire.

However, providing an alternative account is not always a solution to the problem. Providing an alternative may be helpful in simple scenarios with a straightforward cause-and-effect chain (e.g., arson, not negligence, caused the fire), but it may be potentially less useful in scenarios with many alternatives and complex interactions. In particular, if the alternative account is more complicated than the original misinformation-based account, the alternative may not be fully embraced. People generally prefer simple explanations to those which require more cognitive effort to understand and remember (Lombrozo, 2007). For example, Heit and Rotello (2012) reported that valid explanations are considered stronger when they are short whereas, ironically, illogical explanations are considered more convincing when they are long. Those results mesh well with Chater's (1999) proposal that finding the simplest explanatory pattern from complex data is a fundamental principle of cognition that guides perception, learning, memory, and reasoning. Chater argued that simplicity was not only a crucial factor in describing people's behavior across a range of cognitive domains but that the application of a simplicity principle was also normatively justified (meaning essentially that all other variables being equal, simple explanations are more likely to be correct and therefore helpful in making predictions and decisions). On that basis, a simple mental model of an event is not only easy to understand, efficiently stored and remembered, but it is also likely to be adequate. Hence, plausible and simple explanations will be more readily accepted, remembered, and utilized than a correct but overcomplicated account.

To summarize, misinformation effects are usually not an issue when there is a simple and plausible alternative to fill the gap created by a retraction in a person's mental model of an event or links between concepts. When there is no simple alternative available, however, people often continue to rely on retracted misinformation. To better understand this reliance on outdated or incorrect information, it is useful to consider the relevant memory processes in more detail. We frame our discussion within a view that proposes two distinct sets of memory processes: one based on familiarity and one based on a more targeted, strategic memory search to recollect contextual details.

A Dual-Process Account of Misinformation Effects

Familiarity is considered a quick and automatic appraisal process. When people encounter a statement, they judge its familiarity automatically and independently of the recollection of its source and its validity assessment (Begg, Anas, & Farinacci, 1992; Hintzman, 2010; Jacoby, 1991; Zimmer & Ecker, 2010). For example, unfounded statements such as "The Great Wall of China can be seen from the moon," "Sugar causes hyperactivity in children," or "Humans use only 10% of their brain" will be immediately familiar to many people even if they can also recollect having learned that these statements are, in fact, myths. Nonetheless, familiarity can lead to errors of judgment because it is often difficult to determine *why* a piece of information is familiar. Hence, the simple fact that an item is familiar can lead to its acceptance as true (Schwarz, Sanna, Skurnik, & Yoon, 2007) or the impression that the item had been encountered just recently. An example of the latter can be seen in the "mirror effect" in episodic recognition studies, where unstudied but highly familiar items (e.g., high-frequency words) typically attract more false alarms than less familiar items; cf. Reder, Angstadt, Cary, Erickson, & Ayers, 2002; Reder, Nhouyvanisvong, Schunn, Ayers, Angstadt, & Hiraki, 2000). In this case, people misattribute a sense of familiarity that arises from an item's high natural-language frequency (i.e., its general long-term familiarity) to its presumed occurrence in an experiment's study phase (i.e., a specific short-term familiarity or recency).

Likewise, a question about an event or the relationship among concepts will automatically activate related memory representations, some of which will be relevant and valid but some of which may supply irrelevant, incorrect, or subsequently invalidated information (Ayers & Reder, 1998). For example, in the well-studied *postevent misinformation* literature (Loftus & Hoffman, 1989; Loftus & Palmer, 1974), people may retrieve information suggested to them after witnessing an event because that suggestive misinformation is more recent and hence potentially more familiar at retrieval (Ayers & Reder, 1998; Lindsay & Johnson, 1989). It might be suggested to a crime witness, for instance, that the victim's arm was hurt during a theft when, in actual fact, the witness saw the victim's neck being hurt. Because of the suggestion, the witness may later remember seeing the victim's arm, rather than the victim's neck, being hurt (Okado & Stark, 2003).

The reliance on familiarity alone is therefore insufficient for accurate information processing. This implies the need for strategic memory processes: There needs to be a filter or monitoring process that can scrutinize the retrieved memory output and that can direct a potentially more targeted memory search process with the aim of recollecting specific contextual details (M. Johnson, Hashtroudi, & Lindsay, 1993; Schacter, Norman, & Koutstaal, 1998; Zimmer & Ecker, 2010). This filter and directed search is the domain of strategic memory processes. For example, recollecting how your Introductory Psychology lecturer showed you the evidence that people (mostly) use more than 10% of their brain will prevent you from accepting the myth to the contrary as true despite its familiarity. Likewise, a specific search for information regarding an item's source (e.g., whether it was actually encountered within the context of an experiment's study list or whether it was actually encountered during a witnessed event) will—if successful—preclude its false acceptance as valid. In other words, if strategic memory processes are utilized and functional, misinformation effects based on familiarity will not occur. Alas, strategic memory processes often fail; they require more executive control and mental effort than automatic memory processes (Herron & Rugg, 2003; Jacoby, 1991), and hence they are more readily compromised by factors such as divided attention (Jennings & Jacoby, 1993; Troyer & Craik, 2000), old age (Jennings & Jacoby, 1993; Spencer & Raz, 1995), alcohol intoxication (Bisby, Leitz, Morgan, & Curran, 2010), or simply a lack of motivation.

It follows that people will utilize misinformation when (1) an invalid memory representation is activated by a cue and (2) strategic memory processes fail (M. Johnson et al., 1993; Okado & Stark, 2003; Roediger & McDermott, 1995; Schacter et al., 1998). This basic idea of a failed strategic memory process contributing to misinformation effects has been applied in various forms. Sometimes, one correctly remembers an aspect of an event but misremembers important details, such as the source of the information. Incorrect recollection of the source may contribute to misinformation effects, for example, when one erroneously remembers receiving a piece of information from a reliable source (e.g., reading it in a scientific review paper) when in fact one received it from an unreliable source such as a blog or, as discussed above, when one remembers witnessing something (e.g., an injury of a crime victim's arm) that was in fact merely suggested (M. Johnson et al., 1993; Ost, Granhag, Udell, & Roos af Hjelmsäter, 2008; Ruffman, Rustin, Garnham, & Parkin, 2001; Zaragoza & Lane, 1994).

Sometimes misinformation effects may arise when people remember the misinformation but do not recollect the retraction. Considering the earlier emphasis on people's *being able to remember* the retraction but not *using* it during inferencing, this may seem like a contradiction. However, because recollection is a controlled process, there is a difference between *being able* to recollect something (in principle) and *actually* recollecting it (cf. Ecker, Zimmer, & Groh-Bordin, 2007). This is why people may use misinformation in their reasoning in response to indirect questions about the cause of an event while still recollecting the correction when questioned directly as to whether a presented report contained any corrections (as discussed above). The assumption that misinformation effects may occur because people remember the misinformation but fail to recollect the retraction in the same context is supported by research on negations. These studies assume that representations of negated information remain intact but the information's impact is usually offset by concurrent retrieval of an associated negation "tag" (Ecker, Lewandowsky, et al., 2011; Gilbert, Krull, & Malone, 1990; Wilson & Park, 2008)—when the tag is lost or is not retrieved alongside "its" negated piece of information, misinformation effects occur.

Some evidence for the importance of strategic monitoring processes for the continued influence effects of misinformation comes from a study by Ecker et al. (2010). In that study, people read news reports containing corrections. Participants relied less on retracted misinformation in their reasoning when they were informed about the basic notion of misinformation effects, and were warned about the possible presence of misinformation, before reading. The authors suggested that warnings put participants into a more strategic processing mode, allowing for both more efficient "tagging" of misinformation at encoding and better strategic monitoring at retrieval (cf. also Echterhoff, Hirst, & Hussy, 2005).

As mentioned above, the efficiency of strategic memory and monitoring processes is known to depend on age, with both children and the elderly having less efficient strategic processes. It is therefore unsurprising that misinformation effects tend to be particularly pronounced in children (Ruffman et al., 2001) and in the elderly (Ansburg & Heiss, 2012; Dehon, 2006; Skurnik, Yoon, Park, & Schwarz, 2005; cf. also Spencer & Raz, 1995).

By the same token, because strategic monitoring is an effortful process, misinformation effects are generally more likely to occur when people operate under high cognitive load or with few cognitive resources available (Ansburg & Heiss, 2012; Dehon, 2006; Gilbert et al., 1990; Wilson & Wolf, 2009). For example, when participants are sleep deprived at retrieval, they are more likely to produce false memories in the Deese–Roediger–McDermott (DRM) paradigm (Diekelmann, Landolt, Lahl, Born, & Wagner, 2008; in the DRM paradigm, participants study the primary associates of a focal word [e.g., cloud, water, storm, etc.] but not the focal word itself [viz., rain], yet participants reliably misremember studying the focal word).

In summary, people will tend to rely on automatically retrieved, familiar information when they do not have the cognitive resources to invest in monitoring their memory and reasoning. Resources might be compromised by many factors, including age and the demands of the situation. Whenever people rely on automatic memory processes alone, the potential for inadvertent reliance on information that is known to be false is greatest.

Why Retractions Fail: The Effects of Repetition and Familiarity

Because of the impact of automatic memory processes, making (mis-)information more familiar is one of the most powerful ways to make people believe and use it. It is for this reason that advertisements are put on high rotation, and this also explains why politicians repeat the same talking points ad infinitum (Singh, Kristensen, & Villaseñor, 2009). Moons, Mackie, and Garcia-Marques (2009) reported that repeating an argument led to stronger agreement with it; if the argument was a weak one, however, repetition led to stronger agreement only in participants with low induced motivation for analytic processing—a finding that supports the link between low cognitive effort/ strategic memory processing and familiarity-based misinformation effects.

It may seem rational to more strongly believe in statements one has heard repeatedly from various sources—in fact, a statement encountered in different contexts will be particularly memorable (e.g., Verkoeijen, Rikers, & Schmidt, 2004), and true information is more likely to be encountered in a large number of contexts than a fabrication. However, even repetition from a single source will make a statement more believable (Weaver, Garcia, Schwarz, & Miller, 2007), and internally repeating a statement by retrieving it from memory may be even more powerful in generating perceived validity than actual (external) repetition (Ozubko & Fugelsang, 2011). It is particularly remarkable that even when people accurately recognize that a statement is familiar simply because it was just encountered in a lab experiment, or when the source is known to be unreliable, the statement's familiarity will still influence people's belief in it (Begg et al., 1992; Henkel & Mattson, 2011).

Given how generally effective repetition seems to be as a memorial agent, it is tempting to assume that the same benefits of repetition and familiarity might also arise for retractions: Perhaps three corrections are better than one? Contrary to that expectation, the repetition of retractions appears to be less powerful than the repetition of initial information. In a study by Ecker, Lewandowsky, et al. (2011), repeating a piece of misinformation strongly increased people's reliance on it, but repeating the retraction only had a limited effect. In their study, three retractions were more effective than a single retraction after misinformation was encoded three times, but three retractions were as (in-)effective as one retraction when a piece of misinformation was encoded only once. The authors explained this in the framework of "retraction-tags," similar to the negation tags introduced earlier. Ecker et al. argued that each repetition of misinformation lays down a separate memory representation, and repetition thus leads to higher overall availability of misinformation in memory (because there are multiple traces, each of which competes for retrieval). However, each representation can only be offset by one retraction, which "tags" the representation as being incorrect. Repeated retractions therefore have only limited efficacy because once a representation has been tagged, additional repetitions of the retraction have no effect on that particular representation. It is only when there are multiple representations that multiple retractions may become more effective because the retraction tags may attach themselves to different representations.

Another explanation for why retractions, and repeated retractions in particular, are so ineffective can be derived from the dual-process perspective. We have already discussed how retractions are often ineffective: It turns out that, paradoxically, retractions may even *increase* an individual's acceptance of incorrect information, a class of phenomena known as "backfire" or "boomerang" effects. One example of this is the "familiarity backfire effect." This counterintuitive phenomenon occurs when a retraction repeats the misinformation, thereby inadvertently increasing its familiarity. For example, the statement "the belief that the MMR vaccine causes autism is false" repeats the association between MMR and autism, and it may therefore make the statement "MMR causes autism" seem more familiar. When the recollection of specific contextual information fails—memory for details such as the source of the information or its "tagging" as false can be expected to deteriorate over time—only the enhanced familiarity of the statement may remain (Skurnik et al., 2005; also see Schwarz et al., 2007). The marketing industry is well aware of this effect: Even negative advertisements and negative publicity can have a positive long-term effect on sales when it serves to make people more familiar with a product or a brand (Berger, Sorensen, & Rasmussen, 2010).

The familiarity backfire effect has been demonstrated most clearly by Skurnik et al. (2005). These authors presented participants with health-related claims such as "Aspirin destroys tooth enamel." Claims were labeled as either valid or invalid (because of ethical concerns with presenting misleading health claims, all claims were actually valid but were not obviously true or false to the nonexpert participants) and were presented once or three times. Thus, an invalid item presented three times would have been identified as invalid three times, as opposed to just once for the once-presented counterpart. The results were intriguing. On the one hand, Skurnik et al. found that repeating claims that were labeled invalid led older adults to misremember them as valid *less* often after a short delay of 30 minutes (17% of those presented three times vs. 28% of those presented once), thus attesting to the success of repeated retractions (young adults had much lower rates, misremembering 7% of invalid claims presented three times and 10% of invalid claims presented once). On the other hand, after a delay of three days, the effect was reversed, with older people misremembering the thrice-repeated invalid items as valid more often (40%) than their once-presented counterparts (28%). (Young adults did not show this effect, with rates for invalid claims presented thrice vs. once at 14% and 24%, respectively.) Skurnik et al. argued that although repetition served to highlight that a claim was invalid, thereby facilitating its immediate rejection, the repetition also increased the claim's familiarity and thus led to higher levels of misinformation acceptance—at least in older participants—after a delay. After a delay, strategic recollection processes were particularly important, lest they be overwhelmed by relatively intact familiarity-based memory. Because strategic processes are generally weaker in the elderly, they were insufficient to counteract the (misleading) familiarity signal arising from the repetition of the invalid information (cf. Prull, Dawes, Martin, Rosenberg, & Light, 2006; Spencer & Raz, 1995).

Wilson and Park (2008) subsequently adapted the statements used by Skurnik et al. (2005). However, rather than labeling statements as valid or invalid, Wilson and Park simply negated some of the statements (e.g., "Aspirin does not destroy tooth enamel"). Again, elderly people were found to be more likely to misremember negated statements as valid, this time after a mere 45 minutes.

Turning to the other end of the adult life span, research on misinformation in younger adults after shorter delays has hitherto yielded inconclusive evidence. Recall that Skurnik et al. (2005) found no evidence for a familiarity backfire effect in young adults after 30 minutes. Likewise, Ecker, Lewandowsky, and Hogan (2012) presented participants with fictional news reports similar to the "warehouse fire" scenario, in which an initially presented cause of an event subsequently turned out to be false and was replaced by a valid cause. Ecker et al. found that repeating the initial, outdated cause during the retraction made the retraction *more*, not less, effective (cf. also Johar & Roggeveen, 2007).

In contrast, Skurnik, Yoon, and Schwarz (2007; as discussed in Schwarz et al., 2007) reported evidence for a familiarity backfire effect even in young adults after only 30 minutes of retention. They presented their participants with a flyer regarding the common flu vaccine, which employed the popular "myths versus facts" format. For example, it stated that "The side effects [of the vaccine] are worse than the flu.—FALSE. The worst side effect you're likely to get […] is a sore arm […]." Skurnik et al. found that retracting (and thereby repeating) common myths led to a marked increase in accepting those myths as true. Interestingly, attitudes toward the vaccine also changed— participants who had read the flyer rated the vaccine less favorably than those who had not. Similarly, Berinsky (2012) reported that corrections of the rumor that U.S. health care changes would promote euthanasia tended to be more effective when the correction did not repeat the rumor.

In summary, with young adults the balance of evidence does not warrant undue concerns about the familiarity backfire effect. By contrast, in old adults, the presence of familiarity backfire effects seems to be well established and must give rise to concern.

We have identified the reliance on automatic memory processes, in the absence of effortful strategic processing, as a key contributing factor to the persistence of misinformation. That is, in the absence of a particular motivation to believe one version of an event, or one set of concept relations, over another, and when there is no reason to doubt the validity of the retraction, people will rely on misinformation to the extent that strategic memory processes fail to retrieve the retraction. This could be due to a genuine failure but could also happen when the retraction information is available in principle but is not retrieved because the retrieval cue is too indirect or people simply do not invest the effort required. The latter variable is particularly relevant because in many circumstances, people *will* be motivated to believe some pieces of information but not others. We therefore next consider the heuristics involved in people's judgment of the believability of incoming information, as well as the role of people's existing beliefs, attitudes, and worldviews in shaping their beliefs and memory.

Misinformation Effects and Social Cognition

It is impossible to critically assess the veracity of each and every piece of information one encounters, which makes the use of heuristics that can yield quick judgments of credibility particularly attractive. Thus people will often assess the validity of a claim by assessing how it fits in with what they (or their peers) already know or believe. This can be a very efficient strategy and is usually adaptive (e.g., anyone would be skeptical about claims of a newly discovered Pacific island on which there is no gravity). In support, Richter, Schroeder, and Wöhrmann (2009) demonstrated how people use relevant preexisting knowledge to reject false assertions quickly and automatically, provided that the preexisting knowledge is accessible and people are certain that the knowledge is accurate.

The Role of Attitudes for Misinformation Effects

Potential problems arise from use of this heuristic when the existing knowledge is false, beliefs are biased, or people hold very strong attitudes that run counter to the evidence. Ecker, Lewandowsky, Fenton, and Martin (2013) showed that preexisting attitudes determine how often a piece of attitude-relevant (mis-)information is used in reasoning, but they also demonstrated that preexisting attitudes do not necessarily compromise the effectiveness of retractions. In their study, people scoring high or low on a racial-prejudice scale read a news report involving either an Aboriginal robber or an Aboriginal hero; the involvement of the Aboriginal was retracted in some conditions. Ecker et al. found that references to retracted racial misinformation covaried with people's racial prejudice (e.g., people with high racial prejudice referred to the Aboriginal robber more often, but to the Aboriginal hero less often, than people lower in prejudice). Ecker et al. also found that people in both high- and low-prejudice groups reduced their reliance on the racial information after a retraction to equivalent degrees, meaning that there was no evidence that people ignored the retraction when it ran counter to their attitudes.

However, this outcome stands in striking contrast to other research which has found that people holding a strong belief may reject *any* information that runs counter to that belief. Thus, attempts to retract attitude-congruent misinformation can be futile with strongly partisan individuals. Indeed, it can even backfire and strengthen the misconception ("the worldview backfire effect"; see Lewandowsky et al., 2012, for a review). For example, Nyhan and Reifler (2010) reported that attempts to refute nonfictitious misconceptions (e.g., that weapons of mass destruction had been found in Iraq after the 2003 invasion) were successful when the retractions were in line with people's worldview, but that worldview-incongruent retractions were ineffective or, ironically, strengthened the misconceptions. It is presently unclear under what circumstances such worldview backfire effects can be observed, but Ecker et al. (2013) argued that it will depend on whether acknowledging the retraction will require a change of attitudes: In the case of an arbitrary incident such as a robbery, one can uphold one's belief (e.g., that most Aboriginals are criminal) even when accepting that the particular incident (e.g., that a particular crime was not committed by an Aboriginal) did not support the belief. In contrast, a refutation will likely not be accepted when it necessitates a change in belief and potentially entails a loss of face. For example, for a person who supported the 2003 invasion of Iraq, acknowledging that no weapons of mass destruction were found in Iraq may require a reassessment of political decisions made at the time, and a reassessment of one's own support.

Motivated Reasoning and Misinformation Effects
The rejection of attitude-incongruent information can be seen as a case of motivated reasoning—biased information processing that seeks to confirm existing beliefs rather than update one's knowledge based on an unbiased assessment of the evidence (for reviews of motivated cognition, see Kunda, 1990; Nickerson, 1998; Redlawsk, 2002). Motivated reasoning behavior is particularly prevalent when the belief or attitude in question is held with confidence and conviction because it is central to a person's value system and defines their identity (Brannon, Tagler, & Eagly, 2007; Hart, Albarracín, Eagly, Brechan, Lindberg, & Merrill, 2009). This means that efforts to correct common misperceptions may have to focus on people with moderate—rather than extremely strong—convictions. Even in people with moderate attitudes, however, motivated reasoning seems sufficiently common (cf. Prasad et al., 2009) to warrant a more detailed examination.

The confirmation bias behind motivated reasoning can lead people to selectively expose themselves only to ("cherry-picked") evidence that supports their prior beliefs. An example of such behavior is the tendency of consumers to choose newspapers that are known to be biased in their reporting, or Internet users to frequent Web sites that they know to support their worldviews (T. Johnson, Bichard, & Zhang, 2009). Other strategies include denying the existence of contrasting evidence or—when presented with such evidence as in the case of misinformation retractions discussed here—deflecting or discrediting the evidence or its source. For example, when an anthropologist corrects the common myth that there is a debate among climate scientists as to whether climate change is anthropogenic, explaining how there is in fact a strong consensus on this (cf. Anderegg, Prall, Harold, & Schneider, 2010; Cook et al., 2013; Doran & Zimmerman, 2009), a frequent strategy of people who oppose the findings from climate science is to deflect and discredit the source by questioning the anthropologist's expertise to speak about climatology. Supporting this anecdotal evidence, derogating the source of the evidence was one of the strategies identified by Jacks and Cameron (2003) in their study on motivated reasoning. The authors presented counterattitudinal messages (arguing against the death penalty) to participants in favor of the death penalty, and they measured people's responses. Participants particularly used the strategy of derogating the source when the source of the counterattitudinal message was perceived as lacking expertise and when participants' pro–death penalty attitudes were particularly strong.

The two most frequently used strategies in the study by Jacks and Cameron (2003), however, were counterarguing and attitude bolstering. Counterarguing refers to the covert or overt generation of arguments to counter the corrective information being presented, a common and principally rational strategy as long as the counterarguments maintain ties to empirical reality. Attitude bolstering means to completely ignore the refutation and focus on supporting evidence.

In a study by Prasad and colleagues (2009), participants were presented with convincing evidence that was incongruent with both a specific misconception they held and their general political worldview (specifically, Republican voters who believed in a link between Saddam Hussein and the terror attacks of 9/11 were presented with contrary evidence including a statement from President G. W. Bush himself). Faced with the evidence, only 2% of participants explicitly acknowledged the inadequacy of their misconception and updated their beliefs. A higher proportion (14%) denied holding the misconception in the first place, a surprising behavior that may have served to avoid "losing face." Most participants, however, displayed some form of motivated reasoning. They utilized strategies such as the above-mentioned counterarguing of facts and attitude bolstering. Prasad et al. identified two further strategies. One was "inferred justification," which describes a form of flawed backward reasoning where people recursively infer the reasons that justify a present situation, ignoring evidence to the contrary. For example, some people argued that there must have been a link between Hussein and 9/11 because there must have been a reason for the U.S. invasion of Iraq. The other strategy identified by Prasad et al. was "disputing rationality"; this is when people insist on their right to an opinion without factual reasoning, often combined with assertions of confidence that nothing could change their mind.

Munro (2010) additionally described a situation in which people discounted evidence by denying the in-principle amenability of a topic to scientific investigation ("scientific impotence discounting"). In that study, participants who believed that homosexuality was (or was not) a mental illness rejected evidence that homosexuals are not (or are) overrepresented in psychological treatment facilities, and they were more likely to agree with the suggestion that the topic could not be studied scientifically. In fact, the rejection of science even generalized to other topics such as the effectiveness of herbal medicine, implying that when given evidence inconsistent with their beliefs, people became more skeptical of the scientific method in general.

Not surprisingly, motivated reasoning tendencies are less prevalent in open-minded people (Hart et al., 2009). Levitan and Visser (2008) asked their participants to rate the heterogeneity of attitudes in their social network by having them list five members of their social network and rate how much they agreed with each of those people's world-views. The study demonstrated that people exposed to diverse attitudes through their social network are more open to changing their attitudes in response to counterattitudinal persuasive arguments, provided arguments are sufficiently strong (i.e., attitude diversity did not lead to attitude change in response to weak arguments).

Some researchers have argued that personality traits such as "social vigilantism"—the tendency to impose one's own beliefs on others—predict greater expressions of belief superiority and increased counterarguing tendencies (Saucier & Webster, 2010). Other researchers have expressed the somewhat contrasting view that motivated reasoning tendencies are linked to low self-esteem (Wiersema, van Harreveld, & van der Pligt, 2012), negative mood (Jonas, Graupmann, & Frey, 2006), and threats of social exclusion (Greitemeyer, Fischer, & Kastenmüller, 2012).

The idea that people with low self-esteem (or people in a situation of reduced emotional or social stability) have a stronger need to defend their identity-defining attitudes is in line with self-affirmation theory. Self-affirmation theory claims that people use a variety of psychological adaptations, strategies, and distortions to protect the self from the threats of perceived failure or deficiencies (cf. Sherman & Cohen, 2006). In the present case, this implies that people with low self-esteem and strong attitudes will find counterattitudinal evidence particularly threatening to their identity and self-worth and are hence more likely to engage in motivated reasoning. Motivated reasoning tendencies can therefore be softened by affirming people's self-worth—for example, by focusing them on personal achievements before confronting them with attitude-incongruent corrective information (Cohen, Bastardi, Sherman, Hsu, McGoey, & Ross, 2007).

The motivated-reasoning research implies that preexisting attitudes can create a major obstacle for attempts to correct misinformation, in particular when corrections are perceived to require attitudinal change. The literature just reviewed suggests that counterattitudinal retractions are more likely to be accepted when people are reminded of attitudinal diversity in their social network, are in a good mood and self-affirmed, and are not threatened by social exclusion.[1]

Correcting Misinformation

We have already discussed that mere retractions (even when repeated) are fairly ineffective in reducing reliance on invalid or outdated information. Further, the earlier discussion of the familiarity backfire effect suggests that at least in older people, repeating misinformation during attempts to correct it carries the inherent risk of ironically strengthening the misconception (Skurnik et al., 2005, 2007). This finding presents a pragmatic challenge because often a correction will require a myth to be repeated; for example, the statement "The Great Wall of China is *not* visible from the moon" may inadvertently strengthen the link between "the Great Wall of China" and "visible from the moon," yet it is unclear how the debunking could be performed in this instance without mentioning the misinformation. Finally, we have discussed how motivated reasoning can make it difficult to correct misconceptions when the correction runs counter to strongly held beliefs. As was mentioned, preexisting beliefs can, in some instances, be so powerful that the presentation of corrective information can, ironically, fortify the misconception (viz., the worldview backfire effect; Nyhan & Reifler, 2010).

In opposition to those concerns involving backfire effects, there is a growing literature on the *deliberate* use of misinformation, and its refutation, as an educational tool. Students acquiring basic knowledge in any subject will typically harbor a variety of misconceptions, and techniques that can effectively reduce these are of interest to all teachers and science communicators. Directly addressing and refuting such misconceptions to introduce the valid information has been shown to be more effective than presenting the same valid information in a "standard" teaching format (Kowalski & Taylor, 2009). Unlike plain retractions, which simply state that some piece of information is not true, a refutational text is more detailed; although it explicitly presents the misinformation, it also provides a comprehensive explanation of why it is incorrect. For the "Great Wall of China" example, a refutation might include supporting evidence such as the narrow width of the wall relative to the distance between the moon and the earth and how that translates into a visual angle too small for the human eye to resolve. A refutational text might also try to explain why the misinformation was presented in the first place. For example, to understand why Andrew Wakefield suggested that autism was linked to the MMR vaccine, it is helpful to know that he received around half a million pounds in undisclosed payments from a lawyer preparing class action against the producers of the compound vaccine, and that there were plans to start a company to sell diagnostic tests (Deer, 2011). Arguably, such explanations will facilitate belief updating because they foster people's skepticism regarding the initial misinformation and its source (cf. Lewandowsky, Stritzke, Oberauer, & Morales, 2005, 2009).

A meta-analysis by Guzzetti, Snyder, Glass, and Gamas (1993) explored the efficacy of different interventions intended to reduce misconceptions in the classroom. Participants ranged from primary school students to university postgraduates, and a wide range of science misconceptions were incorporated. The authors found seven types of intervention being utilized within these studies, with refutational texts and nonrefutational texts (such as simple narratives, or expository texts where new information is presented with no reference to the misconception) being the most common. Refutational texts were found to be the most effective strategy of all interventions, and significantly more effective in producing conceptual change than nonrefutational texts. Several studies included a posttest one or two months later, and use of refutational texts was the only intervention to foster long-term conceptual change.

Efficacy of a refutation is dependent on a number of factors. Guzzetti, Williams, Skeels, and Wu (1997) observed three high school physics classes for an eight-month period, accumulating qualitative data through interviews and questionnaires. They found that students ignored the refutational text and persisted with misinformation if (1) the refutation was poorly constructed and lacked clarity or (2) the students self-reported that they were only skimming the text. When students did not engage with the text, they mistakenly found evidence for their prior misconception within the refutation. It is also important for the misconception to be based upon a lack of knowledge (which may be corrected by a valid explanation) rather than an individual's attitudes or belief system, as previously discussed.

The effectiveness of refutational texts is often explained within the "conceptual change model" proposed by Posner, Strike, Hewson, and Gertzog (1982). This model suggests that there are four stages necessary for conceptual change to take place. The first step is *dissatisfaction* with one's own current understanding, which instigates cognitive conflict. The proposed replacement construct then needs to be *intelligible* (i.e., easily understood), *plausible*, and potentially *fruitful* (i.e., the student should be able to see the relevance of a correct understanding of matters and the potential applicability of the corrected knowledge to future problems).

Yet, considering the first step in Posner et al.'s (1982) model, to become dissatisfied with one's insufficient understanding, one would first need to notice an incongruity between one's current conception and the evidence. In fact, before one can notice such a discrepancy, one's misconception and the presented evidence (and the associated correction) would have to be coactivated and aligned in working memory (cf. McCrudden & Kendeou, 2014; van den Broek & Kendeou, 2008).

McCrudden (2012) looked at students' understanding of the biological term "fitness," which refers specifically to the number of an animal's offspring that survive into adulthood, a meaning quite different from the common interpretation in terms of physical fitness. Based on an analysis of think-aloud protocols and interviews, McCrudden argued that when a refutational text is read, coactivation of the misconception and the corrective evidence may occur automatically, but that the detection of a discrepancy between the two may require strategic monitoring processes (cf. Ecker et al., 2010). Using think-aloud protocols, McCrudden further demonstrated how merely noticing the discrepancy between misconception and evidence is not sufficient for a change in belief—the reader needs to strategically engage in resolving the discrepancy. Kendeou and van den Broek (2007) found that students with prior misconceptions engaged in such "conceptual change strategies" only when reading refutational texts. These conceptual change or resolution strategies were reflected through participants' vocalizing the juxtaposition between their misconception and the correct information, making text-based inferences, and paraphrasing (McCrudden, 2012; Kendeou & van den Broek, 2007).

The preceding discussion implies that one of the main reasons why refutational texts may be particularly effective in reducing misconceptions is that they set the stage for strategic conceptual change processing. That is, refutational texts allow people to coactivate, align, and integrate their misconceptions with corrective evidence, which then facilitates the updating of their beliefs (cf. Ecker et al., 2012; Johar & Roggeveen, 2007).

This view of corrections via refutation is consistent with, although it does not require, the notion of memory reconsolidation, which has gained recent popularity (see Hardt, Einarsson, & Nader, 2010, for a review, but also Ecker & Lewandowsky, 2012, for a critique). Reconsolidation theory proposes that when an item in memory is retrieved, it reenters a transient, labile state, which may allow it to be modified, updated, or weakened before it is then restabilized (i.e., reconsolidated). When a refutation is read, the original misconception is necessarily recalled, and according to reconsolidation, this would render the misconception's representation labile and amenable to be updated and to accommodate the correct information.

Apart from the "aligning" of misconception and correction, the effectiveness of using refutational materials in a classroom setting may have another "operative ingredient": It fosters critical thinking. Refutational texts encourage students to critically appraise what they know, to skeptically assess empirical evidence, and to endeavor to draw valid conclusions from the evidence (cf. Baker & Piburn, 1991; Berland & Reiser, 2008; Kuhn & Crowell, 2011; Manson, Gava, & Boldrin, 2008; ten Dam & Volman, 2004). Bedford (Bedford, 2010; Bedford & Cook, 2013) has suggested that the in-depth study of misinforming materials itself could improve students' understanding of scientific concepts by motivating students to acquire the necessary knowledge and critical thinking skills to convincingly argue against misrepresentations. The explicit study of misinforming materials and the analysis of controversial issues can thus ameliorate students' critical thinking and reasoning skills. That is, reading refutational texts and discussing them in class, building arguments based on evidence, will help students improve both their understanding of the subject matter and their argumentative reasoning skills. Alas, knowledge is often imparted as a set of unequivocal facts, and there is a lack of argument and debate in science classrooms (Osborne, 2010).

To conclude, our analysis of misinformation correction strategies suggests that familiarity backfire effects may only be a concern when there is little explanation regarding the motivation behind the initial misinformation and the countering evidence (i.e., with simple "this is the myth; this is the fact" statements). In situations in which more extensive explanations are possible, taking up and addressing the misinformation seems beneficial. This process allows misconceptions and corrective evidence to be aligned, and it seems to facilitate belief updating, in particular when a "factual wrapper" can be established to encapsulate misinformation. This can be achieved by providing clear-cut evidence and explaining the motivation behind the initial spreading of misinformation (i.e., a "this is the myth; this is why the myth was spread; this is the truth; this is the evidence" approach). Fostering critical thinking, skepticism, and an understanding of science from a young age thus seem crucial educational aims for contemporary information societies.

Acknowledgment

Preparation of this chapter was facilitated by Discovery Grants DP0770666 and DP110101266 from the Australian Research Council and by an Australian Postdoctoral Fellowship and an Australian Professorial Fellowship to the first and last author, respectively.

Note

1. While it goes beyond the scope of this chapter, there are also strategies that aim more at changing behavioral tendencies rather than the attitudes and beliefs per se. These include the design of choice architectures (e.g., opt-in vs. opt-out approaches to superannuation/pension plans or organ donation schemes) and the framing of information with respect to attitude congruence (e.g., persons concerned about climate change might be persuaded to install solar panels on their house by arguments referring to their carbon footprint, but persons who are not concerned about climate change may find economic arguments more convincing). See Lewandowsky et al. (2012) for a brief review.

References

Anderegg, W. R. L., Prall, J. W., Harold, J., & Schneider, S. H. (2010). Expert credibility in climate change. *Proceedings of the National Academy of Sciences of the United States of America, 107*, 12107–12109.

Ansburg, P. I., & Heiss, C. J. (2012). Potential paradoxical effects of myth-busting as a nutrition education strategy for older adults. *American Journal of Health Education, 43*, 31–37.

Ayers, M. S., & Reder, L. M. (1998). A theoretical review of the misinformation effect: Predictions from an activation-based memory model. *Psychonomic Bulletin & Review, 5*, 1–21.

Baker, D. R., & Piburn, M. (1991). Process skills acquisition, cognitive growth, and attitude change of ninth grade students in a scientific literacy course. *Journal of Research in Science Teaching, 28*, 423–436.

Bedford, D. (2010). Agnotology as a teaching tool: Learning climate science by studying misinformation. *Journal of Geography, 109*, 159–165.

Bedford, D., & Cook, J. (2013). Agnotology, scientific consensus, and the teaching and learning of climate change: A response to Legates, Soon and Briggs. *Science & Education.* doi:10.1007/s11191-013-9608-3.

Begg, I. M., Anas, A., & Farinacci, S. (1992). Dissociation of processes in belief: Source recollection, statement familiarity, and the illusion of truth. *Journal of Experimental Psychology. General, 121,* 446–458.

Berger, J., Sorensen, A. T., & Rasmussen, S. J. (2010). Positive effects of negative publicity: When negative reviews increase sales. *Marketing Science, 29,* 815–827.

Berinsky, A. J. (2012). *Rumors, truths, and reality: A study of political misinformation.* Unpublished manuscript, Massachusetts Institute of Technology, Cambridge, MA.

Berland, L. K., & Reiser, B. R. (2008). Making sense of argumentation and explanation. *Science Education, 93,* 26–55.

Bisby, J. A., Leitz, J. R., Morgan, C. J. A., & Curran, H. V. (2010). Decreases in recollective experience following acute alcohol: A dose–response study. *Psychopharmacology, 208,* 67–74.

Brannon, L. A., Tagler, M. J., & Eagly, A. H. (2007). The moderating role of attitude strength in selective exposure to information. *Journal of Experimental Social Psychology, 43,* 611–617.

Chater, N. (1999). The search for simplicity: A fundamental cognitive principle? *Quarterly Journal of Experimental Psychology, Section A: Human Experimental Psychology, 52,* 273–302.

Cohen, G. L., Bastardi, A., Sherman, D. K., Hsu, L., McGoey, M., & Ross, L. (2007). Bridging the partisan divide: Self-affirmation reduces ideological closed-mindedness and inflexibility in negotiation. *Journal of Personality and Social Psychology, 93,* 415–430.

Cook, J., Nuccitelli, D., Green, S. A., Richardson, M., Winkler, B., Painting, R., et al. (2013). Quantifying the consensus on anthropogenic global warming in the scientific literature. *Environmental Research Letters, 8,* 024024. doi:10.1088/1748-9326/8/2/024024.

De Beni, R., & Palladino, P. (2004). Decline in working memory updating through ageing: Intrusion error analyses. *Memory, 12,* 75–89.

Deer, B. (2011). Secrets of the MMR scare: How the vaccine crisis was meant to make money. *BMJ, 342*:c5258, 136–142.

Dehon, H. (2006). Variations in processing resources and resistance to false memories in younger and older adults. *Memory, 14,* 692–711.

DeStefano, F., & Thompson, W. W. (2004). MMR vaccine and autism: An update of the scientific evidence. *Expert Review of Vaccines, 3,* 19–22.

Diekelmann, S., Landolt, H., Lahl, O., Born, J., & Wagner, U. (2008). Sleep loss produces false memories. *PLoS ONE, 3,* e3512. doi:10.1371/journal.pone.0003512.

Doran, P. T., & Zimmerman, M. K. (2009). Examining the scientific consensus on climate change. *Eos, 90,* 21–22.

Echterhoff, G., Hirst, W., & Hussy, W. (2005). How eyewitnesses resist misinformation: Social postwarnings and the monitoring of memory characteristics. *Memory & Cognition, 33*, 770–782.

Ecker, U. K. H., & Lewandowsky, S. (2012). Computational constraints in cognitive theories of forgetting. *Frontiers in Psychology, 3*, 400. doi:10.3389/fpsyg.2012.00400.

Ecker, U. K. H., Lewandowsky, S., & Apai, J. (2011). Terrorists brought down the plane!—No, actually it was a technical fault: Processing corrections of emotive information. *Quarterly Journal of Experimental Psychology, 64*, 283–310.

Ecker, U. K. H., Lewandowsky, S., Fenton, O., & Martin, K. (2013). *Do people keep believing because they want to? The effects of racial attitudes on misinformation processing.* Manuscript submitted for publication.

Ecker, U. K. H., Lewandowsky, S., & Hogan, J. (2012). *Repeating misinformation when retracting it— Help or hindrance?* Unpublished manuscript.

Ecker, U. K. H., Lewandowsky, S., Swire, B., & Chang, D. (2011). Correcting false information in memory: Manipulating the strength of misinformation encoding and its retraction. *Psychonomic Bulletin & Review, 18*, 570–578.

Ecker, U. K. H., Lewandowsky, S., & Tang, D. T. W. (2010). Explicit warnings reduce but do not eliminate the continued influence of misinformation. *Memory & Cognition, 38*, 1087–1100.

Ecker, U. K. H., Zimmer, H. D., & Groh-Bordin, C. (2007). Color and context: An ERP study on intrinsic and extrinsic feature binding in episodic memory. *Memory & Cognition, 35*, 1483–1501.

Editors of the Lancet. (2010). Retraction—Ileal-lymphoid-nodular hyperplasia, non-specific colitis, and pervasive developmental disorder in children (Retraction of Vol. 351, pp. 637–641, 1998). *Lancet, 375*, 445.

Freed, G. L., Clark, S. J., Butchart, A. T., Singer, D. C., & Davis, M. M. (2011). Sources and perceived credibility of vaccine-safety information for parents. *Pediatrics, 127*, S107–S112.

Gilbert, D. T., Krull, D., & Malone, P. (1990). Unbelieving the unbelievable: Some problems in the rejection of false information. *Journal of Personality and Social Psychology, 59*, 601–613.

Greitemeyer, T., Fischer, P., & Kastenmüller, A. (2012). The effects of social exclusion on confirmatory information processing. *European Journal of Social Psychology, 42*, 462–469.

Guzzetti, B. J., Snyder, T. E., Glass, G. V., & Gamas, W. S. (1993). Promoting conceptual change in science: A comparative meta-analysis of instructional interventions from reading education and science education. *Reading Research Quarterly, 28*, 116–159.

Guzzetti, B. J., Williams, W. O., Skeels, S. A., & Wu, S. M. (1997). Influence of text structure on learning counterintuitive physics concepts. *Journal of Research in Science Teaching, 34*, 701–719.

Hardt, O., Einarsson, E. O., & Nader, K. (2010). A bridge over troubled water: Reconsolidation as a link between cognitive and neuroscientific memory research traditions. *Annual Review of Psychology, 61*, 141–167.

Hart, W., Albarracín, D., Eagly, A. H., Brechan, I., Lindberg, M. J., & Merrill, L. (2009). Feeling validated versus being correct: A meta-analysis of selective exposure to information. *Psychological Bulletin, 135,* 555–588.

Health Protection Agency. (2011, 21 October). *Completed primary courses at two years of age: England and Wales, 1966–1977, England only after 1978 onwards.* Retrieved from http://www.hpa.org.uk/web/HPAweb&HPAwebStandard/HPAweb_C/1195733819251

Heit, E., & Rotello, C. M. (2012). The pervasive effects of argument length on inductive reasoning. *Thinking & Reasoning, 18,* 244–277.

Henkel, L. A., & Mattson, M. E. (2011). Reading is believing: The truth effect and source credibility. *Consciousness and Cognition, 20,* 1705–1721.

Herron, J. E., & Rugg, M. D. (2003). Strategic influences on recollection in the exclusion task: Electrophysiological evidence. *Psychonomic Bulletin & Review, 10,* 703–710.

Hintzman, D. L. (2010). How does repetition affect memory? Evidence from judgments of recency. *Memory & Cognition, 38,* 102–115.

Jacks, J. Z., & Cameron, K. A. (2003). Strategies for resisting persuasion. *Basic and Applied Social Psychology, 25,* 145–161.

Jacoby, L. L. (1991). A process dissociation framework: Separating automatic from intentional uses of memory. *Journal of Memory and Language, 30,* 513–541.

Jennings, J. M., & Jacoby, L. L. (1993). Automatic versus intentional uses of memory: Aging, attention, and control. *Psychology and Aging, 8,* 283–293.

Johar, G. V., & Roggeveen, A. L. (2007). Changing false beliefs from repeated advertising: The role of claim-refutation alignment. *Journal of Consumer Psychology, 17,* 118–127.

Johnson, H. M., & Seifert, C. M. (1994). Sources of the continued influence effect: When misinformation in memory affects later inferences. *Journal of Experimental Psychology. Learning, Memory, and Cognition, 20,* 1420–1436.

Johnson, M. K., Hashtroudi, S., & Lindsay, D. S. (1993). Source monitoring. *Psychological Bulletin, 114,* 3–28.

Johnson, T. J., Bichard, S. L., & Zhang, W. (2009). Communication communities or "cyberghettos?": A path analysis model examining factors that explain selective exposure to blogs. *Journal of Computer-Mediated Communication, 15,* 60–82.

Jonas, E., Graupmann, V., & Frey, D. (2006). The influence of mood on the search for supporting versus conflicting information: Dissonance reduction as a means of mood regulation? *Personality and Social Psychology Bulletin, 32,* 3–15.

Kendeou, P., & van den Broek, P. (2007). The effects of prior knowledge and text structure on comprehension processes during reading of scientific texts. *Memory & Cognition, 35,* 1567–1577.

Kowalski, P., & Taylor, A. K. (2009). The effect of refuting misconceptions in the introductory psychology class. *Teaching of Psychology, 36,* 153–159.

Kuhn, D., & Crowell, A. (2011). Dialogic argumentation as a vehicle for developing young adolescents' thinking. *Psychological Science, 22,* 545–552.

Kunda, Z. (1990). The case for motivated reasoning. *Psychological Bulletin, 108,* 480–498.

Levitan, L. C., & Visser, P. S. (2008). The impact of the social context on resistance to persuasion: Effortful versus effortless responses to counter-attitudinal information. *Journal of Experimental Social Psychology, 44,* 640–649.

Lewandowsky, S., Ecker, U. K. H., Seifert, C. M., Schwarz, N., & Cook, J. (2012). Misinformation and its correction: Continued influence and successful debiasing. *Psychological Science in the Public Interest, 13,* 106–131.

Lewandowsky, S., Stritzke, W. G. K., Oberauer, K., & Morales, M. (2005). Memory for fact, fiction, and misinformation: The Iraq War 2003. *Psychological Science, 16,* 190–195.

Lewandowsky, S., Stritzke, W. G. K., Oberauer, K., & Morales, M. (2009). Misinformation and the "War on Terror": When memory turns fiction into fact. In W. G. K. Stritzke, S. Lewandowsky, D. Denemark, J. Clare, & F. Morgan (Eds.), *Terrorism and torture: An interdisciplinary perspective* (pp. 179–203). Cambridge, England: Cambridge University Press.

Lindsay, D. S., & Johnson, M. K. (1989). The eyewitness suggestibility effect and memory for source. *Memory & Cognition, 17,* 349–358.

Loftus, E. F., & Hoffman, H. G. (1989). Misinformation and memory: The creation of new memories. *Journal of Experimental Psychology. General, 118,* 100–104.

Loftus, E. F., & Palmer, J. C. (1974). Reconstruction of automobile destruction: An example of the interaction between language and memory. *Journal of Verbal Learning and Verbal Behavior, 13,* 585–589.

Lombrozo, T. (2007). Simplicity and probability in causal explanation. *Cognitive Psychology, 55,* 232–257.

Madsen, K. M., Anders, H., Vestergaard, M., Schendel, D., Wohlfart, J., Thorsen, P., et al. (2002). A population based study of measles, mumps and rubella vaccination and autism. *New England Journal of Medicine, 347,* 1477–1482.

Manson, L., Gava, M., & Boldrin, A. (2008). On warm conceptual change: The interplay of text, epistemological beliefs and topic interest. *Journal of Educational Psychology, 100,* 291–309.

McCarthy, J. (2012, March 9). MMR doctor exonerated—Who's guilty now? *Generation Rescue.* Retrieved from http://www.generationrescue.org/latest-news/jenny-mccarthy/mmr-doctor-exonerated-who-s-guilty-now/

McCrudden, M. T. (2012). Readers' use of online discrepancy resolution strategies. *Discourse Processes, 49,* 107–136.

McCrudden, M. T., & Kendeou, P. (2014). Exploring the link between cognitive processes and learning from refutational text. *Journal of Research in Reading, 37*, S116–140.

Moons, W. G., Mackie, D. M., & Garcia-Marques, T. (2009). The impact of repetition-induced familiarity on agreement with weak and strong arguments. *Journal of Personality and Social Psychology, 96*, 32–44.

Munro, G. D. (2010). The scientific impotence excuse: Discounting belief-threatening scientific abstracts. *Journal of Applied Social Psychology, 40*, 579–600.

Nickerson, R. S. (1998). Confirmation bias: A ubiquitous phenomenon in many guises. *Review of General Psychology, 2*, 175–220.

Nyhan, B., & Reifler, J. (2010). When corrections fail: The persistence of political misperceptions. *Political Behavior, 32*, 303–330.

Oberauer, K., & Vockenberg, K. (2009). Updating of working memory: Lingering bindings. *Quarterly Journal of Experimental Psychology, 62*, 967–987.

Okado, Y., & Stark, C. (2003). Neural processing associated with true and false memory retrieval. *Cognitive, Affective & Behavioral Neuroscience, 3*, 323–334.

Osborne, J. (2010). Arguing to learn in science: The role of collaborative, critical discourse. *Science, 328*, 463–466.

Ost, J., Granhag, P.-A., Udell, J., & Roos af Hjelmsäter, E. (2008). Familiarity breeds distortion: The effects of media exposure on false reports concerning media coverage of the terrorist attacks in London on 7 July 2005. *Memory, 16*, 76–85.

Ozubko, J. D., & Fugelsang, J. (2011). Remembering makes evidence compelling: Retrieval from memory can give rise to the illusion of truth. *Journal of Experimental Psychology. Learning, Memory, and Cognition, 37*, 270–276.

Posner, G. J., Strike, K. A., Hewson, P. W., & Gertzog, W. A. (1982). Accommodation of a scientific conception: Towards a theory of conceptual change. *Science Education, 66*, 211–227.

Prasad, M., Perrin, A. J., Bezila, K., Hoffman, S. G., Kindleberger, K., Manturuk, K., et al. (2009). "There must be a reason": Osama, Saddam, and inferred justification. *Sociological Inquiry, 79*, 142–162.

Prull, M. W., Dawes, L. L. C., Martin, A. M., III, Rosenberg, H. F., & Light, L. L. (2006). Recollection and familiarity in recognition memory: Adult age differences and neuropsychological test correlates. *Psychology and Aging, 21*, 107–118.

Rapp, D. N., & Kendeou, P. (2007). Revisiting what readers know: Updating text representations during narrative comprehension. *Memory & Cognition, 35*, 2019–2032.

Rapp, D. N., & Kendeou, P. (2009). Noticing and revising discrepancies as texts unfold. *Discourse Processes, 46*, 1–24.

Reder, L. M., Angstadt, P., Cary, M., Erickson, M. A., & Ayers, M. S. (2002). A reexamination of stimulus-frequency effects in recognition: Two mirrors for low- and high-frequency pseudowords. *Journal of Experimental Psychology. Learning, Memory, and Cognition, 28*, 138–152.

Reder, L. M., Nhouyvanisvong, A., Schunn, C. D., Ayers, M. S., Angstadt, P., & Hiraki, K. (2000). A mechanistic account of the mirror effect for word frequency: A computational model of remember–know judgments in a continuous recognition paradigm. *Journal of Experimental Psychology. Learning, Memory, and Cognition, 26*, 294–320.

Redlawsk, D. P. (2002). Hot cognition or cool consideration? Testing the effects of motivated reasoning on political decision making. *Journal of Politics, 64*, 1021–1044.

Richter, T., Schroeder, S., & Wöhrmann, B. (2009). You don't have to believe everything you read: Background knowledge permits fast and efficient validation of information. *Journal of Personality and Social Psychology, 96*, 538–558.

Roediger, H. L., III, & McDermott, K. B. (1995). Creating false memories: Remembering words not presented in lists. *Journal of Experimental Psychology. Learning, Memory, and Cognition, 21*, 803–814.

Ruffman, T., Rustin, C., Garnham, W., & Parkin, A. J. (2001). Source monitoring and false memories in children: Relation to certainty and executive functioning. *Journal of Experimental Child Psychology, 80*, 95–111.

Saucier, D. A., & Webster, R. J. (2010). Social vigilantism: Measuring individual differences in belief superiority and resistance to persuasion. *Personality and Social Psychology Bulletin, 36*, 19–32.

Schacter, D. L., Norman, K. A., & Koutstaal, W. (1998). The cognitive neuroscience of constructive memory. *Annual Review of Psychology, 49*, 289–318.

Schwarz, N., Sanna, L. J., Skurnik, I., & Yoon, C. (2007). Metacognitive experiences and the intricacies of setting people straight: Implications for debiasing and public information campaigns. *Advances in Experimental Social Psychology, 39*, 127–161.

Sherman, D. K., & Cohen, G. L. (2006). The psychology of self-defense: Self-affirmation theory. *Advances in Experimental Social Psychology, 38*, 183–242.

Singh, S., Kristensen, L., & Villaseñor, E. (2009). Overcoming skepticism towards cause related claims: The case of Norway. *International Marketing Review, 26*, 312–326.

Skurnik, I., Yoon, C., Park, D. C., & Schwarz, N. (2005). How warnings about false claims become recommendations. *Journal of Consumer Research, 31*, 713–724.

Skurnik, I., Yoon, C., & Schwarz, N. (2007). *Education about flu can reduce intentions to get a vaccination.* Unpublished manuscript.

Smith, A., & Yarwood, J. (2007). Tracking mothers' attitudes to MMR immunisation 1996–2006. *Vaccine, 25*, 3996–4002.

Spencer, W. D., & Raz, N. (1995). Differential effects of aging on memory for content and context: A meta-analysis. *Psychology and Aging, 10*, 527–539.

ten Dam, G., & Volman, M. (2004). Critical thinking as a citizenship competence: Teaching strategies. *Learning and Instruction, 14*, 359–379.

Troyer, A. K., & Craik, F. I. M. (2000). The effect of divided attention on memory for items and their context. *Canadian Journal of Experimental Psychology, 54*, 161–170.

van den Broek, P., & Kendeou, P. (2008). Cognitive processes in comprehension of science texts: The role of co-activation in confronting misconceptions. *Applied Cognitive Psychology, 22*, 335–351.

van Oostendorp, H., & Bonebakker, C. (1999). Difficulties in updating mental representations during reading news reports. In H. van Oostendorp & S. R. Goldman (Eds.), *The construction of mental representations during reading* (pp. 319–339). Mahwah, NJ: Lawrence Erlbaum Associates.

Verkoeijen, P. P. J. L., Rikers, R. M. J. P., & Schmidt, H. G. (2004). Detrimental influence of contextual change on spacing effects in free recall. *Journal of Experimental Psychology. Learning, Memory, and Cognition, 30*, 796–800.

Wakefield, A., Murch, S. H., Anthony, A., Linnell, J., Casson, D. M., Malik, M., et al. (1998). Ileal-lymphoid-nodular hyperplasia, non-specific colitis, and pervasive developmental disorder in children. [retracted paper]. *Lancet, 351*, 637–641.

Weaver, K., Garcia, S. M., Schwarz, N., & Miller, D. T. (2007). Inferring the popularity of an opinion from its familiarity: A repetitive voice can sound like a chorus. *Journal of Personality and Social Psychology, 92*, 821–833.

Wiersema, D. V., van Harreveld, F., & van der Pligt, J. (2012). Shut your eyes and think of something else: Self-esteem and avoidance when dealing with counter-attitudinal information. *Social Cognition, 30*, 323–334.

Wilkes, A. L., & Leatherbarrow, M. (1988). Editing episodic memory following the identification of error. *Quarterly Journal of Experimental Psychology: Human Experimental Psychology, 52A*, 165–183.

Wilson, E. A. H., & Park, D. C. (2008). A case for clarity in the writing of health statements. *Patient Education and Counseling, 72*, 330–335.

Wilson, E. A. H., & Wolf, M. S. (2009). Working memory and the design of health materials: A cognitive factors perspective. *Patient Education and Counseling, 74*, 318–322.

Zaragoza, M. S., & Lane, S. M. (1994). Source misattributions and the suggestibility of eyewitness memory. *Journal of Experimental Psychology. Learning, Memory, and Cognition, 20*, 934–945.

Zimmer, H. D., & Ecker, U. K. H. (2010). Remembering perceptual features unequally bound in object and episodic tokens: Neural mechanisms and their electrophysiological correlates. *Neuroscience and Biobehavioral Reviews, 34*, 1066–1079.

3   The Continued Influence Effect: The Persistence of Misinformation in Memory and Reasoning Following Correction

Colleen M. Seifert

I can still recall the event that brought the Continued Influence Effect to my attention:

One cold December day, I spent a lunch hour at the local college sportswear store buying sweatshirts as holiday gifts for my many nephews. At the end of the workday, I returned to my car, and was startled to find the bag of shirts missing. Living in a small college town, I always left my car unlocked and never experienced a problem. Shook up, I filed a report with the university police, and I sent an email to warn my colleagues about "How the Grinch Stole Christmas." I cautioned them not to leave their vehicles unlocked in the university parking lot.

The next day, I returned to the store and approached the same clerk behind the counter to tell her what had happened. "There you are!" the clerk immediately said, handing over a large bag, "You forgot your purchases yesterday!" Of course, I let everyone know that the missing bag had been my error. But the next day, when I drove to work and got out of my car, I locked the door behind me—for the first time ever.

Now, I knew for certain that there had been no theft from my car, and I certainly remembered that fact accurately! But the experience had "registered" in my mind, and when I left my car again, the world now seemed a more dangerous place. My judgment about whether I needed to lock my car was changed by information that I knew to be completely *untrue*. This exemplifies an interesting cognitive phenomenon: Misinformation in memory can continue to affect later judgments, an effect we labeled the continued influence effect (CIE) (Johnson & Seifert, 1994).

The Continued Influence Effect

Clearly, we know better than to use false information in our current reasoning. But when it happened to me, I discovered that psychologists had already demonstrated it in the laboratory. In several experiments, Wilkes and Leatherbarrow (1988; also see Wilkes & Reynolds, 1999) introduced readers to a series of short statements described as "on the scene" news updates about a fire in a paper warehouse (see appendix A). The fifth message in the series referred to "cans of oil paint and gas cylinders" that had been stored in a room where the fire had started. Other messages mentioned the presence of "oily smoke and sheets of flames," explosions, and toxic fumes found by firefighters. Then, the eleventh message stated that "the closet reportedly containing cans of paint and gas cylinders had actually been empty before the fire," and the story ended.

The participants provided a summary of the messages and, after a short (10-minute) distractor task, answered a series of questions about the account. Some questions were factual ("What business was the firm in?"), and some required making inferences beyond the given information ("What was a possible cause of the toxic fumes?") (see appendix B). Readers correctly recalled the facts and the correction message. However, those who saw the misinformation were much more likely to make references to it in their answers as compared to those who never saw a message about it. And those who saw the correction did not differ from those who never saw a correction in the numbers of responses they gave related to the misinformation (Wilkes & Leatherbarrow, 1988)! Both groups frequently referred to the volatile materials as potential sources for toxic fumes, explosions, and denying insurance claims for the fire. Even though readers recalled the correction, they still referred to the oil paint and gas cylinders as central elements in the story.

Further research has consistently found that retractions rarely, if ever, have the intended effect of eliminating any reliance on misinformation, even when people believe, understand, and later remember the correction (e.g., Ecker, Lewandowsky, & Tang, 2010; Fein, McCloskey, & Tomlinson, 1997; Gilbert, Krull, & Malone, 1990; Gilbert, Tafarodi, & Malone, 1993; Johnson & Seifert, 1998, 1999; Schul & Burnstein, 1985; Schul & Mazursky, 1990; van Oostendorp, 1996; van Oostendorp & Bonebakker, 1999; Wegner, Coulton, & Wenzlaff, 1985; Wyer & Unverzagt, 1985; Wilkes & Leatherbarrow, 1988; Wilkes & Reynolds, 1999). In fact, a correction will at most reduce the number of references to misinformation by half (Ecker, Lewandowsky, & Apai, 2011; Ecker, Lewandowsky, Swire, & Chang, 2011); in some studies, correction did not reduce reliance on misinformation at all (e.g., Johnson & Seifert, 1994). Because people acknowledge and remember the correction, and yet continue to rely on misinformation in their reasoning, the CIE is a matter of considerable importance.

Editing Misinformation in Memory

Wilkes and Leatherbarrow (1988) attributed the CIE to a failure to edit inferences made while reading the story. For example, when message 8 in a sequence mentioned toxic fumes, the reader may infer that the fumes came from the gas cylinders. Then, when the correction appeared later, the fact of the absence of the cylinders is added into memory while the inferences based on the volatile materials are left intact. As a result, later questions may bring these earlier inferences still in memory to mind. The editing hypothesis suggests we create new inferences using the information *before* it is corrected and then remember these inferences later (Hastie & Park, 1986; Christiaansen & Ochalek, 1983; McKoon & Ratcliff, 1992). While the correction addresses the specific information about the room contents, it may not provide a means to correct all of the inferences made using that information. This suggests the problem lies in successfully updating all related information in memory when a correction is presented. If true, the source of the influence of misinformation may be the memories generated before correction occurs rather than after (Hertel, 1982).

To test whether this "failure to edit" hypothesis could account for the use of misinformation, we changed the message sequence so that the correction occurred *immediately* after the information was introduced (Johnson & Seifert, 1994). In this sequence, there is little opportunity to use the information before you know it is incorrect. By the time you read about toxic fumes and explosions, you already know that the paint cans and gas cylinders were not in the storage room. This would limit the likelihood of using the misinformation because you would already know it is incorrect when the potentially related information is presented later in the sequence. In this study, we included the original paradigm, in which the correction was delayed until Message 11, and a version in which the correction was immediate. We also included a control condition in which no correction was ever presented. In addition, we altered the correction message to emphasize that the volatile materials had never been present: "It stated that there were no cans of paint or gas cylinders in the closet that had reportedly contained them; the closet had actually been empty before the fire."

A coder blind to the experimental conditions scored each summary sheet and open-ended questionnaire. The measures scored included a *thematic-inference* measure and a *direct-reference* measure. The *thematic-inference* measure consisted of "volatile materials" theme responses made on the ten inference questions. These were responses consistent with believing that the warehouse *had* contained carelessly stored volatile materials that caused or contributed to the fire. This theme encompassed references using key words from the discredited message (e.g., *oil, paint, gas(es), cans,* or *cylinders*), mentions of the closet itself without indications that it was empty, and attributions of carelessness or negligence (see table 3.1 for sample answers consistent with the negligence theme). For readers who received no information about the volatile materials, most

Table 3.1
Sample volatile materials theme answers to inference questions (Johnson & Seifert, 1994)

Q: What was the possible cause of the toxic fumes?
A: Burning paint.
Q: Why do you think the fire was particularly intense?
A: Oil fires are hard to put out.
Q: For what reason might an insurance claim be refused?
A: Because flammable items were not kept in a safe place.

answers would likely reflect themes other than these materials, such as intentional setting of the fire, and paper stored at the warehouse.

The *direct-reference* measure counted all direct and uncontroverted references to the volatile materials themselves (paint cans or gas cylinders) over all measures—in the free recall, in answers to fact questions, or in answers to the inference questions. Story, fact, and correction recall were also assessed in the summary or the open-ended questionnaire.

For all of our experiments, the groups did not differ in their summaries of the reports nor in their memory for the facts presented. Consistently, over 80% of those who saw the correction accurately reported it in their summaries. Omitting individuals who did not report it had no effect on the pattern of observed results. Only a small number (8%) of readers who saw a correction named the volatile materials as the direct "cause" of the fire, compared with 5% of the no-reference control readers. Thus, those who saw the correction did accept it and excluded the volatile materials as the fire's direct cause. But did they avoid referencing them as a potential cause for the fire's features on the inference questions?

When we examined readers' responses on those questions, what we found was startling: Providing an immediate correction did not reduce references to the misinformation at test time! (See figure 3.1.)

Whether the information was immediately followed by the correction, or whether it appeared at the end of the story, readers still used the misinformation to answer

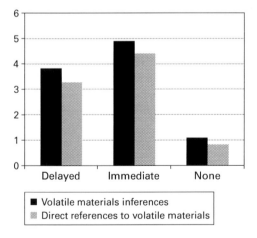

Figure 3.1
Average number of inferences and direct mentions of the misinformation in three reading groups: one in which the correction appeared after a delay, one in which the correction followed immediately, and one in which no correction appeared (from Johnson & Seifert, 1994).

Table 3.2
Examples from three participants' open-ended questionnaires

Participant A:
11. What was the possible cause of the toxic fumes? *"Burning paint...."*
21. What was the point of the second message from the police chief? *"That the storage room didn't have any gas or paint, but was empty."*

Participant B:
13. What was the possible cause of the toxic fumes? *"The paint and gas cylinders...."*
21. What was the point of the second message from the police? *"That the storage room was empty, and didn't have any gas or paint cans."*

Participant C:
12. For what reason might an insurance claim be refused? *"Because of the oil paint and the pressurized gas cylinders that were in the closet...."*
21. What was the point of the second message from the police? *"To state that the gas cylinders and the oil paint cans were not in the closet."*

---

questions about the fire's qualities. This produced puzzling protocols in which a reader would write contradictory information on the same page of questions (see table 3.2).

The readers with the immediate correction remembered the correction, and they had received it well before they heard anything about toxic fumes; however, they "fell back on" the misinformation when they needed it at the time of questioning. In our study, 90% of the readers who saw the correction referred to volatile materials in their answers while only 20% of the control group did so (Johnson & Seifert, 1994). Almost all readers who saw the message about the volatile materials referred to them in their responses about possible explosions, fumes, intensity of the fire, or insurance claims, whether or not they saw the correction. And they were as equally likely to refer to the volatile materials as those who never saw a correction at all! Clearly, the misinformation was correctly perceived to be wrong, but it continued to influence responses well *after* the correction had occurred (Wilkes & Reynolds, 1999).

Availability of Misinformation in Memory

It seems clear readers in these studies know the information is not correct; however, they also know the information itself! In that sense, they are not the same as readers who never see the message about the volatile materials. So perhaps the mere mention of the volatile materials increases their availability in memory, resulting in an increased use when answering questions about the account. Some evidence for this hypothesis is that automatic memory activation of misinformation continues whenever it is referred to, even after a clear correction. For example, after reading, "John played hockey for New York. Actually, he played for Boston," reading "the team" results in both cities' becoming active in memory (Johnson & Seifert, 1998). If both a link to the misinformation and a link to the correct information remain in memory, both may be activated in later processing, and as a result, the misinformation may influence inferences.

To investigate, we introduced the same "volatile materials" content to see if its mere presence in memory motivated readers to use it (Johnson & Seifert, 1994). In one condition, a message referred to "a store across the street selling oil paint and gas cylinders." In this way, the *idea* of volatile materials was presented in the story, but not placed at the scene of the fire. The intention was to make the information available in memory, potentially exerting an influence on judgments (Tversky & Kahneman, 1973). In a second condition, no mention was made of volatile materials, but a distractor task included a word completion task in which "oil paint" and "gas" were answers. This distractor task provided semantic priming of the volatile materials outside of the story context completely. And again, a group was included in which the initial message about the volatile materials was presented with no correction, and a correction group saw the message stating the volatile materials were not in the closet.

The results from the inference questions replicated the CIE again, as the correction group did not differ from the no-correction group in the number of references made to volatile materials in their responses (see figure 3.2).

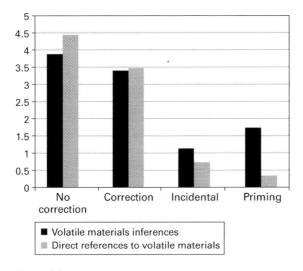

Figure 3.2
Number of inferences and direct references to the misinformation in reading groups provided with no correction, a correction, an incidental reference to the information (about volatile materials not on the premises), or priming of "gas" and "oil" terms during a word completion distractor task (from Johnson & Seifert, 1994).

However, the two groups who saw the volatile materials mentioned incidentally in the story or distractor task showed no effect of the materials on readers' responses. Making the idea of volatile materials more available in memory through a distractor task or through tangential mention in the messages resulted in very few mentions of the volatile materials. We thought it might be more impactful if readers had the opportunity to think about possible causes for warehouse fires, potentially helping them to replace the volatile materials with alternative features. In another study, we asked readers in the correction condition to generate their own ideas for potential causes of the warehouse fire (Johnson & Seifert, 1999). While they were successful in doing so, this had no impact on their answers to the questions. They still fell back on the corrected misinformation when asked about the features of the fire in the story they read. This suggests that the mere presence or activation of the concept of volatile materials does not result in any influence. Rather, the volatile materials had to be *part of the story line* in order to show up in answers to questions about the fire.

Wilkes and Leatherbarrow (1988) had noted that the centrality of the misinformation is important; for example, when tied to the origin of the fire, the volatile materials affected later inferences much more than when they appeared in a noncentral role. Wilkes and Reynolds (1999) manipulated the number of fire features related to the misinformation and found that even just *one* unaccounted for feature resulted in use of the corrected information. This suggested that the corrected misinformation could provide a compelling explanation for a causal "gap" in the story. Explosions, toxic fumes, and intense heat are exceptional features of a fire, and they require some explanation for their presence. In the control version of the story, the volatile materials are never mentioned, so no explanation that would account for these features is provided. In this control condition, readers come up with some answers to the inference questions despite the lack of specifics to help. For example, when asked what might have caused the toxic fumes, one reader in the control condition suggested "toner cartridges from a printer" might be the source. Thus, from the control conditions, it is possible to imagine explanations for these unusual fire features in the absence of hearing about the volatile materials.

However, in the versions in which the volatile materials are introduced, they provide a very good explanation that fits these fire features: exploding gas cylinders, toxic fumes from burning oil paint, and intense heat from the volatile materials not usually found in a warehouse. Once exposed to the idea of the volatile materials as a source for this particular fire, it is apparently very difficult for readers to ignore them when addressing the fire's features. Perhaps readers fall back on the volatile materials because they are such good answers for the inference questions posed. If they were indeed in the closet, they would well account for the fire's toxic fumes, explosions, and intense heat. After the correction, the reader believes and remembers that they were not in the closet. Nevertheless, perhaps the idea of the volatile materials as a source is simply "too good *not* to be true."

The Causal Role of Misinformation

Have you ever heard a story so good, it *should* be true? Suppose that you are a registered Republican voter in the United States, and you very much wish that a contending Democratic candidate for president could be taken out of the race. Then, you read news reports that this candidate is not a U.S. citizen by birth and is therefore ineligible to run. Problem solved! This is such good news, as it really heads off a presidency you don't want to see, and then—oops—sources, increasingly reliable ones, report that the candidate has a U.S. birth certificate. In this case, the story you heard was so good (in your eyes) that it really *should* be true—so you may continue to treasure the thought even as events play out that demonstrate it is not true. If only!

This scenario may illustrate some of what is going on in the continued influence of misinformation. In some settings, information may provide a needed explanation, or fill a causal gap, that is left hanging when the information is corrected (O'Brien & Myers, 1987). Going back to the warehouse fire: If only the volatile materials *had* been in that closet, then these questions would all have answers. Now that it is clear they were not there, the reader is left with questions needing answers.

This suggests that one way to avoid the CIE is to provide an alternative. What if new, different information is introduced that fills the causal gap left hanging by the correction? Perhaps then, the reader will leave the misinformation behind and grasp the new information as the needed explanation. We conducted a further study to test this causal alternative hypothesis. After the correction, a later message introduced evidence of "gasoline-soaked rags near where the bales of paper had been stored," and "empty steel drums of a suspicious nature." This suggests an alternative source for the fire—namely, arson using gasoline. This scenario provides a potential explanation for the fire features such as explosions and is separate from the volatile materials correction. In this study, groups receiving the information about the volatile materials without a correction and with a correction were compared to a group who also saw the correction and then the arson materials and to a group reading about the arson materials alone. However, the results again replicated the CIE, with the no-correction and correction groups referring to the volatile materials in their responses (see figure 3.3).

However, it also showed, for the first time, a significant reduction in references to the volatile materials if the arson materials were included in a later message. These readers referred to the volatile materials as infrequently as readers who only saw the arson materials and never saw the paint and gas cylinders. When a causal account could be constructed with the arson materials, it seemed to obviate the need for readers

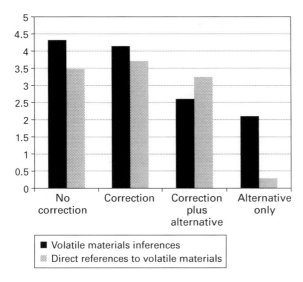

Figure 3.3
Average number of inferences and direct references to the misinformation in the reading groups that never saw a correction, saw the correction only, saw the correction plus an alternative cause, and saw only the alternative (from Johnson & Seifert, 1994).

to fall back on the corrected volatile materials. With a causal alternative, readers finally avoided references to the corrected information.

Providing alternative information that fills the causal gap appears to be an effective method for avoiding the future use of corrected information. Readers were finally able to "let go" of the good explanation in the corrected information and latch onto the equally useful alternative provided. Apparently, when pushed to account for causal gaps in the story, readers fell back on even discredited information when it provided a good account. Replacing the corrected information with a good alternative allowed readers to avoid using the corrected information.

Internal coherence plays a role in truth assessments (Johnson-Laird, 2012; Pennington & Hastie, 1993a, b; Ross, Lepper, & Hubbard, 1975), so a causal gap may motivate the use of the misinformation in spite of the retraction (e.g., "It wasn't the oil and gas, but what else could it be?"). Providing an alternative explanation of the event can fill the gap left behind by retracting misinformation. Similarly, Tenney, Cleary, and Spellman (2009) found that the suggestion of a plausible alternative was successful in reducing "guilty" verdicts (e.g., "The initial suspect may not be guilty as there is an alternative suspect"). However, if the replacement message instead suggested "evidence of water-soaked rags stored in the closet," this alternative seems unlikely to explain the features of the fire; as a consequence, subjects may again be forced to fall back on the misinformation despite the alternative presented.

A puzzling part of this finding is the need to see the causal alternative appear in the story itself. After all, the inference questions were intentionally left open-ended, asking for "what may have" caused explosions, and "possible" reasons insurance claims might be denied. One might generate potential causal explanations of one's own; indeed, there is no need to include only accurate explanations. In the control condition where no explanations for the fire's features are offered, readers sometimes generated their own explanations, such as proposing that toner cartridges for printers may be a potential cause. One might imagine many things in a warehouse (cleaning supplies, bales of paper) that may affect a fire, and one could hypothesize objects even if not likely to be there (even oil paint and gas cylinders). However, readers don't appear to "make up" their own story when an explanation is absent. The idea of oil paint as a cause, if generated by the reader, appears to be less plausible than if mentioned, and corrected, in the story. Even when asked to think about other potential causes of the fire, this activity did not lessen readers' use of the phantom volatile materials (Johnson & Seifert, 1999). There may be some limitation or bias in our thinking about causes that are not "officially" connected with story sources even when it is possible to generate them.

What Makes a Correction Effective?

Often, when attempting to correct misinformation, we don't yet have an alternative to offer. We may know, for example, that a cause is ruled out, as in the warehouse fire scenario, but be left without new information about a different cause: The true cause may be unknown. In the absence of alternatives, is there any way to reduce the use of misinformation?

Correction takes place in a context of communication that includes language conventions, such as offering information believed to be true (maxim of quality) and relevant (maxim of relation) (Grice, 1975). Corrections may be particularly difficult to understand because they seem to violate these conversational conventions (Clark, Schreuder, & Buttrick, 1983). If the correction is truthful, why would a well-intentioned source have presented the misinformation? And if the earlier information is believed to be accurate, how can the correction also be accepted as accurate? Grice's (1975) account of conversational logic suggests that corrections *should* pose problems in interpretation. In particular, two maxims of communication are important in making corrections.

First, conversational contributions are assumed to be *relevant* to the topic under discussion. For corrections, this implies that both the original information and its correction are relevant to the topic. However, since the content of the two are directly contradictory, resolving an interpretation is problematic.

Second, statements are assumed to have informational *quality*. Listeners assume that speakers only provide information when they have good reason to believe it is true

(Haviland & Clark, 1974). In the case of correction, the maxim of quality would imply that the speaker must have had good reason for believing that both the original information and its subsequent correction were true and accurate. Corrections that simply negate the misinformation by saying it is not true do not address these two assumptions. This suggests that corrections addressing only the literal content and not these conventions may be difficult for the reader to interpret (Krosnick, Li, & Lehman, 1990; Schwarz, 1996; Golding, Fowler, Long, & Latta, 1990).

To investigate the comprehension of corrections, we compared several types of corrections intended to minimize the continued influence of misinformation (Seifert, 2002). Using the same warehouse fire paradigm, we altered the correction to address these aspects of conversational convention. In one condition, we explained why the misinformation was no longer *relevant* ("the closet had been empty because a trucker's strike had interfered with an anticipated delivery of paint and gas"). This explains why the information (that a delivery was expected) was initially presented as relevant. In a *quality* condition, we suggested the original information had, outside of the speaker's knowledge, been of poor quality ("the closet contained cans of coffee and soda rather than cans of paint and gas"). This correction explains how the presentation of misinformation may have been made in error. If corrections address these conventions, readers may show less influence from the misinformation.

Another approach to improving the correction message may be to rule out alternative interpretations that readers may generate when trying to reconcile the two statements. For example, readers might resolve the contradiction by inferring that volatile materials were present *somewhere else* on the premises and so are still available to play a role in the fire. This reasoning goes beyond what was stated in the text, so it can be considered part of the CIE. Enhancing the correction statement may be helpful in ruling out alternative accounts not intended by the correction. Finally, we included an *enhanced correction* that asserted "no paint or gas had ever been stored on the premises." Elaborating on the correction may make it easier to avoid the *somewhere else* interpretation but may not help to resolve the contradiction.

As in earlier studies, we observed no differences among the groups for the summary reports or the factual questions, and almost all participants who saw a correction reported it accurately. The written protocols were scored for direct references to the volatile materials, and the results are shown in figure 3.4. Despite the presence of the enhanced information in the corrections, 67% of those who saw them made at least one direct, uncontroverted reference to the volatile materials in their responses.

The no-correction condition resulted in significantly more references to the volatile materials than were observed in the two correction conditions; the two correction conditions resulted in significantly more references than in the two explanatory correction conditions; and the two explanatory correction conditions resulted in significantly more references than the no-information condition. The corrections that attempted

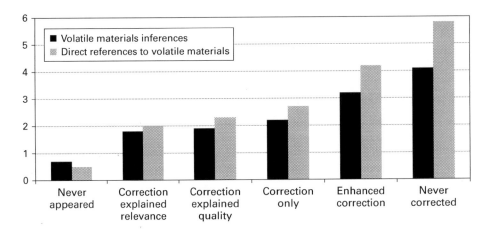

Figure 3.4

Average number of inferences and direct references to volatile materials made by participants as a function of correction type (Seifert, 2002).

to explain the circumstances leading to the misinformation—addressing the relevance or the quality of the initial information—showed only a small (marginally significant) improvement as compared to the standard correction. This suggests that adding explanations as to why a correction was necessary can reduce the use of misinformation. However, even with the explanations, readers who saw corrections still made significantly more inferences and direct references to the volatile materials than did readers who never saw them reported.

The enhanced correction was intended to cut off any attempt to resolve the contradiction by imagining the presence of the volatile materials in some *other* place on the premises. However, the enhanced correction condition appeared to backfire, leading to *more* inferences as compared to the number produced in the simple correction group. If potential ambiguity about the correction was the cause of the CIE, the enhanced correction should have been more successful; however, adding this clarification appeared to make readers even less likely to incorporate the correction into their responses.

In addition, the nature of the correction may affect whether and how subjects express their uncertainty about the misinformation. For example, a subject who said, "*It seems* that there was paint in the closet" would convey more uncertainty than one who said, "There was paint in the closet." To examine differences in uncertainty, we recoded the inferences using the volatile materials as "unhedged" or "hedged." "Hedged" counted all inferences related to the volatile materials that were couched in terms of uncertainty (e.g., "*if* there was paint," "*supposedly* there were explosives in the closet") or that suggested a combination of elements from the original and corrected information (e.g., "gas was *put back* into the closet before the fire"). Inferences using the volatile materials

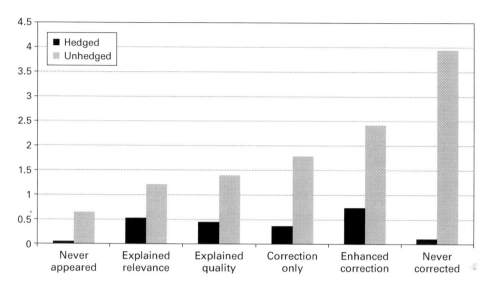

Figure 3.5
Average number of misinformation inferences categorized as "hedged" and "unhedged" as a function of correction type (Seifert, 2002).

without equivocation (unhedged) and those expressing uncertainty about their presence (hedged) were counted for each reader and then averaged by condition, as shown in figure 3.5. A high average count indicates that the readers in that condition made more inferences using the volatile materials.

All of the groups made more unhedged or direct inferences than "hedged" inferences. However, all four correction groups expressed more uncertainty in the form of more "hedged" inferences than did the two control groups. In the simple and enhanced correction conditions, unhedged inferences occurred significantly more often than they did in the no-reference control condition. The two explanation corrections and the enhanced correction groups produced a higher average of hedged responses than did the simple correction group, suggesting they may have incorporated the correction in their inferences by adding words that expressed uncertainty. That is, their use of the misinformation added more qualification.

These results suggest that the contents of a correction can affect how people think and talk about misinformation. Corrections that simply negate the information by saying it is not true are not effective in reducing references to the misinformation. Corrections that address *why* the update was necessary did impact the way readers discussed the corrected information in their reasoning. For the explanatory corrections that addressed the quality or relevance of the original information, references about the volatile materials were made with "hedges" ("If there were [sic] paint in the closet…")

and occurred less often. By addressing the nature of the contradiction between initial misinformation and its correction, the conditions that included explanations about relevance and quality successfully reduced the use of misinformation. Going beyond simple correction of the initial information helps readers to reconcile the contradiction and to adopt a more qualified form of reference to the misinformation. This is consistent with the idea that readers faced with corrections are sensitive to explanations for why the conflict occurred.

Though explanatory corrections show a lessening of the CIE, these readers still frequently referred to the misinformation. However, their references were also qualified with comments about its uncertain status. When readers were offered a suggested explanation with the correction, they rarely directly attributed the cause to the volatile materials without including some qualification. These subjects continued to speak of the discredited information, but in ways that did not literally conflict with the discrediting statement.

These findings are based on variations of a single story account, though an alternative story replicated the findings about the presence of an alternative cause with the correction (Johnson & Seifert, 1998). The CIE may only occur when corrections involve material that is causal in nature or are central to an event (van den Broek, 1990; Trabasso & van den Broek, 1985). Similarly, the CIE may depend upon the reader's assumptions about the validity of the information. It is important to establish that explanations of quality and relevance as pragmatic conventions are helpful in corrections in other types of accounts (Seifert, 2002). If so, corrections may be improved by including information that addresses their inherent contradiction in communication (Schwarz, 1996). Corrections are likely to require additional processing time and effort to integrate into an account (Christianson, Hollingworth, Halliwell, & Feirarra, 2001). This is because corrections are not solely informational but are also interpreted within a pragmatic context of conventions about when and how information is communicated (Grice, 1975). As a consequence, successful correction of misinformation must address not only the informational content but also the reader's experience of contradictory information. Addressing the pragmatics of communication may be key in maintaining the coherence of an account and, as a consequence, the perceived value of the information presented.

Reasoning with Misinformation

What if we could increase people's motivation to avoid the continued influence of misinformation? Of particular interest, jurors may be required to make a decision without regard to some information "stricken" from the official record of legal proceedings. For example, a juror may be instructed to ignore information already presented and not to use it in making a final verdict about a case. When individuals are informed that some information should be "stricken," to what extent, and under what circumstances, can they ignore or discount that information? Ideally, an individual should behave as if he or she had *never* heard the information. The legal system assumes this is what happens in that it routinely allows jurors to hear information that is later stricken. In this section of the chapter, I focus on how research on the CIE proves relevant and informative to work in legal settings.

Dodd and Bradshaw (1980) suggest that the reliability of the source may influence whether information is incorporated into memory. If the source is presumed to be biased, then the information may not be incorporated into memory for an event. However, in circumstances similar to the CIE, experimental studies have found that stricken information is still salient to participants at the time of decision (Carretta & Moreland, 1983). In some situations, people may see the need to correct their judgments; however, Wilson and Brekke (1994) propose that people are often inaccurate in judging whether they will be biased by misinformation and are frequently unwilling or unable to correct their judgments accurately as a result.

In a variety of experimental tasks, corrected information in memory has been shown to affect processing and later judgments in several ways. First, as in Johnson and Seifert's (1994) studies, if information is discredited and no alternative information is available, people will fall back on the original misinformation when seeking causal explanations for events. The misinformation retains explanatory power although it has been shown to be false. A second difficulty is that the mere suggestion of a concept leaves it highly accessible in memory and salient when explanations for subsequent information are sought (Wegner & Erber, 1992). Wegner, Wenzlaff, Kerker, and Beattie (1981) showed participants a newspaper headline reading, "Is Nixon a Crook?" The article later stated that Nixon was not a crook, yet the idea had been planted in the readers' minds, influencing their beliefs about Nixon. As Wegner (1994) reports, the admonition to not think about an idea (such as a white bear) is not sufficient to keep that idea from influencing the participant's thoughts; in fact, the admonition may make it more likely.

Another possibility is that the misinformation biases the interpretation of later information. Lord, Ross, and Lepper (1979) found that people tend to be "confirmation seeking" when testing their hypotheses about people and events in the world. If additional information consistent with the misinformation is presented, then it is more likely to be accepted as it fits in with the existing knowledge base (Anderson, Lepper, & Ross, 1980). Once misinformation is considered, people may be more likely to use that misinformation in subsequent reasoning. In a study by Ross, Lepper, Strack, and Steinmetz (1977), participants were presented with life events and asked to suggest potential antecedents or causes. Although participants were later informed that these events had never occurred, they still viewed the events that they had suggested as more likely to actually happen. These results suggest that the simple process of explaining an event increases its subjective likelihood for the perceiver.

Other factors may make CIE more evident in the courtroom. Sue, Smith, and Caldwell (1973) found that the biasing effect of inadmissible evidence is greatest when there is little other evidence on which to make a decision. When information is ambiguous or contradictory, as often occurs in legal cases, jurors may feel forced to make inferences in order to arrive at a judgment. When misinformation is presented as a part of an impoverished base of knowledge, and a lack of causal information is available, inappropriate inferences are almost certain to follow.

We might expect that explicit knowledge of the importance of corrections will motivate people to avoid the use of the information prior to correction. After all, the legal context clearly dictates what information is admissible as evidence. However, studies of judgment correction suggest that people may have naive theories about when their judgments are biased, but that avoiding bias requires warning (Petty & Wegener, 1993). In a study by Wegener and Petty (1995), individuals asked to correct for any bias that might have affected their judgments were successful in doing so while those not asked to correct for biases did not. Studies by Stapel, Martin, and Schwarz (1998) also found that subjects not warned of potential biases did not correct their judgments. As a result, stricken information may show less persistence in memory because jurors are explicitly instructed to ignore a piece of evidence and not to allow it to affect their decisions.

However, the legal context does offer strategic interventions with regard to jurors' use of corrected information. First, the proceedings are organized so as to immediately strike inadmissible evidence to prevent its further incorporation into a juror's representation of events. When Hatvany and Strack (1980) failed to find perseverance in mock juries' use of inadmissible evidence, they concluded that the rapid presentation of information, including an instruction to disregard some evidence, prevented participants from assimilating stricken information. Prior research has shown that when prevented from making elaborative inferences, participants do not use stricken information in making causal judgments (Wyer & Budesheim, 1987). The "trial schema" may thus successfully change the process of jurors' social judgments from that in other social judgment tasks where people may be less motivated to withhold judgments (Schul & Manzury, 1990).

However, other studies have shown that jurors do make use of stricken evidence. One factor that may encourage jurors to use stricken information is its diagnosticity in the case. In a "weak" prosecution case, the presentation of target information as inadmissible evidence has a significant effect on verdict decisions whereas it has less influence in a "strong" prosecution case (Carretta & Moreland, 1983; Sue, Smith, & Caldwell, 1973; Elliott, Farrington, & Manheimer, 1988). In another study, jurors who received proacquittal inadmissible evidence were less likely to convict than those who received either proconviction inadmissible evidence or no inadmissible evidence (Thompson, Fong, & Rosenhan, 1981). The type of information that is stricken may also influence use, as Loftus (1974) and Saunders, Vidmar, and Hewitt (1983) both found participants fail to disregard discredited eyewitness testimony; however, Weinberg and Baron (1982) found that jurors successfully disregard such testimony.

Given information that is diagnostic of a verdict, evidence suggests participants are reluctant to disregard it even when instructed to do so. For example, participants were found to be unable to disregard an illegally induced confession (Kassin & Sukel, 1997), hearsay (Schuller, 1995), illegally obtained evidence (Kassin & Sommers, 1997), or the prior record of the defendant (Pickel, 1995). In all of these cases, the information was stricken because it was not legal to use; however, it was also "factually" true. In contrast, mock jurors are successful in disregarding information from discredited or recanted testimony (Schul & Manzury, 1990; Hatvany & Strack, 1980; Kassin & Sommers, 1997; Elliott, et al., 1988; Weinberg & Baron, 1982). Perhaps jurors attend to stricken information if it conforms to the goal of finding the truth, rather than following the legal rules of procedure.

There is evidence that instructions asking individuals to disregard information are more or less attended to depending upon the reason given for the instruction. If information is false or irrelevant, it is more likely to be successfully disregarded; information identified as true, but "erroneously" presented, is more likely to be used (Golding & Hauselt, 1994; Golding, Fowler, Long, & Latta, 1990). Kassin & Sommers (1997) sought to establish whether mock jurors would selectively comply with instructions to disregard depending on whether the stricken evidence was identified as "illegally obtained," or simply "unreliable." The results indicated that the reliability of the stricken information was taken into account in participants' verdicts. However, the relationship between "unreliable" and "untrue" is not clear. Participants may have thought the target evidence was untrue information, completely fabricated, inaccurate, random, irrelevant, or nonexistent. From the explanation given for striking the information, it is difficult to determine the reason that participants chose to disregard it.

A Study of CIE in Legal Reasoning

Using a parallel paradigm from the CIE studies (Johnson & Seifert, 1994), we set out to determine if the legal context demonstrates the same effects seen in story comprehension (cf. Mosmann, 1998). Our hypothesis is that participants will intentionally use information in their decision making if they believe that it is true, demonstrating the CIE even in conditions in which they are explicitly warned not to use the corrected information. In addition, it may be possible to observe a CIE effect from stricken information on more indirect measures in addition to verdicts. Pennington and Hastie (1981, 1986, 1993a, b) provide a framework for understanding the potential for bias in jurors' decision making based on stricken information. Jurors may reason about evidence in order to construct a semantic representation with a subjective interpretation in the form of a "story," later used as a basis for a verdict. This story model predicts multiple opportunities for the indirect effects of misinformation to play a major role. In order to assess this possibility, stricken information will be identified as either true or false during the course of a trial, and consequences for the assessment of later evidence will then be measured.

In our study, people were presented with a short description of a crime and trial materials, including a one-page description of a crime, followed by one page of prosecution testimony and one page of defense testimony (appendix C; adapted from Sue, Smith, & Caldwell, 1973). Three versions of each case were created, including target evidence "from a wiretap." In the "Not Stricken" condition, the evidence was presented without objection. In two conditions, the defense objected to the admission of the wiretap evidence, and the judge instructed the jurors to disregard it. In the "Stricken & True" condition, the evidence was immediately stricken because it was illegally obtained, while in the "Stricken & False" condition, the evidence was immediately stricken because it was not the defendant's voice on the wiretap tape. In the "Not Presented" condition, the wiretap evidence did not appear. Following the case description, participants were asked to decide on a verdict and then to rate their beliefs about the defendant—for example, whether he displayed certain personality traits or performed certain actions. Another series of questions evaluated memory for details of the case. Finally, participants were asked to provide verdicts a second time because "people sometimes change their minds after reviewing the evidence."

When aware that discredited information may bias future judgments, people may or may not try to correct for this perceived bias, and they may be more or less accurate in doing so (Wilson & Brekke, 1994). Participants in the Stricken & False condition may be motivated to try to correct for the biasing effects of the stricken evidence either because they believe that it is not relevant to the judgment they are making or because they want to follow the judge's instructions to disregard the stricken evidence. Participants in the Stricken & True condition may believe that the stricken evidence is true and use it in decision making, or they may try to follow the judge's instructions and ignore the information. Test items were designed to assess whether participants attempted to disregard the information and how successful they were in doing so.

There are several alternative models of how participants may respond to the evidence presented. If participants simply follow instructions not to use stricken information, both stricken conditions should resemble the Not Presented condition, indicating that participants were successful in disregarding stricken evidence and behaving as though it had never been presented. A second possibility is that participants in the stricken conditions will simply ignore the instructions to disregard the stricken evidence, as in the CIE. Finally, participants may use the stricken information to the extent that they believe the evidence is true in the current case and would lead to a just outcome; if so, participants in the Stricken & True condition will give responses similar to the Not Stricken condition, and participants in the Stricken & False condition will give responses similar to participants in the Not Presented condition.

Three types of questions were constructed to assess participants' memory for and opinions regarding the defendant and the case presented. First, participants were asked to recall the case material in writing. Next, they selected a verdict: "Guilty beyond a reasonable doubt" or "Not Guilty." Next, participants were asked to read five scenarios with three interpretations to choose from, one consistent with belief in the defendant's guilt, one consistent with an "innocent" representation, and one suggested by the stricken information (see appendix D). Other questions elicited participants' beliefs about various interpretations of the evidence presented during the trial, as well as negative personality traits ascribed to the defendant—for example, "The gunpowder residue on Matthews' hand came from the gun he used while hunting with his son."

The recall test showed that participants tended to report case information consistent with their verdict. Participants rendering a guilty verdict reported significantly more proprosecution statements ($M = 0.75$, $SD = 0.329$) than those voting not guilty ($M = 0.12$, $SD = 0.248$), and significantly fewer prodefense statements as well ($M = 0.04$, $SD = 0.130$; not guilty: $M = 0.58$, $SD = 0.400$). Participants' summaries appeared to reflect their interpretations of the evidence and their belief in either the prosecution's or the defense's version of events.

The verdict results are shown in figure 3.6. The verdicts appear to best match a pattern where the jurors "follow the truth" and use stricken information if it results in a "just" outcome. Participants in the Stricken & True condition ignored the instructions

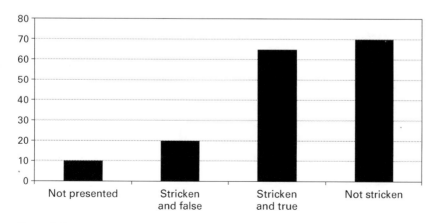

Figure 3.6
Proportion of guilty verdicts rendered by mock jurors as a function of participants' information condition.

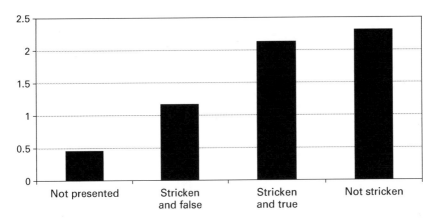

Figure 3.7
Scenario scores showing the average "stricken" interpretation choice as a function of participants' information condition.

to disregard the wiretap evidence and voted "guilty" in proportions similar to those in the Not Stricken condition. The Stricken & False group, on the other hand, is very close to the Not Presented group with respect to conviction rate.

There were no significant differences in conviction rates between the Stricken & True and Not Stricken conditions, nor between the Stricken & False and Not Presented conditions. However, rates between the two pairs of conditions were significantly different. This suggests people were able to make their own judgments about whether to use the stricken information and chose to do so if it was thought to be true.

Each of the five scenario questions had one interpretation suggested by the stricken information; summed together, a score of "5" would indicate a participant chose that interpretation as more likely than the options related to guilt or innocence. Figure 3.7 shows a significant difference in the average "stricken" interpretation choice by condition.

Post hoc analyses showed that participants in both stricken conditions, as well as participants in the Not Stricken condition, rated "stricken" interpretations as "most likely to be true" more often than did participants in the Not Presented condition. Participants in the Stricken & False condition, however, rated these interpretations as "most likely" less often than participants in either the Stricken & True or the Not Stricken conditions. This pattern of results suggests that Stricken & False participants accepted "stricken" interpretations more than participants who had never been presented with the evidence.

This pattern of findings shows people were able to exclude the corrected information when it was false and could limit its influence on their verdicts. However, even

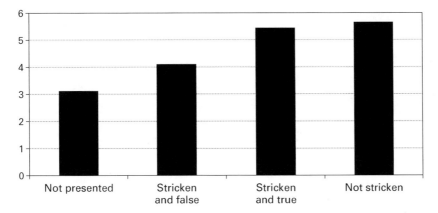

Figure 3.8
Average belief ratings for stricken information as a function of participants' information condition.

though they knew it to be false, it still influenced their assessments of the scenarios. Participants' belief in the truth of the "stricken" information (with 7 as the highest rating) is shown in figure 3.8.

As in the scenario interpretations, a post hoc test (Tukey, $p < 0.05$) comparing all mean pairs showed that participants in the Stricken & True and Not Stricken conditions gave significantly higher ratings than did participants in the Stricken & False and Not Presented condition. Again, the belief in the truth of the stricken information was higher than in the Not Presented condition, suggesting a CIE of the stricken information even when false.

Of course, mock jurors may take their task as experimental subjects less seriously than do jurors in an actual courtroom. In addition, the amount and complexity of case materials is much greater in a legal trial. However, the results of these studies highlight a general failure to disregard stricken information and suggest the CIE may play a role in a wide variety of important decision-making settings. When a source of bias is introduced into the decision-making task, participants may recognize, and attempt to correct, the effects of this perceived bias. However, these results indicate that people may fail to correct their judgments if they believe that stricken information is true. Participants seem to consider the truth of the target evidence before allowing it to affect their verdicts.

Worse yet, there was some evidence that the stricken information influences more indirect judgments even when it was false. Inferences about the defendant's actions and personality traits, as well as interpretations of ambiguous or incomplete information, are often affected regardless of the truth status of the stricken evidence. Specifically, information which is suggested by, or is supported by, the stricken evidence may be perceived as more credible simply as a consequence of its presentation. As a result, the CIE could potentially affect the jurors' construction of a story, the assimilation of evidence, and perhaps final verdict decisions under some circumstances. The continued influence may go unnoticed by jurors and may affect verdict decisions without their intention. The present study shows that the presence and status of stricken evidence may affect evidence interpretations and, in turn, substantially affect the juror's representation of the case as a whole.

The presentation and status of the stricken evidence is a strong predictor of which interpretation is chosen for later information. The stricken evidence, if believed to be true, adds strength to the prosecution's case, making the prosecution's explanations of the other items of evidence more believable. In this way, the juror's overall picture of what "really" happened becomes, and remains, coherent. A story in which the stricken information and the defense's interpretation of the rest of the evidence are believed to be true, for example, would be both incoherent and unbelievable. Thus, these data support Pennington and Hastie's (1993a) "story model," which asserts that jurors engage in integrative processing of the evidence. Our studies have indicated that the presence and status of stricken evidence affects which side is favored, the interpretation of other pieces of evidence, and the manner in which they are assimilated into the story. It is possible that the act of interpreting ambiguous information occurring prior to deciding on a verdict could change participants' verdict decisions.

This study also shows that, if jurors believe that the stricken evidence is true and relevant to the case, and if the stricken evidence is diagnostic of verdict, then they will use stricken information in their interpretations of other evidence, their hypotheses about the defendant, *and* their final verdict decisions. The overall proprosecution ratings given by mock jurors in the Stricken & True condition resemble the "ignore instructions" model, and jurors are true to their own "fact-finding" goals. The results of these studies indicate that jurors consider the truth value of stricken evidence before making their verdict decisions. Of course, jurors may also consider other factors when deciding whether to use stricken information.

The study suggests areas of future research to explore in order to further address the impact of the CIE on judgments. Though people may be made aware of biases resulting from corrections, they may choose to ignore them. In other circumstances, they may be influenced by misinformation that has been corrected even though they are well aware of the value of the correction. Alternatives for promoting careful reasoning following misinformation and correction are needed. One possible intervention is the presence of other people who are also aware of the correction. In the jury setting, it is possible that having a peer group also charged with making careful decisions about information use helps to keep individuals on track. Some prior research has shown that group deliberation prevents the expression of inadmissible evidence in final verdicts (Carretta & Moreland, 1983). Other research, however, indicates that a predeliberation vote among jurors is the best predictor of a jury's final verdict (Kalven & Zeisel, 1966). If so, any stricken information may continue to affect jurors throughout the group deliberation process. Which carries the most weight: the social accountability the group members feel in following the judge's instructions to disregard inadmissible evidence, or the predeliberation verdicts of the majority of jurors? By observing deliberations, we may learn whether, and under what conditions, jurors will overtly advocate the use of stricken evidence in final verdict decisions.

Conclusion

Most strikingly, the only intervention successful in removing CIE involves replacing the misinformation with a causal alternative. This is not always possible because an alternative may not be available at the time of correction. Increasingly, information status is dynamic, and incorrect information may be propagated, and then corrected, over time and sources. Typically, reports about an event from many sources appear over long periods of time, and information continues to unfold about causes. Because available information will be reported, later reports frequently contradict initial information. For the recipient, corrections pose an inherent contradiction: How can one of these pieces of information be wrong? And if the misinformation is central to an account, how can it be omitted without replacing it? As a whole, the previously described studies suggest the direct correction of information is not successful at "removing" misinformation from memory.

The question of *why* misinformation continues to be used *despite* explicit correction appears to be related to its causal role in an account (Johnson & Seifert, 1994). Readers may be uncomfortable with causal gaps in their event knowledge and hence prefer an incorrect model over an incomplete model (Ecker et al., 2010; Ecker, Lewandowsky, & Apai, 2011; Johnson & Seifert, 1994; van Oostendorp & Bonebakker, 1999). Having a plausible answer to a question readily available, but at the same time knowing that it is wrong, may generate contradictory responses that are easier to resolve by sticking to the misinformation. With it, the account at least "makes sense."

Studies of the CIE document its pervasive effects, showing that it is extremely difficult to return readers who see misinformation to a baseline similar to those never exposed to it. You can't "unring the bell," or behave as if the information was never presented. In a real sense, the reader or juror is not the same as he or she was before the information was presented and corrected; instead, the trace of having processed both the misinformation and the correction persists through the consequences of processing their meaning. This seems even more evident when the emotional impact of information is considered (Ecker, Lewandowsky, & Apai, 2011).

Even though I know it never happened, there was a short period of time during which I believed my holiday gifts had been stolen from my car, and that experience remains in my memory, along with the knowledge that it never actually happened. As a result, to me, my college town is not as safe as it once was, back before I was not a victim of theft—a theft, I remind you, that never actually occurred. The CIE is of great interest because it reveals that memory is changed by the processing that takes place, not solely by the present status of that information in memory. As a result, finding ways to address and redress the experience of misinformation is of utmost importance.

Acknowledgments

Many thanks to my former graduate students Hollyn M. Johnson, Julie Bush, and Andrea L. Mosmann for their collaboration on the research reported here.

Appendix A: Fire Story Materials (from Wilkes & Leatherbarrow, 1988)

Message 1: Jan. 25th 8:58 p.m. Alarm call received from premises of a wholesale stationery warehouse. Premises consist of offices, display room, and storage hall.

Message 2: A serious fire was reported in the storage hall, already out of control and requiring instant response. Fire engine dispatched at 9:00 p.m.

Message 3: The alarm was raised by the night security guard, who had smelled smoke and gone to investigate.

Message 4: Jan. 26th 4:00 a.m. Attending fire captain suggests that the fire was started by a short circuit in the wiring of a closet off the main storage hall. Police now investigating.

Message 5 (no-correction and correction groups): 4:30 a.m. Message received from Police Investigator Lucas saying that they have reports that cans of oil paint and pressurized gas cylinders had been present in the closet before the fire.

Message 5 (control group): 4:30 a.m. Message received from Police Investigator Lucas saying that they have reports that the closet was empty before the fire.

Message 6: Firefighters attending the scene report thick, oily smoke and sheets of flames hampering their efforts, and an intense heat that made the fire particularly difficult to bring under control.

Message 7: It has been learned that a number of explosions occurred during the blaze, which endangered firefighters in the vicinity. No fatalities were reported.

Message 8: Two firefighters are reported to have been taken to the hospital as a result of breathing toxic fumes that built up in the area in which they were working.

Message 9: A small fire had been discovered on the same premises, six months previously. It had been successfully tackled by the workers themselves.

Message 10: 10:00 a.m. The owner of the affected premises estimates that total damage will amount to hundreds of thousands of dollars, although the premises were insured.

Message 11 (control and no-correction groups): 10:40 a.m. A second message received from Police Investigator Lucas regarding the investigation into the fire. It stated that the two firefighters taken to the hospital had been released.

Message 11 (correction group): 10:40 a.m. A second message received from Police Investigator Lucas regarding the investigation into the fire. It stated that the closet reportedly containing cans of paint and gas cylinders had actually been empty before the fire.

Message 12: The shipping supervisor has disclosed that the storage hall contained bales of paper; mailing and legal-size envelopes; scissors, pencils, and other school supplies; and a large number of photo-copying machines.

Message 13: 11:30 a.m. Attending fire captain reports that the fire is now out and that the storage hall has been completely gutted.

Appendix B: Open-Ended Questionnaire (from Wilkes & Leatherbarrow, 1988)

Fact Questions

1. What was the extent of the firm's premises?
2. Where did an attending firefighter think the fire started?
3. Where on the premises was the fire located?
4. What features of the fire were noted by the security guard?
5. What business was the firm in?
6. When was the fire engine dispatched?
7. What was in the storage hall?
8. What was the cost of the damage done?
9. How was it thought the fire started?
10. When was the fire eventually put out?

Inference Questions

11. Why did the fire spread so quickly?
12. For what reason might an insurance claim be refused?
13. What was the possible cause of the toxic fumes?
14. What was the relevance of the closet?
15. What aspect of the fire might the police want to continue investigating?
16. Why do you think the fire was particularly intense?
17. What is the most likely cause of the fire that workers successfully put out earlier?
18. What could have caused the explosions?
19. Where was the probable location of the explosions?
20. Is there any evidence of careless management?

Manipulation Check Questions
21. What was the point of the second message from the police?
22. Were you aware of any corrections in the reports that you read?

Appendix C (adapted from Sue, Smith, & Caldwell, 1973)

Jury Service

Case # 37122

Police Report Summary   On Sunday, October 19, 1995, John R. Eldredge, the owner of a small convenience store in Detroit, was confronted by an armed robber who demanded money from the cash register. Mr. Eldredge immediately handed cash amounting to $170 to the robber, who took the money and then fired two shots at Eldredge before fleeing the scene. Eldredge was declared dead when an emergency vehicle arrived on the scene.

The only witness was a clerk, who had been in the storeroom during the robbery. He heard Eldredge pleading, "Take the money, but please don't shoot!" The robber laughed and replied, "I can't leave any witnesses." The clerk then heard two shots fired. After waiting a moment, the clerk cautiously entered the store and caught a glimpse of the robber as he left. The clerk went to the door, looked outside, and saw the robber run into a nearby apartment building. He called "911" and reported the robbery.

The next day, the police arrested the suspect, Daniel A. Matthews. Matthews is charged with one count of robbery and one count of murder in the first degree.

The Prosecution's Case   The defendant, Daniel A. Matthews, had entered an initial plea of "not guilty." The prosecution opened the trial by presenting its case against the defendant. Arguments by the prosecution were prefaced by the comment that the crime was "a most shallow and senseless act." The following are excerpts from the trial transcript:

The clerk of the store hesitantly identified the defendant as the same individual who robbed and shot John Eldredge. The clerk stated that he had caught only a glimpse of the robber as he left the store. The clerk testified that the robber had entered an apartment building located on the same block as the store. The defendant, Matthews, lives in a rented apartment in that same building.

The defendant claimed that he went shopping at the mall on the night of the robbery, but that he had seen no one who knew him. Police officers searching the defendant's apartment found a total of $795 in cash in the top drawer of the dresser.

Crime lab technicians were called to the stand to report on their findings. Traces of ammonia cleaner of the type used to clean the floor of the convenience store were found on the defendant's shoes. However, this type of ammonia is used in other commercial establishments. In addition, paraffin tests were conducted on the day following the murder to determine whether the defendant had residual gunpowder particles on his hand consistent with firing a gun. The results showed that there was a "possibility" that the defendant had fired a gun recently.

The prosecution also revealed that the defendant is a legally registered gun owner.

A tape recording was presented as evidence. Detectives investigating another matter had obtained legal permission to wiretap phone calls made by a suspected drug dealer. The detectives recorded the following call, to the suspected drug dealer: The caller said: "I finally got the money to pay you off... Yeah, I know I've lied to you before, but this time it's really true; I have all the money I owe you and more. It was easy. You'll hear all about it on the news... So call off your collection men! I'm paying it all; everything I owe you. You better believe it... I'm not going to jail again; I've done enough hard time." The detectives both identified the caller as the defendant, Daniel A. Matthews.

The Defense's Case The defendant, Daniel Matthews, took the stand and testified to his innocence. He said that the eyewitness acknowledged having only a brief glimpse of the perpetrator, and so could easily be mistaken in his identification. The money found in his apartment was his; he had been planning on surprising his son with a CD player for his birthday. He also explained that the ammonia tracings on his shoes could have been obtained while he was working, since he worked as a delivery man. The defendant admitted that he owned several guns, and had taken his son hunting on the day before the crime was committed.

In the closing argument, the defense demanded acquittal: "This crime is outrageous, but my client is not to blame for it—Daniel Matthews is innocent of all of the charges. The only real evidence against him is circumstantial, that he lived in the same building that the robber was seen entering. You should not convict Daniel Matthews for living in the wrong place at the wrong time."

Judge's Instructions Judge: "Please bear in mind that you are acting as a juror as you weigh the testimony you have read, and be sure to follow the instructions I have given you.

The charges against Daniel Matthews are one count of robbery and one count of murder. If you believe that the prosecution has shown, beyond a reasonable doubt, that Matthews committed these crimes, then you must return a verdict of 'Guilty'. If you believe that there was not enough evidence to show this, you must return a verdict of 'Not Guilty'."

Manipulations In the Stricken & True condition, participants were informed that the evidence was stricken immediately after its presentation:

The defense objected that the wiretap evidence can only be legally collected and used in matters involving the suspected drug dealer. Thus, any information on the tape could not be presented as evidence in the current case against Mr. Matthews, who is not a suspect in the drug case. The judge ruled that the tape recording evidence be stricken from the record. The jury was then instructed to disregard all of the testimony regarding the tape recording in this case.

In the Stricken & False condition, participants were told that the evidence was stricken because it was found to be untrue. Again, the evidence was stricken immediately after it was presented:

The defense then submitted to the judge and the prosecution the sworn affidavit of a voice print analyst. The prosecution agreed to allow the testimony of the expert witness. This expert witness stated that voice print analysis, which is accurate in 99% of cases, showed that the voice on the tape was NOT that of the defendant, Daniel Matthews. The judge ruled that the tape recording evidence be stricken from the record. The jury was then instructed to disregard all of the testimony regarding the tape recording in this case.

Appendix D (from Mosmann, 1998)

Example Scenario

Suppose the prosecution offered into evidence some pictures of Daniel Matthews meeting with Mark Watson, a known ex-con who has frequently served as an informant in other cases for the state. These pictures clearly show Matthews giving money to Watson. Unfortunately, Watson could not be located to testify at the time of the trial. Given what you know about Matthews, what do you think is the most likely reason for his giving money to Watson?

1: Most likely, 2: Second most likely, 3: Least likely

_____ A. Matthews owed Watson money for illegal drugs.

_____ B. Matthews had lost a bet with Watson and was settling up.

_____ C. Matthews was paying Watson not to testify in the current trial.

(A is consistent with Stricken Information)

References

Anderson, C. A., Lepper, M. R., & Ross, L. (1980). Perseverance of social theories: The role of explanation in the persistence of discredited information. *Journal of Personality and Social Psychology*, *39*, 1037–1049.

Carretta, T. R., & Moreland, R. L. (1983). The direct and indirect effects of inadmissible evidence. *Journal of Applied Social Psychology*, *13*, 291–309.

Christiaansen, R. E., & Ochalek, K. (1983). Editing misleading information from memory: Evidence for the coexistence of original and postevent information. *Memory & Cognition, 11,* 467–475.

Christianson, K., Hollingworth, A., Halliwell, J. F., & Feirarra, F. (2001). Thematic roles assigned along the garden path linger. *Cognitive Psychology, 42,* 368–407.

Clark, H. H., Schreuder, R., & Buttrick, S. (1983). Common ground and the understanding of demonstrative reference. *Journal of Verbal Learning and Verbal Behavior, 22,* 245–258.

Dodd, D. H., & Bradshaw, J. M. (1980). Leading questions and memory: Pragmatic constraints. *Journal of Verbal Learning and Verbal Behavior, 19,* 695–704.

Ecker, U. K. H., Lewandowsky, S., & Apai, J. (2011). Terrorists brought down the plane! —No, actually it was a technical fault: Processing corrections of emotive information. *Quarterly Journal of Experimental Psychology, 64,* 283–310.

Ecker, U. K. H., Lewandowsky, S., Swire, B., & Chang, D. (2011). Correcting false information in memory: Manipulating the strength of misinformation encoding and its retraction. *Psychonomic Bulletin & Review, 18,* 570–578.

Ecker, U. K. H., Lewandowsky, S., & Tang, D. T. W. (2010). Explicit warnings reduce but do not eliminate the continued influence of misinformation. *Memory & Cognition, 38,* 1087–1100.

Elliott, R., Farrington, B., & Manheimer, H. (1988). Eyewitness credible and discredible. *Journal of Applied Social Psychology, 18,* 1411–1422.

Fein, S., McCloskey, A. L., & Tomlinson, T. M. (1997). Can the jury disregard that information? The use of suspicion to reduce the prejudicial effects of pretrial publicity and inadmissible testimony. *Personality and Social Psychology Bulletin, 23,* 1215–1226.

Gilbert, D., Krull, D., & Malone, P. (1990). Unbelieving the unbelievable: Some problems in the rejection of false information. *Journal of Personality and Social Psychology, 59,* 601–613.

Gilbert, D., Tafarodi, R. W., & Malone, P. S. (1993). You can't not believe everything you read. *Journal of Personality and Social Psychology, 65,* 221–233.

Golding, J. M., Fowler, S. B., Long, D. L., & Latta, H. (1990). Instructions to disregard potentially useful information: The effects of pragmatics on evaluative judgments and recall. *Journal of Memory and Language, 29,* 212–227.

Golding, J. M., & Hauselt, J. (1994). When instructions to forget become instructions to remember. *Personality and Social Psychology Bulletin, 20,* 178–183.

Grice, H. P. (1975). Logic and conversation. In P. Cole & J. L. Morgan (Eds.), *Syntax and semantics: Vol. 3. Speech acts* (pp. 41–58). New York: Academic Press.

Hastie, R., & Park, B. (1986). The relationship between memory and judgment depends on whether the judgment task is memory-based or on-line. *Psychological Review, 93,* 258–268.

Hatvany, N., & Strack, F. (1980). The impact of a discredited key witness. *Journal of Applied Social Psychology, 10,* 490–509.

Haviland, S. E., & Clark, H. H. (1974). What's new? Acquiring new information as a process in comprehension. *Journal of Verbal Learning and Verbal Behavior, 13,* 512–521.

Hertel, P. T. (1982). Remembering reactions and facts: The influence of subsequent information. *Journal of Experimental Psychology. Learning, Memory, and Cognition, 8,* 513–529.

Johnson, H. M., & Seifert, C. M. (1994). Sources of the continued influence effect: When discredited information in memory affects later inferences. *Journal of Experimental Psychology. Learning, Memory, and Cognition, 20,* 1420–1436.

Johnson, H. M., & Seifert, C. M. (1998). Updating accounts following a corrections of misinformation. *Journal of Experimental Psychology. Learning, Memory, and Cognition, 24,* 1483–1494.

Johnson, H. M., & Seifert, C. M. (1999). Modifying mental representations: Comprehending corrections. In S. R. Goldman & H. van Oostendorp (Eds.), *The construction of mental representations during reading* (pp. 303–318). Mahwah, NJ: Lawrence Erlbaum Associates.

Johnson-Laird, P. N. (2012). Mental models and consistency. In B. Gawronski & F. Strack (Eds.), *Cognitive consistency: A fundamental principle in social cognition* (pp. 225–243). New York: Guilford Press.

Kalven, H., Jr., & Zeisel, H. (1966). *The American jury.* Boston: Little, Brown.

Kassin, S. M., & Sommers, S. R. (1997). Inadmissible testimony, instructions to disregard, and the jury: Substantive versus procedural considerations. *Personality and Social Psychology Bulletin, 23,* 1046–1054.

Kassin, S. M., & Sukel, H. (1997). Coerced confessions and the jury: An experimental test of the "harmless error" rule. *Law and Human Behavior, 21,* 27–46.

Krosnick, J. A., Li, F., & Lehman, D. R. (1990). Conversational conventions, order of information acquisition, and the effect of base rates and individuating information on social judgment. *Journal of Personality and Social Psychology, 59,* 1140–1152.

Loftus, E. F. (1974). Reconstructing memory: The incredible eyewitness. *Psychology Today, 8*(7), 116–119.

Lord, C. G., Ross, L. D., & Lepper, M. R. (1979). Biased assimilation and attitude polarization: The effects of prior theories on subsequently considered evidence. *Journal of Personality and Social Psychology, 37,* 2098–2109.

McKoon, G., & Ratcliff, R. (1992). Inference during reading. *Psychological Review, 99,* 440–466.

Mosmann, A. L. (1998). "Nothing but the truth": Mock jurors' use of stricken evidence in decision-making. Ann Arbor, Michigan: UMI Dissertation services.

O'Brien, E. J., & Myers, J. L. (1987). The role of causal connections in the retrieval of text. *Memory & Cognition, 15,* 419–427.

Pennington, N., & Hastie, R. (1981). Juror decision-making models: The generalization gap. *Psychological Bulletin*, *89*, 246–287.

Pennington, N., & Hastie, R. (1986). Evidence evaluation in complex decision making. *Journal of Personality and Social Psychology*, *51*, 242–258.

Pennington, N., & Hastie, R. (1993a). The story model for juror decision making. In R. Hastie (Ed.), *Inside the juror* (pp. 192–223). New York: Cambridge University Press.

Pennington, N., & Hastie, R. (1993b). Reasoning in explanation-based decision making. *Cognition*, *49*, 123–163.

Petty, R. E., & Wegener, D. T. (1993). Flexible correction processes in social judgment: Correcting for context-induced contrast. *Journal of Experimental Social Psychology*, *29*, 137–165.

Pickel, K. L. (1995). Inducing jurors to disregard inadmissible evidence: A legal explanation does not help. *Law and Human Behavior*, *19*, 407–424.

Ross, L., Lepper, M. R., & Hubbard, M. (1975). Perseverance in self-perception and social perception: Biased attributional processes in the debriefing paradigm. *Journal of Personality and Social Psychology*, *32*, 880–892.

Ross, L. D., Lepper, M. R., Strack, F., & Steinmetz, J. (1977). Social explanation and social expectation: Effects of real and hypothetical explanations on subjective likelihood. *Journal of Personality and Social Psychology*, *35*, 817–829.

Saunders, D. M., Vidmar, N., & Hewitt, E. C. (1983). Eyewitness testimony and the discrediting effect. In S. M. A. Lloyd-Bostock & B. R. Clifford (Eds.), *Evaluating witness evidence* (pp. 57–78). London: John Wiley.

Schul, Y., & Burnstein, E. (1985). When discounting fails: Conditions under which individuals use discredited information in making a judgment. *Journal of Personality and Social Psychology*, *49*, 894–903.

Schul, Y., & Manzury, F. (1990). The effects of type of encoding and strength of discounting appeal on the success of ignoring an invalid testimony. *European Journal of Social Psychology*, *20*, 337–349.

Schul, Y., & Mazursky, D. (1990). Conditions facilitating successful discounting in consumer decision making. *Journal of Consumer Research*, *16*, 442–451.

Schuller, R. A. (1995). Expert evidence and hearsay: The influence of "secondhand" information on jurors' decisions. *Law and Human Behavior*, *19*, 345–362.

Schwarz, N. (1996). *Cognition and communication: Judgmental biases, research methods, and the logic of conversation*. Hillsdale, NJ: Lawrence Erlbaum Associates.

Seifert, C. M. (2002). The continued influence of misinformation in memory: What makes a correction effective? In B. Ross (Ed.), *The psychology of learning and motivation*, Vol. 41 (pp. 265–292). San Diego: Academic Press.

Stapel, D. A., Martin, L. L., & Schwarz, N. (1998). The smell of bias: What instigates correction processes in social judgments? *Personality and Social Psychology Bulletin, 24,* 797–806.

Sue, S., Smith, R. E., & Caldwell, C. (1973). Effects of inadmissible evidence on the decisions of simulated jurors: A moral dilemma. *Journal of Applied Social Psychology, 3,* 345–353.

Tenney, E. R., Cleary, H. M. D., & Spellman, B. A. (2009). Unpacking the doubt in beyond a reasonable doubt: Plausible alternative stories increase not guilty verdicts. *Basic and Applied Social Psychology, 31,* 1–8.

Thompson, W. C., Fong, G. T., & Rosenhan, D. L. (1981). Inadmissible evidence and juror verdicts. *Journal of Personality and Social Psychology, 40,* 453–463.

Trabasso, T., & van den Broek, P. W. (1985). Causal thinking and the representation of narrative events. *Journal of Memory and Language, 24,* 612–630.

Tversky, A., & Kahneman, D. (1973). Availability: A heuristic for judging frequency and probability. *Cognitive Psychology, 5,* 207–232.

van den Broek, P. (1990). Causal inferences and the comprehension of narrative texts. In A. C. Graesser & G. Bower (Eds.), *The psychology of learning and motivation: Vol. 25. Inferences and text comprehension* (pp. 175–196). San Diego, CA: Academic Press.

van Oostendorp, H. (1996). Updating situation models derived from newspaper articles. *Medienpsychologie, 8,* 21–33.

van Oostendorp, H., & Bonebakker, C. (1999). Difficulties in updating mental representations during reading news reports. In H. van Oostendorp & S. R. Goldman (Eds.), *The construction of mental representations during reading* (pp. 319–339). Mahwah, NJ: Lawrence Erlbaum Associates.

Wegner, D. M. (1994). Ironic processes of mental control. *Psychological Review, 101,* 34–52.

Wegner, D. M., Coulton, G. F., & Wenzlaff, R. (1985). The transparency of denial: Briefing in the debriefing paradigm. *Journal of Personality and Social Psychology, 49,* 338–345.

Wegner, D. M., & Erber, R. (1992). The hyperaccessibility of suppressed thoughts. *Journal of Personality and Social Psychology, 63,* 903–912.

Wegner, D. M., Wenzlaff, R., Kerker, R. M., & Beattie, A. E. (1981). Incrimination through innuendo: Can media questions become public answers? *Journal of Personality and Social Psychology, 40,* 822–832.

Wegener, D. T., & Petty, R. E. (1995). Flexible correction processes in social judgment: The role of naive theories in corrections for perceived bias. *Journal of Personality and Social Psychology, 68,* 36–51.

Weinberg, H. I., & Baron, R. S. (1982). The discredible eyewitness. *Personality and Social Psychology Bulletin, 8,* 60–67.

Wilkes, A. L., & Leatherbarrow, M. (1988). Editing episodic memory following the identification of error. *Quarterly Journal of Experimental Psychology, 40A,* 361–387.

Wilkes, A. L., & Reynolds, D. J. (1999). On certain limitations accompanying readers' interpretations of corrections in episodic text. *Quarterly Journal of Experimental Psychology, 52A*, 165–183.

Wilson, T. D., & Brekke, N. (1994). Mental contamination and mental correction: Unwanted influences on judgments and evaluations. *Psychological Bulletin, 116*, 117–142.

Wyer, R. S., & Budesheim, T. L. (1987). Person memory and judgments: The impact of information that one is told to disregard. *Journal of Personality and Social Psychology, 53*, 14–29.

Wyer, R. S., & Unverzagt, W. H. (1985). Effects of instructions to disregard information on its subsequent recall and use in making judgments. *Journal of Personality and Social Psychology, 48*, 533–549.

4 Failures to Detect Textual Problems during Reading

Douglas J. Hacker

Thirty-six children from grades 1, 2, and 3 were asked by a researcher to help write instructions for a children's alphabet card game and to perform a magic trick (Markman, 1977). The researcher told the children that she needed their help to determine the adequacy of the instructions, and they were to suggest improvements. The researcher explained the card game and told them that the game depended on a "special card," but no mention was made as to what the "special card" was. The children were then asked a series of questions concerning the adequacy of the instructions. They also were shown the magic trick and given instructions on how to perform the trick, but once again, a critical piece of information was withheld from them. After the instructions, the children were again asked a series of questions concerning the adequacy of the instructions. The results of the study indicated that the children had to be asked several questions before they realized that some critical information was lacking from the instructions. Not too surprisingly, older children realized that the given information was incomplete before younger children, but even the older children had to be asked about three questions before realizing the inadequacy of the instructions. Markman speculated that because the children, particularly the youngest, were processing information about the problems at a relatively superficial level, they failed to execute the instructions mentally and consequently had difficulty understanding what information was missing.

However, in a second experiment, children were given a chance to actually see the instructions demonstrated as they were verbally described. The demonstrations helped the children, particularly the oldest, process information about the problem by confronting it more directly, and they were more likely to become aware of their failures to understand; however, even under these circumstances, many children still had difficulty understanding what information was missing. Markman concluded, "If individuals are willing to tolerate such gaps in their knowledge, it is unlikely that they would be moved to search for clarification of material. Thus an awareness of one's own comprehension failure provides a basis for initiating appropriate remedial procedures to ensure that comprehension is achieved" (p. 992).

This study, and others by Markman (e.g., Markman 1979, 1985; Markman & Gorin, 1981), had a seminal effect on the course of nearly 35 years of research that has focused on people's ability, or lack thereof, to monitor their comprehension. During that time, hundreds of investigations of both oral and reading comprehension have been conducted with children to adults, and the consistent finding is that people often do not have an awareness of their comprehension failures and routinely fail to understand textual information or fail to detect blatant gaps, inconsistencies, or inaccuracies in texts. At the same time, they remain highly confident that they have in fact fully and correctly comprehended that textual information. Although people likely do not "tolerate such gaps in their knowledge" as Markman had suggested, which would imply an awareness of a comprehension failure, people likely proceed with listening or reading assuming that comprehension is occurring until some triggering event knocks them into awareness that some component of comprehension has failed (Hacker, 2004). Glenberg, Wilkinson, and Epstein (1982) referred to unconscious failures to comprehend text as "illusions of knowing," but in many cases of reading comprehension, the knowing derived from the text is no illusion. Rather, readers derive a confident and coherent mental representation of the text even though they may have bridged gaps, incorporated inaccuracies, and resolved misunderstandings to get there. As a result, regrettably, the mental representation constructed may bear little semblance to the author's intended text or to another reader's constructed mental representation.

How people bridge gaps, incorporate inaccuracies, or resolve misunderstandings during reading and yet remain confident in their comprehension is the focus of this chapter. Markman's (1977) seminal work did much to identify this persistent and ubiquitous problem with comprehension monitoring of text, and she helped to identify several causes for these failures of awareness. Each of these causes has received considerable study over the past 35 years, and five of the more salient will be addressed in this chapter.

First, at a very basic level, even if readers sense some triggering event that knocks them into an awareness of a comprehension failure, they may lack the requisite knowledge to fix the source of the comprehension failure. Conversely, readers may possess the requisite knowledge to fix the source of comprehension failure but fail to experience the triggering event, that is, they fail to activate that knowledge at times when it is most critical when reading. My colleagues and I have pursued these issues as the knowledge-deficit or processing-deficit hypotheses, respectively (Hacker, Plumb, Butterfield, Quathamer, & Heineken, 1994; Plumb, Butterfield, Hacker, & Dunlosky, 1994).

Second, a great deal of research has been conducted demonstrating that a reader's goals for reading and the problems encountered during reading in pursuit of those goals strongly affect the kinds of reading in which a reader engages (e.g., Baker & Zimlin, 1989; Beal, 1990; Beal, Bonitatibus, & Garrod, 1990; Hacker, 1997, 2004: Hacker et al., 1994; Kaakinen & Hyönä, 2010; Pressley & Afflerbach, 1995; van den Broek,

Bohn-Gettler, Kendeou, Carlson, & White, 2011). In another of Markman's studies (1979), and in other studies that have used the error-detection paradigm, the instructions given to participants may inadvertently create a mismatch between the goals of the reader and the goals of the researcher. Markman asked children to suggest any changes they thought would make essays easier to understand. These young readers may have set for themselves the goal of detecting surface-level corrections whereas the intended goal of the research was to focus on deeper comprehension problems embedded in the texts. Because the readers' goals play an important role in determining how they will process and comprehend or not comprehend the text (Kaakinen & Hyönä, 2010), the children's self-determined goals for reading may not have been the goals necessary for monitoring their comprehension at the levels expected by the researcher (Hacker, 1994).

Third, Markman (1977) appropriately summed up the importance of comprehension monitoring: "[A]n awareness of one's own comprehension failure provides a basis for initiating appropriate remedial procedures to ensure that comprehension is achieved" (p. 992). At the very least, the reader must be aware of a comprehension failure before any action will be taken to repair it. In other words, the reader must monitor ongoing comprehension to gain an awareness of a comprehension failure, and subsequently, the reader must control further reading via remedial procedures to reestablish comprehension. Monitoring and subsequent control of ongoing reading comprehension is a metacognitive process that my colleagues and I have called self-regulated comprehension (Dunlosky & Rawson, 2005; Dunlosky, Rawson, & Hacker, 2002; Hacker, 2004). The monitoring component of self-regulated comprehension, often referred to as metacomprehension, has been the target of an extensive body of research. Disappointingly, this research has clearly established that people across all ages are not particularly accurate at judging their comprehension. As noted in Maki (1998) and reiterated in Dunlosky and Lipko (2007), numerous studies have shown that correlations between judgments of comprehension and actual assessments of comprehension are usually about 0.30.

To investigate why metacomprehension accuracy is so low, we have combined theories of comprehension with theories of metacognition and have hypothesized that metacomprehension accuracy depends on whether the reader experiences disruptions in his or her comprehension processes while reading (Dunlosky & Rawson, 2005; Dunlosky et al., 2002). These disruptions can occur at lexical, textbase, or situation model levels of text representation (Kintsch, 1994). However, because comprehension is predominantly determined by the situation model level of text representation (Kintsch, 1998), disruptions in comprehension at this level are particularly important. Presumably, the more disruptions experienced during comprehension or the more salient the disruptions, the lower the reader's confidence will be in his or her comprehension. Our levels-of-disruption hypothesis (Dunlosky & Rawson, 2005; Dunlosky et al., 2002) states, in part, that disruptions at the situation model level serve as inferential cues that are used by the reader to inform his or her judgments of comprehension. If the judgments indicate poor comprehension, the reader can redirect his or her reading to increase comprehension. If the judgments indicate good comprehension, the reader can simply proceed with reading. Therefore, accurate judgments are critical to self-regulated comprehension. Accurate judgments that are ignored or inaccurate judgments can lead the reader to proceed with reading even though comprehension remains incomplete or inaccurate.

Fourth, Markman (1977) speculated that young readers were "processing material at a relatively superficial level, not really attempting to execute the instructions mentally or determine the relationship between the instructions and goal. As a consequence, they are left unaware of the inadequacy of the instructions" (p. 991). Their superficial processing of the materials and instructions may have been due to the high levels of cognitive effort required both for comprehending the materials and instructions and for engaging in the metacomprehension required to detect textual gaps and inconsistencies (Griffin, Wiley, & Thiede, 2008). Using pupillometric data and response times to measure cognitive effort, Keener and Hacker (2012) showed that questions asking for literal information from a text were easier to answer than questions requiring temporal ordering inferences, which were easier to answer than questions requiring propositional logic inferences. Therefore, the cognitive effort required simply to mentally represent textual information varies by the level of representation, with inferential levels of representation potentially overloading cognitive resources. Moreover, Weaver and Bryant (1995) showed that metacomprehension accuracy is at its greatest when texts are at a moderate level of difficulty. Accuracy is compromised both when texts are too easy and when they are too difficult. Therefore, difficult texts, which require high levels of cognitive effort to comprehend, also produce lower levels of metacomprehension accuracy. The high demands on cognitive processing coupled with poorer monitoring of comprehension could be important contributors to failures to detect textual problems.

Fifth, Markman (1977, 1979) and others (e.g., Adams & Collins, 1979; Bransford, Barclay, & Franks, 1972; Kintsch, 1994) have maintained that comprehension is a constructive process that requires active processing of text. Only by actively engaging in generating a mental representation of a text can the reader gain awareness of comprehension as well as comprehension failures or difficulties. Active processing of text is a necessary ingredient for self-regulated comprehension (Hacker, 2004). Recent advances in the investigation of mindless reading have shown, regrettably, that readers often lapse into periods of reading during which the reader's cognitive processing is decoupled from the text (Schad, Nuthmann, & Engbert, 2012; Reichle, Reineberg, & Schooler, 2010) or the reader is interrupted from task focus by task-unrelated thoughts (Smallwood & Schooler, 2006). During these periods, cognitive processing of text is superseded by processing of potentially anything but the text. Readers can catch themselves and refocus attention on the task at hand, but doubtless, there are significant amounts of reading that occur even though the mind has wandered to other tasks.

In this chapter, more detailed descriptions will be given for each of these five causes for failing to understand that comprehension failures have occurred. In these descriptions, attention will be given to empirical findings and theoretical explanations. Finally, recommendations will be given to combat these ubiquitous failures, and directions for future research will be suggested.

A Knowledge Deficit, Processing Deficit, or Both

My colleagues and I originally were drawn to the problem of readers' failures to detect textual problems via text revision research. Similar to the reading comprehension literature, this body of research indicated that it was not uncommon that 40% to 50% of planted textual errors went unnoticed as writers were rereading and attempting to revise their texts (e.g., Englert, Hiebert, & Stewart, 1988; Hull, 1987), and that this problem was common across elementary school children to college students and beyond. In our preliminary investigations, we had proposed three causes for this problem: (1) Readers/writers lacked knowledge of the textual errors and left them untouched because the errors simply were not perceived as errors (i.e., the knowledge-deficit hypothesis); (2) readers/writers had the knowledge necessary to correct textual errors but were not able to detect them within the text (i.e., the processing-deficit hypothesis); or (3) readers/writers showed a combination of the two causes (Hacker et al., 1994; Plumb et al., 1994). The knowledge-deficit hypothesis assumes that a necessary prerequisite for error detection is knowledge of how to correct the error. However, knowledge of how to correct an error, albeit necessary for error correction, may not be sufficient for its detection. That is, one can have the required knowledge to correct an error, but if that knowledge remains inert or is misapplied during reading, that knowledge is not of much use. Hence, some additional cognitive processing is required to activate and apply that knowledge at appropriate times during reading for detection to occur. If that additional processing is not engaged (i.e., the processing-deficit hypothesis), the error will go undetected despite having the knowledge to correct it.

In our first test of these two hypotheses, Plumb et al. (1994) asked college juniors and seniors and twelfth-grade students to find and correct errors that were implanted in two texts. The errors consisted of spelling, punctuation, word usage, and meaning errors (i.e., errors in logic). Our goal was to separate detection from correction of errors, and we did this by presenting the texts under three conditions. In one condition, the errors were not marked or highlighted in the texts in any way. In the second condition, each error and the surrounding text were highlighted, but the highlighted portion could have been perceived by participants to involve different error possibilities. In the third condition, each error and surrounding text were highlighted as in the second condition, but in this case the correct answer was provided in a multiple-choice format. Our reasoning for the three conditions was that if the highlighted text increased correction over the text that was not highlighted, then a knowledge deficit was not the obstacle to detection. That is, the participant could correct the error but lacked an ability to detect the error in the first place (i.e., a processing deficit). If participants could not correct the errors, even when given multiple choices to do so, then a knowledge deficit was more likely the reason for the lack of detection.

In the unhighlighted and highlighted conditions, participants corrected more spelling, punctuation, and word usage errors than meaning errors. In the multiple-choice condition, approximately the same number of each type of error was corrected. Although not all errors were corrected, participants in the multiple-choice condition corrected about 30 of the 40 errors, reducing the possibility that a knowledge deficit was the cause for not detecting the errors. In addition, a processing deficit was more strongly implicated in that participants corrected nearly twice as many errors in the highlighted text than in the unhighlighted text, indicating that participants had trouble detecting errors they knew how to correct. Not too surprisingly, participants in the multiple-choice condition corrected more errors than participants from the other two conditions; however, when corrected for guessing, the difference between the highlighted condition and the highlighted-with-multiple-choice condition became negligible. Participants either knew how to correct an error or did not, and the additional support provided by the multiple-choice options did not help. We concluded from these results that even when readers have specific knowledge of how to correct an error, that knowledge is not sufficient for its detection in text, and this may be more so for meaning errors than for other error types. Readers need some other cognitive process for successful error detection.

In Hacker et al. (1994), we extended our investigation of the knowledge-deficit and processing-deficit hypotheses and looked more closely at whether knowledge of how to correct an error was either necessary or sufficient for its detection. In this experiment, we had eleventh- and twelfth-grade U.S. students and German college students read two texts that in total contained eight each of punctuation, spelling, usage, and meaning errors. The meaning errors were textual inconsistencies in which inconsistent propositions were within the same sentence or between sentences. One of the texts had the errors highlighted as in Plumb et al. (1994), and the other had no highlighting. Participants received both texts, which were counterbalanced. In the first of two sessions, the participants were told about the kinds of errors to expect in the texts and asked only to identify the errors by circling them as precisely as possible and not to correct them. In the second session, which occurred one week later, the participants were given workbook-like exercises that contained the errors implanted in the texts along with several errors that had not appeared. To disassociate the errors as much as possible from the errors as they had appeared, the contexts in which the errors appeared differed from the contexts of the two texts.

Results again showed that highlighting increased error detection, indicating that participants had the knowledge necessary to detect more errors in the texts but lacked some additional cognitive processing ability to detect them without assistance. We examined whether knowledge of how to correct errors is necessary or sufficient for detection by classifying each error on a participant-by-participant basis according to whether it was detected in the first session and corrected in the second session. Calculating conditional probabilities then allowed us to test four hypotheses. The two hypotheses pertaining to the necessity condition were (1) revisers know how to correct detected errors, and (2) revisers who do not know how to correct errors do not detect them. The two hypotheses pertaining to the sufficiency condition were (3) revisers who know how to correct errors detect them, and (4) revisers do not know how to correct errors that are not detected.

The conditional probabilities for the necessity condition were high. The probabilities that participants knew how to correct detected errors were spelling = 0.91, punctuation = 0.88, usage = 0.93, and meaning = 0.76; the probabilities that uncorrected errors went undetected were spelling = 0.57, punctuation = 0.76, usage = 0.74, and meaning = 0.80. However, the conditional probabilities for the sufficiency condition were low, with the exception of spelling errors. The probabilities of detecting errors that were corrected were spelling = 0.80, punctuation = 0.40, usage = 0.51, and meaning – 0.22; the probabilities of not correcting errors that were not detected were spelling = 0.34, punctuation = 0.20, usage = 0.16, and meaning = 0.25.

In sum, we had speculated that readers do not detect textual errors because they do not have knowledge of them and the errors simply were not perceived as errors (i.e., the knowledge-deficit hypothesis). We showed support for this speculation: Knowledge of the error is a necessary condition for its detection. Figueredo and Varnhagen (2004) also came to this conclusion although they focused only on specific types of spelling errors (orthographic, phonological, and morphological errors). We should note that our conditional probabilities for the necessity hypotheses were not perfect. In other words, there were some errors that could be detected in text and yet the reader did not know precisely how to correct them. This is not unreasonable assuming that a person can sense that something is wrong with a text but have an incorrect notion about how to fix it.

In contrast, knowledge of the error is not a sufficient condition for its detection. Although Figueredo and Varnhagen did find evidence that knowledge of phonological and orthographic spelling errors may be sufficient for detection, a finding not too dissimilar from our finding regarding our mixed-type spelling errors, their support for the sufficiency condition was sporadic at best. In general, something more than simple knowledge of an error is needed for its detection (i.e., the processing-deficit hypothesis). This was shown not only in our tests of necessity and sufficiency but also in our highlighting conditions in which people had knowledge of how to correct errors but simply needed assistance to find them in text. In subsequent research, we showed that the "something more than simple knowledge of an error" involves having access to specific strategies or standards for finding errors.

Reading Goals and Strategies

An abundance of research has shown that a reader's goals for reading strongly affect the kinds of reading in which a reader engages (e.g., Baker & Zimlin, 1989; Beal, 1990; Beal, Bonitatibus, & Garrod, 1990; Hacker, 1997, 2004; Hacker et al., 1994; Kaakinen & Hyönä, 2010; Pressley & Afflerbach, 1995; van den Broek et al., 2011). The kinds of reading will be manifested in the use of different strategies to achieve those goals. If the strategy selected by the reader is appropriate to the goal, he or she stands a better chance of achieving the goal, but an inappropriate strategy will result in partially attained goals or goals that are never achieved. We proposed that failing to detect textual errors or gaps, or incorporating inaccuracies and misunderstandings into one's comprehension of text, may be due to a mismatch between the reader's goals and the goals that are anticipated by the researcher. For instance, if the reader's goal for reading is to develop the gist of a text, and he or she fails to detect spelling errors that he or she knows how to correct, the failure to detect spelling errors is likely due to the fact that detecting spelling errors was not the purpose for reading.

Numerous studies have shown that readers can be quite good at pursuing specific purposes for reading. When given a specific goal for reading, they can adjust their reading behaviors to meet the demands of the goal and successfully accomplish it (e.g., Baker, 1985; Markman, 1979; Pressley & Afflerbach, 1995, Zabrucky & Moore, 1989). Readers also can self-generate goals in the course of reading to meet demands that were not initially specified. In Keener and Hacker (2012), readers were not given specific reading goals, but to be able to answer questions about the texts they were asked to read, they needed, in part, to make a very specific type of inference not often encountered in narrative texts (i.e., propositional logic inferences; Kintsch, 1998). When reading the first of six narrative texts, readers readily made common temporal ordering inferences, but only a few propositional logic inferences were made. However, by the time the second text was read, readers had already self-adjusted their goals for reading and were able to make significantly more propositional logic inferences. Readers had self-generated a strategy for reading to meet the demands of the reading task.

In Hacker (1997), seventh-, ninth-, and eleventh-grade students of widely varying reading abilities participated in a study that investigated how readers respond to multiple goals for reading. All students were asked to read a text that was written at a seventh- to eighth-grade level and contained 24 errors, 8 each of spelling, grammar, and meaning. The meaning errors were once again errors of internal consistency in which a text proposition was inconsistent with or contradicted by another proposition in the same sentence or another sentence. The goals for reading were manipulated in four ways. In condition 1, participants were told only that the text contained errors, and they were asked to find and correct as many of them as possible. In condition 2, participants were told that the text contained meaning errors and "other" kinds of errors. Meaning errors were defined, and an example was given. The participants were told to find and correct as many errors as possible. In condition 3, participants were told that the text contained lexical and syntactic errors and "other" kinds of errors. Examples of lexical and syntactic errors were given. These participants also were told to find and correct as many errors as possible. Finally, in condition 4, participants were told that the text contained all three types of error, and examples of each were given. These participants received the same instruction to find and correct as many errors as possible.

As expected, the results showed that participants who received the lexical/syntactic instructions corrected more spelling and grammar errors than did those who received instructions that did not specify an error type, and participants who received the meaning instructions corrected more meaning errors than did those who received instructions that did not specify an error type. Being provided with a specific goal for reading, the participants were successful at accomplishing that goal. However, participants who received the lexical and syntactic instructions corrected far fewer meaning errors than those who received the general instruction to find and correct errors. These results suggest that pursuing the goal to find lexical and syntactic errors directed readers to find and correct those types of error, but this goal seems to have interfered or distracted them from finding and detecting meaning errors. When given instructions that did not specify an error type, participants directed their attention to meaning and not to lower-level lexical and syntactic features of the text.

When we looked at participants from the three conditions in which participants received instructions to find either meaning errors, lexical and syntactic errors, or all three error types, we found that the participants who received instructions pertaining specifically to meaning errors found and corrected more meaning errors than in the other two conditions; however, there were no differences in the numbers of corrected spelling and grammar errors between this condition and the lexical and syntactic condition. That is, there appeared to be an asymmetry in the effects of goals for reading: Instructions to correct spelling and grammar errors led to higher numbers of corrected spelling and grammar errors but fewer meaning errors, and instructions to correct meaning errors led to higher numbers of corrected meaning errors but in this case the same numbers of corrected spelling and grammar errors as with participants who received the spelling and grammar instructions.

One interpretation of these results is that providing readers with the goal to read for higher semantic levels of text representation may also guarantee pursuit of lower-level goals such as reading for lexical or syntactic levels. Specific goals for reading that do not explicitly involve comprehension may result in overlooking textual problems that require comprehension. However, readers may detect a variety of textual problems simply by being given the goal to read for comprehension (Flower, Hayes, Carey, Schriver, & Stratman, 1986; Kaakinen & Hyönä, 2010; Radach, Huestegge, & Reilley, 2008).

Levels-of-Disruption Hypothesis

In previous work, my colleagues and I proposed the levels-of-disruption hypothesis to explain why metacomprehension of text (i.e., people's judgments regarding their comprehension of text) was so poor (Dunlosky et al., 2002). Maki's (1998) review of the metacomprehension literature indicated that relative accuracy of metacomprehension judgments averaged about 0.27, and Dunlosky and Lipko (2007) reported relative accuracy of about the same low value. Why metacomprehension accuracy is so poor is a question that has proved perplexing. For most proficient readers, reading comprehension is generally taken for granted. You read a text, develop an understanding of the content, discuss the text with others, even perform well on tests of comprehension, and yet, if asked to judge whether you have comprehended the text, your judgment accuracy likely would tend to be low. Experimental attempts have been made to improve accuracy, with more or less success, but there still remains a lack of understanding of the psychology behind comprehension and metacomprehension that has hindered progress.

We maintain that self-regulated comprehension depends on active monitoring and subsequent control of ongoing reading comprehension (Dunlosky & Rawson, 2005; Dunlosky et al., 2002; Hacker, 2004). Further, our levels-of-disruption hypothesis proposes that the monitoring component of self-regulated comprehension, which is the driving psychological process responsible for metacomprehension, depends on whether the reader experiences disruptions in his or her comprehension while reading a text. Because most comprehension of text occurs at the situation model level (i.e., the interface between textual information and the reader's world knowledge via inferential processing; Kintsch, 1994), disruptions at the situation model level should serve as inferential cues that inform judgments of comprehension. If these disruptions are predictive of test performance, then accuracy should be high. That is, if comprehension is disrupted during the processing of information that is subsequently the focus of a test question, then the reader's confidence in answering that test question should be low, reflecting the disruptions in comprehension. Furthermore, if the answer to the question is incorrect, then metacomprehension accuracy would be high.

If we accept the levels-of-disruption hypothesis, then failing to detect textual errors or gaps, or incorporating inaccuracies and misunderstandings into one's comprehension of text, may be due to failures to perceive or failures to respond to disruptions in comprehension. Failures to perceive disruptions assume that a disruption could be occurring, but it is occurring below some threshold level necessary for the reader to be conscious of it. These kinds of unconscious reading behaviors may be prevalent during "mindless reading," which is a topic addressed in a subsequent section of this chapter. Accounts that focus on failures to respond to disruptions assume that a disruption to comprehension has occurred, but that the reader chooses to ignore it or may automatically make inferences to resolve it (Hacker, 1994). As to the former, because disruptions can occur at any level of text representation (e.g., lexical, textbase, situation model level), those occurring at lower levels of text representation may be dismissed as unimportant. As to the latter, research has long established that readers often make bridging inferences concerning ambiguous referents without being aware of making them (Baker, 1979; Vosniadou, Pearson, & Rogers, 1988) or do not detect textual problems because some types of inferences are made that fix them (August, Flavell, & Clift, 1984).

Examinations of the rereading effect have provided additional evidence supporting the levels-of-disruption hypothesis. Rereading has been shown to be an effective strategy to increase comprehension, and one reason why it may be an effective strategy is because rereading increases processing of a text at the situation model level (Millis, Simon, & tenBroek, 1998). The levels-of-disruption hypothesis posits that disruptions at the situation model level serve as inferential cues that inform judgments of comprehension. Processing a text at the situation model level, accordingly, should increase the salience of disruptions and increase the accuracy of the reader's judgments of comprehension. Therefore, rereading should improve not only comprehension but also metacomprehension.

In two experiments, Rawson, Dunlosky, and Thiede (2000) demonstrated that rereading does in fact increase metacomprehension accuracy. Moreover, when rereading is delayed for one week, processing at the situation model level is reduced (Millis et al., 1998). Dunlosky and Rawson (2005) also showed that delayed rereading reduces metacomprehension accuracy. Participants who delayed their rereading for one week attained a level of metacomprehension accuracy that was comparable to the accuracy of the participants who read the texts only once. In sum, rereading does increase comprehension and metacomprehension, but delaying rereading results in a reduction of both.

The failure to detect textual problems may be the result of not experiencing disruptions to one's comprehension, and not experiencing disruptions to comprehension may be the result of not processing a text deeply at a situation model level. Although there is much speculation in this statement, there is sufficient basis to sustain further investigations. If the nexus between comprehension and metacomprehension is the development of a situation model representation of the text, then interventions that encourage reading at this level would be advantageous. For example, asking readers to make multiple judgments concerning their comprehension during reading could be a good strategy to alert readers that a possible disruption in comprehension has occurred, or asking readers to provide self-explanations concerning the meaning and relevance of each sentence or paragraph can improve both comprehension and metacomprehension (Griffin et al., 2008). This online monitoring may encourage greater control of ongoing reading and contribute significantly to self-regulated comprehension (Dunlosky & Rawson, 2005; Dunlosky et al., 2002; Hacker, 2004).

The Cognitive Demands of Comprehension and Metacomprehension

Comprehending text is a resource-demanding task, and the amount of cognitive resources available to readers can constrain comprehension, especially if the texts require higher-order inferential processing. Keener and Hacker (2012), using eye-tracking technology, examined text comprehension by manipulating three types of questions, each designed to probe a specific level of comprehension. The textbase level of representation was probed by asking participants to answer literal questions. The situation model of representation was probed at two levels of inferential processing by asking participants to answer temporal ordering questions, which required inferences dealing with time, and propositional logic questions, which required complex logical-deductive inferences (Kintsch, 1998). Furthermore, metacomprehension was examined by asking readers to provide confidence judgments predicting whether they could correctly answer questions about the text prior to actually answering them and to provide confidence judgments postdicting whether the answers they had given were correct.

Our results showed that participants correctly answered a larger proportion of literal questions ($M = 0.75$) than temporal ordering questions ($M = 0.71$), and a larger proportion of temporal ordering questions than propositional logic questions ($M = 0.67$). Literal questions were answered more quickly ($M = 96.40$ ms/character) than temporal ordering questions ($M = 109.70$ ms/character), and temporal ordering questions were answered more quickly than propositional logic questions ($M = 118.05$ ms/character). Finally, in addition to response time, we used pupil dilation as a measure of cognitive effort, with greater dilation associated with greater cognitive effort. Task-evoked pupillary responses have been shown to provide reliable and sensitive psychophysiological measures of the momentary processing load during performance of cognitive activities (e.g., Ahern & Beatty, 1979; Hess & Polt, 1964; Just & Carpenter, 1993; Kahneman & Beatty, 1966). Pupil dilation was measured by peak amplitude of pupil diameter. Pupil dilation was greater for propositional logic questions than for literal or temporal ordering questions.

The predictive judgments of metacomprehension, as measured by bias scores, showed that participants were nearly perfectly accurate in predicting performance on literal questions ($M = -0.01$; zero indicating perfect accuracy), less accurate in predicting performance on temporal ordering questions ($M = 0.03$), and less accurate in predicting propositional logic questions ($M = 0.08$). Similarly, the postdictive judgments showed greater accuracy with literal questions ($M = 0.03$) and less accuracy with both temporal ordering ($M = 0.06$) and propositional logic questions ($M = 0.05$).

Overall, the deeper into inferential processing that a reader must go to comprehend a text, the more effortful comprehension becomes. Moreover, the metacomprehension judgments showed that the participants were sensitive to the varying degrees of effort needed for comprehension at each level of text representation. Participants modified their confidence judgments according to the type of question being asked, and when greater effort was required to answer questions, participants were less accurate in judging whether they had correctly answered them. In sum, failures to detect textual problems, particularly textual problems involving complex inferences, may be the result of attenuated cognitive resources to comprehend text and lower ability to monitor failures at inferential levels.

Weaver and Bryant (1995) provide additional support for Keener and Hacker's (2012) work concerning both comprehension and metacomprehension. Their results indicated that when texts are more closely matched to the reading abilities of the readers, metacomprehension accuracy was significantly greater than when texts were either more difficult or easy compared to the readers' abilities. To explain these results, Weaver and Bryant proposed the optimum effort hypothesis. That is, when some intermediate level of cognitive effort is required to comprehend a text, sufficient cognitive resources still remain to achieve higher levels of metacomprehension accuracy. However, when high levels of cognitive effort are required to comprehend a difficult text, too few resources remain for adequate metacomprehension, and conversely, too little demand on cognitive resources when reading easy texts places the reader in an "automatic" reading mode (also known as mindless reading). Both conditions lead to poorer metacomprehension accuracy.

Mindless Reading

Most people at one time or another have caught themselves thinking that they were fully engaged in reading but then suddenly realized that not a word of what was read was comprehended. Words, sentences, paragraphs, and sometimes even pages are read, but a coherent idea of the text has not been formed. These mental states in which a person is no longer attending to the task at hand but is instead thinking of something else have been referred to as mind wandering, or mindless reading when applied specifically to reading (Schad et al., 2012; Reichle et al., 2010). Mind wandering is a common psychological phenomenon that may account for as much as 30% of our daily life (Reichle et al., 2010) and may, in fact, be a default mode of operation (Schad et al., 2012). Because active engagement in reading is a necessary ingredient for comprehension and for self-regulated comprehension (Hacker, 2004), mindless reading is antithetical to these purposes. During mindless reading, the reader is interrupted from task focus by task-unrelated thoughts (Smallwood & Schooler, 2006) or decoupled from the text (Schad et al., 2012; Reichle et al., 2010), and cognitive processing of text is superseded by processing of potentially anything but the text. Not too surprisingly, blatant gaps, textual inconsistencies, inaccuracies, or misunderstandings will go unnoticed during these periods.

Eye-tracking technology has provided new opportunities to study mindless reading, affording new insights into the psychological mechanisms contributing to it. For example, Schad et al. (2012) have proposed the levels-of-inattention hypothesis to explain mindless reading. Rather than an all-or-nothing process (i.e., either text processing occurs or all text processing is shut down when mind wandering occurs), the levels-of-inattention hypothesis posits that mindless reading can occur at different hierarchical levels, resulting in graded degrees of weak and deep mindless reading. These hierarchical levels include lexical, syntactic, semantic, and discourse levels. Using an error-detection paradigm, Schad et al. predicted that when deep mindless reading occurs, readers would show little sensitivity to low-level errors, such as lexical errors, and these types of error as well as high-level errors, such as semantic errors, would go undetected; however, when weak mindless reading occurs, readers would maintain a sensitivity to low-level errors and detect them, but high-level errors would go undetected.

Using texts that contained both meaningless sentences and various kinds of errors, mindless reading was operationally defined as reading during which a meaningless sentence is overlooked and the reader shows low sensitivity to errors. The analyses supported predictions: In a deep state of mindless reading, small low-level errors as well as high-level errors were overlooked, but in a weak state of mindless reading, mainly only the high-level errors were overlooked. Eye-movement measures showed that, on average, readers overlooked errors about 40% of the time, and this percentage increased with increased time on task. Moreover, eye movements for as many as 20 words preceding an error could predict whether the upcoming error was to be overlooked. Reading behaviors such as wrap-up effects (i.e., slowing reading at the end of phrases or sentences to integrate words in the sentence) and longer fixation durations on longer or less frequent words, which are typical behaviors for normal reading, were reduced or absent during mindless reading. Therefore, predicting occurrences of mindless reading and when errors will be overlooked is possible by an analysis of eye movements for as much as 5 seconds before the errors appear in the text.

Also using eye-tracking technology, Reichle et al. (2010) provided corroborating evidence for Schad et al.'s (2012) findings. These researchers identified mindless reading from readers' self-reports indicating they were aware that a state of mind wandering had occurred, and from random probes delivered to readers that asked them whether they had been zoning out while reading. Analyses of eye movements showed that first-fixation durations, gaze durations, and total reading times were longer for mind-less reading than for normal reading, and that the longer time periods spent on read-ing can occur for up to 120 seconds prior to readers' catching that they had actually been in a state of mindless reading. In addition, in the 2.5 seconds immediately before catching themselves zoning out, readers were less likely to make first-pass fixations, word fixations, or interword regressions and were more likely looking at something other than the text. Readers' awareness of their extended reading times (i.e., their meta-awareness of reading behaviors) and their atypical reading behaviors may be factors that alert them to being in a mindless reading state.

If readers can routinely fall into states of mindless reading—when mental process-ing that should be directed to comprehension is decoupled from that task and directed elsewhere for periods that can last for approximately 2 minutes—it is perhaps unsur-prising that textual problems can go undetected, even if readers are fully capable of resolving those problems. Although additional research is necessary to more fully investigate states of mindless reading, one can easily speculate that its effects will likely be exaggerated when reading easy or difficult texts (see Weaver & Bryant, 1995), when cognitive resources are being overloaded (see Keener & Hacker, 2012), when multiple goals for reading are being pursued (see Hacker, 1997, 2004), when readers have insuf-ficient knowledge to comprehend (see Hacker et al., 1994; Plumb et al., 1994), or when readers lack motivation to read. Although mindless reading cannot fully explain all the conditions under which textual problems go undetected during reading, the argument that it could be a contributing factor certainly has to be considered.

Conclusion

Why do people often lack an awareness of their comprehension failures and routinely fail to detect blatant gaps, inconsistencies, or inaccuracies in textual information, or misunderstand textual information and yet remain highly confident that they have in fact fully and correctly comprehended it? This question is what intrigued Markman in 1977 and has intrigued many others since—including myself. I have provided five explanations for the lack of awareness of comprehension during reading. Although many more likely exist, these five have caught my attention, and four of the five have been the focus of my research. Very likely, no one explanation can account for all com-prehension failures, and equally as likely, several could be occurring simultaneously.

At a very basic level, readers must have the required knowledge to detect errors. Knowledge of how to correct an error, even if it is an imperfect correction, is necessary for its detection; however, knowledge of how to correct an error is not *sufficient* for its detection. Additional cognitive processing is required for error detection, and one form of that additional cognitive processing involves having a specific goal for read-ing. If readers are provided with specific goals, then lexical, syntactic, semantic, and discourse errors, as well as textual inconsistencies and inaccuracies, can be detected and corrected.

Reading comprehension is a multilayered cognitive process that can and should lead to various levels of text representation, and each of those levels can vary depending on the reader's background knowledge and purpose. Without a specific goal for reading, the constructed text representations can be as variable as the readers constructing them. When given a specific goal, readers are much more likely to construct text representations that are deliberately and intentionally scrutinized to achieve that goal. Deliberate and intentional reading may be the necessary and sufficient conditions for comprehension. There is the possibility that when a reader is given the goal to read for comprehension, a variety of textual problems will become evident; however, this is a possibility in need of further research.

Deliberate and intentional reading may be the cure for mindless reading as well. In experimental settings, the pervasiveness of mindless reading that results in overlooking many kinds of textual problems is disconcerting. If normal reading outside of the lab entails overlooking errors at a rate at least, based on lab data, 40% of the time, this is a major educational problem. Students are routinely asked to read vast quantities of material in short periods of time, material that is usually difficult and at times perhaps too difficult, material that is sometimes unmotivating, and material that is often read under conditions of fatigue and stress. Although researchers need to investigate mindless reading under these various conditions, the possibility that a prevalence of 40% for mindless reading occurs across a variety of conditions and settings does not seem all that far-fetched. Luckily, readers do have the ability to catch themselves when in this mind wandering state. Whatever the mechanism is that alerts readers to this state— abnormal reading behaviors or prolonged reading times—frequently catching oneself in a mindless state could be a good self-regulation cue that the conditions for reading must change to guarantee that comprehension is going to be achieved. Taking a break, engaging in another task, remotivating reading, or reinstating reading goals all could be appropriate responses to decrease this unconscious state.

Responding to self-regulation cues is a part of self-regulated comprehension, which involves monitoring and subsequent control of ongoing reading comprehension. Monitoring is the driving psychological process responsible for metacomprehension, and metacomprehension accuracy, we have theorized, is a function of responding to disruptions in comprehension at the situation model level of text representation. When a reader responds to disruptions, presumably caused by textual problems or breakdowns in comprehension at the situation model level, and then remediates comprehension, and finally is tested on his or her remediated comprehension, metacomprehension accuracy will be high. Thus, comprehension and metacomprehension accuracy depend on the development of a situation model. Research has shown that simple rereading improves both comprehension and metacomprehension. Utilizing this simple strategy could do much to improve students' comprehension. Other proven comprehension strategies, such as questioning, clarifying, discussing, self-explanation, or writing, may work for reasons similar to rereading: Disruptions to comprehension are monitored, the causes of the disruptions are remediated, and a more fully developed situation model of the text is formed.

However, the inferential processing required to construct a situation model can be a stumbling block to comprehension and metacomprehension. Inferential processing requires the reader to combine textual information with his or her world knowledge. Therefore, adequate world knowledge is a necessary prerequisite to comprehension. In addition, some types of inferential processing are highly demanding of cognitive resources. Moreover, readers are less accurate at monitoring their comprehension at inferential levels. With these factors in mind, there is little wonder that textual problems at the inferential level are overlooked, ignored, or resolved in ways that result in inaccurate or incomplete situation models of the text. To assist the reader in overcoming these difficulties with inferential processing, the most basic fix is to learn as much as possible about the world. Research on expertise would attest to the fact that there is no substitute for simply knowing a lot about the world. Inferential processing is demanding of cognitive resources, but there are ways to lessen the demands: decompose complex reading tasks into simpler subtasks, sharing reading in groups in which inferential processing can be scaffolded with other readers, or deliberately making metacomprehension judgments throughout reading and responding appropriately to the judgment (e.g., low confidence is followed up with more strategic reading). Finally, monitoring accuracy can be improved. Rereading has already been discussed, and in addition, Thiede and Anderson (2003) showed that summarizing text improves metacomprehension while Thiede, Dunlosky, Griffin, and Wiley (2005) showed that generating five keywords from a text also can improve metacomprehension.

In sum, Markman (1977) put her finger squarely on the undesirable consequences of failing to detect textual problems: "Consequently individual and developmental differences in sensitivity to one's comprehension failure will result in differences in the quality of comprehension itself" (p. 992). Further research on the role of knowledge, goals and strategies, monitoring accuracy, cognitive demands, and mindless reading will do much to help us understand the importance of "Realizing That You Don't Understand" (p. 986).

References

Adams, M. J., & Collins, A. (1979). A schema-theoretic view of reading. In R. O. Freedle (Ed.), *Discourse processing: Multidisciplinary perspectives* (pp. 486–502). Norwood, NJ: Ablex.

Ahern, S., & Beatty, J. (1979). Pupillary responses during information processing vary with Scholastic Aptitude Test scores. *Science, 205,* 1289–1292.

August, D. L., Flavell, J. H., & Clift, R. (1984). Comparison of comprehension monitoring of skilled and less skilled readers. *Reading Research Quarterly, 20,* 39–53.

Baker, L. (1979). Comprehension monitoring: Identifying and coping with text confusions. *Journal of Reading Behavior, 11,* 363–374.

Baker, L. (1985). How do we know when we don't understand? Standards for evaluating text comprehension. In D. L. Forrest-Pressley, G. E. MacKinnon, & T. G. Waller (Eds.), *Metacognition, cognition, and human performance* (pp. 155–205). New York: Academic Press.

Baker, L., & Zimlin, L. (1989). Instructional effects on children's use of two levels of standards for evaluating their comprehension. *Journal of Educational Psychology, 81,* 340–346.

Beal, C. R. (1990). The development of text evaluation and revision skills. *Child Development, 61,* 247–258.

Beal, C. R., Bonitatibus, G. J., & Garrod, A. C. (1990). Fostering children's revision skills through training in comprehension monitoring. *Journal of Educational Psychology, 82,* 275–280.

Bransford, J. D., Barclay, J. B., & Franks, J. J. (1972). Sentence memory: A constructivist versus interpretive approach. *Cognitive Psychology, 3,* 193–209.

Dunlosky, J., & Lipko, A. R. (2007). Metacomprehension: A brief history and how to improve its accuracy. *Current Directions in Psychological Science, 16,* 228–232.

Dunlosky, J., & Rawson, K. A. (2005). Why does rereading improve metacomprehension accuracy? Evaluating the levels-of-disruption hypothesis for the rereading effect. *Discourse Processes, 40,* 37–55.

Dunlosky, J., Rawson, K., & Hacker, D. J. (2002). Metacomprehension of science text: Investigating the levels-of-disruption hypothesis. In J. Otero, J. A. Leon, & A. C. Graesser (Eds.), *The psychology of science text comprehension* (pp. 255–279). Mahwah, NJ: Lawrence Erlbaum Associates.

Englert, C. S., Hiebert, E. H., & Stewart, S. R. (1988). Detecting and correcting inconsistencies in the monitoring of expository prose. *Journal of Educational Research, 81,* 221–227.

Figueredo, L., & Varnhagen, C. K. (2004). Detecting a problem is half the battle: The relation between error type and spelling performance. *Scientific Studies of Reading, 8,* 337–356.

Flower, L. S., Hayes, J. R., Carey, L., Schriver, K., & Stratman, J. (1986). Detection, diagnosis, and the strategies of revision. *College Composition and Communication, 37,* 16–53.

Glenberg, A. M., Wilkinson, A. C., & Epstein, W. (1982). The illusion of knowing: Failure in the self-assessment of comprehension. *Memory & Cognition, 10,* 597–602.

Griffin, T. D., Wiley, J., & Thiede, K. (2008). Individual differences, rereading, and self-explanation: Concurrent processing and cue validity as constraints on metacomprehension accuracy. *Memory & Cognition, 36,* 93–103.

Hacker, D. J. (1994). Comprehension monitoring as a writing process. In E. C. Butterfield (Ed.), *Children's writing: Toward a process theory of the development of skilled writing.* Greenwich, CT: JAI Press.

Hacker, D. J. (1997). Comprehension monitoring of written discourse across early-to-middle adolescence. *Reading and Writing: An Interdisciplinary Journal, 9*, 207–240.

Hacker, D. J. (2004). Self-regulated comprehension during normal reading. In R. B. Ruddell & N. Unrau (Eds.), *Theoretical models and processes of reading* (5th ed., pp. 775–779). Newark, DE: International Reading Association.

Hacker, D. J., Plumb, C., Butterfield, E. C., Quathamer, D., & Heineken, E. (1994). Text revision: Detection and correction of errors. *Journal of Educational Psychology, 86*, 65–78.

Hess, E. H., & Polt, J. M. (1964). Pupil size in relation to mental activity during simple problem-solving. *Science, 143*, 1190–1192.

Hull, G. (1987). The editing process in writing: A performance study of more skilled and less skilled college writers. *Research in the Teaching of English, 21*, 8–29.

Just, M. A., & Carpenter, P. A. (1993). The intensity of dimension of thought: Pupillometric indices of sentence processing. *Canadian Journal of Experimental Psychology, 47*, 310–339.

Kaakinen, J. K., & Hyönä, J. (2010). Task effects on eye movements during reading. *Journal of Experimental Psychology. Learning, Memory, and Cognition, 36*, 1561–1566.

Kahneman, D., & Beatty, J. (1966). Pupil diameter and load on memory. *Science, 154*, 1583–1585.

Keener, M. C., & Hacker, D. J. (2012). Integration of comprehension and metacomprehension using narrative texts. Doctoral Dissertation, University of Utah.

Kintsch, W. (1994). Text comprehension, memory, and learning. *American Psychologist, 49*, 294–303.

Kintsch, W. (1998). *Comprehension: A paradigm for cognition.* Cambridge: Cambridge University Press.

Maki, R. H. (1998). Test predictions over text material. In D. J. Hacker, J. Dunlosky, & A. C. Graesser (Eds.), *Metacognition in educational theory and practice* (pp. 117–144). Mahwah, NJ: Lawrence Erlbaum Associates.

Markman, E. M. (1977). Realizing that you don't understand: A preliminary investigation. *Child Development, 48*, 986–992.

Markman, E. M. (1979). Realizing that you don't understand: Elementary school children's awareness. *Child Development, 50*, 643–655.

Markman, E. M. (1985). Comprehension monitoring: Developmental and education issues. In S. F. Chipman, J. W. Sega, & R. Glaser (Eds.), *Thinking and learning skills: Vol. 2. Research and open questions* (pp. 275–291). Hillsdale, NJ: Lawrence Erlbaum Associates.

Markman, E. M., & Gorin, L. (1981). Children's ability to adjust their standards for evaluating comprehension. *Journal of Educational Psychology, 73*, 320–325.

Millis, K. K., Simon, S., & tenBroek, N. S. (1998). Resource allocation during the rereading of scientific texts. *Memory & Cognition, 26*, 232–246.

Plumb, C., Butterfield, E. C., Hacker, D. J., & Dunlosky, J. (1994). Error correction in text: Testing the processing-deficit and knowledge-deficit hypotheses. *Reading and Writing: An Interdisciplinary Journal, 6,* 347–360.

Pressley, M., & Afflerbach, P. (1995). *Verbal reports of reading: The nature of constructively responsive reading.* Hillsdale, NJ: Lawrence Erlbaum Associates.

Radach, R., Huestegge, L., & Reilley, R. (2008). The role of global top-down factors in local eye-movement control in reading. *Psychological Research, 72,* 675–688.

Rawson, K. A., Dunlosky, J., & Thiede, K. W. (2000). The rereading effect: Metacomprehension accuracy improves across reading trials. *Memory & Cognition, 28,* 1004–1010.

Reichle, E. D., Reineberg, A. E., & Schooler, J. W. (2010). Eye movements during mindless reading. *Psychological Science, 21,* 1300–1310.

Schad, D. J., Nuthmann, A., & Engbert, R. (2012). Your mind wanders weakly, your mind wanders deeply: Objective measures reveal mindless reading at different levels. *Cognition, 125,* 179–194.

Smallwood, J., & Schooler, J. W. (2006). The restless mind. *Psychological Bulletin, 132,* 946–958.

Thiede, K. W., & Anderson, M. C. M. (2003). Summarizing can improve meta-comprehension accuracy. *Contemporary Educational Psychology, 28,* 129–160.

Thiede, K. W., Dunlosky, J., Griffin, T., & Wiley, J. (2005). Understanding the delayed-keyword effect on metacomprehension accuracy. *Journal of Experimental Psychology. Learning, Memory, and Cognition, 31,* 1267–1280.

van den Broek, P., Bohn-Gettler, C. M., Kendeou, P., Carlson, S., & White, M. J. (2011). When a reader meets a text: The role of standards of coherence in reading comprehension. In M. T. McCrudden, J. P. Magliano, & G. J. Schraw (Eds.), *Text relevance and learning from text* (pp. 123–139). Charlotte, NC: Information Age.

Vosniadou, S., Pearson, P. D., & Rogers, T. (1988). What causes children's failures to detect inconsistencies in text? Representation versus comparison difficulties. *Journal of Educational Psychology, 80,* 27–39.

Weaver, C. A., III, & Bryant, D. S. (1995). Monitoring of comprehension: The role of text difficulty in metamemory for narrative and expository text. *Memory & Cognition, 23,* 2–22.

Zabrucky, K., & Moore, D. (1989). Children's ability to use three standards to evaluate their comprehension of text. *Reading Research Quarterly, 24,* 336–352.

5   Research on Semantic Illusions Tells Us That There Are Multiple Sources of Misinformation

Brenda Hannon

What superhero is associated with bats, Robin, the Penguin, **Metropolis**, *Catwoman, the Riddler, the Joker, and Mr. Freeze?* Did you answer *Batman*? If you did, then you are a victim of a semantic illusion because Batman protects *Gotham City* and not *Metropolis*. In questions like this one, people frequently fail to notice a semantic anomaly even though they know that Batman protects Gotham City and even when they are told in advance that there are questions with semantic errors (Hannon & Daneman, 2001a). But why do people fail to notice semantic anomalies? That is, what are the sources of misinformation that lead people to misread or perhaps even misinterpret semantic anomalies in text like the Batman question? The purpose of this chapter is to identify sources of misinformation. Specifically, I first identify characteristics of the text (i.e., the "Characteristics of the Text that Are Sources of Semantic Illusions" section) and the individual (i.e., the "Characteristics of the Individual that Are Sources of Semantic Illusions" section) that influence detection of semantic anomalies. Next, in the "Theories of Semantic Illusions" section, I review the theoretical explanations for semantic illusions. Then, in the "Summary of Theories" section, I summarize what semantic illusion research tells us about the multisource nature of misinformation. In the concluding section, I identify directions for future research.

Characteristics of the Text That Are Sources of Semantic Illusions

The first empirical investigation of semantic anomalies was conducted by Erickson and Mattson (1981). In their study, participants read aloud a series of nonanomalous and anomalous questions, such as *What country's flag is red, white, and blue?* (nonanomalous) or *How many animals of each kind did* **Moses** *take on the ark?* (anomalous). Participants were instructed to answer the questions with a one-word answer, to say *don't know* if they did not know the answer, or to say *wrong* if they detected something wrong in a question. In spite of being warned that some of the questions had something wrong with them, Erickson and Mattson observed that 80% of their participants failed to detect the anomalous word *Moses*. That is, their participants frequently answered the

Moses question with *two* rather than *wrong* even though a posttest questionnaire indicated that their participants knew that it was *Noah* and not *Moses who took two animals of each kind on the ark.*

Subsequent research has successfully replicated the findings of Erickson and Mattson (1981) using a variety of semantically anomalous questions other than the so-called Moses illusion question (Hannon & Daneman, 2001a; Reder & Kusbit, 1991; Shafto & MacKay, 2000; van Jaarsveld, Dijkstra, & Hermans, 1997; van Oostendorp & de Mul, 1990); see table 5.1 for examples. Although detection failure is not as high as the 80% that is typically observed for the Moses illusion question, studies routinely show that people fail to detect semantic anomalies 35% to 50% of the time (Hannon & Daneman, 2001a). Research also suggests that detection failure is not a consequence of people's simply cooperating with the researcher or withholding a detection response

Table 5.1

Examples of impostor word and number of contextual cues manipulations in anomalous questions

Manipulation	Example
Impostor word	
Strong	1. What superhero is associated with bats, Robin, the Penguin, *Metropolis*, Catwoman, the Riddler, the Joker, and Mr. Freeze?
	2. What country includes the Apache, Cheyenne, Comanche, *Aztec*, Sioux, Mohawk, Shawnee, and Navajo?
	3. What type of mammal includes panda, koala, teddy, *Bengal*, black, brown, pooh, and polar?
Weak	1. What superhero is associated with bats, Robin, the Penguin, *Atlantis*, Catwoman, the Riddler, the Joker, and Mr. Freeze?
	2. What country includes the Apache, Cheyenne, Comanche, *Pygmies*, Sioux, Mohawk, Shawnee, and Navajo?
	3. What type of mammal includes panda, koala, teddy, *labrador*, black, brown, pooh, and polar?
No. of contextual cues	
Many	1. What superhero is associated with bats, Robin, the Penguin, *Metropolis*, Catwoman, the Riddler, the Joker, and Mr. Freeze?
	2. What country includes the Apache, Cheyenne, Comanche, *Aztec*, Sioux, Mohawk, Shawnee, and Navajo?
	3. What type of mammal includes panda, koala, teddy, *Bengal*, black, brown, pooh, and polar?
Few	1. What is the name of the superhero who is associated with bats, Robin, *Metropolis,* Catwoman, and Mr. Freeze?
	2. What is the name of the country that includes the Apache, Cheyenne, *Aztec,* Mohawk, and Navajo?

Note. Impostor words are italicized in the table for illustration purposes.

because they think that errors were inadvertently introduced into the materials by the writer (Reder & Kusbit, 1991; Reder & Cleeremans, 1990). Nor is detection failure a consequence of people's failing to detect the impostor word (e.g., *Moses*) because they skip over it or are processing the text too quickly (Erickson & Mattson, 1981; Reder & Kusbit, 1991). Rather, research suggests that people are genuinely failing to detect the anomalous words (Erickson & Mattson, 1981; van Jaarsveld et al., 1997) even when the presentation speed of the text is slowed down (Fazio & Marsh, 2008) or self-paced (Barton & Sanford, 1993).

There is also evidence that the phenomenon of semantic illusions generalizes over a wide range of stimuli and variety of conditions (e.g., Barton & Sanford, 1993; Bredart & Modolo, 1988; Bredart & Docquier, 1989; Büttner, 2007; Hannon & Daneman, 2001a; Long & Chong, 2001; Reder & Kusbit, 1991; Shafto & MacKay, 2000, 2010; van Jaarsveld et al., 1997; van Oostendorp & Kok, 1990). Semantic illusions can, for instance, occur when the stimuli are either questions or statements (e.g., *How many animals of each kind did* **Moses** *take on the Ark?* or **Moses** *took two animals of each kind on the Ark.*) although detection failure is greater for questions than statements, 47.5% versus 31.5%, respectively (e.g., Büttner, 2007; Erickson & Mattson, 1981; see also Büttner, 2012, and van Jaarsveld et al., 1997). Semantic illusions also occur when anomalies are embedded in multiple lines of text, such as the short passage in table 5.2 that describes the pre- and postevents of a plane crash (Barton & Sanford, 1993; Daneman, Hannon, & Burton, 2006; Daneman, Lennertz, & Hannon, 2007; Hannon & Daneman, 2004). Focus also influences the frequency of semantic illusions inasmuch as more illusions occur when the impostor word/anomaly is not the focus of the text. For example, more illusions occur with the statement *It was* **two animals** *of each kind that Moses took on the Ark.* than with the statement *It was* **Moses** *who took two animals of each kind on the*

Table 5.2
Example of stimulus that includes multiple lines of text

Paragraph:
There was a tourist flight traveling from Vienna to Barcelona. On the last leg of the journey, it developed engine trouble. Over the Pyrenees, the pilot started to lose control. The plane eventually crashed right on the border. Wreckage was equally strewn in France and Spain.
Final sentence of the paragraph was one of the following sentences:
1. The authorities were trying to decide where to bury the *survivors*.
2. The authorities were trying to decide where to bury the *injured*.
3. The authorities were trying to decide where to bury the *surviving injured*.
4. The authorities were trying to decide where to bury the *surviving dead*.
Question following paragraph:
What should the authorities do?

Note. Anomalous impostor words are italicized in the table for illustration purposes. Stimulus example is taken from Barton and Sanford (1993, p. 479).

Ark. because in the former example *Moses* is not the focus of the statement whereas in the latter example he is (e.g., Bredart & Modolo, 1988; Bredart & Docquier, 1989; Sturt, Sanford, Stewart, & Dawydiak, 2004; see Wang, Hagoort, and Yang, 2009, for a similar finding using ERPs).

Another text-based characteristic that influences detection failures of semantic anomalies is the number of semantic features that are common between the impostor word and the correct word (e.g., Hannon & Daneman, 2001a). Indeed, people are less likely to detect an anomaly if the word posing for *Noah* is *Moses* than if it is *Adam* because *Noah* and *Moses* have many more semantic features in common (i.e., old men, long robes, biblical stories about water) than do *Noah* and *Adam* (i.e., Old Testament). On the other hand, people easily detect an anomaly if the word posing for *Noah* is *Obama* because there are few, if any, common semantic features between the two names (e.g., Erickson & Mattson, 1981).

Research also suggests that the greater the number of contextual cues that lead to an illusionary answer, the more likely detection failure will occur (Hannon & Daneman, 2001a). People are, for example, less likely to detect *Metropolis* in the question *What superhero is associated with bats, Robin, the Penguin, **Metropolis**, Catwoman, the Riddler, the Joker, and Mr. Freeze?* than in the question *What is the name of the superhero who is associated with bats, Robin, **Metropolis**, as well as the Penguin, the Riddler, and the Joker?* because the former question has more contextual cues that lead to the illusionary answer *Batman* than does the latter question (i.e., eight vs. six contextual cues). See table 5.1 for more examples.

More recent research in my lab also suggests that the location of the impostor word in an anomalous question influences detection of sematic anomalies. See table 5.3 for examples. In this research, participants read a number of anomalous questions that varied as to whether the impostor word was located early in a question, in the middle of a question, or later in a question. Then they either answered the questions or said "wrong" if they detected something wrong with them. All other properties of the questions such as the impostor words, the length of the questions, and the number and order of the contextual cues were held constant regardless of the location of the impostor words.[1]

The results showed that anomaly detection was greatest when the impostor words were located at the beginning and the end of the questions (i.e., 48% and 54%, respectively) and poorest when they were located in the middle (i.e., 38%). In other words, detection plotted as a function of impostor word location exhibited a U-shaped function. These findings challenge existing theories of semantic illusions inasmuch as no existing theoretical explanation can account for this U-shape function. Moreover, from a theoretical perspective, a U-shape function is often indicative of component processes from two distinct neurological systems (see Glanzer & Cunitz, 1966, for a

Table 5.3

Examples of position manipulation in anomalous questions

Position	Anomalous Question
Early	c **X** c c c c c c c
	1. What superhero is associated with *Metropolis*, bats, Robin, the Penguin, Catwoman, the Riddler, the Joker, and Mr. Freeze?
	2. What country includes the *Aztec*, Apache, Cheyenne, Comanche, Sioux, Mohawk, Shawnee, and Navajo?
	3. What type of mammal includes *Bengal*, panda, koala, teddy, black, brown, pooh, and polar?
Middle	c c c c **X** c c c c
	1. What superhero is associated with bats, Robin, the Penguin, *Metropolis*, Catwoman, the Riddler, the Joker, and Mr. Freeze?
	2. What country includes the Apache, Cheyenne, Comanche, *Aztec*, Sioux, Mohawk, Shawnee, and Navajo?
	3. What type of mammal includes panda, koala, teddy, *Bengal*, black, brown, pooh, and polar?
Late	c c c c c c c **X** c
	1. What superhero is associated with bats, Robin, the Penguin, Catwoman, the Riddler, the Joker, *Metropolis*, and Mr. Freeze?
	2. What country includes the Apache, Cheyenne, Comanche, Sioux, Mohawk, Shawnee, *Aztec,* and Navajo?
	3. What type of mammal includes panda, koala, teddy, black, brown, pooh, *Bengal*, and polar?

Note. Impostor words are italicized in the table for illustration purposes. "c" represents a contextual cue and "x" represents an impostor word.

two-distinct-systems explanation for the serial position curve). See the theoretical section of this chapter for more discussion of these two points.

Other recent research suggests that semantic anomalies are both consciously and unconsciously detected (Hannon, under review). In this research, *conscious detections* of anomalies are assessed using both measures of accuracy and reaction time—for example, when impostor words are explicitly identified and the reading times for detected impostor words are greater than the reading times for undetected impostor words. In contrast, *unconscious detections* of anomalies occur with no overt detections of impostor words (i.e., a reader fails to say wrong after reading an anomalous question). However, *there is* evidence that the reader slowed down while reading the impostor words in the anomalous questions.

In this study, all participants completed a semantic anomaly task that manipulated a priori the location of the impostor words (i.e., early, middle, and late); see table 5.3

for examples. However, only half of the participants followed the standard instructions (i.e., say *wrong* if you detect something wrong in a question, don't know if you did not know the answer, or answer the question); the other half ignored the anomalies and either answered the questions or said "don't know" if they did not know the answer (see Reder & Kusbit, 1991, for a similar procedure). Additionally, the reading time for each word in each question was recorded using Just, Carpenter, and Woolley's (1982) word-by-word *moving window* technique. Reading times for impostor words were used to assess immediate detection of semantic anomalies while reading times of the first and second words following the impostor words were used to assess delayed detection of semantic anomalies.

To assess conscious detection of semantic anomalies, comparisons were made between reading times for detected versus undetected impostor words as a function of impostor word location (early, middle, or late). The prediction was that if people consciously detect semantic anomalies, then the average reading times for detected impostor words should be significantly *slower* than the average reading times for undetected impostor words (Hannon, under review).

The results provided strong support for immediate but not delayed conscious detection of semantic anomalies. As table 5.4 shows, people spent 109 ms longer reading detected versus undetected impostor words (i.e., 1,119 vs. 1,010 ms). This finding clearly suggests that conscious detection of semantic anomalies can be immediate. There was also a marginally significant detection × location interaction such that when impostor words were located earlier in questions, reading times were equivalent for detected versus undetected impostor words (i.e., 921 vs. 923 ms), whereas when impostor words were located in the middle or later in questions, reading times were slower for detected versus undetected impostor words (i.e., 1,260 vs. 1,119 ms and 1,176 vs. 987 ms, respectively). These findings suggest that immediate conscious detection of anomalies occurs when impostor words are located in the middle or later in questions but not when the anomalies are located earlier in questions. In other words, these findings suggest that some of the text has to be processed before immediate conscious detection of impostor words can occur.

On the other hand, there was no evidence for delayed conscious detection of semantic anomalies. Specifically, as table 5.4 shows, regardless of the dependent measure (i.e., the reading time for the first word following an impostor, the reading time for the second word following an impostor, or the combined reading times for the first and second words following an impostor), reading times were equivalent for detected and undetected anomalous questions.

For unconscious detection of semantic anomalies, comparisons were made between reading times for undetected impostor words in anomalous questions versus reading times for impostor words in critical control questions (i.e., the condition in which participants were instructed to ignore impostor words) as a function of impostor word

Table 5.4
Median reading times (and standard errors) for impostor word, first word immediately following impostor, second word immediately following impostor, first and second word immediately following impostor, and total read time as a function of detection and position of impostor word

Position	Dependent Measure									
	Impostor[a]		First[a]		Second[a]		First + Second[a]		Total Read[b]	
Detected Anomalies										
Early	921	(45)	963	(47)	1,001	(43)	2,048	(89)	12.10	(.42)
Middle	1,260	(72)	987	(44)	943	(53)	2,077	(115)	12.02	(.45)
Late	1,176	(72)	615	(31)	1,184	(91)	1,871	(108)	12.41	(.51)
Average	1,119	(56)	855	(30)	1,043	(47)	1,999	(79)	12.18	(.46)
Undetected Anomalies										
Early	923	(63)	979	(44)	914	(37)	1,954	(78)	12.11	(.47)
Middle	1,119	(58)	927	(34)	865	(36)	1,889	(71)	12.38	(.49)
Late	987	(47)	584	(26)	1,223	(92)	1,849	(107)	12.15	(.49)
Average	1,010	(41)	830	(26)	1,000	(46)	1,897	(67)	12.21	(.41)
Critical Control Questions										
Early	846	(40)	825	(31)	851	(33)	1,815	(53)	11.55	(.44)
Middle	934	(40)	858	(31)	777	(32)	1,519	(69)	11.28	(.43)
Late	914	(48)	578	(27)	985	(60)	1,688	(73)	11.25	(.47)
Average	898	(40)	753	(25)	871	(36)	1,674	(39)	11.36	(.42)

Note. Total read time does not include the amount of time needed to answer a question. This table is taken from Hannon (under review).
[a]Values are given in milliseconds. [b]Values are given in seconds.

location (early, middle, late). The prediction was that if people unconsciously detect semantic anomalies, then average reading times for impostor words in undetected anomalous questions should be significantly *slower* than average reading times for impostor words in critical control questions.

The results provided strong evidence for both immediate and delayed unconscious detection of anomalies. As table 5.4 shows, people spent 112 ms longer reading impostor words in undetected anomalous questions than in critical control questions, (1,010 vs. 898 ms). This finding suggests that people immediately detect semantic anomalies unconsciously. Moreover, the lack of a detection × location interaction suggests that immediate detection was not influenced by the number of contextual cues that preceded the impostor words.

For delayed unconscious detection of semantic anomalies, people spent more time reading the first and second words following impostor words in undetected anomalous than in critical control questions (i.e., 830 vs. 753 ms for first words and 1,000 ms vs. 871 ms for second words). This finding suggests that unconscious detection of semantic anomalies can be delayed. There were also two significant detection × location interactions. The first interaction revealed that reading times for the first words following the impostor words located earlier in questions were 154 ms slower in undetected anomalous than in critical control questions (i.e., 979 vs. 825 ms), whereas there were no differences in reading times for first words following impostors located in the middle or later in undetected anomalous and critical control questions. In contrast, the second interaction revealed that there were no differences in reading times for the second words following impostors located either earlier or in the middle of undetected anomalous and critical control questions, whereas the reading times for second words located later in questions were 238 ms slower in undetected anomalous than in critical control questions (i.e., 1,223 vs. 985 ms). Taken as a whole, these two interactions suggest that when the impostor word is located earlier in a question, delayed unconscious detection of a semantic anomaly begins at the first word immediately following the impostor word. However, when the impostor word is located at the end of a question, delayed unconscious detection of a semantic anomaly begins at the second word following the impostor word.

In summary, research examining the influences of text-based characteristics on anomaly detection suggests that there are multiple sources of misinformation. The degree of relatedness between the impostor word and the word it is posing for, for example, is a source of misinformation, especially when the impostor word (e.g., *Moses*) is strongly related to the original word (e.g., *Noah*) (e.g., Erickson & Mattson, 1981; Hannon & Daneman, 2001a). The number of contextual cues that lead to an illusionary answer is also a source of misinformation, especially when there are many cues (e.g., Hannon & Daneman, 2001a). Further, if the misinformation is not the focus of the prose, people are more likely to miss the anomaly (e.g., Bredart & Docquier, 1989; Wang et al., 2009). Research also suggests that the impostor word location is a source of misinformation inasmuch as anomaly detection is greater when impostor words are located at the beginning and end of a text than when they are located in the middle. Finally, research suggests that misinformation is both consciously and unconsciously detected (e.g., Hannon, under review; see Bohan & Sanford, 2008, who used an eye-tracking methodology).

In addition, semantic illusion research suggests that the medium for text-based sources of misinformation is not restricted to questions. Rather, detection failures for misinformation can occur with statements (e.g., Bredart & Docquier, 1989; van Jaarsveld et al., 1997) or short prose passages (e.g., Barton & Sanford, 1993; Hannon & Daneman, 2004; Long & Chong, 2001). Finally, although semantic illusion research has revealed a number of text-based characteristics that influence anomaly detection, most studies have examined a single text-based characteristic. Therefore, one avenue for future research might be to examine the interactive/independent influences of multiple text-based characteristics on the detection of anomalies.

Characteristics of the Individual That Are Sources of Semantic Illusions

To date, only a few studies have examined the influences of characteristics of the individual on anomaly detection. Nevertheless, there is a consensus in the literature that detection failure is greater for less-skilled readers (i.e., readers who score below the mean on a test of reading comprehension) than for skilled readers (i.e., readers who score above the mean on a test of reading comprehension) (e.g., Britt, Kurby, Dandotkar, & Wolfe, 2008; Hannon & Daneman, 2004; Long & Chong, 2001; Todaro, Millis, & Dandotkar, 2010). However, there is little agreement as to which component process of reading might be best for explaining these detection failures. The lack of agreement is not surprising given that reading comprehension is composed of multiple component processes (e.g., lower-level word processes, text memory, text inferencing, knowledge integration, and working memory; see Hannon, 2012; Hannon & Frias, 2012; McNamara & Magliano, 2009, for reviews), and poor performance on one or all of these component processes might influence the frequency of anomaly detection. Todaro and colleagues (2010), for example, argue that less-skilled readers are more influenced than skilled readers by semantic relatedness, whereas skilled readers are more influenced than less-skilled readers by causal relatedness. On the other hand, Long and Chong (2001) argue that poor integration skills are why less-skilled readers fail to detect semantic anomalies more so than their skilled counterparts, and Hannon and Daneman (2004) argue that skill differences in semantic processing explain reading skill differences in anomaly detection.

In Todaro et al.'s (2010) study, skilled and less-skilled readers made judgments about the coherence of passages, which was manipulated in two ways: (1) semantically (e.g., high semantic relatedness: *Susan recognized her baby was sick. She called her family doctor at once.*; low semantic relatedness: *Susan's husband collapsed on the floor. She called her family doctor at once.*) and (2) causally (e.g., high causal relatedness: *Susan's husband collapsed on the floor. She called her family doctor at once.*; low causal relatedness: *Susan recently became a nurse. She called her family doctor at once.*). For semantically related passages, there were greater differences in judgments of coherence for less-skilled readers than for skilled readers, a finding that suggests less-skilled readers are more influenced by semantic relatedness than are skilled readers. On the other hand, for causally related passages, skilled readers had greater differences in judgments of coherence than less-skilled readers, a finding that suggests that skilled readers are more influenced by causal relatedness than are less-skilled readers.

Long and Chong (2001) also showed that reading skill influenced detection of anomalies. Their passages included two manipulations. One manipulation altered the description of a character and his or her action such that the contents were either (1) consistent, like passage 1 in table 5.5 (likes contact sports and signed up for boxing) or (2) inconsistent like passage 2 in table 5.5 (dislikes contact sports but signed up for boxing). The second manipulation altered the proximity of the character's description

Table 5.5

Examples of stimuli used in Long and Chong (2001)

Consistent Character and Character Action

Ken and his friend Mike had been looking for summer hobbies for quite some time. They were both college professors and they had the summers off from teaching. This meant that they both had plenty of time to try new things. Ken was a big man and always tried to keep in shape by jogging and lifting weights. His 250-pound body was solid muscle. Ken loved tough physical contact sports, which allowed him to match his strength against another person. *Ken decided to enroll in boxing classes.*

Inconsistent Character and Character Action (Adjacent)

Ken and his friend Mike had been looking for summer hobbies for quite some time. They were both college professors and they had the summers off from teaching. This meant that they both had plenty of time to try new things. Ken was a small man and didn't worry about staying in shape. His small 120-pound body was all skin and bones. Ken hated contact sports, but enjoyed noncontact sports, such as golf and bowling, which he could practice alone. *Ken decided to enroll in boxing classes.*

Inconsistent Character and Character Action (Distant)

Ken and his friend Mike had been looking for summer hobbies for quite some time. They were both college professors and they had the summers off from teaching. This meant that they both had plenty of time to try new things. Ken was a small man and didn't worry about staying in shape. His small 120-pound body was all skin and bones. Ken hated contact sports, but enjoyed noncontact sports, such as golf and bowling, which he could practice alone. While walking downtown during their lunch break one day, Ken and Mike passed a new gymnasium. They noticed the display in the window. It was an advertisement for the gym's summer sports program. They started looking at the advertisement and were impressed with the long list of activities that the gym sponsored. As they continued to look over the list, they became very excited. It seemed interesting so Ken and Mike went inside. *Ken decided to enroll in boxing classes.*

Note. The character actions are italicized. Examples of stimuli are taken from Long and Chong (2001, p. 1429).

and action such that they were either (1) adjacent in a story (i.e., local anomalies) or (2) separated by intervening sentences (i.e., distant anomalies). Passages 2 and 3 in table 5.5 are examples of this second manipulation.

Long and Chong (2001) observed that when actions and their respective characters' descriptions were adjacent, both skilled and less-skilled readers read inconsistent actions more slowly than consistent actions. On the other hand, when intervening sentences more distally separated the inconsistent actions and their respective character's descriptions, only skilled readers were slower to read the inconsistent actions; the less-skilled readers were not. Long and Chong interpreted this latter finding as evidence that less-skilled readers fail to detect the inconsistencies because of poor integration skills.

Hannon and Daneman (2004) also showed that anomaly detection varied as a function of reading skill. However, they identified shallow semantic processing as the locus of detection failure. In their study, readers read short passages, such as the plane crash passage in table 5.2, and then they answered questions like, *What should the authorities do?* Responses such as *contact living relatives about the dead and go ahead and bury them* were taken as evidence that readers failed to detect the anomalous phrase (e.g., *survivors* or *injured*).

Hannon and Daneman (2004) observed both quantitative and qualitative differences as to how less-skilled and skilled readers processed text. From a quantitative perspective, less-skilled readers detected fewer semantic anomalies than did skilled readers, a finding that suggests that less-skilled readers processed the text more shallowly than the skilled readers. From a qualitative perspective, less-skilled readers detected fewer locally incoherent anomalies (e.g., *surviving dead*) than did skilled readers, even when the two words in the anomalies (e.g., *surviving* and *dead*) had opposite meanings. Hannon and Daneman interpreted this latter finding as evidence that skilled and less-skilled readers processed the text differently.

Besides reading skill, research also suggests that anomaly detection varies as a function of individual differences in more specific cognitive components. In Hannon and Daneman's (2001a) study, for example, participants detected anomalies in questions that manipulated both the strength of the impostor words and the number of contextual cues: (1) strong impostor/few contextual cues, (2) strong impostor/many contextual cues, (3) weak impostor/few contextual cues, and (4) weak impostor/many contextual cues. See table 5.1 for examples. Participants also completed measures that assessed access to semantic information from long term memory and working memory capacity.

Consistent with previous research, strong impostor words (e.g., *Metropolis*) were detected less frequently than weak impostor words (e.g., *Atlantis*). In addition, there were fewer detections when the anomalous questions contained many contextual cues as opposed to few contextual cues. However, Hannon and Daneman also observed that both the individual-differences measures—the ability to access semantic information from long-term memory and working memory—predicted detection of semantic anomalies. Specifically, participants with poorer access to semantic information from long-term memory and/or smaller working memory capacities had more detection failures. This latter finding suggests the possibility that at least two cognitive mechanisms underlie the detection of semantic anomalies.

In subsequent analyses, Hannon and Daneman (2001a) used structural equation modeling (i.e., SEM) to examine the independence/interdependence among the characteristics of the text and the individual. As figure 5.1 shows, whereas the path leading from access to semantic information to the impostor word manipulation was significant, the path leading from access to semantic information to the contextual cue manipulation was not (i.e., $z = 2.80$ vs. $z = 0.65$). In contrast, whereas the path from working memory capacity to the contextual cue manipulation was significant, the path from working memory capacity to the impostor word manipulation was not (i.e., z

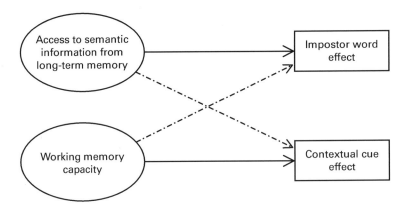

Figure 5.1
Relationships between characteristics of the individual and the text (Hannon & Daneman, 2001a).
Solid lines indicate significant relationships whereas dashed lines indicate nonsignificant relationships.

$= 1.57$ vs. $z = 0.24$). In other words, one cognitive mechanism—the ability to access semantic information from long-term memory—was important for detecting impostor words but not integrating successive contextual cues, whereas a second cognitive mechanism—a reader's working memory capacity—was important for integrating successive contextual cues but not for detecting impostor words.

In summary, research examining the influences of characteristics of the individual on anomaly detection suggests that there are multiple sources of misinformation. For example, reading skill is predictive of susceptibility to misinformation inasmuch as the poorer the reading skill, the greater the susceptibility to misinformation (Hannon & Daneman, 2004; Long & Chong, 2001; Todaro et al., 2010). This research also suggests that the component processes of reading that are responsible for susceptibility to misinformation are (1) the processes that establish semantic or causal connections from text content (e.g., Todaro et al., 2010), (2) the processes that support text integration (e.g., Long & Chong, 2001), and/or (3) the cognitive processes that are used to process semantic information in a text (e.g., Hannon & Daneman, 2004).

It is important to note, however, that one limitation of these studies is that the cognitive processes identified as the sources of reading skill differences in anomaly detection are inferred by the researchers from the manipulations of the text; they are not based on individual differences in performance on psychometric measures of cognitive processes. Consequently, one avenue for future research might be to extend these findings by using psychometric measures that assess individual differences in the processes that form semantic and causal connections in text, integrate text, and process semantic information. One such psychometric measure is Hannon and Daneman's (2001b, 2006) component processes task.

Besides reading skill, other studies have administered psychometric measures to assess individual differences in specific cognitive processes/resources. These studies show that poorer access to semantic information from long-term memory and/or smaller working memory capacities lead to greater susceptibility to misinformation (e.g., Hannon & Daneman, 2001a).

Theories of Semantic Illusions

Currently, there are at least three major theoretical explanations for semantic illusions. Some theoretical explanations, such as *partial matching* (Reder & Kusbit, 1991) and the *structure node theory* (e.g., Shafto & MacKay, 2000, 2010), are based on process-driven memory accounts, such as spread of activation and concept formation. Other theoretical explanations, such as *partial processing* (Barton & Sanford, 1993), are based on theories of language processing, such as local and global processing of words/noun phrases.

Partial Matching

According to Reder and Kusbit (1991), semantic illusions occur because of a *partial matching* or overlap between the semantic features in an anomalous question and its respective concept or schema in memory. Evidence to support partial matching comes from research that shows that the greater the semantic relatedness between the impostor word and the word it is posing for, the less likely readers will detect the impostor word (e.g., Reder & Kusbit, 1991). Consider, for example, the two anomalous questions:

1. What superhero is associated with bats, Robin, the Penguin, **Metropolis**, Catwoman, the Riddler, the Joker, and Mr. Freeze?
2. What superhero is associated with bats, Robin, the Penguin, **Atlantis**, Catwoman, the Riddler, the Joker, and Mr. Freeze?

The semantic contents of both questions have a great deal of overlap with our schema for Batman, yet, question 1 has a greater feature overlap with our Batman schema than does question 2 because the impostor word *Metropolis* (i.e., a fictional city protected by Superman) has more semantic features in common with *Gotham City* (i.e., a fictional city protected by Batman) than does the impostor word *Atlantis* (i.e., a fictional city that sank into the ocean). Thus, detection failure is greater for an anomalous Batman question that includes *Metropolis* rather than *Atlantis* because *Metropolis* has a greater feature overlap with our Batman schema.

In their later work, Reder and colleagues expanded on their idea of partial matching by considering the relationships among (1) the processing of successive contextual cues in an anomalous question, (2) spread of activation of features and/or schema in long-term memory, and (3) the accrued activation of a question's illusionary answer (e.g., Kamas, Reder, & Ayers, 1996; Park & Reder, 2004). Their general idea was that processing each successive contextual cue in an anomalous question increases the activation level and spread of activation of its respective schema in long-term memory. As the activation of the schema spreads, it reaches a high enough activation level that the reader is likely to select the topic of the activated schema in long-term memory as his or her answer for the anomalous question rather than detect a semantic anomaly. Thus, as a reader processes the contextual cues in the Batman anomalous question, the activation level of the Batman schema in long-term memory also increases. Eventually the reader has processed enough contextual cues in the anomalous question that the Batman schema reaches a high activation level and the reader selects Batman as his or her answer to the anomalous question rather than detecting *Metropolis* as a semantic anomaly.

The partial match theory is challenged, however, by research that shows that detection failure is poorest when the impostor word is located in the middle of a question. To reiterate, according to this theory an impostor word located earlier in a question should be detected more frequently than is an impostor word located later in a question because activation accrues with each successive contextual cue. Counter to this prediction, however, detection failure is greatest when the impostor word is located in the middle of a question.

Partial or Shallow Semantic Processing

According to Barton and Sanford (1993), semantic illusions occur because of partial or shallow processing of a text. Consider, for example, the paragraph describing a plane crash in table 5.2. As a reader reads the paragraph, his or her schema for plane crashes in long-term memory begins to activate. By the time a reader reaches the last sentence of the paragraph, the activation level of the plane crash schema is high enough that he or she does not exhaustively check the remaining words in the paragraph. Thus, the reader fails to detect the anomalous impostor word(s) (e.g., *survivors, injured, surviving injured,* or *surviving dead*). Stated another way, the reader has adopted a "good enough" approach to sentence processing (e.g., Christianson, Hollingworth, Halliewell, & Ferreira, 2001; Ferreira, Bailey, & Ferraro, 2002; Todaro et al., 2010), inasmuch as integration of successive words in a text becomes partial rather than exhaustive (e.g., Hannon & Daneman, 2001a, 2004).

Evidence to support the partial processing theory comes from a number of studies (e.g., Barton & Sanford, 1993; Daneman et al., 2006; Daneman et al., 2007; Glenberg, Wilkinson, & Epstein, 1982; Hannon & Daneman, 2001a, 2004). Barton and Sanford's (1993) study, for instance, showed that detection failure is not only prevalent during reading but can also vary as a function of the goodness of fit between the meaning of the impostor word(s) (e.g., *survivors, injured, surviving injured, surviving dead*) and the global theme of the paragraph (e.g., *a plane crash*). Indeed, they observed that the percentages for detection failure were 41% for the baseline *survivors*, 93% for *injured*, 35% for *surviving injured*, and 77% for *surviving dead*. According to the researchers, presumably readers are less likely to detect the impostor word *injured* than the impostor word *survivors* because the meaning of *injured* is more consistent with the plane crash theme of dead victims and plane wreckage. On the other hand, because the meaning of *survivors* includes the feature "is alive," the word *survivors* is contrary to the death and wreckage implied by the plane crash paragraph. Consequently, the impostor word *survivors* is detected more frequently.

Partial processing theory also challenges some influential models of reading comprehension, especially those models that advocate the maintenance of local coherence over retaining global coherence (Hannon & Daneman, 2004). According to the *minimalist hypothesis*, for example, the primary goal of reading is to maintain local coherence and only under rare circumstances do readers refer to global information, such as the passage theme (McKoon & Ratcliff, 1992). Contrary to this assertion, however, research examining partial processing suggests that readers not only frequently fail to detect an impostor word at a local level but they also frequently answer a subsequent question based on the gist or global theme of a passage (e.g., see Sanford & Sturt, 2002, for a review). Barton and Sanford (1993), for example, observed that readers failed to detect the locally incoherent impostor words *surviving dead* 77% of the time presumably because the word *dead* fit the global theme of a plane crash (i.e., bodies of passengers and wreckage strewn everywhere).

Node Structure Theory

The node structure theory proposes that information is stored in a semantic network of interconnected representational units called nodes (Shafto & MacKay, 2000, p. 372). These nodes can be activated in both a bottom-up and a top-down fashion by either semantic or phonological information (Shafto & MacKay, 2000). According to the node structure theory, semantic illusions occur because of three sources of priming: (1) phonological priming from the impostor name in a text, (2) semantic priming from the contextual cues in a text, and (3) semantic priming from semantic similarities in the schema between the impostor name and the name it is posing for. Consider, for example, the anomalous question *What was the famous line uttered by **Louis Armstrong** when he first set foot on the moon? Louis Armstrong* receives one source of phonological bottom-up priming from the *Armstrong question*, whereas *Neil Armstrong* receives two converging sources of semantic priming and one source of phonological priming (Shafto & MacKay, 2000). One source of semantic priming for *Neil Armstrong* occurs when the contextual cues *foot on the moon* activate the *moon landing* and *Neil Armstrong* schema in long-term memory. The other source of semantic priming occurs because the anomalous name *Louis Armstrong* indirectly primes *Neil Armstrong* via shared semantic features between the *Louis Armstrong* schema and the *moon landing/Neil Armstrong* schema in long-term memory (i.e., both are famous people from the 1950s and 1960s, etc.). The third source of priming for the real name occurs when the anomalous name *Louis Armstrong* indirectly phonologically primes *Neil Armstrong* because the two last names are identical. Because the real name *Neil Armstrong* receives more priming than the anomalous name *Louis Armstrong* (i.e., three sources of priming vs. two), *Neil Armstrong* has a greater activation level than does the anomalous name, *Louis Armstrong*. Thus, when readers read the name *Louis Armstrong*, they fail to detect it as anomalous because they believe they read the more highly activated name *Neil Armstrong*.

Support for the node structure theory comes from research that shows both phonological and semantic properties influence the frequency of anomaly detection. In Shafto and MacKay's (2000) study, for example, readers read questions such as the following:

1. The 1868 impeachment trial involving former vice president **Andrew Johnson** followed what major American war? (control)
2. The 1868 impeachment trial involving former vice president **Theodore Roosevelt** followed what major American war? (high semantic similarity)
3. The 1868 impeachment trial involving former vice president **Samuel Johnson** followed what major American war? (high phonological similarity)

They answered the questions by saying don't know, providing the correct answer, or identifying the question as erroneous. Shafto and MacKay observed that readers were just as likely to miss the semantically anomalous name *Theodore Roosevelt* as the phonologically anomalous name *Samuel Johnson*, 33% and 23%, respectively, a finding that provided evidence that both phonological and semantic similarity can influence the detection of semantic anomalies.

In a second experiment, Shafto and MacKay (2000) added one additional condition that included both high phonological and semantic similarity:

4. The 1868 impeachment trial involving former vice president **Lyndon Johnson** followed what major American war? (phonological and semantic similarity)

Performance in the phonologically + semantically similar condition (e.g., *Lyndon Johnson*) was poorer than in either the semantically similar (e.g., *Theodore Roosevelt*) or control (e.g., *Andrew Johnson*) conditions: 49% versus 30% and 9%, respectively. This latter finding was interpreted as evidence that the combined influence of phonological and semantic similarity results in greater detection failure of semantic anomalies than does the influence of semantic similarity alone.

Like the partial match theory, the node structure theory is challenged by research that shows detection of semantic anomalies varies as a function of the location of the impostor word in a question. According to the node structure theory, the location of an impostor word should not influence detection of an anomaly because the amount of phonological and semantic priming accumulated from the three sources of priming (i.e., the impostor word, the contextual cues in a text, and the semantic features in a schema) does not change regardless of the location of the impostor word. As noted earlier, however, detection failure of semantic anomalies varies as a function of the location of the impostor word.

In addition, Shafto and MacKay's (2000) evidence to support phonological similarity is the same evidence used by Barton and Sanford (1993) to support the partial processing theory. For example, Shafto and MacKay argue that the reason why people fail to detect the anomalous name *Samuel Johnson* in the ambiguous impeachment question is because *Samuel Johnson* is phonologically similar to the real name *Andrew Johnson* (i.e., the two last names are the same). On the other hand, Barton and Sanford argue that the reason why people fail to detect the anomalous name *Samuel Johnson* is because *Johnson* fits the question's global theme of a vice president being impeached. In other words, both sets of researchers used the same manipulations to support two separate theories.

Summary of Theories

Table 5.6 briefly summarizes the three theories of semantic illusions—the partial match theory, the partial processing theory, and the node structure theory—as well as some of their strengths and weaknesses. For example, because each theory explains detection failure in terms of a single cognitive mechanism, all three theories are challenged by research that shows detection failure is a consequence of multiple cognitive mechanisms, such as working memory capacity and the ability to access semantic information from long-term memory. Nor can these theories explain why individual-differences research suggests that integration processes (e.g., Long & Chong, 2001), causal relatedness (e.g., Todaro et al., 2010), and semantic relatedness (e.g., Todaro et al., 2010) might also play a role in detection failure. Finally, while each theory explains why detection failure is greater for strong versus weak impostor words, none of these theories explains why detection failure is greatest when the impostor words are located in the middle of an anomalous question rather than the beginning or end.

Rather than attribute detections of semantic anomalies to a single cognitive mechanism or process, perhaps a better approach might be to attribute them to multiple mechanisms. One starting point might be to consider access to semantic information from long-term memory and working memory capacity because these two cognitive mechanisms explain individual differences in the influences that impostor strength and the number of contextual cues have on anomaly detection. Additionally, differences in working memory capacities also account for Long and Chong's finding (2001). To reiterate briefly, Long and Chong argue that the reason why less-skilled readers

Table 5.6
Definitions, strengths, and weaknesses of theories of semantic illusions

Theory	Strengths	Weaknesses
Partial matching: Semantic illusions occur because of a partial overlap at a feature level between an anomalous question and its respective schema in memory	Explains why detection of stronger imposter words is poorer than detection of weaker imposter words Explains why detection of anomalies is poorer when there are more contextual cues that lead to the illusionary answer	Cannot explain why research shows two cognitive mechanisms (access to semantic information in long-term memory and working memory) account for separate text effects Cannot explain why detection of impostors is poorest when they are located in the middle of questions
Partial processing: Readers frequently adopt a "good enough" approach to sentence processing inasmuch as integration of successive words in a text is often partial rather than exhaustive, especially if the impostor words fit the global theme of the passage	Explains why detection of stronger imposter words is poorer than detection of weaker imposter words Explains why locally incoherent imposter words (e.g., *surviving dead*) are poorly detected	Cannot explain why research shows two cognitive mechanisms (working memory, access to semantic information in long-term memory) account for separate text effects Cannot explain why detection of impostors varies as a function of location of impostor words
Node structure theory: This theory proposes a semantic network of interconnected representational units called nodes. The nodes can be activated in both a bottom-up and a top-down fashion by either semantic or phonological information	Explains why detection of stronger imposter words is poorer than detection of weaker imposter words Explains why locally incoherent imposter words (e.g., *surviving dead*) are poorly detected Explains why detection of anomalies is poorer when there are more contextual cues that lead to the illusionary answer	Cannot explain why detection of impostors varies as a function of location of impostor words

failed to detect inconsistencies across multiple lines of text is because they have poor integration processes. However, Daneman and Carpenter (1980) have shown that readers with smaller working memory capacities are poorer than readers with larger working memory capacities at resolving ambiguities across multiple lines of text. Thus, in the context of Long and Chong's study, Daneman and Carpenter's findings suggest that small working memory capacities might also explain the detection failures of the less-skilled readers.

In addition, access to semantic information and working memory capacity might account for the U-shaped function that is a consequence of manipulating the location of the impostor words in anomalous questions. Perhaps, for example, good access to semantic information is most important when an impostor word (e.g., *Metropolis*) appears in the middle or later in a question because the quality/activation level of this later impostor word needs to be high enough so that it can compete with the correct name's (e.g., *Gotham City*'s) activation level, which has accrued from the preceding contextual cues. On the other hand, perhaps a larger working memory capacity is most important when the impostor word appears earlier or in the middle of a question because the activation level of the schema (i.e., Batman), which accrues from the contextual cues that follow the impostor word (e.g., *bats, Robin, the Penguin, Catwoman*), needs to be high enough so that it can compete with the activation level of the earlier impostor word (e.g., *Metropolis*).

Conclusions and Future Directions

Studies examining semantic illusions and misinformation are important theoretically because they challenge a common assumption that "semantic analysis is exhaustive and complete" (e.g., Hannon & Daneman, 2004, p. 188). They also challenge theories of language processing that suggest that local processing of combinations of words/ noun phrases occurs prior to processing the global theme of a text (e.g., Kintsch & van Dijk, 1978; McKoon & Ratcliff, 1992). In addition, the prevalence and pervasiveness of semantic illusions and misinformation make understanding them important for practical reasons (e.g., Fazio & Marsh, 2008). Studies suggest a number of characteristics of the text that influence detection of semantic anomalies, for example, (1) the degree of relatedness between the impostor word and the word it is posing for (e.g., Erickson & Mattson, 1981; van Jaarsveld et al., 1997), (2) the number of contextual cues that lead to an illusionary answer (e.g., Hannon & Daneman, 2001a), (3) whether the impostor word is the primary focus of the anomalous statement or question (e.g., Büttner, 2007, 2012; Wang et al., 2009), (4) the location of the impostor word, and (5) whether the impostor word is consciously or unconsciously detected. Studies also suggest that characteristics of the individual can influence detection of semantic anomalies, for example, (1) the processes responsible for inferring causal relations between information in a text (e.g., Todaro et al., 2010), (2) the processes responsible for encoding the semantic relations between information in a text (e.g., Todaro et al., 2010), (3) integration processes (e.g., Long & Chong, 2001), (4) the ability to access semantic information from long-term memory, and (5) working memory capacity (e.g., Hannon & Daneman, 2001a).

As noted throughout this chapter, there are multiple directions for future research. One important next step would be to design studies that challenge assumptions made by the three theories discussed earlier. For example, there is a need for studies that further challenge the idea that detection failure of semantic anomalies increases with each successive processing of successive contextual cues in an anomalous question (i.e., the partial match theory) or studies that further challenge the idea that weaker integration processes lead to more detection failures of semantic anomalies (Long & Chong, 2001).

In addition, although studies suggest that specific cognitive abilities, such as working memory capacity, predict detection of semantic anomalies and misinformation, these studies are only beginning to inform contemporary theories and explanations. Other specific cognitive processes/abilities, such as monitoring, might also account for detection of semantic anomalies. For example, unlike skilled readers, less-skilled readers often fail to realize that they don't understand large chunks of a text (Garner, 1980). This suggests that measures of monitoring ability might explain individual differences in susceptibility to misinformation.

Finally, another direction for future research would be to continue examining the influences that characteristics of the text and individual exert on detection of semantic anomalies under more naturalistic conditions. Most studies examining semantic illusions have assessed the frequency of detection of semantic anomalies embedded in anomalous questions or statements that were presented via a somewhat artificial detection task (e.g., Bredart & Docquier, 1989; Bredart & Modolo, 1988; Büttner, 2007; Erickson & Mattson, 1981; Hannon & Daneman, 2001a; Reder & Kusbit, 1991; Shafto & MacKay, 2000, 2010; van Oostendorp & de Mul, 1990; van Oostendorp & Kok, 1990). However, it is likely that when the underlying task is not *"detection based"* but is more naturalistic, the frequency of detection failures of semantic anomalies may increase because in a more naturalistic situation readers are not trained to detect anomalies. Nor are readers expecting to encounter them. Although a few studies have used short passages and eye-tracking technology (e.g., Barton & Sanford, 1993; Daneman et al., 2006, 2007), this avenue of research could be expanded to include a wider variety of text-based characteristics and characteristics of the individual.

In conclusion, research on semantic illusions tells us that there are multiple sources of misinformation. This research, as well as future work, should prove informative in distinguishing between and highlighting the valid aspects of contemporary accounts of misinformation, with the goal of better understanding when and how people notice discrepancies.

Note

1. By holding the other properties of the questions constant, any significant difference in frequency of detection of the impostor words among the three locations could therefore be attributed to the impostor word location manipulation rather than some other property of the questions that was inadvertently altered.

References

Barton, S. B., & Sanford, A. J. (1993). A case study of anomaly detection: Shallow semantic processing and cohesion establishment. *Memory & Cognition, 21*, 477–487.

Bohan, J., & Sanford, A. (2008). Semantic anomalies at the borderline of consciousness: An eye-tracking investigation. *Quarterly Journal of Experimental Psychology, 61*, 232–239.

Bredart, S. B., & Docquier, M. (1989). The Moses illusion: A follow-up on the focalization effect. *Cahiers de Psychologie Cognitive, 9*, 357–362.

Bredart, S. B., & Modolo, K. (1988). Moses strikes again: Focalization effect on a semantic illusion. *Acta Psychologica, 67*, 135–144.

Britt, M. A., Kurby, C. A., Dandotkar, S., & Wolfe, C. R. (2008). I agreed with what? Memory for simple argument claims. *Discourse Processes, 45*, 42–84.

Büttner, A. C. (2007). Questions versus statements: Challenging an assumption about semantic illusions. *Quarterly Journal of Experimental Psychology, 60*, 779–789.

Büttner, A. C. (2012). The effect of working memory load on semantic illusions: What phonological loop and central executive have to contribute. *Memory, 20*, 882–890.

Christianson, K., Hollingworth, A., Halliewell, J., & Ferreira, F. (2001). Thematic roles assigned along the garden path linger. *Cognitive Psychology, 42*, 368–407.

Daneman, M., & Carpenter, P. A. (1980). Individual differences in working memory and reading. *Journal of Verbal Learning and Verbal Behavior, 19*, 450–466.

Daneman, M., Hannon, B., & Burton, C. (2006). Age-related differences in detections of semantic anomalies: Evidence from eye movements. *Discourse Processes, 42*, 177–203.

Daneman, M., Lennertz, T., & Hannon, B. (2007). Shallow semantic processing of text: Evidence from eye movements. *Language and Cognitive Processes, 22*, 83–105.

Erickson, T. D., & Mattson, M. E. (1981). From words to meaning: A semantic illusion. *Journal of Verbal Learning and Verbal Behavior, 20*, 540–551.

Fazio, L. K., & Marsh, E. J. (2008). Slowing presentation speed increases illusions of knowledge. *Psychonomic Bulletin & Review, 15*, 180–185.

Ferreira, F., Bailey, K. G. D., & Ferraro, V. (2002). Good-enough representations in language comprehension. *Current Directions in Psychological Science, 11*, 11–15.

Garner, R. (1980). Monitoring of understanding: An investigation of good and poor readers' awareness of induced miscomprehension of text. *Journal of Reading Behavior, 12*, 55–64.

Glanzer, M., & Cunitz, A. R. (1966). Two storage mechanisms in free recall. *Journal of Verbal Learning and Verbal Behavior, 5*, 351–360.

Glenberg, A. M., Wilkinson, A. C., & Epstein, W. (1982). The illusion of knowing: Failure in the self-assessment of comprehension. *Memory & Cognition, 10*, 597–602.

Hannon, B. (2012). Understanding the relative contributions of lower-level word processes, higher-level processes, and working memory to reading comprehension performance in proficient adult readers. *Reading Research Quarterly, 47*, 125–152.

Hannon, B. (under review). Understanding the time course for conscious and unconscious detection of semantic anomalies.

Hannon, B., & Daneman, M. (2001a). Susceptibility to semantic illusions: An individual-differences perspective. *Memory & Cognition, 19*, 449–461.

Hannon, B., & Daneman, M. (2001b). A new tool for measuring and understanding individual differences in the component processes of reading comprehension. *Journal of Educational Psychology, 93*, 103–128.

Hannon, B., & Daneman, M. (2004). Shallow semantic processing of text: An individual-differences account. *Discourse Processes, 37*, 187–204.

Hannon, B., & Daneman, M. (2006). What do tests of reading comprehension ability such as the VSAT really measure? A componential analysis. In A. V. Mittel (Ed.), *Focus on educational psychology* (pp. 105–146). New York: Nova Science Publishers.

Hannon, B., & Frias, S. (2012). A new measure for assessing the contributions of higher-level processes to language comprehension in preschoolers. *Journal of Educational Psychology, 104*, 897–921.

Just, M. A., Carpenter, P. A., & Woolley, J. D. (1982). Paradigms and processes in reading comprehension. *Journal of Experimental Psychology. General, 111*, 228–238.

Kamas, E. N., Reder, L. M., & Ayers, M. S. (1996). Partial matching in the Moses illusion: Response bias not sensitivity. *Memory & Cognition, 24*, 687–699.

Kintsch, W., & van Dijk, T. A. (1978). Towards a model of text comprehension and production. *Psychological Review, 85*, 363–394.

Long, D. L., & Chong, J. L. (2001). Comprehension skill and global coherence: A paradoxical picture of poor comprehenders' abilities. *Journal of Experimental Psychology. Learning, Memory, and Cognition, 27*, 1424–1429.

McKoon, G., & Ratcliff, R. (1992). Inference during reading. *Psychological Review, 99*, 440–466.

McNamara, D. S., & Magliano, J. P. (2009). Towards a comprehensive model of comprehension. In B. Ross (Ed.), *The psychology of learning and motivation* (Vol. 51, pp. 297–384). New York: Elsevier Science.

Park, H., & Reder, L. M. (2004). Moses illusion: Implication for human cognition. In R. F. Pohl (Ed.), *Cognitive illusions* (pp. 275–291). Hove, England: Psychology Press.

Reder, L. M., & Cleeremans, A. (1990). The role of partial matches in comprehension: The Moses illusion revisited. In A. Graesser & G. Bower (Eds.), *The psychology of learning and motivation* (Vol. 25, pp. 233–258). New York: Academic Press.

Reder, L. M., & Kusbit, G. W. (1991). Locus of the Moses illusion: Imperfect encoding, retrieval, or match? *Journal of Memory and Language, 30,* 385–406.

Sanford, A. J., & Sturt, P. (2002). Depth of processing in language comprehension: Not noticing the evidence. *Trends in Cognitive Sciences, 6,* 382–386.

Shafto, M., & MacKay, D. L. (2000). The Moses, mega-Moses, and Armstrong illusions: Integrating language comprehension and semantic memory. *Psychological Science, 11,* 372–378.

Shafto, M. A., & MacKay, D. G. (2010). Miscomprehension, meaning, and phonology: The unknown and phonological Armstrong illusions. *European Journal of Cognitive Psychology, 22,* 529–568.

Sturt, P., Sanford, A. J., Stewart, A., & Dawydiak, E. (2004). Linguistic focus and good-enough representations: An application of the change detection paradigm. *Psychonomic Bulletin & Review, 11,* 882–888.

Todaro, S., Millis, K., & Dandotkar, S. (2010). The impact of semantic and causal relatedness and reading skill on standards of coherence. *Discourse Processes, 47,* 421–446.

van Jaarsveld, H. J., Dijkstra, T., & Hermans, D. (1997). The detection of semantic illusions: Task specific effects for similarity and position of distorted terms. *Psychological Research, 59,* 219–230.

van Oostendorp, H., & de Mul, S. (1990). Moses beats Adam: A semantic relatedness effect on a semantic illusion. *Acta Psychologica, 74,* 35–46.

van Oostendorp, H., & Kok, I. (1990). Failing to notice errors in sentences. *Language and Cognitive Processes, 5,* 105–113.

Wang, L., Hagoort, P., & Yang, Y. (2009). Semantic illusion depends on information structure: ERP evidence. *Brain Research, 1282,* 50–56.

6 Sensitivity to Inaccurate Argumentation in Health News Articles: Potential Contributions of Readers' Topic and Epistemic Beliefs

Jason L. G. Braasch, Ivar Bråten, M. Anne Britt, Brent Steffens, and Helge I. Strømsø

What are the health benefits of daily exercise? Would a vaccination reduce the likelihood that I get the flu this season? Are there health risks associated with cell phone use? In our day-to-day lives, we have frequent concerns about health topics that can drive us to seek out relevant, high-quality information. The development of the Internet has made it possible to rapidly and easily acquire a wealth of information about such health topics, affording opportunities to increase the depth and breadth of our understandings. However, the Internet brings about an unbridled access to information, where virtually anyone can publish without adherence to verification standards. Health articles on the Internet often present "arguments," in the sense that the text's author makes assertions about the world and provides support for his or her assertions. There are increasing concerns about the kinds of arguments individuals might come across when reading health information for which they have little prior knowledge upon which to draw (Adelhard & Obst, 1999; Andreassen & Strømsø, 2012; Cline & Haynes, 2001; Fox, 2006; Freeman & Spyridakis, 2004). As such, perhaps now more than ever, given the ubiquity and easy access of the Internet, readers must be able to carefully evaluate the accuracy of the arguments they read to differentiate those that seem tenable from those that are not.

At the same time, features of the information sources themselves can be informative regarding message quality and credibility. Readers could opt to critically scrutinize the sources proposing arguments to decide on credibility (e.g., Who wrote this argument? Where was it published? Do they have a particular agenda in distributing this argument?). Although a source may draw an inaccurate conclusion simply based on naïveté (e.g., imprecision in language use, low knowledge on the criteria one needs to establish causation), the source might also have a purposeful, calculated agenda in providing an incorrect proposal. For example, an author might argue that cell phone use causes brain tumors to seek solace for a loved one's recent affliction.

Examples like these highlight that readers should critically evaluate both the conclusions that authors draw (are they warranted based on the empirical evidence?), and the available source features (does the author seem knowledgeable?). If readers uncritically accept faulty arguments they come across and change their behavior accordingly, there could be consequences for their health and well-being. In this chapter, we investigate the ways in which college students' preexisting beliefs relate to their memory for simple scientific arguments found in health news articles and the sources presenting them. What we intend to demonstrate is that readers will use their preexisting beliefs to help determine whether an author has made unwarranted conclusions given the available evidence, which will, in turn, relate to a reader's memory for inaccurate arguments and their information sources.

By way of an introduction to our specific research questions, we briefly review four separate but related research literatures. These include (1) argumentation, (2) the role of source information in text comprehension, (3) the relationships between reading texts on controversial scientific topics and topic-specific beliefs, and (4) the relationships between reading texts on controversial scientific topics and beliefs concerning the ways one can justify knowledge claims in science. The overarching goal in presenting these literatures is to provide clearer specifications of the ways that reader beliefs might relate to memory for popular press scientific reports, with a specific focus on belief–memory relationships when sources present inaccurate versus accurate arguments.

Argumentation

Argumentation concerns identifying and weighing positive and negative attributes of conflicting perspectives on a particular topic or issue, as well as considering relevant reasons and evidence for the different perspectives when making decisions (Kuhn & Crowell, 2011). Argumentation may refer to both the process of creating an argument and the resulting product, as well as to the process of considering arguments for the purpose of understanding a phenomenon (Nussbaum, Sinatra, & Poliquin, 2008). In its basic form, an argument consists of a main claim that takes a stance on a controversial issue (e.g., whether living close to power lines may increase the risk of contracting cancer), with at least one reason or piece of evidence provided as support for the claim (Toulmin, 1958). Claims can be supported by a mechanistic explanation that make it clear how the claim could be true (e.g., "Power lines create electromagnetic fields, and electromagnetic fields disturb normal cell development") or by *evidence* serving as proof that testifies to the accuracy of the claim (e.g., "People living in houses near electromagnetic fields have a higher incidence of developing cancer") (Kuhn, 2001).

While a reasonable explanation and evidential proof may both be used as legitimate support for a claim, research indicates that generating and understanding evidence may be more difficult than generating and understanding reasons for a claim (Glassner, Weinstock, & Neuman, 2005; Kuhn, 1991). Evidential support for a claim is particularly emphasized within the disciplinary epistemology of science (Kuhn, 1993) and is, thus, essential to consider when reading about science issues both in formal and informal contexts. While formal conditions include the practices of scientists and students of science, informal experiences include everyday situations in which people have to make rational judgments about social-scientific issues, such as whether to restrict their cell phone use (Kuhn, 1991; Shtulman, 2013; Yang & Tsai, 2010). Science education researchers have also highlighted the challenges of processing popular reports of science, especially when they deal with controversial scientific issues (Linn & Eylon, 2006; Yang & Tsai, 2010). For example, Norris and colleagues (Norris, Phillips, & Korpan, 2003; Phillips & Norris, 1999) have shown that both high school and university students may read media reports about scientific topics uncritically, readily accepting the claims without thoroughly analyzing the degree to which the evidence provided supports the claim.

A less thorough analysis of arguments is especially problematic given that popular reports of science often contain claims that are poorly coordinated with the evidence provided. That is, readers seeking relevant health information may come across arguments that, at times, overstate findings—for example, providing weak evidence accompanied by a strong claim—perhaps to persuade the reader toward their stance. In other instances, popular media reports offer a more guarded approach, understating the findings by presenting strong evidence in support of a weak claim, possibly to take the sting out of a stance with which the journalist disagrees. Such lack of coordination between claim and evidence creates conditions for inaccurate argumentation, in contrast to the accurate argumentation that occurs when the strength of the claim and the type of evidence are aligned (Kuhn, 1991).

Source Information

At the core of most theories of text comprehension is a basic assumption that readers strive to maintain globally coherent representations of the information they read (for a review, see McNamara & Magliano, 2009). Inference generation serves as one— and perhaps the most frequently applied—way to maintain coherence during reading (Blanc, Kendeou, van den Broek, & Brouillet, 2008; Hakala & O'Brien, 1995; Graesser, Singer, & Trabasso, 1994; van den Broek, Lorch, Linderholm, & Gustafson, 2001; Wiley & Myers, 2003). However, some comprehension difficulties are simply unresolvable via inferential processing.

Several researchers have highlighted the functionality of the information sources themselves in (re)establishing coherence in both single and multiple document reading contexts (Braasch, Rouet, Vibert, & Britt, 2012; Britt & Rouet, 2012; Macedo-Rouet, Braasch, Britt, & Rouet, 2013; Strømsø, Bråten, Britt, & Ferguson, 2013). That is, rather than generating inferences to reduce comprehension difficulties at the level of the content information, readers may incorporate source–content links into their mental representations of what was read. Doing so helps to define contradictory information as representing different perspectives rather than a break in coherence per se, thus serving as a means of reducing any unwanted confusion (Bråten, Britt, Strømsø, & Rouet, 2011; Perfetti, Rouet, & Britt, 1999). Several recent think-aloud studies have demonstrated that, indeed, spontaneous sourcing responses often emerge from experienced comprehension difficulties (Anmarkrud, Bråten, & Strømsø, in press; Goldman, Braasch, Wiley, Graesser, & Brodowinska, 2012; Strømsø et al., 2013), which were, in turn, related to more integrated understandings of multiple documents. In related single text comprehension research, Braasch et al. (2012) experimentally manipulated the presence or absence of contradictory claims between two authors. The findings showed that, when two sources contradicted one another in news reports, readers attended to and recalled them better than when the sources agreed. Much like with multiple documents, readers appeared to index the discrepant claims onto the respective sources as a way to structure their memory of the text, thereby resolving discrepancy-induced comprehension difficulties.

For the single and multiple text examples outlined above, the oppositional nature of the claims dictates that at least one must be inaccurate. That is, cell phone use cannot *be unrelated to* and at the same time *cause* brain tumors. In the current chapter, we extend these investigations to consider whether comprehension problems stemming from other kinds of textual inaccuracies also stimulate a greater attention to and memory for source feature information. In the same vein, readers might experience comprehension difficulties that raise their awareness of the need to more closely consider the available source information as a way to maintain a coherent mental representation of the text. It is a main assumption in the current work that students' memory for the content may differ when they read inaccurate arguments versus accurate arguments about controversial scientific topics. More specifically, student beliefs may play a larger role in the former condition.

As we clarify in the next two sections, we examined students' beliefs about the topic of the texts and their epistemic beliefs concerning the justification of knowledge claims in science. When encountering inaccurate arguments, stronger beliefs about the topic in question may make it important for readers to turn to source information for support. Furthermore, justification-for-knowing beliefs may become functional to a greater extent to compensate for the lack of convincing arguments.

Topic Beliefs

Topic beliefs reflect what individuals accept as or want to be true about a particular topic. They may, more or less consciously, prime or guide particular reading goals, processing activities, and the understandings that are ultimately derived from reading experiences (Bråten, Ferguson, Strømsø, & Anmarkrud, 2013; Murphy & Mason, 2006). Thus, when people read about controversial issues or topics, the strength of their topic beliefs prior to reading (e.g., how strongly they believe prior to reading that radiation from cell phones causes brain tumors) may guide their processing and postreading text memory. In demonstratively seminal work by Lord, Ross, and Lepper (1979), people read and evaluated conflicting research evidence regarding the efficacy of capital punishment as a criminal deterrent. Participants who held strong initial beliefs on the topic, regardless of whether they believed capital punishment does or does not deter crime, evaluated evidence that supported their views as more convincing and substantiating than they did conflicting evidence. Reading conflicting evidence also actually strengthened their initial views on the topic. Kardash and Scholes (1996) investigated the degree to which people's preexisting beliefs about the HIV–AIDS relationship was reflected in the written conclusions that they produced after reading a text presenting arguments for different positions on the topic (HIV is the sole cause of AIDS vs. HIV does not cause AIDS). Results showed that the stronger the preexisting beliefs that students held about this topic, the more certain conclusions the students wrote from the inconclusive text favoring their own initial beliefs. In the same vein, Murphy and Alexander (2004) found that students reading single texts—each presenting arguments as well as counterarguments for a particular position—strengthened their own preexisting beliefs about the topic discussed in the text. Finally, Kahan et al. (2012) showed that people's perceptions of risks related to climate change were not dependent on their science literacy or their technical reasoning capacities (i.e., numeracy) but, rather, on their preexisting beliefs and values stemming from their cultural groups.

Thus, evidence indicates that readers frequently use their preexisting topic beliefs to interpret arguments in texts. They appear to place a greater value on belief-compatible arguments compared to belief-incompatible arguments, even when the argument materials are carefully designed to ensure similar believability, strength of evidence, and—of interest for the current work—appropriateness of the conclusions given the available evidence. Regarding this last point, the previous experiments all represent reading situations in which the arguments were "accurate," in the sense that none involved unwarranted claims given the available evidence. Moreover, very few studies included information about the sources presenting the arguments. As alluded to above, source feature information could be an additional cue that helps readers support their preexisting beliefs, especially when the arguments themselves are suboptimally supportive of those beliefs (i.e., inaccurate).

Justification Beliefs

Readers, of course, hold a number of different beliefs with different degrees of endorsements. Above, we posited a potential role concerning beliefs specific to the topic. Several studies suggest that more broadly operative beliefs, such as those stemming from readers' personal epistemologies, also prime or guide reading goals, processing activities, and the understandings that are ultimately derived from reading experiences (Bråten et al., 2011). Research efforts in personal epistemology have focused on individuals' views and understandings of knowledge and the process of knowing (Hofer & Pintrich, 1997). Recently, Greene, Azevedo, and Torney-Purta (2008) posited that beliefs concerning justifications for knowing are the only beliefs that deserve to be labeled epistemic. They also suggested that justifications for knowing should be a primary research focus and that the construct should be further separated into more than one dimension. This is because individuals can justify knowledge claims using both internal and external sources. In their proposed model, they emphasized two dimensions: *justification based on personal opinion* (internal) and *justification by authority* (external). Justification by personal opinion reflects whether or not readers believe it is appropriate to evaluate knowledge claims in a domain based on personal views and opinions; justification by authority reflects whether or not it is appropriate to evaluate knowledge claims in a domain simply because authoritative sources—teachers, textbooks, and scientists—reported the information. In addition to those two dimensions, Ferguson and colleagues (Ferguson, Bråten, & Strømsø, 2012; Ferguson, Bråten, Strømsø, & Anmarkrud, 2013) recently identified a third dimension, *justification by multiple sources*. This dimension reflects whether or not it is appropriate to evaluate knowledge claims in a domain on the basis of cross-checking, comparing, and corroborating across several sources of information.

Researchers have begun to investigate relationships between preexisting justification-for-knowing beliefs concerning the domain of science and understandings derived from multiple conflicting documents about socioscientific issues. Investigating the three dimensions outlined above, Bråten and colleagues (Bråten, Ferguson, Strømsø, & Anmarkrud, 2013, in press; Bråten, Strømsø, & Samuelstuen, 2008) showed that beliefs in both justification by authority and justification by multiple sources positively predict performance on measures reflecting readers' generation of inferences within and across documents. Beliefs in personal justification were negatively related to the same performance measures.

Thus, evidence supports the assumption that readers use their justification-for-knowing beliefs when interpreting multiple conflicting claims presented across different documents. It is important to note that, in the above-described studies, postreading measures were all completed from memory. As such, performance may reflect the degree to which content information is integrated in readers' mental representations. In the current work, we investigated whether justification beliefs differentially relate to postreading memory performance when students read single texts presenting inaccurate or accurate arguments.

The Present Study

Informed by these theoretical and empirical literatures, we sought to address two research questions. First, to what extent do students' topic beliefs and justification beliefs predict their memory for the *arguments* presented in the texts? We hypothesized that justification beliefs would be related to argument memory when reading inaccurate arguments, but not when reading accurate arguments, whereas topic beliefs would be unrelated to argument memory in both conditions. When arguments are accurate, the justification of claims, whether weak or strong, can be considered to be inherent in the texts. When the arguments are inaccurate, however, readers might rely more on their preexisting beliefs to help to evaluate the new knowledge claims. For readers who typically appeal to authoritative sources, inaccuracy-induced comprehension difficulties might result. Additional processing of the inaccurate arguments might ultimately result in better memory for them. Readers relying on their personal opinions, however, might dismiss inaccurate arguments outright. Given assumptions of shallow processing, one would expect poorer memory for these dismissive readers. Thus, we expected that beliefs in justification by authority would positively predict memory for inaccurate arguments while beliefs in personal justification would negatively predict them. Given that students did not read multiple conflicting texts on the same issue in the present study, we considered beliefs in justification by multiple sources less relevant in single text contexts and did not entertain any specific hypothesis regarding their relationship with argument or source memory.

We also addressed a second research question: To what extent are students' topic beliefs and justification beliefs related to their memory for *information sources* when reading inaccurate and accurate arguments concerning controversial issues? Given that readers appear to strengthen their preexisting beliefs when reading about controversial issues (Kardash & Scholes, 1996; Lord et al., 1979; Murphy & Alexander, 2004), two potential sources of support for those beliefs are source information (e.g., about the author) and the evidence presented in the texts. When the arguments are insufficient because they are not convincing (i.e., an inaccurate interpretation is made given the evidence), readers holding stronger beliefs about the topic may turn to source information (e.g., a reliable author, a well-respected publication venue) to bolster their initial beliefs whereas individuals reading accurate arguments may have less need for source information. This is because the argument, in and of itself, is sufficient to support their prior topic beliefs. Accordingly, we hypothesized that readers' topic beliefs would positively predict source memory for inaccurate but not accurate arguments whereas justification beliefs would be unrelated to source memory in both conditions.

Method

Participants
One-hundred thirty-three college undergraduate students (49% male, 51% female) with a mean age of 19.5 years ($SD = 1.69$) enrolled in an introductory psychology course at a large midwestern university participated for course credit.[1] Demographic

characteristics reflected a diverse sample of students: 58% Caucasian, 31% African American, 9% Hispanic, and 2% Asian American. Regarding science background, the mean number of high school science classes completed was 2.49 ($SD = 0.65$) and the mean number of college science classes completed or in progress was 0.69 ($SD = 0.73$). There were no significant differences across the argument accuracy manipulation on any of these variables.

Materials

Topic Beliefs Measure   Topic beliefs were measured with a list of six health belief statements (sample items: *Radiation from cell phones may cause brain tumors, Sunrays may cause skin cancer, Electro-magnetic fields released from power lines may cause cancer*), two for each of the three health articles that participants read (see below). Instructions asked participants to rate the extent to which they agreed or disagreed with each statement on a 10-point Likert-type scale with anchors of *strongly disagree* (1) and *strongly agree* (10). Because all items concerned the degree of participants' beliefs that radiation may cause serious illness in humans, we used a composite score based on the average of all six items to assess participants' preexisting beliefs. The Cronbach's alpha reliability for scores on this six-item measure was 0.99.

Justification Beliefs Measures   Participants' justification beliefs were measured with the Justification for Knowing Questionnaire (JFK-Q; Bråten et al., 2013; Ferguson et al., 2013). The JFK-Q contains 18 items focusing on three different points of reference: justification by authority (JA), justification by personal opinion (JPO), and justification by multiple sources (JMS). In the current study, all items were targeting the domain of natural science. JA items focus on the reliability of statements or claims based on scientific research and conveyed by teachers, textbooks, and scientists (sample item: *If a scientist says something is a fact, then I believe it*). Higher scores on these items indicate that students believe knowledge claims can be justified by appealing to an authoritative external source or evidence derived from scientific research. JPO items focus on the extent to which students consider it appropriate to evaluate knowledge claims in natural science based on personal views and opinions (sample item: *What is fact in natural science depends on one's personal views*). Higher scores on these items indicate that students believe knowledge claims can be justified by appealing to subjective, internal means of justification. Finally, JMS items focus on cross-checking and corroborating claims across several sources of information (sample item: *To detect incorrect claims in texts about natural science, it is important to check several information sources*). Higher scores on these items represent stronger beliefs in the importance or necessity of justifying knowledge claims in natural science by checking multiple external sources for consistency. Each item was rated on a 10-point Likert scale (anchored 1 = *disagree completely*, 10 = *agree completely*).

We factor-analyzed participants' scores on the JFK-Q using maximum likelihood exploratory factor analysis with oblique rotation. This analysis resulted in three factors with high loadings (> 0.45) and no overlap for any item. The three factors had eigenvalues of 3.35, 2.35, and 1.55, respectively, and explained 60.5% of the total sample variation. In accordance with the conceptualization underlying the JFK-Q, a first factor included five JA items, a second factor included two JPO items, and a third factor included four JMS items. We used three composite justification belief measures based on this factor analysis in subsequent statistical analyses. The reliability estimates (Cronbach's alpha) for the JA, JPO, and JMS scores were 0.87, 0.62, and 0.73, respectively.

Health Articles   We developed three short health articles (approximately 200 words each) that all focused on radiation as a potential contributor to cancer. The articles discussed everyday contexts of cell phone usage, exposure to the sun's rays, and proximity to electromagnetic radiation released from power lines. We constructed four different versions of each article by manipulating claim strength and type of evidence (see table 6.1 for an example). Thus, in one version, a strong claim was combined with experimental evidence, which resulted in an accurate argument. In another version, a weak claim was combined with correlational evidence, also resulting in an accurate argument. The two versions containing inaccurate arguments involved mismatches between the strength of the claim and the type of evidence. In these conditions, a strong claim was combined with correlational evidence or a weak claim was combined with experimental evidence.

For all versions of each article, the title (e.g., "Cell Phones and Cancer") was followed by source information including the author's name, occupation, place of work or affiliation, the magazine venue that published the article, and the year of publication (e.g., "By Dr. Bradford Franks, Neurosurgeon at the University of Memphis, Tennessee. Published in *Newsweek* Magazine, Week 26, 2011"). A seven-to-eight-sentence research report with a standard structure followed. Three sentences introduced the topic, which were also held constant across the four versions. The remainder of table 6.1 demonstrates the manipulation of claim strength and type of evidence. Whereas strong claims used causal language with definitive qualifiers, weak claims used correlational language with probabilistic hedges. That is, claim strength was manipulated by varying the predicates (e.g., *causes* vs. *is linked to*) and the hedges (e.g., *clearly demonstrated* vs. *likely suggests*) together. Type of evidence was manipulated in the three sentences that followed the main claim. The first sentence reported on participant assignment (the experimental cases reported random assignment; the correlational cases reported preexisting groups). The second sentence included an interpretation statement of the method for participant assignment, as our sample had not had a course in research methods prior to participation in the experiment. The third sentence provided the results of the study. A final sentence of the article restated the main claim. The structure and manipulation of claim strength and type of evidence were the same for all three articles.

Table 6.1
Example stimulus demonstrating manipulation of claim strength (strong, weak) and type of evidence (causal, correlational)

Title: Cell Phones and Cancer
By Dr. Bradford Franks, Neurosurgeon at the University of Memphis, Tennessee.
Published in *Newsweek* Magazine, Week 26, 2011

Introduction	The rise in technology has led to greater cell phone use, but that doesn't come without concerns about potential risks associated with using them. When a cell phone is being used, it creates a radiofrequency (RF) current that is used to stay connected with the network. The RF levels vary from phone to phone; many have high levels, while a smaller set of phones have low levels.	
	Strong Claim	**Weak Claim**
Claim statement	My research has **clearly demonstrated** that cell phone use **causes** brain tumors.	My research **likely suggests** that cell phone use **is linked to** brain tumors.
	Causal Evidence	**Correlational Evidence**
Participant assignment	In this study, I **randomly assigned 30 people to use** high RF-emitting phones, while 30 were given low RF-emitting phones to use.	In this study I **interviewed 60 patients with brain tumors.**
Interpretation statement	Random assignment is a gold standard for experiments, because **it rules out alternative explanations.**	This procedure **does not allow us to rule out alternative explanations.**
Result statement	The results showed that 90% of the people in the high RF-emitting phone group reported the presence of brain tumors after 5 years, while only 20% in the low RF-emitting phone group reported brain tumors.	The results showed that 90% of these cancer patients had been using high RF-emitting cell phones for the past 5 years.
	Strong Claim	**Weak Claim**
Claim restatement	**Clearly** my research **demonstrates** that cell phones cause brain tumors.	My research **likely suggests** that cell phone use **is linked to** brain tumors.

Argument Memory Measure After reading the set of articles, participants were prompted to recall each author's main claim and the details of the study described. To measure argument memory, we counted the number of arguments (claim–evidence pairs) that participants correctly recalled from the three articles. Verbatim or close synonyms of the wordings of the article were accepted. Claims were scored as strong if the response used a causal term (e.g., *causes, was due to*) and were scored as weak if the response used a predicate that indicated a correlational relationship (e.g., *related, is linked to*) or a probable hedge (e.g., *possibly, may*). To score evidence statements, participants had to mention something about how conditions were formed or how the study could be interpreted. A response was scored as experimental evidence if the participant mentioned random assignment or the corresponding interpretive statement (e.g., rules out alternative explanations). A response was scored as correlational evidence if relevant participant assignment (e.g., interviewed, surveyed) or the limits on interpretation (e.g., does not allow ruling out alternative explanations) were mentioned.

Recalls were scored blind to reading condition; accuracy was then determined in relation to the particular version of the articles that were read. Thus, if either the claim strength or the type of evidence recalled did not match those presented in the versions of the articles that were read, argument memory was considered incorrect. Given that participants read three articles each, they could potentially recall three arguments. Two raters independently classified a 20% randomly selected sample of the argument recall protocols. A Cohen's Kappa reliability index of 0.88 was obtained. Disagreements were resolved in discussion, and one rater coded the remaining protocols.

Source Memory Measure Source memory was measured in terms of the number of source features that participants accurately recalled from each of the three articles. Because five source features were presented for each of three articles (i.e., author name, occupation, affiliation, magazine venue, and year of publication), scores on this measure could range from 0 to 15. Author names were considered correct if the student wrote down the author's first, last, or both names. For occupation, verbatim matches (e.g., neurosurgeon) or closely related words (e.g., neuroscientist) were considered correct. For affiliation, responses were considered correct if the student wrote down the city, state, or both. For magazine venue, verbatim matches or closely related titles were accepted, and for year of publication, only the exact year was coded as correct. Two raters independently classified a 20% randomly selected sample of the source recall protocols. A Cohen's Kappa reliability index of 0.90 was obtained. Disagreements were resolved by discussion, and one rater coded the remaining protocols.

Procedure

Participants were randomly assigned to one of four conditions. Two conditions presented health articles containing accurate arguments (i.e., strong claims using experimental evidence as support or weak claims using correlational evidence as support), and two conditions presented health articles containing inaccurate arguments (i.e., strong claims using correlational evidence as support or weak claims using experimental evidence as support). For our analysis, we collapsed the four conditions into two to create an argumentation accuracy variable (accurate vs. inaccurate arguments). Average word length (154.3 vs. 153.2), Flesch–Kincaid grade level (9.8 vs. 9.9), and Flesch reading ease values (57 vs. 56.8) were comparable for articles presented in the accurate and inaccurate argument conditions.

The group-administered experimental session lasted 60 minutes. Participants completed the topic and epistemic beliefs surveys for 10 minutes. Afterwards, they read the three health articles in their argument condition for 20 minutes. Topic presentation order was counterbalanced; however, participants were instructed that they could read the articles in any order they wished. The instructions asked participants to "read carefully as if you were trying to make a decision about your own behavior. After you are done reading, you will be asked questions about what you read. So it is important that you try to remember what you read in these articles." When the participants had finished reading or time had expired, they performed a 5-minute filler task. Participants were then provided with the source memory test. For each article, participants were provided with the title and the five distinct source feature cues (i.e., author name, occupation, affiliation, magazine venue, and year of publication) and asked to identify as much information as they could for each text. They were allotted 5 minutes to complete this task. The argument memory task immediately followed; participants had 10 minutes to complete this task. For each article, participants were asked to recall the main conclusion and the details of the study. Finally, participants were allotted 10 minutes to complete a demographic and academic background survey.

Results

Table 6.2 presents descriptive statistics (means, standard deviations, and values of skewness and kurtosis) for all variables for all participants. First, we conducted a repeated-measures analysis of variance to check whether there were differences between participants' scores on the three justification beliefs measures. Using the Huynh–Feldt correction due to a violation of the sphericity assumption, results indicated that participants endorsed some of the means of justifying knowledge claims in science more than others, $F(1.89, 249.91) = 88.20$, $p = 0.000$, $\eta_p^2 = 0.40$. Follow-up paired-sample t tests with Bonferroni adjustment showed that participants agreed significantly more

Table 6.2

Descriptive statistics for all participants

	M	SD	Skewness	Kurtosis
Topic beliefs	6.58	1.33	–.41	1.89
Justification by authority	5.73	1.90	.05	–.69
Justification by personal opinion	5.04	1.93	.00	–.39
Justification by multiple sources	7.77	1.42	–.44	–.40
Source memory	1.19	1.78	2.04	4.69
Argument memory	.70	.90	1.13	.34

Note. The topic beliefs scale ranged from 0–10 with 10 as *strongly agree*. Justification scales ranged from 0–10 with 10 as *agree completely*. Source memory ranged from 0–15. Argument memory ranged from 0–3.

with the justification by multiple sources statements (M = 7.77, SD = 1.42) than the justification by authority (M = 5.73, SD = 1.90), $t(132)$ = 10.59, p = 0.000, Cohen's d = 1.23, and the justification by personal opinion statements (M = 5.04, SD = 1.93), $t(132)$ = 13.26, p = 0.000, Cohen's d = 1.63. Moreover, participants' scores on the measure of justification by authority were significantly higher than their scores on the measure of justification by personal opinion, $t(132)$ = 2.86, p = 0.005, Cohen's d = 0.36. The participants in this study, thus, seemed to differ from lower- and upper-secondary-school students participating in other studies using the JFK-Q, who have previously been shown to endorse justification by authority most often, followed by justification by multiple sources and justification by personal opinion (Bråten et al., 2013; Strømsø, Bråten, Anmarkrud, & Ferguson, 2012).

There were no statistically significant differences between participants in the accurate and inaccurate argument conditions on any of the justification beliefs measures, $ts(131) < 1.30$, $ps > 0.20$, nor were there differences on the topic beliefs measure, $t(131)$ = 1.12, p = 0.26. In fact, the only statistically significant difference between the two conditions was observed on the source memory measure, Mann–Whitney U, $Z = -2.87$, $p < 0.01$, $r = -0.25$, indicating that participants in the accurate argument condition tended to recall more source features than did participants in the inaccurate argument condition (see table 6.3 for descriptive information regarding each of the two conditions).

Because the descriptive statistics indicated that the score distribution for source memory was positively skewed, we corrected those scores toward normality by means of standard transformation techniques (Tabachnick & Fidell, 2007) before performing

Table 6.3
Descriptive statistics and Pearson correlations between topic beliefs, justification beliefs, and postreading memory for source features and arguments from health news articles

Variable	1	2	3	4	5	6	M	SD
1. Topic beliefs	—	-.02	-.06	.08	.23*	-.04	6.46	1.47
2. Authority	.12	—	-.03	.15	.02	.24*	5.81	1.81
3. Personal opinion	.18	-.05	—	-.06	-.15	-.22*	4.83	1.91
4. Multiple sources	.14	.06	.09	—	.20	-.03	7.69	1.36
5. Source memory	.13	.06	-.16	.12	—	-.02	0.79	1.47
6. Argument memory	-.04	.02	-.03	.16	.14	—	0.55	0.82
M	6.72	5.64	5.26	7.85	1.59	0.85		
SD	1.18	2.00	1.94	1.48	1.97	0.97		

Note. Accurate argument readers' correlations are below the diagonal; inaccurate argument readers' correlations are above the diagonal.
*p < .05, one-tailed.

correlational and multiple regression analyses to examine our two major research questions. Specifically, we improved the deviation from normality through log transformation, resulting in acceptable skewness (0.79) and kurtosis (–0.55) values for these participants. Please note that the log transformed source memory variable was used for the Pearson correlations computed separately for the two conditions, which are reported in table 6.3. The multiple regression analyses conducted for each condition (see below) also used the log transformed source memory variable. Given our specific directional hypotheses regarding relationships of student beliefs to argument memory and source memory, we conducted one-tailed tests (Levin, 1985; Tabachnick & Fidell, 2007).

Our first research question examined the extent to which students' topic beliefs and justification beliefs related to memory for the inaccurate versus accurate arguments presented in health news articles. We expected that justification beliefs would correlate with argument memory when reading inaccurate arguments, but not when reading accurate arguments, whereas topic beliefs would be unrelated to argument memory in both conditions. As can be seen in table 6.3, for participants reading articles presenting inaccurate arguments, preexisting beliefs about the topic did not correlate with memory for arguments ($r = -0.04$, ns). However, justification of knowledge claims by personal opinion was negatively correlated with memory for arguments, $r = -0.22$, $p = 0.038$. Moreover, justification of knowledge claims by appealing to authority showed a positive correlation with memory for inaccurate arguments, $r = 0.24$, $p = 0.027$. Justification by multiple sources showed no relationship with argument memory, $r = -0.03$, ns. As a point of contrast, when articles presented accurate arguments, neither the topic beliefs nor any of the justification-for-knowing indices related to memory for arguments embedded within the content of the health news articles. Thus, the more students considered it appropriate to evaluate knowledge claims in natural science based on their personal views and opinions, the more they disregarded inaccurate arguments in the texts (as evidenced by their poorer memory). On the other hand, the more students evaluated knowledge claims in natural science through appeals to authoritative external sources or evidence derived from scientific research, the better their memory for inaccurate arguments. Although process data was not collected in the current study, these memory products may reflect that students holding authority beliefs more "deeply" scrutinized arguments, especially when they involved conclusions that did not match the available evidence.

Our second research question examined the extent to which students' topic beliefs and justification beliefs related to memory for source information after reading inaccurate and accurate arguments. We expected that justification beliefs would correlate with argument memory when reading inaccurate arguments, but not when reading accurate arguments, whereas topic beliefs would be unrelated to argument memory in both conditions. As expected, for participants reading news articles presenting inaccurate arguments, preexisting beliefs about the topic positively correlated with memory for source features ($r = 0.23$, $p = 0.031$). On the other hand, the same pattern was not present for participants reading news articles presenting accurate arguments: Topic beliefs did not correlate with source memory ($r = 0.13$, *ns*). Thus, the more students believed that environmental factors could lead to health risks associated with radiation, the better they remembered the articles' source features. This was only the case, however, when the content of the argumentation signaled that information sources were presenting unwarranted conclusions based on the supporting evidence (i.e., under- or overstating the findings). This was obtained, importantly, irrespective of the fact that source features were held constant across the text versions.

None of the justification beliefs, in general, related to memory for source features associated with inaccurate or accurate arguments.

Table 6.3 also signifies that, for participants reading either type of argument, there were no relationships between the two indices of memory performance (inaccurate: $r = -0.02$, *ns*; accurate: $r = 0.14$, *ns*). The ratings on topic beliefs and justification beliefs were also unrelated or only weakly related for participants in either reading condition. This suggests that the previously described significant relationships reflect isolable belief contributions to memory for sources and for inaccurate arguments.

To further examine this issue, we conducted two multiple regression analyses for each reading condition, one with argument memory as the dependent variable and another with source memory as the dependent variable. In each analysis, participants' topic beliefs and the three justification beliefs measures were entered simultaneously as predictors. When memory for inaccurate arguments was the dependent variable, the model explained 11% of the variance. For this measure, both justification by personal opinion, $\hat{a} = -0.22$, $p = 0.038$, and justification by authority, $\hat{a} = 0.24$, $p = 0.027$, emerged as unique predictors. The four predictors together explained 10% of the variance in source memory, but only topic beliefs emerged as a unique predictor, $\hat{a} = 0.21$, $p = 0.046$. For participants reading accurate arguments, however, only 3% and 7% of the variance in argument and source memory, respectively, were explained; no variables emerged as unique predictors.

Discussion

This chapter contributes uniquely to research on readers' contemplations of inaccurate information in texts. Whereas other chapters in this volume focus on the comprehension of and memory for factual inaccuracies, we focused on a subtler—yet frequently encountered—type of inaccuracy: inaccurate argumentation, which regularly appears in popular press scientific reports. When readers can interpret that a source has drawn an accurate conclusion given the empirical results, their preexisting beliefs do not predict memory for either the information sources or the arguments reports put forth.

Beliefs seem to become important when there is a conflict between the author's interpretation and the type of research study that was reported. That is to say, relationships between readers' beliefs and memory measures depended on the accuracy of the arguments that were read.

Readers might have considered accurate arguments, instances where the interpretations were logically derived from the available empirical evidence, as "internally justifiable." In this sense, readers may not have needed to activate and use their preexisting beliefs on the topic or the ways one can justify knowledge claims in science, more generally. In this sense, the text does all of the "heavy lifting." In cases in which the evidence does not logically support the interpretation, that is, when arguments are not "internally justifiable," readers appear to utilize their preexisting beliefs to support memory for different aspects of the articles.

For example, readers may not be able to use the textual evidence to strengthen their preexisting beliefs on the topic, which they often want to do, when a misinterpretation is present (Kardash & Scholes, 1996; Lord et al., 1979; Murphy & Alexander, 2004). Accordingly, readers might instead more "deeply" process source information (e.g., author credentials and affiliation). This increased attention to the source features of the articles may have, in turn, facilitated memory. Correlations provide initial support for such a characterization. Topic beliefs predicted memory for source features associated with inaccurate but not accurate arguments, irrespective of the fact that all readers received the same source features.

The findings also seem to support that claim–evidence misalignment might stimulate activation and the use of different justification-for-knowing beliefs in support of argument processing. On one hand, stronger beliefs that knowledge claims can be justified based on personal opinion seemed to make it more likely that readers disregarded inaccurate arguments, as evidenced by their relatively poorer memory compared to the accurate argument conditions. On the other hand, stronger beliefs that knowledge claims can be justified through appeals to authoritative sources appeared to relate to a deeper processing of the details of the study as well as the author's misinterpretation, perhaps reflecting an attention to the lack of "scientificness" (Thomm & Bromme, 2012). This increased attention may have, in turn, facilitated memory for the inaccurate arguments.

Thus, the recall measures—taken as evidence of the memory "products" of reading—indicated that college students activate preexisting beliefs to deal with the different facets of popular press science reports depending on the quality (in this case the accuracy) of the argumentation. It is unclear, however, *when* they made these decisions. Future work could track reading behaviors to examine whether readers with different topic-specific and justification belief profiles differentially attend to and process the news articles *during reading* (e.g., more rereading and reanalysis of the arguments, more scrutinizing of the source features). Such indices could confirm that the different memory effects reflect that moment-by-moment changes in text processing occurred during reading. These reading time analyses could more directly pinpoint which specific text features stimulated a deeper processing of the articles, and for which types of readers.

Of course, our findings are potentially constrained not only by the undergraduate sample that participated but also by the particular text materials and tasks that were presented to them. Future work examining the role of reader beliefs in argument memory should probe the generalizability of our findings. Such extensions could include populations working with unwarranted conclusions for other controversial health topics (e.g., "causes" of childhood obesity). It would also be interesting to incorporate additional outcome measures that more closely mirror the use of previously read information in making future decisions (e.g., "Given what you read, would you change your child's diet? Why, and in what ways?"). Moreover, because the current analyses were correlational in nature, the findings do not warrant causal conclusions. Further experimental work is needed to more firmly establish causal relations between students' beliefs and aspects of their postreading memory for texts. For example, future work might experimentally induce different justification beliefs to more directly assess their impact on comprehension and decision making.

Finally, although readers should cautiously consider the quality of the arguments that they come across, especially since many, if not most, people use the Internet to inquire about topics of interest, such consideration appears to depend on the beliefs that are brought to bear during reading. Across a life span, a reader will no doubt make a number of important health decisions based primarily on independent research on a variety of issues (i.e., without consulting a medical professional directly). In practice, this means some of the texts the individual comes across will contain conclusions that are poorly coordinated with the evidence provided, both intentionally and unintentionally. A passive, uncritical acceptance of faulty arguments could merely result in someone's being ill-informed on the topic, but it is the more drastic consequences that are most concerning (e.g., a negative impact on a person's health and well-being). As such, future research in this area may have important implications for understanding why some people succumb to maladies based on knowledge-based decisions and others are more critical and seemingly savvy about which sources and arguments to trust when their health is on the line. Informing oneself to make health decisions is, at the very least, a pervasive activity that warrants concentrated research efforts.

Acknowledgments

This book chapter was funded by a Norwegian Research Council grant to Ivar Bråten and Helge I. Strømsø and an Institute for Educational Sciences grant (No. R305F100007) to the University of Illinois at Chicago.

Note

1. The sample of students in the current work is a subset of students who also contributed data reported by Steffens et al. (2014), particularly in experiment 1. Accordingly, the participants used the same materials and followed the same procedure as reported there.

References

Adelhard, K., & Obst, O. (1999). Evaluation of medical Internet sites. *Methods of Information in Medicine, 39*, 75–79.

Andreassen, R., & Strømsø, H. I. (2012). Reading about health risks: Who and what to trust? A research review. In K. P. Knutsen, S. Kvam, P. Langemeyer, A. Parianou, & K. Solfjeld (Eds.), *Narratives of risk: Interdisciplinary studies* (pp. 255–274). Münster: Waxman.

Anmarkrud, Ø., Bråten, I., & Strømsø, H. I. (in press). Multiple-documents literacy: Strategic processing, source awareness, and argumentation when reading multiple conflicting documents. *Learning and Individual Differences*.

Blanc, N., Kendeou, P., van den Broek, P., & Brouillet, D. (2008). Updating situation models during reading of news reports: Evidence from empirical data and simulations. *Discourse Processes, 45*, 103–121.

Braasch, J. L. G., Rouet, J.-F., Vibert, N., & Britt, M. A. (2012). Readers' use of source information in text comprehension. *Memory & Cognition, 40*, 450–465.

Bråten, I., Britt, M. A., Strømsø, H. I., & Rouet, J.-F. (2011). The role of epistemic beliefs in the comprehension of multiple expository texts: Toward an integrated model. *Educational Psychologist, 46*, 48–70.

Bråten, I., Ferguson, L. E., Strømsø, H. I., & Anmarkrud, Ø. (2013). Justification beliefs and multiple-documents comprehension. *European Journal of Psychology of Education, 28*, 879–902.

Bråten, I., Ferguson, L. E., Strømsø, H. I., & Anmarkrud, Ø. (in press). Students working with multiple conflicting documents on a scientific issue: Relations between epistemic cognition while reading and sourcing and argumentation in essays. *British Journal of Educational Psychology*.

Bråten, I., Strømsø, H. I., & Samuelstuen, M. S. (2008). Are sophisticated students always better? The role of topic-specific personal epistemology in the understanding of multiple expository texts. *Contemporary Educational Psychology, 33*, 814–840.

Britt, M. A., & Rouet, J.-F. (2012). Learning with multiple documents: Component skills and their acquisition. In M. J. Lawson & J. R. Kirby (Eds.), *The quality of learning: Dispositions, instruction, and mental structures* (pp. 276–314). New York: Cambridge University Press.

Cline, R. J. W., & Haynes, K. M. (2001). Consumer health information seeking on the Internet: The state of the art. *Health Education Research, 16*, 671–692.

Ferguson, L. E., Bråten, I., & Strømsø, H. I. (2012). Epistemic cognition when students read multiple documents containing conflicting scientific evidence: A think-aloud study. *Learning and Instruction, 22*, 103–120.

Ferguson, L. E., Bråten, I., Strømsø, H. I., & Anmarkrud, Ø. (2013). Epistemic beliefs and comprehension in the context of reading multiple documents: Examining the role of conflict. *International Journal of Educational Research, 62*, 100–114.

Fox, S. (2006). *Online health search 2006*. Washington, DC: Pew Internet & American Life Project.

Freeman, K. S., & Spyridakis, J. H. (2004). An examination of the factors that affect the credibility of online health information. *Technical Communication, 51*, 239–263.

Glassner, A., Weinstock, M., & Neuman, Y. (2005). Pupils' evaluation and generation of evidence and explanation in argumentation. *British Journal of Educational Psychology, 75*, 105–118.

Goldman, S. R., Braasch, J. L. G., Wiley, J., Graesser, A. C., & Brodowinska, K. (2012). Comprehending and learning from Internet sources: Processing patterns of better and poorer learners. *Reading Research Quarterly, 47*, 356–381.

Graesser, A., Singer, M., & Trabasso, T. (1994). Constructing inferences during narrative comprehension. *Psychological Review, 101*, 371–395.

Greene, J. A., Azevedo, R., & Torney-Purta, J. (2008). Modeling epistemic and ontological cognition: Philosophical perspectives and methodological directions. *Educational Psychologist, 43*, 142–160.

Hakala, C. M., & O'Brien, E. J. (1995). Strategies for resolving coherence breaks in reading. *Discourse Processes, 20*, 167–185.

Hofer, B. K., & Pintrich, P. R. (1997). The development of epistemological theories: Beliefs about knowledge and knowing and their relation to learning. *Review of Educational Research, 67*, 88–140.

Kahan, D. M., Peters, E., Wittlin, M., Slovic, P., Ouellette, L. L., Braman, D., et al. (2012). The polarizing impact of science literacy and numeracy on perceived climate change risks. *Nature Climate Change, 2*, 732–735.

Kardash, C. M., & Scholes, R. J. (1996). Effects of preexisting beliefs, epistemological beliefs, and need for cognition on interpretation of controversial issues. *Journal of Educational Psychology, 88*, 260–271.

Kuhn, D. (1991). *The skills of argument*. Cambridge, England: Cambridge University Press.

Kuhn, D. (1993). Science as argument: Implications for teaching and learning scientific thinking. *Science Education, 77*, 319–337.

Kuhn, D. (2001). How do people know? *Psychological Science, 12*, 1–8.

Kuhn, D., & Crowell, A. (2011). Dialogic argumentation as a vehicle for developing young adolescents' thinking. *Psychological Science, 22,* 545–552.

Levin, J. R. (1985). Some methodological and statistical "bugs" in research on children's learning. In M. Pressley & C. Brainerd (Eds.), *Cognitive learning and memory in children* (pp. 205–233). New York: Springer.

Linn, M. C., & Eylon, B.-S. (2006). Science education: Integrating views of learning and instruction. In P. A. Alexander & P. H. Winne (Eds.), *Handbook of educational psychology* (2nd ed., pp. 511–544). Mahwah, NJ: Lawrence Erlbaum Associates.

Lord, C. G., Ross, L., & Lepper, M. R. (1979). Biased assimilation and attitude polarization: The effects of prior theories on subsequently considered evidence. *Journal of Personality and Social Psychology, 37,* 2098–2109.

Macedo-Rouet, M., Braasch, J. L. G., Britt, M. A., & Rouet, J.-F. (2013). Teaching fourth and fifth graders to evaluate information sources during text comprehension. *Cognition and Instruction, 31,* 204–226.

McNamara, D. S., & Magliano, J. (2009). Toward a comprehensive model of comprehension. *Psychology of Learning and Motivation, 51,* 297–384.

Murphy, P. K., & Alexander, P. A. (2004). Persuasion as a dynamic, multidimensional process: An investigation of individual and intraindividual differences. *American Educational Research Journal, 41,* 337–363.

Murphy, P. K., & Mason, L. (2006). Changing knowledge and beliefs. In P. A. Alexander & P. H. Winne (Eds.), *Handbook of educational psychology* (pp. 305–324). Mahwah, NJ: Lawrence Erlbaum Associates.

Norris, S. P., Phillips, L. M., & Korpan, C. A. (2003). University students' interpretation of media reports of science and its relationship to background knowledge, interest, and reading difficulty. *Public Understanding of Science (Bristol, England), 12,* 123–145.

Nussbaum, E. M., Sinatra, G. M., & Poliquin, A. (2008). Role of epistemic beliefs and scientific argumentation in science learning. *International Journal of Science Education, 30,* 1977–1999.

Perfetti, C. A., Rouet, J.-F., & Britt, M. A. (1999). Towards a theory of documents representation. In H. van Oostendorp & S. R. Goldman (Eds.), *The construction of mental representations during reading* (pp. 99–122). Mahwah, NJ: Lawrence Erlbaum Associates.

Phillips, L. M., & Norris, S. P. (1999). Interpreting popular reports of science: What happens when the reader's world meets the world on paper? *International Journal of Science Education, 21,* 317–327.

Shtulman, A. (2013). Epistemic similarities between students' scientific and supernatural beliefs. *Journal of Educational Psychology, 105,* 199–212.

Steffens, B., Britt, M. A., Braasch, J. L. G., Strømsø, H. I., & Bråten, I. (2014). Memory for scientific arguments and their sources: Claim-evidence consistency matters. *Discourse Processes, 51,* 117–142.

Strømsø, H. I., Bråten, I., Anmarkrud, Ø., & Ferguson, L. E. (2012). *Relationships between beliefs about justification for knowing and multiple-documents comprehension among language-majority and language-minority Norwegian students*. Paper presented at the annual meeting of the Society for Text and Discourse, Montreal, Canada.

Strømsø, H. I., Bråten, I., Britt, M. A., & Ferguson, L. E. (2013). Spontaneous sourcing among students reading multiple documents. *Cognition and Instruction, 31*, 176–203.

Tabachnick, B. G., & Fidell, L. S. (2007). *Using multivariate statistics* (5th ed.). Boston: Allyn & Bacon.

Thomm, E., & Bromme, R. (2012). "It should at least seem scientific!" Textual features of "scientificness" and their impact on lay assessment of online information. *Science Education, 96*, 187–211.

Toulmin, S. E. (1958). *The uses of argument*. Cambridge, England: Cambridge University Press.

van den Broek, P., Lorch, R. F., Linderholm, T., & Gustafson, M. (2001). The effects of readers' goals on inference generation and memory for texts. *Memory & Cognition, 29*, 1081–1087.

Wiley, J., & Myers, J. L. (2003). Availability and accessibility of information and causal inferences from scientific text. *Discourse Processes, 36*, 109–129.

Yang, F. Y., & Tsai, C. C. (2010). An epistemic framework for scientific reasoning in informal contexts. In L. D. Bendixen & F. C. Feucht (Eds.), *Personal epistemology in the classroom* (pp. 124–162). Cambridge, England: Cambridge University Press.

7 Conversational Agents Can Help Humans Identify Flaws in the Science Reported in Digital Media

Arthur C. Graesser, Keith K. Millis, Sidney K. D'Mello, and Xiangen Hu

It is widely believed that information in print, spoken, and digital media is replete with inaccuracies, especially now that there is less editing of content in most media outlets. Inaccurate information may range from a single sentence that conveys a fact or claim to lengthy discourse that incorporates a deeply flawed mental model. Sometimes there are explicit contradictions within a text or between texts. At other times the contradictions require inferences and careful scrutiny with respect to prior knowledge. This is impossible or difficult for readers who have low knowledge about the subject matter. They cannot identify false information or resolve contradictions without conceptual knowledge about the domain. Individuals respond in a variety of ways to these inaccuracies. The most gullible readers accept virtually all content as true and miss most contradictions. The most skeptical readers question the veracity of most content and are on the lookout for contradictions. Most individuals undoubtedly fall somewhere in between these two extremes on the gullible–skeptical continuum.

Most of the chapters in this volume investigate how individuals by themselves process and respond to the inaccurate information. Do readers notice such information? Do they ask questions about it? Do they discard it? Do they abandon the information source altogether? Do they read a different information source to check it out? Do they challenge the author? This chapter stretches beyond individual responses to inaccurate information. Our research incorporates conversational computer agents (called *agents* for short) that interact with the human while the human comprehends information sources. The agents hold conversations with the human that scrutinizes the reliability, accuracy, validity, and completeness of the content expressed in information sources. The hope is that these social interactions between humans and agents will help the human learn strategies of identifying inaccuracies and to automatize such skills. Ideally the human will shift a bit from the gullible to the skeptical end of the continuum and will possibly converge on a sweet spot of intelligent scrutiny. ·

The chapter discusses two classes of agent-based computer systems. The next section describes systems that have a single agent interacting with a human during the course of reading science content from the Web (such as SEEK Web Tutor) or evaluating whether a scientific experiment has an ethical problem (such as HURA Advisor). The subsequent section describes a system called Operation ARIES! that has two or more agents interacting with a human while evaluating whether a science news report in the media does or does not have flawed scientific methodology. Sometimes two agents contradict each other; sometimes two agents agree on a false claim. We examine how the human learner responds (both cognitively and emotionally) to the agents as they express inaccurate information. The materials in all of these studies involve science, technology, engineering, and mathematics (STEM) content.

Single Agents Interacting with the Human

Learning environments with pedagogical agents have been developed to serve as substitutes for humans who range in expertise from peers to subject matter experts with pedagogical strategies. Agents can guide the interaction with the learner, instruct the adult learner in what to do, and interact with other agents to model ideal behavior, strategies, reflections, and social interactions (Baylor & Kim, 2005; Graesser, Jeon, & Dufty, 2008; Millis et al., 2011). Some agents generate speech, gestures, body movements, and facial expressions in ways similar to people, as exemplified by Betty's Brain (Biswas, Jeong, Kinnebrew, Sulcer, & Roscoe, 2010), Tactical Language and Culture System (Johnson & Valente, 2008), iSTART (McNamara, Boonthum, Levinstein, & Millis, 2007; McNamara, O'Reilly, Best, & Ozuru, 2006), Crystal Island (Rowe, Shores, Mott, & Lester, 2010), and My Science Tutor (Ward et al., 2011). Systems like AutoTutor and Why-Atlas can interpret the natural language of the human that is generated in spoken or typed channels and can respond adaptively to what the student expresses (Graesser et al., 2012; D'Mello, Dowell, & Graesser, 2011; VanLehn et al., 2007). These agent-based systems have frequently demonstrated value in improving students' learning and motivation (Graesser, Conley, & Olney, 2012; VanLehn, 2011), but it is beyond the scope of this chapter to review the broad body of research on agents in learning environments.

This section describes two learning environments with single agents that assist the student in handing inaccuracies and problematic content in STEM topics. SEEK Web Tutor (Graesser et al., 2007) was designed to directly teach students how to take a critical stance when evaluating science content on the Internet. HURA Advisor (Hu & Graesser, 2004) was designed to train students on the fundamentals of research ethics and to identify ethical flaws in scientific research. After discussing the successes and failures of these two systems, we speculate on how more powerful systems can be designed to help students acquire intelligent scrutiny.

SEEK (Source, Evidence, Explanation, and Knowledge) Web Tutor
Critical thinking about science requires learners to actively evaluate the truth and relevance of information, the quality of information sources, the plausibility of causal

systems, and the implications of evidence (Braasch et al., 2009; Bråten, Strømsø, & Britt, 2009; Britt & Aglinskas, 2002; Goldman et al., 2012; Halpern et al., 2012; Rouet, 2006; Wiley et al., 2009). A deep understanding is needed to construct causal reasoning, integration of the components in complex systems, and logical justifications of claims. This is very difficult to achieve without sufficient prior knowledge about a domain and reasoning skills (Kendeou & van den Broek, 2007). However, a major start is for the student to acquire a thinking strategy with a *critical stance*—essentially, the skeptic. An individual with a critical stance considers the possibility that there may be problems with the truth, relevance, or quality of the information that is received. A critical stance toward scientific information is especially important in the digital age.

SEEK Web Tutor (Graesser, Wiley, et al., 2007) was designed to improve college students' critical stance while they search Web pages on the topic of plate tectonics. Some of the Web sites were reliable information sources on the topic, written by professionals in the National Aeronautics and Space Administration, the Public Broadcasting Service, and Scientific American. Others were erroneous accounts of earthquakes and volcanoes that appealed to the stars, the moon, and oil drilling. The student's goal in the experiments was to search the Web for the purpose of writing an essay on what caused the eruption of the Mount St. Helens volcano in 1980.

SEEK Web Tutor took a direct approach to training students on critical stance by implementing three facilities with different instruction methods. The first was a *Hint* button on the Google search engine page that contained suggestions on how a student can strategically search and read a set of Web sites. This page was a mock Google page with titles and URLs for reliable and unreliable Web sites, which could be accessed and explored if the student so desired. When a student clicked the Hint button, spoken messages gave reminders of the goal of the task (i.e., writing an essay on the causes of the Mount St. Helens volcano eruption in the state of Washington) and suggestions on what to do next (i.e., reading Web sites with reliable information). The agent in one version of the SEEK Tutor had a talking head, but the final version had "voice only" facility because there was a worry that the visual animation of the head would create a distraction from the Web material to be learned. Research has subsequently revealed that such worries are unwarranted if the talking heads are designed appropriately (Graesser, Moreno, et al., 2003; Louwerse, Graesser, McNamara, & Lu, 2009). Viewers of learning technologies in the modern world are quite adept at attending to conversational agents at appropriate moments.

It should be noted that the spoken messages of this first facility were presented only if the student decided to click the Hint button. In reflection, this was an unfortunate design decision because students rarely ask for help (Graesser, McNamara, & VanLehn, 2005; Graesser & Person, 1994) unless they are gaming the system to avoid learning, a condition that does not apply here.

The second computer facility was a pop-up *Rating and Justification* that asked students to evaluate the expected reliability of the information in a site. Figure 7.1 shows

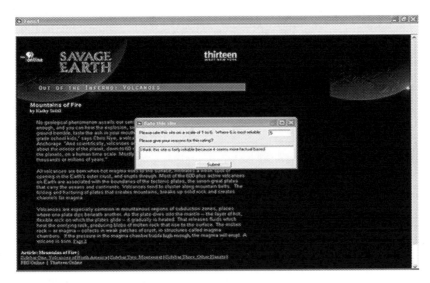

Figure 7.1
Web page with Pop-Up Rating and Justification for the SEEK Web Tutor (from Graesset et al., 2007).

an example Web page and the associated pop-up Rating and Justification. This facility deterministically appeared after the students first viewed a particular Web site for 20 seconds. The student rated the reliability of the information and typed in a verbal justification of the rating.

The third computer facility consisted of a pop-up *Journal* that had five questions about the reliability of the site that the learner had just visited. These questions were designed to address some of the core aspects of critical stance: *Who authored this site? How trustworthy is it? What explanation do they offer for the cause of volcanic eruptions? What support do they offer for this explanation? Is this information useful to you, and if so, how will you use it?* Each of the questions had a Hint button that could be pressed to receive spoken hints on answering each question. The pop-up Journal was launched whenever the learner left one of the Web sites. It forced learners to think about each of the five core aspects of critical stance. They not only gave a rating for each question but also typed in a verbal justification for each rating.

The three computer facilities were expected to automatize a habit of mind with a critical stance by direct didactic training and application of the principles to the exemplar Web sites. We conducted some experiments to test the effectiveness of this approach (Graesser, Wiley, et al., 2007).

College students explored the Web sites for approximately 1 hour with the goal of writing an essay on the causes of the eruption of Mount St. Helens. Participants were randomly assigned to either the SEEK Web Tutor condition or to a *navigation* condition that had no training on critical stance. The 1-hour training with the Tutor was expected to enhance a critical stance, as assessed by over a dozen measures, including an essay on the causes of a volcano. Unfortunately, we were quite mistaken. An hour of intense training on critical stance had very little impact on college students. SEEK Web Tutor did not improve learners' ability to detect reliable versus unreliable information sources during training, the amount of study time they allocated to reliable versus unreliable sites, their judgments of the truth/falsity of 30 statements about plate tectonics after the training was completed, and the articulation of core ideas about plate tectonics in the essays. After assessing over a dozen measures, there was only one measure that showed a benefit of the SEEK Web Tutor over the navigation control. Namely, we found that students had more expressions in the essay with language about causal explanations (such as "cause" and "explanation") compared to navigation controls. We concluded that the SEEK Web Tutor did influence the causal language in their essays but had no noticeable influence on critical stance during the learning processes, on articulation of critical stance principles, on detection of truth versus falsity, and on the acquisition of a deep mental model of science.

There are of course many reasons why the direct approach to instruction was unimpressive. One explanation is that much more training is needed. Perhaps dozens of hours of SEEK Web Tutor on multiple topics and problems are needed before benefits are realized for deep science learning and the application of a critical stance. Another explanation is that there has to be a more adaptive, intelligent, tailored interaction with the student in the context of specific cases before more noticeable improvements will occur. Expertise does not simply fall out from time on task but rather requires expert tutoring on critical constructs and milestones in the context of specific experiences. This raises the bar for both computer and human learning environments.

Human Use Regulatory Affairs Advisor (HURA Advisor)

HURA Advisor (HURAA) was a comprehensive learning environment on the Web that helped adults learn the policies on the ethical use of human subjects in research. The system had a full suite of facilities: (1) didactic lessons that resemble PowerPoint lectures, (2) a technical document repository, (3) hypertext at a deep hierarchically nested grain size, (4) multimedia (including an engaging video), (5) lessons with concrete scenarios to assess case-based reasoning on research ethics, (6) query-based information retrieval, and (7) an animated agent that served as a navigational guide (Hu & Graesser, 2004).

The agent navigational guide provided coherence on the entire learning experience. Figure 7.2 shows the layout of the interface of the learning environment. The animated conversational agent of HURAA appeared in the upper left of the Web page and

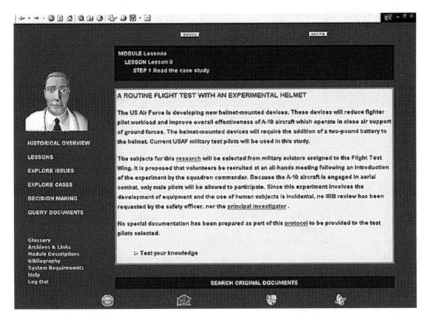

Figure 7.2
Interface of the HURA Advisor (from Hu & Graesser, 2004).

served as a navigational guide to the student. The agent suggested what to do next and answered student questions that matched entries in a frequently asked questions database. Below the agent was a column with labels for the major learning modules that spanned a broad array of learning technologies (1–6 above). An intelligent agent could direct the student on which of these facilities to use, but the system we ended up designing did not have that adaptive intelligence. Perhaps interactivity, adaptation, and intelligence of the system matters, but we could not assess that with this instantiation of HURAA.

One component that did have adaptive intelligence is the case study module. Students were presented with a series of cases and asked to identify ethical flaws. For example, the experiment described in figure 7.2 may have violated one or more of the seven principles: social or scientific value, scientific validity, fair subject selection, favorable risk–benefit ratio, independent review, informed consent, and respect for enrolled subjects. The participants rated the extent to which each case had problems with each of the seven dimensions. The system then gave feedback on their ratings and presented what a panel of experts would say. To be adaptive, the selection of case N was expected to be sensitive to performance on the prior case, such that the new case should have unresolved problems of the past.

HURAA was evaluated in experiments that contrasted it with conventional computer-based instruction containing the same content that controlled for information equivalence as best it could. Such controls on content between interventions are equally important as time on task; time on task is irrelevant without an information theoretical analysis of content. The results of Hu and Graesser (2004) were both positive and negative after collecting dozens measures of retention, reasoning, and inquiry. Memory for core concepts was enhanced by HURAA compared to the conventional Web software, with effect sizes averaging 0.78. HURAA's answers to students' questions in the information retrieval facilities were impressive, with 95% of the answers being judged as relevant by the learner and 50% judged as being informative. Unfortunately, however, HURAA had no significant increment for several measures compared with the control condition: case-based reasoning, the speed of accessing information when trainees were given difficult questions that required information search, and perceptions of the system with respect to interest, enjoyment, amount learned, and ease of learning. Interestingly, no significant differences occurred in any of the measures we collected when we conducted an experiment that compared the agent's messages being presented in different media, that is, the full animated conversational agent, text only, voice only, and text + voice (Graesser, Ventura, Jackson, Mueller, Hu, & Person, 2003). Simply concluded, it is the content of what the agent says in the conversation that matters rather than the medium of message delivery.

One of the painful lessons from our research on single agents is that there are very limited outcomes of single agents on an ensemble of training methods in a 1-hour period. There needs to be much more extensive training and diversity of experiences to compete with a 20-year-old who has had 20 years of life's experiences.

Multiple Agents Interacting with the Human

The incremental value of multiple agents is that the human can see how others respond and adjust knowledge accordingly. The social world opens up a large array of possibilities in acquiring a critical stance. A student can learn vicariously by observing one agent interacting with another agent and exhibiting strategies with a critical stance. Two agents can disagree, contradict each other, and hold an argument, periodically turning to the student to solicit the student's perspective. The agents can correct each other or the student when false information is expressed. And vice versa, the student can correct the agents when they express false information or faulty reasoning. This section describes some studies with agents in learning environments that have false information, faulty reasoning, and various barriers to comprehension. The studies involve two agents interacting with a human student in what is called a *trialog*.

Trialogs with Contradictions in Operation ARIES! and Operation ARA
The trialog studies involved two agents and a student critiquing case studies of scientific research with respect to scientific methodology. The design of the case studies and trialog critiques were inspired by a serious game called Operation ARIES! (Forsyth et al., 2013; Millis et al., 2011), which was subsequently commercialized by Pearson Education as *Operation ARA* (Halpern et al., 2012). Players learn how to critically evaluate research they encounter in various media, such as the Web, TV, magazines, and newspapers. ARIES is an acronym for Acquiring Research Investigative and Evaluative Skills. The game teaches how to critically evaluate aspects of scientific investigations (e.g., the need for control groups, adequate samples of observations, operational definitions, etc.) and how to ask appropriate questions in order to uncover problems with design or interpretation. Scientific inquiry is crucial because it comprises the necessary steps of "science as process," the steps that scientists follow in establishing and critiquing causal claims. Figure 7.3 shows the interface of ARIES, showing multiple agents, a case to be evaluated and other components of the learning environment.

It could be argued that scientific reasoning and inquiry are core skills of citizens in the information age. The public is constantly being exposed to causal claims made by scientists, advertisers, coworkers, friends, and the press via a variety of media (blogs,

Figure 7.3
Interface of Operation ARIES! (from Millis et al., 2011).

TV, Web, print, word of mouth). Of course, some of the claims have relatively solid scientific evidence for support whereas others do not. In some cases, the research is well executed, but the interpretation or conclusion drawn by the press is inappropriate. For example, consider a headline that makes a causal claim that "wine lowers heart attack risk in women," based on a correlational design which does not support a cause–effect interpretation. In other cases, a claim is unfounded because the design of the study itself is flawed or nonexistent. Consider a TV news report that concludes that teenagers are too immature to drive, with a film depicting irresponsible teens and a statistic that reports how many automobile accidents they had in a given year. There is no comparison group, operational definition, and systematic collection of data. An informed viewer should be able to identify the problems with such a flimsy news report. There can be costly consequences to the misinformation. According to the U.S. National Institutes of Health (NIH), approximately four million U.S. adults and one million U.S. children used homeopathy and other alternative medicines in 2006 even though there is little or no benefit of these medicines beyond placebo effects.

We have conducted a series of studies that plant false information and contradictions in the trialogs as case studies are critiqued (D'Mello, Lehman, Pekrun, & Graesser, 2014; Lehman, D'Mello, & Graesser, 2012). A three-way trialog conversation transpired between the human student, a tutor agent, and a student agent. The tutor agent was an expert on scientific inquiry whereas the student agent was a peer of the human learner. A series of cases were presented to the student that described experiments that may have had a number of flaws with respect to scientific methodology. For example, one case study described a new pill that purportedly helps people lose weight, but the sample size was small and there was no control group. The goal of the participants in the trialog was to identify the flaws and express them in natural language.

Lehman et al. (2012) attempted to plant cognitive disequilibrium by manipulating whether or not the tutor agent and the student agent contradicted each other during the trialog and expressed points that are incorrect. Each case study had a description of a research study that was to be critiqued during the trialogs. That is, the tutor agent and student agent engaged in a short exchange about (1) whether there was a flaw in the study and (2) if there *was* a flaw, which part of the study was flawed. The tutor agent expressed a correct assertion and the student agent agreed with the tutor in the *True–True* control condition. In the *True–False* condition, the tutor expressed a correct assertion but the student agent disagreed by expressing an incorrect assertion. In the *False–True* condition it was the student agent who provided the correct assertion and the tutor agent who disagreed. In the *False–False* condition, the tutor agent provided an incorrect assertion and the student agent agreed.

The human student was asked to intervene after particular points of possible contradiction in the conversation. For example, the agents turned to the human and asked "Do you agree with Chris (student agent) that the control group in this study was flawed?" The human's response was coded as correct if he or she agreed with the agent who had made the correct assertion about the flaw of the study. If the human experienced uncertainty and was confused, this should be reflected in the incorrectness and/or uncertainty of the human's answer. This uncertainty would ideally stimulate thinking and learning.

The data indeed confirmed that the contradictions and false information had an impact on the humans' answers to these Yes–No questions immediately following a contradiction. The proportion of correct student responses showed the following order: True–True > True–False > False–True > False–False conditions. These findings indicated that learners were occasionally confused when both agents agreed and were correct (True–True, no contradiction), became more confused when there was a contradiction between the two agents (True–False or False–True), and were either confused or simply accepted the incorrect information when the agents incorrectly agreed (False–False). Confusion would be best operationally defined as occurring if both (1) the student manifests uncertainty/incorrectness in their decisions when asked by the agents and (2) the student either reports being confused or the computer automatically detects confusion (through technologies that track discourse interaction, facial expressions, and body posture that are beyond the scope of this article to discuss; D'Mello & Graesser, 2010; Graesser & D'Mello, 2012).

The ARIES-inspired trialog studies also showed that contradictions, confusion, and uncertainty caused more learning at deeper levels of mastery, as reflected in a delayed test on scientific reasoning. The results indicated that contradictions in the False–True condition produced higher performance on multiple choice questions that tapped deeper levels of comprehension than performance in the True–True condition. Identification of flaws on far-transfer case studies in a delayed test also showed significant benefits over the True–True condition without contradictions. Thus, the results indicated that the most uncertainty occurred when the tutor agent made false claims that the student agent disagreed with, that the contradictions stimulated thought and reasoning at deeper levels, and that scores on a delayed posttest were improved by this experience. These data suggest that there may be a causal relationship between contradictions (and the associated cognitive disequilibrium) and deep learning, with confusion playing either a mediating, moderating, or causal role in the process. The results and interpretation are compatible with those of other researchers who have emphasized the role of confusion as a necessary early step in conceptual change (Posner, Strike, Hewson, & Gertzog, 1982) and the role of cognitive conflict as crucial for deeper learning (van den Broek & Kendeou, 2008). It is indeed compatible with Piagetian theory of intellectual development (Piaget, 1952).

It is illuminating that the False–False condition did not engender much uncertainty and confusion. The students pretty much accepted what the tutor and student agents expressed when they agreed even if the claims were false. An alternative possibility could have been that the claims of the two agents would clash with the reasoning and belief system of the human. However, that rarely occurred among the college students who participated in this study. This result is compatible with models that predict that it takes a large amount of world knowledge before students can detect what they don't know (knowledge gaps) (Miyake & Norman, 1979), false information (Rapp, 2008), and contradictory information (Baker, 1985; O'Brien, Rizzella, Albrecht, & Halleran, 1998). A strategic, skeptical, critical stance is the only hope for the human when the person is not fortified with sufficient subject matter knowledge.

There was a need for the two agents to directly contradict each other in a conversation before the humans experienced an appreciable amount of uncertainty and confusion. We suspect that the contradiction would have to be contiguous in time before the contradiction would be detected. That is, the contradiction is likely to be missed if one agent makes a claim and then another agent makes a contradictory claim 10 minutes later. This is compatible with research in text comprehension that has shown that the contradictory claims must be copresent in working memory before they get noticed (Baker, 1985; Otero & Kintsch, 1992) unless there is a high amount of world knowledge. It is also compatible with the observation that it is difficult for many students to integrate information from multiple texts and spot contradictions (Bråten et al., 2009; Britt & Aglinskas, 2002; Goldman et al., 2012; Rouet, 2006) unless there is a high amount of world knowledge. A strategic attempt to integrate information from multiple texts would be needed to draw such connections unless the person is fortified with sufficient subject matter knowledge (Goldman et al., 2012; Graesser et al., 2007; Wiley et al., 2009).

Our research on trialogs with agent contradictions has illustrated the benefits of learning at deep levels when putting students in cognitive disequilibrium. The result is compatible with our research on the AutoTutor agent that helps students learn by holding a conversation in natural language and that tracks their moment-by-moment emotions (i.e., cognitive–affective mixtures) during the learning process (D'Mello & Graesser, 2012; Graesser & D'Mello, 2012). The common emotions during learning are boredom, engagement/flow, frustration, confusion, delight, and surprise in a wide range of learning environments (Baker, D'Mello, Rodrigo, & Graesser, 2010). The learning-centered emotion that best predicts learning at deeper levels is confusion, a cognitive–affective state associated with thought and deliberation (Craig et al., 2004; D'Mello & Graesser, 2012; D'Mello et al., 2014; Graesser & D'Mello, 2012).

We have been investigating a cognitive disequilibrium framework that integrates a number of psychological processes: confusion (and other learning-centered emotions), question asking (inquiry), deliberative thought, and deeper learning. Cognitive disequilibrium is a state that occurs when people face obstacles to goals, interruptions, contradictions, incongruities, anomalies, impasses, uncertainty, and salient contrasts (Barth & Funke, 2010; D'Mello & Graesser, 2012; Festinger, 1957; Graesser, Lu, Olde,

Cooper-Pye, & Whitten, 2005; Mandler, 1999; Piaget, 1952; Schwartz & Bransford, 1998). Initially, the person experiences various emotions when beset with cognitive disequilibrium, but notably confusion, surprise, or curiosity (D'Mello & Graesser, 2012; D'Mello et al., 2014; Graesser & D'Mello, 2012; Lehman, D'Mello, & Graesser, 2012). This elicits question asking and other forms of inquiry (Graesser & McMahen, 1993; Graesser, Lu, et al., 2005; Otero & Graesser, 2001), such as social interaction, physical exploration of the environment, or the monitoring of focal attention. The person engages in problem solving, reasoning, and other thoughtful cognitive activities in an attempt to resolve the impasse and restore cognitive equilibrium. The consequence is deeper learning.

There are, of course, individual differences in the handling of cognitive disequilibrium. Relevant traits tap constructs of motivation, self-concept, and goal orientations (Deci & Ryan, 2002; Dweck, 2002; Pekrun, 2006; Meyer & Turner, 2006). Responses to cognitive disequilibrium depend on the learners' appraisal or reappraisal of their own abilities, their goals, the event that triggered the disequilibrium, and the context (Ortony, Clore, & Collins, 1988). For example, some students enjoy high levels of disequilibrium, confusion, and frustration over a lengthy time span when playing games; other students are not comfortable with the disequilibrium even in game environments. Some students give up and conclude they are not good at the subject matter or skill whereas others see it as a challenge to be conquered with an investment of effort (Dweck, 2002).

There are other systems with trialogs and multiple agents that train students on cognitive and metacognitive skills that have relevance to the detection and handling of incorrect information. Four of these systems are briefly described next.

MetaTutor Training on Self-Regulated Learning
MetaTutor trains students on 13 strategies that are theoretically important for self-regulated learning (SRL; Azevedo, Moos, Johnson, & Chauncey, 2010). The SRL process theoretically involves the learners' constructing a plan, monitoring metacognitive activities, implementing learning strategies, and reflecting on their progress and achievements. The MetaTutor system has a main agent (Gavin) that coordinates the overall learning environment and three satellite agents that handle three phases of SRL: planning, monitoring, and applying learning strategies. Each of these phases can be decomposed further under the guidance of the assigned conversational agent. For example, metacognitive monitoring can be decomposed into judgments of learning, feeling of knowing, content evaluation, monitoring the adequacy of a strategy, and monitoring progress toward goals. Examples of learning strategies include searching for relevant information in a goal-directed fashion, taking notes, drawing tables or diagrams, rereading, elaborating the material, making inferences, and coordinating information sources (text and diagrams). Each of these metacognitive and SRL skills

has associated measures that are based on the student's actions, decisions, ratings, and verbal input. The frequency and accuracy of each measured skill is collected throughout the tutoring session and hopefully increases as a function of direct training. The MetaTutor training would be expected to improve a person's detection of incorrect information through the monitoring component and also the strategies that compare information in different documents and media.

Teachable Agents with Betty's Brain

Betty's Brain (Biswas et al., 2010; Schwartz et al., 2009) requires the human student to teach an agent named Betty about causal relationships in a biological system that is depicted in a conceptual graph. Betty has to get the conceptual graph correct in order to pass a multiple-choice test. When she fails, the human interacts with Betty to improve her conceptual graph and thereby improve her scores. Another mentor agent guides this interaction through comments, hints, and suggestions to the human learner. The trialogs utilize learning-through-teaching and also precise accountability on the quality of the teacher's actions. The human student teaches the student agent, with the tutor agent periodically entering the conversation to guide a productive interaction. It takes a sufficient amount of knowledge to produce the content to teach the student agent. Betty will fail the test if the teacher does not set up the correct graph so incorrect links are detected.

iDRIVE (Instruction with Deep-Level Reasoning Questions in Vicarious Environments)

iDRIVE has two agents train students to learn science content by modeling deep reasoning questions in question–answer dialogues (Craig, Sullins, Witherspoon, & Gholson, 2006; Gholson et al., 2009). A student agent asks a series of deep questions about the science content, and the teacher agent immediately answers each question. Approximately 30 good questions are asked (by the student agent) and answered (by the tutor agent) per hour in this learning environment, so high quality inquiry is weathered into the students' thinking habits. There is evidence that learning gains are higher and students ask better questions for those students who have the mind-set of asking deep questions (*why, how, what-if, what-if-not*) that tap causal structures, complex systems, and logical justifications (Graesser & Olde, 2003). When students are trained how to ask good questions, the frequency of good questions increases and their text comprehension improves (Gholson et al., 2009; Rosenshine, Meister, & Chapman, 1996). We expect that sophisticated inquiry skills will help them detect misinformation and also to compare different information sources when contradictions arise.

iSTART (Interactive Strategy Trainer for Active Reading and Thinking)

This strategy trainer helps students become better readers by monitoring comprehension at deep levels and constructing self-explanations of the text (McNamara, O'Reilly,

Rowe, Boonthum, & Levinstein, 2007). The construction of self-explanations during reading is known to facilitate deep comprehension (Chi et al., 1989), particularly when there is some context-sensitive feedback on the explanations that get produced (McNamara, O'Reilly, Best, & Ozuru, 2006). The iSTART interventions focus on five reading strategies that are designed to enhance self-explanations: *monitoring comprehension* (i.e., recognizing comprehension failures and the need for remedial strategies), *paraphrasing* explicit text, making *bridging inferences* between the current sentence and prior text, making *predictions* about the subsequent text, and *elaborating* the text with links to what the reader already knows. The accuracy of applying these metacognitive skills is measured and tracked throughout the tutorial session.

Groups of agents scaffold these strategies in three phases of training. In an *Introduction Module*, a trio of agents (an instructor and two students) collaboratively describes self-explanation strategies with each other. In a *Demonstration Module*, two agents demonstrate the use of self-explanation in the context of a science passage and then the student identifies the strategies being used. A measure of metacognitive skill is the accuracy of the students' identifying the correct strategy exhibited by the student agent. In a final *Practice* phase, an agent coaches and provides feedback to the student one-to-one while the student practices self-explanation reading strategies. That is, for particular sentences in a text, the agent reads the sentence and asks the student to self-explain it by typing a self-explanation. The iSTART system then attempts to interpret the student's contributions, gives feedback, and asks the trainee to modify unsatisfactory self-explanations (McNamara, Boonthum, Levinstein, & Millis, 2007). Improved skills with comprehension monitoring and self-explanation would be expected to help students detect misinformation and explain how to resolve discrepancies among claims and information sources.

Closing Comments

This chapter has described some learning environments with agents that are designed to help students detect misinformation and incompatibilities among different information sources. Many students are gullible and accept the information presented in different sources, so they need to be trained to have a critical stance. The skeptical students are more vigilant in detecting false claims, faulty reasoning, and contradictions among sources. It is, of course, healthy to adopt a skeptical stance when comprehending some genres of documents, such as editorials, blogs, Web sites, and social media messages. However, a critical stance is also needed for virtually all documents in the information age, including those in print, particularly as editors are less likely to scrutinize the content.

The learning environments with agents can help humans acquire a critical stance that helps inoculate them from misinformation. Systems with agents train students to evaluate the quality of Web sites (SEEK Web Tutor), identify problematic ethics in research studies (HURA Advisor), identify science news articles with faulty research methods (Operation ARIES! and ARA), acquire metacognitive skills for self-regulated learning (MetaTutor), identify gaps and faulty links in knowledge representations (Betty's Brain), ask deep questions (iDRIVE), and monitor comprehension and self-explain during reading (iSTART). Some of these trainers have a single computer agent whereas others have two or more agents that take on different roles. All of these trainers are intelligent and flexibly interact with students in ways that attempt to adapt to individual needs of the learners. All of them have been tested on humans and have shown improvements in metacognitive skills, reasoning, and/or deeper knowledge of the subject matter—all of which allegedly help the learner detect misinformation.

The agents are needed to train most students on how to handle misinformation because their habits of mind are not reliably geared to spot information pollution. According to the cognitive disequilibrium model discussed in this chapter, a number of processes would occur when a person receives information that either contradicts another claim or clashes with what a person knows: (1) detection of the misinformation neurally, as manifested by the N400 (Kutas & Federmeier, 2000), (2) surprise, curiosity, or another cognitive–affective process, (3) muscular tension, (4) eye movements for exploration, (5) confusion, (6) inquiry and question asking, (7) reasoning and problem solving, (8) explicit acknowledgment of the misinformation, (9) physical actions, and (10) social interactions for help. We are uncertain about the specific ordering of these processes, which are no doubt interactive, but the higher numbers tend to be later in the psychological timeline. Nevertheless, we are certain that agents or other forms of training are needed to help students intelligently execute the processes associated with the higher numbers.

References

Azevedo, R., Moos, D., Johnson, A., & Chauncey, A. (2010). Measuring cognitive and metacognitive regulatory processes used during hypermedia learning: Issues and challenges. *Educational Psychologist, 45*, 210–223.

Baker, L. (1985). Differences in standards used by college students to evaluate their comprehension of expository prose. *Reading Research Quarterly, 20*, 298–313.

Baker, R. S., D'Mello, S. K., Rodrigo, M. T., & Graesser, A. C. (2010). Better to be frustrated than bored: The incidence, persistence, and impact of learners' cognitive–affective states during interactions with three different computer-based learning environments. *International Journal of Human–Computer Studies, 68*, 223–241.

Barth, C. M., & Funke, J. (2010). Negative affective environments improve complex solving performance. *Cognition and Emotion, 24*, 1259–1268.

Baylor, A. L., & Kim, Y. (2005). Simulating instructional roles through pedagogical agents. *International Journal of Artificial Intelligence in Education, 15*, 95–115.

Biswas, G., Jeong, H., Kinnebrew, J., Sulcer, B., & Roscoe, R. (2010). Measuring self-regulated learning skills through social interactions in a teachable agent environment. *Research and Practice in Technology-Enhanced Learning, 5*, 123–152.

Braasch, J. L. G., Lawless, K. A., Goldman, S. R., Manning, F. H., Gomez, K. W., & MacLeod, S. M. (2009). Evaluating search results: An empirical analysis of middle school students' use of source attributes to select useful sources. *Journal of Educational Computing Research, 41*, 63–82.

Bråten, I., Strømsø, H. I., & Britt, M. A. (2009). Trust matters: Examining the role of source evaluation in students' construction of meaning within and across multiple texts. *Reading Research Quarterly, 44*, 6–28.

Britt, M. A., & Aglinskas, C. (2002). Improving students' ability to identify and use source information. *Cognition and Instruction, 20*, 485–522.

Chi, M. T. H., Bassok, M., Lewis, M., Reimann, P., & Glaser, R. (1989). Self-explanations: How students study and use examples in learning to solve problems. *Cognitive Science, 13*, 145–182.

Craig, S. D., Graesser, A. C., Sullins, J., & Gholson, B. (2004). Affect and learning: An exploratory look into the role of affect in learning. *Journal of Educational Media, 29*, 241–250.

Craig, S. D., Sullins, J., Witherspoon, A., & Gholson, B. (2006). Deep-level reasoning questions effect: The role of dialog and deep-level reasoning questions during vicarious learning. *Cognition and Instruction, 24*, 563–589.

Deci, E., & Ryan, R. (2002). The paradox of achievement: The harder you push, the worse it gets. In J. Aronson (Ed.), *Improving academic achievement: Impact of psychological factors on education* (pp. 61–87). Orlando, FL: Academic Press.

D'Mello, S., Dowell, N., & Graesser, A. C. (2011). Does it really matter whether students' contributions are spoken versus typed in an intelligent tutoring system with natural language? *Journal of Experimental Psychology. Applied, 17*, 1–17.

D'Mello, S., & Graesser, A. C. (2010). Multimodal semi-automated affect detection from conversational cues, gross body language, and facial features. *User Modeling and User-Adapted Interaction, 20*, 147–187.

D'Mello, S. K., & Graesser, A. C. (2012). Dynamics of affective states during complex learning. *Learning and Instruction, 22*, 145–157.

D'Mello, S., Lehman, B., Pekrun, R., & Graesser, A. C. (2014). Confusion can be beneficial for learning. *Learning and Instruction, 29*, 153–170.

Dweck, C. S. (2002). The development of ability conceptions. In A. Wigfield & J. S. Eccles (Eds.), *Development of achievement motivation: A volume in the educational psychology series* (pp. 57–88). San Diego, CA: Academic Press.

Festinger, L. (1957). *A theory of cognitive dissonance.* Stanford, CA: Stanford University Press.

Forsyth, C. M., Graesser, A. C., Pavlik, P., Cai, Z., Butler, H., Halpern, D. F., et al. (2013). Operation ARIES! methods, mystery and mixed models: Discourse features predict affect in a serious game. *Journal of Educational Data Mining, 5,* 147–189.

Gholson, B., Witherspoon, A., Morgan, B., Brittingham, J. K., Coles, R., Graesser, A. C., et al. (2009). Exploring the deep-level reasoning questions effect during vicarious learning among eighth to eleventh graders in the domains of computer literacy and Newtonian physics. *Instructional Science, 37,* 487–493.

Goldman, S. R., Braasch, J. L. G., Wiley, J., Graesser, A. C., & Brodowinska, K. (2012). Comprehending and learning from Internet sources: Processing patterns of better and poorer learners. *Reading Research Quarterly, 47,* 356–381.

Graesser, A. C., Conley, M., & Olney, A. (2012). Intelligent tutoring systems. In K. R. Harris, S. Graham, & T. Urdan (Eds.), *APA educational psychology handbook: Vol. 3. Applications to learning and teaching* (pp. 451–473). Washington, DC: American Psychological Association.

Graesser, A., & D'Mello, S. K. (2012). Emotions during the learning of difficult material. In B. Ross (Ed.), *Psychology of learning and motivation* (Vol. 57, pp. 183–225). New York: Elsevier.

Graesser, A. C., D'Mello, S. K., Hu, X., Cai, Z., Olney, A., & Morgan, B. (2012). AutoTutor. In P. McCarthy & C. Boonthum-Denecke (Eds.), *Applied natural language processing: Identification, investigation, and resolution* (pp. 169–187). Hershey, PA: IGI Global.

Graesser, A. C., Jeon, M., & Dufty, D. (2008). Agent technologies designed to facilitate interactive knowledge construction. *Discourse Processes, 45,* 298–322.

Graesser, A. C., Lu, S., Olde, B. A., Cooper-Pye, E., & Whitten, S. (2005). Question asking and eye tracking during cognitive disequilibrium: Comprehending illustrated texts on devices when the devices break down. *Memory & Cognition, 33,* 1235–1247.

Graesser, A. C., & McMahen, C. L. (1993). Anomalous information triggers questions when adults solve problems and comprehend stories. *Journal of Educational Psychology, 85,* 136–151.

Graesser, A. C., McNamara, D. S., & VanLehn, K. (2005). Scaffolding deep comprehension strategies through Point&Query, AutoTutor, and iSTART. *Educational Psychologist, 40,* 225–234.

Graesser, A. C., Moreno, K., Marineau, J., Adcock, A., Olney, A., & Person, N. (2003). AutoTutor improves deep learning of computer literacy: Is it the dialog or the talking head? In U. Hoppe, F. Verdejo, & J. Kay (Eds.), *Proceedings of Artificial Intelligence in Education* (pp. 47–54). Amsterdam: IOS Press. (Finalist for Outstanding Paper Award)

Graesser, A. C., & Olde, B. A. (2003). How does one know whether a person understands a device? The quality of the questions the person asks when the device breaks down. *Journal of Educational Psychology, 95,* 524–536.

Graesser, A. C., & Person, N. K. (1994). Question asking during tutoring. *American Educational Research Journal, 31,* 104–137.

Graesser, A. C., Ventura, M., Jackson, G. T., Mueller, J., Hu, X., & Person, N. (2003). The impact of conversational navigational guides on the learning, use, and perceptions of users of a Web site. *Proceedings of the AAAI Spring Symposium 2003 on Agent-Mediated Knowledge Management* (pp. 9–14). Palo Alto, CA: AAAI Press.

Graesser, A. C., Wiley, J., Goldman, S. R., O'Reilly, T., Jeon, M., & McDaniel, B. (2007). SEEK Web tutor: Fostering a critical stance while exploring the causes of volcanic eruption. *Metacognition and Learning, 2*, 89–105.

Halpern, D. F., Millis, K., Graesser, A. C., Butler, H., Forsyth, C., & Cai, Z. (2012). Operation ARA: A computerized learning game that teaches critical thinking and scientific reasoning. *Thinking Skills and Creativity, 7*, 93–100.

Hu, X., & Graesser, A. C. (2004). Human Use Regulatory Affairs Advisor (HURAA): Learning about research ethics with intelligent learning modules. *Behavior Research Methods, Instruments, & Computers, 36*, 241–249.

Johnson, L. W., & Valente, A. (2008). Tactical language and culture training systems: Using artificial intelligence to teach foreign languages and cultures. In M. Goker & K. Haigh (Eds.), *Proceedings of the Twentieth Conference on Innovative Applications of Artificial Intelligence* (pp. 1632–1639). Menlo Park, CA: AAAI Press.

Kendeou, P., & van den Broek, P. (2007). The effects of prior knowledge and text structure on comprehension processes during reading of scientific texts. *Memory & Cognition, 35*, 1567–1577.

Kutas, M., & Federmeier, K. D. (2000). Electrophysiology reveals semantic memory use in language comprehension. *Trends in Cognitive Sciences, 4*, 463–470.

Lehman, B., D'Mello, S. K., & Graesser, A. C. (2012). Confusion and complex learning during interactions with computer learning environments. *Internet and Higher Education, 15*, 184–194.

Louwerse, M. M., Graesser, A. C., McNamara, D. S., & Lu, S. (2009). Embodied conversational agents as conversational partners. *Applied Cognitive Psychology, 23*, 1244–1255.

Mandler, G. (1999). Emotion. In B. M. Bly & D. E. Rumelhart (Eds.), *Cognitive science handbook of perception and cognition* (2nd ed., pp. 367–384). San Diego, CA: Academic Press.

McNamara, D. S., Boonthum, C., Levinstein, I. B., & Millis, K. (2007). Evaluating self-explanations in iSTART: Comparing word-based and LSA algorithms. In T. Landauer, D. S. McNamara, S. Dennis, & W. Kintsch (Eds.), *Handbook of latent semantic analysis* (pp. 227–241). Mahwah, NJ: Lawrence Erlbaum Associates.

McNamara, D. S., O'Reilly, T., Best, R., & Ozuru, Y. (2006). Improving adolescent students' reading comprehension with iSTART. *Journal of Educational Computing Research, 34*, 147–171.

McNamara, D. S., O'Reilly, T., Rowe, M., Boonthum, C., & Levinstein, I. B. (2007). iSTART: A web-based tutor that teaches self-explanation and metacognitive reading strategies. In D.S. McNamara (Ed.), *Reading comprehension strategies: Theories, interventions, and technologies*. Mahwah, NJ: Erlbaum

Meyer, D. K., & Turner, J. C. (2006). Re-conceptualizing emotion and motivation to learn in class-room contexts. *Educational Psychology Review, 18,* 377–390.

Millis, K., Forsyth, C., Butler, H., Wallace, P., Graesser, A., & Halpern, D. (2011). Operation ARIES! A serious game for teaching scientific inquiry. In M. Ma, A. Oikonomou, & J. Lakhmi (Eds.), *Serious games and edutainment applications* (pp. 169–196). London: Springer-Verlag.

Miyake, N., & Norman, D. A. (1979). To ask a question one must know enough to know what is not known. *Journal of Verbal Learning and Verbal Behavior, 18,* 357–364.

O'Brien, E. J., Rizzella, M. L., Albrecht, J. E., & Halleran, J. G. (1998). Updating a situation model: A memory-based text processing view. *Journal of Experimental Psychology: Learning, Memory, & Cognition, 24,* 1200–1210.

Ortony, A., Clore, G., & Collins, A. (1988). *The cognitive structure of emotions.* New York: Cambridge University Press.

Otero, J., & Graesser, A. C. (2001). PREG: Elements of a model of question asking. *Cognition and Instruction, 19,* 143–175.

Otero, J., & Kintsch, W. (1992). Failures to detect contradictions in a text: What readers believe versus what they read. *Psychological Science, 3,* 229–235.

Pekrun, R. (2006). The control-value theory of achievement emotions: Assumptions, corollaries, and implications for educational research and practice. *Educational Psychology Review, 18,* 315–341.

Piaget, J. (1952). *The origins of intelligence.* New York: International University Press.

Posner, G. J., Strike, K. A., Hewson, P. W., & Gertzog, W. A. (1982). Accommodation of a scientific conception: Toward a theory of conceptual change. *Science Education, 66,* 211–227.

Rapp, D. N. (2008). How do readers handle incorrect information during reading? *Memory & Cognition, 36,* 688–701.

Rosenshine, B., Meister, C., & Chapman, S. (1996). Teaching students to generate questions: A review of the intervention studies. *Review of Educational Research, 66,* 181–221.

Rowe, J., Shores, L., Mott, B., & Lester, J. (2010). Integrating learning and engagement in narrative-centered learning environments. In J. Kay & V. Aleven (Eds.), *Proceedings of 10th International Conference on Intelligent Tutoring Systems* (pp. 166–177). Berlin/Heidelberg: Springer.

Rouet, J.-F. (2006). *The skills of document use.* Mahwah, NJ: Lawrence Erlbaum Associates.

Schwartz, D., & Bransford, D. (1998). A time for telling. *Cognition and Instruction, 16,* 475–522.

Schwartz, D. L., Chase, C., Chin, D., Oppezzo, M., Kwong, H., Okita, S., et al. (2009). Interactive metacognition: Monitoring and regulating a teachable agent. In D. J. Hacker, J. Dunlosky, & A. C. Graesser (Eds.), *Handbook of metacognition in education* (pp. 340–358). Routledge.

Van den Broek, P., & Kendeou, P. (2008). Cognitive processes in comprehension of science texts: The role of co-activation in confronting misconceptions. *Applied Cognitive Psychology, 22,* 335–351.

VanLehn, K. (2011). The relative effectiveness of human tutoring, intelligent tutoring systems and other tutoring systems. *Educational Psychologist, 46*, 197–221.

VanLehn, K., Graesser, A. C., Jackson, G. T., Jordan, P., Olney, A., & Rose, C. P. (2007). When are tutorial dialogues more effective than reading? *Cognitive Science, 31*, 3–62.

Ward, W., Cole, R., Bolaños, D., Buchenroth-Martin, C., Svirsky, E., Van Vuuren, S., et al. (2011). My Science Tutor: A conversational multimedia virtual tutor for elementary school science. *ACM Transactions of Speech and Language Processing, 13*, 4–16.

Wiley, J., Goldman, S. R., Graesser, A. C., Sanchez, C. A., Ash, I. K., & Hemmerich, J. A. (2009). Source evaluation, comprehension, and learning in Internet science inquiry tasks. *American Educational Research Journal, 46*, 1060–1106.

II   Mechanisms of Inaccurate Knowledge Acquisition

8 Knowledge Neglect: Failures to Notice Contradictions with Stored Knowledge

Elizabeth J. Marsh and Sharda Umanath

Why do students often think that Toronto is the capital of Canada and that vitamin C wards off colds? Misconceptions are common across domains, including physics (e.g., Brown, 1992; McCloskey, 1983), health (e.g., Lee, Friedman, Ross-Degnan, Hibberd, & Goldmann, 2003; Wynn, Foster, & Trussell, 2009), chemistry (e.g., Nakhleh, 1992), gambling (e.g., Ferland, Ladouceur, & Vitaro, 2002), and ecology (e.g., Munson, 1994), among many others. Part of the problem is that there are many potential sources of misconceptions, including (but not limited to) misleading content in textbooks (e.g., Cho, Kahle, & Nordland, 1985), logical errors on the part of the learner (e.g., Clement, Narode, & Rosnick, 1981), other people such as family and friends (e.g., Landau & Bavaria, 2003), and fictional sources like movies and novels (e.g., Gouvier, Prestholdt, & Warner, 1988). In many cases, students learn a misconception because they have no knowledge with which to combat that misconception; for example, the average viewer knows little about amnesia and traumatic brain injury and thus finds no fault with movies depicting release from amnesia following a blow to the head. In such situations, the only solutions involve either avoiding the misconceptions in the first place (a nearly impossible task) or correcting the errors after the fact, when they can often prove quite tenacious (e.g., Butler, Fazio, & Marsh, 2011; Chi, 2008; Landau & Bavaria, 2003; Simons & Chabris, 2011).

In contrast, one might expect that having relevant prior knowledge would insulate the learner from picking up misconceptions. For example, it seems plausible that knowing that Neil Armstrong was the first astronaut on the moon would protect one from believing a story or movie claiming that John Glenn was the first astronaut on the moon. Prior knowledge often benefits learning and memory and specifically supports new learning (Anderson, 1981; Ausubel & Blake, 1958; Chiesi, Spilich, & Voss, 1979; Dooling & Mullet, 1973; Kole & Healy, 2007; Rapp, 2008). Thus, it seems intuitive that prior knowledge should make factual inaccuracies so obvious that one would dismiss them immediately and never reproduce them. Yet, surprisingly, the effects of exposure to misconceptions are not limited to cases where people are ignorant of the true state of the world. That is, having accurate knowledge does not guarantee that one will notice an error (something inconsistent with one's stored knowledge), and furthermore, it does not protect the learner from later repeating that error. It is this particular problem that will be the focus of this chapter. We refer to this problem as *knowledge neglect* and use the term to refer to cases where people fail to retrieve and apply stored knowledge appropriately. For example, consider the reader who, after reading a short passage about a plane crash, answers the question "Where were the survivors buried?" (Barton & Sanford, 1993). This example demonstrates knowledge neglect because the reader has failed to retrieve and apply stored knowledge of the word "survivor" (successfully doing so would make this question an impossible one). Knowledge neglect goes beyond the immediate failure to notice a contradiction, as will be described below, and has consequences for later remembering.

In this chapter, we will describe experimental paradigms that demonstrate knowledge neglect and then discuss the memorial consequences of failing to retrieve and apply stored knowledge. Because error detection is key, we will consider how to promote monitoring, which is more challenging than it seems. We will then discuss how knowledge neglect and the resulting suggestibility compare to what we know about episodic memory, where there is a much larger literature about how people come to misremember events.

Two Examples of Knowledge Neglect

We begin by briefly overviewing two situations that we believe demonstrate knowledge neglect, with learners failing to retrieve and/or apply stored knowledge to a situation where it is highly relevant.

Example 1

Our initial work on knowledge neglect involved a laboratory analogue of learning from fictional sources. Novels, movies, and other fictional works often take place in familiar places and time periods and contain references to real people and events—and as such, can be sources of information about the world. However, fictional works, by definition, are not necessarily accurate, meaning that they can also be sources of misinformation about the world. To explore this situation, we use short stories that contain developed characters, dialogue, and plot and critically refer to facts about the world (Marsh, 2004). Some references are accurate (correct), others are plausible but incorrect (misleading), and the rest refer generally to facts without explicitly stating them (neutral). For example, a correct reference would refer to *"paddling across the largest ocean, the Pacific,"* a neutral reference would simply allude to *"paddling across the largest ocean,"* and a misleading reference would state *"paddling across the largest ocean, the Atlantic."* Critical for present purposes, we manipulated the preexperimental likelihood that readers would be familiar with the target facts, based on the Nelson and Narens

Table 8.1

Proportion of misleading, correct, and neutral sentences labeled as containing errors

	Misleading (Hits)	Neutral (False Alarms)	Correct (False Alarms)
Well-known facts	.23	.09	.10
Obscure facts	.24	.10	.15
M	.23	.10	.13

Note. Data from the story paradigm (Fazio & Marsh, 2008a).

(1980) norms. For the "well-known" facts, students in the norming study were able to answer about 70% of short-answer questions about these facts (and we would expect recognition to be higher). In contrast, the "obscure" facts were correctly produced by 15% of norming participants on average. Thus, if readers bring their stored knowledge to bear, they should be able to spot more of the errors that contradict well-known facts.

For present purposes, our focus is on whether participants noticed the errors in the stories (successful error detection), or missed them (knowledge neglect). To measure this, participants were explicitly instructed to look for errors while reading the stories and asked to press a key each time they noticed an error. Across experiments, participants did worse than predicted by the norms. For example, consider data from Fazio and Marsh (2008a), as presented in table 8.1. As a reminder, only sentences in the misleading condition actually contained factual inaccuracies. Readers did show some ability to discriminate accurate from erroneous sentences, but the hit rate (*M* = 0.23) was not much higher than the false-alarm rate (which ranged from 0.09 to 0.15, depending upon condition). Two points are crucial for present purposes. First, the detection rate is much lower than would be predicted by the norms; the norms predict that individuals would be able to correctly answer questions about 42% of items, and we would expect recognition rates to be higher. That is, we would expect more subjects to be able to recognize the largest ocean on Earth than would be able to produce the answer to the question "What is the largest ocean?" Second, the detection rate is similar regardless of whether misinformation contradicts well-known or obscure facts; 23% of the errors were successfully detected with no difference as a function of prior knowledge.

In short, readers of fictional stories experienced knowledge neglect because they struggled to identify errors that contradicted information likely to be stored in memory.

Example 2

A second example of knowledge neglect involves the Moses illusion, a semantic illusion in which people fail to notice erroneous presuppositions in questions (Erickson & Mattson, 1981). For example, when asked "How many animals of each kind did Moses take on the ark?" people often answer "two" even though they later demonstrate that they know the biblical reference should be to *Noah*. In a typical Moses illusion experiment, readers are explicitly warned that some of the questions will contain errors, and for each question, the task is to note if a question is unanswerable (because it contains an incorrect presupposition) or to answer it if the question is a valid one (Büttner, 2007; Kamas, Reder, & Ayers, 1996; Reder & Kusbit, 1991). Readers encounter a series of questions, including distorted ones that contain plausible but incorrect references (like the example above) and *un*distorted ones that contain correct references (e.g., "How many animals of each kind did Noah take on the ark?"). The illusion is measured by people's willingness to answer the distorted questions (Erickson & Mattson, 1981). Most critically for present purposes, readers complete a knowledge check at the end of the experiment, so that the experimenter knows exactly what knowledge an individual subject does versus does not have stored in memory (Baker & Wagner, 1987; Bredart & Docquier, 1989; Bredart & Modolo, 1988; Kamas, et al., 1996). This knowledge check typically takes the form of a multiple-choice test (e.g., "Who took two animals of each kind on the Ark": "Moses," "Noah," or "Don't Know"?) and normally includes a "don't know" option as the goal is to be sure of what an individual knows (as opposed to what he or she can guess; e.g., Büttner, 2007; Hannon & Daneman, 2001; van Oostendorp & de Mul, 1990). Strong demonstrations of the Moses illusion conditionalize the results so that the illusion is only examined for questions for which the subject successfully demonstrated knowledge on the final test.

For example, consider data from Bottoms et al. (2010). Readers were able to discriminate between distorted and undistorted questions, correctly saying "wrong" to distorted questions ($M = 0.42$; hits) much more often than mistakenly doing so for undistorted questions ($M = 0.02$; a low false-alarm rate). However, the Moses illusion was robust, with participants answering 35% of distorted questions as if the questions were unproblematic. We want to emphasize that answering distorted questions represents an illusion because we know participants had knowledge stored in memory which could have been used to detect the contradiction (the analysis only includes the 67% of items for which participants demonstrated accurate knowledge on the knowledge check). Overall, the Moses illusion is robust, with readers answering from 14% (van Jaarsveld, Dijkstra, & Hermans, 1997) to 40% (Hannon & Daneman, 2001) to 52% (Erickson & Mattson, 1981) to 77% (Barton & Sanford, 1993) of distorted questions, depending upon the particular experiment.

Why Does Knowledge Neglect Occur?

Why would people be so poor at detecting contradictions with their stored knowledge? Gilbert and colleagues have argued that people automatically believe information when they read it and that a second processing step is required to "unbelieve" information and label it as false (see Gilbert, 1991, for a review). This claim is supported with data from experiments like the following: Subjects learn translations of Hopi words (e.g., *A twyrin is a doctor*), each of which is labeled as correct or incorrect immediately after its presentation. Critically, sometimes there is a dual task during the presentation of the true/false label; a tone sounds, and the subject has to press a button registering that tone. The question is whether completing a secondary task systematically affects later truth judgments (*Is a twyrin a doctor? true, false, no information, never seen*). That is, how do subjects later reconstruct the truth of the statements, given that the secondary task presumably disrupts their ability to process (encode) the true/false label? The key result is that subjects are much more likely to incorrectly say "true" to statements previously labeled as false than they are to say "false" to statements previously labeled as true (Gilbert, Krull, & Malone, 1990). That is, when the secondary task disrupts that second step of "unbelieving," subjects show a bias to call a statement "true" rather than to say that they did not have any knowledge about it.

When reading stories or detecting/answering distorted questions, the participant is doing a lot and may not have the processing resources available to assess the truth value of what is being read. The reader of a story is processing a plot line, keeping track of characters, and more generally, building a mental model of the text (e.g., Bower & Morrow, 1990; Johnson-Laird, 1983); catching contradictions with stored knowledge is not the main focus of the reader. Similarly, the subject in a Moses experiment is focused on answering general knowledge questions, and deciding not to answer a question (because it contains a contradiction with stored knowledge) requires inhibiting one's natural impulse to answer. In both situations, we argue that the monitoring task is not the primary one, if only because errors are relatively infrequent. At least some data suggest that making the task easier (freeing resources for monitoring) may help. For example, Moses subjects are more likely to notice distortions when the task is to verify statements rather than answer questions. That is, people are better at saying "false" to "Snow White slept for a hundred years after she pricked her finger" than at refusing to answer the question "For how many years did Snow White sleep after she pricked her finger?" (Büttner, 2007). Of course, the illusion was not eliminated in the statement condition, but it was smaller when the processing load was reduced.

Even if subjects do engage in evaluation (the assessment stage, using Gilbert's terms), they may not be successful. We will return to this problem later in the chapter. However, briefly, we can draw on the partial match hypothesis (Reder & Kusbit, 1991) to explain why subjects sometimes fail to successfully evaluate the information they encounter. The partial match hypothesis is a theory developed to explain the Moses illusion but is one that can be applied more broadly to other situations that appear to involve knowledge neglect. The idea is that the Moses illusion occurs when the subject fails to notice a mismatch between what is retrieved from memory (e.g., details related to the biblical story of Noah and the ark) and what one is reading (e.g., a reference to Moses). When what is retrieved is very similar to what one is reading, the match is close enough and is accepted, with the result that highly related (plausible) errors go unnoticed. The reader is much more likely to notice a problem with "How many animals of each kind did Nixon take on the ark?" because there is no partial match, whereas an incorrect reference to Moses overlaps with Noah in multiple ways (e.g., both are men who appeared in the Old Testament of the Bible), and thus, the match is close enough to accept (Erickson & Mattson, 1981; van Oostendorp & de Mul, 1990). A similar idea is that language processing is often shallow and incomplete, leading to distorted but often "good enough" semantic representations (Ferreira, Bailey, & Ferraro, 2002). In the case of knowledge neglect, these incomplete representations are not, in fact, good enough but slip through anyway.

Finally, there are situations that may discourage monitoring or otherwise make noticing factual inaccuracies more difficult, even without a concurrent processing load. Consider the specific case of consuming fiction; readers and moviegoers often enjoy novels and films that contradict the true state of the world (e.g., science fiction) or for which they already know the ending (e.g., that JFK was assassinated). One by-product of this behavior involves what Gerrig (1989) calls "the suspension of disbelief." Gerrig's subjects were slower to verify the well-known fact *"George Washington was elected first president of the United States"* after reading statements that created some doubt about this outcome (e.g., *Washington wanted to retire…*). In such cases, it is almost as if readers/viewers are insulated from their prior knowledge, so that they can enjoy themselves (see also Horton & Rapp, 2003, for a demonstration of the consequences of a reader's taking the point of view of a character). To measure people's involvement in a story (transportation), Green and Brock (2000) developed a scale that includes items such as *"I found myself thinking of ways the narrative could have turned out differently"* and *"I found my mind wandering while reading the narrative"* (reverse scored). Readers who reported greater transportation into a narrative were less likely to indicate that parts of the narrative "rung false" to them (see also Gerrig & Rapp, 2004). In short, some situations may encourage knowledge neglect because participation means ignoring one's general knowledge.

Overall, whether knowledge is inferred from norms (the story paradigm) or directly measured from individual performance on a knowledge check (the Moses illusion), individuals are often poor at noticing errors that contradict information stored in memory. This problem (knowledge neglect) may occur because the situation discourages monitoring (i.e., to allow enjoyment of fictional materials) or because the monitoring is difficult and careful processing is not possible. Monitoring may also fail when the information being evaluated is similar enough to what is stored in memory. The larger issue is that such lapses have consequences for memory, as we will describe in the next section.

Memorial Consequences of Knowledge Neglect

Knowledge neglect is more than a momentary lapse in attention; knowledge neglect has memorial consequences. That is, when the reader fails to notice a contradiction between what he or she is reading and his or her stored knowledge, this failure results in the error's being stored in memory. Because this error was recently encountered, it is accessible in memory and comes to mind fluently on later general knowledge tests. The relative ease with which something comes to mind at test is interpreted as confidence in one's response (Kelley & Lindsay, 1993), meaning that an error that pops to mind quickly is likely to be interpreted as a correct answer. Such memorial consequences are observed in both of the situations described earlier. When a general knowledge test follows the story-reading phase (fiction paradigm) or question-answering phase (Moses illusion), prior exposure to errors affects subjects' responses on the general knowledge test.

For example, figure 8.1 shows the use of the story errors on later memory tests (suggestibility) in the story paradigm. After the story-reading phase, participants answer general knowledge questions, including ones that can be answered with information from the stories (e.g., *"What is the largest ocean on Earth?"*). Readers are very suggestible, meaning that they later use story errors to answer the general knowledge questions

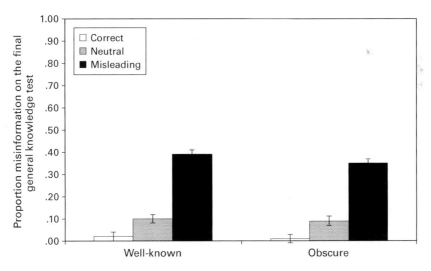

Figure 8.1

The proportion of final general knowledge questions answered with target misinformation as a function of fact framing during story reading (correct, neutral, misleading). The left portion shows responses to questions about well-known facts and the right portion shows responses to questions about lesser-known facts. Data from young adults in Umanath and Marsh (2012).

(e.g., answering *Atlantic*; see Marsh & Fazio, 2007, for a review). As shown in figure 8.1, people answer some questions with the target misinformation even after reading neutral references, likely because the errors are plausible ones and there is some pre-experimental belief in them. However, this baseline is low, and the production of mis-information errors increases dramatically after reading misinformation in the stories. Warning readers that authors of fiction often take liberties with the truth does nothing to reduce this pattern of suggestibility (Marsh & Fazio, 2006, experiment 1), although it does make readers a bit more conservative overall on the final test. Critically, sug-gestibility is similar regardless of (estimated) prior knowledge. That is, participants are just as likely to later incorrectly claim that the Atlantic is the largest ocean on Earth as they are to state that Jefferson invented dynamite, even though it is much more likely that they know that the Pacific is the largest ocean than that Nobel invented dynamite.

While it is possible that norms (especially old ones like the Nelson and Narens norms, which were published in 1980) may not be the best measure of what a given individual knows, similar results are obtained when individual knowledge is directly measured. To establish knowledge, we simply administered a pretest to measure what each individual participant knew two weeks before reading the stories. Participants were just as likely to later answer general knowledge questions with story errors regardless of whether or not they had demonstrated correct knowledge two weeks earlier (Fazio, Barber, Rajaram, Ornstein, & Marsh, 2013). The results were similar when the analyses were limited to facts produced on the pretest with the highest level of confidence. Of course, knowl-edge on this pretest was measured two weeks earlier, leaving open the possibility that for some reason knowledge was forgotten before the experimental session where the stories were read (although this possibility seems quite unlikely for the highest-con-fidence responses). However, in a recent experiment, participants still showed robust suggestibility when the pretest was administered immediately before exposure to the stories, meaning that the relevant knowledge was highly accessible (Mullet, Umanath, & Marsh, 2012). Thus, even when we are sure participants have stored knowledge and are highly confident in those facts, they still reproduce story errors.

Only a handful of studies have examined the memorial consequences of exposure to distorted questions in the Moses illusion, but with these cases a similar pattern occurs (Bottoms et al., 2010; Umanath, Dolan, & Marsh, 2014; see also Kamas et al., 1996). In a typical study, after the initial question-answering phase (where the task is to detect errors and answer valid questions), participants take a general knowledge test contain-ing questions that can be answered with information from the initial questions (e.g., "Who took two animals of each kind on the Ark?"). As in the story paradigm, partici-pants are suggestible, using previously seen errors to answer the later general knowl-edge questions (e.g., answering *Moses* about 6% of the time; Umanath et al., 2014). Participants rarely answer with the target errors if they have not seen the distorted question during the initial phase (1%). Critically, both analyses are limited to items for

Table 8.2

Probability that an error was reproduced on the final general knowledge test as a function of whether it was detected or missed during the initial phase of the experiment

	Detected	Missed (Knowledge Neglect)
Story paradigm	.09	.36
Moses illusion	.00	.09

Note. The Moses illusion data are conditional on participants having demonstrated knowledge of the correct answer on a later test. Data from Umanath and Marsh (2012) and Bottoms et al. (2010).

which participants are able to select the correct answer on the knowledge check, meaning that suggestibility occurs despite participants' ability to demonstrate the correct knowledge on another test. These results are consistent with evidence of the memorial consequences of knowledge neglect in the story paradigm.

In both paradigms, suggestibility is primarily driven by instances where participants suffered knowledge neglect, meaning they failed to notice the errors initially during the encoding phase (Bottoms et al., 2010; Fazio & Marsh, 2008a; Umanath & Marsh, 2012; Umanath et al., 2014). Table 8.2 shows the probabilities that an error (either in a story or a distorted Moses question) was reproduced as a function of whether or not the reader caught the error during the initial phase of the experiment (successful error detection) or missed it (knowledge neglect). Story readers reproduced about a third of missed errors, but less than 10% of errors they had caught previously. Moses subjects showed lower suggestibility overall but demonstrated the same pattern: They only reproduced errors they had missed, not ones they noticed during the initial phase of the experiment.

Reducing Suggestibility

How do we reduce the likelihood that people will pick up and later reproduce incorrect information that contradicts what they already know? It is clear that warnings alone will not suffice even though pre-encoding warnings often reduce suggestibility in episodic memory paradigms where people are misled about the content of videos or other stimuli (e.g., Loftus, 1979) and can also help readers avoid irrelevant details in texts (Peshkam, Mensink, Putnam, & Rapp, 2011). In both the story paradigm and the Moses illusion, learners are explicitly told that they will be exposed to errors and yet still reproduce some subset of those errors on later tests. One problem may be that readers forget to critically analyze material as they read, especially when they are engrossed in a narrative or other ongoing task. A general warning imposes a prospective memory load upon the reader (he or she needs to keep that goal in mind while doing something else). Although no study (to our knowledge) has examined the effects of reminding the reader to monitor, increasing the frequency of errors may serve that function, leading to a reduction in the Moses illusion (although this benefit was too small to translate into a reduction in later suggestibility; Bottoms, Eslick, & Marsh, 2010). Similarly, the instruction to explicitly mark errors (via key press) during the story-reading phase reduces later suggestibility by about 5% (Fazio & Marsh, 2008a), likely because it keeps the monitoring task salient. Two points are relevant. First, the drop in suggestibility is modest, because (as alluded to earlier), readers miss the majority of the errors (and eye-tracking data also suggest that readers miss many errors; Bohan & Sanford, 2008). Second, the fact that detection instructions reduce suggestibility means that without this instruction, participants are likely missing even more errors (hence the higher resulting suggestibility).

Given the relationship between error detection and later suggestibility, one obvious solution is to improve the reader's monitoring, as that should reduce later suggestibility. The problem is that manipulations aimed at increasing monitoring sometimes help and sometimes hurt the learner. Consider the perceptual salience of the errors during the initial phase of the experiment. At first glance, the literature suggests that making errors physically salient will make them more noticeable, hence reducing knowledge neglect. For example, when the incorrect presupposition (as opposed to another word in the question) is capitalized and underlined, the Moses illusion is reduced (Bredart & Docquier, 1989; see also Kamas et al., 1996, experiment 1). Participants are also more likely to detect errors in the Moses paradigm when they are syntactically salient in the questions (e.g., placed in the main clause vs. a subordinate clause; Baker & Wagner, 1987; Bredart & Modolo, 1988).

However, drawing attention to errors can have *ironic* effects such that participants become even *more* likely to acquire and reproduce them. Returning to the story paradigm, in an effort to facilitate monitoring and detection of errors, Eslick, Fazio, and Marsh (2011) highlighted some of the general knowledge references in the stories using red font. Thus, readers no longer had to search for the factual information to evaluate it but were just charged with the task of evaluating the references' accuracy. Yet, instead of helping readers notice and later avoid reproducing the errors, the red font actually led readers to reproduce more of those story errors on the final general knowledge test, as compared to ones that were not highlighted. Drawing attention to the specific errors, in this case, increased suggestibility.

How do we resolve such results? The explanation is somewhat unsatisfactory, but the best we can offer is to say that perceptual salience draws attention to the errors, and then the end result depends upon whether readers actually catch the errors or not (which was not directly measured in the Eslick et al. study, unfortunately). If the salient errors are caught, then suggestibility will decrease. However, if the reader suffers from knowledge neglect, then suggestibility will either be constant or even increase (due to the increased attention to the errors). What is lacking from this analysis, of course, is an a priori way of knowing which manipulations will help monitoring and error detection, and in which situations.

In other words, the problem is that many manipulations designed to promote monitoring may not actually do so, and thus their memorial consequences will depend upon how much (indiscriminate) attention they direct toward the errors. Consider the effects of slowing processing; the original idea was that slowed presentation would provide readers with more time and resources to catch inaccuracies embedded in stories (with the idea being that the slower reader is a more careful one; Tousignant, Hall, & Loftus, 1986). To avoid individual differences in reading speed, the materials from the story paradigm were translated to a book-on-tape format and then played in either a faster or slower version, and all subjects later took a general knowledge test. Surprisingly, subjects in the slowed condition were more likely to use story errors to answer the final general knowledge questions even though all participants were warned that the stories might contain errors. This experiment also contained conditions where subjects pressed a key whenever they noticed errors, so there was an explicit measure of the impact of slowing on monitoring and error detection. Critically, even though the slowed version allowed more time for monitoring, readers were equally (un)likely to notice the story errors regardless of presentation speed. Slowing presumably increased attention to the errors, but attention without detection only served to increase suggestibility.

In short, overcoming knowledge neglect is a challenge since it is difficult to predict a priori which manipulations will successfully increase error detection versus simply increasing attention to errors (and, thereby, potentially increasing suggestibility).

Connections to Research on Episodic Memory

Thus far, we have focused on failures to apply knowledge appropriately, both when initially encountering contradictory information and later when one needs to retrieve related knowledge from memory (e.g., when asked general knowledge questions). In this section, we consider the role of episodic memory (remembering past events) in these failures of memory. In addition, we compare the results reviewed here to the large literature examining how people come to misremember events from their lives; in what ways is knowledge neglect different from and similar to failures of episodic memory? Because these two phenomena have not been directly compared in experiments, this section will necessarily be speculative, but we think the comparison raises important directions for future research.

To frame this discussion, we will focus on possible age differences in the memorial consequences of knowledge neglect. First, we describe children's learning from stories. Age-appropriate stories were modified to contain references to facts known to most first graders; some facts were presented in correct frames and others in misleading frames (e.g., referring to autumn as "…another word for fall" versus "…another word for spring"). The stories were presented in a book-on-tape format (with pictures paired with the narrative), so no assumptions about reading ability were made. Of interest was performance on a later general knowledge test. Robust suggestibility was observed, with children using story errors to answer general knowledge questions. However, the key point is that *older* children (age 7) were more suggestible than younger ones (ages 5–6; Fazio & Marsh, 2008b). That is, after hearing an error like *"Mount Washington is the tallest mountain in the world,"* older children were more likely to later repeat that error. Similar results were found when the final test contained multiple-choice questions (e.g., *"What is another word for autumn: fall, spring, summer, winter, or I don't know?"*) instead of open-ended questions (Goswick, Mullet, & Marsh, 2013).

At the other end of the life span, consider older adults' learning from stories. College students and older adults (ages 65–85) listened to book-on-tape versions of the stories while also reading them (in large font). Again, the stories contained correct and misleading references, and of interest was performance on a final general knowledge test. The key finding for present purposes is that older adults were *less* suggestible than younger adults (Marsh, Balota, & Roediger, 2005; Umanath & Marsh, 2012). That is, older adults were less likely than younger adults to use story errors like *"Saturn, the largest planet"* when answering later general knowledge questions.

Both of these individual differences contrast with the age differences in suggestibility typically observed in episodic memory experiments. That is, younger children are normally *more* suggestible than older ones, and older adults are typically *more* suggestible than college students. For example, younger children are more likely than older ones to accept experimenter suggestions about mock eyewitness situations (see Ceci & Bruck, 1993, for a review) and to develop false memories for entire events, like riding in a hot air balloon (Ceci, Huffman, Smith, & Loftus, 1994). Similarly, older adults are more likely than college students to be influenced by postevent suggestions and experiences when asked to judge the preexperimental fame of names (Dywan & Jacoby, 1990), remember events portrayed in videos and photographs (Loftus, Levidow, & Duensing, 1992; Schacter, Koutstaal, Johnson, Gross, & Angell, 1997), or recollect experiences from the lab (Mueller-Johnson & Ceci, 2004; Cohen & Faulkner, 1989).

We will use these data on age differences in suggestibility to explore three points about the role of episodic memory. First, these results highlight that the two types of memory errors are not always the same: Age effects may be different for errors of episodic memory than for memorial consequences of knowledge neglect. Other manipulations also appear (at least based on the limited data sets available) to dissociate the two types of memory errors. For example, test instructions that require one to identify the sources of one's memories reduce errors of episodic memory (e.g.,. in mock eyewitness scenarios; Lindsay & Johnson, 1989) but have little impact on use of story errors to answer general knowledge questions (Marsh, Meade, & Roediger, 2003). Similarly, pre-encoding warnings and slower encoding reduce eyewitness suggestibility (Greene, Flynn, & Loftus, 1982; Tousignant, Hall, & Loftus, 1986), but not the learning of story errors (Marsh & Fazio, 2006; Fazio & Marsh, 2008a). On the other hand, there are also variables that have similar effects on both types of errors. For example, repeated exposure to misinformation tends to increase suggestibility across paradigms. Readers who read the same error-filled stories twice are more likely to use story errors to answer later general knowledge questions (Marsh et al., 2003), and mock eyewitnesses who are exposed to misinformation twice are later more likely to rely upon it (Zaragoza & Mitchell, 1996). As we will unpack below, these similarities likely arise because episodic memory is involved when errors enter the knowledge base. However, the fact that dissociations are also observed suggests that these two types of errors are not likely to be identical in mechanism, a point we will also return to later in this section.

Second, as just alluded to, episodic memory is likely to be involved in encoding and later remembering the misinformation. Learning the misinformation can be thought of as encoding a new association (e.g., the association between "the tallest mountain" and "Mount Washington"), a standard episodic memory task. Episodic memory improves across childhood (Ghetti & Lee, 2011) and declines in old age (Craik & Jennings, 1992). Thus, younger children will have poorer memory for the misinformation than will older children, and older adults will have worse memory for the misinformation than will the college students (see Brainerd, Reyna, & Ceci, 2008, and Mitchell, Johnson, & Mather, 2003, for similar arguments in the episodic memory domain). Episodic memory deficits also likely explain why older adults with mild cognitive impairment are even less likely to reproduce story errors on later tests, as compared to healthy older adults (Marsh et al., 2005). In addition, episodic memory mechanisms provide a clear explanation for the effects of manipulations like repeated reading, initial testing, and delaying the final test. Repeated reading increases encoding of the story errors, an initial test provides retrieval practice of the error (something known to benefit memory; Roediger & Karpicke, 2006; Roediger & Butler, 2011), and delaying the final test reduces memory for errors read in the stories due to forgetting. Consistent with this analysis, repeated reading and initial testing increase suggestibility but delaying the final test decreases suggestibility (Marsh et al., 2003; Barber, Rajaram, & Marsh, 2008).

Our final point about episodic memory involves the role of source monitoring in the two memory errors. While there are many differences across false memory paradigms, one commonality is that children and older adults tend to perform worse on memory tasks that depend upon source memory, meaning that they struggle when the task requires participants to identify the origin of their memories (Johnson, Hashtroudi, & Lindsay, 1993). For example, the successful eyewitness would be able to identify which details were actually observed versus only heard about in later media coverage or alluded to in a police interview. When an eyewitness claims to remember seeing a detail that was suggested in a postevent interview, it is a failure of source memory because that detail is misattributed to the original event rather than correctly sourced to the interview. Because older adults often struggle with source memory, they are more likely than college students to become confused between what they thought and what they actually did (Rabinowitz, 1989) or to confuse what they saw presented visually with something someone else said (McIntyre & Craik, 1987). Similarly, the suggestibility of young eyewitnesses has been linked to source problems, such as distinguishing between what was seen in a movie from what was included in an experimenter's subsequent narrative (Giles, Gopnik, & Heyman, 2002). However, with the story paradigm, failure to remember the story source does not drive suggestibility (Marsh et al., 2003). In fact, older children are better able to identify which answers had been encountered in the stories, as compared to younger children (Fazio & Marsh, 2008b). Similarly, college students are better able to identify which answers had been encountered in the stories, as compared to older adults (Marsh et al., 2005). In these studies, the groups with best memory for the story source were the ones who were the most suggestible, instead of the least suggestible, as might be expected based on the large literature showing source memory as protecting against suggestion. This is not to say that subjects had perfect source memory in the story experiments, but that they made a very specific type of source error. Critically, readers experienced an *illusion of prior knowledge*, whereby they believed that they knew the story errors prior to the experiment, even though baseline belief in the errors was low. It does a reader no good to remember that a fact was read in a story if he or she also attributes it to prior experience and, thereby, assumes it is true.

In short, episodic memory is necessarily involved in learning and storing false facts, but illusions of knowledge do not appear to be identical to episodic memory errors. The two types of memory errors can be dissociated.

Conclusions and Future Directions

This chapter makes a simple point: People often have information stored in memory that they fail to apply successfully. We used the term knowledge neglect to refer to people's failures to bring to bear relevant stored knowledge. We believe such failures to be common. They may occur because the reader is not focused on monitoring (e.g., because of processing load) or because monitoring fails when a plausible error is close enough to the correct answer to register as a match. Regardless, a failure to notice an error has repercussions for memory. The problem is that this recently encountered error is more available in memory than the original knowledge, meaning that it is the error that later comes to mind fluently; this fluency is misinterpreted as truth. Thus, people reproduce the errors even though they have stored knowledge that contradicts those errors.

There remain a number of open questions and directions for future research. For instance, we discussed the mixed literature aimed at improving monitoring, with the goal of reducing knowledge neglect and subsequent suggestibility; future research should pinpoint the specific circumstances under which monitoring and detection of errors can be successfully improved, so that we can predict this a priori. It is unsatisfying to claim after the fact that "monitoring was poor" because suggestibility increased, even when a manipulation was designed to increase monitoring.

Theoretically, the most interesting open question involves whether "knowledge neglect" is specific to knowledge or if this behavior is an example of a broader phenomenon that includes episodic memory. That is, one can easily imagine a situation where one has stored personal memories that are relevant to the current situation and yet fails to bring them to bear. To what extent is there likely to be something different about knowledge? Unlike episodic memories, much knowledge is retrieved without a feeling of projecting oneself backward in time to a specific time and place; much knowledge is sourceless and labeled as "known" rather than "remembered" (e.g., you simply "know" that George Washington was the first president of the United States; Conway, Gardiner, Perfect, Anderson, & Cohen, 1997). The result is that learners often judge the veracity of retrieved knowledge by how fluently or easily it comes to mind (Kelley & Lindsay, 1993). Fluency misattributions can also lead to errors of episodic memory, of course (e.g., Jacoby, Kelley, & Dywan, 1989), but we believe people are particularly reliant on fluency when the content involves knowledge. Because of this, readers may be more likely to suffer from knowledge neglect, as opposed to neglecting other types of memories. More generally, future research should directly compare errors of episodic memory to the errors observed following knowledge neglect. We presented cross-experimental evidence for the similarities and differences between these types of errors, but a direct comparison is needed.

Overall, a lot is known about how people come to misremember events, but less is known about how errors enter the knowledge base, especially when the errors contradict stored knowledge. Clearly, there are connections between episodic memory and the knowledge base, but there are differences as well. Future research should better connect these two areas of research, with the goal of better understanding knowledge neglect and the resultant illusions of knowledge.

Acknowledgment

The writing of this chapter was supported in part by a collaborative activity award from the James S. McDonnell Foundation.

References

Anderson, J. R. (1981). Effects of prior knowledge on memory for new information. *Memory & Cognition, 9,* 237–246.

Ausubel, D. P., & Blake, E. (1958). Proactive inhibition in the forgetting of meaningful school material. *Journal of Educational Research, 52,* 145–149.

Baker, L., & Wagner, J. L. (1987). Evaluating information for truthfulness: The effects of logical subordination. *Memory & Cognition, 15,* 247–255.

Barber, S. J., Rajaram, S., & Marsh, E. J. (2008). Fact learning: How information accuracy, delay, and repeated testing change retention and retrieval experience. *Memory, 16,* 934–946.

Barton, S. B., & Sanford, A. J. (1993). A case study of anomaly detection: Shallow semantic processing and cohesion establishment. *Memory & Cognition, 21,* 477–487.

Bohan, J., & Sanford, A. (2008). Semantic anomalies at the borderline of consciousness: An eye-tracking investigation. *Quarterly Journal of Experimental Psychology, 61,* 232–239.

Bottoms, H. C., Eslick, A. N., & Marsh, E. J. (2010). Memory and the Moses illusion: Failures to detect contradictions with stored knowledge yield negative memorial consequences. *Memory, 18,* 670–678.

Bower, G. H., & Morrow, D. G. (1990). Mental models in narrative comprehension. *Science, 247,* 44–48.

Brainerd, C. J., Reyna, V. F., & Ceci, S. J. (2008). Developmental reversals in false memory: A review of data and theory. *Psychological Bulletin, 134,* 343–382.

Bredart, S., & Docquier, M. (1989). The Moses illusion: A follow-up on the focalization effect. *European Bulletin of Cognitive Psychology, 9,* 357–362.

Bredart, S., & Modolo, K. (1988). Moses strikes again: Focalization effect on a semantic illusion. *Acta Psychologica, 67,* 135–144.

Brown, D. E. (1992). Using examples and analogies to remediate misconceptions in physics: Factors influencing conceptual change. *Journal of Research in Science Teaching, 29,* 17–34.

Butler, A. C., Fazio, L. F., & Marsh, E. J. (2011). The hypercorrection effect persists over a week, but high confidence errors return. *Psychonomic Bulletin & Review, 18,* 1238–1244.

Büttner, A. C. (2007). Questions versus statements: Challenging an assumption about semantic illusions. *Quarterly Journal of Experimental Psychology, 60,* 779–789.

Ceci, S. J., & Bruck, M. B. (1993). Suggestibility of the child witness: A historical review and synthesis. *Psychological Bulletin, 113,* 403–439.

Ceci, S. J., Huffman, M. L. C., Smith, E., & Loftus, E. F. (1994). Repeatedly thinking about a non-event: Source misattributions among preschoolers. *Consciousness and Cognition, 3,* 388–407.

Chi, M. T. H. (2008). Three types of conceptual change: Belief revision, mental model transformation, and categorical shift. In S. Vosniadou (Ed.), *Handbook of research on conceptual change* (pp. 61–82). Hillsdale, NJ: Lawrence Erlbaum Associates.

Chiesi, H. L., Spilich, G. J., & Voss, J. F. (1979). Acquisition of domain-related information in relation to high and low domain knowledge. *Journal of Verbal Learning and Verbal Behavior, 18,* 257–274.

Cho, H.-H., Kahle, J. B., & Nordland, F. H. (1985). An investigation of high school biology text-books as sources of misconceptions and difficulties in genetics and some suggestions for teaching genetics. *Science Education, 69*, 707–719.

Clement, J., Narode, R., & Rosnick, P. (1981). Intuitive misconceptions in algebra as a source of math anxiety. *Focus on Learning Problems in Mathematics, 3*, 36–45.

Cohen, G., & Faulkner, D. (1989). Age differences in source forgetting: Effects on reality monitoring and on eyewitness testimony. *Psychology and Aging, 4*, 10–17.

Conway, M. A., Gardiner, J. M., Perfect, T. J., Anderson, S. J., & Cohen, G. M. (1997). Changes in memory awareness during learning: The acquisition of knowledge by psychology undergraduates. *Journal of Experimental Psychology. General, 126*, 393–413.

Craik, F. I. M., & Jennings, J. M. (1992). Human memory. In F. I. M. Craik & T. A. Salthouse (Eds.), *The handbook of aging and cognition* (pp. 51–110). Hillsdale, NJ: Lawrence Erlbaum Associates.

Dooling, D. J., & Mullet, R. L. (1973). Locus of thematic effects in retention of prose. *Journal of Experimental Psychology, 97*, 404–406.

Dywan, J., & Jacoby, L. (1990). Effects of aging on source monitoring: Differences in susceptibility to false fame. *Psychology and Aging, 5*, 379–387.

Erickson, T. D., & Mattson, M. E. (1981). From words to meaning: A semantic illusion. *Journal of Verbal Learning and Verbal Behavior, 20*, 540–551.

Eslick, A. N., Fazio, L. K., & Marsh, E. J. (2011). Ironic effects of drawing attention to story errors. *Memory, 19*, 184–191.

Fazio, L. K., Barber, S. J., Rajaram, S., Ornstein, P. A., & Marsh, E. J. (2013). Creating illusions of knowledge: Learning errors that contradict prior knowledge. *Journal of Experimental Psychology. General, 142*, 1–5

Fazio, L. K., & Marsh, E. J. (2008a). Slowing presentation speed increases illusions of knowledge. *Psychonomic Bulletin & Review, 15*, 180–185.

Fazio, L. K., & Marsh, E. J. (2008b). Older, not younger, children learn more false facts from stories. *Cognition, 106*, 1081–1089.

Ferland, F., Ladouceur, R., & Vitaro, F. (2002). Prevention of problem gambling: Modifying misconceptions and increasing knowledge. *Journal of Gambling Studies, 18*, 19–29.

Ferreira, F., Bailey, K. G. D., & Ferraro, V. (2002). Good-enough representations in language comprehension. *Current Directions in Psychological Science, 11*, 11–15.

Gerrig, R. J. (1989). Suspense in the absence of uncertainty. *Journal of Memory and Language, 28*, 633–648.

Gerrig, R. J., & Rapp, D. N. (2004). Psychological processes underlying literary impact. *Poetics Today, 25*, 265–281.

Ghetti, S., & Lee, J. (2011). Children's episodic memory. *Wiley Interdisciplinary Reviews: Cognitive Science, 2,* 365–373.

Gilbert, D. T. (1991). How mental systems believe. *American Psychologist, 46,* 107–119.

Gilbert, D. T., Krull, D. S., & Malone, P. S. (1990). Unbelieving the unbelievable: Some problems in the rejection of false information. *Journal of Personality and Social Psychology, 59,* 601–613.

Giles, J. W., Gopnik, A., & Heyman, G. D. (2002). Source monitoring reduces the suggestibility of preschool children. *Psychological Science, 13,* 288–291.

Goswick, A. E., Mullet, H. G., & Marsh, E. J. (2013). Suggestibility from stories: Can production difficulties and source monitoring explain a developmental reversal? *Journal of Cognition and Development, 14,* 607–616.

Gouvier, W. D., Prestholdt, P. H., & Warner, M. S. (1988). A survey of common misconceptions about head injury and recovery. *Archives of Clinical Neuropsychology, 3,* 331–343.

Green, M. C., & Brock, T. C. (2000). The role of transportation in the persuasiveness of public narratives. *Journal of Personality and Social Psychology, 79,* 701–721.

Greene, E., Flynn, M. S., & Loftus, E. F. (1982). Inducing resistance to misleading information. *Journal of Verbal Learning and Verbal Behavior, 21,* 207–219.

Hannon, B., & Daneman, M. (2001). Susceptibility to semantic illusions: An individual-differences perspective. *Memory & Cognition, 29,* 449–461.

Horton, W. S., & Rapp, D. N. (2003). Out of sight, out of mind: Occlusion and the accessibility of information in narrative comprehension. *Psychonomic Bulletin & Review, 10,* 104–110.

Jacoby, L. L., Kelley, C. M., & Dywan, J. (1989). Memory attributions. In H. L. Roediger, III, & F. I. M. Craik (Eds.), *Varieties of memory and consciousness: Essays in honour of Endel Tulving* (pp. 391–422). Hillsdale, NJ: Lawrence Erlbaum Associates.

Johnson, M. K., Hashtroudi, S., & Lindsay, D. S. (1993). Source monitoring. *Psychological Bulletin, 114,* 3–28.

Johnson-Laird, P. N. (1983). *Mental models.* Cambridge, MA: Harvard University Press.

Kamas, E. N., Reder, L. M., & Ayers, M. S. (1996). Partial matching in the Moses illusion: Response bias not sensitivity. *Memory & Cognition, 24,* 687–699.

Kelley, C. M., & Lindsay, D. S. (1993). Remembering mistaken for knowing: Ease of retrieval as a basis for confidence in answers to general knowledge questions. *Journal of Memory and Language, 32,* 1–24.

Kole, J. A., & Healy, A. F. (2007). Using prior knowledge to minimize interference when learning large amounts of information. *Memory & Cognition, 35,* 124–137.

Landau, J. D., & Bavaria, A. J. (2003). Does deliberate source monitoring reduce students' misconceptions about psychology? *Teaching of Psychology, 30,* 311–314.

Lee, G. M., Friedman, J. F., Ross-Degnan, D., Hibberd, P. L., & Goldmann, D. A. (2003). Misconceptions about colds and predictors of health service utilization. *Pediatrics, 111*, 231–236.

Lindsay, D. S., & Johnson, M. K. (1989). The eyewitness suggestibility effect and memory for source. *Memory & Cognition, 17*, 349–358.

Loftus, E. F. (1979). Reactions to blatantly contradictory information. *Memory & Cognition, 7*, 368–374.

Loftus, E. F., Levidow, B., & Duensing, S. (1992). Who remembers best? Individual differences in memory for events that occurred in a science museum. *Applied Cognitive Psychology, 6*, 93–107.

Marsh, E. J. (2004). Story stimuli for creating false beliefs about the world. *Behavior Research Methods, Instruments, & Computers, 36*, 650–655.

Marsh, E. J., Balota, D. A., & Roediger, H. L., III. (2005). Learning facts from fiction: Effects of healthy aging and early-stage dementia of the Alzheimer type. *Neuropsychology, 19*, 115–129.

Marsh, E. J., & Fazio, L. K. (2006). Learning errors from fiction: Difficulties in reducing reliance on fictional stories. *Memory & Cognition, 34*, 1140–1149.

Marsh, E. J., & Fazio, L. K. (2007). Learning from fictional sources. In J. Nairne (Ed.), *The foundations of remembering: Essays in honor of Henry L. Roediger III* (pp. 397–413). New York: Psychology Press.

Marsh, E. J., Meade, M. L., & Roediger, H. L., III. (2003). Learning facts from fiction. *Journal of Memory and Language, 49*, 519–536.

McCloskey, M. (1983). Intuitive physics. *Scientific American, 248*, 122–130.

McIntyre, J. S., & Craik, F. I. M. (1987). Age differences in memory for item and source information. *Canadian Journal of Psychology, 41*, 175–192.

Mitchell, K. J., Johnson, M. K., & Mather, M. (2003). Source monitoring and suggestibility to misinformation: Adult age-related differences. *Applied Cognitive Psychology, 17*, 107–119.

Mueller-Johnson, K., & Ceci, S. J. (2004). Memory and suggestibility in older adults: Live event participation and repeated interview. *Applied Cognitive Psychology, 18*, 1109–1127.

Mullet, H. G., Umanath, S., & Marsh, E. J. (November 2012). Accessibility of knowledge and susceptibility to semantic illusions. Poster presented at the 53rd Annual Meeting of the Psychonomic Society, Minneapolis, MI.

Munson, B. H. (1994). Ecological misconceptions. *Journal of Environmental Education, 25*, 30–35.

Nakhleh, M. B. (1992). Why some students don't learn chemistry. *Journal of Chemical Education, 69*, 191–196.

Nelson, T. O., & Narens, L. (1980). Norms of 300 general-information questions: Accuracy of recall, latency of recall, and feeling-of-knowing ratings. *Journal of Verbal Learning and Verbal Behavior, 19*, 338–368.

Peshkam, A., Mensink, M. C., Putnam, A. L., & Rapp, D. N. (2011). Warning readers to avoid irrelevant information: When being vague might be valuable. *Contemporary Educational Psychology*, *36*, 219–231.

Rabinowitz, J. C. (1989). Judgments of origin and generation effects: Comparisons between young and elderly adults. *Psychology and Aging*, *4*, 259–268.

Rapp, D. N. (2008). How do readers handle incorrect information during reading? *Memory & Cognition*, *36*, 688–701.

Reder, L. M., & Kusbit, G. W. (1991). Locus of the Moses illusion: Imperfect encoding, retrieval, or match? *Journal of Memory and Language*, *30*, 385–406.

Roediger, H. L., III, & Butler, A. C. (2011). The critical role of retrieval practice in long-term retention. *Trends in Cognitive Sciences*, *15*, 20–27.

Roediger, H. L., III, & Karpicke, J. D. (2006). Test-enhanced learning: Taking memory tests improves long-term retention. *Psychological Science*, *17*, 249–255.

Schacter, D. L., Koutstaal, W., Johnson, M. K., Gross, M. S., & Angell, K. E. (1997). False recollection induced by photographs: A comparison of older and younger adults. *Psychology and Aging*, *12*, 203–215.

Simons, D. J., & Chabris, C. F. (2011). What people believe about how memory works: A representative survey of the U.S. population. *PLoS ONE*, *6*, e22757.

Tousignant, J. P., Hall, D., & Loftus, E. F. (1986). Discrepancy detection and vulnerability to misleading postevent information. *Memory & Cognition*, *14*, 329–338.

Umanath, S., Dolan, P. O., & Marsh, E. J. (2014). Aging and the Moses illusion: Older adults fall for Moses but if asked directly, stick with Noah. *Memory*, *22*, 481–492.

Umanath, S., & Marsh, E. J. (2012). Aging and the memorial consequences of catching contradictions with prior knowledge. *Psychology and Aging*, *27*, 1033–1038.

van Jaarsveld, H. J., Dijkstra, T., & Hermans, D. (1997). The detection of semantic illusions: Task-specific effects for similarity and position of distorted terms. *Psychological Research*, *59*, 219–230.

van Oostendorp, H., & de Mul, S. (1990). Moses beats Adam: A semantic relatedness effect on a semantic illusion. *Acta Psychologica*, *74*, 35–46.

Wynn, L. L., Foster, A. M., & Trussell, J. (2009). Can I get pregnant from oral sex? Sexual health misconceptions in e-mails to a reproductive health website. *Contraception*, *79*, 91–97.

Zaragoza, M. S., & Mitchell, K. J. (1996). Repeated exposure to suggestion and the creation of false memories. *Psychological Science*, *7*, 294–300.

9 Mechanisms of Problematic Knowledge Acquisition

David N. Rapp, Matthew E. Jacovina, and Jessica J. Andrews

Careful scrutiny is an invaluable activity. When crafting written materials, proofreading our productions can catch spelling and grammatical mistakes, as well as more egregious logical inconsistencies. Fact-checking is considered so important to journalistic activity that editors and their assistants are assigned the specific task of deliberating over contributions to ensure their accuracy. Classroom assignments in grades K–12 and beyond similarly require students to critique the validity of theories, positions, and viewpoints, sometimes with accompanying coursework intended to train those necessary evaluative skills (e.g., Toth, Klahr, & Chen, 2000). And our mundane everyday activities regularly benefit from carefully monitoring for errors, whether it involves assessing the components and ingredients of a recipe before following it, prescreening a route before relying on driving directions, or reconsidering whether we really know the answer to a trivia question. Across these situations, scrutiny and evaluation can help us notice errors to avoid reproducing them or letting them influence subsequent judgments and decisions.

However, the level of scrutiny necessary to detect errors and avoid their problematic influence does not seem to be regularly applied. Several accounts have been offered that provide informative, theoretical explanations for when and why readers (1) fail to detect inaccuracies (Bottoms, Eslick, & Marsh, 2010; Green & Brock, 2000; Otero & Kintsch, 1992) and (2) regularly rely on inaccurate content (Ayers & Reder, 1998; Wilkes & Leatherbarrow, 1988). The goal of the current chapter is to review prevailing accounts and to reconsider an explanation that perhaps has not received the attention it should. The main premise of this explanation is that individuals default to accepting information they read, only engaging in critical evaluation under specific circumstances, and only after initially encoding potentially inaccurate information. This explanation was originally discussed in social and cognitive psychological work from the 1990s (Gilbert, Krull, & Malone, 1990) but has clear historical antecedents from philosophical and literary traditions much earlier than that. An important feature of this default processing assumption is that it does not obviate other accounts; explanations derived from recent findings can usefully (and in some cases necessarily) invoke readers' willing acceptance in their theoretical accounts. In this chapter, we present evidence from two recent lines of work that indicates individuals exhibit a general tendency to accept what is presented or, at least, to use information they have recently received, even when it is wrong. The findings have important implications for establishing the boundary conditions associated with when and how individuals evaluate information.

Encoding and Relying on Inaccurate Information

Inaccurate information appears regularly in books, Web sources, newspapers, and our everyday conversations. These inaccuracies can have important consequences if readers accept the problematic content as true or fail to discount it as false. A variety of projects have shown that readers seem to respond to inaccurate information as they would to accurate facts: They encode the information they read and subsequently recall the information in attempts to complete postreading tasks (Seifert, 2002; Wilkes & Reynolds, 1999). These behaviors would be effective and useful for texts containing accurate information but are clearly problematic when texts contain inaccuracies (Marsh, Butler, & Umanath, 2012). And readers seem to rely on inaccuracies not just when they are unaware that the information they are being presented with is wrong but also when they should know a priori that the inaccurate information is obviously incorrect (Fazio, Barber, Rajaram, Ornstein, & Marsh, 2013).

In general, studies demonstrating these effects ask participants to read texts that include accurate, inaccurate, or unspecified information in their contents. For example, participants might read one of three statements describing the assassination of President Abraham Lincoln: a true version stating "…an actor named Booth has killed Lincoln"; a false version stating "…an actor named Oswald has killed Lincoln"; or a neutral version stating "…an actor has killed Lincoln." Presentation of these statements is varied to determine the kinds of understandings readers subsequently exhibit about Lincoln's assassination. As another example, participants might be presented with an assertion stating the true idea that "…too little tooth brushing leads to gum disease," or the false idea that "…too much tooth brushing leads to gum disease." After reading is completed, participants are asked to answer questions or make judgments about information that may have appeared in the stories as a test of their subsequent knowledge.

Across studies employing these materials and methods, two disheartening findings have emerged. First, people who read inaccurate information sometimes reproduce it when tested later (Barber, Rajaram, & Marsh, 2008; Marsh, Meade, & Roediger, 2003; Strange & Leung, 1999). Participants show an increased likelihood of producing inaccurate responses (e.g., responding "Oswald" when asked "Who assassinated Abraham Lincoln?") after having read inaccurate as compared to accurate or neutral information. Second, participants can exhibit difficulty judging the validity of related statements, as measured with response latencies and accuracy measures, after reading inaccurate as compared to accurate information (Albrecht & O'Brien, 1993; Gerrig, 1989; Gerrig & Prentice, 1991; Rapp, 2008). For example, participants exhibit slowdowns identifying the statement "Frequent toothbrushing prevents gum disease" as true after reading a false assertion decrying the practice as a problem.

These two findings, that people use what they have read even when it is wrong, and that wrong information can lead to processing decrements on subsequent tasks for which people *should* know the correct information, characterize the problematic consequences of reading inaccurate information. The findings suggest people do not routinely scrutinize what they read and consider false information on tasks for which its use indicates misunderstandings and confusion. And again, these decrements are observed for information that should be well-known and easily retrieved from memory given readers' familiarity with the conveyed ideas.

Text Features Can Encourage Reliance on Inaccurate Content

Several accounts have been offered to explain why readers exhibit patterns of performance that exemplify gullibility rather than evaluation. One view has contended that text statements can have qualities that make it difficult to avoid relying on their contents, potentially leading readers to defer to inaccurate information. When inaccuracies offer causal explanations for events and situations, or fit easily into existing causal frameworks that individuals are familiar with and hold in memory, their problematic influence can prove difficult to counteract (Bush, Johnson, & Seifert, 1994; Johnson & Seifert, 1998; O'Brien, Cook, & Guéraud, 2010; O'Brien, Rizzella, Albrecht, & Halleran, 1998; van Oostendorp & Bonebakker, 1999). Even explicit warnings to discount explanations seem to fail when misinformation offers causal structure (Ecker, Lewandowsky, & Tang, 2010).

Evidence for this explanation derives from projects by Johnson and Seifert (1994), in which participants were presented with a series of messages that conveyed a fire report. Statements included in the report clearly indicated the fire was caused by negligence, with discarded oil cans and rags a likely origin of the fire. In one condition, participants read a subsequent message that refuted the original cause, indicating that the room containing those materials was actually empty. In another condition, no refutation was offered at all. After reading the messages, participants were asked questions about the fire and to recall the information from the report. While participants easily recalled reading the refutations, those recollected refutations were ineffective at reducing references to and reliance on the original cause when answering questions about the fire. One explanation for this surprising effect is that the original cause was both reasonable and informative, making it difficult for individuals to discount that cause even in the face of counterclaims. Despite a refutation suggesting otherwise, participants found the earlier cause informative for framing the events described in the report.

Causal explanations are so important, they prove critical for constructing *effective* refutations designed to obviate encoded understandings (Rapp & Kendeou, 2007, 2009). In follow-up experiments to the previously mentioned project, participants learned the original cause of the fire was unlikely and were provided with an alternative causal explanation for the event (i.e., it was a result of arson rather than negligence, which allows the oil cans and rags to continue to play an instrumental role; Johnson & Seifert, 1994). This encouraged readers to update their account of the fire, in contrast to the responses of participants who received an uninformative discounting statement or no alternative information. These findings are consistent with the view that readers, in their attempts to establish coherence across text sentences, build causal networks that encode how events lead to or emerge from other events (Trabasso & van den Broek, 1985). These representational networks include explicitly stated information (e.g., reading "The fire was caused by negligence"), and inferences connecting text propositions and informing causality (e.g., inferring "The fire was caused by negligence" after reading "cans of oil paint and pressurized gas cylinders had been present..."). Causal explanations therefore prove crucially informative for readers' understandings of texts. However, that influence is a challenge to overcome when causal models contain incorrect explanations and details.

We have focused our discussion here on causality, but other aspects of text content might analogously encourage reliance when they offer clear explanations, support the generation of relevant inferences, and connect with reader expectations. These effects can be driven, for instance, by the plausibility or typicality of misinformation (i.e., plausible statements and typical explanations are more likely to be endorsed than are implausible and atypical ones; Hinze, Slaten, Horton, Jenkins, & Rapp, 2014), the consistency of inaccurate information with personal beliefs (i.e., people are less likely to correct false information if it matches their viewpoint; Lewandowsky, Stritzke, Oberauer, & Morales, 2005), and reader familiarity with text content (i.e., people are more likely to trust information that feels familiar as compared to information that seems new; Reber & Schwarz, 1999).

Ordinary Cognition Encourages Reliance on Misinformation

Reliance on text information can also emerge as an ordinary consequence of the mechanisms underlying memory. The critical evaluations that readers *ought* to regularly undertake require contrasting relevant knowledge with the information offered by unfolding discourse. However, the processes associated with retrieving prior knowledge can influence the use of inaccurate information. Consider that, during reading, individuals encode momentary traces of what was just read, which, if sufficiently compelling, relevant, or rehearsed, may get stored in long-term memory. But before being consolidated into more permanent stores, those traces influence comprehension (e.g., Albrecht & Myers, 1995; Cook, Halleran, & O'Brien, 1998). Their recent encoding often makes them easy to retrieve, and people's feelings about the ease of accessing recently encoded traces can foster beliefs about the validity of that information. The result is that information that is fluently recalled from memory is believed to be more valid than information that is a struggle to recall, even when those beliefs are undergirded by inaccurate or irrelevant information (Schwarz, Sanna, Skurnik, & Yoon, 2007).

A compelling example of these *fluency effects* comes from work by McGlone and Tofighbakhsh (2000). In their study, participants read unfamiliar aphorisms presented in rhyming (e.g., "What sobriety conceals, alcohol reveals") or nonrhyming forms (e.g., "What sobriety conceals, alcohol unmasks"). Participants were tasked with judging whether presented aphorisms accurately described human behavior. They tended to judge rhyming aphorisms as more true than their nonrhyming forms. However, being aphorisms, the statements should be more or less true depending on the contexts within which they are described, and these aphorisms were presented outside of any supportive context. Explanations of these results appealed to the fluency perspective, contending that rhyming aphorisms were easier to retrieve from memory than their nonrhyming counterparts. This ease of retrieval encourages a potentially misleading attribution that the information is obvious, clear, and true. When information can be easily brought to mind, people feel it is relevant and accurate.

Processes associated with learning and memory have been invoked in other ways to account for readers' reliance on inaccurate information. Consider reading a false statement like "Oswald killed Lincoln." New memory traces might be encoded for this information despite its being false. Those traces could become reactivated when individuals later read about Lincoln, including when they answer questions related to the subject. Contemporary accounts of memory have indicated that encoded traces are necessarily reactivated when related information is encountered. This reactivation process is automatic, unguided, and far-reaching, which could lead to the retrieval of various kinds of information (Gerrig & McKoon, 1998; McKoon, Gerrig, & Greene, 1996; O'Brien, 1995). The result is that false information that was previously encountered has the potential to become available again. While those retrieved traces might be successfully discounted before they are actually used, their reactivations can have processing consequences, including the judgment slowdowns identified in the earlier mentioned studies.

Theories of memory and comprehension have highlighted that people routinely reactivate information related to what they are reading, even when such reactivations include irrelevant, outdated, and incorrect information (O'Brien et al., 1998). And if those memories are easily retrieved, beliefs about that retrieval can influence expectations about the information's validity (Begg, Armour, & Kerr, 1985; Kelley & Lindsay, 1993). The spontaneous retrieval of information from memory and inferential beliefs about the ease of retrieval exemplify how the routine functioning of human memory can encourage reliance on misinformation.

Failing to Identify Misinformation

A third view appeals to the notion that any influence might involve failures to tag information as wrong. If readers neglect to identify information as inaccurate, they should be just as likely to use that information as they would potentially relevant or true details. This explanation relates to a large body of work on source monitoring, which has shown that people have difficulty identifying where and from whom they initially acquired information (Johnson, Hashtroudi, & Lindsay, 1993). Consider that participants who encode and rely on inaccurate content are sometimes unable to accurately indicate how they learned it (Marsh et al., 2003; Meade & Roediger, 2002). Even when participants report knowing that experimental texts contained misinformation, they can also report having known the information before reading—even when the information is patently wrong, and even though participants were unlikely to have encountered the inaccuracies at any point prior to the experiment (Marsh et al., 2003)! For instance, while Oswald, like Booth, is associated with the assassination of a U.S. president, it is doubtful that anyone has ever read or heard that Oswald pulled the trigger that ended Abraham Lincoln's life. The overconfidence people exhibit with respect to what they think they know can encourage reliance on information they should know better than to use.

A related strategy for supporting more critical evaluation of text content might require readers to tag information as inaccurate, to motivate the clear rejection of misinformation before it can influence postreading behaviors. Participants might be asked to monitor for any instance of an error, or every error might be explicitly distinguished for them with a particular font color. Unfortunately, projects using these approaches have not proven beneficial. Asking readers to take note when information is wrong (by pressing a key on a keyboard) has led to little reduction in use of that information later (Marsh & Fazio, 2006). And identifying information for readers as wrong can actually lead to *greater* reliance on misinformation (Eslick, Fazio, & Marsh, 2011).

Why do these sourcing activities fail? One explanation is that drawing attention to inaccuracies might make misinformation more salient, increase focus on and consideration of the material, support continued reflection on the inaccuracies, and increase the material's ready accessibility from memory (Henkel & Mattson, 2011; Lewandowsky, Ecker, Seifert, Schwarz, & Cook, 2012; Mitchell & Zaragoza, 1996; Seifert, 2002). Because these tasks only ask readers to take note of things that are wrong without operating on them, such noticing might actually encourage the encoding and use of misinformation. Recent work from our own lab has shown that tasks requiring students not just to notice but also to act on inaccuracies prove more successful at reducing reliance (Rapp, Hinze, Kohlhepp, & Ryskin, 2014). Tasks that require the activation of correct information, in competition with encoded but inaccurate traces, help emphasize contradictions between discrepant information. Contemporaneous activation of the correct and encoded yet inaccurate concepts is a necessary condition for noticing conflicts, and in taking the appropriate steps to reconcile them (van den Broek & Kendeou, 2008). We note, though, that even with tasks that encourage careful monitoring, we still observe instances in which participants problematically rely on the inaccurate information they should have discounted. The mind-sets encouraged by evaluative instructions are clearly effective, but not entirely so.

Overall, previous work indicates that any identification process, even when enacted through task instructions, (1) may be insufficient to ensure inaccuracies are tagged, (2) may be ignored during subsequent processing and decision making, or (3) may not matter given the contingencies of the task (Ecker et al., 2010; Fazio & Marsh, 2008; Umanath, Butler, & Marsh, 2012). With respect to this third consideration, it is possible that participants actually have tagged the information but still rely on it given expectations they should use what they just read (McCloskey & Zaragoza, 1985). These types of task demands could be invoked through expectations about performance or beliefs that what was read will be relevant for what will be tested. Lab investigations might thus overestimate the likelihood of reliance on inaccurate information given participants' expectations about whether and how they should use what an experimenter has asked them to read. However, these demands do not obviate the relevance of previous findings: Individuals *more often than not* have expectations about what they are doing, and as such, the expectations engendered during real-world experiences could analogously encourage reliance on inaccurate information. Consider, for example, a child who repeats the uninformed claims a role model publicly states, or members of a team holding the party line even in the face of contrary information.

General Acceptance

We suspect all of the above explanations, sometimes interactively and sometimes separately, prove valid when considering people's use of misinformation. Here we focus on another mechanism that might drive the encoding and use of inaccuracies: People can exhibit a default propensity toward accepting, or at least not rejecting, incoming information. A strong form of this view contends that the kinds of evaluations that reflect skepticism and rejection only emerge after initial processing, during which misinformation has had time to become encoded into memory, to establish connections to previous knowledge, and to support the construction of inferences (Gilbert, 1991). Early acceptance of incoming information creates the necessary conditions for incorrect material to influence processing that, when examined with subsequent testing, reveals evidence of comprehension decrements. This view, while not new, has failed to receive sufficient attention in explanatory accounts of the effects of misinformation.

The notion that individuals might default toward accepting what they read has classic philosophical roots. Several contemporary investigations have used those roots to motivate their examinations of knowledge acquisition. Work examining people's evaluations of false information (Gilbert et al., 1990; Gilbert, Tafarodi, & Malone, 1993) has framed the issue around two philosophical approaches. One approach, associated with the philosopher Descartes (1641/1984), contends that incoming information must be comprehended before it can be evaluated for truth. Before this evaluation process, information is stored in memory without an associated truth value. If it is perceived as inaccurate *after* initial comprehension, it can be rejected. A second approach, associated with the philosopher Spinoza (1677/1982), argues that people implicitly agree with all incoming information, only afterwards subjecting the accepted propositions to potential scrutiny. For this approach, acceptance occurs at the outset.

To distinguish between these two views, Gilbert and colleagues tested whether information is initially represented in memory as true or whether it can be represented in an unassessed form. In their paradigm, participants were presented with unfamiliar information accompanied by a cue indicating whether it was true or false. On some trials, participants were interrupted with a secondary task that imposed a cognitive burden, making it more difficult to contemplate the presented information. After reading, participants were presented with questions that probed for the validity of the previous information. A Spinozan view predicts that interrupted false information should frequently be mistaken as true because propositions are initially accepted and further evaluation would be difficult given interference by the secondary task. However, true information, even with such interference, should not be mistaken as false if people are indeed defaulting to true interpretations. In contrast, a Cartesian view contends that information is unassessed until subsequent reflection, thus receiving no default true or false determination. Because the secondary task would disrupt any evaluation, participants should be just as likely to mistake interrupted false information as true as they are to mistake interrupted true information as false.

In one version of this task, participants learned the ostensible meanings of foreign language words (e.g., "A twyrin is a doctor"), marked as true or false, and accompanied by or omitting a secondary task (i.e., press a button when you hear a tone). After reading sets of propositions, participants were asked to answer questions about the meanings of the words (e.g., "Is a twyrin a doctor?"). The results indicated that when participants made errors, they most often misremembered false information as true when a secondary task interrupted their comprehension. Interrupted false propositions were incorrectly remembered as true 33% of the time whereas interrupted true propositions were incorrectly remembered as false only 17% of the time—in contrast, error rates for uninterrupted false propositions (21%) and uninterrupted true propositions (22%) were identical (Gilbert et al., 1990). These data are more consistent with a Spinozan than a Cartesian view: Participants seemed to initially encode information as true, so when information labeled as false was interrupted, they defaulted to also remembering that information as true. True information, however, was unlikely to be labeled as false.

The types of materials employed above, and from other projects, have utilized decontextualized, propositional facts quite different from the kinds of materials we commonly encounter. We traditionally read expository and narrative texts that provide coherent, extended descriptions of real-world (i.e., newspapers, textbooks) and imagined (i.e., fictional novels) events. If readers willingly accept information only when it is presented as separated idea units lacking an overarching causal event structure, it would be a stretch to argue that such willingness regularly occurs across discourse experiences. Other projects have directly tested this issue using narrative stories (e.g., Appel & Richter, 2007; Butler, Dennis, & Marsh, 2012).

In a series of experiments, Gerrig and Prentice (1991) examined whether the false information included in fictional narratives can have direct consequences for subsequent decisions. Participants were tasked with reading a 20-page story describing a single day in the life of two college students. Over the course of their day, the story characters had conversations that included a variety of assertions. For example, a character might assert the accurate statement, "Frequent toothbrushing prevents gum disease," or the inaccurate version of that same statement, "Toothbrushing frequently leads to gum disease." Each statement included supporting ideas to cohere with the general nature of the conversation and to avoid appearing as if random statements had been inserted into the narrative. The assertions represented ideas that people presumably already know are either true or false. After reading the story containing an equal number of true and false assertions, participants were tasked with judging the validity of individually presented statements. This judgment task included statements unmentioned in the story but, more importantly for the experiment, also included statements conveying true or false summarizations of the assertions that had appeared in the text.

The results revealed a problematic effect of incorrect information. Participants exhibited slowdowns when judging false statements (e.g., "Brushing your teeth can lead to gum disease") after having previously read assertions conveying those false ideas. However, participants did not reveal similar slowdowns after reading accurate assertions in the story or when making judgments of correct statements (e.g., "Not brushing your teeth can lead to gum disease."). This pattern indicates that participants were influenced by the inaccurate information they had previously read that conflicted with their prior knowledge. If readers had neglected the influence of the false information, the aforementioned slowdowns should not have been obtained.

One question derived from this work is whether such reliance is a general consequence of comprehending text. In a subsequent study, Prentice, Gerrig, and Bailis (1997) asked participants to read the same story, this time set at one of two locations. Specifically, participants from either Yale or Princeton read a version of the story set at either Yale or Princeton. The hypothesis was that readers would be more likely to spontaneously evaluate text contents when they were familiar with story settings. This familiarity would free up the resources necessary for building models of the story locations and events, allowing for more attention to be devoted to evaluating content. In addition, the relevance of the material to participants' lives might encourage careful reading. Differential effects as a function of setting would indicate reliance on misinformation can be mediated by text content and reader responses to that content.

After reading the story, participants were asked to judge whether they agreed or disagreed with statements, some of which included summarizations of the assertions made in the text. Overall, participants tended to rely on what they read: They agreed more with inaccurate statements after reading inaccurate as compared to accurate assertions, and they agreed more with accurate statements after reading accurate as compared to inaccurate assertions. However, these effects were most prominent following stories set at unfamiliar locations. For stories set in familiar locations, the influence of the assertions was reduced (Prentice et al., 1997). Familiarity with the story setting may have afforded easier processing of the text descriptions, allowing for resources to be devoted specifically to evaluating assertions made by characters. Additionally, readers may have become invested in the materials when the stories were set in familiar places, prompting careful reading and evaluation of content. But regardless of explanation, it is worth emphasizing that participants used content from stories set in unfamiliar locales for which they lacked expertise. Given that we encounter a considerable amount of material during our everyday experiences for which we are not experts, liberal acceptance might still be the norm.[1]

Although the above studies suggest that people tend to accept what they read as true, other lines of work have argued that people automatically and efficiently monitor incoming information (e.g., Isberner & Richter, 2013; Richter, Schroeder, & Wöhrmann, 2009). These studies provide evidence that readers notice implausible information even when engaging in evaluation might be detrimental to performance in a secondary task. While the results of these recent projects are provocative, they are not necessarily incompatible with a Spinozan view of general acceptance: Readers might initially accept inaccurate information and then proceed, possibly through automatic processes, to evaluation and rejection. A propensity to accept information before rejection is therefore still an important consideration, given its potential for biasing memory and subsequent behavior. This influence would be especially harmful when monitoring is made imperfect because of relevant knowledge's being less accessible or following contexts that support inaccurate ideas.

Overall, the findings described in this section provide evidence that people tend to rely on what they read, potentially discounting information only after additional evaluation is relevant or required. However, these findings are also consistent with another view that allows for readers' overarching processing decisions to guide evaluation. Rather than default acceptance, people might *choose* to adopt a liberal acceptance of incoming information, sometimes termed "a willing suspension of disbelief." This notion has its roots in literary–philosophical discussions by Coleridge (1817), subsequently discussed in classic and contemporary accounts of writing, filmmaking, and narrative experience (Ferri, 2007; Gerrig & Rapp, 2004; Iser, 1978; Prentice et al., 1997; Radford & Weston, 1975). Individuals opting to suspend disbelief could also obtain the patterns of results described previously, as they would willingly use what was read to make subsequent judgments and decisions. These effects might therefore represent a choice opted for by the reader, or encouraged by skilled authors' constructions, rather than a necessary by-product of cognitive processing (Gerrig, 1993; Green & Brock, 2000). For example, people might decide that because they are participating in an experiment, what they read should be treated differently than real-world materials, and as such, inaccuracies are permissible. This decision could result in a reliance on text content but overestimate the degree to which this regularly occurs. Thus, individuals might modify processing so that inaccurate information is afforded a more reasonable status than it normally receives, which differentiates from an account indicating these effects are a general processing tendency beyond reader control or are so well-practiced as to be regularized.

Work attempting to discern between these two accounts cannot rely on product-specific measures like judgments of validity or analyses of text recall. These measures provide insight into the consequences of a learning experience but do not provide direct evidence concerning what goes on spontaneously *during* learning. In the next section, we describe some of our own work that attempts to examine readers' processing of inaccurate information *as* they read, to help begin distinguishing between general processing tendencies and strategic decisions.

Processing Misinformation

Examining how learners process inaccurate information during reading can help describe the time course of any subsequent influence. One possibility is that readers rarely notice inaccurate information during reading and fluently process even the most obviously fallacious statements. Although this would explain why inaccurate information influences memory, previous work calls this view into question given that readers regularly show processing difficulties to text inconsistencies and implausible information (e.g., Albrecht & O'Brien, 1993; Matsuki et al., 2011; Rapp, Gerrig, & Prentice, 2001). A second possibility is that readers' processing is always disrupted by inaccurate information, as a consequence of routinely scrutinizing incoming information using prior knowledge (e.g., Isberner & Richter, 2013; Richter et al., 2009; Singer, 2006). This would mean that any processing consequences of inaccurate information (e.g., using inaccuracies on subsequent tests) emerge *despite* readers noticing problems. A third possibility is that the magnitude of processing disruptions varies as a function of other factors, including the context in which inaccurate information appears. Results supporting this view would indicate that while people *can* monitor incoming information for its veracity, their tendency or success at doing so is moderated by features of their text experiences. Processing measures are particularly useful not just for addressing these specific hypotheses but also because they are less likely to be driven solely by deliberate strategies. For example, potential differences in sentence reading times are unlikely to reflect strategic decisions about word-by-word slowdowns and speedups (Cook et al., 1998; O'Brien et al., 1998). While task demands could certainly influence responses to texts, more implicit processing measures can provide insight into effects that might emerge outside of strategic control.

Implementing this approach, Rapp (2008) asked participants to read short expository texts, each describing a well-known event that included a historically accurate or inaccurate outcome. The contexts preceding these outcomes were of two types: Unambiguous contexts supported the likely occurrence of accurate outcomes, whereas ambiguous contexts were less certain, instead potentially supporting inaccurate outcomes. Consider one of the stories, which described George Washington's decision about running for president of the United States. The unambiguous context detailed his credentials and the endorsements he received from others. The ambiguous context, however, described him as tired and reluctant to seek office. These contexts were followed by either an accurate ("George Washington was elected first President of the United States") or inaccurate outcome ("George Washington was not elected first President of the United States"). Reading times to outcome sentences were used to measure (1) whether participants exhibited difficulty reading inaccurate as compared to accurate outcomes and (2) whether story contexts might drive any such difficulty. If readers evaluate incoming information, inaccurate historical outcomes should always incur processing difficulty (i.e., reading slowdowns), as compared to accurate ones. If, however, context can influence the degree to which information is carefully evaluated, slowdowns should be more pronounced following unambiguous as compared to ambiguous contexts.[2]

Participants overall demonstrated processing difficulties when reading inaccuracies, taking 552 ms longer to read inaccurate than accurate outcomes. However, the magnitude of this effect was influenced by preceding contexts. Following unambiguous contexts, participants took 693 ms longer to read inaccurate than accurate outcomes; following ambiguous contexts, this difference was reduced to 410 ms. Participants noticed when text content ran counter to their prior knowledge, but the processing disruption that resulted was moderated by the biasing influence of story contexts. These results are useful for considering whether readers might strategically toggle between being more or less accepting of inaccuracies during processing. If they had opted to treat stories as inappropriate or wrong, overall slowdowns should have been obtained rather than disruptions emerging from particular kinds of preceding contexts. Text content guided the effects despite participants having knowledge about the events, and despite the problematic consequences of failing to scrutinize inaccurate historical events (e.g., encoding that Washington was not elected first president).

One important issue concerns the pervasiveness of any biasing effects; another is whether familiarity with stories reduces the influence of inaccurate presentations. To assess these issues, a new set of participants was asked to read a subset of the same texts twice, with a one-week delay between their readings (Jacovina, Hinze, & Rapp, in press). During rereading, participants are aware of the content of the texts, how they will unfold, and whether they will end in expected or unexpected ways. This knowledge might change the pattern of results if people strategically shift their tolerance for inaccuracies across readings, scrutinizing texts differently when they are aware of the eventual outcome. They might also defer more or less to prior knowledge when they are aware a story will present a recurring (and only previously surprising) inaccuracy.

The reading times for participants' first experiences with the stories replicated Rapp (2008). Participants took 441 ms longer to read inaccurate than accurate outcomes, with this difference larger following unambiguous (a 770-ms difference) than ambiguous contexts (a 112-ms difference). As before, contexts influenced the ease with which readers processed the story outcomes. But what about during their second reading? Readers were overall faster to read the texts a second time, consistent with past research on multiple exposures (e.g., Raney, Therriault, & Minkoff, 2000). Besides this effect, though, the same general pattern previously observed was obtained for second readings: Participants took 133 ms longer to read inaccurate than accurate outcomes, with this difference larger following unambiguous (a 290-ms difference) as compared to ambiguous contexts (a 24-ms difference in the opposite direction). This pattern was also replicated with a 5-minute delay between readings, indicating any observed effects were not a function of poor memory for what was previously presented. To call back to the theme of this chapter, one contributor to the evaluative deficit following ambiguous contexts might be a general tendency to accept incoming information. And such a tendency would have problematic consequences when contexts bias inaccurate interpretations and expectations.

The studies we have described up until this point have relied on participants' encoding information from written sources. One concern might be whether the written materials utilized in lab studies, or more generally from a variety of kinds of texts, are inherently identified as credible sources. If so, any general reliance on misinformation might be caused by a perception that the source is credible. Studies in our lab have indicated that credibility can influence comprehension, but only when readers are made explicitly aware of and tasked with considering it (Sparks & Rapp, 2011). How might the credibility of a source influence reliance on misinformation?

Responses to Sources of Potential Misinformation

We have begun addressing whether sources can influence reliance on misinformation by examining whether people consider the credibility of others during interactive tasks. If partners in a task utilize each other's productions, even when those productions provide incorrect information, it would further support the view that general acceptance is a default. However, if actual interactions with others fail to reveal a liberal reliance on information, it would indicate that the effects previously described are restricted to texts.

In one experiment (Andrews & Rapp, in press), we set up conditions in which individuals could learn accurate and inaccurate information from a partner while they worked together to complete an interactive task. The experiment utilized the social contagion paradigm in which a participant studies information, completes a collaborative recall with a confederate partner, and then completes a second recall individually (Roediger, Meade, & Bergman, 2001). The paradigm allows for testing whether the information provided during the collaborative recall contaminates subsequent individual recalls, which is a concern when the collaborative recalls include inaccurate productions. We modified the paradigm to implement a source credibility manipulation focused specifically on the competency of a partner. Competency can provide a useful cue toward the reliability, intelligence, and credibility of others (Hovland, Janis, & Kelley, 1953; McCroskey & Young, 1981; Rieh & Danielson, 2007). When participants arrived at the lab, they met another participant who, unbeknownst to them, was actually a member of the research team. Participants then completed a task designed to invoke beliefs about the credibility of the confederate partner. Each person was tasked with circling as many instances of the letter F in a one-page passage as they could find in 1 minute. The confederate circled either many or few instances, and the pair exchanged papers to count up their successes. The experimenter also highlighted the performance of each member of the pair. This design was intended to encourage participants to infer that their partner was highly competent or not. In a control condition, the pair completed the task but never assessed each other's performance.

After this initial task, the members of the pair were separated and asked to study the same sets of categorized word lists. When they were finished, the lists were taken away and the pair came together to recall the studied words, taking turns producing items from each of the studied lists. Occasionally the confederate would incorrectly recall items that had not appeared during the initial study session but were plausible given the categories. After the collaborative activity, the pair separated again, and the participant completed an individual recall of the studied items.

The results demonstrated a clear effect of social contagion. On the final individual recalls, participants produced a greater proportion of incorrect items when they had been suggested by the confederate partner as compared to when those incorrect items were not suggested.[3] This provides evidence that individuals relied on the information they received regardless of its veracity. However, critically, that reliance was dependent upon the exhibited competency of the conference partner. Participants were *less* likely to rely on misinformation provided by a partner they perceived as being less credible, as compared to misinformation provided by partners who were credible, or when no insight was available with respect to partner credibility. These results, consistent with earlier work focused on text experiences, indicate that reliance on presented information is also observed during more interactive tasks. This reliance can be moderated by the quality of a source: When participants had evidence for their partner's not being particularly competent, they were more careful in their use of the information that the partner provided. When they felt their partner was competent, they relied on their partner's productions. And interestingly, when little information was offered as to partner competence, participants also relied on what they heard. This latter finding suggests that people seem to hold a general propensity toward using the information they are presented with, especially when they have some confidence in the source of that information. Perhaps, then, the materials and conditions inherent to a variety of experimental designs might include characteristics that imply they involve credible sources.

Conclusion

The review offered here was intended to highlight mechanisms potentially underlying people's use of misinformation. Based on the findings from a variety of studies, readers (and listeners) seem to exhibit a general reliance on what is presented to them. This liberal encoding can have problematic consequences when the presented information is inaccurate. While people can certainly opt to carefully evaluate information they receive with respect to what they know, such activity is not guaranteed. The nature of particular tasks that bias reliance on inaccurate information and the effort required to engage in critical evaluation does little to dissuade such a liberal approach. Work from our own lab has begun identifying some of the ways in which readers can be encouraged to engage in critical evaluation, based on instructional strategies that necessitate being mindful of problematic content. For example, when participants are asked to fact-check text contents (Rapp, Hinze, Kohlhepp, & Ryskin, 2014) or to read texts set in fantasy locales (Rapp, Hinze, Slaten, & Horton, 2014), their use of inaccurate information contained in stories is reduced. However, even with such interventions, we still observe instances in which participants rely on information that they should know is wrong.

One issue of considerable theoretical and applied importance involves identifying whether any use of misinformation means participants have incorporated inaccuracies into existing knowledge, or rather compartmentalized those inaccuracies into a separable store (Gerrig & Prentice, 1991; Potts & Peterson, 1985; Potts, St. John, & Kirson, 1989). This distinction is crucial for gaining a better understanding of the scope of readers' reliance on inaccurate information. If participants encode inaccuracies in a representation that is separate from general memory structures, compartmentalization might offer a form of tagging that prevents contaminating prior knowledge with false information. Of course, this might not have the intended benefits if readers liberally rely on even compartmentalized information.

Related to these issues, it remains unclear whether people's reliance on misinformation should be taken to mean that they have changed their beliefs concerning presented facts or assertions. At first blush this seems unlikely, particularly with respect to information that was presumably already known. For instance, we doubt that participants would change their understandings of historical events so as to *believe* that Lee Harvey Oswald was actually President Lincoln's assassin. However, with respect to newly learned information, it remains possible that misinformation can be incorporated such that reliance during future tasks reflects changes in memory and beliefs. Previous work examining misinformation effects in eyewitness contexts has shown that after one experiences a new event, inaccuracies that are related to the event tend to persist or even increase in influence over time (e.g., Frost, Ingraham, & Wilson, 2002; Paz-Alonso & Goodman, 2008). Interestingly, this persistence is marked by changes in the subjective quality of people's memories and increased confidence concerning the veracity of the information (Mudd & Govern, 2004). With a retention interval as short as one week, Frost (2000) showed that individuals' reports of their memories for misinformation changed from merely being known (reflecting familiarity but not actual recollection) to actually being remembered, a quality associated with real memories. Given the frequency with which people encounter new information on a daily basis, the potential for incomplete, misleading, or inaccurate information to influence memory and beliefs may be quite far-reaching.

Moreover, while we have a good grasp of the more immediate responses that participants have to questions and tasks related to previously read information, we know much less about how any unfolding understandings and beliefs might influence subsequent decisions (e.g., "Maybe I *won't* brush my teeth every day!"). Thus, while this work proves informative for clarifying theoretical accounts of memory and text processing, future projects should focus on the actual behaviors that can arise as a consequence of our text experiences. Investigations along these lines are necessary to fully understand the consequences of reading inaccurate information.

Notes

1. Subsequent work by Wheeler, Green, and Brock (1999) attempted to replicate these location-based effects with a different sample of participants: Ohio State University (OSU) students read stories set either at OSU or at Yale University. While a general influence of text content on reader judgments was observed, no effect of story setting was obtained. These results are consistent with the claim that readers rely on text information regardless of its veracity. However, the difference between this study and Prentice et al. (1997) raises the possibility that factors besides familiarity influence whether readers will be sufficiently invested to critically evaluate content (Van Der Wege, Kurivchack, & Rapp, 2005).

2. The story outcomes were balanced so that half of the accurate outcomes included a negation and half did not while half of the inaccurate outcomes included a negation and half did not. This ensured that any slowdowns could not be attributed to the effects of negated statements.

3. We note that the effects described in this experiment are different from the earlier discussed studies in that individuals were not neglecting prior knowledge from long-term memory in favor of a recent memory trace but rather neglecting a recent episodic memory in favor of an even more recent memory trace. Nevertheless, the effects in both experiments are analogous, as they indicate a problematic reliance on inaccurate memory traces provided by other sources.

References

Albrecht, J. E., & Myers, J. L. (1995). Role of context in accessing distant information during reading. *Journal of Experimental Psychology. Learning, Memory, and Cognition, 21*, 1459–1468.

Albrecht, J. E., & O'Brien, E. J. (1993). Updating a mental model: Maintaining both local and global coherence. *Journal of Experimental Psychology. Learning, Memory, and Cognition, 19*, 1061–1070.

Andrews, J. J., & Rapp, D. N. (in press). Partner characteristics and social contagion: Does group composition matter? *Applied Cognitive Psychology*.

Appel, M., & Richter, T. (2007). Persuasive effects of fictional narratives increase over time. *Media Psychology, 10*, 113–134.

Ayers, M. S., & Reder, L. M. (1998). A theoretical review of the misinformation effect: Predictions from an activation-based memory model. *Psychonomic Bulletin & Review, 5*, 1–21.

Barber, S. J., Rajaram, S., & Marsh, E. J. (2008). Fact learning: How information accuracy, delay, and repeated testing change retention and retrieval experience. *Memory, 16*, 934–946.

Begg, I., Armour, V., & Kerr, T. (1985). On believing what we remember. *Canadian Journal of Behavioural Science, 17*, 199–214.

Bottoms, H. C., Eslick, A. N., & Marsh, E. J. (2010). Memory and the Moses illusion: Failures to detect contradictions with stored knowledge yield negative memorial consequences. *Memory, 18*, 670–678.

Bush, J. G., Johnson, H. M., & Seifert, C. M. (1994). The implications of corrections: Then why did you mention it? In A. Ram & K. Eiselt (Eds.), *Proceedings of the 16th annual conference of the Cognitive Science Society* (pp. 112–117). Hillsdale, NJ: Lawrence Erlbaum Associates.

Butler, A. C., Dennis, N. A., & Marsh, E. J. (2012). Inferring facts from fiction: Reading correct and incorrect information affects memory for related information. *Memory, 20*, 487–498.

Coleridge, S. T. (1817). *Biographia literaria; or biographical sketches of my literary life and opinions*. London: Rest Fenner.

Cook, A. E., Halleran, J. G., & O'Brien, E. J. (1998). What is readily available during reading? A memory-based view of text processing. *Discourse Processes, 26*, 109–129.

Descartes, R. [1641] (1984). Fourth meditation. In J. Cottingham, R. Stoothoff, & D. Murdoch (Eds.), *The philosophical writings of Descartes* (Vol. 2, pp. 37–43). Cambridge, England: Cambridge University Press.

Ecker, U. K. H., Lewandowsky, S., & Tang, D. T. W. (2010). Explicit warnings reduce but do not eliminate the continued influence of misinformation. *Memory & Cognition, 38*, 1087–1100.

Eslick, A. N., Fazio, L. K., & Marsh, E. J. (2011). Ironic effects of drawing attention to story errors. *Memory, 19*, 184–191.

Fazio, L. K., Barber, S. J., Rajaram, S., Ornstein, P., & Marsh, E. J. (2013). Creating illusions of knowledge: Learning errors that contradict prior knowledge. *Journal of Experimental Psychology. General, 142*, 1–5.

Fazio, L. K., & Marsh, E. J. (2008). Slowing presentation speed increases illusions of knowledge. *Psychonomic Bulletin & Review, 15*, 180–185.

Ferri, A. (2007). *Willing suspension of disbelief: Poetic faith in film*. Lanham, MD: Lexington Books.

Frost, P. (2000). The quality of false memory over time: Is memory for misinformation "remembered" or "known"? *Psychonomic Bulletin & Review, 7*, 531–536.

Frost, P., Ingraham, M., & Wilson, B. (2002). Why misinformation is more likely to be recognised over time: A source monitoring account. *Memory, 10*, 179–185.

Gerrig, R. J. (1989). Suspense in the absence of uncertainty. *Journal of Memory and Language, 28*, 633–648.

Gerrig, R. J. (1993). *Experiencing narrative worlds*. New Haven, CT: Yale University Press.

Gerrig, R. J., & McKoon, G. (1998). The readiness is all: The functionality of memory-based text processing. *Discourse Processes, 26*, 67–86.

Gerrig, R. J., & Prentice, D. A. (1991). The representation of fictional information. *Psychological Science, 2*, 336–340.

Gerrig, R. J., & Rapp, D. N. (2004). Psychological processes underlying literary impact. *Poetics Today, 25*, 265–281.

Gilbert, D. T. (1991). How mental systems believe. *American Psychologist, 46*, 107–119.

Gilbert, D. T., Krull, D. S., & Malone, P. S. (1990). Unbelieving the unbelievable: Some problems in the rejection of false information. *Journal of Personality and Social Psychology, 59*, 601–613.

Gilbert, D. T., Tafarodi, R. W., & Malone, P. S. (1993). You can't not believe everything you read. *Journal of Personality and Social Psychology, 65*, 221–233.

Green, M. C., & Brock, T. C. (2000). The role of transportation in the persuasiveness of public narratives. *Journal of Personality and Social Psychology, 79*, 701–721.

Henkel, L. A., & Mattson, M. E. (2011). Reading is believing: The truth effect and source credibility. *Consciousness and Cognition, 20*, 1705–1721.

Hinze, S. R., Slaten, D. G., Horton, W. S., Jenkins, R., & Rapp, D. N. (2014). Pilgrims sailing the Titanic: Plausibility effects on memory for facts and errors. *Memory & Cognition, 42*, 305–324.

Hovland, C. I., Janis, I. L., & Kelley, M. M. (1953). *Communication and persuasion.* New Haven, CT: Yale University Press.

Isberner, M.-B., & Richter, T. (2013). Can readers ignore implausibility? Evidence for nonstrategic monitoring of event-based plausibility in language comprehension. *Acta Psychologica, 142*, 15–22.

Iser, W. (1978). *The act of reading: A theory of aesthetic response.* Baltimore, MD: The Johns Hopkins University Press.

Jacovina, M. E., Hinze, S. R., & Rapp, D. N. (in press). Fool me twice: The consequences of reading (and rereading) inaccurate information. *Applied Cognitive Psychology.*

Johnson, H. M., & Seifert, C. M. (1994). Sources of the continued influence effect: When misinformation in memory affects later inferences. *Journal of Experimental Psychology. Learning, Memory, and Cognition, 20*, 1420–1436.

Johnson, H. M., & Seifert, C. M. (1998). Updating accounts following a correction of misinformation. *Journal of Experimental Psychology. Learning, Memory, and Cognition, 24*, 1483–1494.

Johnson, M. K., Hashtroudi, S., & Lindsay, D. S. (1993). Source monitoring. *Psychological Bulletin, 114*, 3–28.

Kelley, C. M., & Lindsay, D. S. (1993). Remembering mistaken for knowing: Ease of retrieval as a basis for confidence in answers to general knowledge questions. *Journal of Memory and Language, 32*, 1–24.

Lewandowsky, S., Ecker, U. K. H., Seifert, C. M., Schwarz, N., & Cook, J. (2012). Misinformation and its correction: Continued influence and successful debiasing. *Psychological Science in the Public Interest, 13*, 106–131.

Lewandowsky, S., Stritzke, W. G. K., Oberauer, K., & Morales, M. (2005). Memory for fact, fiction, and misinformation: The Iraq War 2003. *Psychological Science, 16*, 190–195.

Marsh, E. J., Butler, A. C., & Umanath, S. (2012). Using fictional sources in the classroom: Applications from cognitive psychology. *Educational Psychology Review, 24*, 449–469.

Marsh, E. J., & Fazio, L. K. (2006). Learning errors from fiction: Difficulties in reducing reliance on fictional stories. *Memory & Cognition, 34*, 1140–1149.

Marsh, E. J., Meade, M. L., & Roediger, H. L., III. (2003). Learning facts from fiction. *Journal of Memory and Language, 49*, 519–536.

Matsuki, K., Chow, T., Hare, M., Elman, J. L., Scheepers, C., & McRae, K. (2011). Event-based plausibility immediately influences on-line language comprehension. *Journal of Experimental Psychology. Learning, Memory, and Cognition, 37*, 913–934.

McCloskey, M., & Zaragoza, M. S. (1985). Misleading postevent information and memory for events: Arguments and evidence against memory impairment hypotheses. *Journal of Experimental Psychology. General, 114*, 1–16.

McCroskey, J. C., & Young, T. J. (1981). Ethos and credibility: The construct and its measurement after three decades. *Communication Studies, 32*, 24–34.

McGlone, M. S., & Tofighbakhsh, J. (2000). Birds of a feather flock conjointly (?): Rhyme as reason in aphorisms. *Psychological Science, 11*, 424–428.

McKoon, G., Gerrig, R. J., & Greene, S. B. (1996). Pronoun resolution without pronouns: Some consequences of memory-based text processing. *Journal of Experimental Psychology. Learning, Memory, and Cognition, 22*, 919–932.

Meade, M. L., & Roediger, H. L., III. (2002). Explorations in the social contagion of memory. *Memory & Cognition, 30*, 995–1009.

Mitchell, K. J., & Zaragoza, M. S. (1996). Repeated exposure to suggestion and false memory: The role of contextual variability. *Journal of Memory and Language, 35*, 246–260.

Mudd, K., & Govern, J. M. (2004). Conformity to misinformation and time delay negatively affect eyewitness confidence and accuracy. *North American Journal of Psychology, 6*, 227–238.

O'Brien, E. J. (1995). Automatic components of discourse comprehension. In E. P. Lorch & E. J. O'Brien (Eds.), *Sources of coherence in reading* (pp. 159–176). Hillsdale, NJ: Lawrence Erlbaum Associates.

O'Brien, E. J., Cook, A. E., & Guéraud, S. (2010). Accessibility of outdated information. *Journal of Experimental Psychology. Learning, Memory, and Cognition, 36*, 979–991.

O'Brien, E. J., Rizzella, M. L., Albrecht, J. E., & Halleran, J. G. (1998). Updating a situation model: A memory-based text processing view. *Journal of Experimental Psychology. Learning, Memory, and Cognition, 24*, 1200–1210.

Otero, J., & Kintsch, W. (1992). Failures to detect contradictions in a text: What readers believe versus what they read. *Psychological Science, 3*, 229–235.

Paz-Alonso, P. M., & Goodman, G. S. (2008). Trauma and memory: Effects of post-event misinformation, retrieval order, and retention interval. *Memory, 16*, 58–75.

Potts, G. R., & Peterson, S. B. (1985). Incorporation versus compartmentalization in memory for discourse. *Journal of Memory and Language, 24,* 107–118.

Potts, G. R., St. John, M. F., & Kirson, D. (1989). Incorporating new information into existing world knowledge. *Cognitive Psychology, 21,* 303–333.

Prentice, D. A., Gerrig, R. J., & Bailis, D. S. (1997). What readers bring to the processing of fictional texts. *Psychonomic Bulletin & Review, 4,* 416–420.

Radford, C., & Weston, M. (1975). How can we be moved by the fate of Anna Karenina? *Proceedings of the Aristotelian Society, Supplementary Volumes, 49,* 67–93.

Raney, G. E., Therriault, D., & Minkoff, S. (2000). Repetition effects from paraphrased text: Evidence for an integrative model of text representation. *Discourse Processes, 28,* 61–81.

Rapp, D. N. (2008). How do readers handle incorrect information during reading? *Memory & Cognition, 36,* 688–701.

Rapp, D. N., Gerrig, R. J., & Prentice, D. A. (2001). Readers' trait-based models of characters in narrative comprehension. *Journal of Memory and Language, 45,* 737–750.

Rapp, D. N., Hinze, S. R., Kohlhepp, K., & Ryskin, R. A. (2014). Reducing reliance on inaccurate information. *Memory & Cognition, 42,* 11–26.

Rapp, D. N., Hinze, S. R., Slaten, D. G., & Horton, W. S. (2014). Amazing stories: Acquiring and avoiding inaccurate information from fiction. *Discourse Processes, 1–2,* 50–74.

Rapp, D. N., & Kendeou, P. (2007). Revising what readers know: Updating text representations during narrative comprehension. *Memory & Cognition, 35,* 2019–2032.

Rapp, D. N., & Kendeou, P. (2009). Noticing and revising discrepancies as texts unfold. *Discourse Processes, 46,* 1–24.

Reber, R., & Schwarz, N. (1999). Effects of perceptual fluency on judgments of truth. *Consciousness and Cognition, 8,* 338–342.

Richter, T., Schroeder, S., & Wöhrmann, B. (2009). You don't have to believe everything you read: Background knowledge permits fast and efficient validation of information. *Journal of Personality and Social Psychology, 96,* 538–558.

Rieh, S. Y., & Danielson, D. (2007). Credibility: A multidisciplinary framework. In B. Cronin (Ed.), *Annual review of information science and technology* (Vol. 41, pp. 307–364). Medford, NJ: Information Today.

Roediger, H. L., III, Meade, M. L., & Bergman, E. T. (2001). Social contagion of memory. *Psychonomic Bulletin & Review, 8,* 365–371.

Schwarz, N., Sanna, L. J., Skurnik, I., & Yoon, C. (2007). Metacognitive experiences and the intricacies of setting people straight: Implications for debiasing and public information campaigns. *Advances in Experimental Social Psychology, 39,* 127–161.

Seifert, C. M. (2002). The continued influence of misinformation in memory: What makes a correction effective? In B. H. Ross (Ed.), *The psychology of learning and motivation: Advances in research and theory* (Vol. 41, pp. 265–292). San Diego, CA: Academic Press.

Singer, M. (2006). Verification of text ideas during reading. *Journal of Memory and Language, 54*, 574–591.

Sparks, J. R., & Rapp, D. N. (2011). Readers' reliance on source credibility in the service of comprehension. *Journal of Experimental Psychology. Learning, Memory, and Cognition, 37*, 230–247.

Spinoza, B. [1677] (1982). S. Feldman (Ed.), *The Ethics and selected letters* (Shirley, S., Trans.). Indianapolis, IN: Hackett.

Strange, J. J., & Leung, C. C. (1999). How anecdotal accounts in news and in fiction can influence judgments of a social problem's urgency, causes, and cures. *Personality and Social Psychology Bulletin, 25*, 436–449.

Toth, E. E., Klahr, D., & Chen, Z. (2000). Bridging research and practice: A cognitively based classroom intervention for teaching experimentation skills to elementary school children. *Cognition and Instruction, 18*, 423–459.

Trabasso, T., & van den Broek, P. (1985). Causal thinking and the representation of narrative events. *Journal of Memory and Language, 24*, 612–630.

Umanath, S., Butler, A. C., & Marsh, E. J. (2012). Positive and negative effects of monitoring popular films for historical inaccuracies. *Applied Cognitive Psychology, 26*, 556–567.

van den Broek, P., & Kendeou, P. (2008). Cognitive processes in comprehension of science texts: The role of co-activation in confronting misconceptions. *Applied Cognitive Psychology, 22*, 335–351.

Van Der Wege, M. M., Kurivchack, A., & Rapp, D. N. (2005). Changing beliefs based on information in fictional narratives. Presented at the 46th annual meeting of the Psychonomic Society, Toronto, Ontario, Canada.

van Oostendorp, H., & Bonebakker, C. (1999). Difficulties in updating mental representations during reading news reports. In H. van Oostendorp & S. R. Goldman (Eds.), *The construction of mental representations during reading* (pp. 319–339). Mahwah, NJ: Lawrence Erlbaum Associates.

Wheeler, S. C., Green, M. C., & Brock, T. C. (1999). Fictional narratives change beliefs: Replications of Prentice, Gerrig, & Bailis (1997) with mixed corroboration. *Psychonomic Bulletin & Review, 6*, 136–141.

Wilkes, A. L., & Leatherbarrow, M. (1988). Editing episodic memory following the identification of error. *Quarterly Journal of Experimental Psychology: Human Experimental Psychology, 52A*, 165–183.

Wilkes, A. L., & Reynolds, D. J. (1999). On certain limitations accompanying readers' interpretations of corrections in episodic text. *Quarterly Journal of Experimental Psychology: Human Experimental Psychology, 52A*, 165–183.

10 Discounting Information: When False Information Is Preserved and When It Is Not

Yaacov Schul and Ruth Mayo

Although people often assume that communicators are cooperative (Grice, 1975), they are also well prepared for deception. Evolutionary theory assumes that deception is inherent to living in groups, and there are empirical demonstrations indicating that lying is common in everyday interactions (DePaulo, Kashy, Kirkendol, Wyer, & Epstein, 1996; DePaulo & Kashy, 1998; Feldman, Forrest, & Happ, 2002). It is therefore not surprising that consumers distrust product information provided by sellers (e.g., Dyer & Kuehl, 1978; Prendergast, Liu, & Poon, 2009) or that voters are suspicious of messages coming from political candidates (Schyns & Koop, 2010). Hence, it seems reasonable to conclude that in many, if not most, of their dealings with others, people are aware of the possibility of being misled (Schul & Burnstein, 1998; Schul, Mayo, & Burnstein, 2004).

After so many generations of coping with the need to identify deception, one might think that human beings would have evolved into highly accurate social perceivers. Yet, as dozens of studies suggest, the accuracy of interpersonal perception is modest at best. In particular, as a recent review suggests (Hartwig & Bond, 2011), liars seem to win the Darwinian "arms race" between senders (who attempt to deceive) and receivers (who strive to detect deception).

Because using false information from others might be very costly, and at the same time, the detection of falsehoods communicated by others proves very difficult, one expects that receivers would have developed skills that allow them to discount false information once such information is identified. However, as past research suggests, the success of discounting such information is limited. This chapter discusses the obstacles that prevent people from attaining the discounting challenge, as well as the conditions that promote successful discounting.

Overview

We start by providing a very brief review of past research on discounting that emphasizes the importance of the nature of encoding and the strength of the request to discount for successful discounting. We note that receivers might be motivated to discount a particular testimony based on what they know about the source's motivations or abilities. That is, people attempt to discount when they discover that the source of a testimony attempts to deceive them or when the source appears to be incompetent (e.g., Eagly, Wood, & Chaiken, 1978). Notwithstanding, we remark that discounting success might differ in the two cases because the reason for discounting matters. Then, we view the discounting challenge from three perspectives. First, we consider the literature on negations that offers some insight into the cognitive routes that might be taken when people attempt to discount. We continue by describing research on implicit truth, which suggests that failure to discount might be more likely when the to-be-discounted information feels true, even when the receiver knows it to be false. We end by considering the mind-set of receivers. Specifically, we compare the states of trust and distrust and argue that when one distrusts, discounting might be more successful than when one trusts. The trust/distrust comparison provides some understanding of the obstacles to discounting.

Early Research on the Success of Discounting

Early explorations into the phenomenon of information discounting run along two main lines: research about the success of discounting of invalid testimonies in court settings (e.g., Elliott, Farrington, & Manheimer, 1988; Hatvany & Strack, 1980; Kassin & Wrightsman, 1980, 1981; Thompson, Fong, & Rosenhan, 1981; Wolf & Montgomery, 1977) and research about belief perseverance (see reviews in Anderson, New, & Speer, 1985; Schul & Burnstein, 1985). Interestingly, whereas the bulk of the early research on discounting in court settings suggests that individuals can successfully ignore an invalid testimony, studies done within the belief perseverance paradigm suggest the opposite. This inconsistency points to several key differences between the two paradigms which are important in understanding the process of information discounting. The two paradigms differ in the nature of the encoding of the to-be-used (TBU) and the to-be-discounted (TBD) information, the strength of the request to discount, and the motivations of the decision makers to succeed in appropriate discounting. These key factors will be discussed below. A more comprehensive analysis of the success of discounting in court settings published recently by Steblay, Hosch, Culhane, and McWethy (2006) shows that in contrast to the conclusion gleaned from the early studies, inadmissible evidence has a reliable impact on verdicts or judgments of guilt, that is, that discounting fails even in courtroom simulations. Still, their meta-analysis reveals that a strong admonition by a judge to disregard the inadmissible evidence can nullify this effect so that discounting of invalid testimonies succeeds.

What is so unique in the discounting phenomenon relative to other cases in which people have to avoid biases? In the typical discounting situation, the receiver does not know at the time the information is encoded whether it would have to be used (TBU) or discounted (TBD) at the time the judgment will be made.[1] In contrast, in the cases of having to avoid known biases such as those associated with stereotypes, one can identify the bias-related information and its implications very early in the process, even before that information has been fully processed. Therefore, receivers are better able to prepare themselves, if they are motivated to do so, to discount the biased information. For example, receivers might be aware of their tendency to treat others differently because of the way they speak (e.g., when foreigners have poor command of the language). If they so desire, they can overcome the bias by considering the essential aspects of the communication (e.g., its content) while effortfully ignoring the incidental aspects (e.g., the style) at the time of encoding. Although by itself this challenge might be very hard to attain, the challenge of information discounting is even harder. This is because the biases in the typical discounting situation are discovered only *after* encoding because during encoding one does not know which piece of information would have to be discounted (see Schul, Burnstein, & Bardi, 1996).

Still, in spite of the difficulty of the challenge to discount, there are conditions that facilitate people's attempts to remove the influence of the TBD information from their judgments. Research suggests that when people are aware of the potential influence of TBD testimony, and especially its direction of strength, when they have cognitive resources to operate on this knowledge, and when they have the motivation to avoid the bias, they can avoid the impact of the TBD testimony (e.g., Martin, Seta, & Crelia, 1990; Schwarz et al., 2007; Strack & Hannover, 1996; Wilson & Brekke, 1994), at least when they make explicit judgments. This is done by mentally "subtracting" the bias from the initial judgment response. Going back to our previous example, if one knows that he or she tends to discriminate against foreigners with poor command of English, he or she can mentally add positive valence to an initial (negatively biased) impression of the foreigner, thereby attempting to overcome the bias. The example illustrates that discounting can be achieved by a correction at the response level.

The response-level correction is one of the major mechanisms that might be used for discounting. Research shows that under well-specified conditions people might be able to undo the bias brought about by the TBD information in making their judgments. However, it is important to note that the correction is made at the response (judgment) level rather than through reinterpretation of the information. As a consequence, what appears to be a successful discounting in judgments that are made in close temporal proximity to the discounting request turns out to be failure to discount in judgments made when the request to discount is no longer active in memory. Later on, we shall describe other mechanisms of discounting and discuss the shortcomings of correction in more detail. However, before doing so, let us describe three studies from our laboratory that demonstrate how predictions derived from considering the correction mechanism can shed light on the success of discounting.

Schul and Goren (1997) found that individuals who were asked to ignore a strong testimony adjusted their judgments more than those asked to ignore a testimony with a milder persuasive impact. They proposed that as individuals consider the implication of a testimony for the judgment that they are making, they also create a metacognitive assessment of the impact of that testimony. When a testimony has to be discounted, the metacognitive assessment of its impact is utilized, and the judgment is adjusted (corrected) accordingly. The findings reveal that when a critical testimony was weak, participants tended to underestimate its persuasive impact. As a result, they undercorrected and consequently failed to discount when instructed to ignore it. In contrast, when the critical testimony was strong, participants tended to slightly overestimate its persuasive impact. Consequently, discounting succeeded.

The research reported in Schul and Manzury (1990) highlights the importance of the reminders of the requirement to discount. Participants in their study were asked to discount a testimony and make three types of judgments with respect to the guilt of the accused, his aggressiveness, and his likability. The question of interest has to do with the differences between the three judgments. Making a judgment of guilt is the essence of the decision maker's activity in court. Therefore, the norms of judgments imposed by the court setting become maximally relevant. Judgments of likability or aggressiveness are less central to court decision making. Therefore, the pressure to conform to the standards of judgments in court becomes weaker. Indeed, the participants failed to discount the TBD testimony properly when they made judgments about the aggressiveness and likability of the accused person. However, when the same participants were making judgments of guilt, they were unaffected by the TBD testimony; that is, discounting succeeded. Schul and Manzury interpreted this finding to mean that although people know what they need to do, they act on this knowledge only when the judgment reminds them of the need to correct (see also Schul, 1993).

The third example we describe involves the nature of the motivation of participants to discount appropriately. Saar and Schul (1996) manipulated this motivation in two complementary ways. First, they reasoned that decision makers should be more motivated to discount when they are held publicly accountable for their answers (see Lerner & Tetlock, 1999, 2003, for a more comprehensive analysis of the conditions under which accountability is likely to reduce biases). Second, they noted that the motivation to discount properly is stronger when the reasons given for discounting are substantive rather than procedural (see Golding & Hauselt, 1994; Kassin, & Sommers, 1997; Steblay et al., 2006; see also Demaine, 2008).

In order to investigate the joint impact of these two motivational forces, respondents were randomly assigned to one of six cells. There were two conditions in which respondents were given reasons (either procedural or substantive) to ignore an argument. Respondents in a third condition (termed the *no-request* control condition) received the same TBD argument but were not asked to ignore it. These three conditions were crossed with an accountability manipulation. Half the respondents were told at the onset of the experiment that they would be asked to explain their responses to the experimenter. These respondents were also instructed to write their name on the questionnaire. The remaining respondents were not instructed to identify themselves on the questionnaire, nor did they anticipate having to explain their responses.

The stimulus material involved a fictional protocol of a meeting whereby the decision about a fee reduction at the university's recreation center was discussed. The center's head trainer presented the TBD argument, arguing against a fee reduction. The substantive request to ignore his testimony attacked the cogency of the TBD argument by showing that the center's head trainer omitted important details, which would have made his argument false. The procedural request challenged the formal qualifications of the head trainer to present financial data. In both cases the chair of the meeting instructed the meeting discussants to ignore the TBD argument. Participants were asked to assume the role of someone in the meeting and rate their agreement with fee reduction. Table 10.1 presents the mean judgments after standardization. Higher positive numbers reflect more agreement with fee reduction.

Participants who used all the information (no-request control condition) found the fee reduction request relatively unacceptable, indicating that the critical testimony (that was discounted in the other conditions) was by itself persuasive. Participants in the two other conditions who were asked to discount the critical testimony found the proposal for fee reduction acceptable. Notwithstanding, whereas the accountability manipulation had no effect on participants who received the substantive request to discount, it affected those who received the procedural request to discount. That is, participants who received a request to discount based on procedural grounds *and* were not held accountable managed to discount the TBD argument, and thus they agreed with fee reduction. In contrast, when the participants who received the procedural request anticipated having to justify their judgment (the accountability condition), they were reluctant to ignore the TBD testimony, and therefore these participants opposed the proposal of fee reduction. This pattern of findings is consistent with the suggestion that accountability sensitizes decision makers to the goal they want to satisfy (Lerner &

Table 10.1

Participants' agreement with fee reduction

	No Accountability	Accountability
Use all information (including TBD argument)	−.69	−.32
Substantive request to discount	.43	.59
Procedural request to discount	.23	−.31

Note. More positive numbers indicate more agreement. TBD, to be discounted.

Tetlock, 2003). The goal of making an appropriate judgment dictates that TBD information should be disregarded when there are good reasons for doing so but should not be disregarded when the reasons are unconvincing.

Summary

Taken together, the three studies described above are consistent with the suggestion that the task of discounting could be done through a deliberate process of correction whereby decision makers assess their potential biases and their incentive to avoid them. Discounting succeeds when (1) people have a good estimate of the size and direction of the bias that the TBD information induces, (2) they are motivated to remove the bias, and (3) they have the cognitive resources to do so.

In the reminder of this chapter, we offer three extensions to the conceptualization of discounting as deliberate correction. First, we apply findings from research on the processing of negations in an attempt to shed light on the cognitive activity enacted when people discover that a particular message should be discounted. In particular, we examine the role of an alternative schema for the success of discounting. Second, we examine the properties of the outcome measures (e.g., judgment of guilt). Specifically, we emphasize differences between corrections done superficially, at a response level, and reinterpretation done at the level of representation. Finally, we discuss the readiness of individuals to cope with the challenge of invalid messages. We argue that some mental states, and particularly a state of distrust, facilitate successful handling of false information. Facilitation is manifested not only by discounting success but also by the spontaneity of the discounting process.

Negation and Discounting

The correction perspective discussed above suggests that under well-specified conditions people might be able to undo the bias brought about by the TBD information. However, as we noted earlier, the correction is superficial—it is done at the response (judgment) level rather than through reinterpretation of the information. The research on negation is informative about the potential for reinterpretation of the information.

Instructions to discount tell a person that a particular claim, X, is suspect (or even false), and thus it should be ignored. To illustrate, consider a description of a political candidate. After learning about her positions on ten issues, you are informed that the information about the third issue comes from an unreliable source and therefore you should disregard it when evaluating her. What do respondents do when they are asked to ignore the third issue? Ideally, respondents should place themselves in an alternative world in which they reprocess the information without receiving the TBD issue. Indeed, a control condition which is used as a benchmark for discounting success had just this format. Unfortunately, however, the alternative-world scenario is only possible in a between-respondents design. For better or worse, our mental system is affected by past exposure, so that the bias that the TBD information causes to the interpretation of the TBU information during the original encoding cannot be undone by merely asking people to reprocess the information *as if* the TBD information had never been shown (Ecker, Lewandowsky, Swire, & Chang, 2011; Schul & Burnstein, 1985; Schul & Mayo, 1999; Schul & Mazursky, 1990).

As an illustration of the nature of this bias in interpretation, imagine that Jim is applying for the position of copywriter at an advertising agency. The members of the selection committee are considering two recommendations about Jim. One indicates that Jim is hardworking while the other states that Jim is uncooperative. Normally, when two testimonies about Jim are processed, they are interpreted jointly so that their meanings become interdependent (Schul, Burnstein, & Martinez, 1983; Schul & Mayo, 1999). To illustrate, the positive characteristic "hardworking" might be fitted with the testimony about Jim's uncooperativeness by interpreting hardworking as a somewhat negative characteristic, projecting, for example, an image of a person who is not willing to learn from others and as a result often has to rediscover the wheel. Accordingly, if later the respondents consider "hardworking" by itself (e.g., because the testimony about "uncooperativeness" has been declared inadmissible), their judgments become overly unfavorable compared to respondents that received only the "hardworking" recommendation. Parenthetically, simply trying to reprocess the TBU information without doing anything about the TBD information is like trying to avoid thinking about a white bear (Wenzlaff & Wegner, 2000)—it is not likely to work.

This bias in encoding reflects the selection of meaning of the TBU information, which occurs during the early encoding of the information. In this sense it resembles a primacy effect. Can such a bias be nullified when people are told to re-encode the information as if the TBD had never been presented? The answer is "yes." It can be achieved through correction processes, as we have suggested earlier. But our focus in this section is on effects that have to do with the interpretation of the TBU information. Specifically, we ask about reinterpretation, namely, whether the original interpretation afforded to the TBU information by the TBD information can be changed upon learning that the TBD testimony is false. Our lesson from the research on negation is that the answer to this question is "it depends." Successful reinterpretation depends on the nature of the TBD testimony and the way it is encoded.

Prior to discovering that the TBD testimony is false, one thinks about the TBD testimony as an affirmation—a testimony that is phrased in a positive way. An affirmation (abstractly, "A is X") tends to activate the core of the message (X) with its associations. For example, the assertion "John is intelligent" activates associations of intelligence and the assertion "Jim is hardworking" triggers associations of industriousness. However, what happens when the request to discount is introduced? For example, one is told that the testimony about John's intelligence is based on a completely invalid test. Some people may infer that the opposite of the assertion is true—that is, that John is stupid. Others may entertain both possibilities—that is, the possibility that the oppo-site of the assertion is true and the possibility that the original assertion is true. Still, there are cases (see below) in which receivers may maintain the original set of associa-tions. The research on negations offers predictions about the prevalence of these alter-natives and their consequences for the challenge of discounting.

Mayo, Schul, and Burnstein (2004) explored the kind of associations that come to mind when one process negations. To illustrate, imagine being told that "John is sim-ply not a romantic person." Do you think about associations that are congruent with the intended meaning of the negation (e.g., unromantic gestures that John makes) or associations congruent with what is being negated (e.g., romantic gestures that John doesn't make)? Mayo et al. (2004) distinguished between two types of negation pro-cesses: fusion and schema-plus-tag.

Negation through a process of fusion is performed by activating an affirmative schema that entails the meaning of the negated message. For example, upon being told that "John is not smart," receivers may activate spontaneously inferences and impli-cations that are congruent with being stupid. Thus, when negating according to the fusion model, receivers are able to accommodate the intended meaning of the negation as a whole. Note, however, that a necessary condition for the utilization of the fusion model is having in mind an affirmative alternative schema that entails the meaning of the negation.

Negation through the schema-plus-tag model is different. The receiver does not access an opposite schema, but rather represents the negation as "A is Not(X)." For example, John is Not(romantic). Here, one thinks of romantic associations and negat-ing each of them. Consequently, a boomerang effect might occur (Mayo et al., 2004). Because receivers activate during comprehension associations that are opposite to the intended meaning of the negation (e.g., romantic), in the long run receivers of the negated description might remember the description as if it had not been negated (e.g., "John is NOT(romantic)" is remembered as "John is romantic"). In short, whereas the fusion model of negation leads to reinterpretation (e.g., instead of thinking about not-intelligent, one thinks about stupid), the schema-plus-tag model, in contrast, resembles correction. One thinks about being romantic and adds a negation marker—a mental instruction to modify the judgment.

The schema-plus-tag encoding is particularly likely when one negates a unipolar description, namely, in the case of negation of messages that have no clear alternative schema. To illustrate, consider the message "John harassed the secretary." What is the alternative schema? Not harassing can take many forms, and no form is particularly dominant. Therefore, upon being asked to negate the message, receivers are likely to activate various associations of harassment and negate each of them. Consequently, they will actually have multiple associations and inferences related to harassment in mind. Negation markers often become dissociated from the core attribute. When this happens, John would be incorrectly remembered as someone who *did* harass the secretary. It is important to note that most negative behaviors are unipolar, as there is no clear-cut alterative schema to represent their negation.

Returning to the issue of discounting success, we can rephrase our question: Can receivers reinterpret the TBU information when they process the request to discount the TBD information? We have highlighted the challenge of reinterpretation which stems from bias in the interpretation of the TBU information that the TBD information induces. Our theoretical analysis suggests that reinterpretation can occur when an alternative interpretation of the TBD testimony is readily available. The research on negation suggests that an alternative schema might be activated when the receiver thinks about the discounting request according to a fusion model, that is, with a schema that can accommodate the alternative of the TBD information. Accordingly, we propose that discounting of messages that have clear opposites (bipolar messages) is more likely to be successful than discounting of messages that do not (unipolar messages). This is because thinking about the negation of the unipolar TBD message brings to mind inferences that are congruent with that message and incongruent with its negation. Therefore, in such cases the likelihood of reinterpretation of the TBU information during discounting becomes small.

The analysis of negation might have important implications for the well-known "sleeper effect" (Cook & Flay, 1978; Mazursky & Schul, 1988; Pratkanis, Greenwald, Leippe, & Baumgardner, 1988). Research shows that a persuasive message attributed to an untrustworthy source is completely discounted in the immediate judgment condition. However, when the impact of such a message is not measured immediately, the message is dissociated from the source and discounting fails. Our analysis suggests that when the message which comes from an untrustworthy source can be interpreted within a well-defined schema with an alternative meaning (as in the case of bipolar negations), a sleeper effect would be less likely to occur than when the untrustworthy source provides a unipolar message. In that case, the immediate negation of the message may still leave behind inferences associated with the message rather than its negation. The later dissociation of the message and the source, therefore, is likely to bring about a strong sleeper effect.

Finally, let us explicitly caution the reader that having the alternative schema is not a sufficient condition for successful discounting. Rather, we consider discounting as a struggle between competing schemata so that the schema that has an accessibility advantage at the time of judgment wins. To illustrate this struggle, we showed participants in a recent experiment two versions of the same face that differed in one feature: One version had narrow eyes while the other version had round eyes. Past research suggests that narrow (vs. round) eyes tend to be associated with untrustworthiness (Schul et al., 2004; Zebrowitz, 1997). After being shown one version of the face, participants were shown the other version and were told how the version of the face they were seeing differed from the original version and how it might affect their impressions from the faces. After a short filler task, all participants were shown one of the two versions of each face, that is, either the original or the modified. They were instructed to move forward if the *original* version was trustworthy and to move backward if the *original* face was untrustworthy. The findings revealed that participants' movements were dominated by the face they were seeing at the time of movement rather than by the original version of the face. This failure, however, was not a failure of memory. Participants were highly accurate when they were asked to identify which of the two faces was the original face. We interpret these findings to mean that when people are making judgments, they tend to rely on the most highly accessible schema information (in the above research, the face they see). Accordingly, in the battle between what they were seeing and what they knew, the former won. The lesson to those who wish to trigger an appropriate discounting is clear. It is not sufficient to highlight the nature of the bias that should be undone in order to undo the impact of a TBD testimony. Rather, the alternative has to be fully available and made at least as accessible as the TBD version.

Implicit and Explicit Senses of Truth

The outcome of the battle between the two interpretations of the TBU information, one that contains the meanings implied by the TBD and the other without it, might be influenced by feelings of truth with respect to the TBD version. We have already noted this when we discussed the importance of the reason given for discounting. That is, discounting is less successful when it is motivated by procedural concerns than when the reason is substantive (e.g., Kassin & Sommers, 1997; Saar & Schul, 1996; Sommers & Kassin, 2001). The procedural/substantive comparison highlights a reasoning process: Because a request on procedural grounds implies that the TBD testimony might be actually true, whereas a request on substantive grounds implies that it is false, substantive requests lead to more successful discounting. However, as the research described below suggests, the feeling of truth might impact the ease of discounting through non-reasoning processes as well.

Let us start with a simple example. Assume that you try to ascertain if Bob told you that you are self-centered. Did he actually do it? Is it your imagination? Research conducted within the source-monitoring framework (see review in Johnson, 2006; see also Johnson & Raye, 1981) suggests two routes through which questions of this sort might be answered. Truth might be uncovered by reasoning. You might consider the situation involving Bob's statement, the details of interaction, your reaction to Bob, and the provocation that triggered his unkind assertion. You may also try to compare this statement to Bob's past behaviors toward you and others and/or to the ways people other than Bob evaluate you. In a sense, you are trying to determine whether the assertion is reasonable within whatever else you know about the interaction. Research on reasoning (Evans, 2008; Johnson-Laird, 2006) and causal attribution (see Jaspars, Fincham, &

Hewstone, 1983) provides important insights into the systematic reasoning processes that allow people to evaluate the truth value.

Still, in trying to determine whether it is true that Bob made the assertion, you might also be influenced by the properties of the active representation, based on a toolbox of heuristic rules (Gigerenzer, 2001). These properties do not involve the content of the information. Instead, they are based on features of the representation that the mental system learns implicitly while processing externally generated facts and internally generated fiction. The source-monitoring model suggests that people capitalize on these properties in separating truth (memories reflecting facts) from falsehoods (internally generated memories). Thus, for example, rich memory representations, or an absence of cues about the operations that gave rise to the representation, might cause perceivers to err and evaluate an internally generated image as an actual or "real" experience (e.g., Johnson et al., 1993; Fiedler et al., 1996).

One of the strongest heuristic cues for inducing a bias of truth is the fluency of processing (e.g., Begg et al., 1992; Hansen et al., 2008; Henkel & Mattson, 2011; Winkielman et al., 2003). It has been repeatedly shown that other things being equal, statements which are easy to process (e.g., due to perceptual or conceptual facilitation) are rated as more true than less fluent statements. This effect ties well with the findings of Mayo and Schul discussed above. It is much easier to process the face you see than to reconstruct a face from memory. Such differences may make the seen face "more real," allowing respondents to react to it as if it were true.

The research briefly reviewed above indicates conditions and processes responsible for the failure of people to separate truth from fiction. Shidlovski, Schul, and Mayo (under review) have recently begun investigating a complementary question. Assume we focus only on events that have been recognized explicitly as false; do these events vary in their propensity to be felt as true? Stated differently, can an explicitly false event feel like a true event?

The short answer is "yes." Shidlovski et al. investigated imagined events and assessed their truth value both explicitly and implicitly. Explicit truth was assessed by judgments on a true/false continuum, as is typically done in research on veracity. Implicit truth was assessed in a variant of the autobiographical Implicit Association Test (see Sartori et al., 2008) that has been developed recently as a lie-detection tool. This procedure enabled us to test the extent to which it is easier to associate sentences about an imagined event with true sentences than with false ones and, therefore, the extent to which it is easier to associate the sentences about the imagined event with truth rather than with falsehood. Note that the implicit truth value (ITV) of events indicates the perceiver's tendency to categorize events that are implicitly true together with other events solely on the basis of their truth value. Without going into details, it was found that the imagined event (as well as an event that was actually experienced) gave rise to a higher ITV compared to a similar event that was not experienced or imagined.

Significantly, this effect occurred even when participants acknowledged explicitly that the imagined event was false. Finally, it was found that the influence of the imagination manipulation on the ITV is mediated by the vividness of the representation of that event.

At the most general level, the dissociation between implicit and explicit senses of truth implies that perceivers who cognize (explicitly) that a specific act was false might still be influenced by it as if it were true, and conversely, people who acknowledge something as true might be unable to accept it as such and react to it as if it were false. Accordingly, the distinction between the explicit and the implicit senses of truth may help us understand the huge array of phenomena in which people behave as if they are inconsistent or irrational.

In particular, discounting can fail because people may feel that the narrative which contains the TBD is implicitly truer, even though they acknowledge explicitly that the TBD is false. To cope with this, one can either make the alternative narrative—the one without the TBD—feel more implicitly true, or one can weaken the tendency of decision makers to rely on their feelings of implicit truth (e.g., Pham, Lee, & Stephen, 2012).

Trusting versus Distrusting States of Mind

Our introduction refers to the duality of motivations that participants in social interactions have: They need to cooperate with each other, and at the same time they need to protect themselves from being exploited by the other. The former need is associated with trust, the latter with distrust. In this section we propose that the mental states of trust and distrust trigger cognitive processes that have opposite implications for the success of discounting. Specifically, trust impairs successful discounting and distrust facilitates it.

Trust connotes safety and transparency; individuals believe there is nothing to be feared in transactions between themselves and others. Distrust, in contrast, is associated with the perception that the other person intends to mislead the perceiver (Schul, Mayo, Burnstein, & Yahalom, 2007). Therefore, unlike situations that trigger trust, when people distrust they attempt to search for signs that the other's behavior is departing from what is normal in the situation and prepare to act upon finding out that deception has occurred.

What are the implications of this for the thought processes triggered under trust and distrust? Other things being equal, when a state of trust is active, one tends to believe; to follow the immediate implications of the given information. As a result, information is encoded in an integrative fashion, whereby early information influences the narrative within which later information is being processed. Moreover, when they trust, perceivers do not question their gut reactions. They trust not only others but also their internal cues (Schul, Mayo, & Burnstein, 2008). Accordingly, trust might impair successful discounting for two main reasons. First, it enhances integrative encoding, which makes it difficult to separate the TBD from the TBU information. Second, it leads one to trust gut feelings and, in particular, the implicit sense of truth of the narrative that contains the TBD testimony.

In contrast, when a state of distrust is active, one tends to search for alternative interpretations of the given information. This spontaneous activity is a generalization of receivers' habitual responses to the situation of distrust, which is associated with concealment of truth (cf. Fein, 1996; Schul, Burnstein, & Bardi, 1996; Schul et al., 2008). Thus, in distrust, the mental system becomes more open to the possibility that the ordinary schema typically used to interpret the ongoing situation may need to be adjusted.

We investigated these conjectures by comparing contexts of trust versus distrust with respect to the associative links they activated in processing messages (Schul, Mayo, & Burnstein, 2004). It was predicted that when receivers trust, they bring to mind thoughts that are congruent with the message. In contrast, when receivers distrust, they tend to look for hidden or nonroutine associations, which are typically incongruent with the message. This prediction was tested using single words as messages and priming facilitation to indicate the associative structure activated in response to a prime word. We triggered trust or distrust by showing faces that were associated either with trust or with distrust. We found, as predicted, that the standard congruent priming effect was flipped in a distrust context: When a prime word appeared together with a face which signaled *distrust*, it facilitated associations that were *incongruent* with it. Thus, incongruent target words were facilitated more than congruent target words (e.g., "light" activated "night" more than "dark" activated "night"). The opposite pattern was found in the context of trust: Now the prime activated associations that were *congruent* with it (e.g., "dark" activated "night") more than associations that were incongruent with it (e.g., "light" activating "night"). This has been extended by Mayer and Mussweiler (2011) and generalized to nonverbal stimuli by Schul et al. (2008).

It should be noted that the states of trust and distrust differ not only in terms of their impact on encoding processes but also in the motivational forces that they trigger. Suspicion and distrust may raise the need to discern and identify falsehoods from truth, or, put differently, the concern for information accuracy. Accordingly, individuals concerned with information accuracy (i.e., under distrust) may seek to find out whether a witness has the ability and the incentive to report accurately or whether the testimony fits with other reports. Moreover, trust and distrust may also differ with respect to concerns for outcome accuracy. In particular, compared with conditions of trust, conditions of distrust might trigger a greater concern with judgment accuracy. Concern with judgment accuracy can lead to increased information search, to a stronger tendency to analyze the information systematically, and to a higher likelihood of being influenced by the diagnosticity of the information (Chaiken et al., 1989; Krug-lanski, 1989; Thompson et al., 1994).

The differences in encoding and in motivation suggest that a state of distrust (vs. trust) allows receivers to discount information more appropriately for several related reasons. First, during encoding, those who distrust may encode messages with incongruent as well as congruent associations. By creating narratives that contain multiple interpretations of the message, which either are consistent with the given information or are inconsistent with it, receivers can prepare for discounting. In this sense, a state of distrust might function as a trigger for spontaneous negation, whereby the given messages are encoded together with alternative schemata that entail their negations. Such encoding prevents the tight associative structure created by integrative encoding and therefore allows more successful discounting. Second, those who distrust might have higher motivation for veridical processing of messages and for arriving at unbiased judgments. Indeed, Schul, Burnstein, and Bardi (1996) showed that people who were warned about the possibility of being misled discounted information more successfully than those who were not warned (see also Ecker, Lewandowsky, & Tang, 2010).

Final Notes

More often than not, discounting fails. The mental system seems to prefer construction to reconstruction. Accordingly, as the literature on belief perseverance shows, interpretations tend to stick, even when the evidential basis of them is undermined (see Guenther & Alicke, 2008, for a fuller discussion). The research we described above suggests some reasons for this phenomenon. We tend to create mental structures that are well integrated, and in doing so we try to account for everything that we know. We are not very good with introspecting and assessing the impact of individual messages or cues on our judgments, and we often do not care that much about being accurate. When we do correct, however, we act superficially; namely, we use various shortcuts or heuristic rules in trying to remove a bias at a response level. Although such correction might provide decision makers with a sense of competence in being able to control biases, the biases may surface if measured by alternative means.

One may consider replacing the attempts at correction with attempts at reinterpretation. The research described above offers several ways in which reinterpretation might be achieved. However, it should be noted that attempts at reinterpretation may also induce a bias. The admonition to ignore the testimony about Bill's stupidity should not be taken as a license to assume Bill's smartness. Assuming the opposite might do as much injustice as assuming the original interpretation.

The challenge of proper discounting, therefore, involves finding a way to lead decision makers to think in a more complex way, to entertain both possibilities: Bill might be smart or stupid; one does not know. Such complex thinking requires one to delay arriving at closure, to be tolerant of ambiguities, and to resist resolving inconsistencies

(Kruglanski et al., 2006). In a world of information overload and high time pressure, habitual decision-making strategies tend to work in the opposite way, to lead to immediate resolution of inconsistencies and to early freezing of conclusions. No wonder, therefore, that discounting often fails.

Acknowledgments

Preparation of this manuscript was funded by the Israel Science Foundation (ISF) grants 124/08 (YS) and 594/12 (RM).

Note

1. As suggested later on, a state of distrust may lead receivers to encode information spontaneously as if it is TBD information.

References

Anderson, C. A., New, L. B., & Speer, J. R. (1985). Argument availability as a mediator of social theory perseverance. *Social Cognition, 3*, 235–249.

Begg, I. M., Anas, A., & Farinacci, S. (1992). Dissociation of processes in belief: Source recollection, statement familiarity, and the illusion of truth. *Journal of Experimental Psychology. General, 121*, 446–458.

Chaiken, S., Liberman, A., & Eagly, A. H. (1989). Heuristic and systematic processing within and beyond the persuasion context. In J. S. Uleman & J. A. Bargh (Eds.), *Unintended thought* (pp. 212–252). New York: Guilford Press.

Cook, T. D., & Flay, B. R. (1978). The persistence of experimentally induced attitude change. In L. Berkowitz (Ed.), *Advances in experimental social psychology* (Vol. 11, pp. 1–57). New York: Academic Press.

Demaine, L. J. (2008). In search of an anti-elephant: Confronting the human inability to forget inadmissible evidence. *George Mason Law Review, 16*, 99–140.

DePaulo, B. M., & Kashy, D. H. (1998). Everyday lies in close and casual relationships. *Journal of Personality and Social Psychology, 74*, 63–79.

DePaulo, B. M., Kashy, D. H., Kirkendol, S. E., Wyer, M. M., & Epstein, J. A. (1996). Lying in everyday life. *Journal of Personality and Social Psychology, 70*, 979–993.

Dyer, R. F., & Kuehl, P. G. (1978). A longitudinal study of corrective advertising. *Journal of Marketing Research, 15*, 39–48.

Eagly, A. H., Wood, W., & Chaiken, S. (1978). Causal inferences about communicators and their effect on opinion change. *Journal of Personality and Social Psychology, 36*, 424–435.

Ecker, U. K. H., Lewandowsky, S., Swire, B., & Chang, D. (2011). Correcting false information in memory: Manipulating the strength of misinformation encoding and its retraction. *Psychonomic Bulletin & Review, 18,* 570–578.

Ecker, U. K. H., Lewandowsky, S., & Tang, D. T. W. (2010). Explicit warnings reduce but do not eliminate the continued influence of misinformation. *Memory & Cognition, 38,* 1087–1100.

Elliott, R., Farrington, B., & Manheimer, H. (1988). Eyewitnesses credible and discredible. *Journal of Applied Social Psychology, 18,* 1411–1422.

Evans, J. St. B. T. (2008). Dual-processes accounts of reasoning. *Annual Review of Psychology, 59,* 255–278.

Fein, S. (1996). Effects of suspicion on attributional thinking and the correspondence bias. *Journal of Personality and Social Psychology, 70,* 1164–1184.

Feldman, R. S., Forrest, J. A., & Happ, B. R. (2002). Self-presentation and verbal deception: Do self-presenters lie more? *Basic and Applied Social Psychology, 24,* 163–170.

Fiedler, K., Walther, E., Armbruster, T., Fay, D., & Naumann, U. (1996). Do you really know what you have seen? Intrusion errors and presuppositions effects on constructive memory. *Journal of Experimental Social Psychology, 32,* 484–511.

Gigerenzer, G. (2001) The adaptive toolbox: Toward a Darwinian rationality. In J. A. French, A. C. Kamil, & D. W. Leger (Eds.), *Evolutionary psychology and motivation (Nebraska Symposium on Motivation,* Vol. 48, pp. 113–143). Lincoln: University of Nebraska Press.

Golding, J. M., & Hauselt, J. (1994). When instructions to forget become instructions to remember. *Personality and Social Psychology Bulletin, 20,* 178–183.

Grice, H. P. (1975). Logic and conversation. In P. Cole & J. Morgan (Eds.), *Syntax and semantics* (Vol. 3, pp. 43–58). New York: Academic Press.

Guenther, C. L., & Alicke, M. D. (2008). Self-enhancement and belief perseverance. *Journal of Experimental Social Psychology, 44,* 706–712.

Hansen, J., Dechêne, A., & Wänke, M. (2008). Discrepant fluency increases subjective truth. *Journal of Experimental Social Psychology, 44,* 687–691.

Hartwig, M., & Bond, C. F. (2011). Why do lie-catchers fail? A lens model meta-analysis of human lie judgments. *Psychological Bulletin, 137,* 643–659.

Hatvany, N., & Strack, F. (1980). The impact of a discredited key witness. *Journal of Applied Social Psychology, 10,* 490–509.

Henkel, L. A., & Mattson, M. E. (2011). Reading is believing: The truth effect and source credibility. *Consciousness and Cognition, 11,* 1705–1721.

Jaspars, J., Fincham, F., & Hewstone, M. (Eds.). (1983). *Attribution theory and research: Conceptual, developmental and social dimensions.* London: Academic Press.

Johnson, M. K. (2006). Memory and reality. *American Psychologist, 61,* 760–771.

Johnson, M. K., Hashtroudi, S., & Lindsay, D. S. (1993). Source monitoring. *Psychological Bulletin*, *114*, 3–28.

Johnson, M. K., & Raye, C. L. (1981). Reality monitoring. *Psychological Review*, *88*, 67–85.

Johnson-Laird, P. N. (2006). *How we reason*. Oxford, England: Oxford University Press.

Kassin, S. M., & Sommers, S. R. (1997). Inadmissible testimony, instructions to disregard, and the jury: Substantive versus procedural considerations. *Personality and Social Psychology Bulletin*, *23*, 1046–1055.

Kassin, S. M., & Wrightsman, L. S. (1980). Prior confessions and mock-jury verdicts. *Journal of Applied Social Psychology*, *10*, 133–146.

Kassin, S. M., & Wrightsman, L. S. (1981). Coerced confessions, judicial instruction, and mock juror verdicts. *Journal of Applied Social Psychology*, *11*, 489–506.

Kruglanski, A. W. (1989). The psychology of being "right": On the problem of accuracy in social perception and cognition. *Psychological Bulletin*, *106*, 395–409.

Kruglanski, A. W., Pierro, A., Manetti, L., & DeGrada, E. (2006). Groups as epistemic providers: Need for closure and the unfolding of group centrism. *Psychological Review*, *113*, 84–100.

Lerner, J. S., & Tetlock, P. E. (1999). Accounting for the effects of accountability. *Psychological Bulletin*, *125*, 255–275.

Lerner, J. S., & Tetlock, P. E. (2003). Bridging individual, interpersonal, and institutional approaches to judgment and choice: The impact of accountability on cognitive bias. In S. Schneider & J. Shanteau (Eds.), *Emerging perspectives on judgment and decision research* (pp. 431–457). Cambridge, England: Cambridge University Press.

Martin, L. L., Seta, J. J., & Crelia, R. A. (1990). Assimilation and contrast as a function of people's willingness and ability to expend effort in forming an impression. *Journal of Personality and Social Psychology*, *59*, 27–37.

Mayer, J., & Mussweiler, T. (2011). Suspicious spirits, flexible minds: When distrust enhances creativity. *Journal of Personality and Social Psychology*, *101*, 1262–1277.

Mayo, R., Schul, Y., & Burnstein, E. (2004). "I am not guilty" versus "I am innocent": Successful negation may depend on the schema used for its encoding. *Journal of Experimental Social Psychology*, *40*, 433–449.

Mazursky, D., & Schul, Y. (1988). The effects of advertisement encoding on the failure to discount information: Implications for the sleeper effect. *Journal of Consumer Research*, *15*, 24–36.

Pham, M. T., Lee, L., & Stephen, A. T. (2012). Feeling the future: The emotional oracle effect. *Journal of Consumer Research*, *39*, 461–477.

Pratkanis, A. R., Greenwald, A. G., Leippe, M. R., & Baumgardner, M. H. (1988). In search of a reliable persuasion effect: III. The sleeper effect is dead. Long live the sleeper effect. *Journal of Personality and Social Psychology*, *54*, 203–218.

Prendergast, G., Liu, P. Y., & Poon, D. T. Y. (2009). A Hong Kong study of advertising credibility. *Journal of Consumer Marketing, 26*, 320–329.

Saar, Y., & Schul, Y. (1996). The effect of procedural versus substantive instructions to disregard information. Unpublished manuscript.

Sartori, G., Agosta, S., Zogmaister, C., Ferrara, S. D., & Castiello, U. (2008). How to accurately detect autobiographical events. *Psychological Science, 19*, 772–780.

Schul, Y. (1993). When warning succeeds: The effect of warning on success of ignoring invalid information. *Journal of Experimental Social Psychology, 29*, 42–62.

Schul, Y., & Burnstein, E. (1985). When discounting fails: Conditions under which individuals use discredited information in making a judgment. *Journal of Personality and Social Psychology, 49*, 894–903.

Schul, Y., & Burnstein, E. (1998). Suspicion and discounting: Ignoring invalid information in an uncertain environment. In J. M. Golding & C. MacLeod (Eds.), *Intentional forgetting: Interdisciplinary approaches* (pp. 321–348). Mahwah, NJ: Lawrence Erlbaum Associates.

Schul, Y., Burnstein, E., & Bardi, A. (1996). Dealing with deceptions that are difficult to detect: Encoding and judgment as a function of preparing to receive invalid information. *Journal of Experimental Social Psychology, 32*, 228–253.

Schul, Y., Burnstein, E., & Martinez, J. (1983). The informational basis of social judgments: Under what conditions are inconsistent trait descriptions processed as easily as consistent ones? *European Journal of Social Psychology, 13*, 143–151.

Schul, Y., & Goren, H. (1997). When strong evidence has less impact than weak evidence: Bias, adjustment, and instructions to ignore. *Social Cognition, 15*, 133–155.

Schul, Y., & Manzury, F. (1990). The effect of type of encoding and strength of discounting appeal on the success of ignoring an invalid testimony. *European Journal of Social Psychology, 20*, 337–349.

Schul, Y., & Mayo, R. (1999). Two sources are better than one: The effects of ignoring one message on using a different message from the same source. *Journal of Experimental Social Psychology, 35*, 327–345.

Schul, Y., Mayo, R., & Burnstein, E. (2004). Encoding under trust and distrust: The spontaneous activation of incongruent cognitions. *Journal of Personality and Social Psychology, 86*, 668–679.

Schul, Y., Mayo, R., & Burnstein, E. (2008). The value of distrust. *Journal of Experimental Social Psychology, 44*, 1293–1302.

Schul, Y., Mayo, R., Burnstein, E., & Yahalom, N. (2007). How people cope with uncertainty due to chance or deception. *Journal of Experimental Social Psychology, 43*, 91–103.

Schul, Y., & Mazursky, D. (1990). Conditions facilitating successful discounting in consumer decision making: Type of discounting cue, message encoding, and kind of judgment. *Journal of Consumer Research, 16*, 442–451.

Schwarz, N., Sanna, L., Skurnik, I., & Yoon, C. (2007). Metacognitive experiences and the intricacies of setting people straight: Implications for debiasing and public information campaigns. *Advances in Experimental Social Psychology*, *39*, 127–161.

Schyns, P., & Koop, C. (2010). Political distrust and social capital in Europe and the USA. *Social Indicators Research*, *96*, 145–167.

Shidlovski, D., Schul, Y., & Mayo, R. (under review). If I can imagine it, then it happened: The implicit truth value of imaginary representations.

Sommers, S. R., & Kassin, S. (2001). On the many impacts of inadmissible testimony: Selective compliance, need for cognition, and the overcorrection bias. *Personality and Social Psychology Bulletin*, *26*, 1368–1377.

Steblay, N., Hosch, H. M., Culhane, S. E., & McWethy, A. (2006). The impact on juror verdicts of judicial instruction to disregard inadmissible evidence: A meta-analysis. *Law and Human Behavior*, *30*, 469–542.

Strack, F., & Hannover, B. (1996). Awareness of influence as a precondition for implementing correctional goals. In P. M. Gollwitzer & J. A. Bargh (Eds.), *The psychology of action: Linking motivation and cognition to behavior* (pp. 579–596). New York: Guilford Press.

Thompson, E. P., Roman, R. J., Moskowitz, G. B., Chaiken, S., & Bargh, J. A. (1994). Accuracy motivation attenuates covert priming: The systematic reprocessing of social information. *Journal of Personality and Social Psychology*, *66*, 474–489.

Thompson, W. C., Fong, G. T., & Rosenhan, D. L. (1981). Inadmissible evidence and juror verdicts. *Journal of Personality and Social Psychology*, *40*, 453–463.

Wenzlaff, R. M., & Wegner, D. M. (2000). Thought suppression. In S. T. Fiske (Ed.), *Annual review of psychology* (Vol. 51, pp. 59–91). Palo Alto, CA: Annual Reviews.

Wilson, T. D., & Brekke, N. (1994). Mental contamination and mental correction: Unwanted influences on judgments and evaluations. *Psychological Bulletin*, *116*, 117–142.

Winkielman, P., Schwarz, N., Fazendeiro, T., & Reber, R. (2003). The hedonic marking of processing fluency: Implications for evaluative judgment. In J. Musch & K. C. Klauer (Eds.), *The psychology of evaluation: Affective processes in cognition and emotion* (pp. 189–217). Mahwah, NJ: Lawrence Erlbaum Associates.

Wolf, S., & Montgomery, D. A. (1977). Effects of inadmissible evidence and level of judicial admonishment to disregard on the judgment of mock jurors. *Journal of Applied Social Psychology*, *7*, 205–219.

Zebrowitz, L. A. (1997). *Reading faces: Window to the soul?* Boulder, CO: Westview Press.

11   The Ambivalent Effect of Focus on Updating Mental Representations

Herre van Oostendorp

Common to most theoretical approaches to text comprehension is that readers construct a representation of incoming text information at different levels: a representation of the exact wording of the text (surface representation), a propositional representation of the text's meaning (textbase), and a model of the situation described by the text (situation model; van Dijk & Kintsch, 1983; Kintsch, 1998). When a text is read, these construction processes have to be synchronized as they proceed in a dynamic way. Readers appear to initiate a new structure when a new episode begins (global updating) and then map new information incrementally throughout the episode (incremental or local updating) (Kurby & Zacks, 2012). This chapter describes research on the integration or mapping of new information onto the existing representation in working memory and subsequent storage in episodic memory (Albrecht & O'Brien, 1993). We will mainly be concerned with the processing of information that is *new and discrepant* compared to what was already known to the reader on a situation-model level. This process is called updating.

Several types of situation-model updating are distinguished by Dutke et al. (2010): (1) constraint-driven updating, (2) change-driven updating, and (3) inconsistency-driven updating. Constraint-driven updating concerns the situation where new incoming information constrains the situation model. For example, the sentence "Tom is sitting next to Jim" does not specify whether Tom is sitting on the right or left of Jim.

Encountering subsequent information that further specifies the described situation may require updating of the original situation model, for example, when reading a later sentence "Tom is turning rightward to look at Jim" (Dutke et al., 2010). Change-driven updating corresponds to updating due to explicit changes in the current situation described by the text. For instance in news reports, developments can describe a situation in the world, for example, the state of affairs in "Somalia," and the current model of the situation in "Somalia" may thus demand a modification of the old situation model (van Oostendorp, 1996; van Oostendorp, Otéro, & Campanario, 2002). Inconsistency-driven updating relates to situations in which later text information is introduced that is inconsistent with the model constructed so far. For instance, in the context of a text about a chemical method to harden the strength of ceramic materials, it might first be mentioned in the text that "the process takes some days," but later on that "the process can be carried out in a few minutes" (cf. van Oostendorp, 2002).

I will focus on the latter two classes of problems (change-driven and inconsistency-driven updating) because they represent a strict form of updating. In the first part of the text, a particular situation with its characteristics is introduced. In a second part (later in the text or in a subsequent text) some of the characteristics of the original situation are changed. The issue is how both situations are encoded and what the nature of the final representation might be. Here I focus on situations in which new information is introduced that deviates in some way from previously encountered information. Specifically, my first aim is to gain more insight into the strategies that readers apply toward encoding the new discrepant information, that is, information that deviates from information read before on a situation-model level. My second goal is to more closely examine the mental representation that remains in episodic memory after processing the new discrepant information. I will investigate what happens with the central part of the representation, particularly when it is relevant to the focus of reading. However, I will first briefly describe some background work on updating of mental representations.

Updating of Mental Representations

During reading, readers can construct a textbase and situation model as indicated above. Regarding the textbase construction, readers monitor for local and global coherence. In the research literature there has been much debate on the degree to which these coherence criteria are always monitored and achieved. For instance, Graesser, Singer, and Trabasso (1994) assume that readers construct a coherent representation on a local level and also on a global level even when there is no break in local coherence. In opposition, McKoon and Ratcliff (1992) take a more minimalist position: They assume that connections needed for maintaining global coherence are only made when local coherence fails. This issue is not pursued further here, except to mention that an important moderating role is likely determined by the coherence standards that readers maintain during reading on a textbase level (van den Broek, Virtue, Everson, Tzeng, & Sung, 2002; van Oostendorp, 1994).

Regarding the construction of a situation model and the mapping or integrating of new information onto the existing model, similar processes contributing to local and global coherence have been assumed. For instance Albrecht and O'Brien's (1993) account of updating a situation model distinguishes between establishing local and global coherence when reading text information that is inconsistent with information presented earlier. The difference between local and global coherence is here mainly a matter of whether preceding information is still in working memory (local), or presumably no longer in working memory (global), having been presented in more distant sections of text. Albrecht and O'Brien showed that readers indeed try to build a single, locally and globally coherent representation. They demonstrated this on the basis of reading times and free recall data. For the current discussion, it is sufficient to note that their results did not demonstrate that readers actually resolved global inconsistencies that were encountered. Furthermore, their results seem to reflect mainly differences on a (local and global) textbase level. Thus, the results on this matter did not directly relate to the issue of the extent of updating on a situation-model level.

We cannot a priori assume that situation-model effects will be similar to those found on a textbase level. For instance, Tapiero and Otéro (1999) showed that the effect of contradictions on recall was different from their effect on answers to inference questions probing the situation model that readers had created. And inference questions seem to be necessary to probe situational representations as opposed to textbase representations (Fletcher & Chrysler, 1990). In fact, across a number of studies, readers do not differ in free recall after reading contradictions but differ in their performance on inference questions after reading new information that is discrepant with old information. Readers given old information, as well as new but discrepant information appearing later in the text, hold on more strongly to the old information and use less new information than do control readers who only receive new information (Blanc et al., 2008, 2011; Johnson & Seifert, 1993, 1994, 1999; van Oostendorp & Bonebakker, 1999, Wilkes & Leatherbarrow, 1988; Wilkes & Reynolds, 1999). All of these studies demonstrate that updating does not seem to occur on a situation-model level even if the new discrepant information is plausible.

The updating process seems also to be affected by the level of certainty with which information is presented. For example, in previous work, the certainty of old information was manipulated to be described as certain, suspected, or not presented (control) at all (Blanc et al., 2011). Updating appeared to be specifically sensitive to the certainty of old information. When the old information was presented as certain, participants' reading times were slowed when they encountered the new discrepant information, and their recall of the old information also improved. These results suggest that the more certain the old information is represented in memory, the more difficult the updating process.

In a study I did some years ago (van Oostendorp, 1996), I found a similar pattern of results, although that project was not concerned with the certainty of information but rather with the relevance of information to the situation described. I had participants read a news report about a military intervention in Somalia that actually occurred (the U.S. operation "Restore Hope") and presented participants with a second, related text some time later. This second text contained *transformations* of facts mentioned in the first text. These transformations were changes of the original information following developments in the real world, so they included changes in the situation described by the text that should initiate a change-driven updating (cf. Dutke et al., 2010). For example the first text mentioned that "...*operation Restore Hope began under the supreme command of the United States.*" In the second text the command structure of the operation had been changed: "... *the United Nations took over command in Somalia.*" Note here that the current command is in hands of the United Nations (UN) and no longer in the hands of the United States. A correct updating of the situation model necessitates that the old information is replaced by new information or perhaps pushed into the background. After reading each text, participants received an inference judgment task. For instance, after reading the second text, participants judged the test item "*The US troops operate under the UN-flag*" as true or false. Readers were asked to judge the accuracy of the presented statements in light of the text they had just read. In a separate norming study, the relevance or importance of items to the situation described by the texts was determined. Subjects indicated relevance using a 5-point rating scale with the texts available during judgments. On the basis of the median judgment, items were divided into (eight) low- and (eight) high-relevant inference items.

Because I was interested in participants' updating of their mental representations after reading the first text, I examined first how well the original model was represented, given that based on a strict definition of updating the original information has to be correctly represented in the first place. Subsequently, performance on the second inference task was analyzed given that participants correctly knew the corresponding information in the first text. It appeared in this conditional analysis that the original model strength (measured on the basis of the score on the first test) had a significant influence on updating, that is, on performance on the second test. Participants with a strong original model were more likely to update than were participants with a weak original model. Thus, in general, we might expect that participants with more background knowledge are able to better update, that is, better incorporate new information. This result might seem to be contradictory to results of, for instance, Johnson and Seifert (1993), which indicate that updating of an old model is difficult in light of a new one. However, I think it is not. Updating is difficult but still easier for participants who have a well-defined original model available. The better represented variables and features are in memory, characterizing a better model, the easier it is in general to replace them with new values and to update.

More importantly, it also appeared that changes that were *more important*, as in more relevant to the situation described, were *less* updated than were less important transformations (see figure 11.1). The interaction of model strength and relevance was not significant ($p > .05$).

It is worthwhile to note that I found this effect of relevance in two studies with different materials (for details, see van Oostendorp, 1996). The difficulty in updating highly relevant information could be caused by the centrality of that information in the situation model. Highly relevant information has more or stronger links in the

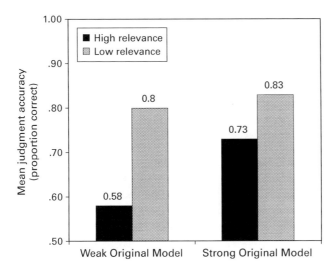

Figure 11.1
Mean judgment accuracy on the second test.

model, which would make the model more difficult to update or would necessitate building a completely new model. These results confirm the pattern of results Blanc et al. (2011) previously found. Thus, it seems that the central part of a situation model may be less easily updated than the peripheral parts. This result also aligns with what Chinn and Brewer (1993) called, in their work on the domain of science and the evolution of theories, "peripheral theory change." This involves a repair strategy to account for anomalous data by reinterpreting the data and making peripheral changes to the theory. Central propositions cannot easily be altered without scrapping the whole theory (or situation model) while peripheral propositions can be altered while preserving the kernel. Central propositions likely align with highly relevant information while peripheral propositions align with less relevant details.

Explanations for the Difficulties in Updating

One can envision a number of reasons that readers might find it difficult to update their initially constructed representations rather than fully taking into account new, discrepant information. Firstly, readers tend to take in new information more superficially; in other words, they sometimes "skip" the new information because they (erroneously) think that they already possess relevant information. I will call this the *skipping hypothesis*. This strategy more or less matches a strategy identified by Chinn and Brewer (1993) termed "ignoring the data." Alternatively, it may be that readers "reject" the modifications contained in new information—for instance, because information that constitutes the central part of their situation model is hard to change even if the text requires a change. In other words, readers may actively hold on to their first perspective once it is established. In this case readers have processed the discrepancy but reject it. I will refer to this explanation as the *rejection hypothesis*. The study presented next attempts to provide direct evidence for these two explanations.

Think-Aloud Experiment: How Do Readers Process New, Discrepant Information?

The present study examines the occurrence of skipping or rejection processes by asking participants to think aloud while reading (Suh & Trabasso, 1993; Trabasso, Suh, Payton & Jain, 1995). Such a procedure affords opportunities to examine the mental operations participants perform while processing information. An important assumption is that their utterances can provide valid insight into what participants are doing during reading (Suh & Trabasso, 1993; Trabasso, Suh, Payton, & Jain, 1995; and see van Soomeren, Barnard, & Sandberg, 1994, for an extensive guide for using the think-aloud method). The focus of this study was on the way readers process the transformations occurring in the second text of the two Somalia reports described above.

Method
As described above, the second text contained 16 transformations of facts that were mentioned in the first text. The texts were presented in fragments of one to three sentences on separate pages in a booklet. Twenty-four undergraduates from Utrecht University read the text at their own reading speed. They were asked to talk aloud about their understanding of the sentences in the context of the story. The resulting protocols were analyzed with the same method of coding as used by Suh and Trabasso (1993) and Trabasso, Suh, Payton, and Jain (1995). The think-aloud protocols were scored in terms of occurrences of the (six) categories described below, particularly at the locations of the (16) transformation sentences. After reading each text, participants had to indicate on an inference judgment task whether a statement related to the transformative information, had it been accurately updated, was true or not.

Hypotheses
This study examined whether a low degree of updating is caused by superficial reading ("skipping") *or* by a refusal to change the model through rejection of the information provided in the second text ("rejecting"). If superficial processing (skipping) is the cause of poor updating, then we might expect that think-aloud activities including "incomplete repetitions," "incorrect repetitions," and "careless metacomments" will be of great importance (and will occur frequently). (See also table 11.1 for examples.) If skipping occurs, we might expect to observe a negative relation between the frequency of these activities and test performance (i.e., specifically high frequency and low test performance). If, however, active refusal (rejecting) is the cause of poor updating, then

Table 11.1
Examples of the different types of activities identified for the skipping and rejection categories

Category	Activity	Example
Skipping	Incomplete repetition	"One year after the invasion on the beach of Mogadishu…" (The text mentions here "More than a year after the invasion of American soldiers on the beach of Mogadishu…")
Skipping	Incorrect repetition	"After the invasion of the international force on the beach …" (The text mentions here "More than a year after the invasion of American soldiers on the beach of Mogadishu…")
Skipping	Careless metacomment	"I don't care" etc.
Rejection	Rejecting comment	"That is not true" etc.
Rejection	Questioning own understanding	"Did I see that right?"
Rejection	Retrieval from previous text	"Before it was mentioned that the operation was under American command…" (Information from the first text is mentioned.)

we might expect to see think-aloud activities including "rejecting comments," "questioning own understanding," and "retrieval from previous text" reflecting an active and opposing point of view (for details, see van Oostendorp, 2001). These activities would therefore be negatively related to test performance.

Results and Conclusion
A multiple linear regression between the observed frequencies on the above-mentioned six variables (activities or utterances that reflect certain mental operations) and test performance showed that these variables together had a significant relationship with test performance: Multiple $R = 0.76$, or 57% explained variance of test performance, $F(5, 18) = 4.78$, $p < 0.01$. Furthermore, skipping variables appeared to be better predictors of test performance than rejection variables. In particular, the careless-metacomments activity was significantly related to test performance ($Beta = -0.46$, $p < 0.05$). Some of the rejection variables also had significant Beta weights, but in an unexpected positive direction, specifically involving the activities of questioning own understanding ($Beta = 0.44$, $p < 0.05$) and retrieval from previous text ($Beta = 0.35$, $p < 0.06$). These mental operations are indeed relevant for performance, but instead of hurting performance they contribute to it. A higher frequency of these mental operations thus corresponds to a better performance and could be better interpreted as "actively trying to integrate" the transformative information into the situation model.

All in all, these results indicate that skipping of transformations rather than rejecting them led to low performance on the judgment test. Skipping could thus be a main contributor of failing to update, perhaps because readers erroneously think they already know the information that is being communicated.

The Effect of Focus on Updating Mental Representations

Previously I suggested that central parts of a mental representation are more difficult to update as compared to peripheral parts (Chinn & Brewer, 1993; Blanc et al., 2011). Wilkes and Leatherbarrow (1988) offered a similar suggestion, examining the role of the relevance of information in updating. Their results showed that readers tend to hold on to old, discredited information if that information is highly relevant to a change in the situation. Recall that the earlier presented Somalia study (van Oostendorp, 1996) directly supported this idea. Relevance here reflected the importance of the information with respect to the situation, which can be coupled with the finding that readers exhibit a tendency to skip discrepant new, central information. Despite these clear findings, though, we do not know what might occur when information is also important from the viewpoint of the reader, rather than just from importance *within* the text. Is information also less likely to be updated when it corresponds to a reader's focus?

In the next study, I examined whether the central part of a mental representation is less likely to be updated when new, discrepant information is in focus—that is, relevant to the perspective of the reader. Focus was manipulated by letting readers compare one text with another along some dimension. A control, nonfocus reading group received no specific reading instruction. A second aspect that I wanted to study here was the nature of the mental representation itself. By examining the episodic network of concepts that is constructed after reading the texts, I hoped to derive more direct evidence of the shift or constancy of the structure of the mental representation, as an indication of the degree of updating.

Assessing the Structure of the Mental Representation

I examined the change or updating of the mental representation based on a *cued association* task, a method introduced by Ferstl and Kintsch (1999). The basic assumption underlying this task is that background knowledge as well as text memory is represented in the form of associative networks (Kintsch, 1998). The nodes in these networks correspond to concepts or propositions whereas the associative links connecting them are directed and vary in strength. With the cued association task, participants are presented with a keyword (a "cue") and are asked to provide an association to it. The number of times a keyword is given as a response to another keyword is used as a measure of relatedness between the two words. Based on these data, an asymmetrical proximity matrix is calculated for each participant, which is formally equivalent to a network structure. The keywords represent the nodes, and the strengths of links are determined by their response order, that is, the sequence of responding to a keyword.

Table 11.2

Example association matrices A and B for four keywords for one participant

Keyword	Matrix A					Matrix B				
	1	2	3	4	Out-degree	1	2	3	4	Out-degree
1	—	1	.5	.33	1.83	—	1	.5	.33	1.83
2	.5	—	.33	0	.83	1	—	.5	.33	1.83
3	.33	0	—	0	.33	.5	.33	—	0	.83
4	0	.33	0	—	.33	.5	0	0	—	.5
In-degree	.83	1.33	.83	.33	3.32	2	1.33	1	.66	4.99

Note. Matrix A is the matrix constructed, based on the first cued association task, before the participant read the target (second) text; matrix B is the matrix constructed, based on the second cued association task, after the participant read the target (second) text.

The participants in this study received a list of 64 keywords and were instructed to write down next to each word the three words that first came to mind. Similar to Ferstl and Kintsch (1999), the first answer to a keyword received a connection strength of 1, the second one mentioned received one half, and the third one received one third. Before and after reading the target text, the cued association task was presented. Table 11.2 shows a simple example of two matrices, matrix A before reading the target text and matrix B after reading the target text, for 4 keywords of one participant. For instance, stimulus keyword 1 receives keyword 2 as first association (strength 1), keyword 3 as second association (strength 0.5), and keyword 4 as third association (strength 0.33), and so on.

In these network structures it is possible to discern concepts that are highly related to each other, as well as concepts that are less strongly related. Useful notions for measures of centrality include the *in-degree* and *out-degree* of concepts, that is, the summation of all links going *into* a node or *out of* a node, respectively (see Ferstl & Kintsch, 1999). The in-degree of a word corresponds roughly to a measure of how often a word was mentioned as an answer to any keyword (in-degree $(k) = \Sigma_i a_{ik}$) while the out-degree reflects the number of answers to this word from the list of selected keywords (out-degree $(k) = \Sigma_j a_{kj}$). The first (in-degree) indicates how many other concepts point to a certain concept and how strongly they do so while the second (out-degree) reflects the number and strength of links departing from this concept. Table 11.2 also shows a simple example of the overall connection strengths, in terms of in-degrees and out-degrees, for 4 keywords from one participant.

Both matrices also show the overall connection strengths between keywords that were given as stimuli *and* keywords given as responses; for example, the in-degree of keyword 1 = 0.83, and the out-degree = 1.83 in matrix A. In this example, keywords

1 and 2 are more strongly connected to other keywords than are keywords 3 and 4 because the in- and out-degrees for keywords 1 and 2 are higher than for keywords 3 and 4.

I focused on the central parts of the representation—that is, the areas with the highest inner cohesion in the networks, having the highest number of links between selected concepts based on the highest in-degrees and out-degrees. Subsequently I analyzed the *similarity* of the central parts of the networks of the participants in the focus group before and after reading the target text and compared that with the similarity for participants in the nonfocus group. Similarity scores were calculated for each participant, defined as the inner products between two matrices A (the network before reading the second text) and B (the network after reading the second text), and normalized so that the range fell between 0 (not sharing any links) and 1 (for identical networks). Consider the overlap between matrix A and matrix B, $(A, B) = 2\Sigma(a_{ij} b_{ij})/(\Sigma a_{ij}^2 + \Sigma b_{ij}^2)$, with A as the association matrix that was constructed at the first cued association task, and B as the second matrix (see table 11.2). For this formula, a_{ij} = link strength a in matrix A between keyword i and j, and b_{ij} = link strength b in matrix B between keyword i and j (see Goldsmith & Davenport, 1990; Ferstl & Kintsch, 1999, for a discussion on similarity measures between matrices). In the above example the overlap between matrix A and B can be computed based on the 12 inner products; applying the formula to the example in table 11.2, a_{21} = .5 (meaning that on stimulus keyword 2 the response keyword 1 came as second response (0.5) at the first cued association task); and b_{21} = 1 (meaning that on keyword 1 as stimulus, keyword 2 came as the first response at the second cued association task), with the inner product $a_{21}b_{21} = 0.5 \times 1 = 0.5$ and so forth for the other 11 inner products. The overlap in this artificial case is 0.83.

Similarity measures have proven to be predictive of performance in a variety of domains such as with naval decision tasks (Kraiger et al., 1995), learning statistics (Goldsmith et al., 1991), learning a computer programming language (Trumpower et al., 2010), and transfer after learning a complex skill in a video game (Day et al., 2001). Previously, in the domain of learning a complex skill such as doing a medical triage in the context of a serious game, structural assessment of mental representations has been usefully applied (Wouters, van der Spek, & van Oostendorp, 2011). This work showed that similarity measures using a Pathfinder algorithm generated useful information, for example, that the representations of novice learners became more similar to an expert referent structure after playing the game.

Finally, Ferstl and Kintsch (1999) successfully used the *network size* of each reader as an indication of the amount of his or her background knowledge. I also used network size as an index of prior knowledge and computed for this purpose the sum of all the link strengths between keywords in the first association matrix (Netsize (A) = $\Sigma_{ij}a_{ij}$). In other words, the more answers a reader produced consisting of keywords from the list presented before reading the target text, the greater the network (more and higher values present in the cells of the matrix). In the above example, for table 11.2, in the first matrix the network size for this person would be 3.32, and in the second matrix 4.99. In other words, more answers from the list, and higher in order, were given after reading the target text than before reading it.

Hypotheses

In line with the previously mentioned studies (Blanc et al., 2011; van Oostendorp, 1996; Wilkes & Leatherbarrow, 1988), I hypothesized that the central part of the mental representation would be *less* likely to be updated when that information is *in reader focus and is corrected* by text information, as compared to when the information is not in focus.

Because we saw in the Somalia study that prior knowledge is a relevant variable to updating, I also included network size as an assessment of prior knowledge. I predicted that the overlap of the central part of the network structures after reading both texts would be *higher* when this representation is in focus than when it is not in focus. Thus, focus should lead to less updating. Furthermore, I expected that readers with low prior knowledge would update less. This would be in line with the results of the previously mentioned Somalia study and also with the results of Kintsch and Franzke (1995), who showed that the availability of an appropriate situation model positively influences the application of it when reading new information.

Method

Participants and Materials   Forty Utrecht University students received two related texts about the Spanish terrorist movement ETA. ETA is an acronym for "Euskadi Ta Askatasuna," which means "Basque Homeland and Freedom." It was an armed Basque separatist militant movement and a very active group in Spain some years ago. The second text indicating "ETA not responsible for attacks" contained a number of important changes or corrections of facts as compared to the first ETA text which indicated "ETA renews attacks after surge of arrests." The texts were made up specifically for this study using information from a number of different news sources. A number of changes were inserted in the second ETA text, including that the responsibility for a recent attack was not associated with the ETA anymore but rather with the son-in-law of a murdered police officer and so on. See table 11.3 for a number of example sentences from both ETA texts.

Each text was presented as a typical newspaper article and also had the layout of a newspaper contribution (about 500 words each). Both texts contained two kinds of information. First, they contained information about attacks and violence. I categorized this information as *action concepts*. Secondly, they contained information about political standpoints and reactions, which we categorized as *political concepts*. Focus was introduced by first providing the focus group with a text about the Irish terrorist movement IRA, also containing political information and thus focusing on political

Table 11.3

Example sentences from both ETA texts (originally in Dutch)

ETA Text 1 (500 words)

ETA renews attacks after surge of arrests
From our correspondent Cees Zoon
Madrid

....Spanish authorities claim that the new murders are the reaction of ETA on the recent series of arrests....

....The top of the ETA would have given the signal to reinforce attacks to members of city councils of the party in office, the *Partido Popular*....

ETA Text 2 (500 words)

ETA not responsible for attacks
From our correspondent Jop Cortez
Barcelona

....Son-in-law of the killed police officer now held responsible....

....ETA denies starting a new increase of violence as was suggested before....

....ETA suspects a media campaign of the Spanish government against the ETA in order to obstruct the peace process....

---

concepts. Participants in the focus condition were asked to compare the political situations in Northern Ireland and Spain, thus bringing the political information to the foreground. Participants in the nonfocus (control) group received a neutral text about Spain without any specific reading instructions. After reading this text, participants received the first and second ETA text. They read these texts at their own pace (for a maximum of 10 minutes per text) and were instructed to read the articles as they would normally read a newspaper article.

Before and after reading the second ETA text, the cued association task was presented. Participants read a list of 64 keywords twice and were instructed to write down next to each word one, two, or three words that first came to mind. The list contained 20 words that were important to the domain based on a pilot study but were not mentioned in the text, with the other 44 keywords derived from the text. The first answer to a keyword received a connection strength of 1, the second one mentioned received one half, and the third received one third, at least when the answers consisted of keywords from the list. Synonyms were similarly counted. Answers that did not come from the list were ignored. I focused on the central part of the representations, that is, the areas with the highest inner cohesion. The procedure to select these was based on (20) concepts with the highest in-degrees and out-degrees from and to other selected concepts, respectively, common to both conditions. Examples of the action concepts were "violence," "attack," and "murder"; examples of the political concepts were "declaration," "peace plan," and "conflict." The in- and out-degrees are based on the summation of all the links going *into* a node or *out of* a node, respectively. So, in fact, I selected a specific area, that is, the area with the highest cohesion.

To assess the amount of updating, that is, the degree of change in the networks, I computed the overlap of these central parts of the networks for the participants in the focus group before and after reading the second ETA text. I compared that with similarity (or overlap) with the nonfocus group. A high degree of similarity corresponds, thus, to a low degree of updating. In this case the network before corresponds to a high degree with the network after reading the second ETA text.

At the end of the session, participants were presented with textbase-oriented true/false recognition questions. The purpose of including this test was to be able to make a distinction between updating on a situation-model level and corrections on a textbase level (see Tapiero & Otéro, 1999).

Results

Because I hypothesized that the extent of updating would also be influenced by the background knowledge of the participant, in addition to the effect of focus on updating, I first determined the *network size* of each reader on the first cued association task that was presented before reading the second ETA text. Based on the mean score, I distinguished participants with an initially small and initially large network size.

A 2×2 analysis of variance (with focus and initial network size as between-subjects factors) on the updating (i.e., $1 -$ overlap) scores of the central parts of the networks showed a significant interaction effect, $F(1, 37) = 4.04$, $p < 0.05$. (See figure 11.2.) For participants with a small initial network, less updating was observed in the focus group

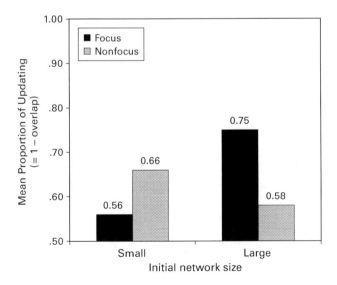

Figure 11.2
Mean proportion of updating (i.e., $1 -$ overlap).

as compared to the nonfocus group while, in contrast, for participants with a large initial network, the focus group showed a significant increase in updating as compared to the nonfocus group. Both differences were significant ($p < 0.05$).

In a secondary analysis I examined more specifically what happened with the political concepts that were corrected in the text. These concepts were specifically part of the focus of reading for participants in the focus group. I examined whether the political concepts that were part of discrepant facts would obtain more connections to other political concepts or would become more disconnected to other political concepts (including fewer associations to each other). For this purpose I checked whether the connectedness of corrected political concepts in relation to the other political as well as to action concepts changed more in the nonfocus group than in the focus group after reading the last ETA text. This connectedness is based on the in-degrees, that is, the summation of links with other concepts, and it expresses the connectedness of concepts to other concepts—for example, the political concepts to other political concepts—in the cognitive network.

It appeared that for participants with an initially small network, the connectedness of political concepts to other political concepts (see figure 11.3a) significantly increased in the nonfocus group as compared to the focus group after reading the last ETA text, $F(1, 17) = 7.09$, $p < 0.05$. In contrast, for participants with an initially large network, focus group as compared to nonfocus group participants showed a significant decrease in connectedness of political concepts to action concepts (see figure 11.3b), $F(1, 17) = 5.27$, $p < 0.05$.

There were no significant main or interaction effects of focus on the textbase-oriented recognition questions that were presented at the end of the session.

Conclusions

Two conclusions can be drawn from these results. First, for participants with initially small networks, in other words, readers with little background knowledge before reading the target text (i.e., the second ETA text), there is indeed some resistance to updating of concepts relevant to the focus of reading. Participants with initially small networks update less, and they embed the correcting political concepts less even though these concepts were part of their reading focus. With focus there was, for these participants, less change in the central part of the network and fewer connections among the political concepts after reading the last ETA text. These results reveal a low degree of updating with a focus instruction and correspond to work mentioned in the introduction (cf. van Oostendorp, 1996; Blanc et al., 2011; Chinn & Brewer, 1993): Changes in important information can be updated less easily when that information is part of a reader's focus. This holds specifically for participants with less background knowledge.

Second, participants with an initially large network, probably due to extensive background knowledge, are able to update to a high degree when they read with a specific

(a)

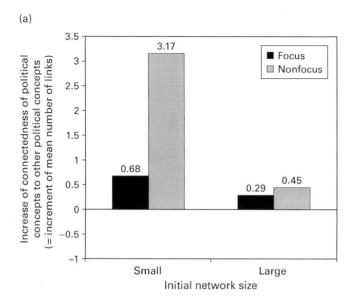

(b)

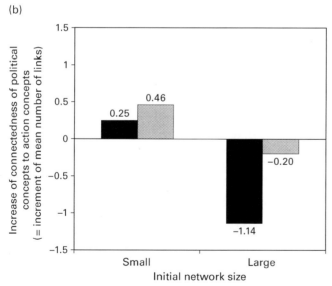

Figure 11.3
(a) Increase of connectedness of political concepts to other *political* concepts. (b) Increase of connectedness of political concepts to *action* concepts.

focus. Furthermore, they show a strong *decrease* in connections of political concepts to action concepts. It seems like they are beginning to construct two differentiated knowledge clusters, in this particular case due to their specific reading focus: one for political concepts and one for action concepts.

General Discussion and Conclusions

Based on the results of the first, think-aloud study, I concluded that skipping of transformations containing new discrepant information leads to low performance on an inference judgment test. Thus, the process of skipping this information could be a main contributor to failing to update. In the second study I examined what happened with the central part of the representation when readers processed new information discrepant with old information, particularly when it aligned with their focus of reading. I concluded that readers with sufficient background knowledge updated the central part of their mental representations when the focus of their reading encouraged them to do so. However, readers with little background knowledge seemed unable to do that: They updated their representation to a lesser extent than did readers who did not have a specific reading focus. Also, readers with little background knowledge failed to strengthen the connectedness of their political concepts to other political concepts when these concepts were in focus; readers with little background knowledge seemed unable to further connect them when they read with focus. The political concepts, despite being part of that focus, became loosely interconnected. In contrast, readers with sufficient background knowledge did not connect political concepts to other political concepts; rather these readers were engaged in differentiating political concepts from other (action) concepts, also exhibiting a higher degree of updating.

All in all, it seems that based on the work presented, updating of new discrepant information is indeed laborious when that information is relevant to the perspective of reading and belongs to the central part of the representation, but specifically for readers with little background knowledge. These readers experienced problems with elaborating the political network structure that was in focus in the materials and in bringing about changes in existing connections between concepts. Readers with sufficient background knowledge do indeed update (in line with van Oostendorp, 1996), and they differentiate the specific episodic network representation, when their reading focus demands that. They seem to organize their knowledge structure into several connected clusters of concepts (see also Wouters et al., 2011).

Regulation Mechanism

There clearly is evidence that readers tend to use old, discredited information and have difficulties updating their mental representations (Johnson & Seifert, 1993, 1994, 1999; Wilkes & Leatherbarrow, 1988; Wilkes & Reynolds, 1999; van Oostendorp & Bonebakker, 1999; Blanc et al., 2008, 2011). This resistance to correction has been found in many topic areas, including information about governments, politicians, the Internet, public information campaigns, and so on (Lewandowsky, Ecker, Seifert, Schwarz, & Cook, 2012). Similar effects emerge when people learn about characters through short texts describing those characters in a stereotypical manner (Baadte & Dutke, 2013; Rapp & Kendeou, 2009). Similar patterns are also found when both older and younger participants are examined (Guillory & Geraci, 2010). At the same time, however, there are limits within which old information may obstruct the updating of previously formed mental representations. For instance, van Oostendorp (2002) presented readers with texts containing rather strong contradictions between old and new information (so-called inconsistency-driven updating situations; cf. Dutke et al., 2010). Confronted with such explicit and strong contradictions, readers edited their mental representations and frequently used the new information to answer inference questions. The updating process seems to consist of a regulation mechanism that is based on weighing evidence in favor of old and new sources of information. According to the outcomes of this evaluation process, readers choose one or the other point of view, the old or new source of information, and use that for making inferences.

In terms of the construction-integration model (Kintsch, 1998) and the Landscape model (van den Broek, 2010; van den Broek & Kendeou, 2008; Blanc et al., 2008; Blanc et al., 2011), the exact balance between the strengths of the old and new sources may influence the degree of updating. Strong support for one source causes an increased activation of this source in the network of propositions as compared with the other source. The exact balance of activation values of old and new information in the final representation after processing both sources determines which interpretation receives priority. Subtle reinforcement, directly or indirectly, of old or new information can lead to differences in the exact balance of activation values of old and new information, thereby activating qualitatively different updating strategies by readers such as holding on to the old information or rejecting the new information (Johnson & Seifert, 1993, 1994, 1999; Blanc et al., 2008, 2011; Wilkes & Leatherbarrow, 1988; Wilkes & Reynolds, 1999; van Oostendorp & Bonebakker, 1999) or even switching to a new perspective (van Oostendorp, 2002; Rapp & Kendeou, 2009; Baadte & Dutke, 2013). For instance, Baadte and Dutke (2013) showed that participants updated their initial situation model more effectively when a second text additionally provided a plausible explanation for conflicting information.

Coactivation of both sources seems to be an essential step to successful updating, but it is probably not sufficient to fully explain the actual degree of updating (van den Broek & Kendeou, 2008). Individual characteristics like motivation and personal involvement with the topic of the text are relevant too. It seems that strategic considerations are also involved, such as epistemic beliefs (Bråten et al., 2013; Maier & Richter, 2013). For instance, readers with an epistemic belief that ideas should be connected and consistent will try to integrate information from old and new sources to a greater extent even when they are discrepant (Rukavina & Daneman, 1996). Because these readers aim for a higher degree of coherence of the representation, more inferences and further knowledge activation will be generated, leading to a higher degree of incorporating new discrepant information and updating the representation. It could also be that the decision to skip information that is discrepant with existing ideas or models as described above is a strategic consideration. In order to limit resource-intensive construction processes like inference construction, which is necessary to integrate the new discrepant information, readers prefer for the time being to stay with old points of view.

The general message of the work presented here regarding updating mental representations is twofold. First, updating by incorporating new discrepant information can be difficult. New and discrepant information relevant to (1) the situation described by the text and/or (2) the focus of reading is difficult to integrate for readers with little background knowledge. Focusing these readers on new and discrepant information seems even to generate a negative effect regarding updating. High prior knowledge readers do better: They update information and seem to construct specialized knowledge clusters. Second, mental operations like active processing (by questioning one's own understanding), chunking of information, and integrating new information (by retrieving information from previous text in order to contrast that with present information) seem relevant to updating a situation model and enhancing performance, as was observed in the think-aloud study. Focusing instruction or training on these kinds of mental operations may be helpful to foster better updating.

References

Albrecht, J. E., & O'Brien, E. J. (1993). Updating a mental model: Maintaining both local and global coherence. *Journal of Experimental Psychology. Learning, Memory, and Cognition*, *19*, 1061–1070.

Baadte, C., & Dutke, S. (2013). Learning about persons: The effects of text structure and executive capacity on conceptual change. *European Journal of Psychology of Education*, *28*, 1045–1064. doi:10.1007/s10212-012-0153-2.

Blanc, N., Kendeou, P., van den Broek, P., & Brouillet, D. (2008). Updating situation models during reading of news reports: Evidence from empirical data and simulation. *Discourse Processes*, *45*, 103–121.

Blanc, N., Stiegler-Balfour, J. J., & O'Brien, E. J. (2011). Does the certainty of information influence the updating process? Evidence from the reading of news articles. *Discourse Processes*, *48*, 387–403.

Bråten, I., Ferguson, L. E., Strømsø, H. I., & Anmarkrud, O. (2013). Justification beliefs and multiple-documents comprehension. *European Journal of Psychology of Education*, *28*, 879–902. doi:10.1007/s10212-012-0145-2.

Chinn, C. A., & Brewer, W. F. (1993). The role of anomalous data in knowledge acquisition: A theoretical framework and implications for science instruction. *Review of Educational Research, 63,* 1–49.

Day, E. A., Arthur, W., Jr., & Gettman, D. (2001). Knowledge structures and the acquisition of a complex skill. *Journal of Applied Psychology, 86,* 1022–1033.

Dutke, S., Baadte, C., Hähnel, A., von Hecker, U., & Rinck, M. (2010). Using diagnostic text information to constrain situation models. *Discourse Processes, 47,* 510–544.

Ferstl, E. C., & Kintsch, W. (1999). Learning from text: Structural knowledge assessment in the study of discourse comprehension. In H. van Oostendorp & S. R. Goldman (Eds.), *The construction of mental representations during reading* (pp. 247–277). Mahwah, NJ: Lawrence Erlbaum Associates.

Fletcher, C. R., & Chrysler, S. T. (1990). Surface forms, textbases, and situation models: Recognition memory for three types of textual information. *Discourse Processes, 13,* 175–190.

Goldsmith, T. E., & Davenport, D. M. (1990). Assessing structural similarity of graphs. In R. Schvaneveldt (Ed.), *Pathfinder associative networks: Studies in knowledge organization* (pp. 75–88). Norwood, NJ: Ablex.

Goldsmith, T. E., Johnson, P. J., & Acton, W. H. (1991). Assessing structural knowledge. *Journal of Educational Psychology, 86,* 601–618.

Graesser, A. C., Singer, M., & Trabasso, T. (1994). Constructing inferences during narrative text comprehension. *Psychological Review, 101,* 371–395.

Guillory, J. J., & Geraci, L. (2010). The persistence of inferences in memory for younger and older adults: Remembering facts and believing inferences. *Psychonomic Bulletin & Review, 17,* 73–81.

Johnson, H. M., & Seifert, C. M. (1993). Correcting causal explanations in memory. *Proceedings of the 15th annual conference of the Cognitive Science Society* (pp. 5011–5016). Hillsdale, NJ: Lawrence Erlbaum Associates.

Johnson, H. M., & Seifert, C. M. (1994). Sources of the continued influence effect: When misinformation in memory affects later inferences. *Journal of Experimental Psychology. Learning, Memory, and Cognition, 20,* 1420–1436.

Johnson, H. M., & Seifert, C. M. (1999). Modifying mental representations: Comprehending corrections. In H. van Oostendorp & S. R. Goldman (Eds.), *The construction of mental representations during reading* (pp. 303–318). Mahwah, NJ: Lawrence Erlbaum Associates.

Kintsch, W. (1998). *Comprehension: A paradigm for cognition.* Cambridge, England: Cambridge University Press.

Kintsch, W., & Franzke, M. (1995). The role of background knowldege in the recall of a news story. In R. F. Lorch & E. J. O'Brien (Eds.), *Sources of coherence in reading* (pp. 321–333). Mahwah, NJ: Lawrence Erlbaum Associates.

Kraiger, K., Salas, E., & Cannon-Bowers, J. A. (1995). Measuring knowledge organization as a method for assessing learning during training. *Human Factors*, *37*, 804–814.

Kurby, C. A., & Zacks, J. M. (2012). Starting from scratch and building brick by brick in comprehension. *Memory & Cognition*, *40*, 812–826.

Lewandowsky, S., Ecker, U. H., Seifert, C., Schwarz, N., & Cook, J. (2012). Misinformation and its correction: Continued influence and successful debiasing. *Psychological Science in the Public Interest*, *13*, 106–131.

Maier, J., & Richter, T. (2013). How non-experts understand conflicting information on social science issues: The role of perceived plausibility and reading goals. *Journal of Media Psychology: Theories, Methods, and Applications*, *25*(1), 14–26.

McKoon, G., & Ratcliff, R. (1992). Inferences during reading. *Psychological Review*, *99*, 440–466.

Rapp, D. N., & Kendeou, P. (2009). Noticing and revising discrepancies as texts unfold. *Discourse Processes*, *46*, 1–24.

Rukavina, I., & Daneman, M. (1996). Integration and its effect on acquiring knowledge about competing scientific theories from text. *Journal of Educational Psychology*, *88*, 272–287.

Suh, S., & Trabasso, T. (1993). Inference during reading: Converging evidence from discourse analysis, talk-aloud protocols, and recognition priming. *Journal of Memory and Language*, *32*, 279–300.

Tapiero, I., & Otéro, J. (1999). Distinguishing between textbase and situation model in the processing of inconsistent information: Elaboration versus tagging. In H. van Oostendorp & S. R. Goldman (Eds.), *The construction of mental representations during reading* (pp. 341–365). Mahwah, NJ: Lawrence Erlbaum Associates.

Trabasso, T., Suh, S., Payton, P., & Jain, R. (1995). Explanatory inferences and other strategies during comprehension and their effect on recall. In R. F. Lorch & E. J. O'Brien (Eds.), *Sources of coherence in reading* (pp. 219–239). Mahwah, NJ: Lawrence Erlbaum Associates.

Trumpower, D. L., Sharara, H., & Goldsmith, T. E. (2010). Specificity of structural assessment of knowledge. *Journal of Technology, Learning, and Assessment*, *8*, 1–31.

van den Broek, P. (2010). Using texts in science education: Cognitive processes and knowledge representation. *Science*, *328*, 453–456.

van den Broek, P., & Kendeou, P. (2008). Cognitive processes in comprehension of science texts: The role of co-activation in confronting misconceptions. *Applied Cognitive Psychology*, *22*, 335–351.

van den Broek, P., Virtue, S., Everson, M. G., Tzeng, Y., & Sung, Y. (2002). Comprehension of science texts: Inferential processes and the construction of a mental representation. In J. Otéro, J. A. Leon, & A. C. Graesser (Eds.), *The psychology of science text comprehension* (pp. 131–154). Mahwah, NJ: Lawrence Erlbaum Associates.

van Dijk, T. A., & Kintsch, W. (1983). *Strategies of discourse comprehension*. New York: Academic Press.

van Oostendorp, H. (1994). Text processing in terms of semantic cohesion monitoring. In H. van Oostendorp & R. A. Zwaan (Eds.), *Naturalistic text comprehension* (pp. 35–56). Norwood, NJ: Ablex.

van Oostendorp, H. (1996). Updating situation models derived from newspaper articles. *Medienpsychologie, 8*, 22–33.

van Oostendorp, H. (2001). Holding onto established viewpoints during processing news reports. In W. van Peer & S. Chatman (Eds.), *New perspectives on narrative perspective* (pp. 173–188). Albany, NY: State University of New York Press.

van Oostendorp, H. (2002). Updating mental representations during reading scientific text. In J. ·Otéro, J. Leon, & A. Graesser (Eds.), *The psychology of science text comprehension* (pp. 309–329). Mahwah, NJ: Lawrence Erlbaum Associates.

van Oostendorp, H., & Bonebakker, C. (1999). Difficulties in updating mental representations during reading news reports. In H. van Oostendorp & S. R. Goldman (Eds.), *The construction of mental representations during reading* (pp. 319–339). Mahwah, NJ: Lawrence Erlbaum Associates.

van Oostendorp, H., Otéro, J., & Campanario, J. (2002). Conditions of updating during reading. In M. Louwerse & W. van Peer (Eds.), *Thematics: Interdisciplinary studies* (pp. 55–76). Amsterdam: Benjamins.

van Soomeren, M., Barnard, Y., & Sandberg, J. (1994). *The think aloud method: A practical guide to modeling cognitive processes*. London: Academic Press.

Wilkes, A. L., & Leatherbarrow, M. (1988). Editing episodic memory following the identification of error. *Quarterly Journal of Experimental Psychology, 40A*, 361–387.

Wilkes, A. L., & Reynolds, D. J. (1999). On certain limitations accompanying readers' interpretations of corrections in episodic text. *Quarterly Journal of Experimental Psychology, 52A*, 165–183.

Wouters, P., Van der Spek, E., & van Oostendorp, H. (2011). Measuring learning in serious games: A case study with structural assessment. *Educational Technology Research and Development, 59*, 741–763.

12 Comprehension and Validation: Separable Stages of Information Processing? A Case for Epistemic Monitoring in Language Comprehension

Maj-Britt Isberner and Tobias Richter

How and when do we realize that something we comprehend is inconsistent with our knowledge about the world? Is this realization a part of comprehension, or is it a voluntary decision process subsequent to comprehension? Is it strategic—that is, dependent on an evaluative processing goal—or nonstrategic—that is, relatively fast, effortless, and difficult to suppress? Clearly, we cannot properly judge the truth or plausibility of something we do not comprehend. But can we comprehend something without also judging its truth or plausibility?

Evaluation of information is widely considered an offline, downstream, voluntary process that is subsequent to comprehension (e.g., Gilbert, Krull, & Malone, 1990; Gilbert, Tafarodi, & Malone, 1993; Herbert & Kübler, 2011; Sparks & Rapp, 2011; Wiswede, Koranyi, Müller, Langner, & Rothermund, 2013). Underlying this conception is a two-step model of comprehension and evaluation, in which comprehension is nonevaluative and any knowledge-based (epistemic) evaluation of information is strategic and delayed until after comprehension has finished.

Consistent with this idea, there has been an implicit division of epistemic labor in psychological research: Whereas cognitive psychology mainly focuses on investigating phenomena of comprehension, processes of information evaluation are primarily investigated in social psychology (e.g., in the framework of the elaboration likelihood model; Petty & Cacioppo, 1986; Petty & Wegener, 1999). In contrast, evaluative processing is often used in psycholinguistic research to *measure* comprehension in the first place: In studies on the organization of semantic memory, the time it takes to verify a sentence is often taken as an indicator of how long it takes to comprehend it (e.g., Kintsch, 1980; Kounios, Osman, & Meyer, 1987). This approach is consistent with the idea that meaning is conveyed when the truth conditions of a sentence are understood (e.g., Davidson, 2001). Moreover, readers' ability to evaluate information fast and incrementally with regard to their world knowledge is often utilized (seemingly naturally) in psycholinguistic studies to investigate a variety of phenomena, such as the time course of availability of different kinds of information during comprehension (e.g., Fischler, Childers, Achariyapaopan, & Perry, 1985; Hagoort, Hald, Bastiaansen,

& Petersson, 2004; O'Brien, Rizzella, Albrecht, & Halleran, 1998; Rayner, Warren, Juhasz, & Liversedge, 2004), memory-based processing in situation-model updating (e.g., Albrecht & O'Brien, 1993; O'Brien et al., 1998), the processing of negation (e.g., Nieuwland & Kuperberg, 2008), the question of when a sentence's meaning is integrated with its context (Nieuwland & van Berkum, 2006; van Berkum, Zwitserlood, Hagoort, & Brown, 2003), or syntactic analysis (e.g., Pickering & Traxler, 1998; Speer & Clifton, 1998; Staub, Rayner, Pollatsek, Hyönä, & Majewski, 2007; Traxler & Pickering, 1996; van Gompel, Pickering, & Traxler, 2001), to name just a few topics. Many of the results reported in these studies call the two-step model into question although this is often overlooked or taken for granted in interpretations of the findings. It seems thus that the relationship between comprehension and evaluation of information, which is rarely explicitly addressed in the literature, merits a closer examination.

In this chapter, we would like to provide a systematic overview of studies that allow conclusions regarding this issue. From our point of view, many of these studies support the assumption that comprehension comprises a routine, nonstrategic validation process that detects knowledge violations, which we will term *epistemic monitoring* (Richter, 2011; Richter, Schroeder, & Wöhrmann, 2009). Our literature review will span violations of factual world knowledge (e.g., *Soft soap is edible*), implausibility (e.g., *Frank has a broken leg. He calls the plumber*), inconsistencies with antecedent text (e.g., *Mary is a vegetarian.... She orders a cheeseburger*), and semantic anomalies (e.g., *Dutch trains are sour*). Moreover, we will briefly touch on the validation of self-referential statements (e.g., *My name is Ira*) and of statements that refer to a person's value system (e.g., *Euthanasia is acceptable/unacceptable*). We will also consider the role of negation, predictability, and typicality in both comprehension and validation.

We will start by proposing a framework for integrating the findings on these various topics by projecting them onto the common dimension of plausibility. We will then review evidence which demonstrates the sensitivity of early comprehension processes to plausibility, challenging the two-step model's assumption of a nonevaluative comprehension stage. In doing so, we will integrate research from studies spanning three decades that have used a variety of dependent variables (reading times, response latencies, eye movements, and event-related potentials or ERPs) to investigate a variety of phenomena (e.g., semantic integration, syntactic analysis, situation-model construction, and prediction). Finally, we will try to reconcile the assumption of nonstrategic validation in language comprehension with findings that show people's failure to notice even blatant violations of their knowledge under certain circumstances by discussing the limitations of epistemic monitoring.

The Role of Knowledge-Based Validation in Language Processing

With knowledge-based (or epistemic) validation, we mean the evaluation of information with regard to its consistency with stored knowledge, which entails the detection of knowledge violations. These knowledge violations can take several forms: They may comprise information that is clearly false (based on semantic or world knowledge), information that is merely implausible, or information that is not false or implausible per se but inconsistent with antecedent text.

It is difficult to draw clear distinctions between these types of knowledge violations. First of all, whether something is perceived as clearly false or merely as implausible depends on the knowledge of the reader and on the certainty of that knowledge. For example, a reader can only recognize a particular sentence as false if he or she possesses the specific knowledge required to assess its truth, while plausibility judgments can be based on less specific or certain knowledge.

Moreover, the detection of inconsistencies with antecedent text sometimes requires the reactivation of not only previous text information but also of relevant semantic or world knowledge. Thus, this type of violation seems to be a subtype of false or implausible information in which the discourse context becomes part of the background against which incoming information is evaluated (in line with the notion that information is immediately related to the widest available context during language comprehension; e.g., Hagoort & van Berkum, 2007; Just & Carpenter, 1980; Nieuwland & van Berkum, 2006; van Berkum, Hagoort, & Brown, 1999; van Berkum et al., 2003). For example, in a classic study by O'Brien et al. (1998), participants first read that either *Mary is a vegetarian* or *Mary is a fast food lover*, and later in the text read that *she orders a cheeseburger*. Reading times were longer when the behavior was inconsistent with the previously described trait, which is generally taken as evidence that the trait is reactivated by a passive memory-based retrieval process. However, it is important to note that the inconsistency only becomes apparent when relevant world knowledge is also activated—namely, that cheeseburgers usually contain meat and that vegetarians usually do not eat any meat whatsoever (see also Cook & Guéraud, 2005).

For the purpose of integrating the findings reviewed in this chapter, it seems to us that the best way of systematizing the various kinds of knowledge violations is to project them onto the dimension of plausibility. In the extant literature, plausibility has been defined as the goodness of fit with prior knowledge (Connell & Keane, 2004) or as the "relative potential truthfulness of incoming information compared to our existing mental representations" (Lombardi, 2012, p. 3). Some researchers use "plausibility" synonymously with "sensibility" (e.g., Speer & Clifton, 1998) while others have obtained plausibility judgments by asking participants to rate how "realistic" (e.g., van Gompel et al., 2001) or how "likely" (e.g., Matsuki et al., 2011; Warren & McConnell, 2007) a described situation is. According to Matsuki et al. (2011),

...plausibility, in its most general form, can be defined as the acceptability or likelihood of a situation or a sentence describing it, as a whole. Plausibility usually is measured by asking participants to rate, on a Likert scale, "How likely it is [sic] that the described event occurs in the real world?" (p. 926)

Their definition points to the interesting phenomenon that plausibility of linguistic information is influenced not only by its content but also by the pragmatic felicity of the utterance itself. Even a true sentence, if it is pragmatically infelicitous, will be perceived as implausible, such as in the case of implausible negatives for which it is difficult to imagine a context in which they are plausibly uttered (e.g., *A sparrow is not a vehicle*; Fischler, Bloom, Childers, Roucos, & Perry, 1983; Wason, 1965).

Effects of plausibility on language processing have been widely acknowledged and well-documented in the literature; however, it is still a point of contention whether these effects reflect downstream, offline, strategic processing or online, nonstrategic processing.

Two-Step Models of Comprehension and Validation

Why is the view that evaluative processing is delayed with regard to comprehension so widespread? One major reason for this is the popularity of two-step models of comprehension and validation, which differentiate between separate comprehension and evaluation stages (e.g., Connell & Keane, 2006; Gilbert, 1991; Herbert & Kübler, 2011; Wiswede et al., 2013). According to these models, the evaluation of information comes in only after the (nonevaluative) comprehension stage is completed. Moreover, evaluation is usually assumed to be an intentional and therefore optional decision process. This assumption is based on a theoretical distinction between linguistically relevant lexical knowledge (e.g., knowledge about selectional restrictions), which is assumed to be accessed for comprehension, and world knowledge, which is assumed to be accessed for evaluation (e.g., Chomsky, 1965; Rayner et al., 2004).

In line with the two-step model, effects of world knowledge on language processing are sometimes found to be delayed in comparison to effects of semantic knowledge (Rayner et al., 2004; Warren & McConnell, 2007). Moreover, evidence has been presented which suggests that people are bound to believe everything they read at first and can only effortfully "unbelieve" it at a later point if they have the motivation and cognitive resources to do so (Gilbert et al., 1990, 1993). Consistent with this idea, there are findings suggesting that people sometimes fail to use their general world knowledge adequately even when they are explicitly instructed to do so (e.g., Rapp, 2008) and, under some conditions, fall victim to even blatant inaccuracies (e.g., Marsh, Meade, & Roediger, 2003). Moreover, response latencies and ERPs associated with verifying or reading negated sentences have often been found to be more sensitive to semantic mismatches than to a sentence's truth value, suggesting that word-level matches are privileged over message-level truth or plausibility, at least at an early stage of comprehension (Clark & Chase, 1972; Fischler et al., 1983; Wiswede et al., 2013). Finally, much evaluative processing is indeed offline and deliberate, generally when relevant knowledge for judging truth or plausibility is not (easily) available.

However, from a theoretical perspective, the conceptualization of a nonevaluative comprehension stage is problematic. First of all, the distinction between semantic and world knowledge has been called into question by a number of researchers (e.g., Hagoort et al., 2004; Jackendoff, 2002; Matsuki et al., 2011; this will be discussed in more detail at a later point).

Secondly, modern theories of language comprehension, like the situation-model approach (Johnson-Laird, 1983; van Dijk & Kintsch, 1983), assume that world knowledge is already activated in the course of comprehension: Situation models (or mental models) are conceptualized as referential representations of the state of affairs described in the text, which are constructed by integrating text information with prior knowledge, including relevant world knowledge (e.g., Zwaan & Radvansky, 1998). In this way, situation models specify how linguistic expressions relate to the world and thus represent extensional aspects of meaning, that is, reference and truth (Johnson-Laird, Herrmann, & Chaffin, 1984).

The construction of a situation model has been found to entail the monitoring of multiple dimensions such as time, space, or characters' goals (e.g., Zwaan, Langston, & Graesser, 1995; Zwaan, Magliano, & Graesser, 1995; Zwaan & Radvansky, 1998). Discontinuities (e.g., time shifts) or inconsistencies (e.g., conflicts between characters' goals and their actions) in these dimensions have been shown to slow down processing, which is usually interpreted as comprehension or integration difficulty. This is also the case when inconsistencies arise between the currently processed text information and antecedent text information that is no longer active in working memory, suggesting that situation models require global coherence, and that previous text information can be reactivated by a passive resonance process (memory-based processing; e.g., Albrecht & O'Brien, 1993; Gerrig & McKoon, 1998; Gerrig & O'Brien, 2005; McKoon, Gerrig, & Greene, 1996; McKoon & Ratcliff, 1998; O'Brien, 1995; O'Brien & Albrecht, 1992; O'Brien et al., 1998; Ratcliff, 1978).

An Alternative Two-Step Model: Epistemic Monitoring Followed by Epistemic Elaboration

Based on the assumption that comprehension entails the construction of a situation model, our central claim in this chapter is that comprehenders monitor incoming information routinely, nonstrategically, and online during comprehension with respect to its internal consistency and its consistency with their knowledge and beliefs about the world (Richter, 2003).

In line with Singer (2006), we assume that this monitoring process relies on the activation of knowledge through memory-based processing: "The passive retrieval associated with the memory-based analysis ... affords the reader with the opportunity to evaluate each discourse constituent in the context of referent text and knowledge" (Singer, 2006, p. 587). However, it is important to note that not all knowledge that is potentially relevant for evaluation will be activated during situation-model construction; rather, the activation will be a function of accessibility. It is reasonable to assume that the accessibility of knowledge will, among other things, be influenced by how recently it was previously activated, by its typicality given the reader's experience of the world (e.g., Matsuki et al., 2011), by how well connected it is with other stored knowledge (e.g., Kendeou, Smith, & O'Brien, 2013), by how the currently processed text information is phrased (resulting in more or less surface overlap with knowledge in long-term memory; e.g., Albrecht & O'Brien, 1993; O'Brien et al., 1998), by how focused the information is in the text (e.g., Sanford, 2002), and by the depth of processing required by the task (e.g., Sanford & Sturt, 2002). Thus, violations of knowledge that is not activated for situation-model construction may well go unnoticed.

Accordingly, we do not propose that comprehension entails a full analysis of the (potential) truth of information but rather a quick and incomplete analysis based on the knowledge that is activated for situation-model construction. If an inconsistency with the activated knowledge is detected, the incoming information is initially rejected to protect the situation model from contamination with false information (Richter et al., 2009). However, if the reader's motivation and cognitive capacity are high, or if the reader pursues an explicit evaluation goal (e.g., a patient reading about his or her medical condition), the detection of implausibility may be followed by a deliberate attempt to resolve the conflict. We call this kind of offline deliberation *epistemic elaboration* (Richter, 2011). It may range from reasoning about the conflicting information (plausible reasoning; e.g., Collins & Michalski, 1989) to attempts to ascertain its validity with the help of external sources (e.g., looking up information in a textbook or encyclopedia or searching the Internet). In this way, epistemic elaboration allows for taking more factors into account than just the immediately accessible knowledge and thereby making a more elaborate (and probably more justified) judgment about the plausibility of information.

Thus, we propose an alternative two-step model of an evaluative comprehension stage (comprising epistemic monitoring) followed by an optional stage of epistemic elaboration (depending on the reader's goals and motivations). In particular, we would like to argue against the still very prevalent idea that any effects of plausibility on language processing are downstream and reflect intentional evaluative processing. For example, Connell and Keane (2004) proposed a two-step model with a comprehension and a subsequent assessment stage:

For example, if someone is asked to assess the plausibility of the statement *The bottle rolled off the shelf and smashed on the floor*, he or she might make the inference that the bottle rolling off the shelf *caused* it to smash on the floor. Then he or she might consider this elaborated description to be highly plausible because past experience has suggested that falling fragile things often end up breaking when they hit floors. In short, the description has a certain conceptual coherence. (p. 186)

However, it seems more reasonable to us to assume that, rather than making the inference and then judging its plausibility, the plausibility of the inference (based on world knowledge) is the reason *why* it is made in the first place. In this way, plausibility already influences the comprehension stage of the assumed two-step model by affecting which inferences are drawn during text comprehension (e.g., Thorndyke, 1976). Moreover, to the extent that plausibility affords online prediction (DeLong, Urbach, & Kutas, 2005; van Berkum et al., 2005), it can exert effects even *prior* to comprehension of a particular linguistic input (for instance, in the form of predictive inferences; e.g., Cook, Limber, & O'Brien, 2001).

In fact, the idea that the validity or plausibility of information is monitored during language comprehension is not entirely new. Some researchers have at least alluded to the idea that such a process may exist. For example, according to Fischler et al. (1983), "The negativity [in the ERPs] associated with anomalous sentences ... suggests that a basic process in sentence comprehension is the monitoring of the consistency or validity of the propositions asserted by the sentence, with a negativity associated with the disruption of that process" (p. 401). Similarly, West and Stanovich (1982) found that words which are incongruent in their context (e.g., *The accountant balanced the people*) lead to slower yes–responses in making a lexical decision and suggested that "responses in the lexical-decision task are affected by postlexical message-level processes that detect incongruity" (p. 385). Fischler and Bloom (1980) pointed out that the interference produced by a detection of incongruity "would be of value to the reader, as a signal that perception or comprehension has failed, and that some reanalysis is called for" (p. 224). In a similar vein, Murray and Rowan (1998) argued that plausibility effects in eye movements reflect "Early, Mandatory, Pragmatic processing" (p. 1), in contrast with the view that "factors like pragmatic plausibility are ... extralinguistic, outside the language module and optional in their operation" (p. 3). Rather, they concluded that "plausibility effects are not restricted to low-level phrasal units and that they appear to arise as a necessary consequence of the process responsible for deriving basic sentence meaning" (p. 1).

Furthermore, Singer and colleagues (Singer, 1993, 2006; Singer, Halldorson, Lear, & Andrusiak, 1992) have provided evidence that readers routinely validate the causal relationships implied by a text (e.g., *Dorothy poured the bucket of water on the fire. The fire went out/grew hotter—Does water extinguish fire?*), and that in self-paced reading, reading times are sensitive to truth and negation, which are factors that have been shown to influence overt sentence verification (e.g., Carpenter & Just, 1975). Based on these findings, Singer (2006) proposed that fully comprehending text entails its verification, and that verification emerges not from an evaluative processing goal but from "the fundamentals of the cognition of reading" (p. 589).

Nonetheless, the two-step model of comprehension and validation is still very prevalent in psycholinguistic research. In the following, we will present a summary of what we perceive as the greatest challenges for this conceptualization.

Challenges for a Two-Step Model of Comprehension and Validation

Findings by Gilbert and Colleagues

Evidence for the view that validation is subsequent, optional, and cognitively effortful primarily comes from studies by Gilbert and colleagues, which show a so-called "affirmation bias" in sentence verification: When people learn sentences and their associated truth values under speeded conditions or when they are distracted by a secondary task, they have a tendency to later judge false sentences as true, but not vice versa (Gilbert et al., 1990, 1993). This finding is explained by the two-step model of comprehension and validation: First, the linguistic message is understood, that is, its meaning is computed based purely on semantic knowledge. Then, in the second step, the computed meaning can be compared with real-world knowledge to assess its truth value and—if necessary—"unbelieve" the message. This second step, however, is assumed to be cognitively demanding and therefore only carried out when the reader has the motivation and the cognitive resources to do so. Thus, under speeded conditions, or when readers are put under additional cognitive load, this "unbelieving" is disrupted, leading to a higher amount of falsely accepted sentences. Gilbert et al. (1990, 1993) found support for these assumptions in several studies, using fictitious facts with arbitrarily assigned truth values—for example, fictitious Hopi word definitions such as *A monishna is a star*, which were presented to the participants as being either true or false.

However, multiple arguments against the generality of Gilbert et al.'s (1990, 1993) findings have been raised. For example, Richter et al. (2009) pointed out the fact that Gilbert et al. eliminated effects of prior knowledge by using fictitious facts, which limits the applicability of their findings. In contrast, when people do have prior knowledge, this may enable them to reject false statements even when they are distracted by a secondary task. To test this assumption, Richter et al. replicated Gilbert et al.'s (1990) study with facts for which participants had either weak (e.g., *Toothpaste contains sulfur*) or strong knowledge (e.g., *Perfume contains scents*) and showed that cognitive load produces an affirmation bias only for facts associated with weak knowledge. Sperber et al. (2010) also raised the question of relevance:

Even if the participants could muster some interest for statements about the meaning of Hopi words (and there is nothing in either the experimental situation or the participants' background knowledge which makes it likely that they would), the information that one of these statements (e.g. 'A Monishna is a star') is false would still be utterly irrelevant to them. From the knowledge that such a statement is false, nothing follows. With other statements, things may be different. If you had prior reasons for thinking that a certain statement was true, or if it described a normal state of affairs, it is easy to see how you might find it relevant to be told that it is false. (p. 363)

In line with this objection, an experiment by Hasson, Simmons, and Todorov (2005) showed that there is no affirmation bias when the false version of a statement is informative. From this, the authors concluded that it does in fact appear to be possible to suspend belief in comprehended statements, in contrast to what Gilbert et al. (1990, 1993) claimed. In conclusion, it seems that the two-step model proposed by Gilbert and colleagues only applies to the processing of certain kinds of information, but certainly not to all.

Semantic versus World Knowledge Violations—Is Semantic Knowledge Temporally Privileged?

Another main reason for the widespread assumption of a two-step model of comprehension and validation is that some research has suggested that the integration of world knowledge in language comprehension is delayed relative to semantic knowledge. However, as we will show in the following, it is debatable whether the two types of violations can actually be clearly distinguished on a theoretical basis and whether their operationalization in psycholinguistic studies has been appropriate.

From a theoretical point of view, the distinction between semantic knowledge and world knowledge is based on a distinction between meaning and truth, or in other words, on the distinction between the construction of meaning and the verification of that meaning (Hagoort et al., 2004). Meaning construction is assumed to rely purely on semantic knowledge whereas verification also draws on (extralinguistic) world knowledge. Semantic violations are assumed to be violations of purely semantic knowledge: They arise when a word or phrase violates the selectional restrictions placed by the context. For example, as Hagoort et al. (2004) pointed out, the sentence *The favorite palace of the present queen of England is divorced* violates the selectional restrictions of the predicate *is-divorced* because being divorced requires an animate object as its argument. Therefore, this sentence is semantically malformed. This malformation, according to different definitions, causes the sentence to be incapable of having a sense ("Senseless Sentences"; Kutas & Hillyard, 1980, p. 203), of being true ("Selectional restriction violations lead to impossibility"; Warren & McConnell, 2007, p. 770), or of having a truth value because their truth conditions are unclear (Asher, 2011). In contrast, world knowledge violations are perfectly sensible and could therefore theoretically be true, but it is the (current) state of affairs in the real world that renders them false (e.g., *The present queen of England is divorced*; Hagoort et al., 2004).

However, the problem is that not all stimuli clearly fall into one category or the other. For example, Kutas and Hillyard (1980) used "strongly anomalous" sentence completions (e.g., *You can't make a silk purse out of a cow's chair* or *He took a sip from the transmitter*) and "moderately anomalous" completions (e.g., *You can't make a silk purse out of a cow's skin* or *He took a sip from the waterfall*). It is important to note, however, that the latter examples seem to violate world knowledge rather than selectional restrictions. Similarly, van Berkum et al. (1999) referred to words that were implausible in their context (e.g., *Jane told her brother that he was exceptionally _slow_*, when the brother had previously been described as having been very quick) as "discourse-dependent semantic anomalies" (p. 657) although these words did not render the context sentences senseless. Likewise, the so-called Moses illusion (i.e., the often overlooked error in the question "How many animals of each kind did Moses take on the ark?"; Erickson & Mattson, 1981) has often been described as a semantic anomaly when it is clearly world knowledge that renders it false (it should be Noah instead of Moses). As these examples show, the terminology in the literature has at the very least been blurry. Matsuki et al. (2011) point toward a similar problem by remarking that some of the selectional restriction violations that have been used in psycholinguistic studies (e.g., Warren & McConnell, 2007) involve violations of highly verb-specific restrictions such as *inflatable*, *catchable*, *cookable*, *mixable*, or *edible*, rather than of abstract verb-general features such as *animacy* or *humanness*. However, as they point out, knowing which objects fulfill these verb-specific requirements seems to qualify as world or event knowledge rather than as specifically semantic knowledge.

An additional problem is that different definitions of semantic violations exist in linguistics and psycholinguistics: A sentence such as *He spread the warm bread with socks* (Kutas & Hillyard, 1980), which has been considered a semantic violation in psycholinguistics, would be categorized as a typical world knowledge violation in linguistics because "it follows all the semantic rules of English, and the reason it sounds odd is simply that socks do not have the right chemical make-up to function as a spread" (Pylkkänen, Oliveri, & Smart, 2009, p. 1314).

Moreover, it is always possible to construct a context—at least a fictional or metaphorical one—in which an anomaly can appear perfectly sensible. For example, it is not unusual for waiters to refer to their customers by the names of the dishes they ordered, so the utterance *The ham sandwich is getting impatient* would not be perceived as anomalous in this context (Asher, 2011). This notion is supported by results showing that animacy violations which are consistent with the discourse context (e.g., a peanut described as being in love in a cartoon-like discourse) elicit a smaller N400 (an ERP component that indexes semantic integration) than information which is consistent with world knowledge but does not fit well with the context (e.g., the same peanut described as being salted; Nieuwland & van Berkum, 2006; see also Filik & Leuthold, 2008). Consequently, the context can obviously override local animacy requirements.

Moreover, Hagoort et al. (2004) found that the time course and amplitude of the N400 are highly similar for the processing of world knowledge violations (e.g., *Dutch trains are white*) and semantic violations (e.g., *Dutch trains are sour*) as compared to correct controls (e.g., *Dutch trains are yellow*). Thus, whether or not a clear distinction is feasible, the kinds of knowledge usually separated into semantic and world knowledge in psycholinguistics appear to be integrated simultaneously during language comprehension. This speaks against a two-step model of comprehension and validation in which first meaning and then truth value is computed.

However, not all studies support this conclusion. Using eye-tracking technology, Warren and McConnell (2007) and Rayner et al. (2004) found that semantic violations have immediate disruptive effects on reading whereas those of world knowledge violations are delayed. Matsuki et al. (2011) tried to reconcile the contradictory results by proposing that the typicality of the items used may be key. They hypothesized that in order to find early effects of plausibility, it is crucial that the plausible items be typical of the reader's experience, and that the plausible items used by Warren and McConnell (2007) and Rayner et al. (2004) may not have been typical enough given participants' real-world-event knowledge (e.g., items about dusting miniatures or catching a goose with a trap). To ensure typicality, Matsuki et al. (2011) based their stimuli on production norms in addition to plausibility ratings (e.g., by asking "what do you cut with a knife?", p. 916). With these stimuli, they found immediate effects of plausibility (or typicality) in both eye-tracking and self-paced reading. These results suggest that the goodness of fit with readers' knowledge and experience (and consequently, the accessibility of knowledge) may be the key variable, rather than the type of knowledge necessary for validation.

However, semantic and world knowledge may gradually differ on the dimensions of commonality, stability, and accessibility: Knowledge which is at the core of word meanings tends to be shared by many language users, tends to be more stable, and may therefore be, on average, more easily accessible. Moreover, the verification of world knowledge violations may, on average, require more specialized knowledge. To verify the sentence *The favorite palace of the present queen of England is divorced*, one merely needs to draw on the (rather general) knowledge that a palace is a building and buildings cannot be divorced. However, to verify the sentence *The present queen of England is divorced,* one needs to possess and invoke more specific knowledge about the present queen of England and her biography.

Nonetheless, it is unclear at this point whether a clear distinction between semantic and world knowledge violations is possible and useful. It is not our goal in this chapter to advance this debate, but we do find it worthy of noting here because we think that the heterogeneous use·and blurry operationalizations of terms obscure the relevance of some existent studies for validation in language comprehension. For the present purpose, it seems both fruitful and parsimonious to view the different types of violations on a continuous dimension of plausibility rather than trying to separate them into different categories. This may seem like an oversimplification at first glance, but plausibility ratings obtained in various studies (e.g., Rayner et al., 2004; Warren & McConnell, 2007) support the idea that both semantic and world knowledge violations can be adequately arranged on a continuum of plausibility, with semantic violations usually receiving lower plausibility ratings. It is also in line with the terminology chosen by Warren (2011), who uses implausibility and anomaly virtually interchangeably and locates different kinds of knowledge violations on a dimension of "plausibility violation severity" (p. 914). Moreover, as we hope to show in this chapter, the results of these seemingly different types of knowledge violations can be integrated into a surprisingly coherent picture, supporting the idea that there is a common underlying dimension (e.g., Fischler, Bloom, Childers, Arroyo, & Perry, 1984).

Immediate Effects of Plausibility on Comprehension

A highly consistent finding in the literature is that implausible information is processed more slowly as compared to plausible information. Specifically, it leads to longer reading times in self-paced reading (e.g., Albrecht & O'Brien, 1993; O'Brien et al., 1998; Singer, 2006) and longer fixations in eye-tracking (e.g., Cook & Myers, 2004; Murray & Rowan, 1998; Rayner et al., 2004; Staub et al., 2007; Warren & McConnell, 2007), as well as to more regressions and rereading (e.g., Braze, Shankweiler, Ni, & Palumbo, 2002). Processing difficulties due to implausibility are immediate, suggesting an incremental assessment of the plausibility of linguistic input (Staub et al., 2007; Traxler & Pickering, 1996), which is unaffected by the distance and structural relationship between the words cueing the implausibility (Patson & Warren, 2010). Moreover, the reading time penalty caused by an implausibility correlates with offline plausibility ratings (Staub et al., 2007), suggesting that the plausibility judgment— which can be computed in an intentional, offline decision process—is in fact in some form immediately available during online comprehension (see also Isberner & Richter, 2013a).

In line with the findings demonstrating implausibility-related comprehension disruptions, Black, Freeman, and Johnson-Laird (1986) have shown that the more implausible a text is, the more it is judged as surprising and as difficult to comprehend, and the less it is remembered. Implausible information has also been shown to be less likely to be integrated into the situation model (Maier & Richter, 2013; Schroeder, Richter, & Hoever, 2008). Other work from our own lab (Isberner & Richter, 2013a, 2013b; Richter et al., 2009) as well as results obtained in lexical decision tasks (e.g., West & Stanovich, 1982) also suggest that implausibility makes any kind of subsequent positive responses more difficult, even if the task that requires them is completely unrelated to plausibility. Moreover, plausibility guides the knowledge-based inferences that are generated during comprehension, such as thematic or predictive inferences (e.g., Federmeier & Kutas, 1999; Hannon & Daneman, 1998; Long, Oppy, & Seely, 1994; Peracchi & O'Brien, 2004; Thorndyke, 1976).

Furthermore, plausibility has been found to influence syntactic analysis and reanalysis. For example, it can bias analysis in syntactically ambiguous sentences (van Gompel et al., 2001). In the so-called "garden path" phenomena, it affects the commitment to the initial analysis, and therefore recovery from an implausible misanalysis is faster than from a plausible one (Pickering & Traxler, 1998). Plausibility has also been present in everyday reasoning contexts (plausible reasoning; e.g., Collins & Michalski, 1989) and has been shown to be used as a shortcut in recognition when the retrieval of an exact memory match is difficult or costly (Lemaire & Fayol, 1995; Reder, 1982; Reder, Wible, & Martin, 1986).

Another finding that has been associated with implausibility is an elevated N400 ERP (Ferretti, Singer, & Patterson, 2008; Fischler et al., 1984, 1985; Hagoort et al., 2004; Nieuwland & Kuperberg, 2008; van Berkum et al., 1999, 2003). This ERP component was elevated for all types of knowledge violations that we discussed in the previous sections, supporting our decision to subsume them on a single dimension of plausibility. In addition, violations of self-referential knowledge (e.g., *My name is Ira*; Fischler et al., 1984) and statements contradicting (moral) beliefs (e.g., *I think euthanasia is an acceptable/unacceptable course of action;* van Berkum, Holleman, Nieuwland, Otten, & Murre, 2009) have also been found to elicit an elevated N400, suggesting that these types of knowledge are also accessed during comprehension and used for validation. In line with this idea, van Berkum et al. (2009) concluded from their data that "strong disagreement rapidly influences the ongoing analysis of meaning, which indicates that even very early processes in language comprehension are sensitive to a person's value system" (p. 1092). As Lombardi (2012) has pointed out, "Plausibility judgments do not rely on absolute definitions of and distinctions between knowledge and belief" (p. 4), suggesting that there may be little difference between the processing of information that is inconsistent with one's knowledge and the processing of information that is inconsistent with one's beliefs.

We propose that these findings should not merely be seen as showing the processing costs of implausibility but rather as evidence for a purposeful online and nonstrategic validation process (*epistemic monitoring*) which protects the system from false information and thereby—in general—promotes accurate and stable mental representations (Schroeder et al., 2008).

Does the N400 Index Validation or Detection of Semantic Mismatches? Evidence from Studies on Negation, Self-Referential Statements, and Knowledge Acquired in the Lab

A finding which has often been interpreted as evidence for a two-step model of comprehension and validation is that in tasks crossing truth value and negation, the N400 has been found to be more sensitive to semantic matches versus mismatches than to truth value (e.g., Fischler et al., 1983; Wiswede et al., 2013). However, the problem with many of the negated sentences that have been used in these studies is that they violate pragmatic rules. According to Wason (1965), negation is typically used to deny an assumption that the recipient is assumed to hold—for example, to point out exceptions to a rule or deny plausible misconceptions (e.g., *A whale is not a fish*). In contrast, denying something that makes no sense in the first place violates the conversational maxim to be informative (Grice, 1975; Sperber & Wilson, 1995). Against this background, a sentence such as *A sparrow is not a vehicle* (Fischler et al., 1983), which is representative of the kind of stimuli used in these studies, seems pragmatically implausible. Fischler et al. (1983) also refer to these types of negated sentences as implausible negatives to point out that the negative itself is implausible, even if the overall sentence is true according to formal logic. Thus, in this particular case, the plausibility of the utterance per se runs counter to the formal truth value of its content.

Unlike most other studies on the processing of negation, Nieuwland and Kuperberg (2008) used negated sentences that were pragmatically licensed (e.g., *With proper equipment, scuba diving is not very dangerous*). Under these conditions, the N400 was modulated by truth value rather than by semantic matches or mismatches, which speaks against a two-step model of comprehension and validation, in which "nonpropositional semantic processes precede the decision processes that compute sentence truth value" (Nieuwland & Kuperberg, 2008, p. 1213). Rather, under these conditions, people appear to be able to validate the negated sentences without any delay.

Fischler and colleagues used two other methods to avoid confounds between semantic mismatch and truth value. In one of their studies (Fischler et al., 1984), they investigated the verification of statements that referred to facts about the participants themselves, such as *My name is Ira*. Although these stimuli contained neither semantic mismatches nor semantic anomalies, false statements were marked by a larger N400 than true statements. In another study, Fischler et al. (1985) investigated the processing of knowledge acquired in the lab, whose truth and falsity were determined arbitrarily. An elevated N400 distinguished false from true sentences, regardless of whether the participants were explicitly asked to verify the sentences, or to "continue to look at the statement and read the words, but not make any decision or response about its truth value or meaning" (p. 87), or to respond incorrectly (i.e., respond with "false" to a true statement, and vice versa). Based on these results, the authors concluded that comprehension is automatic: "It is concluded that attending to a presented word results in an automatic analysis of its meaning in the context of a preceding verbal input, and that ERPs can indicate the nature of the output of that analysis" (p. 83). It is important to note, however, that this conclusion is actually based on the automaticity of the true/false discrimination. Thus, Fischler et al. directly equated analysis of meaning with the determination of truth value, consistent with Singer's (2006) proposal that fully comprehending a sentence entails its verification.

Prediction: Readers Use Their World Knowledge to Predict Upcoming Words before They Appear

Knowledge-based prediction in language comprehension represents another phenomenon that speaks against two-step models of comprehension and validation. For example, many studies suggest that people make predictive inferences based on their world knowledge (e.g., Cook et al., 2001; Peracchi & O'Brien, 2004). These experiments usually have participants read texts which strongly imply a particular consequence (e.g., a person falling from the 15th story of a building) and then test for the activation of the predictive inference by having readers name or perform lexical decision on a word which is assumed to represent the inference (e.g., "dead"). Faster naming or lexical decisions compared to a baseline condition are taken as evidence that the inference was indeed activated. However, few studies are conclusive regarding the question of whether this processing advantage may simply reflect easier postlexical integration rather than prediction. An exception is a study by van Berkum et al. (2005) on online prediction of specific upcoming words. Using an ingenious paradigm, they were able to show effects of prediction before the predicted word actually appeared by making use of the fact that adjectives in Dutch are gender inflected and positioned before the noun. If readers or listeners predict a particular word in a certain context, they should struggle when they encounter an adjective whose gender does not match that of the expected word. Van Berkum et al. found evidence for this disruption both in ERPs and reading times, and both for reading and listening. These results clearly show that world knowledge not only exerts an influence after comprehension has terminated, but that readers use it online during comprehension to predict what will be said (or written) next. Thus, the fit between their world knowledge and unfolding discourse immediately affects subsequent processing.

Evidence for Nonstrategic Validation

One may raise the concern that many of the above studies may have triggered evaluative processing by repeatedly exposing participants to knowledge violations. However, this concern can be rejected on the basis of the results of studies reporting early effects of local implausibility despite using globally plausible stimuli (e.g., Pickering & Traxler, 1998; Matsuki et al., 2011; Staub et al., 2007). This suggests a nonstrategic, fast, word-by-word plausibility assessment that is not triggered by repeated exposure to unusual stimuli. Moreover, in a study by Fischler and Bloom (1979, experiment 2), effects of implausibility on lexical decision latencies disappeared when all of the stimuli were implausible, suggesting that a large proportion of implausible stimuli in an experiment reduces validation rather than encouraging it, at least when participants are not explicitly instructed to validate. Thus, it is unlikely that epistemic monitoring is merely triggered by implausible or anomalous stimuli.

Evidence from Our Own Lab: The Epistemic Stroop Effect

The aforementioned studies suggest that evaluative processing during comprehension is the default mode of processing (i.e., whenever readers are instructed to read for comprehension), but they still leave open the possibility that readers can "switch off" validation when it is strategically useful to do so. However, there is evidence from our own lab that speaks against this possibility.

To test whether it is possible for readers to ignore validity or plausibility when it is irrelevant to a task, we used a Stroop-like paradigm (Stroop, 1935) in which participants were required to respond positively or negatively after reading true (plausible) or false (implausible) sentences. Crucially, the actual experimental task did not require or encourage validation: It involved an orthographic task in which participants were asked to indicate whether a particular word was spelled correctly or not (Richter et al., 2009; Isberner & Richter, 2013a), a nonlinguistic color judgment task in which participants judged whether or not a word had changed color (Isberner & Richter, 2013a), or a simple probe task in which participants were required to respond to the words "true" and "false" (as introduced by Wiswede et al., 2013; Isberner & Richter, 2013b). Participants were presented with the sentences word by word using rapid serial visual presentation and were prompted to perform the assigned task at varying points during sentence presentation. In experimental items, which varied in validity or plausibility, the prompt always appeared immediately after the end of the sentence. We predicted that if validation is a nonstrategic process, it should be more difficult to respond positively after reading invalid/implausible information because the validation process should bias the system toward a negative response (see figure 12.1). In line with this prediction, a consistent finding in all of the tasks was that task-irrelevant plausibility affected response latencies, resulting in a significant interaction of plausibility and required response (figure 12.2 shows representative data from two of our experiments). This was the case regardless of whether the stimuli used were true or false sentences (referring to factual knowledge), whether they were plausible or implausible scenarios (referring to event-based knowledge), and whether plausibility was manipulated by the intrasentential (e.g., *Soft soap is edible*) or extrasentential context (e.g., *Frank has a broken pipe/leg. He calls the plumber.*). In particular, positive responses were always much slower after reading implausible stimuli, which suggests that implausible information elicits a negative response tendency which interferes with any kind of positive response.

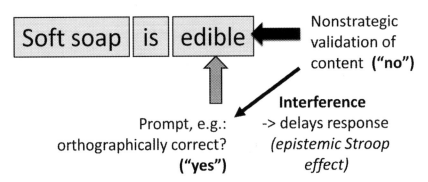

Figure 12.1
Rationale of our epistemic Stroop paradigm.

(a)

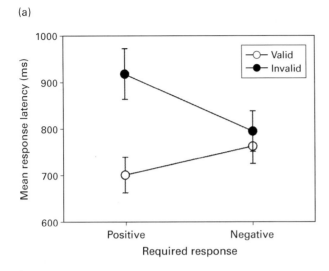

(b)

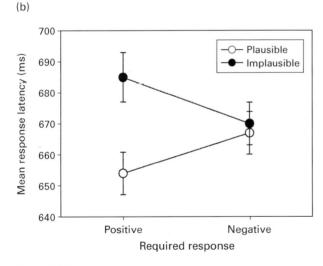

Figure 12.2

Mean correct response latency as a function of required response (positive, negative) (a) when participants were required to judge the orthographical correctness of the last word of valid versus invalid sentences (adapted from "You Don't Have to Believe Everything You Read: Background Knowledge Permits Fast and Efficient Validation of Information," by T. Richter, S. Schroeder, and B. Wöhrmann, 2009, *Journal of Personality and Social Psychology*, *96*, pp. 538–558. Copyright 2009 by the American Psychological Association. Adapted with permission) and (b) when participants were required to indicate whether the last word of plausible versus implausible sentences had changed color (reprinted from *Acta Psychologica*, *142*, M.-B. Isberner and T. Richter, "Can Readers Ignore Implausibility? Evidence for Nonstrategic Monitoring of Event-Based Plausibility in Language Comprehension," pp. 15–22. Copyright 2013, with permission from Elsevier). Error bars correspond to ± 1 standard error of the mean.

In fact, similar interference has been found in lexical decisions for "yes" responses to words that are incongruous in their context (e.g., Fischler & Bloom, 1979; West & Stanovich, 1982), the difference being that these incongruous completions, unlike ours, mostly comprised more severe plausibility violations which some might classify as semantic violations (e.g., *We stayed until the pants*). Moreover, in lexical decision, validation processes are confounded with access to word meaning (West & Stanovich, 1982). Therefore, tasks that are nonsemantic or even nonlinguistic, such as the tasks we have used so far in our Stroop-like paradigm, appear to be better suited for directly investigating nonstrategic validation. Nonetheless, the consistency of our findings with these previous results (despite using very different stimuli and tasks) is noteworthy. Moreover, this effect was present even when participants were instructed to treat the context reading and lexical decision as different tasks (Fischler & Bloom, 1979, experiment 5), suggesting that epistemic monitoring is difficult to suppress. However, the effect disappeared when the participants only saw incongruous (or implausible) sentences (Fischler & Bloom, 1979, experiment 2), suggesting that epistemic monitoring can be reduced by strong manipulations of the task context.

Are the Effects of Validation due to Prediction?   Another question we have attempted to answer in our experiments is whether the effects of plausibility may be due to prediction rather than validation. As previously discussed, readers can exploit their world knowledge and situation model to predict upcoming words during online comprehension (DeLong et al., 2005; van Berkum et al., 2005), and words that are implausible in their context are often surprising, that is, not predictable (Black et al., 1986). Therefore, the disruptive effects of implausibility may be simply due to the fact that the implausible completion is unexpected.

Plausibility and predictability are empirically very difficult to disentangle (see also Matsuki et al., 2011), as they are both related to the goodness of fit with what one knows about the world. However, implausible completions are always unpredictable while unpredictable completions are not necessarily implausible. Taking advantage of this fact, we tried to disentangle effects of plausibility and predictability in our own experiments by varying the predictability of the target words in the plausible condition (Isberner & Richter, 2013a). To do so, we obtained cloze norms for sentence pairs (e.g., *Frank has a broken pipe. He calls the...*) which were strongly biased toward a particular completion (*plumber*) but at the same time permitted other plausible completions (e.g., *tradesman*). Based on these norms, we selected completions that had either a high (M = 75%) or a low (M = 6%) cloze value in the plausible context but were equally plausible when paired with the plausible context sentence (e.g., *Frank has a broken pipe. He calls the plumber/tradesman*) and equally implausible when paired with the implausible context sentence (e.g., *Frank has a broken leg. He calls the plumber/tradesman*). If the epistemic Stroop effect reported in the previous section was due to disconfirmations of

specific lexical predictions, then it should emerge only for highly predictable completions, resulting in a three-way interaction with predictability. Alternatively, a two-way
interaction of predictability and required response analogous to the predicted interaction of plausibility and required response might emerge. Contrary to these notions, the
epistemic Stroop effect was not modulated by predictability, suggesting that it hinges
on message-level implausibility rather than on the disconfirmation of a specific lexical
prediction.

These results are consistent with results presented by West and Stanovich (1982),
who found that "yes" responses in a lexical decision task are delayed when the word
is presented in an incongruous context. Given that there is no such delay in naming
tasks, they interpreted that it is not a delay (or inhibition) of lexical access but rather
a bias toward a "no" response because incongruity is detected on the message level.
They were also able to confirm that it is congruity at the message level rather than "a
mismatch between the stimulus word and lexical-level expectations" (p. 385) which
produces this effect because there was no such inhibition for unexpected but congru-
ous words. Thus, these convergent findings suggest differential effects of plausibility
and predictability.

Open Questions—Future Directions   In future studies, it would be desirable to establish more clearly to what extent interference and facilitation contribute to the observed
Stroop-like effect, as the present results are not fully conclusive regarding this question.
For this purpose, it would be useful to introduce an adequate neutral condition into
the design. It would also be interesting to investigate the processing of self-referential
or belief-related statements with our paradigm. There are ERP studies suggesting validation also occurs rapidly in these types of sentences (Fischler et al., 1984; van Berkum
et al., 2009), and we would assume that our behavioral measures should be sensitive to
these types of violations as well.

In any case, our paradigm has proven to be a useful tool for investigating nonstrategic validation in language comprehension. As such, it can be used to investigate
how validation is affected by context and task demands (e.g., by the text genre or the
required depth of comprehension). It could also shed light on (gradual or categorical)
differences in the processing of knowledge violations, for example, in the time course
or strength of the interference effects of semantic and world knowledge violations.

Does Validation Always Work?

The studies presented in the previous sections may foster the impression that validation is, so to speak, "infallible." However, this conclusion would be inconsistent with a
large number of studies where validation appears to be absent. The most extreme examples are so-called semantic illusions, in which a blatant violation of world knowledge

(which should be easily accessible) goes unnoticed, such as *The authorities were trying to decide where to bury the survivors* (Barton & Sanford, 1993). But there are also less extreme examples of people's susceptibility to false information. For example, Marsh and colleagues have reported evidence suggesting that readers sometimes rely on previously read information which they should know to be false to later answer general knowledge questions (e.g., Bottoms, Eslick, & Marsh, 2010; Fazio, Barber, Rajaram, Ornstein, & Marsh, 2013; Fazio & Marsh, 2008; Marsh & Fazio, 2006; Marsh et al., 2003). Similarly, findings by Rapp (2008) suggest that prior knowledge does not protect readers from being affected by false information. Warning readers about this in advance or explicitly encouraging them to use their prior knowledge does not seem to eliminate these effects (e.g., Marsh & Fazio, 2006; Rapp, 2008).

More evidence that seemingly contradicts the notion of nonstrategic validation comes from a study by Wiswede et al. (2013). They used a Stroop-like paradigm similar to ours in which participants were asked to respond to a "true" or "false" probe presented after a true or false sentence (orthogonal to its truth value). Two groups of participants performed the same probe task, but for each group, it was randomly intermixed with a second task: The experimental group performed a truth evaluation task ("Is the sentence true or false?") whereas the control group performed a sentence comparison task ("Is this the sentence that you've just seen?"). Until the prompt appeared (1,500 ms after the final word), the participants did not know which task they would have to perform. Thus, for the experimental group, evaluation of the sentences was strategically useful on half of the trials, whereas for the control group, it was never useful. For the experimental group, Wiswede et al. found a compatibility effect in the probe task similar to our Stroop-like effect, with responses being faster when the required response matched the actual truth value of the sentence. For the control group, however, there was no such effect. Wiswede et al. thus concluded that validation is only conditionally automatic, that is, depending on an evaluative mind-set of the reader, which they assume to be induced by an evaluative task such as the orthographic task we used in our studies.

We think, however, that alternative interpretations of the results are conceivable: Unlike the study by Nieuwland and Kuperberg (2008) discussed above, Wiswede et al. (2013) used pragmatically unlicensed negatives (Wason, 1965). Therefore, the plausibility of the negative sentences themselves ran counter to their formally derived truth value. Second, it is possible that the sentence comparison task reduced not only evaluative but also semantic processing in general. Notice that it would be possible to perform this task in a foreign language on a purely perceptual level. This interpretation is supported by an attenuation of the influence of semantic mismatches on the amplitude of the N400 in the control group in Wiswede et al.'s (2013) study. This suggests that epistemic monitoring is closely tied to the depth of comprehension. We will discuss this issue in more detail in the following section.

Limits of Epistemic Monitoring—Reconciling the Contradictory Findings

We hope we have been able to show in this book chapter that routine validation can protect the mental system from false/implausible information to some extent (epistemic vigilance; Sperber et al., 2010) but also that this protection is far from perfect. The biggest challenge at the present time seems to be the integration of findings showing people's resistance to correcting information when they have acquired false knowledge on the one hand (continued influence of misinformation; Ross, Lepper, & Hubbard, 1975; Johnson & Seifert, 1994)—which is in line with the notion that previously acquired knowledge is used for validating new information—and people's apparent susceptibility to false information on the other hand, even when they have relatively strong and certain knowledge which should prevent this. However, in light of the abundance of evidence for validation in language comprehension, we would agree with Singer (2006) that the conditions under which validation fails "tend to specify the factors that regulate text verification rather than diagnose readers' systematic failure to scrutinize text" (p. 588). He identified factors on the part of the text, the reader, and the task, some of which we will reiterate here.

1. *Validation can be based on false/subjective beliefs and, hence, contribute to the persistence of such beliefs.* We suggested that prior knowledge and beliefs are used for validating incoming information in order to protect the mental system from contamination with false information. However, this conversely implies that in the case of false beliefs, validation can actually hinder the acquisition of correct knowledge (e.g., Maier & Richter, 2013) because prior beliefs immediately influence the analysis of meaning (van Berkum et al., 2009). This may also explain people's resistance to revising their beliefs or previously acquired knowledge in the face of correcting information (Ross et al., 1975; Johnson & Seifert, 1994).

2. *Validation is moderated by available knowledge/beliefs.* Naturally, only knowledge that is available and activated during comprehension can be used for validation. Knowledge can be activated either through memory-based processes (independent of reading goals; O'Brien & Myers, 1999) or through strategic memory retrieval (dependent on reading goals). For the detection of inconsistencies in a text, the coactivation of the conflicting information is crucial (van den Broek & Kendeou, 2008). As a consequence, inconsistencies will not be detected if conflicting information is not coactivated (e.g., Otero & Kintsch, 1992). Thus, a reader characteristic that is likely to play a role for validation is working memory capacity, as it limits the extent to which information can be coactivated (e.g., Hannon & Daneman, 2001; Singer, 2006). Daneman and colleagues also showed that reading skill (Daneman, Lennertz, & Hannon, 2007) and the ability of readers to access prior knowledge from long-term memory (Hannon & Daneman, 2001) moderate the detection of semantic anomalies. However, characteristics of the text also play a role: False information is particularly likely to be missed when it is

semantically strongly related to its context (Hannon & Daneman, 2001). Moreover, to the extent that readers cannot memorize all of the details mentioned in a text (Kintsch & van Dijk, 1978), inconsistencies with antecedent text may go unnoticed when the text is complex (Glenberg, Sanocki, Epstein, & Morris, 1987; Otero & Kintsch, 1992) or when it does not provide sufficient retrieval cues (e.g., lack of surface overlap with antecedent text; Albrecht & Myers, 1995). Similarly, implausibility may be overlooked in syntactically complex sentences, such as *No head injury is too trivial to be ignored* (Wason & Reich, 1979), whose exact meaning is so difficult to compute that readers may rely on a shallow analysis. In fact, it seems that in shallow semantic processing, pragmatics in the form of situation-specific plausibility can actually *override* local semantic or syntactic processing (Sanford, 2002; Sanford & Sturt, 2002), which is clearly at odds with a two-step model of comprehension and validation.

3. *Routine validation processes may be conditionally automatic* (Wiswede et al., 2013). Validation is assumed to be routine in the sense of conditionally automatic processes (Bargh & Chartrand, 1999). As such, it is nonstrategic (involuntary, i.e., it does not require specific processing goals). Nevertheless, it still depends on certain conditions: It may be modulated by mind-sets (e.g., it may be influenced by text genre or by perceived credibility of the text source), but further research is necessary to elucidate the modulating conditions. For example, readers seem to be particularly susceptible to misinformation and persuasion when they read narratives (e.g., Appel & Richter, 2007; Gerrig & Prentice, 1991; Green & Brock, 2000), which suggests that epistemic monitoring of incoming information might be suppressed to some extent in this text genre.

4. *Readers can fall victim to false information when it is sufficiently plausible.* It must be noted that studies demonstrating readers' susceptibility to misinformation usually probe knowledge that is, on average, not held with high certainty among the participants, and they always use lures that are relatively plausible (e.g., Marsh et al., 2003). Since plausibility judgments correlate with effects of plausibility on online comprehension (Staub et al., 2007), it seems possible that the more plausible false information is, the less likely it is to be reliably rejected by epistemic monitoring. In line with this idea, the plausibility of false information has been shown to affect the probability with which readers accept it as (potentially) correct (Hinze, Slaten, Horton, Jenkins, & Rapp, 2014). Moreover, epistemic monitoring is based on easily accessible knowledge, not on a complete analysis of all principally available knowledge. Unfortunately, this makes it prone to error by changes in the accessibility of inaccurate knowledge. It has been shown that episodic memory traces of false information can interfere with the retrieval of correct information from long-term memory when the false information is more readily available, even if the correct information is held with a relatively strong degree of certainty (e.g., Marsh et al., 2003). As Fazio et al. (2013) point out, it seems that the false information does not overwrite the correct knowledge but that the two representations coexist in memory and that temporarily higher accessibility of the false

information (e.g., because it was more recently encountered) explains why readers may inaccurately rely on this information. In line with this idea, readers' reliance on the false information decreases as its activation fades over time (e.g., Barber, Rajaram, & Marsh, 2008; Marsh et al., 2003).

5. *Validation is based on a quick and incomplete analysis.* Naturally, we are not suggesting that all kinds of evaluative processes occur as part of comprehension or that epistemic monitoring allows a complete analysis of the (potential) truth of information. Rather, epistemic monitoring only detects (and initially rejects) inconsistencies with easily accessible knowledge. Whether a reader then elaborates on a detected inconsistency (epistemic elaboration) depends on his or her goals and strategies (Maier & Richter, 2013; Richter, 2011).

6. *Readers perform validation to the extent that they understand a linguistic message.* It is important to note that we do not propose validation to be a routine component of listening or reading per se, but of comprehension. Language is often processed in a shallow manner (Barton & Sanford, 1993), which can lead to "good-enough" representations but sometimes also to false representations (Ferreira, Bailey, & Ferraro, 2002). Shallow processing of language can lead to failures to notice even blatant errors, as in the case of the previously mentioned semantic illusions. For example, in the case of the Moses illusion (Erickson & Mattson, 1981), the wrong kind of knowledge seems to be activated and used for interpretation as well as for validation, causing both comprehension and validation to fail and resulting in an inaccurate representation of what is being asked. Moreover, linguistic focus is likely to have an influence on the success of epistemic monitoring: False or implausible information that is not in linguistic focus, especially when it is marked as presupposed or "given" (Haviland & Clark, 1974) as in the Moses illusion, is more likely to be missed by the monitoring process. Consistent with this idea, detection rates are much higher when the implausible information is focalized (e.g., *It was Moses who put two of each kind of animal on the ark*; Bredart & Modolo, 1988). Linguistic focus has been suggested to affect the specificity of the mental representation constructed during comprehension (Sanford & Garrod, 2005). Thus, failures to notice such errors may be due to the construction of an underspecified mental representation (Bohan & Sanford, 2008; Sanford, 2002; Sanford & Graesser, 2006; Sanford, Leuthold, Bohan, & Sanford, 2011).

Because of this close relationship between comprehension and validation, one may ask whether epistemic monitoring may not be more accurately termed comprehension monitoring. However, it is important, then, to keep in mind that comprehension itself already seems to comprise evaluative processing with regard to world knowledge, as we have hopefully been able to show in this chapter. Moreover, it is the detection of implausibility that prompts people to reanalyze a syntactically or semantically ambiguous sentence when they have initially chosen the wrong interpretation (e.g., when reading the ambiguous sentence *He gave her cat food*)—*not* because of a failure to extract any meaning at all, but because of a failure to extract a meaning that is plausible with regard to world knowledge and the current situation model. In this way, validation seems to serve as a means for preserving the usefulness of language for its primary purpose: successful communication about states of affairs in the real world.

Summary

We propose that the disruption of comprehension by implausible information, which has been shown in many studies, does not just reflect processing costs of implausibility but rather a highly purposeful validation process that protects the mental system from false information. This validation process (termed *epistemic monitoring*) appears to be incremental, immediate, context-sensitive, and nonstrategic. However, the protection it provides is far from perfect, given that epistemic monitoring relies on easily accessible knowledge and seems to hinge on a minimum depth of processing.

Acknowledgments

The research reported in this chapter was supported by the German Research Foundation (Deutsche Forschungsgemeinschaft, DFG, grants RI 1100/4–2 and RI 1100/5–2).

References

Albrecht, J. E., & Myers, J. L. (1995). Role of context in accessing distant information during reading. *Journal of Experimental Psychology. Learning, Memory, and Cognition, 21*, 1459–1468.

Albrecht, J. E., & O'Brien, E. J. (1993). Updating a mental model: Maintaining both local and global coherence. *Journal of Experimental Psychology. Learning, Memory, and Cognition, 19*, 1061–1070.

Appel, M., & Richter, T. (2007). Persuasive effects of fictional narratives increase over time. *Media Psychology, 10*, 113–134.

Asher, N. (2011). *Lexical meaning in context: A web of words*. Cambridge, England: Cambridge University Press.

Barber, S. J., Rajaram, S., & Marsh, E. J. (2008). Fact learning: How information accuracy, delay and repeated testing change retention and retrieval experience. *Memory, 16*, 934–946.

Bargh, J. A., & Chartrand, T. L. (1999). The unbearable automaticity of being. *American Psychologist, 54*, 462–479.

Barton, S. B., & Sanford, A. J. (1993). A case study of anomaly detection: Shallow semantic processing and cohesion establishment. *Memory & Cognition, 21*, 477–487.

Black, A., Freeman, P., & Johnson-Laird, P. N. (1986). Plausibility and the comprehension of text. *British Journal of Psychology*, *77*, 51–62.

Bohan, J., & Sanford, A. (2008). Semantic anomalies at the borderline of consciousness: An eye-tracking investigation. *Quarterly Journal of Experimental Psychology*, *61*, 232–239.

Bottoms, H. C., Eslick, A. N., & Marsh, E. J. (2010). Memory and the Moses illusion: Failures to detect contradictions with stored knowledge yield negative memorial consequences. *Memory*, *18*, 670–678.

Braze, D., Shankweiler, D., Ni, W., & Palumbo, L. C. (2002). Readers' eye movements distinguish anomalies of form and content. *Journal of Psycholinguistic Research*, *31*, 25–44.

Bredart, S., & Modolo, K. (1988). Moses strikes again: Focalization effect on a semantic illusion. *Acta Psychologica*, *67*, 135–144.

Carpenter, P. A., & Just, M. A. (1975). Sentence comprehension: A psycholinguistic processing model of verification. *Psychological Review*, *82*, 45–73.

Chomsky, N. (1965). *Aspects of the theory of syntax*. Cambridge, MA: MIT Press.

Clark, H. H., & Chase, W. G. (1972). On the process of comparing sentences against pictures. *Cognitive Psychology*, *3*, 472–517.

Collins, A., & Michalski, R. (1989). The logic of plausible reasoning: A core theory. *Cognitive Science*, *13*, 1–49.

Connell, L., & Keane, M. T. (2004). What plausibly affects plausibility? Concept coherence and distributional word coherence as factors influencing plausibility judgments. *Memory & Cognition*, *32*, 185–197.

Connell, L., & Keane, M. T. (2006). A model of plausibility. *Cognitive Science*, *30*, 95–120.

Cook, A. E., & Guéraud, S. (2005). What have we been missing? The role of general world knowledge in discourse processing. *Discourse Processes*, *39*, 265–278.

Cook, A. E., Limber, J. E., & O'Brien, E. J. (2001). Situation-based context and the availability of predictive inferences. *Journal of Memory and Language*, *44*, 220–234.

Cook, A. E., & Myers, J. L. (2004). Processing discourse roles in scripted narratives: The influences of context and world knowledge. *Journal of Memory and Language*, *50*, 268–288.

Daneman, M., Lennertz, T., & Hannon, B. (2007). Shallow semantic processing of text: Evidence from eye movements. *Language and Cognitive Processes*, *22*, 83–105.

Davidson, D. (2001). *Inquiries into truth and interpretation* (2nd ed.). Oxford, England: Oxford University Press.

DeLong, K. A., Urbach, T. P., & Kutas, M. (2005). Probabilistic word pre-activation during language comprehension inferred from electrical brain activity. *Nature Neuroscience*, *8*, 1117–1121.

Erickson, T. D., & Mattson, M. E. (1981). From words to meaning: A semantic illusion. *Journal of Verbal Learning and Verbal Behavior, 20,* 540–551.

Fazio, L. K., Barber, S. J., Rajaram, S., Ornstein, P. A., & Marsh, E. J. (2013). Creating illusions of knowledge: Learning errors that contradict prior knowledge. *Journal of Experimental Psychology. General, 142,* 1–5.

Fazio, L. K., & Marsh, E. J. (2008). Slowing presentation speed increases illusions of knowledge. *Psychonomic Bulletin & Review, 15,* 180–185.

Federmeier, K. D., & Kutas, M. (1999). A rose by any other name: Long-term memory structure and sentence processing. *Journal of Memory and Language, 41,* 469–495.

Ferreira, F., Bailey, K. G. D., & Ferraro, V. (2002). Good enough representations in language comprehension. *Current Directions in Psychological Science, 11,* 11–15.

Ferretti, T. R., Singer, M., & Patterson, C. (2008). Electrophysiological evidence for the time-course of verifying text ideas. *Cognition, 108,* 881–888.

Filik, R., & Leuthold, H. (2008). Processing local pragmatic anomalies in fictional contexts: Evidence from the N400. *Psychophysiology, 45,* 554–558.

Fischler, I., & Bloom, P. A. (1979). Automatic and attentional processes in the effects of sentence contexts on word recognition. *Journal of Verbal Learning and Verbal Behavior, 18,* 1–20.

Fischler, I., & Bloom, P. A. (1980). Rapid processing of the meaning of sentences. *Memory & Cognition, 8,* 216–225.

Fischler, I., Bloom, P. A., Childers, D. G., Arroyo, A. A., & Perry, N. W. (1984). Brain potentials during sentence verification: Late negativity and long-term memory strength. *Neuropsychologia, 22,* 559–568.

Fischler, I., Bloom, P. A., Childers, D. G., Roucos, S. E., & Perry, N. W. (1983). Brain potentials related to stages of sentence verification. *Psychophysiology, 20,* 400–409.

Fischler, I., Childers, D. G., Achariyapaopan, T., & Perry, N. W. (1985). Brain potentials during sentence verification: Automatic aspects of comprehension. *Biological Psychology, 21,* 83–105.

Gerrig, R. J., & McKoon, G. (1998). The readiness is all: The functionality of memory-based text processing. *Discourse Processes, 26,* 67–86.

Gerrig, R. J., & O'Brien, E. J. (2005). The scope of memory-based processing. *Discourse Processes, 39,* 225–242.

Gerrig, R. J., & Prentice, D. A. (1991). The representation of fictional information. *Psychological Science, 2,* 336–340.

Gilbert, D. T. (1991). How mental systems believe. *American Psychologist, 46,* 107–119.

Gilbert, D. T., Krull, D. S., & Malone, P. S. (1990). Unbelieving the unbelievable: Some problems in the rejection of false information. *Journal of Personality and Social Psychology, 59,* 601–613.

Gilbert, D. T., Tafarodi, R. W., & Malone, P. S. (1993). You can't not believe everything you read. *Journal of Personality and Social Psychology, 65*, 221–233.

Glenberg, A. M., Sanocki, T., Epstein, W., & Morris, C. (1987). Enhancing calibration of comprehension. *Journal of Experimental Psychology. General, 116*, 119–136.

Green, M. C., & Brock, T. C. (2000). The role of transportation in the persuasiveness of public narratives. *Journal of Personality and Social Psychology, 79*, 701–721.

Grice, P. (1975). Logic and conversation. In P. Cole & J. L. Morgan (Eds.), *Syntax and semantics: Vol. 3. Speech acts* (pp. 41–58). New York: Academic Press.

Hagoort, P., Hald, L., Bastiaansen, M., & Petersson, K. M. (2004). Integration of word meaning and world knowledge in language comprehension. *Science, 304*, 438–441.

Hagoort, P., & van Berkum, J. J. A. (2007). Beyond the sentence given. *Philosophical Transactions of the Royal Society. Series B: Biological Sciences, 362*, 801–811.

Hannon, B., & Daneman, M. (1998). Facilitating knowledge-based inferences in less-skilled readers. *Contemporary Educational Psychology, 23*, 149–172.

Hannon, B., & Daneman, M. (2001). Susceptibility to semantic illusions: An individual-differences perspective. *Memory & Cognition, 29*, 449–461.

Hasson, U., Simmons, J. P., & Todorov, A. (2005). Believe it or not: On the possibility of suspending belief. *Psychological Science, 16*, 566–571.

Haviland, S. E., & Clark, H. H. (1974). What's new? Acquiring new information as a process in comprehension. *Journal of Verbal Learning and Verbal Behavior, 13*, 512–521.

Herbert, C., & Kübler, A. (2011). Dogs cannot bark: Event-related brain responses to true and false negated statements as indicators of higher-order conscious processing. *PLoS ONE, 6*, e25574.

Hinze, S. R., Slaten, D. G., Horton, W. S., Jenkins, R., & Rapp, D. N. (2014). Pilgrims sailing the Titanic: Plausibility effects on memory for misinformation. *Memory & Cognition, 42*, 305–324.

Isberner, M.-B., & Richter, T. (2013a). Can readers ignore implausibility? Evidence for nonstrategic monitoring of event-based plausibility in language comprehension. *Acta Psychologica, 142*, 15–22.

Isberner, M.-B., & Richter, T. (2013b). Does validation during language comprehension depend on an evaluative mindset? *Discourse Processes.* Advance online publication. doi:10.1080/01638 53X.2013.855867

Jackendoff, R. (2002). *Foundations of language: Brain, meaning, grammar, evolution.* Oxford, England: Oxford University Press.

Johnson, H. M., & Seifert, C. M. (1994). Sources of the continued influence effect: When misinformation in memory affects later inferences. *Journal of Experimental Psychology. Learning, Memory, and Cognition, 20*, 1420–1436.

Johnson-Laird, P. N. (1983). *Mental models: Towards a cognitive science of language, inferences, and consciousness*. Cambridge, England: Cambridge University Press.

Johnson-Laird, P. N., Herrmann, D. J., & Chaffin, R. (1984). Only connections: A critique of semantic networks. *Psychological Bulletin, 96*, 292–315.

Just, M. A., & Carpenter, P. A. (1980). A theory of reading: From eye fixations to comprehension. *Psychological Review, 87*, 329–354.

Kendeou, P., Smith, E. R., & O'Brien, E. J. (2013). Updating during reading comprehension: Why causality matters. *Journal of Experimental Psychology. Learning, Memory, and Cognition, 39*, 854–865.

Kintsch, W. (1980). Semantic memory: A tutorial. In R. Nickerson (Ed.), *Attention and performance* (Vol. 8, pp. 595–620). Hillsdale, NJ: Lawrence Erlbaum Associates.

Kintsch, W., & van Dijk, T. A. (1978). Toward a model of text comprehension and production. *Psychological Review, 85*, 363–394.

Kounios, J., Osman, A. M., & Meyer, D. E. (1987). Structure and process in semantic memory: New evidence based on speed–accuracy decomposition. *Journal of Experimental Psychology. General, 116*, 3–25.

Kutas, M., & Hillyard, S. A. (1980). Reading senseless sentences: Brain potentials reflect semantic incongruity. *Science, 207*, 203–205.

Lemaire, P., & Fayol, M. (1995). When plausibility judgments supersede fact retrieval: The example of the odd–even effect on product verification. *Memory & Cognition, 23*, 34–48.

Lombardi, D. A. (2012). *Students' conceptions about climate change: Using critical evaluation to influence plausibility reappraisals and knowledge reconstruction*. (Unpublished doctoral dissertation). University of Nevada, Las Vegas.

Long, D. L., Oppy, B. J., & Seely, M. R. (1994). Individual differences in the time course of inferential processing. *Journal of Experimental Psychology. Learning, Memory, and Cognition, 20*, 1456–1470.

Maier, J., & Richter, T. (2013). Text belief consistency effects in the comprehension of multiple texts with conflicting information. *Cognition and Instruction, 31*, 151–175.

Marsh, E. J., & Fazio, L. K. (2006). Learning errors from fiction: Difficulties in reducing reliance on fictional stories. *Memory & Cognition, 34*, 1140–1149.

Marsh, E. J., Meade, M. L., & Roediger, H. L. (2003). Learning facts from fiction. *Journal of Memory and Language, 49*, 519–536.

Matsuki, K., Chow, T., Hare, M., Elman, J. L., Scheepers, C., & McRae, K. (2011). Event-based plausibility immediately influences on-line language comprehension. *Journal of Experimental Psychology. Learning, Memory, and Cognition, 37*, 913–934.

McKoon, G., Gerrig, R. J., & Greene, S. B. (1996). Pronoun resolution without pronouns: Some consequences of memory-based text processing. *Journal of Experimental Psychology. Learning, Memory, and Cognition, 22*, 919–932.

McKoon, G., & Ratcliff, R. (1998). Memory-based language processing: Psycholinguistic research in the 1990s. *Annual Review of Psychology, 49*, 25–42.

Murray, W. S., & Rowan, M. (1998). Early, mandatory, pragmatic processing. *Journal of Psycholinguistic Research, 27*, 1–22.

Nieuwland, M. S., & Kuperberg, G. R. (2008). When the truth is not too hard to handle: An event-related potential study on the pragmatics of negation. *Psychological Science, 19*, 1213–1218.

Nieuwland, M. S., & van Berkum, J. J. A. (2006). When peanuts fall in love: N400 evidence for the power of discourse. *Journal of Cognitive Neuroscience, 18*, 1098–1111.

O'Brien, E. J. (1995). Automatic components of discourse comprehension. In R. F. Lorch & E. J. O'Brien (Eds.), *Sources of coherence in reading* (pp. 159–176). Hillsdale, NJ: Lawrence Erlbaum Associates.

O'Brien, E. J., & Albrecht, J. E. (1992). Comprehension strategies in the development of a mental model. *Journal of Experimental Psychology. Learning, Memory, and Cognition, 18*, 777–784.

O'Brien, E. J., & Myers, J. L. (1999). Text comprehension: A view from the bottom up. In S. R. Goldman, A. C. Graesser, & P. van den Broek (Eds.), *Narrative comprehension, causality, and coherence: Essays in honor of Tom Trabasso* (pp. 35–53). Mawah, NJ: Lawrence Erlbaum Associates.

O'Brien, E. J., Rizzella, M. L., Albrecht, J. E., & Halleran, J. G. (1998). Updating a situation model: A memory-based text processing view. *Journal of Experimental Psychology. Learning, Memory, and Cognition, 24*, 1200–1210.

Otero, J., & Kintsch, W. (1992). Failures to detect contradictions in a text: What readers believe versus what they read. *Psychological Science, 3*, 229–235.

Patson, N. D., & Warren, T. (2010). Eye movements when reading implausible sentences: Investigating potential structural influences on semantic integration. *Quarterly Journal of Experimental Psychology, 63*, 1516–1532.

Peracchi, K. A., & O'Brien, E. J. (2004). Character profiles and the activation of predictive inferences. *Memory & Cognition, 32*, 1044–1052.

Petty, R. E., & Cacioppo, J. T. (1986). *Communication and persuasion: Central and peripheral routes to attitude change.* New York: Springer.

Petty, R. E., & Wegener, D. T. (1999). The elaboration likelihood model: Current status and controversies. In S. Chaiken & Y. Trope (Eds.), *Dual-process theories in social psychology* (pp. 41–72). New York: Guilford Press.

Pickering, M. J., & Traxler, M. J. (1998). Plausibility and recovery from garden paths: An eye-tracking study. *Journal of Experimental Psychology. Learning, Memory, and Cognition, 24*, 940–961.

Pylkkänen, L., Oliveri, B., & Smart, A. J. (2009). Semantics vs. world knowledge in prefrontal cortex. *Language and Cognitive Processes, 24*, 1313–1334.

Rapp, D. N. (2008). How do readers handle incorrect information during reading? *Memory & Cognition, 36,* 688–701.

Ratcliff, R. (1978). A theory of memory retrieval. *Psychological Review, 85,* 59–108.

Rayner, K., Warren, T., Juhasz, B. J., & Liversedge, S. P. (2004). The effect of plausibility on eye movements in reading. *Journal of Experimental Psychology. Learning, Memory, and Cognition, 30,* 1290–1301.

Reder, L. M. (1982). Plausibility judgments versus fact retrieval: Alternative strategies for sentence verification. *Psychological Review, 89,* 250–280.

Reder, L. M., Wible, C., & Martin, J. (1986). Differential memory changes with age: Exact retrieval versus plausible inference. *Journal of Experimental Psychology: Learning, Memory, and Cognition, 12,* 72–81.

Richter, T. (2003). *Epistemologische Einschätzungen beim Textverstehen.* Lengerich, Germany: Pabst.

Richter, T. (2011). Cognitive flexibility and epistemic validation in learning from multiple texts. In J. Elen, E. Stahl, R. Bromme, & G. Clarebout (Eds.), *Links between beliefs and cognitive flexibility* (pp. 125–140). Berlin: Springer.

Richter, T., Schroeder, S., & Wöhrmann, B. (2009). You don't have to believe everything you read: Background knowledge permits fast and efficient validation of information. *Journal of Personality and Social Psychology, 96,* 538–558.

Ross, L., Lepper, M. R., & Hubbard, M. (1975). Perseverance in self-perception and social perception: Biased attributional processes in the debriefing paradigm. *Journal of Personality and Social Psychology, 32,* 880–892.

Sanford, A. J. (2002). Context, attention and depth of processing during interpretation. *Mind & Language, 17,* 188–206.

Sanford, A. J., & Garrod, S. C. (2005). Memory-based approaches and beyond. *Discourse Processes, 39,* 205–224.

Sanford, A. J., & Graesser, A. C. (2006). Shallow processing and underspecification. *Discourse Processes, 42,* 99–108.

Sanford, A. J., Leuthold, H., Bohan, J., & Sanford, A. J. S. (2011). Anomalies at the borderline of awareness: An ERP study. *Journal of Cognitive Neuroscience, 23,* 514–523.

Sanford, A. J., & Sturt, P. (2002). Depth of processing in language comprehension: Not noticing the evidence. *Trends in Cognitive Sciences, 6,* 382–386.

Schroeder, S., Richter, T., & Hoever, I. (2008). Getting a picture that is both accurate and stable: Situation models and epistemic validation. *Journal of Memory and Language, 59,* 237–255.

Singer, M. (1993). Causal bridging inferences: Validating consistent and inconsistent sequences. *Canadian Journal of Experimental Psychology, 47,* 340–359.

Singer, M. (2006). Verification of text ideas during reading. *Journal of Memory and Language, 54,* 574–591.

Singer, M., Halldorson, M., Lear, J. C., & Andrusiak, P. (1992). Validation of causal bridging inferences in discourse understanding. *Journal of Memory and Language, 31,* 507–524.

Sparks, J. R., & Rapp, D. N. (2011). Readers' reliance on source credibility in the service of comprehension. *Journal of Experimental Psychology. Learning, Memory, and Cognition, 37,* 230–247.

Speer, S. R., & Clifton, C., Jr. (1998). Plausibility and argument structure in sentence comprehension. *Memory & Cognition, 26,* 965–978.

Sperber, D., Clément, F., Heintz, C., Mascaro, O., Mercier, H., Origgi, G., & Wilson, D. (2010). Epistemic vigilance. *Mind & Language, 25,* 359–393.

Sperber, D., & Wilson, D. (1995). *Relevance: Communication and cognition.* Oxford, England: Blackwell.

Staub, A., Rayner, K., Pollatsek, A., Hyönä, J., & Majewski, H. (2007). The time course of plausibility effects on eye movements in reading: Evidence from noun–noun compounds. *Journal of Experimental Psychology. Learning, Memory, and Cognition, 33,* 1162–1169.

Stroop, J. R. (1935). Studies of interference in serial verbal reactions. *Journal of Experimental Psychology, 18,* 643–662.

Thorndyke, P. W. (1976). The role of inferences in discourse comprehension. *Journal of Verbal Learning and Verbal Behavior, 15,* 437–446.

Traxler, M. J., & Pickering, M. J. (1996). Plausibility and the processing of unbounded dependencies: An eye-tracking study. *Journal of Memory and Language, 35,* 454–475.

van Berkum, J. J. A., Brown, C. M., Zwitserlood, P., Kooijman, V., & Hagoort, P. (2005). Anticipating upcoming words in discourse: Evidence from ERPs and reading times. *Journal of Experimental Psychology. Learning, Memory, and Cognition, 31,* 443–467.

van Berkum, J. J. A., Hagoort, P., & Brown, C. M. (1999). Semantic integration in sentences and discourse: Evidence from the N400. *Journal of Cognitive Neuroscience, 11,* 657–671.

van Berkum, J. J. A., Holleman, B., Nieuwland, M. S., Otten, M., & Murre, J. (2009). Right or wrong? The brain's fast response to morally objectionable statements. *Psychological Science, 20,* 1092–1099.

van Berkum, J. J. A., Zwitserlood, P., Hagoort, P., & Brown, C. M. (2003). When and how do listeners relate a sentence to the wider discourse? Evidence from the N400 effect. *Cognitive Brain Research, 17,* 701–718.

van den Broek, P., & Kendeou, P. (2008). Cognitive processes in comprehension of science texts: The role of co-activation in confronting misconceptions. *Applied Cognitive Psychology, 22,* 335–351.

van Dijk, T. A., & Kintsch, W. (1983). *Strategies of discourse comprehension.* New York: Academic Press.

van Gompel, R. P. G., Pickering, M. J., & Traxler, M. J. (2001). Reanalysis in sentence processing: Evidence against current constraint-based and two-stage models. *Journal of Memory and Language, 45*, 225–258.

Warren, T. (2011). The influence of plausibility and anomaly on eye movements in reading. In S. P. Liversedge, I. Gilchrist, & S. Everling (Eds.), *The Oxford handbook on eye movements* (pp. 911–923). New York: Oxford University Press.

Warren, T., & McConnell, K. (2007). Investigating effects of selectional restriction violations and plausibility violation severity on eye-movements in reading. *Psychonomic Bulletin & Review, 14*, 770–775.

Wason, P. C. (1965). The contexts of plausible denial. *Journal of Verbal Learning and Verbal Behavior, 4*, 7–11.

Wason, P. C., & Reich, S. S. (1979). A verbal illusion. *Quarterly Journal of Experimental Psychology, 31*, 591–597.

West, R. F., & Stanovich, K. E. (1982). Source of inhibition in experiments on the effect of sentence context on word recognition. *Journal of Experimental Psychology. Learning, Memory, and Cognition, 8*, 385–399.

Wiswede, D., Koranyi, N., Müller, F., Langner, O., & Rothermund, K. (2013). Validating the truth of propositions: Behavioral and ERP indicators of truth evaluation processes. *Social Cognitive and Affective Neuroscience, 8*, 647–653.

Zwaan, R. A., Langston, M. C., & Graesser, A. C. (1995). The construction of situation models in narrative comprehension: An event-indexing model. *Psychological Science, 6*, 292–297.

Zwaan, R. A., Magliano, J. P., & Graesser, A. C. (1995). Dimensions of situation model construction in narrative comprehension. *Journal of Experimental Psychology: Learning, Memory, and Cognition, 21*, 386–397.

Zwaan, R. A., & Radvansky, G. A. (1998). Situation models in language comprehension and memory. *Psychological Bulletin, 123*, 162–185.

III Epistemological Groundings

13 An Epistemological Perspective on Misinformation

Andrea A. diSessa

My aim in this chapter is to bring a slightly exotic perspective, that of epistemology (the study of knowledge, per se), to the study of misinformation. How is it that humans suffer the effects of believing things that are not true? Where does misinformation come from, what are its properties and consequences, and how might we mitigate the acquisition or consequences of misinformation?

My personal research specialty is the study of conceptual change, particularly in learning science (physics). It has long been known that some curricular topics are particularly challenging at least in part because students start with intuitive ideas that seem rather far from normative ways of thinking. These "false" intuitive notions are usually called "misconceptions." Students (most everyone, actually) seem to believe such "strange" things as "Instigated motion always dies away" (Newton says things continue moving forever, without a good reason to stop), "Things move with a speed proportional to the force propelling them" (again, Newton says force creates acceleration, not speed), and "Ducks acquired webbed feet so that they could swim efficiently" (the purpose does not create the structure; it only validates it). The study of misinformation often includes reference to the misconceptions identified in conceptual change research, analogizing them to other kinds of misinformation (Rapp, 2008). Indeed, it is often assumed that the means to overcome such ideas might be similar to that needed to overcome other kinds of misinformation.

A presumption of my discussion, here, is that misconceptions might *not* be misinformation—or possibly, that misconceptions are a *very particular kind* of misinformation. This, it turns out, is a major element of this chapter. The epistemological inquiry is to investigate the forms of knowledge involved in misconceptions and misinformation, and, if they are different, to compare and contrast. A word of warning: I use the term "knowledge" in a very broad sense, encompassing but extending beyond both misconceptions and misinformation.

Since I do not study other kinds of misinformation, I am not going to try to solve other researchers' problems directly. Instead, I am going to explicate my own perspective on misconceptions, generalize it slightly into a more flexible epistemological perspective, and hope this can be valuable to researchers of misinformation. In short, I hope to make suggestions toward an epistemological research program that can illuminate misinformation of many kinds, including what are called misconceptions. This is a program of study that, as far as I know, has not been pursued to deal with misinformation. But I think it should be.

Epistemology and "Knowledge in Pieces"

Epistemology

Like any enduring and fundamental inquiry, the study of knowledge, historically, has been approached in many different ways. The common element is to problematize knowledge, this thing that is pervasive in our everyday lives (Does John know my telephone number? Does my partner really understand me?) and also particularly ingrained in education (What knowledge constitutes high school physics?). Like fish swimming in water, just because we encounter it every day does not mean we know very much about knowledge. My attitude is that, professionally, we know a bit more about knowledge than did the ancient philosophers. In fact, I believe we have a good critical perspective on most historical analyses of knowledge. However, we are far from having solved the problem of knowledge sufficiently to give good answers to questions such as these: What exactly is the knowledge learned in school, and what are the general processes by which it is acquired? That is precisely where my program of studies focuses.

Our natural language and common sense provide resources for thinking about knowledge. We have a large lexicon of knowledge terms—fact, idea, concept, true, false, questionable, certain, and so on—and even more professional-sounding terms, like hypothesis and theory. Each term embodies assumptions and potential inferences about the relevant knowledge type. Facts, for example, are just there, they do not depend on things like personal point of view, and we can investigate and find out whether a purported fact is true or false. Whether any of these knowledge terms are adequate to a scientific theory of knowledge and whether the assumptions about them are valid are things to investigate.

To cut a long story very short, I do not believe that any of these terms can survive scrutiny as adequate scientific tools, not even if they are modestly improved. We need models and theories of kinds of knowledge and knowledge properties and processes that, at minimum, cleanly transcend common understanding. And we need entirely new terms, as well, to pursue adequate understanding of knowledge. To sharpen this claim, I believe that even scientific-sounding terms such as "concept" require very substantial reworking to be helpful in understanding key learning phenomena. This is ironic, given that the very term for my research specialty, "conceptual change," would seem to be predicated on knowing what concepts are. (See diSessa & Sherin,

1998, with regard to the literature on what "concept" means in the field of conceptual change.)

The stepping-off point for the epistemological explorations here is not generic. It is, instead, a point of view that I call "knowledge in pieces" (KiP), which I have cultivated over the last decades.

Knowledge in Pieces

In keeping with the spirit of this chapter, I avoid more technical aspects of this point of view but just sketch main points that will be useful here. There is plenty of literature for readers to pursue a deeper understanding. (Some good starting places for this chapter are, in rough order of accessibility, diSessa, 1983, 1996; diSessa & Wagner, 2005; diSessa, 1993.) The main point is fairly big and complicated. However, one can start with a simple assertion: Knowledge is in its essence diverse and complicated and, as yet, ill understood; KiP provides some direction for improving our understanding of it.

A Complex Systems Approach to Knowledge

Elements and Knowledge Terms   The big presumption of KiP is that, in order to describe knowledge in any detail, we need, in principle, to describe systems of hundreds or thousands of elements, or more. This should not be, by itself, much of a surprise: The working vocabulary of adults consists of many thousands of words ("concepts," very roughly speaking). However, when we look at research focusing on naive knowledge in physics, for example, many researchers have aimed for very compact descriptions, attempting to capture what people know in just a few sentences of text (see relevant discussion in diSessa, Gillespie, & Esterly, 2004). In fact, naive ideas in various areas are often characterized as "naive theories," which are presumed to be statable in brief, natural language descriptions.

If KiP is correct, however, such simplifications are doubly wrong. First, I believe naive physics contains hundreds or thousands of individually important pieces—a large vocabulary, similar to natural language lexicon. We need to engage that complexity and not just make generalizations about it. Here are two reasons for engaging the complexity. Many of the misconceptions that have been identified can be explained, one at a time, as the result of one or, possibly, a few naive elements taken together. However, the relevant elements are different from one misconception to the next. So, in all, we cannot reduce our analysis to one element, or even just a few. Second, when it comes time to learn normative physics, a significant variety of elements one at a time or in small clusters become involved in learning at various stages in various ways. (See later discussion on this point.) Glossing the naive state as a single incorrect theory, thus, does a great disservice to the complexity of naive knowledge (many naive ideas are, in fact, productive in learning), and it makes it nearly impossible to trace how old ideas become part of new understandings. Indeed, the moniker "misconception" entails the assumption that these ideas are all "mis" conceptions; they are all categorically wrong. My suggestion that naive ideas become involved in learning correct science puts the categorical characterization as "wrong" in doubt. We shall see soon how bad an idea sorting into right and wrong is, from a KiP perspective. The extension to "*mis*information" might be illuminating.

The second oversimplification of the simple-and-compact descriptions presumption about naive knowledge is that it is even appropriate to use common categories, such as "theory" or "concept," at all, without technical refinement. Indeed, on the high end, we may need a completely different set of knowledge terms (along with appropriate theories and models of each of them), and possibly even quite a large set of such terms. In this chapter, I'll briefly explain two "new" knowledge terms—p-prims and coordination classes—that I have found tremendously helpful.

System and Systematicity   If one has hundreds of elements in a system, the question immediately arises, what are the relations among them? "Theory" implies a pretty tight set of relations among various well-defined elements. As explained above, I take "theory" as a rather seriously awkward, if not incorrect, way to describe naive ideas in physics. An alternative description is necessary. In fact, I believe that elements of naive physics have substantially independent developmental trajectories, so "a loosely coupled system" is far more apt than "theory." One thing that this implies, once again, is that there really is no substitute for describing the many elements of naive physics in order to track their influence during learning.

Processes of Use and Development   How do we describe what happens when an element of knowledge is used? How does a knowledge element come to take the shape that it finally has in students or adults, generally? Even more important, how do mature intuitive elements get reshaped and combined to help construct more normative ideas? This may be the most exotic part of the KiP epistemology, and luckily, for these purposes, we do not need to say very much about it.

Examples: P-prims and Coordination Classes

P-prims as Elements   Under the epistemological circumstances described above, I have found it useful to introduce two new knowledge terms. The first new knowledge term—p-prim—will be, by far, the most important for our discussion here. P-prims (phenomenological primitives) are small and simple elements of intuitive causality. They are phenomenological in the sense that they grow out of "easy," everyday descriptions of common phenomena. There are two senses of "primitive" involved. The first is that people see them as primitively explanatory: When a p-prim fits a real-world situation, what happens in that situation seems natural and to demand no more explanation. For example, one of the most important p-prims asserts that more effort begets greater result. If you push harder, of course things go faster or farther. There's nothing more to say. The other sense of primitive is that p-prims, by themselves, cannot really be disassembled in the way that one might think that a theory can be disassembled into, for example, basic concepts and relations among them.[1] Individual p-prims get evoked and used as a whole.

The System of P-prims   As I've already hinted, there are hundreds or thousands of p-prims, and they are, in significant degree, independent; they are "loosely coupled." The first technical paper on the subject (diSessa, 1993) documented a couple of scores of p-prims. Recent work has documented that many individual p-prims become active and consequential in students' learning of topics like thermal equilibration. Again, be alert to later development of this idea.

Real-Time and Developmental Processes for P-prims   We do not need to say much about the local processing of p-prims, except to note that they act over short timescales (a few seconds to several minutes), and they do not connect easily to language. People are unaware of their p-prims; there are no common words to describe them; and putting them into language is, indeed, very difficult. Development is particularly interesting. The origins of p-prims seem fairly simple. They are just simple "descriptions" (as in some internal language) of common situations that are found to be more generally explanatory. They work by asserting fairly general connections between causes and consequences (e.g., effort and result). But the path is long for p-prims to be sorted into their most general form, and to become reliably connected to appropriate circumstances—that is, so that they are activated (mostly) in appropriate circumstances, and not in others.

P-prims and Misconceptions   The relationship between p-prims and what are called misconceptions in the conceptual change literature is slightly complicated. In a nutshell, p-prims account for many (but not all) misconceptions, but in several different ways. Here is an example. The prototypical p-prim, Ohm's p-prim, prescribes a direct relationship between agentive "effort" or impetus and some kind of result. When this idea is used in everyday situations, say, pushing an object, muscular effort is easy to interpret as generic agentive impetus. And the corresponding "result" may be taken as the speed of the object. Sure enough, in many or even most everyday situations, it takes greater "effort" to effect greater "result" (speed): personal effort in running, the level of "power" (controlled by the accelerator) with a car engine. Unfortunately for learners of science, Newton's laws take these phenomena to be derived from a more fundamental law, that motion perpetuates itself, and only change in motion is caused by force. So, the typical use of Ohm's p-prim with respect to motion works properly in everyday situations (thus to use the word "wrong" is already a bit suspect as a way to characterize it), but, since it disagrees with Newton's conception of basic principles, it is regarded as a "misconception."

Similarly, another misconception, which is known as the "impetus theory" (a proposed "naive theory of physics"; see McCloskey, 1983) seems to be the result of a particular confluence of p-prims in a particular class of circumstances. For an extended exposition, see the decomposition of the impetus theory into p-prims in diSessa (1996). So, p-prims are not even in one-to-one correspondence with misconceptions but can be many-to-one. "Wrong" has gotten seriously muddied here; is each of the p-prims "wrong" because it is sometimes used in a situation that correctly describes what happens in experience, but it affords a different explanation than scientists prefer? How do we summarize the various "correct" or "incorrect" usages of the several, separate p-prims?

Even more troublesome (for the term "misconception"), individual p-prims sometimes appear perfectly correct in some scientific circumstances, and, in all likelihood, become surreptitious parts of knowing "real physics." Ohm's p-prim, for example, makes Ohm's law (that current flow in an electrical circuit is proportional to the "impetus" that is voltage) almost intuitively obvious. No doubt, the p-prim becomes part of how students know the official scientific law.

All in all, p-prims used in particular circumstances result in student explanations that are regarded as misconceptions, but the same p-prims in other circumstances work just fine, or even can be integrated into completely scientific understandings. These epistemological subtleties will continue to be explored in this chapter.

Coordination Classes as Elements   I can be much briefer with this next new knowledge term—coordination class. This is because it is, in a sense, more familiar. In fact, it involves a technically refined model of a certain kind of "concept." (With a careful epistemological treatment, it turns out that we must distinguish among various kinds of concepts. See the discussion in the next footnote.) On the other hand, saying a few words about this new kind of knowledge type makes several important points. First, it serves as a token of the fact that we need diverse terms to describe knowledge. Second, its nature contrasts markedly with the idea of p-prims, and that makes the point that we must be very careful not to confuse different knowledge types. Third, it provides a precise model of how things like p-prims become involved in normative understanding.

A *coordination class* is a model aimed at capturing the main properties of many technical concepts in science. It is not obviously apt for more everyday concepts, like "dog" or "book."[2] Coordination classes are defined by how it is that we "see" them in the world. How do we see the location, direction, and magnitude—that is, the defining properties—of a force? Sometimes more or less direct sensory access does the job. For example, we can kinesthetically feel the tension in our arms when we deliberately push an object. At other times, there are complex inferential chains that connect observations to our determination of the force's properties. For example, an often-serviceable model of a spring is that it exerts a force proportional to its deformation (stretching or compression). Thus, we can see and measure deformation, and infer from it the amount of force.

In net, the two major components of a coordination class are (1) the set of things that one actually observes (called extraction or readout strategies), and (2) the set of inferences (called the inferential net) that one uses to get from observations to characteristic features of the coordination class.

A critical observation is that, in general, one must use different extractions and inferences in different circumstances. For example, if you are not in a position to feel a force, you must use other means to determine it. For the forces that affect distant planets or stars, complex inferences are often needed. As a result of these complications, it is evident that a well-formed coordination class requires the property that all possible chains from observation to determination of its core properties give the same result. If not, we would have an incoherent concept, which changes according to how you "observe" it. This coherence property is called *alignment*. One can summarize: In general, it turns out that the most critical problems in acquiring a coordination class are (1) collecting a sufficient set of relevant extractions, (2) collecting a sufficient set of inferencing strategies, which interpolate from observation to property determination, and (3) making sure that every possible path from observation to property yields the same result. Empirical work shows that novices can fail to have a particular coordination class in any of these ways: They may not know what to look for in some situations (relevant extractions); they may use commonsense inferencing strategies in some circumstances in place of scientific ones, and thus determine incorrect properties; and they may shift their attention subtly even in the same situation, thus following different chains of determination and, consequently, determining different things at different points of time (thus appearing to be "incoherent"). Three representative studies of the development of proper coordination classes are as follows: Parnafes (2007) for the coordination class "speed"; Levrini and diSessa (2008) for the coordination class "time" in Einstein's special relativity; and diSessa (2004), diSessa and Wagner (2005), and Wagner (2006) for several coordination classes involved in the "law of large numbers" in statistics.

Coordination classes are very complex subsystems, certainly compared with p-prims. Indeed, p-prims may become parts of a coordination class in very particular ways. For example, a p-prim can provide relevant and proper inferences in particular circumstances. As important, p-prims, when slightly revised and properly incorporated, can provide a sense of understanding to students concerning the meaning of the coordination class under consideration. One of the important changes to p-prims that supports normative thinking is that they become active in different circumstances than they do before instruction. (See earlier discussion of Ohm's p-prim with respect to Ohm's law in electricity, and, also, later discussion of Ohm's p-prim with respect to thermal equilibration.) This is one important aspect of the general idea of *contextuality*, understanding knowledge by understanding exactly when it is activated and how it "responds" to different contexts.

Misconceptions and Misinformation

In this section, I examine and compare the epistemology of misconceptions (in the form of their underlying p-prims) and misinformation.

A Default View of Misinformation

Since I know of no professionally done epistemological analysis of misinformation, I provide a rough and ready sketch, trying to capture what I imagine are something like the common cultural assumptions about misinformation. I organize these points according to a scheme designed to connect well with some of the core questions examined in this volume.

Source   There must be a variety of sources for misinformation, which may provide different challenges for dealing with it. First, social/cultural sources might exist; people might simply be told wrong things. A second source might be in misreadings of reality. Although not widespread, occasionally one finds this idea in the conceptual change literature. For example, McCloskey, Washburn, and Felch (1983) proposed that some misconceptions are due to visual illusions. According to McCloskey et al., in watching a scene where an object falls in a moving frame of reference (say, a walking person drops an apple), the observer might just take the frame of reference of the walker (not the frame of reference fixed relative to the ground) and "conclude" that dropped things fall straight down, which is a well-documented misconception.[3] In general, it is pretty well established that people often do not see happenings in the world with high accuracy, and therefore it seems certain that some bits of misinformation arise in this way.

Another general class of possible sources of misinformation lies in cognitive processing difficulties. For example, people might be prone to misremembering things, or—a more interesting phenomenon—they might be prone to make up "facts" that fit their broader assumptions about the world.

Status   How should one describe the nature of misinformation? Although it might easily be contested, let us postulate that misinformation is fact-like and propositionally encodable. That is, people can assert their beliefs pretty well in natural language.

"Berlin is on the border of former West Germany and East Germany." "Immigration to the U.S. is on the order of tens of millions of people per year, and illegal immigration is the majority of the influx." "Italians are lazy." "Force results in a speed proportional to its magnitude."

Preventing Misinformation   This depends, of course, at least somewhat on the source. We might educate the populace, and thus attempt to stamp out culturally provided misinformation. This might either be at the level of the information itself, or we might attempt to educate students to be more critical of sources of information. Misinformation based on cognitive processing limitations might be more difficult to prevent.

Remediating Misinformation   On this "popular" view of misinformation, there is no particular reason to believe individual bits should be difficult to correct. Indeed, Ranney (Ranney et al., 2008) proposes that correcting factual misinformation (or improving far-off-base numerical estimates) might be an easy path to changing more substantial conceptual things, like decisions on public policy. An exception to "easy to change" might be, for example, misinformation generated on the basis of more substantial and persistent points of view. However, this probably transcends misinformation construed as information, per se, and begins to look like conceptual change, where "entrenched" frameworks are demonstrably "stubborn and difficult to remove." One really needs a different epistemological theory (see below) to understand how to deal with misinformation when it is generated by stubborn intellectual frameworks.

Now I turn to comparing misinformation to p-prims, which might, under some interpretations, simply count as misinformation. Let us see how that goes. For simplicity, I start with a transitional but analogically relevant analysis of a more familiar kind of knowledge, proverbs. Thereafter, I provide a little more elaborated treatment of p-prims, per se, vis-à-vis misinformation.

A Cautionary (Epistemological) Tale
• Absence makes the heart grow fonder.
• Out of sight, out of mind.

What are we to make of these two bits of wisdom? One seems to contradict the other; will we or will we not miss individuals when we are away from them? At first blush, we may be prone to think that the existence of both these proverbs is an indication of the fact that people may accept contradictory bits of information, a core processing limitation.

However, we can easily be more generous. I would defend the proposition that each of these proverbs represents a useful insight. *Sometimes* (possibly unpredictably), each of these things may happen. "Out of sight..." forewarns us, for example, about potential problems in relationships on the basis of separation, even if it turns out, in retrospect, that the opposite effect transpires. Similarly, it seems perfectly sensible to recognize that a loved one may miss us when away, and we might take ameliorative actions.

To put it a bit more technically, we need to unpack contextuality. The proverbs do not tell us when one or the other will apply, even if it is useful to know that both *can* happen, sometimes. As things stated simply in natural language tend to do, they masquerade as universal propositions, with no exceptions. Now, things get particularly interesting. Suppose that each of these proverbs comes to mind exactly when it is most likely to happen, even if we cannot say, out loud, how we distinguish relevant from irrelevant circumstances. That is, we must admit that the patterns of activation of the idea contain a good bit of its usefulness, even though there is no corresponding saying that can help us with that. The proverb, by itself, may not be wise, but, together with whatever mental processes bring it to mind, we might have a completely adequate "conceptualization" of the effects of absence on emotional binding. It might not be good science (where we are obligated to describe contextuality, when principles apply), but it may be perfectly functional for us as human agents.

Here we have some nice, subtle, epistemological distinctions. One is that we can know things and use them effectively in governing our lives but still be far short of the clarity and articulateness that science requires. Another is that "knowledge elements" (e.g., proverbs) can be very different depending on connected but invisible knowledge processing, such as activation possibilities. We need to evaluate knowledge differently depending on such subtleties. A proverb, by itself, might be useless unless we are sensitized to the particular contexts in which it is apt.

To sum up, we started with two ideas—proverbs—that seem, on the surface, contradictory. Thus, it would seem, at least one must be "misinformation." However, with just a bit of epistemological subtlety, we realize that both might be productive ideas, and that the key is contextuality: when each is worth attending to, and when we do instinctively attend to it. Further, we understand that this kind of information can be improved—moved toward scientific status—if we can get the relevant contextuality under adequate control. Optimally, we should be able to say exactly when each applies.

P-prims as Knowledge versus P-prims as Misinformation

As far as I analyzed proverbs, precisely the same observations apply to p-prims. However, we can go much further since p-prims have a substantial empirical and theoretical basis in the literature, unlike proverbs. Some of what I say below, of course, reiterates and extends our earlier discussion of p-prims, but now it is organized so as to compare directly to misinformation.

Source and Status   It is illuminating to back up and consider the function of p-prims in human cognition. This will afford a broader epistemological framing of them. Broadly speaking, p-prims are abstracted causal relations that help us understand and efficiently operate in our world. In this context, the contention that they might arise from mis-readings of reality is bizarre. When we recognize that we are not walking fast enough, we "work harder" to gain greater results (Ohm's p-prim). We naturally expect a book placed on a table just to stay there and not to fall (a "blocking" p-prim), but if the table disintegrates, we know the book will fall (an "unsupported objects fall" p-prim).

Because they have this practical niche, p-prims must satisfy the "real-time con-straint." That is, unless they are rapid, they are useless. If you have to sit and think for a minute to decide what to do in a given situation, the tiger will eat you (as it were). This accounts, in a way, for the fact that p-prims are generally easy to recognize, certainly in most everyday contexts of use. This is one reason for describing p-prims as "phenom-enological"; they should be quickly present to us in everyday observation.

Science is not much like this. Science is precisely to handle the very wide array of problems that defy common sense or require a precision far beyond what suffices for everyday human action. We expect to pay for these luxuries by relaxing the real-time constraint; we get to (are required to!) think hard and long in order to apply scientific principles for the real work they do.

From this view, it is completely understandable that p-prims are more "superficial" than scientific principles. This is true in terms of swiftness of seeing the p-prims, in con-trast to scientific principles, in real-world situations. After activation, p-prims' "conclu-sions" are similarly rapid, compared to the long chains of inference that we engage in in solving problems with scientific knowledge. With these considerations in mind, it might even be surprising how abstract and general p-prims are. However, the move toward generality is highly evolutionarily adaptive, so, apparently, nature has accom-modated us with the ability to attain some degree of generality in our ideas, while continuing to satisfy the real-time constraint in the face of a tremendously diverse and complex world. One simply needs a large number of ideas to manage the multitudes of everyday situations quickly and efficiently. Science can afford to produce "deeper" ideas, with a more precise sense for when they do or do not apply, at the expense of foregoing the real-time constraint.

As we have described for proverbs, a lot of the "intelligence" in p-prims is in their contextuality. However, p-prims are even more unscientific than proverbs; people sim-ply cannot put p-prims, per se, into natural language. Hence one cannot observe, as we did with proverbs, that some p-prims might appear to contradict others (if we treat them—probably incorrectly—as universally true). So, as a knowledge system, we should expect them to be even less organized than any cultural set of proverbs. In this regard, they approximate the property of information/misinformation as independent bits.

P-prims are useful, and fluently so (the real-time constraint). As with proverbs, it really does not do us much good to try to consider them true or false. To make this point dramatically, I think it is fair to say that it is a category error to try to think of p-prims as "right" or "wrong." In this respect, they are definitively different from the above model of misinformation. P-prims work for us fine in everyday life, and that is all they need to do (in most circumstances). But, then, we start learning science, and greater demands are placed on our ideas of causality. P-prims, as the basis of our causal thinking, must be surpassed.

Prevention   It makes little sense to try to "prevent" p-prims from forming. I see no reason to expect humans to be able to survive—certainly as well as they have—without p-prims or the machinery that generates them. It borders on idle speculation to imagine humans better adapted to operate in their everyday physical and social worlds without p-prims (although it might be an interesting theoretical thought experiment).

On the other hand, it is worth considering how students digest the instruction they are given in school. It seems likely that p-prim-generating mechanisms operate there (in fact, it's reasonably well documented—why do students think that multiplication always makes numbers larger? [Fischbein, Deri, Nello, & Marino, 1985]). I do not feel this is likely to be a serious problem, with good instruction. Still, overall, one wants schooled learning to include the capacity to operate, sometimes, in ways more strictly in accord with rigorous scientific thought, with greater reliance on articulate principles, explicit contextuality, and, generally, more critical consideration. So, here, in fact, is a place to contemplate not *eliminating* p-prim-like knowledge but rather helping students embed that substrate within a stronger, more systematic basis for thinking. In this regard, it is helpful for students to understand their own nature as knowers and the status of various ways of knowing. Thus, "intuitive epistemology" (what people implicitly think knowledge is, and what its properties are) is a good target for cultivating general expertise. It is a target that does not attempt to do the undoable, eliminating p-prim-like knowledge, but merely puts it in its place, seeking systematically to extend "superficial" ways of knowing. There is a large literature generally following these directions (e.g., Hofer & Pintrich, 2002; Sinatra & Pintrich, 2002).

"Remediation"   This is the big and inescapable educational issue. What do we do about the body of naturally developed p-prims? To start, it is important to observe that some simplicities of the misinformation model are simply gone. P-prims are not just right or wrong. So, even if we could (which is extremely doubtful, given their functionality in everyday thought), it makes little sense to imagine eliminating "the wrong ones," like bits of misinformation.

Because of the centrality of this point to this chapter, elaboration will be helpful. Early on in the history of conceptual change, in the KiP view, researchers made a deep epistemological mistake (diSessa, 2013). They treated students' naive ideas as systematic enough to be viewed as, structurally, competitive with instructed theories. Some even considered them to be "surprisingly articulate" (McCloskey, 1983), that is, expressible fairly directly in natural language. In this model, then, one could focus attention on naive "theories" and directly refute them, even if this might be more difficult than with isolated bits of misinformation (e.g., because these ideas are supposedly "entrenched," unlike bits of misinformation).

There are many things wrong with this refutational model of dealing with misconceptions. First, and maybe foremost, again, p-prims, the root of many misconceptions, are not right or wrong. Thus, eliminating the wrong ones does not even make sense. If one genuinely succeeded in eliminating many p-prims from a human's conceptual ecology, one will have produced a crippled ability to deal with the physical world. Second, since p-prims are many, one has the "fly-swatting" problem. With hundreds or thousands of elements to contest, how could one possibly organize a practical curriculum around the idea of eliminating (even a reasonable proportion of) naive p-prims?

As with proverbs, contextuality is a key consideration. Perhaps one could just let p-prims be, allow them to continue to account for everyday action capabilities, but keep them out of scientific understanding. It is not clear that this is possible. After all, how do we "turn off" their activation in the context of considering a physical setup in a physics class? Luckily, as suggested earlier in our description of coordination classes, it is possible (and maybe even necessary) actually to use p-prims as positive resources in learning.

Now, this is as revolutionary an idea as the judgment that the use of "right" and "wrong" to describe p-prims is a category error. The entire edifice built around characterizing all naive physics ideas as "misconceptions" is chimera. P-prims are productive, adaptive; they work (mostly), but do not satisfy some criteria we might expect of scientific knowledge. So the judgment of *productivity* is the critical judgment in the pursuit of more scientific understanding. If they are not right or wrong, might they still be helpful in developing scientific thinking?

This is, in part, an engineering problem. Can we construct ways of understanding science that productively engage the rich supply of naturally occurring p-prims? For some of us, this is an old pursuit (diSessa, 1980). However, the best evidence for the possibility is recent. In diSessa (in press), I produce an essentially p-prim-by-p-prim analysis of how a small group of students constructed Newton's laws of thermal equilibration. There is no space here for an extensive recounting, but it is worth remarking that the core causality—that temperature changes in proportion to the difference between temperatures of a body and its surround—came from Ohm's p-prim. That is, students came to interpret a difference in temperature as a kind of impetus or driving force toward equilibrium, and the resulting "effect" was taken to be, just as Newton had it, the rate of change of temperature. The trick here is contextuality, or more precisely put, change in contextuality. Ohm's p-prim came *newly* to apply in one specific (scientific) context. Good scientific understanding can result from p-prims' finding surprising new contexts in which to function.

Another recent analysis (Kapon & diSessa, 2012) looks in detail at processes of learning concerning a well-documented misconception—that a table does *not* apply a force upward on an object resting on it. The analysis looks at the specific trajectories of individual students as their personal "swarm" of p-prims[4] gets selected and massaged (recontextualized) in order to produce a more scientific understanding. The paper also shows how, depending on details of a student's individual repertoire of p-prims, this can fail.

Summary

This section considered in what respects and to what degree one may consider p-prims to be misinformation. To do this, we provided a rough model of misinformation and systematically compared and contrasted the properties of p-prims, as revealed in detailed empirical and theoretical work. In one respect, p-prims seem like misinformation in that both come in many "bits" and are only loosely organized, if at all, by higher principles. But p-prims work! Their function is to help us understand and manage our actions in the everyday world. Some bits of misinformation may well prescribe actions, but it seems safest to believe that most misinformation does not exist because it helps us cope better with the world (although exceptions to the lack of higher-order principles and lack of deep functionality for what might be taken as misinformation should be scrutinized carefully; see below).

Arguably the central epistemological difference between p-prims and misinformation is with respect to the judgments of "true" and "false." Usefulness, as a property of p-prims, simply does not entail any judgment of scientifically correct or not. Thus, p-prims cannot be sorted according to this principle, unlike the assumption that information comes in positive (information) and negative (misinformation) forms.

Eliminating p-prims is inappropriate on the basis of their epistemological status. First, of course, the very basis for wanting to eliminate depends on being able to separate the good ones from the bad ones, which sorting, as above, cannot be done cogently. However, as well, eliminating p-prims also eliminates their productive function. Why would we want to make people less fluently competent in everyday situations? In addition, even if one wanted to eliminate p-prims, their problematic relationship to language means that one cannot even formulate language to say "This is not so."

Instead, the key observation is that contextuality plays an enormous role in how p-prims work. If they come to mind in a certain class of situations, they can be quite helpful; if they come to mind in other situations, they may be viewed as misconceptions, competing with proper scientific ideas. However, changing contextuality seems relatively easy, based on studies to date, and it can result in p-prims' serving the function of helping students understand scientific principles. To do so, they must come to mind in properly scientific ways, and also, we do need to ensure that some p-prims that consistently adhere unproductively to scientific contexts get "displaced" (not replaced, as the p-prim will continue to be used in other contexts, perhaps even in ways that enhance understanding of other scientific principles). In short, p-prims are not scientific principles, but, by shifting contextuality, they can become involved in knowing such principles, and they can be "nudged out" of situations in which they appear as misconceptions.

Finally, how to make optimal use of p-prims, and to minimize their unproductive instantiations, is an essentially complicated affair. The garden path (which is probably a good, if not optimal, path) is to know the various p-prims that get activated in instructional situations. Then, one needs to know or design productive roles for those p-prims that can be made compatible with the relevant science. Finally, of course, one needs to design specific instruction in order to carry out the contextual shifting necessary to adapt p-prims to science. In all this, understanding the mechanisms by which p-prims are developed, used, and may be changed underlies effective instructional design. These constitute a relevant learning theory, specifically for p-prims.

This kind of instructional design is quite intensive and detailed. Are there any simpler, more general principles that may be as or even more effective? For example, can we simply teach students to be more discerning, more critical, more properly "metacognitive"? I think this question is beyond the state of the art to answer. My suspicion is that the microanalysis I have proposed above will always be more effective, if we have the time to do it thoroughly, than more homogeneous methods of instruction, even if such methods help. However, I do not think that we are, right now, in a position to know for sure.

Conclusion: Looking Forward

I have proposed taking an epistemological look at the problem of misinformation. In order to do this, I used a case study of what I believe to be a good theory of what are called "misconceptions" in conceptual change. Misconceptions look to many to be obstructive misinformation that plagues students in learning many things, science in particular. The immediate questions that follow from this view are these: (1) Can we prevent misconceptions from happening in the first place, and (2) when we cannot prevent their occurrence, how do we minimize or eliminate their negative impact? However, a proper epistemological view of misconceptions (p-prims theory) reveals a very different picture. P-prims are not right or wrong, but they are best looked at as productive (*in certain contexts*) or not (in other contexts). In any case, eliminating them is not a sensible option for several reasons. In contrast, it appears that shifting contexts of application of p-prims is not all that difficult. Then, the instructional task is finding productive contexts in which to invoke p-prims (or possibly even to create new p-prims; they are not that hard to manufacture!) and, sometimes, to marginalize an unproductive p-prim (displace it) from scientific consideration of certain contexts. With all this, the task of instruction of difficult concepts does not get easy, in part because it is often true that many p-prims require massaging. But the path to learning is foreseeable.

The generalization of these observations to misinformation more broadly provides an agenda that looks to me very productive for future work. Simply said, we need a proper epistemology of misinformation, as, I argue, p-prims provide a pretty good theory of misconceptions. The rough and ready sketch I provided, "a default view of misinformation," is a small start, but more is needed. To begin, my strong suspicion is that "misinformation" is a highly inhomogeneous class of ideas. That is, there are fundamentally different kinds of misinformation that originate and work in rather different ways. Therefore, the way we answer those basic questions of source, status, prevention, and mitigation may be different, from one kind of misinformation to another.

Using the case of p-prims for inspiration, these are the sorts of things that need inquiry:

• What are the basic units of misinformation, and what are their properties?
• How do units of misinformation arise? Those that arise in different ways (social spread vs. individual invention vs. misreading or misremembering) may very well behave differently, so we may need multiple epistemological models.
• How do instances of those units relate to each other? Are they, in fact, nearly discrete and separable, or is there some fabric of inference that ties them strongly together or to some other part of our conceptual ecology, such as a pervasive theory or some set of core principles?
• How do they work in intellectually important contexts? Are they tied to linguistic forms (as proverbs are), or may they *become* articulated in language, possibly with productive consequences (such as explicit, critical consideration)?
• Are they hard to change, and if so, why? (P-prims are no more "entrenched" than other ideas that do constant, productive work for us. In fact, their contextuality seems quite malleable, a bit at a time. The appearance of great stability stems from the fact that conceptual change requires a great number of changes to many p-prims.)

This is, as I mentioned from the start, an unfamiliar program. However, I do not believe it is an inordinately difficult program toward getting better purchase on the problem of misinformation. Creating and differentiating a set of rough models of a few principal kinds of misinformation may well be all we need. In fact, the greatest impediment to the program may well be that our common sense tell us that there is only one kind of misinformation, and that we already know, well enough, what its epistemological properties are.

Acknowledgments

I thank the editors of this volume for considering that my expertise with intuitive conceptions in science instruction might have some relevance to the rather different-appearing study of misinformation. I certainly found the inquiry engaging, and I welcomed the opportunity to try to make my work comprehensible and useful to a different community. The debt I owe to collaborators in the knowledge in pieces perspective is deep and wide; many of them appear in the references.

Notes

1. Think "force," "mass," and "acceleration," and then "F = ma," which are the basic concepts and core relational principle of Newton's laws of motion.

2. Learning coordination classes almost by definition takes a long time and requires one to see different things in the world. Consider a made-up concept such as "A 'guare' is anything that is both green and square." If you can already see green and square, you can learn this concept instantly without changing any of your ways of seeing. Similarly, children, during their peak vocabulary learning periods, learn perhaps a dozen words per week. It seems immensely implausible that these innovations involve new ways to see, that is, new coordination classes.

3. Things do fall straight down in the frame of reference in which they are released, such as the frame of reference of the walker. However, dropped things will then be moving sideways, too, with the walker, and thus they will be swooping sideways and down with respect to the ground.

4. Technically speaking, the cited paper introduces a slight generalization of p-prims, so not every element tracked is, in all its specifics, a p-prim.

References

diSessa, A. A. (1980). Momentum flow as an alternative perspective in elementary mechanics. *American Journal of Physics, 48*, 365–369.

diSessa, A. A. (1983). Phenomenology and the evolution of intuition. In D. Gentner & A. Stevens (Eds.), *Mental models* (pp. 15–33). Hillsdale, NJ: Lawrence Erlbaum Associates.

diSessa, A. A. (1993). Toward an epistemology of physics. *Cognition and Instruction, 10*, 105–225.

diSessa, A. A. (1996). What do "just plain folk" know about physics? In D. R. Olson & N. Torrance (Eds.), *Handbook of education and human development: New models of learning, teaching, and schooling* (pp. 709–730). Oxford, England: Blackwell.

diSessa, A. A. (2004). Contextuality and coordination in conceptual change. In E. Redish & M. Vicentini (Eds.), *Proceedings of the International School of Physics "Enrico Fermi": Research on physics education* (pp. 137–156). Amsterdam: ISO Press/Italian Physics Society.

diSessa, A. A. (2013). A bird's eye view of "pieces" vs. "coherence" controversy. In S. Vosniadou (Ed.), *Handbook of conceptual change research* (2nd ed., pp. 31–48). New York: Routledge.

diSessa, A. A. (in press). The construction of causal schemes: Learning mechanisms at the knowledge level. *Cognitive Science*.

diSessa, A. A., Gillespie, N., & Esterly, J. (2004). Coherence vs. fragmentation in the development of the concept of force. *Cognitive Science, 28*, 843–900.

diSessa, A. A., & Sherin, B. (1998). What changes in conceptual change? *International Journal of Science Education, 20*, 1155–1191.

diSessa, A. A., & Wagner, J. F. (2005). What coordination has to say about transfer. In J. Mestre (Ed.), *Transfer of learning from a modern multi-disciplinary perspective* (pp. 121–154). Greenwich, CT: Information Age Publishing.

Fischbein, E., Deri, M., Nello, M. S., & Marino, M. S. (1985). The role of implicit models in solving verbal problems in multiplication and division. *Journal for Research in Mathematics Education, 16*, 3–17.

Hofer, B., & Pintrich, P. (2002). *Personal epistemology*. Mahwah, NJ: Lawrence Erlbaum Associates.

Kapon, S., & diSessa, A. A. (2012). Reasoning through instructional analogies. *Cognition and Instruction, 30*, 261–310.

Levrini, O., & diSessa, A. A. (2008). How students learn from multiple contexts and definitions: Proper time as a coordination class. *Physical Review Special Topics: Physics Education Research, 4*, 010107.

McCloskey, M. (1983). Naive theories of motion. In D. Gentner & A. Stevens (Eds.), *Mental models* (pp. 299–324). Hillsdale, NJ: Lawrence Erlbaum Associates.

McCloskey, M., Washburn, A., & Felch, L. (1983). Intuitive physics: The straight-down belief and its origin. *Journal of Experimental Psychology. Learning, Memory, and Cognition, 9*, 636–649.

Parnafes, O. (2007). What does "fast" mean? Understanding the physical world through computational representations. *Journal of the Learning Sciences, 16*, 415–450.

Ranney, M., Rinne, L., Yarnall, L., Munich, E., Miratrix, L., & Schank, P. (2008). Designing and assessing numeracy training for journalists: Toward improving quantitative reasoning among media consumers. In P. A. Kirschner, F. Prins, V. Jonker, & G. Kanselaar (Eds.), *International perspectives in the learning sciences: Proceedings of the Eighth International Conference for the Learning Sciences* (Vol. 2, pp. 2–246 to 2–253). International Society of the Learning Sciences.

Rapp, D. N. (2008). How do readers handle incorrect information during reading? *Memory & Cognition, 36*, 688–701.

Sinatra, G., & Pintrich, P. (2002). *Intentional conceptual change*. Mahwah, NJ: Lawrence Erlbaum Associates.

Wagner, J. F. (2006). Transfer in pieces. *Cognition and Instruction, 24*, 1–71.

14 Percept–Concept Coupling and Human Error

Patricia A. Alexander and Peter Baggetta

The purpose of this edited volume is to tackle the pervasive and perplexing problem of errors in human information processing, including the well-documented tendency of individuals to embrace information that is unsubstantiated, flawed, or even contradictory (Ayers & Reder, 1998; Lewandowsky, Ecker, Seifert, Schwarz, & Cook, 2012; Modell, Michael, & Wenderoth, 2005; Pfundt & Duit, 1994; Rapp, 2008). The goal is to understand why such unsatisfactory situations occur and what can be done to rectify or ameliorate this all-too-common but less-than-optimal human condition. What we intend to demonstrate in this theoretical and empirical analysis is that the deeper understanding of the continuous and reciprocal interplay of perception and conception—what we label the percept–concept coupling—affords critical insights into human error. Further, deeper understanding of the percept–concept coupling can suggest effective mechanisms for not only reducing initial error but also transforming misguided, naive, or unscientific ideas that continue to complicate subsequent learning and performance.

To achieve our intended goal, we first consider a long-raging debate within the literature on conceptual change—"pieces" versus "coherence"—that speaks directly to our interest. Then, we seek to reframe that debate in terms of broader notions of percepts and concepts. Once this reframing has occurred, we offer a theoretical model that demonstrates the interplay of percepts and concepts in human learning and performance. As part of this coupling model, we discuss the ideas of relational thinking and relational reasoning and their potential for contributing to or inhibiting human error. Finally, we close the chapter with discussion of several key principles for enhanced learning and performance drawn from the preceding empirical and theoretical analysis.

The "Pieces" versus "Coherence" Debate

Within cognitive and educational psychology, an extensive literature dealing with conceptual change has accumulated over decades examining such questions as why erroneous ideas take hold and how such malformed or misconstrued notions pollute new information that is encountered (Chi, 2013; Confrey, 1990; Murphy & Alexander,

2013; Smith, diSessa, & Roschelle, 1993). A plethora of empirical studies in this literature have investigated why individuals apparently rely on primitive and unsubstantiated beliefs or use inaccurate information and inappropriate sources to solve learning tasks and problems, understand scientific concepts, and engage in decision making (Chi, 2005; Hogarth & Kunreuther, 1997; Taylor & Kowalski, 2004).

Many of the aforementioned studies point to the role of incomplete, inaccurate, or naive prior knowledge and how such knowledge creates challenges and difficulties in present and future learning (Griffin, Dodds, Placek, & Tremino, 2001; Hare & Graber, 2007; Vosniadou 1999). They also indicate how various epistemic principles and ontological beliefs distort and misguide individuals engaged in learning and problem solving (Chi, 1992; Gill, Ashton, & Algina, 2004; Mason, Gava, & Boldrin, 2008; Qian & Alvermann, 1995). Indeed, the first and second editions of the *International Handbook of Research on Conceptual Change* (Vosniadou, 2008, 2013a) provide ample evidence of these continuing influences on subsequent errors in learning and performance. Interestingly, the opening two chapters of the more recent *Handbook* (Vosniadou, 2013a) highlight a significant debate among conceptual change researchers as to the "real" source of human error (diSessa, 2013; Vosniadou, 2013b), referred to as the "pieces-versus-coherence" debate.

The "Pieces" Argument

Specifically, representing the "pieces" side of this debate, diSessa (2013) argues for those who hold that error (or success) in human processing occurs largely *in mundi*, or in the moment, as one's epistemic and ontological principles shape what is seen, understood, and done. These "pieces" are believed to be innumerable and incoherent, although relevant to given domains and disciplines, and to configure spontaneously as conditions arise. So conceived, this situated orientation to human learning and performance demands no explicit or additional justification (Firth, 1950; Rosenthal, 1969).

Where human error arises from the "pieces" side of this fence is from the faulty or nonscientific principles, beliefs, and perceptions upon which individuals operate. What individuals "pick up" at a particular time and place frames what they discern and how they respond in that moment. If their perception and attention is misdirected, or if their epistemic or ontological beliefs are less than competent, then they will arrive at flawed determinations, institute inappropriate procedures, or derive unacceptable solutions to problems (diSessa, 1988; Endsley, 2006; Salthouse, 1991). Thus, whether the focus is on middle-school Earth science students engaged in learning about the rock cycle (Russ, Scherr, Hammer, & Mikeska, 2008) or college health and life science majors participating in an algebra-based physics course (Scherr & Hammer, 2009), there is evidence that their less-than-facilitative epistemic and ontological frames and perceptivity contribute to nonoptimal thinking and performance.

But, still, this bottom-up perspective on human learning and performance does not mean that the outcome is erroneous or misguided by default. To the contrary, there are competent individuals or experts in fields whose in-the-moment perceptions are disciplined and influenced by the ontologies and practices characteristic of their specific domains (Goodwin, 1994), what Stevens and Hall (1998) called *disciplined perception*. The goal for educators is to make individuals more aware of the "pieces" that they are bringing into play within a problem-solving or domain context and to reshape or to align those pieces in more suitable and scientific ways so that the outcome is more acceptable.

The "Coherence" Perspective

On the other side of the conceptual change fence, there are those who argue from a more top-down orientation to human learning and performance. For these researchers, errors in understanding and performance derive from individuals' prior knowledge and from the nonscientific or problematic mental models into which this knowledge is organized. As Carey (2000a) stated, "the main barrier to learning the curricular materials is not what the student lacks but what the student has, namely, alternative conceptual frameworks" (p. 14). These conceptual models or "theories" are *in mente*, global in character, and formed over time. According to theory-theory (Carey, 1985, 2009; Wellman & Gelman, 1992) or framework theory (Vosniadou, 2013b) perspectives, for instance, individuals come to any given situation already having acquired ideas, knowledge, or epistemic orientations formed by their everyday or formal educational experiences (Chi, 1992; Ioannides & Vosniadou, 2002; Vosniadou & Brewer, 1992). These less-than-ideal models then frame the present situation so as to interfere with or block more scientific or sophisticated understandings and more accurate performance.

What is essential to this viewpoint is that these "coherence" perspectives, even naive or nonscientific ones, meet the criterion of internal consistency (Ozdemir & Clark, 2007; Vosniadou, 2013b). That is to say, the models and frames that individuals develop are not fragmented or spur-of-the-moment creations. Rather, they have an explanatory quality that derives from the fact that their conceptual elements adhere to some degree. In effect, the conceptual elements work together to provide a cursory explanation that may or may not hold up under more critical scrutiny. The primitive explanations offered for the day/night cycle, for example, work for young children and their experiences with the world, even if those explanations are highly flawed from a scientific standpoint (Vosniadou & Brewer, 1994). Precisely because these mental models are internally consistent, they can become a barrier to dealing with new or even conflicting information. Thus, until these naive and "synthetic" models are abandoned, errors in understanding, decision making, or performance will persist (Modell et al., 2005; Vosniadou, 2007).

Percepts and Concepts: Reframing the Debate

As we have seen within the literature on conceptual change, there are those who attribute flawed or misconstrued ideas or problem solving to imperfect ways of seeing and reasoning about the world (diSessa, 2013; Smith et al., 1993) while others emphasize individuals' existing mental models as explanatory factors for the inaccurate processing of information (Vosniadou, 2013b). However, neither side of this debate offers a comprehensive or complete vista on the potential sources of error in human performance. For one, those espousing the "pieces" argument have difficulty explaining how more expert-like or disciplined perceptions take shape when their framing remains *in munde* and "in the moment." For another, theory-theory or framework theory researchers struggle to explain how or why mental models take shape in the first place or what stands as a barrier to their dismantling or reformation.

But what is gained and what is lost if this continuing debate is left unresolved for another quarter century? Even the leading proponents of the two positions understand that the need for reconciliation, if not consilience (Wilson, 2000), is warranted if the study of human learning and performance is to progress. As diSessa (2013) noted:

I believe that the fragmentary vs. coherent issue is manifestly epistemologically and empirically fundamental. Our very sense of the nature of knowledge and how it changes is at stake. If we cannot settle on a broad characterization of naïve knowledge, how can we expect to settle other more subtle issues, such as tracking conceptual change in detail? I believe that the state of the art in theoretical sophistication and empirical methodology has advanced far since the early days of conceptual change research. It is time to push toward a consensus on the nature of naïve ideas. (p. 31)

Reconciling these two alternative sides of the conceptual fence may result in a more informative framework to understanding how and why errors arise in human performance. Schneider and Hardy (2012) offered one such attempt at reconciliation, arguing that knowledge could be both fragmented and integrated depending on different time points of *when* and *how* individuals acquire that knowledge. While we agree with Schneider and Hardy (2012) that knowledge can be both coherent and fragmented, our approach to reconciliation seeks to recast the debate in terms of percept and concepts— which comes with a long and rich history within the philosophical and psychological literatures. Once we have looked in depth at percepts and concepts individually, we will turn to a model that allows for their coupling in ascertaining patterns in human error.

Percepts

The focus on percepts reaches well back into the history of psychological research (e.g., James, 1890; Köhler, 1958; Wertheimer, 1923). According to Charles Peirce (1955), "the starting point of all our reasoning is our percepts; it is the external world we directly observe" (p. 308). Simply defined, percepts are the mental impressions formed in the present moment from sensory receptor systems data (Ernst & Bülthoff, 2004; Gallese & Lakoff, 2005; Medin & Smith, 1984; Portas, Strange, Friston, Dolan, & Frith, 2000). Percepts are configurations, most often fleeting in nature, that arise from humans' sensory experiences with the world around them.

Percepts are not singular or isolated in nature; quite to the contrary. At any given moment, there are innumerable percepts that present themselves to the human mind (Mandler, 2008), and they provide a continuous and rapid flow of ever-changing stimuli and information from the world (Schyns, 1997). The percepts we observe are largely felt or sensed, and most are processed outside of our awareness (Mandler, 2008); thus, as with "pieces," there is no justification required. Moreover, percepts are not copies of sensory impressions but are the actual impressions of things in the world (Meloy, 1985); what Peirce characterized as *presentation* of the world without objective reference or predictive meaning (Bergman, 2007; Rosenthal, 1969). Regardless of the individual's will, judgment, or knowledge, percepts are constantly present. Most often, these perceptual units form at an unconscious or involuntary level of awareness although there may be some percepts that are consciously accessible (Carey, 2009; Mandler, 2008).

Percepts give us our first contact with the world as they are formed from observational properties and provide us with physical descriptions such as color, shape, texture, and spatiotemporal descriptions (Carey, 2009). Percepts can be thought of as "bottom-up" processing or the initial inputs to the development of knowledge, conceptual or procedural (Meloy, 1985; Weiskopf, 2008). However, alone percepts remain only the first analytic level of interpretation, almost purely impressionistic. We intentionally qualify these configurations as "almost" purely impressionistic because there is some evidence that percepts can begin to organize and form more collective units; what Peirce (1955) called *generalized percepts*.

I see an inkstand on the table: that is a percept. Moving my head, I get a different percept of the inkstand. It coalesces with the other. What I call the inkstand is a generalized percept, a quasi-inference from percepts, perhaps I might say a composite-photograph of percepts.... Of course, in being real and external, [the inkstand] does not in the least cease to be a purely psychical product, a generalized percept, like everything of which I can take any sort of cognizance. (p. 308)

In more contemporary literature, others have addressed the potential combining or generalization of percepts through the notion of *perceptual schema* (Mandler, 2004). Perceptual schema formation does not require conscious, rational thought per se but is simply a realization of associations about information about the physical dimensions of the percept. As is evident in Peirce's example of the inkstand, discernible patterns take shape either through repeated exposures over time or through convergence among rapidly occurring percepts (Gibson, 1960; Gibson & Gibson, 1955). McClelland

and Rumelhart (1985) called these convergences *prototypes*. Whether we are dealing with generalized percepts, perceptual schemata, or prototypes, these manifestations of percepts begin to blur the boundaries between percepts and concepts, which we consider next. Nonetheless, they suggest how percepts and concepts may meaningfully interface in human learning and performance.

Building on the foundational literatures in philosophy and psychology, including the writings of James (1911/1996), Peirce (1955), Gibson (1960), and others (Carey, 2000b; Keil, 1992; Mandler, 2004), we have sought to capture the physical environment and individual characteristics that seemingly have a role to play in percept formation. These influences are visually summarized in figure 14.1.

Physical Environment   Specifically, Gibson (1979/1986) and contemporary situated learning theorists and researchers (Greeno, 1994; Roth, 2001; Young & Barab, 1999) argue that every physical context may simultaneously constrain and afford human perception. Constraints, in essence, limit what can be discerned by the senses and the ensuing impressions that can form. Conversely, each physical environment presents affordances or aids to human perception and, as with constraints, those affordances

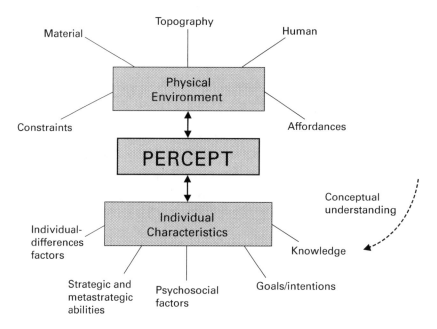

Figure 14.1
The environmental and person factors that influence what and how percepts are formed at any given time and place.

may pertain to the humans or to the material objects that populate that particular environment. Even the physical landscape or configuration itself can play an important role in the percepts that arise.

Let's consider the case of a player on a rugby field to illustrate the way environmental components work together in the formation of percepts. In team sports such as rugby, players have to make fast and effective decisions in a complex and dynamic environment. This environment is a source of continuous and quickly changing percepts that provides players with visual, spatial, and temporal information. These sources include the ball, teammates, opponents, the referee, areas of space, and the playing area. Each of these environmental cues has the potential to either afford or constrain the percepts a player notices.

Individual Characteristics As critical as the physical environment to the percepts that form in the moment is the array of cognitive and noncognitive characteristics unique to individuals (see figure 14.1). Specifically, there are the individual-differences factors, such as working memory, which involves attentional and perceptual abilities, that can influence what learners can discern within any environment (Bell & Calkins, 2012; Bredemeier & Simons, 2012; Kane & Engle, 2002; Prabhakaran, Smith, Desmond, Glover, & Gabrieli, 1997). There are also the strategies or metastrategies that have become part of individuals' reasoning repertoires or their thinking dispositions (Alexander, 1997; Stanovich & West, 2008)—their ways of moving effectively through any problem space. As suggested, however, not all individual characteristics that matter are cognitive in nature. There are also psychosocial factors like personality traits or dispositions that can strongly influence the impressions that form in the moment. For instance, individuals' tendency toward performance anxiety and distractibility are just two psychosocial characteristics that can shape what is perceived (Balcetis & Dunning, 2006).

Also, the goals and intentions that individuals bring with them into any problem space has been repeatedly shown to matter to what that environment may afford or constrain (Bekkering & Neggers, 2002; Cañal-Bruland & van der Kamp, 2009). Those goals or intentions can sharpen focus on features within the environment that coincide with those goals or intentions, but they could simultaneously obstruct elements that are not in concert. Finally, one of the most potent individual characteristics to influence the formation of percepts is prior knowledge. What individuals know about the immediate situation or context colors what they may pick up in the moment (Cook, 2006; Ernst & Bülthoff, 2004; Williams, Hodges, North, & Barton, 2006). That existing knowledge includes individuals' conceptual understanding, as figure 14.1 suggests. We now turn to a deeper consideration of concepts in this reframing of the persistent "pieces-versus-coherence" debate.

Table 14.1
Comparison of percepts and concepts

| Points of comparison | | |
Attribute	Percept	Concept
Nature	Presentation	Re-presentation
Locus	*In mundi*	*In mente*
Time frame	Immediate	Over time
Justification	Impressionistic; largely felt or sensed	Can be examined or justified
Changeability	Continually in flux	Open to change
Base abilities	Reliant on individual differences	Reliant on individual differences
Relatedness	Requires relational thinking	Requires relational thinking and relational reasoning

Concepts   As illustrated in table 14.1, there are significant similarities and differences between concepts and percepts that merit consideration in the discussion of performance error. For example, the very nature of concepts in comparison to percepts matters. In essence, precisely because concepts are not *of the moment* or *in the moment* in the way percepts are, Peirce (Bergman, 2007) regarded them as *re-presentations* of experiences rather than real-time *presentations*. Another marked difference pertains to the locus of these phenomena in that concepts are *in mente* whereas percepts can be characterized as *in mundi*. That is, concepts are presumed to have structure and some degree of durability within the mind while percepts remain nested in the world from which they arise.

Further, compared to percepts, which remain immediate in-the-moment impressions, concepts are generalized understandings derived over time and across multiple experiences in and with the world (Gallese & Lakoff, 2005; Mandler, 2007; Rosch, 1999). Concepts are broader than percepts because they consist of knowing what something is—they constitute our representational system (Bedny, Caramazza, Grossman, Pascual-Leone, & Saxe, 2008; Carey, 2009; Keil, 1992; Medin & Smith, 1984). As such, they allow humans to categorize and reflect on experiences or aspects of those experiences (Mervis & Rosch, 1981; Sloutsky, 2010). Through the formation of concepts, individuals have the means to describe, recall, and think about something, not simply recognize it as occurs with percepts. Further, the development of concepts allows individuals to understand the meaning of an object and put it into some type of context (Mandler, 2004; Meloy, 1985).

What needs to be appreciated about concepts is that they cannot divorce themselves from the reality or the world without. However, there are no assurances that the concepts richly, completely, or accurately describe what is "true" or "real." In fact, there is strong evidence that conceptual knowledge, especially in the case of complex ideas, is inherently incomplete and fraught with misinterpretations or inaccuracies (Carey, 2000b; Mandler, 2004; Vosniadou, 1999; Weiskopf, 2008). This is true whether one is young or new to some field of study (i.e., novices) or regarded as competent or expert in that field (Adelson, 1984; Ericsson & Lehmann, 1996; Sternberg, 1996). This is why so much focus within the conceptual change literature is devoted to ways to ascertain what notions individuals seem to form from everyday or formal experiences and what can be done to enhance or alter those concepts that have been found to be particularly problematic (Chi, 2013; Vosniadou, 2013a).

These aforementioned attributes of concepts clearly move them beyond the impressionistic characteristic of percepts. As such, there is more opportunity and more demand to justify what is known conceptually—to seek evidence that the ideas formed and reformed are based on evidence that is accurate or scientifically legitimate. Of course, whether such justification ultimately occurs has been the focus of much of the conceptual change literature (Mason et al., 2008; Murphy, Alexander, Greene, & Hennessey, 2012).

Further, even though there may be more durability to concepts than to percepts, concepts remain continually open to change, whether modestly and imperceptively or dramatically and evidently, and are the result of an active process that is central to cognition and learning (Alexander, 2003; Alexander & Murphy, 1999; Bransford, Brown, & Cocking, 2000). They are central to cognition and learning because humans carry their conceptual structures with them into each and every situation, and these structures have the power to shape or distort those moment-by-moment perceptions and to guide or misguide human processing.

To this point, we have been emphasizing the differences between concepts and percepts. However, there are two important ways in which these two phenomena are similar. For one, what is evident for concepts, as with percepts, is that they are influenced by the unique abilities and characteristics of the individual (Gentner & Smith, 2012; Stanovich & West, 2000). Cognitive differences in memory, perception, attention, spatial reasoning, to say nothing about personality traits like curiosity, persistence, or temperament, are ever present in humans' interactions with the world at any given time or over time (Blanchette & Richards, 2010; Schmitt & Lahroodi, 2008). Consequently, what concepts are formed from experiences reflect one's humanness and individuality.

In addition, there is another critical feature that percepts and concepts share. Both rely on the process of perceiving or discerning relations or associations among information that is otherwise fragmented or "in pieces." Whether we are dealing with the in-the-moment percepts or the in-the-mind concepts, it is evident that neither form or reform without *relational thinking* and its more intentional or purposeful partner, *relational reasoning*. At its simplest, relational thinking can be conceived as the ability to perceive associations between and among pieces of seemingly unrelated sensory data or information (Alexander & the Disciplined Reading and Learning Research Laboratory [DRLRL], 2012). As with much of perception, relational thinking is an automatic cognitive process that can occur with or without conscious awareness. By comparison, relational reasoning is the intentional harnessing of relational thinking processes as a means of enhancing one's understanding and performance (Alexander & the DRLRL, 2012).

What will become evident in the discussion of the "coupling" model that follows is the belief that relational thinking and relational reasoning are foundational to human cognition and human performance—whether that thinking and doing results in successful or erroneous outcomes. Without relational thinking, "pieces" remain pieces and never assemble into impressions or rudimentary understandings that influence cognition and behavior. Likewise, without relational reasoning, there are no mechanisms available for enhancing perception and attention, for activating relevant concepts, or for recognizing gaps or weaknesses in those percepts and concepts. We will elaborate further on the roles of relational thinking and reasoning as we describe the critical interplay between percepts and concepts that occur in the "coupling" model that follows.

Modeling the Percept–Concept Coupling

While much can be learned from the individual examination of percepts and concepts as key components in human learning and performance, and the errors that arise therein, we hold that the systematic exploration of how percepts and concepts work together can prove even more enlightening. Moreover, the "coupling" model we put forward here reflects both the commonalities and the distinctions between percepts and concepts just discussed. William James (1911/1996) provided a compelling argument for the coupling of percept and concept in achieving understanding of human learning and performance when he wrote the following:

We thus see clearly what is gained and what is lost when percepts are translated into concepts. Perception is solely of the here and now: conception is of the like and unlike, of the future, of the past, and of the far away. But this map of what surrounds the present, like all maps, is only a surface: its features are but abstract signs and symbols of things that in themselves are concrete bits of sensible experience. We have but to weigh extent against content, thickness against spread, and we see that for some purposes the one, for other purposes the other, has the higher value. Who can decide off-hand which is absolutely better to live or to understand life? We must do both alternately, and a man can no more limit himself either than a pair of scissors can cut with a single one of its blades. (p. 74)

As displayed in the model (figure 14.2), we argue that there are two dimensions of percept–concept coupling where the potential for human error and, concurrently, enhanced cognitive performance exist: in-formation and re-formation.

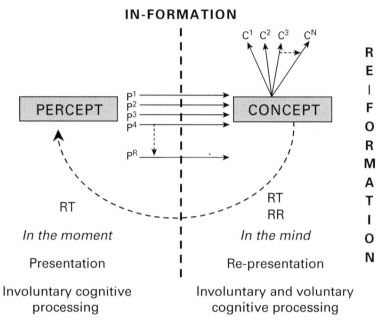

Figure 14.2
A model of the coupling of percept and concepts in human learning and performance.

In-Formation

As discussed, individuals are continuously exposed to, awash in, and in touch with sensory information from the physical environment in which they are presently situated. However, human nature does not leave such sensory information "in pieces." Rather, immediately and in the moment these data configure into percepts, which for better or worse turn what would otherwise be sensory chaos into conditions or contexts in which humans can function (Mandler, 2004; Schyns, 1997). For the most part, this configuration happens at an involuntary and nonintentional level through relational thinking, without individuals' awareness or regulation (Carey, 2009; Mandler, 2004).

Further, not only are there are innumerable percepts that form at any moment in time (see P^1 to P^n in figure 14.2), but there is also unfettered progression from one percept to the next. Consider Peirce's example of the inkstand. Shift your head slightly, and the vantage point afforded shifts, altering the percepts that are potentially formed (Gibson, 1960; Peirce, 1955). What is significant about this multitude of percepts arising at one time point or across time points is that it fuels the conceptual knowledge base, even if the process remains below the level of consciousness. This occurs as the mind is cued by the perceptual, bottom-up system and relevant concepts and procedures are thus instantiated (Gallese & Lakoff, 2005). It also occurs as the percepts themselves begin to configure and reach a more global and, thus, somewhat more durable state, as with generalized percepts (Peirce, 1955) or perceptual schema (Mandler, 2004). Yet, as we contend, these percepts are never completely independent of individuals' preexisting knowledge structures, as marked by the intrusion of conceptual understanding into the knowledge factor in figure 14.1. The degree to which the bottom-up (percepts) or top-down (concepts) components of the model are exerting greater influence depends on the particular context or the problem at hand (Keil, 1992; Weiskopf, 2008).

This play-off between the percepts and concepts side of the coupling model can be effectively illustrated by juxtaposing a rather stable problem-solving space to a much more dynamic environment, where percepts change so quickly and are continually in flux. Compare a game of chess, where the pieces on the board remain fairly frozen in time until acted upon, to a game of rugby, where the problem space and the elements within are in perpetual motion. For the chess game, one can ponder the placement of the pieces and call to mind prior games and maneuvers. Chess players can even plan out a series of moves and contemplate their opponent's likely responses. In dynamic environments, in contrast, individuals must quickly connect and make associations between rapidly occurring and changing sensory information in the environment in order to grasp what is happening and to react accordingly (Ward, Suss, & Basevitch, 2009).

Prior knowledge exerts itself into both aforementioned situations, as noted in figure 14.1, but the emphasis on the dynamic and situated perceptual elements are apt to play a more significant role in the rugby game (Carling, Reilly, & Williams, 2009; Vaeyens, Lenoir, Williams, & Philippaerts, 2008; Ward & Williams, 2003; Williams & Ericsson, 2005). Those in this environment who are more attentive and perceptive and with more attuned sensory abilities are more apt to pick up critical information or to form percepts that are facilitative to performance. For instance, unlike the words on a page of print, the players on a field are in constant motion with continuously shifting patterns of play. Automatic relational thinking permits individuals to pick up and respond effectively to environmental cues as the action is unfolding. Of course, with such a fluid problem space, failure to quickly notice and attend to relevant informational cues may well lead to insufficiently or inaccurately processed information or nonoptimal behavioral response (Novick, 1988; Williams et al., 2006).

Re-formation

Human learning and performance are not only driven by the percepts that are continually *in formation* but also flow reciprocally from the concept side of this dynamic system. Even the primitive concepts that begin to develop in the re-formation phase are invariably re-presentations of percepts that are generalized or configured—perhaps through repeated exposure or some more formal intervention (Bedny et al., 2008; Fodor, 1981). As Vygotsky (1934/1986) stated, it is "the mental elaboration of the sensory material that gives birth to the concept" (p. 96). This process of re-presentation may be either an involuntary process occurring through relational thinking or a voluntary cognitive process resulting from relational reasoning. In effect, concepts assemble, to some extent, without human intention or awareness (Carey, 2009; Mandler, 2004). Yet, there is a body of theoretical and empirical work that supports the notion of intentional conceptual change (Sinatra & Pintrich, 2003)—suggesting that individuals can play a very conscious and effortful part in their own learning and performance. Such intentionality demands strategic and metastrategic processing, including the deployment of relational reasoning strategies.

As illustrated in figure 14.2, concepts also undergo change (see C^1 to C^N in figure 14.2), although not with the same rapidity or mutability as percepts. While conceptual change researchers are most invested in the study of "misconceptions"—those naive or misconceived ideas that become significant barriers to more sophisticated or more scientific concepts (Murphy & Alexander, 2013)—many changes to conceptual knowledge are neither dramatic nor radical in form (Chan, Burtis, & Bereiter, 1997; Eimas, 1994). Such subtle changes may entail the assimilation of new information that may not even rise to the level of conscious awareness (Carey, 2009; Piaget, 1964/1997). Thus, the early re-formation of concepts can encompass involuntary and unconscious cognitive processes via relational thinking and can be described as simple associations or organizations of conceptual similarities (Fodor, 1981; Keil, 1992; Mandler, 2004; Murphy, 2007; Vosniadou, 1994).

Just like percepts, this early conceptual development relies heavily on simple perceptual comparisons and associations that are dependent on relational thinking. However, association is not enough for sophisticated concept formation and, eventually, theory development to occur (Medin & Smith, 1984; Murphy, 2007; Rosch, 1999). That is, the act of simply adding or strengthening the associations among pieces of information will not necessarily lead to the development of more "sophisticated" or scientific concepts (Vosniadou & Brewer, 1987). For the initial concepts to potentially develop into more enriched, more complete, and more accurate understandings, these concepts need to cluster around specific properties or theories about how the world operates (Fodor, 1981; Hartman & Stratton-Salib, 2007; Keil, 1992)—properties and theories that may rest upon formal educational experiences. As seen in the model, as the concepts start to cluster more and more, they shift from simple association to a more systematic organization based on principled and specific relations that start to become organized theoretically (Keil, 1992; Vygotsky, 1934/1986).

What we hopefully have demonstrated is that the percept–concept coupling is not a fixed or linear process but rather a dynamic, reciprocal, continuous interplay between the external environment and the information it affords, and the internal universe of the mind and the knowledge and abilities that reside therein. At the same time as concepts are clustering with each other, they also influence what percepts individuals notice and then attend to in the environment depending on the context, affordances, objectives, and constraints of the situation or task. The percept–concept coupling occurs continually and helps learners notice and attend to relevant information in the environment while ignoring information that is either irrelevant or distracting. Through the processes of noticing, attending, and relational thinking and reasoning, individuals create understanding or meaning from what they notice and to what they attend. As individuals combine, interpret, and create relations and patterns from this coupling, they then store and retain the information for future use. As a consequence of these processes and their orchestration, human error is possible at each step in the process—be it during the in-formational or re-formational phases of coupling.

The Role of Relational Thinking and Reasoning in Human Learning and Performance

Throughout the discussion of percepts and concepts and the examination of a model depicting their coupling, we have made periodic reference to relational thinking and relational reasoning. As should be evident, we regard both of these cognitive processes as foundational to human learning and performance and, thereby, contributors to errors that occur therein. By their very nature, relational reasoning strategies require individuals to engage in a deeper processing of information than would otherwise occur (Stephens, 2006). Moreover, such strategies serve as a counter to learners' tendency to treat information in a piecemeal or isolated manner, and they thereby contribute to the likelihood of processing information accurately and developing more principled knowledge (van Gog, Paas, & van Merriënboer, 2004). While there are various relational reasoning strategies that might be examined, we wish to mention four that we regard as fundamental for forging associations between and among pieces of information and as having potential applications to the development of concepts and theories: analogy, anomaly, antinomy, and antithesis. In what follows, we define these four relational reasoning strategies and then illustrate their role in the acts of learning how to play a game of rugby to demonstrate their versatility to human learning and performance.

The basis for association in *analogical reasoning* is a *relational similarity* between two seemingly disparate ideas, objects, representations, or situations (Gentner & Landers, 1985; Glynn, 2007; Holyoak, 2012; Bassok, Dunbar, & Holyoak, 2012; Nersessian & Chandrasekharan, 2009). In analogical reasoning, there is the effort to construct meaningful associations via this relational similarity between objects or events that initially appear dissimilar (Hesse, 1959). Of the four relational reasoning strategies, *analogies* and *analogical reasoning* are perhaps the most empirically studied (Cosgrove, 1995;

Gentner & Markman, 1997; Glaser, 1984; Hong & Liu, 2003; Novick, 1988). In fact, there are those in the research community who would argue that analogical reasoning is the very basis for concept formation or knowledge transfer (Alexander & Murphy, 1998; Salomon & Perkins, 1989).

We can see the utility of analogical reasoning as novice rugby players attempt to understand this unfamiliar game by drawing on their knowledge of American football. What the novice players come to recognize is that both games are territorial or invasion games that have similar surface and structural features (Butler & McCahan, 2005). These include analogous features such as the main objective of the game of invading the opponents' area to score while protecting home turf, offensive concepts of keeping possession of the ball and invading the opposition territory, and defensive concepts such as defending players in an area or defending a specific player.

By comparison, *anomalous reasoning* involves the recognition of *discrepancies* or *deviations* in one idea, object, representation, or situation from an established rule or trend in another (Chinn & Brewer, 1993; Singer & Gagnon, 1999). The ability to detect and analyze dissimilarities or aberrations in typical patterns is also invaluable for concept formation. An *anomaly* is defined as any occurrence or object that is strange, unusual, or unique (Chinn & Brewer, 1993). The awareness of and response to anomalous data are also critical to conceptual restructuring (Chinn & Brewer, 1993; Chinn & Malhotra, 2002) and, thus, to the development of principled knowledge in a number of domains. Returning to novice rugby players' understanding of the game, these players may fail to recognize that the 80 points just scored by the winning side is clearly an outlier since rugby scores rarely reach 40 points. Consequently, a final score of 80 was overlooked as an anomaly in this instance.

Antinomous reasoning, which entails the recognition that two ideas, objects, representations, or situations are *incompatible* (Berlin, 1990; Chi & Roscoe, 2002), is another invaluable relational reasoning strategy. Unlike analogical thinking, where the intention is to forge some similarity, or anomalous reasoning, where the point is that some fact or observation appears aberrant from others, the goal in antinomous reasoning is to understand what something *is* by ascertaining what it *is not*. *Antinomy* refers to multiple principles or statements that are apparently contradictory but nonetheless true (Mosenthal, 1988). By extension, antinomy also encompasses the type of mutual exclusivity involved in distinguishing different conceptual categories and the paradox that arises when they are brought together.

For example, the idea that we both change and remain the same over time involves such an antinomy-based paradox (Chandler, Lalonde, Sokol, Hallett, & Marcia, 2003). This can be demonstrated by novice rugby players' efforts to understand what is or is not a tackle. After being penalized on multiple occasions for not properly executing a tackle, these inexperienced players may recognize that they have missed the salient attribute of holding the opponent to the ground once that player has been brought down. Without both the ball carrier's being held by the tackler and both players' going to the ground, there is no tackle in rugby.

Finally, *antithetical reasoning* requires the recognition that two representations are set in *direct contrast or opposition* (Nussbaum, Kardash, & Graham, 2005). While antithetical comparisons, like antinomies, involve conflicting information, the contrast is much sharper and entails apparent opposites viewed in a mutually exclusive, either/or relation. Specifically, an *antithesis* arises when two propositions, principles, or explanations are set in direct contrast or direct opposition (Merriam-Webster, 2010). Antithetical reasoning is central to the work done in argumentation and in persuasion (Felton & Kuhn, 2001; Kuhn & Udell, 2001, 2007). For instance, some of the interesting research in refutational text, where two sides of an argument are developed with one's being summarily dismantled, draws heavily on the principle of thesis and antithesis (Fives, Alexander, & Buehl, 2001; Hynd, 2003).

Consider how antithetical reasoning is positioned in helping novice rugby players understand the game better. In rugby, the ball is passed backward, which is directly antithetical to how the ball is passed forward in American football. This is a key concept for inexperienced players to grasp, as it helps them to understand why it is so important to be behind the ball in rugby instead of in front of the ball as in American football.

As we have defined them, relational reasoning processes are metastrategies since they entail recognizing or deriving meaningful relations or patterns between and among pieces of information that would otherwise appear unrelated (Bulloch & Opfer, 2009; Holyoak, 2012; Van der Henst, Sperber, & Politzer, 2002). They promote cross-task and cross-domain thinking, thereby helping to promote the transfer of knowledge from one specific situation or context to another (Bereby-Meyer & Kaplan, 2005). Further, since they require consideration of the attributes or features of information in its many forms, relational reasoning strategies have the potential to heighten individuals' attentional and perceptual processes (e.g., Dunbar & Fugelsang, 2005).

The essential nature of relational thinking and reasoning to intentional learning, including conceptual change, leaves open the door to direct intervention. However, relational thinking, as we have argued, largely operates below the level of human consciousness as a rather instinctive, involuntary response to the physical world and the information it affords. Consequently, it becomes difficult, if not impossible, to directly affect individuals' relational thinking. Rather, it would appear that one possible path to more effective and enhanced relational thinking is through the more effortful and intentional form of this patterning ability, relational reasoning, which relies on such cognitive processes as sensing, noticing, and attending (James, 1911/1996; Ward et al., 2009).

For instance, for relational thinking to be augmented, individuals need to take full advantage of their sensorial abilities by watching and listening more intently. When individuals are inattentive or distracted, or their attention is fragmented, they may be less apt to take notice of what is present and ongoing within their surroundings; thus, their perceptions may be negatively affected and the potential for error increased. Likewise, through training, individuals may be helped to identify relevant versus irrelevant information within the environment and to grasp what those informational cues may suggest about what is transpiring or about to transpire (Endsley, 2006; Farrow & Raab, 2008). Further, when individuals become familiar with a certain situation, such as playing chess or rugby, they can filter through the common or routine stimuli that arise (e.g., the shape of pieces or sounds from the fans) and focus greater attention on those sights and sounds that are apt to influence them and the outcome (e.g., the pieces their opponents eye or touch, or the body movements of the ball carrier; Poplu, Ripoll, Mavromatis, & Baratgin, 2008; McPherson & Vickers, 2004).

Overall, it is our contention that the explicit attention to the processes underlying relational thinking (e.g., noticing and attending) and to the four relational reasoning strategies of analogy, anomaly, antinomy, and antithesis constitute a two-pronged approach to enhancing the coupling of percept and concept. Understanding how this coupling unfolds during concept formation and re-formation and how to utilize the power of relational thinking and reasoning in those in-formation and re-formation phases can go a long way to reduce human error and optimize human performance.

Implications and Concluding Thoughts

As the editors of this important volume, Rapp and Braasch made a compelling case that there is an active and expanding group of cognitive and educational researchers who have picked up the gauntlet of investigating errors in human information processing. These editors thoughtfully argued that responding to such a challenging question has clear implications for learning and performance, whether in a formal setting such as a classroom or informally in the world at large. We applaud these editors' efforts and agree that it is critical to ascertain the multitude of reasons why students persist in the processing of inappropriate, irrelevant, contradictory, and even blatantly incorrect information, even when they should likely know better.

What we wanted to contribute to this examination extended beyond the well-investigated concerns over prior knowledge as the principal culprit in human error in learning and performance. Of course, individuals' existing knowledge—complete with its flaws and gaps—matters to more or less successful learning outcomes. However, our intention was to probe into the nature of percepts and concepts, and especially their coupling, as an understudied yet fertile avenue not only for investigating human error but also for promoting more competent, less error-filled performance. Toward that end, we forward four statements of principle that we believe speak to future research and informed instructional practice in this arena.

Principle 1: Any concerted effort to understand and intervene in nonoptimal human learning and performance must pay homage to both percepts and concepts and their continual coupling.

We return to James's astute observation and powerful admonition: "Perception is solely of the here and now: conception is of the like and unlike, of the future, of the past, and of the far away.... We must do both alternately, and a man can no more limit himself either than a pair of scissors can cut with a single one of its blades" (p. 74). This is precisely our contention herein. Both percepts and concepts play significant parts in the drama of human learning and performance. While those long invested in the study of conceptual change and misconceptions have debated the relative importance of these "in-the-moment" or "in-the-mind" facets, the reality of accurate and effective cognitive processing cannot ignore either. Further, it will be the interplay of person, context, and task that will ultimately determine whether percepts *or* concepts, in-formation *or* re-formation, are more pertinent in that instance. Thus, we hope that the theoretical model of percept–concept coupling we offered can serve as a starting point for the empirical study of their interrelations and suggest ways in which the foundational processes or instantiation of each can be targeted within the learning environment.

Principle 2: A greater focus on the nature of percepts and their influence on human learning and performance seems warranted.

Although we have just argued that both the percepts and concepts side of our coupling model matter to more competent learning and performance, the weight of empirical research and practical interventions has been on conceptual development and conceptual change for the last 25 years. As diSessa (2013), long associated with the pieces side of the piece–coherence debate, recently argued,

> I believe that there is a large family of sub-conceptual elements—multiple elements that play a role in the construction of scientific concepts—and the structure of that family of elements and their contributions to instructed concepts must be charted in order to understand conceptual change. Coherence advocates, to the extent they do not recognize or articulate any sub-conceptual structure, are simply playing a different game. (p. 35)

We do agree that, for the percept–concept pairing, it has too long been percepts, and what diSessa called "sub-conceptual elements" (p. 34), that seem somewhat neglected. The significance of this problem is heightened in our opinion by the conditions facing today's learners. As we have argued elsewhere (Alexander & the DRLRL, 2012), the informational onslaught students encounter almost continuously, coupled with what has been shown to be their general lack of epistemic competence (Bromme, Kienhues, & Stahl, 2008; Muis, 2004; Wood & Kardash, 2002), make it all the more important to understand how percepts form and feed into students' conceptual understanding. To what do these individuals attend, what potentially relevant cues and signals within the immediate context do they overlook or misinterpret, and why? These are the types of questions that merit careful consideration when we tackle perplexing concerns over students' inaccurate or misguided information processing and, consequently, the errors that result.

Thankfully, with the growing interest in neuroscience and with the enhanced technologies and experimental procedures that allow for the investigation of basic cognitive abilities like attention and relational thinking, it may be the time to refocus *our* attention on percepts and their underlying cognitive elements.

Principle 3: The systematic investigation of effective versus ineffective or accurate versus inaccurate processing of information must move beyond static or stable re-presentations of problems or conditions to fluid or dynamic problems and conditions present both in classrooms and in out-of-school contexts.

Throughout this chapter, we have revisited two forms of problems and conditions that seemingly stand in sharp contrast; playing chess and playing rugby. We have done so for various reasons. While neither typifies traditional "school" problems, the task of playing chess has historically been used as a means of examining novice versus expert differences (Simon & Chase, 1973; DeGroot 1965). Chess has long afforded a rich context for exploring the workings of the human mind and for ascertaining why some individuals are better equipped to plan a series of moves well in advance, anticipate the actions of their opponents, and maneuver deftly through the problem space (Didierjean, 2003; McGregor & Howes, 2002; Reingold, Charness, Schultetus, & Stampe, 2001). Those studying chess have also found a means of investigating the effects of explicit training or deliberate practice on those who are new or less than competent at the game (Charness, Krampe, & Mayr, 1996).

Yet, in the minute-by-minute and day-to-day rhythms of humans' lives, there are incalculable problems or situations that cannot be held stable, that cannot be thoughtfully examined or reflected upon. They require immediate response. This manner of problem is evident in a game of rugby. A player on the opposition shifts to your right, even as her teammates cluster to the ball as it moves to the left. This requires the player to react immediately to the creation of the space by the simultaneous movements of her teammates and the opposition player. If she takes the time to try to analyze or reflect on what is happening, it may be too late, and the opportunity to possibly score, or prevent an opponent from scoring, may already have passed.

Like the movements on the rugby field, such fluidity and dynamism is certainly present within any learning context, even if we forget that it is so. The words and actions of teachers, the interactions among peers in the room—the myriad of noises, smells, and sights that invade the mind as individuals participate in learning—alter whatever seemingly static or stable task is set before them. Perhaps some of the growing interest in classroom discourse (Anderson, Chinn, Waggoner, & Nguyen, 1998; Chinn, O'Donnell, & Jinks, 2000; Murphy, Wilkinson, Soter, Hennessey, & Alexander, 2009) reflects the appreciation that the learning environment remains dynamic and that some interjection of words or questions from another can shift the focus of participants or position the "problem" differently. Thus, we cannot limit or constrain the study of human learning and performance to problem sets that are frozen in time or on the page. We must also position problems in more fluid contexts that parallel the more dynamic environments that confront learners continuously. Those committed to the learning sciences appear to have embraced such a notion and feel at home in the "moments" of learning and performance (Sawyer, 2005).

However, we do not intend to privilege the in-the-moment problem solving or reasoning over the more traditional manner of problem investigation; to do so would be to advocate for one blade of the scissors or the other. As we argued with regard to the coupling of percepts and concepts, we contend that both have a place in the study of how learning and performance unfold—for better or for worse.

Principle 4: The intentional incorporation of relational reasoning strategies in empirical research and instructional practice may well afford a much-needed mechanism for promoting enhanced learning and performance.

The final segment of our chapter dealt with four relational reasoning strategies that we regard as viable means of promoting the formation and reformation of conceptual understanding. Recently, we have undertaken a multitiered examination of relational reasoning and, more specifically, the four As—analogy, anomaly, antinomy, and antithesis—to better understand how to instantiate the aforementioned principle in research and practice. For instance, we have collaborated with colleagues to scour the psychological and educational literatures to ascertain how these processes have manifested in prior research and the conclusions that can be drawn from that expanding body of evidence (Dumas, Alexander, & Grossnickle, 2013). As well, we are conducting several studies investigating the role of relational reasoning in a number of complex cognitive tasks, both static and dynamic.

What we learn from these ongoing and soon-to-occur studies should enlighten us about the nature of relational reasoning and suggest what could be done to intervene in the relational thinking and reasoning of adolescents and adults. While it would unquestionably be a move forward to understand better how performance in both in-school and out-of-school contexts unfolds and the role that relational thinking and reasoning can play in those contexts, we want to use that knowledge to make a difference in individuals' learning and performance. That is to say, we not only want to determine why and how errors may arise in the processing of in-the-moment information and in-the-mind knowledge but also want to take steps to increase accuracy in learning and performance.

We accept that errors will always be with us—they are a hallmark of our humanness after all. Indeed, we are not troubled by errors per se. To the contrary, we see errors as important and useful steps toward deeper and more "educated" understandings. Thus, it is ludicrous and even unproductive to desire the elimination of errors. Yet, we do hold that it is a laudable goal to seek learners who are more perceptive and attentive; who notice relevant and discount irrelevant data; who discern meaningful patterns within the immediate context; who are able to grasp similarities, dissimilarities, contradictions, and incompatibilities among otherwise discrete "pieces" of information or ideas; and who use that relational understanding to guide their subsequent thinking or actions. Perhaps understanding the coupling between percepts and concepts and the manner in which humans' ability to discern patterns within and across them will provide the means to make such goals a reality. We hope so.

Acknowledgments

A version of this paper was presented at the European Association for Research on Learning and Instruction's 8th International Conference on Conceptual Change, Trier, Germany.

The authors wish to thank Sandra M. Loughlin for her thoughtful comments on an earlier version of this chapter.

References

Adelson, B. (1984). When novices surpass experts: The difficulty of a task may increase with expertise. *Journal of Experimental Psychology. Learning, Memory, and Cognition, 10,* 483–495.

Alexander, P. A. (1997). Mapping the multidimensional nature of domain learning: The interplay of cognitive, motivational, and strategic forces. In M. L. Maehr & P. R. Pintrich (Eds.), *Advances in motivation and achievement* (Vol. 10, pp. 213–250). Greenwich: JAI Press.

Alexander, P. A. (2003). The development of expertise: The journey from acclimation to proficiency. *Educational Researcher, 32,* 10–14.

Alexander & the Disciplined Reading and Learning Research Laboratory. (2012). Reading into the future: Competence for the 21st century. *Educational Psychologist, 47,* 259–280.

Alexander, P. A., & Murphy, P. K. (1998). The research base for APA's learner-centered psychological principles. In N. M. Lambert & B. L. McCombs (Eds.), *How students learn: Reforming schools through learner-centered education* (pp. 25–60). Washington, DC: American Psychological Association.

Alexander, P. A., & Murphy, P. K. (1999). Nurturing the seeds of transfer: A domain-specific perspective. *International Journal of Educational Research, 31,* 561–576.

Anderson, R. C., Chinn, C., Waggoner, M., & Nguyen, K. (1998). Intellectually stimulating story discussions. In J. Osborn & F. Lehr (Eds.), *Literacy for all: Issues in teaching and learning* (pp. 170–186). New York: Guilford Press.

Ayers, M., & Reder, L. (1998). A theoretical review of the misinformation effect: Predictions from an activation-based memory model. *Psychonomic Bulletin & Review, 5,* 1–21. doi:10.3758/BF03209454.

Balcetis, E., & Dunning, D. (2006). See what you want to see: Motivational influences on visual perception. *Journal of Personality and Social Psychology, 91,* 612–625. doi:10.1037/0022-3514.91.4.612.

Bassok, M., Dunbar, K. N., & Holyoak, K. J. (2012). Introduction to the special section on the neural substrate of analogical reasoning and metaphor comprehension. *Journal of Experimental Psychology. Learning, Memory, and Cognition, 38,* 261.

Bedny, M., Caramazza, A., Grossman, E., Pascual-Leone, A., & Saxe, R. (2008). Concepts are more than percepts: The case of action verbs. *Journal of Neuroscience, 28,* 11347–11353. doi:10.1523/jneurosci.3039-08.2008.

Bekkering, H., & Neggers, S. F. W. (2002). Visual search is modulated by action intentions. *Psychological Science, 13,* 370–374.

Bell, M. A., & Calkins, S. D. (2012). Attentional control and emotion regulation in early development. In M. I. Posner (Ed.), *Cognitive neuroscience of attention* (2nd ed., pp. 322–330). New York: Guilford Press.

Bereby-Meyer, Y., & Kaplan, A. (2005). Motivational influences on transfer of problem-solving strategies. *Contemporary Educational Psychology, 30,* 1–22. doi:10.1037/0882-7974.20.2.341.

Bergman, M. (2007). Representationism and presentationism. *Transactions of the Charles S. Peirce Society, 43,* 53–89.

Berlin, S. (1990). Dichotomous and complex thinking. *Social Service Review, 64,* 46–59.

Blanchette, I., & Richards, A. (2010). The influence of affect on higher level cognition: A review of research on interpretation, judgment, decision making and reasoning. *Cognition and Emotion, 24,* 561–595. doi:10.1080/02699930903132496.

Bransford, J. D., Brown, A. L., & Cocking, R. R. (Eds.). (2000). *How people learn: Brain, mind, experience, and school.* Washington, DC: National Academy Press.

Bredemeier, K., & Simons, D. J. (2012). Working memory and inattentional blindness. *Psychonomic Bulletin & Review, 19,* 239–244. doi:10.3758/s13423-011-0204-8.

Bromme, R., Kienhues, D., & Stahl, E. (2008). Knowledge and epistemological beliefs: An intimate but complicated relationship. In M. S. Khine (Ed.), *Knowing, knowledge and beliefs: Epistemological studies across diverse cultures* (pp. 423–441). New York: Springer Science.

Bulloch, M. J., & Opfer, J. E. (2009). What makes relational reasoning smart? Revisiting the perceptual-to-relational shift in the development of generalization. *Developmental Science, 12,* 114–122.

Butler, J. I., & McCahan, B. J. (2005). Teaching games for understanding as a curriculum model. In L. L. Griffin & J. I. Butler (Eds.), *Teaching games for understanding* (pp. 33–54). Champaign, IL: Human Kinetics.

Cañal-Bruland, R., & van der Kamp, J. (2009). Action goals influence action-specific perception. *Psychonomic Bulletin & Review, 16*, 1100–1105. doi:10.3758/pbr.16.6.1100.

Carey, S. (1985). *Conceptual change in childhood*. Cambridge, MA: MIT Press.

Carey, S. (2000a). Science education as conceptual change. *Journal of Applied Developmental Psychology, 21*, 13–19.

Carey, S. (2000b). The origin of concepts. *Journal of Cognition and Development, 1*, 37–41.

Carey, S. (2009). *The origin of concepts*. New York: Oxford University Press.

Carling, C., Reilly, T., & Williams, A. M. (2009). *Performance assessment for field sports*. New York: Routledge.

Chan, C., Burtis, J., & Bereiter, C. (1997). Knowledge building as a mediator of conflict in conceptual change. *Cognition and Instruction, 15*, 1–40.

Chandler, M. J., Lalonde, C. E., Sokol, B. W., Hallett, D., & Marcia, J. E. (2003). Personal persistence, identity development, and suicide. *Monographs of the Society for Research in Child Development, 68*(2), 1–138.

Charness, N., Krampe, R., & Mayr, U. (1996). The role of practice and coaching in entrepreneurial skill domains: An international comparison of life-span chess skill acquisition. In K. A. Ericsson (Ed.), *The road to excellence: The acquisition of expert performance in the arts and sciences, sports, and games* (pp. 51–80). Mahwah, NJ: Lawrence Erlbaum Associates.

Chi, M. (1992). Conceptual change in and across ontological categories: Examples from learning and discovery in science. In R. Giere (Ed.), *Cognitive models of science* (pp. 129–160). Minneapolis, MN: University of Minnesota Press.

Chi, M. T. H. (2005). Commonsense conceptions of emergent processes: Why some misconceptions are robust. *Journal of the Learning Sciences, 14*, 161–199.

Chi, M. T. H. (2013). Two kinds and four sub-types of misconceived knowledge, ways to change it, and the learning outcomes. In S. Vosniadou (Ed.), *International handbook of research on conceptual change* (2nd ed., pp. 49–70). New York: Routledge.

Chi, M. T. H., & Roscoe, R. D. (2002). The processes and challenges of conceptual change. In M. Limon & L. Mason (Eds.), *Reframing the process of conceptual change: Integrating theory and practice* (pp. 3–27). Dordrecht, the Netherlands: Kluwer Academic.

Chinn, C. A., & Brewer, W. F. (1993). The role of anomalous data in knowledge acquisition: A theoretical framework and implications for science instruction. *Review of Educational Research, 63*, 1–49. doi:10.2307/1170558.

Chinn, C. A., & Malhotra, B. A. (2002). Children's responses to anomalous scientific data: How is conceptual change impeded? *Journal of Educational Psychology, 94*, 327–343. doi:10.1037/0022 -0663.94.2.327.

Chinn, C. A., O'Donnell, A. M., & Jinks, T. S. (2000). The structure of discourse in collaborative learning. *Journal of Experimental Education, 69*, 77–97.

Confrey, J. (1990). A review of the research on student conceptions in mathematics, science, and programming. *Review of Research in Education, 16*, 3–56.

Cook, M. (2006). Visual representations in science education: The influence of prior knowledge and cognitive load theory on instructional design principles. *Science Education, 90*, 1073–1091.

Cosgrove, M. P. (1995). The fruit of integration: Results in the teaching of psychology. *Journal of Psychology and Theology, 23*, 289–295.

de Groot, A. D. (1965). *Thought and choice in chess*. The Hague: Mouton.

Didierjean, A. (2003). Is case-based reasoning a source of knowledge generalisation? *European Journal of Cognitive Psychology, 15*, 435–453. doi:10.1080/09541440244000247.

diSessa, A. A. (1988). Knowledge in pieces. In G. Forman & P. B. Pufall (Eds.), *Constructivism in the computer age* (pp. 49–69). Hillsdale, NJ: Lawrence Erlbaum Associates.

diSessa, A. A. (2013). A bird's-eye view of the "pieces" vs. "coherence" controversy (from the "pieces" side of the fence). In S. Vosniadou (Ed.), *International handbook of research on conceptual change* (2nd ed., pp. 31–48). New York: Routledge.

Dumas, D., Alexander, P. A., & Grossnickle, E. M. (2013). *Relational reasoning and its manifestations in the educational context: A systematic review of the literature*. Manuscript submitted for publication.

Dunbar, K., & Fugelsang, J. (2005). Scientific thinking and reasoning. In K. J. Holyoak & R. Morrison (Eds.), *Cambridge handbook of thinking and reasoning* (pp. 705–726). New York: Cambridge University Press.

Eimas, P. (1994). Categorization in early infancy and the continuity of development. *Cognition, 50*, 83–93.

Endsley, M. R. (2006). Expertise and situation awareness. In K. A. Ericsson, N. Charness, P. J. Feltovich, & R. R. Hoffman (Eds.), *The Cambridge handbook of expertise and expert performance* (pp. 633–651). New York: Cambridge University Press.

Ericsson, K., & Lehmann, A. (1996). Expert and exceptional performance: Evidence of maximal adaptation to task constraints. *Annual Review of Psychology, 47*, 273–305.

Ernst, M., & Bülthoff, H. (2004). Merging the senses into a robust percept. *Trends in Cognitive Sciences, 8*, 162–169. doi:10.1016/j.tics.2004.02.002.

Farrow, D., & Raab, M. (2008). A recipe for expert decision making. In D. Farrow, J. Baker, & C. MacMahon (Eds.), *Developing sport expertise: Researchers and coaches put theory into practice* (pp. 137–154). New York: Routledge.

Felton, M., & Kuhn, D. (2001). The development of argumentive discourse skill. *Discourse Processes, 32*, 135–153. doi:10.1080/0163853X.2001.9651595.

Firth, R. (1950). Sense-data and the percept theory. *Mind, 59*, 35–56.

Fives, H. L., Alexander, P. A., & Buehl, M. M. (2001). Teaching as persuasion: Approaching classroom discourse as refutational text. In J. V. Hoffman, D. L. Schallert, C. M. Fairbanks, J. Worthy, & B. Maloch (Eds.), *Fiftieth yearbook of the National Reading Conference* (pp. 200–212). Chicago: National Reading Conference.

Fodor, J. A. (1981). *Representations*. Cambridge, MA: MIT Press.

Gallese, V., & Lakoff, G. (2005). The brain's concepts: The role of the sensory–motor system in conceptual knowledge. *Cognitive Neuropsychology, 22*, 455–479. doi:10.1080/02643290442000310.

Gentner, D., & Landers, R. (1985). Analogical reminding: A good match is hard to find. *Proceedings of the International Conference on Systems, Man, and Cybernetics*. Tuscon, AZ.

Gentner, D., & Markman, A. B. (1997). Structure mapping in analogy and similarity. *American Psychologist, 52*, 45–56. doi:10.1037/0003-066X.52.1.45.

Gentner, D., & Smith, L. (2012). Analogical reasoning. In V. S. Ramachandran (Ed.), *Encyclopedia of human behavior* (2nd ed., pp. 130–136). Oxford, England: Elsevier.

Gibson, J. J. (1960). The concept of the stimulus in psychology. *American Psychologist, 15*, 694–703.

Gibson, J. J. (1979/1986). *The ecological approach to visual perception*. Hillsdale, NJ: Lawrence Erlbaum Associates.

Gibson, J. J., & Gibson, E. J. (1955). Perceptual learning: Differentiation or enrichment? *Psychological Review, 62*, 32–41.

Gill, M. G., Ashton, P., & Algina, J. (2004). Changing preservice teachers' epistemological beliefs about teaching and learning in mathematics: An intervention study. *Contemporary Educational Psychology, 29*, 164–185.

Glaser, R. (1984). Education and thinking: The role of knowledge. *American Psychologist, 39*, 93–104. doi:10.1037/0003-066X.39.2.93.

Glynn, D. (2007). Iconicity and the grammar–lexis interface. In E. Tabakowska, C. Ljungberg, & O. Fischer (Eds.), *Insistent images: Iconicity in language and literature* (Vol. 5, pp. 269–288). Amsterdam: John Benjamins.

Goodwin, C. (1994). Professional vision. *American Anthropologist, 96*, 606–633.

Greeno, J. G. (1994). Gibson's affordances. *Psychological Review, 101*, 336–342. doi:10.1037//0033-295X.101.2.336.

Griffin, L. L., Dodds, P., Placek, J. H., & Tremino, F. (2001). Middle school students' conceptions of soccer: Their solutions to tactical problems. *Journal of Teaching in Physical Education, 20*, 324–340.

Hare, M. K., & Graber, K. C. (2007). Investigating knowledge acquisition and developing misconceptions of high school students enrolled in an invasion games unit. *High School Journal*, *90*(4), 1–14.

Hartman, M., & Stratton-Salib, B. C. (2007). Age differences in concept formation. *Journal of Clinical and Experimental Neuropsychology*, *29*, 198–214. doi:10.1080/13803390600630294.

Hesse, M. B. (1959). On defining analogy. *Proceedings of the Aristotelian Society, 60,* 79–100.

Hogarth, R. M., & Kunreuther, H. (1997). Decision making under ignorance: Arguing with yourself. In W. M. Goldstein & R. M. Hogarth (Eds.), *Research on judgment and decision making* (pp. 482–508). New York: Cambridge University Press.

Holyoak, K. J. (2012). Analogy and relational reasoning. In K. J. Holyoak & R. G. Morrison (Eds.), *The Oxford handbook of thinking and reasoning* (pp. 234–259). Oxford, England: Oxford University Press.

Hong, J., & Liu, M. (2003). A study on thinking strategy between experts and novices of computer games. *Computers in Human Behavior, 19,* 245–258. doi:10.1016/S0747-5632(02)00013-4.

Hynd, C. R. (2003). Conceptual change in response to persuasive messages. In G. M. Sinatra & P. R. Pintrich (Eds.), *Intentional conceptual change* (pp. 291–315). Mahwah, NJ: Lawrence Erlbaum Associates.

Ioannides, C., & Vosniadou, S. (2002). Exploring the changing meanings of force: From coherence to fragmentation. *Cognitive Science Quarterly, 2,* 5–61.

James, W. (1890). *The principles of psychology* (Vol. 1). New York: Henry Holt.

James, W. [1911] (1996). *Some problems of philosophy: A beginning of an introduction to philosophy.* Lincoln, NE: University of Nebraska Press.

Kane, M. J., & Engle, R. W. (2002). The role of prefrontal cortex in working-memory capacity, executive attention, and general fluid intelligence: An individual-differences perspective. *Psychonomic Bulletin & Review, 9,* 637–671.

Keil, F. C. (1992). *Concepts, kinds, and cognitive development.* Cambridge, MA: MIT Press.

Köhler, W. (1958). Perceptual organization and learning. *American Journal of Psychology, 71,* 311–315.

Kuhn, D., & Udell, W. (2001). The path to wisdom. *Educational Psychologist, 36,* 261–264. doi:10.1207/s15326985ep3604_6.

Kuhn, D., & Udell, W. (2007). Coordinating own and other perspectives in argument. *Thinking & Reasoning, 13,* 90–104. doi:10.1080/13546780600625447.

Lewandowsky, S., Ecker, U. K. H., Seifert, C. M., Schwarz, N., & Cook, J. (2012). Misinformation and its correction: Continued influence and successful debiasing. *Psychological Science in the Public Interest, 13,* 106–131. doi:10.1177/1529100612451018.

Mandler, J. M. (2004). Two kinds of knowledge acquisition. In J. Lucariello, J. A. Hudson, R. Fivush, & P. J. Bauer (Eds.), *The development of the mediated mind: Sociocultural context and cognitive development. Essays in honor of Katherine Nelson* (pp. 13–32). Mahwah, NJ: Lawrence Erlbaum Associates.

Mandler, J. M. (2007). On the origins of the conceptual system. *American Psychologist, 62,* 741–751.

Mandler, J. M. (2008). On the birth and growth of concepts. *Philosophical Psychology, 21,* 207–230. doi:10.1080/09515080801980179.

Mason, L., Gava, M., & Boldrin, A. (2008). On warm conceptual change: The interplay of text, epistemological beliefs, and topic interest. *Journal of Educational Psychology, 100,* 291–309.

McClelland, J. L., & Rumelhart, D. E. (1985). Distributed memory and the representation of general and specific information. *Journal of Experimental Psychology. General, 114,* 159–188.

McGregor, S. J., & Howes, A. (2002). The role of attack and defense semantics in skilled players' memory for chess positions. *Memory & Cognition, 30,* 707–717.

McPherson, S., & Vickers, J. N. (2004). Cognitive control in motor expertise. *International Journal of Sport & Exercise Psychology, 2,* 274–300.

Medin, D. L., & Smith, E. E. (1984). Concepts and concept formation. *Annual Review of Psychology, 35,* 113–138.

Meloy, J. (1985). Concept and percept formation in object relations theory. *Psychoanalytic Psychology, 2,* 35–45.

Merriam-Webster. (2010). *Antithesis.* Merriam-Webster Online Dictionary. Retrieved April 1, 2010, from http://www.merriam-webster.com/dictionary/antithesis

Mervis, C. B., & Rosch, E. (1981). Categorization of natural objects. *Annual Review of Psychology, 32,* 89–115.

Modell, H., Michael, J., & Wenderoth, M. (2005). Helping the learner to learn: The role of uncovering misconceptions. *American Biology Teacher, 67*(1), 20–26.

Mosenthal, P. B. (1988). Research views: Anopheles and antinomies in reading research. *Reading Teacher, 42,* 234–235.

Muis, K. R. (2004). Personal epistemology and mathematics: A critical review and synthesis of research. *Review of Educational Research, 74,* 317–377. doi:10.3102/00346543074003317.

Murphy, P. K. (2007). The eye of the beholder: The interplay of social and cognitive components in change. *Educational Psychologist, 42,* 41–53.

Murphy, P. K., & Alexander, P. A. (2013). Situating text, talk, and transfer in conceptual change: Concluding thoughts. In S. Vosniadou (Ed.), *International handbook of research on conceptual change* (2nd ed., pp. 603–621). New York: Routledge.

Murphy, P. K., Alexander, P. A., Greene, J. A., & Hennessey, M. N. (2012). Examining epistemic frames in conceptual change research: Implications for learning and instruction. *Asia Pacific Education Review*, *13*, 475–486. doi:10.1007/s12564-011-9199-0.

Murphy, P. K., Wilkinson, I. A. G., Soter, A. O., Hennessey, M. N., & Alexander, J. F. (2009). Examining the effects of classroom discussion on students' high-level comprehension of text: A meta-analysis. *Journal of Educational Psychology*, *101*, 740–764.

Nersessian, N. J., & Chandrasekharan, S. (2009). Hybrid analogies in conceptual innovation in science. *Cognitive Systems Research*, *10*, 178–188. doi:10.1016/j.cogsys.2008.09.009.

Novick, L. R. (1988). Analogical transfer, problem similarity, and expertise. *Journal of Experimental Psychology. Learning, Memory, and Cognition*, *14*, 510–520.

Nussbaum, E. M., Kardash, C. A. M., & Graham, S. E. (2005). The effects of goal instructions and text on the generation of counterarguments during writing. *Journal of Educational Psychology*, *97*, 157–169. doi:10.1037/0022-0663.97.2.157.

Ozdemir, G., & Clark, D. B. (2007). An overview of conceptual change theories. *Eurasia Journal of Mathematics, Science & Technology Education*, *3*, 351–361.

Peirce, C. (1955). *Philosophical writings of Peirce*. Mineola, NY: Courier Dover.

Pfundt, H., & Duit, R. (1994). *Students' alternative frameworks and science education: Bibliography*. Kiel, Germany: Institut für die Pädagogik der Naturwissenschaften an der Universität Kiel (IPN), Institute for Science Education.

Piaget, J. [1964] (1997). Development and learning. In M. Gauvin & M. Cole (Eds.), *Readings on the development of children* (pp. 7–20). New York: W. H. Freeman.

Poplu, G., Ripoll, H., Mavromatis, S., & Baratgin, J. (2008). How do expert soccer players encode visual information to make decisions in simulated game situations? *Research Quarterly for Exercise and Sport*, *79*, 392–398.

Portas, C. M., Strange, B. A., Friston, K. J., Dolan, R. J., & Frith, C. D. (2000). How does the brain sustain a visual percept? *Proceedings of the Royal Society of Biological Sciences*, *267*, 845–850. doi:10.1098/rspb.2000.1080

Prabhakaran, V., Smith, J. A., Desmond, J. E., Glover, G. H., & Gabrieli, J. D. (1997). Neural substrates of fluid reasoning: An fMRI study of neocortical activation during performance of the Raven's Progressive Matrices Test. *Cognitive Psychology*, *33*, 43–63. doi:10.1006/cogp.1997.0659.

Qian, G., & Alvermann, D. (1995). Role of epistemological beliefs and learned helplessness in secondary school students' learning science concepts from text. *Journal of Educational Psychology*, *87*, 282–292. doi:10.1037/0022-0663.87.2.282.

Rapp, D. N. (2008). How do readers handle incorrect information during reading? *Memory & Cognition*, *36*, 688–701. doi:10.3758/MC.36.3.688.

Reingold, E. M., Charness, N., Schultetus, R. S., & Stampe, D. M. (2001). Perceptual automaticity in expert chess players: Parallel encoding of chess relations. *Psychonomic Bulletin & Review, 8,* 504–510.

Rosch, E. (1999). Reclaiming concepts. *Journal of Consciousness Studies, 11,* 61–77.

Rosenthal, S. (1969). Peirce's theory of the perceptual judgment: An ambiguity. *Journal of the History of Philosophy, 7,* 303–314. doi:10.1353/hph.2008.1194.

Roth, W. (2001). Situating cognition. *Journal of the Learning Sciences, 10,* 27–61.

Russ, R. S., Scherr, R. E., Hammer, D., & Mikeska, J. (2008). Recognizing mechanistic reasoning in student scientific inquiry: A framework for discourse analysis developed from philosophy of science. *Science Education, 92,* 499–525.

Salomon, G., & Perkins, D. (1989). Rocky roads to transfer: Rethinking mechanisms of a neglected phenomenon. *Educational Psychologist, 24,* 113–142.

Salthouse, T. A. (1991). Expertise as the circumvention of human processing limitations. In K. A. Ericsson & J. Smith (Eds.), *Toward a general theory of expertise: Prospects and limits* (pp. 286–300). Cambridge, England: Cambridge University Press.

Sawyer, R. K. (2005). The new science of learning. In R. K. Sawyer (Ed.), *The Cambridge handbook of the learning sciences* (pp. 1–16). Cambridge, England: Cambridge University Press.

Scherr, R. E., & Hammer, D. (2009). Student behavior and epistemological framing: Examples from collaborative active-learning activities in physics. *Cognition and Instruction, 27,* 147–174.

Schmitt, F., & Lahroodi, R. (2008). The epistemic value of curiosity. *Educational Theory, 58,* 125–148.

Schneider, M., & Hardy, I. (2012). Profiles of inconsistent knowledge in children's pathways of conceptual change. *Developmental Psychology.* Advance online publication. doi:10.1037/a0030976

Schyns, P. G. (1997). Categories and percepts: A bi-directionnal framework for categorization. *Trends in Cognitive Sciences, 1,* 183–189.

Simon, H. A., & Chase, W. G. (1973). Skill in chess: Experiments with chess-playing tasks and computer simulation of skilled performance throw light on some human perceptual and memory processes. *American Scientist, 61,* 394–403.

Sinatra, G. M., & Pintrich, P. R. (Eds.). (2003). *Intentional conceptual change.* Mahwah, NJ: Lawrence Erlbaum Associates

Singer, M., & Gagnon, N. (1999). Detecting causal inconsistencies in scientific text. In S. R. Goldman, A. C. Graesser, & P. van den Broek (Eds.), *Narrative comprehension, causality, and coherence: Essays in honor of Tom Trabasso* (pp. 179–194). Mahwah, NJ: Lawrence Erlbaum Associates.

Sloutsky, V. M. (2010). From perceptual categories to concepts: What develops? *Cognitive Science, 34,* 1244–1286. doi:10.1111/j.1551-6709.2010.01129.x.

Smith, J. P., diSessa, A. A., & Roschelle, J. (1993). Misconceptions reconceived: A constructivist analysis of knowledge in transition. *Journal of the Learning Sciences*, *3*, 115–163.

Stanovich, K. E., & West, R. F. (2000). Individual differences in reasoning: Implications for the rationality debate? *Behavioral and Brain Sciences*, *23*, 645–665.

Stanovich, K. E., & West, R. F. (2008). On the relative independence of thinking biases and cognitive ability. *Journal of Personality and Social Psychology*, *94*, 672–695.

Stephens, A. C. (2006). Equivalence and relational thinking: Preservice elementary teachers' awareness of opportunities and misconceptions. *Journal of Mathematics Teacher Education*, *9*, 249–278. doi:10.1007/s10857-006-9000-1.

Sternberg, R. J. (1996). Costs of expertise. In K. A. Ericsson (Ed.), *The road to excellence: The acquisition of expert performance in the arts and sciences, sports, and games* (pp. 347–354). Mahwah, NJ: Lawrence Erlbaum Associates.

Stevens, R., & Hall, R. (1998). Disciplined perception: Learning to see in technoscience. In M. Lampert & M. L. Blunk (Eds.), *Talking mathematics in school: Studies of teaching and learning* (pp. 107–148). Cambridge, England: Cambridge University Press.

Taylor, A. K., & Kowalski, P. (2004). Naive psychological science: The prevalance, strength, and sources of misconceptions. *Psychological Record*, *54*, 15–25.

Vaeyens, R., Lenoir, M., Williams, A. M., & Philippaerts, R. M. (2008). Talent identification and development programmes in sport: Current models and future directions. *Sports Medicine (Auckland, N.Z.)*, *38*, 703–714.

Van der Henst, J. B., Sperber, D., & Politzer, G. (2002). When is a conclusion worth deriving? A relevance-based analysis of indeterminate relational problems. *Thinking & Reasoning*, *8*, 1–20.

van Gog, T., Paas, F., & van Merriënboer, J. J. G. (2004). Process-oriented worked examples: Improving transfer performance through enhanced understanding. *Instructional Science*, *32*, 83–98. doi:10.1023/B:TRUC.0000021810.70784.b0.

Vosniadou, S. (1994). Capturing and modeling the process of conceptual change. *Learning and Instruction*, *4*, 45–69.

Vosniadou, S. (1999). Conceptual change research: State of the art and future directions. In W. Schnotz, S. Vosniadou, & M. Carretero (Eds.), *New perspectives on conceptual change* (pp. 3–13). Oxford, England: Elsevier.

Vosniadou, S. (2007). Conceptual change and education. *Human Development*, *50*, 47–54. doi:*10.1159/000097684*.

Vosniadou, S. (2008). *International handbook of research on conceptual change*. New York: Routledge.

Vosniadou, S. (2013a). *International handbook of research on conceptual change* (2nd ed.). New York: Routledge.

Vosniadou, S. (2013b). Conceptual change in learning and instruction: The framework theory approach. In S. Vosniadou (Ed.), *International handbook of research on conceptual change* (2nd ed., pp. 11–30). New York: Routledge.

Vosniadou, S., & Brewer, W. F. (1987). Theories of knowledge restructuring in development. *Review of Educational Research, 57,* 51–67.

Vosniadou, S., & Brewer, W. F. (1992). Mental models of the earth: A study of conceptual change in childhood. *Cognitive Psychology, 24,* 535–585.

Vosniadou, S., & Brewer, W. F. (1994). Mental models of the day/night cycle. *Cognitive Science, 18,* 123–183. doi:10.1207/s15516709cog1801_4.

Vygotsky, L. S. [1934] (1986). *Thought and language* (Kozulin, A., Trans.). Cambridge, MA: MIT Press.

Ward, P., Suss, J., & Basevitch, I. (2009). Expertise and expert performance-based training (ExPerT) in complex domains. *Cognition and Learning, 7,* 121–146.

Ward, P., & Williams, A. M. (2003). Perceptual and cognitive skill development in soccer: The multidimensional nature of expert performance. *Journal of Sport & Exercise Psychology, 25,* 93–111.

Weiskopf, D. A. (2008). First thoughts. *Philosophical Psychology, 21,* 251–268. doi:10.1080/09515080801980211.

Wellman, H. M., & Gelman, S. A. (1992). Cognitive development: Foundational theories of core domains. *Annual Review of Psychology, 43,* 337–375.

Wertheimer, M. (1923). Principles of perceptual organization. Translated. In D. C. Beardslee & M. Wertheimer (Eds.), *Readings in perception* (pp. 115–135). New York: Van Nostrand.

Williams, A. M., & Ericsson, K. A. (2005). Perceptual–cognitive expertise in sport: Some considerations when applying the expert performance approach. *Human Movement Science, 24,* 283–307. doi:10.1016/j.humov.2005.06.002.

Williams, A. M., Hodges, N. J., North, J. S., & Barton, G. (2006). Perceiving patterns of play in dynamic sport tasks: Investigating the essential information underlying skilled performance. *Perception, 35,* 317–332. doi:10.1068/p5310.

Wilson, R. A. (2000). The mind beyond itself. In D. Sperber (Ed.), *Metarepresentations: A multidisciplinary perspective* (pp. 31–52). New York: Oxford University Press.

Wood, P., & Kardash, C. A. (2002). Critical elements in the design and analysis of studies of epistemology. In B. K. Hofer & P. R. Pintrich (Eds.), *Personal epistemology: The psychology of beliefs about knowledge and knowing* (pp. 231–260). Mahwah, NJ: Lawrence Erlbaum Associates.

Young, M. F., & Barab, S. A. (1999). Perception of the raison d'être in anchored instruction: An ecological psychology perspective. *Journal of Educational Computing Research, 20,* 119–141. doi:10.2190/43cd-l0cr-h1hf-kr95.

15 Cognitive Processing of Conscious Ignorance

José Otero and Koto Ishiwa

Encoding and utilizing inaccurate information is a way of being ignorant. This and other manifestations of ignorance, such as errors or biases in judgments, have been of interest to researchers in psychology, education, and several other disciplines. In fact, the study of ignorance dates back to at least 1440, when Nicholas of Cusa, a German cardinal and philosopher, wrote a treatise on God, the Universe, and Jesus Christ entitled "De Docta Ignorantia." Nicholas of Cusa examined the limitations of human understanding and what is now termed "conscious ignorance." However, the explicit and systematic study of ignorance in its various forms did not enjoy much popularity until recent times, with some notable exceptions such as Duncan and Weston-Smith's (1977) *The Encyclopaedia of Ignorance*. More recently, the situation is quickly changing. The roles of ignorance and of a plethora of associated concepts, such as those treated in this volume around the idea of inaccurate information, are being explicitly examined in several areas. Psychological studies have focused on ignorance as it emerges in a variety of forms such as with anomalies (Chinn & Brewer, 1993), biases in judgment and reasoning (Gilovich, 1991; Gilovich, Griffin, & Kahneman, 2002; Kahneman, Slovic, & Tversky, 1982; Tversky & Fox, 1995), errors (Sloman, 1999), illusions of explanatory depth (Mills & Keil, 2004; Rozenblit & Keil, 2002), inappropriate judgments of learning (Koriat, 1997; Nelson & Dunlosky, 1991; Schneider, Vise, Lockl, & Nelson, 2000), misconceptions (Kendeou & van den Broek, 2005), or, more generally, in metacognitive failures in knowledge monitoring and comprehension monitoring (Dunlosky, Rawson, & Hacker, 2002; Hacker, Dunlosky, & Graesser, 1998, 2009; Nelson, 1992). Also, the awareness of ignorance has been studied in educationally relevant processes such as question asking (Graesser, Person, & Huber, 1992), help seeking (Nelson-Le Gall, 1981, 1985), or problem finding, understood as "the ability to discover discrepancies (problem sensitivity) and to render explicit a felt problem (problem formulation), with the implication of a strong intrinsic motivation" (Brugman, 1995, p. 42; Runco, 1994).

A growing attention to ignorance is also emerging in other disciplines such as sociology and the history of science (for basic theoretical perspectives, see Bammer & Smithson, 2008; Merton, 1987; or Smithson, 1989), anthropology (Hobart, 1993), economics and management (Jauch & Kraft, 1986; Modica & Rustichini, 1999), engineering (Ayyub, 2004), and education (Bedford, 2010; Doerr, 2009). This interest has given rise to the relatively recent field of "agnotology" (Proctor & Schiebinger, 2008), focusing on the cultural roles and production of ignorance.

In this chapter we take a relatively broad view of ignorance, examining some of its roles and the processes involved in its production. To do this, we start by examining the meaning of ignorance in some detail, drawing a distinction between two main types: conscious ignorance and meta-ignorance. The first kind basically corresponds to what is known not to be known or understood while the second consists of what is unknown without knowing that it is unknown. Then, we analyze some of the roles of ignorance, with an emphasis on those that are positive. Understandably, researchers in psychology and education have traditionally focused on forms of meta-ignorance, such as errors or misconceptions, with the intention of overcoming its adverse effects. In the main section of this chapter we rather focus on conscious ignorance, expressed as the awareness of lack of knowledge or of understanding, and its positive roles. We discuss the process by which this awareness is individually built, and we examine some of the variables influencing this process.

Definition and Types of Ignorance

Anyone reviewing some of the studies mentioned in the previous section will be struck by the confusion of terminology and definitions. The literature on ignorance, especially in the sociological area, "lacks an agreed-on nomenclature" (Smithson, 2008a, p. 209) and uses a variety of different terms in relation to it: error (Smithson, 1989), unknowns (Kerwin, 1993), uncertainty (Jauch & Kraft, 1986), unawareness (Modica & Rustichini, 1999), nonknowledge and nescience (Gross, 2007), negative knowledge (Knorr-Cetina, 1999), conscious ignorance and meta-ignorance (Smithson, 1989), ignorance of ignorance (Ravetz, 1993), or unrecognized ignorance and specified ignorance (Merton, 1987). In some studies, ignorance is defined as the absence or distortion of "true knowledge" (Smithson, 1989), but this immediately leads to epistemological problems linked to the definition of knowledge.

One way to clarify the concept is to distinguish between different kinds of ignorance so that research may focus on a particular type. The distinctions that have been made to date are varied (Einsiedel & Thorne, 1999; Gross, 2007; Smithson, 1989). Kerwin (1993) makes a fine-grained distinction by splitting ignorance into six types. Different states of ignorance can arise depending on the existence of entities (1) known not to be known (known unknowns), (2) not known not to be known (unknown unknowns), (3) thought to be known but actually not known (errors), (4) thought not to be known but actually known (tacit knowledge), (5) not supposed to be known but possibly useful (taboos), and (6) too painful to be known so instead suppressed (denial).

Table 15.1

A categorization of ignorance (adapted from Bammer, Smithson, and the Goolabri Group, 2008)

Primary Level	Metalevel	
	Known	Unknown
The known	Known knowns: conscious knowledge	Unknown knowns: tacit knowledge
The unknown	Known unknowns: conscious ignorance	Unknown unknowns: meta-ignorance

The first two categories offered by Kerwin capture essential features of ignorance. They provide what is now a widespread and basic distinction between kinds of ignorance, subsequently synthesized by Bammer, Smithson, and the Goolabri Group (2008) and summarized here in table 15.1. This elaborates further on our previous descriptions. The distinction is based on two levels—a primary level, used to differentiate between what is in fact known and what is unknown, and a metalevel, describing the awareness of the primary level. At the primary level, there may exist knowledge or, alternatively, lack of knowledge, that is, unknowns. At the metalevel there may be awareness or unawareness of the two previous elements. Therefore, there is knowledge one is aware of, known knowns, as well as lack of knowledge one is aware of, known unknowns. The latter results in conscious ignorance. Then, there is knowledge one is unaware of, that is, tacit knowledge, as well as lack of knowledge one is unaware of, that is, unknown unknowns. The latter is termed "meta-ignorance" by Smithson (1989), and it is basically equivalent to what Gross (2007) calls nescience. Unknown unknowns include errors, Kerwin's third category (Kerwin, 1993), as an important subcategory. Errors may be regarded as unknown unknowns hidden under false beliefs.

Conscious Ignorance

Conscious ignorance and meta-ignorance are complementary components of ignorance. Ignorance, in relation to an individual or to a social group, could be conceived as composed of a relatively small segment of conscious ignorance (known unknowns), together with a possibly infinite area of meta-ignorance (unknown unknowns). Conscious ignorance includes all that is known not to be known, or, more broadly, not to be understood (although a precise definition of understanding may not be easy). Early studies of the cognitive processes involved in knowing when one knows or does not know were conducted by Glucksberg and McCloskey (1981) and Gentner and Collins (1981). Many others followed, examining conscious ignorance and its relation to knowing (Klin, Guzmán, & Levine, 1997; Radecki & Jaccard, 1995; Scholnick & Wing, 1988; Zechmeister, Rusch, & Markell, 1986).

Conscious ignorance was termed by Merton (1971) "specified ignorance," which is "the express recognition of what is not yet known but needs to be known in order to lay the foundation for still more knowledge" (p. 191). It should be distinguished from general or diffuse ignorance: "In workaday science, it is not enough to confess one's ignorance; the point is to specify it. That, of course, amounts to instituting, or finding, a new, worthy, and soluble scientific problem" (Merton, 1987, p. 7). Thus, as pointed out by Merton, research in any area focuses on turning conscious ignorance into knowledge. As examples, the process of organ regeneration as well as the precise structure of mental representations are topic areas that involve conscious ignorance. The journal *Science* celebrated its 125th anniversary by gathering 25 "Big Questions" along with 100 smaller ones, providing a nice map of conscious ignorance in science (Kennedy & Norman, 2005).

Meta-ignorance

The range of frequencies for visible radiation was unknown to Aristotle. In addition, he did not know that this was unknown to him since he lacked the very concept of electromagnetic radiation. Therefore, the range of frequencies for visible radiation was a component of meta-ignorance for Aristotle. Meta-ignorance, for a particular individual, consists of the possibly infinite set of all that is not known beyond the person's conscious ignorance. Therefore meta-ignorance, like conscious ignorance, should be considered relative to individuals or to social groups. The unknowns identified by the editors of the anniversary issue of *Science* mentioned above are most probably meta-ignorance for primary school students.

As previously pointed out, errors or misconceptions may be considered a form of meta-ignorance where the lack of awareness of the unknown is associated with an erroneous belief. This and the more evident type of meta-ignorance, the potentially infinite set of all that is unknown and never was known nor consciously unknown, conform more clearly to the naive view of ignorance as a passive construct (Proctor, 2008). Therefore, meta-ignorance seems not to require an active production, in contrast to conscious ignorance. However, there are some situations for which meta-ignorance can also be the product of deliberate processes. The use of faulty metacognitive control strategies represents an instance of meta-ignorance's being produced by turning known unknowns into unknown unknowns. Starting with the early work of Abelson (1968) on strategies to repair dissonance and inconsistency, a number of researchers (e.g., Baker, 1979; Chinn & Brewer, 1993; Lightfoot & Bullock, 1990) have studied inappropriate "fix-up" strategies used by individuals to solve information-processing problems. The ultimate result of these processes, unfortunately, involves turning conscious ignorance into meta-ignorance. For instance, the subjects studied by Baker (1979) or Otero and Campanario (1990) discounted inconsistencies or contradictions that constituted conscious ignorance at some point by fixing the anomaly through inadequate inferences.

Students in the latter study who read a paragraph including "Until now [superconductivity] had only been obtained by cooling certain materials to low temperatures..." and, in the same paragraph, "Until now superconductivity had been obtained by considerably increasing the temperature of certain materials" explained away the contradiction by interpreting that "Some time ago superconductivity was only achieved by using low temperatures but nowadays some high temperature process could have been discovered" (Otero & Campanario, 1990, p. 453). Therefore they are moving from an initial situation of conscious ignorance, corresponding to an evaluation phase when the coherence of the texts fails to meet a standard of intelligibility (see the "Standards of Coherence" section below), to a situation of meta-ignorance, where a conscious comprehension problem is turned into a false belief. As a result, for the study example, the relation between superconductivity and temperature remains unknown but without the learner's awareness of its being so.

Conscious ignorance and meta-ignorance play significant roles in cognition, both at the individual level and at the social level. As indicated above, psychological and educational research has been primarily focused on the negative role of ignorance, searching for ways to eliminate or to alleviate it. However there are positive benefits of ignorance, especially when it is conscious. In the next section we pay attention to these positive roles.

Roles of Ignorance

Ignorance has traditionally been associated with negative functions (Smithson, 2008a), and it has been regarded as an unavoidable shortcoming accompanying the generation of knowledge. The complexity of human behavior, of social systems, or of natural systems represent sources of ignorance in scientific research. Error and uncertainty are introduced also in the production of other types of knowledge, such as historical knowledge, due to limitations in the compilation of material traces or textual traces or in inferring something about the past from such evidence (Wylie, 2008).

However, sociological studies have unveiled many other roles of ignorance when considered as an active construct, in contrast to the traditional view of ignorance as the passive result of a lack of knowledge. Ignorance appearing in social contexts may sometimes be a deliberate choice of individuals. For instance, many people do not want to take genetic marker tests about hereditary risks (Smithson, 2008b) or do not seek information about the health risks of atomic power plants (Stocking, 1998; Wynne, 1995). In these instances, citizens choose to remain ignorant, actively deciding not to know. A disinterest about complex scientific or technical issues affecting citizens' lives may be caused not solely by passive scientific illiteracy but also by people's deliberate decisions to remain ignorant. Bensaude-Vincent (1995) maintains that the growing gap between scientists and the public cannot be solved by popularization because people in fact often do not want to know. They choose to live under intellectual tutelage, expecting experts to decide for them on complex matters. The reason may lie in their understanding of the division of labor or on a desire to avoid unsettling uncertainties (Stocking, 1998). Journalists readily respond to this disposition of the public by removing the unknowns and uncertainties that accompany many scientific reports because their audience presumably has a low tolerance for complexity and uncertainty (Whitley, 1985): "In the case of phenomena that have been defined as hazardous, for example, journalists often want black-and-white answers. 'Is it risky or not?' they ask scientists, with little attention to the constructed nature of the claims and their unknowns and uncertainties" (Stocking & Holstein, 1993, p. 202).

However, there is also social production of ignorance, independent of any willingness of citizens to remain ignorant or not. Meta-ignorance may be purposefully created by deliberately limiting access to knowledge as in censorship regarding national security issues (Galison, 2008). Areas of ignorance are deliberately set up by scientists, also, by searching for knowledge in certain areas and not in others (Hess, 2007; Kleinman & Suryanarayanan, 2012). For instance, cancer researchers have put emphasis on knowledge gaps related to biological mechanisms, compared to knowledge gaps about social or environmental causes of the disease (Proctor, 1995). Other, more controversial examples of the deliberate production of ignorance can be found in the programs put into effect by the tobacco industry to generate doubt about the health risks of smoking (Proctor, 1995, 2008), in actions of the pharmaceutical industry to withhold data from regulators (McGoey & Jackson, 2009), or in the attempts made by several individuals and organizations to introduce controversy about the environmental dangers of global warming (Oreskes & Conway, 2010). The motivations behind this purposeful, active production of meta-ignorance and conscious ignorance may be varied, but many social groups build ignorance so that it may serve their own interests (Scitovsky, 1950). For instance, ignorance may fulfill the social function of preserving privileged positions of individuals and organizations. Specialists in medicine, law, and other technical fields actively promote ignorance, for example, by using a specialized or esoteric vocabulary or using special instruments removed from public access (Moore & Tumin, 1949).

However, not all of the social functions of ignorance should be considered negative. The most obvious positive role of conscious ignorance is found in its ability to motivate the generation of problems in scientific research. Discovery in science, according to Kuhn's (1969) well-known work, starts with the recognition of ignorance in the form of an anomaly, that is, the discovery of an unknown. A different type of discovery from that involved in the production of new knowledge is considered here. The discovery of conscious ignorance is probably less studied and understood than the discovery of knowledge although both may have essential roles in the development of science.

Other positive roles of ignorance may be found in secrecy, a form of virtuous ignorance defended by all democratic states, or politeness that is based on uncertainty and vagueness in order to protect the feelings of others (Smithson, 2008b). Vagueness or ambiguity may also be used in science and elsewhere for the purpose of avoiding making mistakes. A vague statement has a higher probability of being true than a precise one because there are a greater number of states of affairs that would verify the former compared to the latter (Russell, 1923).

Ignorance appears to play a somewhat ambivalent role in education and educational research. On the one hand, ignorance is considered negative, as educational systems deliberately try to increase students' knowledge and understanding, and not their ignorance. In accordance with this, educational assessment methods traditionally share the "choice procedure" that Acredolo and O'Connor (1991) identify as characterizing assessment in research on children's reasoning. These methods imply that every question or problem has a single answer or solution, and that evaluation is based on whether subjects are able to provide the answer or the solution to the problem. This pedagogical approach offers little room for the manifestation of conscious ignorance. Also, some research explicitly focusing on ignorance in the form of error, such as the numerous studies on students' misconceptions in science and other disciplines (Wandersee, Mintzes, & Novak, 1994), focuses on ignorance as a pathological outcome, searching for ways to turn it into scientific knowledge.

However, the positive roles that ignorance plays in education are increasingly being considered. Conscious ignorance is a significant, positive element of students' thinking in approaches to learning by inquiry (Minner, Levy, & Century, 2010): Being aware of problems or anomalies is the basis for further learning activities. Also, the recognition of uncertainty in scientific data and theories is a basic component of scientific research, and several studies have analyzed its conceptualization by science students (Kirch, 2010; Metz, 2004; Nicholls & Nelson, 1992). Rowell and Pollard (1995) examined uncertainties and inconsistencies in teachers' understanding of the nature of science and designed an addendum to courses in the history and the philosophy of science aimed at increasing awareness of this uncertainty. Nicholls and Nelson (1992) found that elementary school students are able to recognize uncertainty and disagreement both in an empirical matter and in an ethical one, as well as to recognize the cultural variability of the controversial topics. Bedford (2010) suggested that the analysis of inaccurate or misleading statements on global warming found in popular media may be a teaching tool to learn the basic science involved, to achieve a better understanding of the processes of scientific inquiry, and to strengthen students' critical thinking skills. In sum, all of the previous studies exemplify a positive stance in regard to the educational role of conscious ignorance.

Questioning has been a traditional topic in educational and psychological studies where conscious ignorance also plays an important, positive role. Conscious ignorance, in the form of recognized anomalies, gaps, or inconsistencies, is at the root of questioning, particularly with information-seeking questions (Otero, 2009). Although many studies on question asking have been descriptive, or focused mainly on relations between questioning and other variables such as comprehension (Olson, Duffy, & Mack, 1985; Ozgungor & Guthrie, 2004; Taboada & Guthrie, 2006), a number of them have addressed the conscious ignorance underlying question generation. Kemler Nelson, Egan, and Holt (2004) carried out a study on young children with the purpose of finding out what type of information children seek when they ask an ambiguous *What is X?* question on artifacts. Their analysis of follow-up questions showed that children were more likely to inquire about what an artifact is for rather than asking about its name. Results consistent with these findings were reported by Greif, Kemler Nelson, Keil, and Gutierrez (2006) in a study on the different kinds of conscious ignorance that motivate preschool children's questions about animals and artifacts. Ignorance about functions was most frequent when asking about artifacts but did not occur when asking about animals. Therefore, functions appear to be a central component of conscious ignorance of artifacts for children at this age. The result, as discussed below, may be generalized to other age levels.

Ishiwa, Sanjosé, and Otero (2012) also attempted to identify the conscious ignorance responsible for question generation, particularly on expository texts with scientific content. Three types of unknowns may underlie questioning in this situation. First there may be association obstacles or unknowns; that is, difficulties in representing the objects and processes described or explained in a text, together with their features. They are usually made explicit through *Who, What, How, When,* and *Where* questions. Secondly, there are explanation unknowns that concern justifications for or explanations about the entities mentioned in a text. They are frequently expressed as *Why* questions. Finally, there are prediction unknowns that relate to difficulties in generating predictions about the objects or processes appearing in the text. They correspond to *What happens next* or *What if* questions.

Studies on the conscious ignorance underlying questioning, such as Ishiwa et al.'s, suggest first that a certain structure may be identified in conscious ignorance and, therefore, point to the inadequacy of conceiving of such ignorance as an undifferentiated lack of knowledge or comprehension. Secondly, studies such as those of Greif et al. (2006) and Kemler Nelson et al. (2004) indicate there are mechanisms for tuning conscious ignorance depending on the target entity that the questioner is considering. This suggests that conscious ignorance, as in the case of knowledge, is actively constructed and points also to the existence of variables that may influence this construction. We turn now to the discussion of these variables.

Generation of Conscious Ignorance

Philosophers have dealt with some of the puzzling problems involved in the transition from meta-ignorance to conscious ignorance: "So far as we *know* there is something of which we are ignorant, [then] we are not ignorant of it. And so far as we are ignorant of it, how can we know that there is something for us yet to know?" (Weiss, 1934, p. 403). Learning that there is something for us yet to know or to understand, that is, discovering conscious ignorance, may range from a simple process, as in noticing that we do not know how to reach a meeting point in an unknown city, to creative and original acts, such as problem finding that characterizes the work of outstanding scientists (Mackworth, 1965). Identifying both interesting and remediable unknowns in science involves finding, in the vast repository of meta-ignorance, problems that could be solvable with the intellectual tools available at the moment (Kuhn, 1969). However, problem finding in science often proves far from straightforward. Many problems that seem obvious in retrospect, such as the reason for the relative shapes of Africa and South America, altruistic behavior in animals, or the equivalence of inertial mass and gravitational mass, were invisible or ignored by geologists, biologists, and physicists, respectively, at some point in time (Lightman & Gingerich, 1992).

At a relatively simpler level, conscious ignorance is involved in common processes of problem finding and question generation on daily issues. Regarding these processes, asking how we may be aware of what we do not know, or do not understand, is most relevant. This includes asking about the variables involved in the consciousness of ignorance, as did Dillon (1982) some time ago in regard to problem finding. Hoover and Feldhusen (1994) considered this issue by proposing a general model of problem finding and problem solving that included individual variables such as memory organization, cognitive and metacognitive skills, motivation, and interest. We will focus on a reduced range of individual variables—namely, goals, standards of coherence, and domain knowledge—that operate in the production of conscious ignorance in a variety of tasks, especially in discourse processing. It is not our intention to provide a model of the generation of conscious ignorance but only some cognitive variables that need to be taken into account in such a model. The role of these variables is illustrated in studies on discourse processing and question asking, as well as in analyses of problem finding. The operation of goals, standards of coherence, and domain knowledge in other situations where conscious ignorance may also appear remains an open question.

Goals

Conscious ignorance depends on one's purpose for knowing in situations such as question asking on texts. As indicated above, researchers on questioning conceptualize sincere information-seeking questions as triggered by the recognition of obstacles found by a questioner. However, the identification of the obstacles found when processing a text depends on reading goals. This is because readers construct different representations of discourse in memory depending on their reading purpose. For instance, reading with a study goal results in more explanatory and predictive inferences than reading with an entertainment goal (van den Broek, Lorch, Linderholm, & Gustafson, 2001). Also, reading a short scientific text with an understanding goal results in more explanatory inferences than reading the same text with a simple problem-solving goal (Ishiwa et al., 2012). The attempts to build these different representations result in different obstacles found and different conscious ignorance made explicit through questioning (Otero, 2009; Otero & Graesser, 2001). This was demonstrated in a study by Graesser, Langston, and Bagget (1993) that examined learning by questioning. Students had to explore a computer database on woodwind instruments and ask questions when needed. Causal questions, and therefore conscious ignorance on causal relations, were more frequent and increased over time in a condition in which the goal was to design a wind instrument. However, these questions were less likely to emerge, and remained constantly low over time, in a condition in which the goal was simply to assemble a band to play at a party—a goal requiring superficial knowledge. This latter goal prompted subjects to mainly identify ignorance related to taxonomic-definitional knowledge.

Ishiwa et al. (2012) also found an effect of reading goals on conscious ignorance expressed through questioning. In this study, reading goals were manipulated through two different tasks: reading a short paragraph for understanding versus reading the same paragraph to solve a simple problem. The mental representations that subjects attempted to build in the two conditions were different: Explanation inferences were found to be more frequent in the understanding condition than in the simple problem-solving condition. Different unknowns were also identified in the two conditions: Readers generated significantly more causal questions, associated with causal unknowns, in the understanding goal condition than in the problem-solving goal condition.

The influence of processing goals on conscious ignorance is reflected not only in question asking on texts but also in some studies of problem finding. Problem finding, as described previously, involves the discovery of discrepancies or anomalies, a form of lack of understanding. This process has received some attention in research on creativity (Reiter-Palmon, Mumford, Boes, & Runco, 1997; Runco, 1994) and in policy studies and management studies. In the latter area, Cowan's (1986) model of problem recognition provided a detailed account of how individuals in organizations recognize problems. A central element in this model is the comparison between information gathered in a "scanning" process that depicts a perceived state, and the goals an individual possesses with respect to defining a desired state. This comparison may lead to the recognition of performance gaps that result in the detection of a problem or the awareness of this type of ignorance.

As explained above in relation to question asking on texts, the influence of goals in the recognition of ignorance is closely related to the features of the mental representation that a learner attempts to build. One feature of this representation that is especially related to the recognition of ignorance is its coherence. The relation between coherence and conscious ignorance may be described in terms of standards of coherence that determine the acceptability of mental representations. These standards are the second type of variables influencing conscious ignorance that we consider next.

Standards of Coherence

The influence of standards of coherence on conscious ignorance may be seen in the detection of comprehension obstacles in discourse processing. Early work on the processing of dissonant information had already showed that individuals have varying degrees of tolerance for inconsistencies (Miller & Rokeach, 1968). As a result, what is not understood by some readers may be acceptable to others. This variability in the standards for appraising coherence in text processing has been addressed by several researchers in the area of discourse comprehension. Van Oostendorp (1994) proposed that readers monitor the semantic cohesion of a text by comparison with internal standards, generating inferences when reading low-relatedness sentences until they reach the standard. Therefore, readers with a low standard may not be aware of a lack of relations that may be considered unacceptable to other readers. Van den Broek, Risden, and Husebye-Hartmann (1995) also examined the role of standards of coherence in defining what is not understood. They suggest that readers employ standards of coherence that influence the types of inferences they might make. For instance, a reader's standards of coherence determine whether an adequate causal explanation exists for a presented event. When these standards are not met, readers recognize their lack of understanding and engage in control processes that include inferential activity to achieve adequate understanding. Otero (2002) synthesized these and other related findings in a model of readers' regulation of text comprehension. Readers' conscious ignorance with respect to a failure to understand a text is seen as dependent on a parameter representing the coherence or intelligibility standard used by the reader. Conscious comprehension problems depend on the relative value of the self-assessed coherence of the mental representation of a text and on a coherence standard that depends on individual, textual, or contextual variables.

The role of these standards in defining what may not be known or understood is also apparent when comparing the identification of anomalies in scientific thinking and everyday thinking. Standards of coherence in the representations of the world produced by science are quite different from those used in laypersons' thinking (Reif & Larkin, 1991). Standards for scientific comprehension require mental representations including rigorous deductions of the observed phenomena from a small number of basic premises. This is not the case in everyday thinking, especially when using abstract concepts, which usually involves fragmented, relatively inconsistent, and sometimes vague beliefs. In fact, some of the conceptual errors committed by science novices are caused by interrelating abstract scientific concepts in the loose ways in which abstract nonscientific concepts are used in everyday thinking (Mateus & Otero, 2011). Imprecise relations and vague notions used in everyday thinking, as pointed out above, have the property of being compatible with a great number of facts. Therefore violation of the lax coherence standards in everyday thinking is more difficult than a violation of the stringent coherence standards used in science (Russell, 1923). This implies that conscious ignorance, in the form of recognized anomalies, is more likely to appear in the latter system than in the former, assuming that all the other factors remain equal.

Domain Knowledge

What one already knows is a central variable defining what one may consciously ignore. Consider that a widely accepted premise of sociological and historical studies about the unknown is that the active production of conscious ignorance by scientists and scholars is based on what is already known: As perceived knowledge increases, questions and uncertainties may increase as well (Einsiedel & Thorne, 1999; Jaeger, Renn, Rosa, & Webler, 2001; Stocking & Hollstein, 1993). This view has been synthesized using an island metaphor for the production of ignorance (Smithson, 2008b): Knowledge is conceived as an island surrounded by an ocean of meta-ignorance. Conscious ignorance is found at the borders of the island and becomes more extensive, rather than smaller, as the island (i.e., known information) grows in size.

Studies in several areas dealing with different forms of conscious ignorance lend credibility to this metaphor. Knowledge is considered a key variable in the recognition of ignorance that leads to questioning (Flammer, 1981; Miyake & Norman, 1979). Although studies on the relation between knowledge and quantity of questions have produced inconsistent results (Van der Meij, 1990), a positive relation between knowledge and question quality has generally been reported. In a study on questioning by elementary school students, Scardamalia and Bereiter (1992) found that students adjusted the kind of questions that they asked to their perceived level of knowledge. Children who were unfamiliar with the topic of fossil fuels produced a majority of questions involving basic unknowns, such as *What are fossil fuels?* or *What are fossil fuels made of?* However, these basic unknowns were less frequent in questioning about the more familiar topic of endangered species. Children in this latter situation produced more elaborated unknowns through "wonderment questions," that is, questions of a challenging kind reflecting knowledge-based speculation. In the same vein, Van der Meij (1990) compared the questioning of low-knowledge versus high-knowledge fifth-grade students. The results showed more global, low-specificity questions than high-specificity questions asked by low-knowledge students, but not from students with more knowledge. Paradis and Peverly (2003) also found differences in the quality of questions asked by fifth-grade students as they worked in cooperative groups, depending on the amount of mathematical knowledge that members of the groups possessed. Low-knowledge students, unlike their more knowledgeable peers, failed to ask the questions necessary to improve their knowledge of fractions.

Studies on the comprehension of malfunctioning devices by Graesser and Olde (2003) and Graesser, Lu, Olde, Cooper-Pye, and Whitten (2005) also illustrate how knowledge affects the recognition of unknowns. Students with variable technical knowledge read texts describing malfunctioning everyday devices, such as a cylinder lock. Participants were instructed to ask questions in order to identify the components responsible for the malfunctions. The results showed an important effect of technical knowledge on the quality of questions asked and, therefore, on the unknowns identified. Technical knowledge enabled students to identify appropriate unknowns, focusing on likely malfunctioning parts. In contrast, low-knowledge students asked diffuse questions, generating unknowns on components that would not explain the breakdown.

Knowledge also influences the generation of conscious ignorance in problem finding and in the perception of uncertainty. Lee and Cho (2007) studied factors that affect problem finding by fifth-grade students depending on the structure of the problem situation. An ill-structured problem situation involved students finding original research problems when provided with a naturalistic scenario about the ebb and flow of the sea. In contrast, in a moderately structured problem situation, the information and data were provided by the teachers. Prior scientific knowledge was found to be the most important predictor of original unknowns in the ill-structured situation where little relevant information was provided. Also consider work by Powell, Dunwoody, Griffin, and Neuwirth (2007) that studied factors that influence perceived uncertainty about an environmental risk. A strong positive correlation was found between perceived current knowledge and sufficient protection knowledge. The latter is defined as additional knowledge that people find necessary to deal adequately with a risk beyond what they already know. The results showed that as perceived knowledge increases, people tend to feel they need to know more about the risk; that is, they recognize more conscious ignorance.

Vaz, Morgado, Fernandes, Monteiro, and Otero (2013) directly studied the influence of knowledge on the conscious ignorance that primary level and secondary level students have about objects. The study used a questioning procedure to elicit unknowns about natural objects, such as "intestine," or artifacts, such as "battery." The generated unknowns were classified into a few basic categories that corresponded to the kinds of knowledge that lexicographers distinguish in word definitions. These categories included unknowns on functions of the object or on features such as parts or composition. There was also a general category, "What," consisting of unspecified unknowns expressed through ambiguous "What is X?" questions. Two main results showed a correspondence between knowledge and the types of unknowns generated by the students. First, "What is X?" questions, corresponding to unspecified "What" unknowns, were more frequently asked on the less known objects—a result consistent with the findings of questioning studies such as Scardamalia and Bereiter's (1992) mentioned above. Secondly, function unknowns were more frequently generated on artifacts than on natural objects, across the grade levels, aligning with the results of Kemler Nelson et al. (2004) and Greif et al. (2006) mentioned above. This finding is in correspondence with the importance of functional features in the *knowledge* of artifacts (but not of natural objects) that has been found in categorization studies (Barton & Komatsu, 1989; Gelman, 1988; Keil, 1989).

Final Comments

Conscious ignorance, under the form of a conscious lack of knowledge or lack of understanding, plays an important role both in academic and in everyday comprehension experiences. Conscious ignorance should not be considered a passive and unstructured construct that emerges from meta-ignorance. On the contrary, it is actively built and may be elaborated to varying degrees depending, at least, on the goals, standards of coherence, and domain knowledge of the learner. The way in which learners notice and deal with inaccurate or inconsistent information, especially when it cannot be easily converted into unproblematic knowledge or understanding, depends on this constructive process. Therefore, the characterization of the generation of conscious ignorance reveals itself as a critical task. The convenience of a theory of problem finding was pointed out some time ago (Dillon, 1982). In view of the present absence, to our knowledge, of articulated models of the generation of conscious ignorance, their development would constitute a significant psychological and educational contribution. It would open pathways to achieve a better understanding of, and develop responses to, challenges such as the following: figuring out the conditions that encourage asking deep-level questions (Graesser & Person, 1994); knowing how to help readers to turn detected text inconsistencies into recognized comprehension problems, instead of explaining them away by means of Inadequate inferencing or suppressing them (Otero, 2002; Otero & Kintsch, 1992); and helping students to generate original unknowns in a learning by inquiry situation or in a problem-finding task (Lee & Cho, 2007). A response to these concerns is closely dependent on an improved understanding of the mechanisms that produce conscious ignorance. In fact, the lack of this understanding remains one of the interesting elements that make up our own conscious ignorance.

Acknowledgments

This research was funded by grant EDU2008–05359 of the Ministry of Education, Spain. We are grateful to Adolfo López Otero for the linguistic revision of the manuscript.

References

Abelson, R. (1968). *Theories of cognitive consistency theory*. Chicago: Rand McNally.

Acredolo, C., & O'Connor, J. (1991). On the difficulty of detecting cognitive uncertainty. *Human Development, 34*, 204–223.

Ayyub, B. M. (2004). From dissecting ignorance to solving algebraic problems. *Reliability Engineering & System Safety, 85*, 223–238.

Baker, L. (1979). Comprehension monitoring: Identifying and coping with text confusions. *Journal of Reading Behavior, 11*, 365–374.

Bammer, G., & Smithson, M. (Eds.). (2008). *Uncertainty and risk: Multidisciplinary perspectives.* London: Earthscan.

Bammer, G., Smithson, M., & the Goolabri Group. (2008). The nature of uncertainty. In G. Bammer & M. Smithson (Eds.), *Uncertainty and risk: Multidisciplinary perspectives* (pp. 289–303). London: Earthscan.

Barton, M. E., & Komatsu, L. K. (1989). Defining features of natural kinds and artifacts. *Journal of Psycholinguistic Research, 18*, 433–447.

Bedford, D. (2010). Agnotology as a teaching tool: Learning climate science by studying misinformation. *Journal of Geography, 109*, 159–165.

Bensaude-Vincent, B. (1995). The savants and the rest. *Diogenes, 43*, 133–151.

Brugman, G. M. (1995). The discovery and formulation of problems. *European Education, 27*, 38–57.

Chinn, C. A., & Brewer, W. F. (1993). The role of anomalous data in knowledge acquisition: A theoretical framework and implications for science instruction. *Review of Educational Research, 63*, 1–49.

Cowan, D. A. (1986). Developing a process model of problem recognition. *Academy of Management Review, 11*, 763–776.

Dillon, J. T. (1982). Problem finding and solving. *Journal of Creative Behavior, 16*, 97–111.

Doerr, N. M. (2009). Introduction: Knowledge, ignorance, and relations of dominance. *Critical Studies in Education, 50*, 289–294.

Duncan, R., & Weston-Smith, M. (Eds.). (1977). *The encyclopaedia of ignorance.* Oxford, England: Pergamon Press.

Dunlosky, J., Rawson, K. A., & Hacker, D. J. (2002). Metacomprehension of science texts: Investigating the levels-of-disruption hypothesis. In J. Otero, J. A. León, & A. C. Graesser (Eds.), *The psychology of science text comprehension* (pp. 255–279). Mahwah, NJ: Lawrence Erlbaum Associates.

Einsiedel, E. F., & Thorne, B. (1999). Public responses to uncertainty. In S. M. Friedman, S. Dunwoody, & C. L. Rogers (Eds.), *Communicating uncertainty: Media coverage of new and controversial science* (pp. 43–58). Mahwah, NJ: Lawrence Erlbaum Associates.

Flammer, A. (1981). Towards a theory of question asking. *Psychological Research, 43*, 407–420.

Galison, P. (2008). Removing knowledge: The logic of modern censorship. In R. N. Proctor & L. Schiebinger (Eds.), *Agnotology: The making and unmaking of ignorance* (pp. 37–54). Stanford, CA: Stanford University Press.

Gelman, S. A. (1988). The development of induction within natural kind and artifact categories. *Cognitive Psychology, 20,* 65–95.

Gentner, D., & Collins, A. (1981). Studies of inference from lack of knowledge. *Memory & Cognition, 9,* 434–443.

Gilovich, T. (1991). *How we know what isn't so: The fallibility of human reason in everyday life.* New York: The Free Press.

Gilovich, T., Griffin, D., & Kahneman, D. (Eds.). (2002). *Heuristics and biases: The psychology of intuitive judgment.* Cambridge, England: Cambridge University Press.

Glucksberg, S., & McCloskey, M. (1981). Decisions about ignorance: Knowing that you don't know. *Journal of Experimental Psychology. Human Learning and Memory, 7,* 311–325.

Graesser, A. C., Langston, M. C., & Bagget, W. B. (1993). Exploring information about concepts by asking questions. In G. V. Nakamura, R. M. Taraban, & D. Medin (Eds.), *The psychology of learning and motivation: Categorization by humans and machines* (Vol. 29, pp. 411–436). Orlando, FL: Academic Press.

Graesser, A. C., Lu, S., Olde, B., Cooper-Pye, E., & Whitten, S. N. (2005). Question asking and eye tracking during cognitive disequilibrium: Comprehending illustrated texts on devices when the devices break down. *Memory & Cognition, 33,* 1235–1247.

Graesser, A. C., & Olde, B. A. (2003). How does one know whether a person understands a device? The quality of the questions the person asks when the device breaks down. *Journal of Educational Psychology, 95,* 524–536.

Graesser, A. C., & Person, N. K. (1994). Question asking during tutoring. *American Educational Research Journal, 31,* 104–137.

Graesser, A. C., Person, N. K., & Huber, J. D. (1992). Mechanisms that generate questions. In T. Lauer, E. Peacock, & A. C. Graesser (Eds.), *Questions and information systems* (pp. 167–187). Hillsdale, NJ: Lawrence Erlbaum Associates.

Greif, M. L., Kemler Nelson, D. G., Keil, F. C., & Gutierrez, F. (2006). What do children want to know about animals and artifacts? Domain-specific requests for information. *Psychological Science, 17,* 455–459.

Gross, M. (2007). The unknown in process: Dynamic connections of ignorance, nonknowledge and related concepts. *Current Sociology, 55,* 742–759.

Hacker, D., Dunlosky, J., & Graesser, A. C. (Eds.). (1998). *Metacognition in educational theoy and practice.* Mahwah, NJ: Lawrence Erlbaum Associates.

Hacker, D., Dunlosky, J., & Graesser, A. (Eds.). (2009). *Handbook of metacognition in education.* New York: Routledge.

Hess, D. (2007). *Alternative pathways in science and industry: Activism, innovation and the environment in an era of globalization.* Cambridge, MA: MIT Press.

Hobart, M. (Ed.). (1993). *An anthropological critique of development: The growth of ignorance*. London: Routledge.

Hoover, S. M., & Feldhusen, J. F. (1994). Scientific problem solving and problem finding: A theoretical model. In M. A. Runco (Ed.), *Problem finding, problem solving, and creativity* (pp. 201–219). Westport, CT: Ablex.

Ishiwa, K., Sanjosé, V., & Otero, J. (2012). Generation of information-seeking questions on scientific texts under different reading goals. *British Journal of Educational Psychology*. Advance online publication. doi:10.1111/j.2044-8279.2012.02079.x.

Jaeger, C. C., Renn, O., Rosa, E. A., & Webler, T. (2001). *Risk, uncertainty, and rational action*. Sterling, VA: Earthscan.

Jauch, L. R., & Kraft, K. L. (1986). Strategic mangement of uncertainty. *Academy of Management Review, 11*, 777–790.

Kahneman, D., Slovic, P., & Tversky, A. (Eds.). (1982). *Judgment under uncertainty: Heuristics and biases*. New York: Cambridge University Press.

Keil, F. C. (1989). *Concepts, kinds, and cognitive development*. Cambridge, MA: MIT Press.

Kemler Nelson, D. G., Egan, L. C., & Holt, M. B. (2004). When children ask, "What is it?" what do they want to know about artifacts? *Psychological Science, 15*, 384–389.

Kendeou, P., & van den Broek, P. (2005). The effects of readers' misconceptions on comprehension of scientific text. *Journal of Educational Psychology, 97*, 235–245.

Kennedy, D., & Norman, C. (2005). What we don't know? *Science, 309*, 78–102.

Kerwin, A. (1993). None too solid, medical ignorance. *Knowledge: Creation, Diffusion, Utilization, 15*, 166–185.

Kirch, S. A. (2010). Identifying and resolving uncertainty as a mediated action in science: A comparative analysis of the cultural tools used by scientists and elementary science students at work. *Science Education, 94*, 308–335.

Kleinman, D., & Suryanarayanan, S. (2012). Dying bees and the social production of ignorance. *Science, Technology and Human Values*. Advance online publication. doi:10.1177/0162243912442575

Klin, C. M., Guzmán, A. E., & Levine, W. H. (1997). Knowing that you don't know: Metamemory and discourse processing. *Journal of Experimental Psychology. Learning, Memory, and Cognition, 23*, 1378–1393.

Knorr-Cetina, K. (1999). *Epistemic cultures: How the sciences make knowledge*. Cambridge, MA: Harvard University Press.

Koriat, A. (1997). Monitoring one's knowledge during study: A cue-utilization approach to judgments of learning. *Journal of Experimental Psychology. General, 126*, 349–370.

Kuhn, T. S. (1969). *The structure of scientific revolutions*. Chicago: Chicago University Press.

Lee, H., & Cho, Y. (2007). Factors affecting problem finding depending on degree of structure of problem situation. *Journal of Educational Research*, *101*, 113–124.

Lightfoot, C., & Bullock, M. (1990). Interpreting contradictory communications: Age and context effects. *Developmental Psychology*, *26*, 830–836.

Lightman, A., & Gingerich, O. (1992). When do anomalies begin? *Science*, *255*, 690–695.

Mackworth, N. H. (1965). Originality. *American Psychologist*, *20*, 51–66.

Mateus, G., & Otero, J. (2011). Memory content of scientific concepts in beginning university science students. *Educational Psychology*, *31*, 675–690.

McGoey, L., & Jackson, E. (2009). Seroxat and the suppression of trial data: Regulatory failure and the uses of legal ambiguity. *Journal of Medical Ethics*, *35*, 107–112.

Merton, R. K. (1971). The precarious foundation of detachment in sociology. In E. A. Tiryakian (Ed.), *The phenomenon of sociology* (pp. 188–199). New York: Appleton-Century-Crofts.

Merton, R. K. (1987). Three fragments from a sociologist's notebooks: Establishing the phenomenon, specified ignorance, and strategic research materials. *Annual Review of Sociology*, *13*, 1–28.

Metz, K. (2004). Children's understanding of scientific inquiry: Their conceptualization of uncertainty in investigations of their own design. *Cognition and Instruction*, *22*, 219–290.

Miller, G. R., & Rokeach, M. (1968). Individual differences and tolerance for inconsistency. In R. Abelson, E. Aronson, W. McGuire, T. Newcomb, M. Rosenberg, & P. Tannenbaum (Eds.), *Thories of cognitive consistency: A sourcebook* (pp. 624–632). Chicago: Rand McNally.

Mills, C. M., & Keil, F. C. (2004). Knowing the limits of one's understanding: The development of an awareness of an illusion of explanatory depth. *Journal of Experimental Child Psychology*, *87*, 1–32.

Minner, D., Levy, A. J., & Century, J. (2010). Inquiry-based science instruction—What is it and does it matter? Results from a research synthesis years 1984 to 2002. *Journal of Research in Science Teaching*, *47*, 474–496.

Miyake, N., & Norman, D. A. (1979). To ask a question one must know enough to know what is not known. *Journal of Verbal Learning and Verbal Behavior*, *18*, 357–364.

Modica, S., & Rustichini, A. (1999). Unawareness and partitional information structures. *Games and Economic Behavior*, *27*, 265–298.

Moore, W. E., & Tumin, M. M. (1949). Some social functions of ignorance. *American Sociological Review*, *14*, 787–795.

Nelson, T. O. (Ed.). (1992). *Metacognition: Core readings*. Cambridge, MA: MIT Press.

Nelson, T. O., & Dunlosky, J. (1991). The delayed-JOL effect: When delaying your judgements of learning can improve the accuracy of your metacognitive monitoring. *Psychological Science*, *2*, 267–270.

Nelson-Le Gall, S. (1981). Help-seeking: An understudied problem-solving skill in children. *Developmental Review, 1,* 224–246.

Nelson-Le Gall, S. A. (1985). Help-seeking in learning. In E. Gordon (Ed.), *Review of research in education* (Vol. 12, pp. 55–90). Washington, DC: American Educational Research Association.

Nicholls, J. G., & Nelson, J. R. (1992). Students' conceptions of controversial knowledge. *Journal of Educational Psychology, 84,* 224–230.

Olson, G. M., Duffy, S. A., & Mack, R. L. (1985). Question asking as a component of text comprehension. In A. C. Graesser & J. B. Black (Eds.), *The psychology of questions* (pp. 219–226). Hillsdale, NJ: Lawrence Erlbaum Associates.

Oreskes, N., & Conway, E. (2010). *Merchants of doubt: How a handful of scientists obscured the truth on issues from tobacco smoke to global warming.* New York: Bloomsbury Press.

Otero, J. (2002). Noticing and fixing difficulties in understanding science texts. In J. Otero, J. A. León, & A. Graesser (Eds.), *The psychology of science text comprehension* (pp. 281–307). Mahwah, NJ: Lawrence Erlbaum Associates.

Otero, J. (2009). Question generation and anomaly detection in texts. In D. Hacker, J. Dunlosky, & A. Graesser (Eds.), *Handbook of metacognition in education* (pp. 47–59). New York: Routledge.

Otero, J., & Campanario, J. M. (1990). Comprehension evaluation and regulation in learning from science texts. *Journal of Research in Science Teaching, 27,* 447–460.

Otero, J., & Graesser, A. (2001). PREG: Elements of a model of question asking. *Cognition and Instruction, 19,* 143–175.

Otero, J., & Kintsch, W. (1992). Failures to detect contradictions in a text: What readers believe versus what they read. *Psychological Science, 3,* 229–235.

Ozgungor, S., & Guthrie, J. T. (2004). Interactions among elaborative interrogation, knowledge, and interest in the process of constructing knowledge from text. *Journal of Educational Psychology, 96,* 437–443.

Paradis, L., & Peverly, S. (2003). The effects of knowledge and task on students' peer-directed questions in modified cooperative learning groups. *Child Study Journal, 33,* 117–136.

Powell, P., Dunwoody, S., Griffin, R., & Neuwirth, K. (2007). Exploring lay uncertainty about an environmental health risk. *Public Understanding of Science (Bristol, England), 16,* 323–343.

Proctor, R. N. (1995). *Cancer wars: How politics shapes what we know and don't know about cancer.* New York: Basic Books.

Proctor, R. N. (2008). Agnotology: A missing term to describe the cultural production of ignorance (and its study). In R. N. Proctor & L. Schiebinger (Eds.), *Agnotology: The making and unmaking of ignorance* (pp. 1–33). Stanford, CA: Stanford University Press.

Proctor, R. N., & Schiebinger, L. (2008). *Agnotology: The making and unmaking of ignorance.* Stanford, CA: Stanford University Press.

Radecki, C. M., & Jaccard, J. (1995). Perceptions of knowledge, actual knowledge, and information search behaviour. *Journal of Experimental Social Psychology, 31*, 107–138.

Ravetz, J. R. (1993). The sin of science: Ignorance of ignorance. *Knowledge: Creation, Diffusion, Utilization, 15*, 157–165.

Reif, F., & Larkin, J. (1991). Cognition in scientific and everyday domains: Comparison and learning implications. *Journal of Research in Science Teaching, 28*, 733–760.

Reiter-Palmon, R., Mumford, M. D., Boes, J. O. C., & Runco, M. A. (1997). Problem construction and creativity: The role of ability, cue consistency, and active processing. *Creativity Research Journal, 10*, 9–23.

Rowell, J. A., & Pollard, J. M. (1995). Raising awareness of uncertainty: A useful addendum to courses in the history and philosophy of science for science teachers? *Science & Education, 4*, 87–97.

Rozenblit, L. R., & Keil, F. C. (2002). The misunderstood limits of folk science: An illusion of explanatory depth. *Cognitive Science, 26*, 521–562.

Runco, M. A. (1994). *Problem finding, problem solving and creativity*. Norwood, NJ: Ablex.

Russell, B. (1923). Vagueness. *Australasian Journal of Philosophy and Psychology, 1*, 84–92. (Reprinted in *Vagueness: A reader*, pp. 61–68, by R. Keefe & P. Smith, Eds., 1997, Cambridge, MA: MIT Press.)

Scardamalia, M., & Bereiter, C. (1992). Text-based and knowledge-based questioning by children. *Cognition and Instruction, 9*, 177–199.

Schneider, W., Vise, M., Lockl, K., & Nelson, T. O. (2000). Developmental trends in children's memory monitoring: Evidence from a judgment-of-learning (JOL) task. *Cognitive Development, 15*, 115–134.

Scholnick, E. K., & Wing, C. S. (1988). Knowing when you don't know: Developmental and situational considerations. *Developmental Psychology, 24*, 190–196.

Scitovsky, T. (1950). Ignorance as a source of oligopoly power. *American Economic Review, 40*, 48–53.

Sloman, S. A. (1999). Rational versus arational models of thought. In R. J. Sternberg (Ed.), *The nature of cognition* (pp. 557–586). Cambridge, MA: MIT Press.

Smithson, M. (1989). *Ignorance and uncertainty: Emerging paradigms*. New York: Springer.

Smithson, M. (2008a). Social theories of ignorance. In R. N. Proctor & L. Schiebinger (Eds.), *Agnotology: The making and unmaking of ignorance* (pp. 209–229). Stanford, CA: Stanford University Press.

Smithson, M. (2008b). The many faces and masks of uncertainty. In G. Bammer & M. Smithson (Eds.), *Uncertainty and risk: Multidisciplinary perspectives* (pp. 13–26). London: Earthscan.

Stocking, S. H. (1998). On drawing attention to ignorance. *Science Communication, 20*, 165–178.

Stocking, S. H., & Holstein, L. S. (1993). Constructing and reconstructing scientific ignorance. *Knowledge: Creation, Diffusion, Utilization, 15*, 186–210.

Taboada, A., & Guthrie, J. T. (2006). Contributions of student questioning and prior knowledge to construction of knowledge from reading information text. *Journal of Literacy Research, 38*, 1–35.

Tversky, A., & Fox, C. R. (1995). Weighing risk and uncertainty. *Psychological Review, 109*, 269–283.

van den Broek, P., Lorch, R. F., Linderholm, T., & Gustafson, M. (2001). The effects of readers' goals on inference generation and memory for texts. *Memory & Cognition, 29*, 1081–1087.

van den Broek, P., Risden, K., & Husebye-Hartmann, E. (1995). The role of readers' standards for coherence in the generation of inferences during reading. In R. F. Lorch & E. J. O'Brien (Eds.), *Sources of coherence in reading* (pp. 353–373). Hillsdale, NJ: Lawrence Erlbaum Associates.

Van der Meij, H. (1990). Question asking: To know that you do not know is not enough. *Journal of Educational Psychology, 82*, 505–512.

van Oostendorp, H. (1994). Text processing in terms of semantic cohesion monitoring. In H. van Oostendorp & R. A. Zwaan (Eds.), *Naturalistic text comprehension* (pp. 35–55). Norwood, NJ: Ablex.

Vaz, P., Morgado, J., Fernandes, P., Monteiro, A., Otero, J. (2013). *Students' unknowns about natural objects and artifacts*. Manuscript submitted for publication.

Wandersee, J. H., Mintzes, J. J., & Novak, J. D. (1994). Research on alternative conceptions in science. In D. L. Gabel (Ed.), *Handbook of research in science teaching and learning* (pp. 17–210). New York: Macmillan.

Weiss, P. (1934). Metaphysics: The domain of ignorance. *Philosophical Review, 43*, 402–406.

Whitley, R. (1985). Knowledge producers and knowledge acquirers: Popularisation as a relation between scientific fields and their publics. In T. Shinn & R. Whitley (Eds.), *Expository science: Forms and functions of popularization* (pp. 3–28). Dordrecht, the Netherlands: Reidel.

Wylie, A. (2008). Mapping ignorance in archaelogy: The advantages of historical hindsight. In R. N. Proctor & L. Schiebinger (Eds.), *Agnotology: The making and unmaking of ignorance* (pp. 183–205). Stanford, CA: Stanford University Press.

Wynne, B. (1995). Public understanding of science. In S. Jasanoff, G. E. Markle, J. C. Petersen, & T. Pinch (Eds.), *Handbook of science and technology studies* (pp. 361–388). Thousand Oaks, CA: Sage.

Zechmeister, E. B., Rusch, K. M., & Markell, K. A. (1986). Training college students to assess accurately what they know and don't know. *Human Learning, 5*, 3–19.

IV   Emerging Models and Frameworks

16 The Knowledge Revision Components (KReC) Framework: Processes and Mechanisms

Panayiota Kendeou and Edward J. O'Brien

In formal and informal settings we continually encode, use, integrate, and manipulate information that becomes a part of our long-term knowledge base. It is a common problem that often when we first encode information about a particular topic, initial information turns out to be incomplete or even factually incorrect. Nevertheless, that information resides in our knowledge base unhindered until and/or unless on a subsequent occasion we encode new information related to this topic. Newly encoded information may extend or deepen the existing knowledge base by adding information that builds on it. Alternatively, the new information may directly conflict with information in the existing knowledge base. Independent of the exact relation between the newly encoded information and the current knowledge base, when new information is encoded, the knowledge base is updated/modified/revised to accommodate this newly encoded information. The exact revisions that will occur will depend on the specific relation that exists between the newly encoded information and the preexisting knowledge base. The goal of the present chapter is to specify both the processes and mechanisms necessary for knowledge revision via a proposed theoretical framework, the Knowledge Revision Components (KReC) framework.

We restrict our definition of knowledge revision to the modification of the existing knowledge base in memory to accommodate newly acquired information. A core assumption is that the knowledge revision process can only occur when newly acquired information makes contact with, and activates, the preexisting knowledge base so that both pieces of information are in working memory at the same time (Kendeou & van den Broek, 2007; van den Broek & Kendeou, 2008). We conceptualize the knowledge revision process as incremental, conservative, and slow. As new information is encoded, it is integrated into, and becomes a part of, the already-existing knowledge base. Thus, by definition, in the early stage of the knowledge revision process, the knowledge base will be dominated by preexisting knowledge; evidence that any sort of knowledge revision has occurred will be subtle and difficult to measure. It is only after the amount, and quality, of new information integrated into the knowledge base crosses some threshold that overt evidence of knowledge revision will become evident.

Because a core process in the comprehension of text also involves the continual revision of text representations in memory to accommodate each incoming piece of information, models that have been developed to capture this process (e.g., Graesser, Singer, & Trabasso, 1994; Kintsch, 1988; Kintsch & van Dijk, 1978; Langston & Trabasso, 1999; O'Brien & Myers, 1999; Myers & O'Brien, 1998; Sanford & Garrod, 1998; van den Broek, Rapp, & Kendeou, 2005) also lend themselves to understanding the process of knowledge revision more broadly. By investigating the basic processes involved in knowledge revision within a well-defined context such as that of reading comprehension, we will be better positioned to propose a broader theory of knowledge revision that can generalize to a wide variety of situations. Thus, our goal in this chapter is to outline a theoretical framework of knowledge revision that aligns itself with what we know about knowledge revision in the context of reading comprehension. We first review basic memory processes that form the central core of most models of reading comprehension and memory in general; we then review several findings within the reading comprehension literature that constitute a basic form of knowledge revision; we then extend and generalize those findings to knowledge revision in other domains; and finally, we conclude with the discussion of the core principles of our proposed theoretical account of knowledge revision, the KReC framework.

Basic Memory Assumptions

We adopt the view that inactive information in long-term memory (e.g., previously acquired information) becomes active and available relying on passive processing assumptions derived from more global models of memory (e.g., Gillund & Shiffrin, 1984; Hintzman, 1986; Kintsch, 1988; Ratcliff, 1978; Ratcliff & McKoon, 1988). One instantiation of a model that captures these assumptions, especially as they relate to the activation process during reading, is the *resonance model* (Myers & O'Brien, 1998; O'Brien & Myers, 1999), a model that is consistent with the basic passive memory activation components of several other models and accounts relevant to reading comprehension (e.g., Kintsch, 1988, 1998; Sanford & Garrod, 1981, 1998, 2005; van den Broek, Young, Tzeng, & Linderholm, 1999; van den Broek et al., 2005). The core assumption of the resonance model is that newly encoded information, in combination with the current contents of working memory, serves as a signal to all of long-term memory, including both earlier portions of the text representation as well as general world knowledge (e.g., Cook & Guéraud, 2005; Garrod & Terras, 2000; Gerrig & McKoon, 1998; Gerrig & O'Brien, 2005; Guéraud & O'Brien, 2005; Lassonde, Smith, & O'Brien, 2011; McKoon & Ratcliff, 1998; Myers & O'Brien, 1998; O'Brien & Albrecht, 1991; O'Brien & Myers, 1999; Rizzella & O'Brien, 2002). The intensity of the signal that emanates will depend on the degree of attention given to information currently in active memory, but the signal proceeds autonomously and is unrestricted. Concepts from inactive portions of the text representation, as well as information from general world knowledge, resonate as a function of the degree of match to input. The match depends primarily on the overlap of semantic features. Memory elements that are contacted by the initial signal in turn signal other elements in memory. During this resonance process, activation builds, and when the process stabilizes, information that has the highest level of activation enters working memory. Because this activation process is unrestricted, it proceeds without regard for the information that is activated; any information related to the signal that is sufficiently activated will be returned to working memory, independent of whether that information will ultimately facilitate or hinder further processing.

Knowledge Revision in Narratives: An Incremental Process

Comprehension of narrative text requires the continual integration of incoming information into the evolving discourse representation in readers' memory. Integrating new information during reading results in the updating or revision of the emerging discourse representation. Indeed, that readers continually update their discourse representation is an uncontroversial component of most models of reading comprehension (e.g., Gernsbacher, 1990; Gerrig & McKoon, 1998; Gerrig & O'Brien, 2005; Goldman & Varma, 1995; Graesser et al., 1994; Kintsch & van Dijk, 1978; Magliano, Trabasso, & Graesser, 1999; McNamara & Magliano, 2009; O'Brien & Myers, 1999; Rapp & van den Broek, 2005; Tzeng, van den Broek, Kendeou, & Lee, 2005; van den Broek et al., 1999; Zwaan, Magliano, & Graesser, 1995). Often, however, updating involves not only the incorporation of new information but also the discounting, changing, or outdating of previously read information (Blanc, Kendeou, van den Broek, & Brouillet, 2008; Cook, Halleran, & O'Brien, 1998; Hakala & O'Brien, 1995; Johnson & Seifert, 1998; Kendeou & van den Broek, 2007; Kendeou, Smith, & O'Brien, 2013; O'Brien, Rizzella, Albrecht, & Halleran, 1998; O'Brien, Cook, & Guéraud, 2010; O'Brien, Cook, & Peracchi, 2004; Rapp & Kendeou, 2007, 2009).

Outdating of information in a narrative constitutes a basic form of knowledge revision. It occurs whenever the integration of newly encoded information produces a conflict with information encoded earlier. Typically, knowledge revision during the reading of a narrative occurs whenever information is introduced that indicates a change in the state of affairs of a character, an object, or a scenario that requires the "negation" of earlier information. For example, a reader may initially learn that "Mary is a vegetarian" but then subsequently read that this is no longer correct (e.g., O'Brien et al., 1998, 2004, 2010). Or readers may infer that "Albert is sloppy" because he is described as living in a messy apartment but then subsequently read that his apartment is messy only because he had just moved (e.g., Rapp & Kendeou, 2007, 2009). In each of these cases, knowledge revision would involve incorporating this new information into the discourse representation as well as outdating of the initially encoded information because it is no longer correct and/or relevant. The information that has been outdated (i.e., revised) remains a part of the long-term memory representation, but, as a function of having been revised, the outdated information would lose activation, would become less accessible, and should not impact the comprehension of subsequent text.

However, even when readers have engaged in knowledge revision, there is considerable evidence indicating that the knowledge revision process may not be sufficient to stop the outdated information from being reactivated and disrupting comprehension (e.g., Guéraud, Harmon, & Peracchi, 2005; Hakala & O'Brien, 1995; Kendeou, Smith, & O'Brien,, 2013; Kendeou & van den Broek, 2007; O'Brien et al., 1998, 2010; Rapp & Kendeou, 2007, 2009). Consider the following example in table 16.1 taken from O'Brien, et al. (1998). Participants read an initial description that served to establish the story line of the passage. This was followed by one of three elaboration conditions: consistent, inconsistent, and qualified. The consistent elaboration condition described characteristics of the protagonist (e.g., Mary loves junk food and does not care about her diet) that were consistent with the target sentence that followed (e.g., "Mary ordered a cheeseburger and fries"). The inconsistent elaboration condition described

Table 16.1
Sample passage from O'Brien et al. (1998)

Introduction
Today, Mary was meeting a friend for lunch. She arrived early at the restaurant and decided to get a table. After she sat down, she started looking at the menu.

Consistent Elaboration
This was Mary's favorite restaurant because it had fantastic junk food. Mary enjoyed eating anything that was quick and easy to fix. In fact, she ate at McDonald's at least three times a week. Mary never worried about her diet and saw no reason to eat nutritious foods.

Inconsistent Elaboration
This was Mary's favorite restaurant because it had fantastic health food. Mary, a health nut, had been a strict vegetarian for 10 years. Her favorite food was cauliflower. Mary was so serious about her diet that she refused to eat anything which was fried or cooked in grease.

Qualified Elaboration
As she was waiting, Mary recalled that this had been her favorite restaurant because it had fantastic health food. Mary recalled that she had been a health nut and a strict vegetarian for about 10 years but she wasn't anymore. Back then, her favorite food had been cauliflower. At that time, Mary had been so serious about her diet that she had refused to eat anything which was fried or cooked in grease.

Filler
After about 10 minutes, Mary's friend arrived. It had been a few months since they had seen each other. Because of this they had a lot to talk about and chatted for over a half hour. Finally, Mary signaled the waiter to come take their orders. Mary checked the menu one more time. She had a hard time deciding what to have for lunch.

Target Sentence
Mary ordered a cheeseburger and fries.

---

characteristics of the protagonist that were inconsistent (e.g., Mary is a health nut and a strict vegetarian) with the target sentence that followed. The qualified-elaboration section contained information that outdated the initial character trait; that is, it required readers to revise what they knew and understood about the protagonist (e.g., "Mary recalled that she had been a health nut and a strict vegetarian for about 10 years but she wasn't anymore"). Across five experiments, O'Brien et al. showed that reading times on the target sentence were significantly slower following the inconsistent elaboration than following the consistent elaboration. However, the critical test involved reading times for the qualification condition. Across all five experiments, reading times indicated that the target sentence was read more slowly in the qualified condition than in the consistent condition, but reading times on the target sentence were also faster in the qualified condition than in the inconsistent condition. O'Brien et al. concluded that even though the readers had encoded the qualifying information, and therefore revised their understanding of the protagonist, the outdated information continued to be reactivated and disrupted comprehension.

Similarly, O'Brien et al. (2010) demonstrated that even when the knowledge revision necessary in the qualified conditions involved encoding an irreversible change in state of a primary object in a narrative (e.g., a once standing tree was cut down and no longer present), reading times on a target sentence (e.g., "All that remained of the tree was the stump") continued to be disrupted by previously-mentioned-but-outdated information (e.g., that the tree had been standing). Consider how these findings fit with the passive activation mechanism described earlier: Whenever readers encoded a target sentence, information in that sentence served as a signal to all of memory; anything that was related to the target sentence had the potential to be reactivated and returned to working memory, independent of whether that information was correct or even relevant. In the qualified conditions, both the updated and outdated information would draw activation from this signal and both would be returned to working memory. Because the reader has available both the updated and outdated information, the outdated information will continue to disrupt comprehension, but not as severely as in the inconsistent condition in which no updated information is available. Thus, the reduced disruption in reading times in the qualified conditions (when compared to the slowdowns in the inconsistent conditions) reflects the early stages of knowledge revision; outdated or previously-acquired-but-no-longer-correct information still has the potential to compete with the revised knowledge for activation that can impact comprehension and memory processes.

Because the outdated information continued to disrupt comprehension in the qualified conditions, it could be argued that readers never really engaged in knowledge revision. However, there are two findings that reject this possibility. First, reading times in the qualified condition were always significantly faster than in the inconsistent condition; if readers had not encoded the qualification and revised their understanding accordingly, reading times in the qualified condition would have been the same as in the inconsistent condition. Second, participants were asked direct questions about the updating information to ensure that they engaged in knowledge revision and understood that the outdated information was no longer correct (e.g., "Was the tree cut down?"). With an accuracy level of over 95%, the findings confirmed that readers had updated their understanding of the passages, outdated the appropriate information, and maintained the updated information as the correct information. Taken together, the results of O'Brien et al. (1998, 2010) confirm that even when readers engage in knowledge revision, they remain at risk for interference from knowledge prior to correction.

Although the findings described above make clear that knowledge revision is not all-or-none, and that outdated information can continue to disrupt comprehension, the conditions under which this will occur must be limited; otherwise, readers/learners would never be able to fully revise what they know without continual interference from earlier acquired, but incorrect, information. In order for the outdated information to disrupt comprehension, it must first be reactivated; that is, it must be reintroduced into the active portion of the discourse model, thereby becoming an active component of the ongoing integration process. For that to occur, the reader must encode information that is related to the outdated information. However, it is important to note that simply reactivating outdated information does not necessarily mean that the comprehension process will be disrupted. Whether disruption occurs depends on the complete pattern of activated information in working memory, and the pattern of outdated information that is activated and becomes a part of working memory will depend largely on how the outdated information was initially outdated. For example, Guéraud et al. (2005) found that increasing the amount of updating information eliminated the disrupting impact of outdated information on the comprehension process; however, the outdated information continued to be reactivated. Similarly, Rapp and Kendeou (2007, 2009) found that when information was outdated with a simple refutation, the outdated information continued to disrupt comprehension of subsequent information. When information was outdated using a refutation that included an explanation, however, its impact was eliminated.

Kendeou, Smith, and O'Brien (2013) argued that one way to increase the effectiveness of knowledge revision—and by definition reduce the impact of outdated information—was to provide the reader with causal explanations that supported updating and therefore the knowledge revision process in general. They noted that causal information inherently provides a rich elaborated network of information, as well as additional connections to readers' background knowledge (e.g., Albrecht & O'Brien, 1995; Lombrozo, 2006; O'Brien & Myers, 1987; Rizzella & O'Brien, 1996; Trabasso & Suh, 1993; Trabasso & van den Broek, 1985). This highly interconnected network, when combined with updating information, would provide additional competition with outdated information for reactivation when the reader encodes related information. The structural richness of the causal network (i.e., multiple connections, multiple retrieval routes) would increase the amount of activation that the updated/revised information drew, thereby ensuring that it would be returned to active memory. At the same time that it drew increased activation to itself, the updated/revised information would also draw activation away from the outdated information, thereby decreasing its negative impact. To test this, Kendeou, Smith, and O'Brien modified the materials from O'Brien et al. (1998) by adding increasing amounts of causal information to the qualified elaboration. In one experiment they added a simple one-sentence causal explanation (e.g., explaining why Mary was no longer a vegetarian). The addition of just one causal sentence was enough to eliminate any disruption in reading time on the target sentence; however, subsequent tests showed that, although the outdated information was no longer disrupting comprehension, it was still being reactivated. Thus, in a subsequent experiment, they increased the amount of causal information in the qualified condition from one causal sentence to three causal sentences. With three causal sentences, any measurable disruption in reading was again eliminated; more important, there was no longer any measurable activation of the outdated information.

In subsequent experiments, Kendeou, Smith, and O'Brien (2013) tested whether it was merely the sheer amount of additional information that eliminated the reactivation of the outdated information or if it was due to the nature/quality of that information. They directly compared the three-sentence causal qualification to a three-sentence qualification that simply elaborated and expanded on the updated information. They found that even though both types of qualifications were sufficient to eliminate the disruption in comprehension caused by the outdated information, only the causal qualification was sufficient to eliminate its reactivation. However, as Kendeou et al. noted, the critical difference between the two qualification elaborations was not causality per se. The critical difference was the richer, more interconnected network of information provided by the three causal sentences relative to the three elaborative sentences. This rich, interconnected network drew increased activation to itself and away from the outdated information relative to the amount of activation drawn by the more impoverished network provided by the three elaborative sentences. The advantage of causality is that, by definition, it requires the connection of one piece of information to another through a causal link, allowing for the easy, efficient, and effective development of integrated networks (O'Brien & Myers, 1987; Trabasso & Suh, 1993; Trabasso & van den Broek, 1985).

To summarize, the work conducted with narratives suggests that knowledge revision is a slow and incremental process. Whenever a reader encodes information designed to initiate knowledge revision (i.e., update his or her understanding of a narrative), that updating information is integrated into the evolving network representation of the narrative. More important, that information is also integrated *with* the information that is being outdated. That is, both the updated "state of affairs" and the outdated "state of affairs" *coexist in memory*. At any later point, whenever a reader encodes related information, that information sends a signal to all of memory. Both the updated information and the outdated information have the potential to draw activation (i.e., resonate) and become reactivated in response to that signal. When outdated information draws sufficient activation to be returned to working memory, it can produce interference (i.e., a disruption in reading), even under conditions in which both online and offline evidence have made clear that basic knowledge revision has occurred (e.g., O'Brien et al., 1998, 2010). Systematically strengthening the knowledge revision process by adding increasing amounts of causal information to the updating information can systematically decrease the potential interference from outdated information (Kendeou, Smith, & O'Brien, 2013). As the amount of causal information added to the updated information increases, the structural richness of the resulting network increases. This, in turn, increases the amount of activation it will draw to itself. At the same time that it is drawing activation to itself, it is also drawing activation away from any outdated information, thereby reducing the potential for any interference. Thus, the evidence regarding knowledge revision within the context of narratives demonstrates that even after a reader has engaged in knowledge revision, outdated information still resides in memory and can interfere with later comprehension. The knowledge revision process becomes more evident as the strength of updated knowledge is increased—through the building of integrated networks of information—and the impact or interference created by outdated knowledge is decreased.

Co-activation

One of the limitations of research examining the knowledge revision process within the context of narratives is that the updating information and the outdating information have often been presented proximal to each other; that is, they generally co-occurred in working memory. Indeed, one of the critical assumptions regarding the knowledge revision process is that for knowledge to be revised, both the outdated information and the updated information must be integrated together. When considering knowledge revision in the context of revising general world knowledge, this does not often occur naturally; texts must be written in a way such that both the updated "state of affairs" and the outdated "state of affairs" coexist in memory. This necessary condition for knowledge revision is best captured by the co-activation hypothesis proposed by Kendeou and colleagues (Kendeou, Muis, & Fulton, 2011; Kendeou & van den Broek, 2005, 2007; van den Broek & Kendeou, 2008). According to the co-activation hypothesis, when texts are employed as a means of knowledge revision, the targeted information in general world knowledge will typically not be active in memory unless/until the text contains information that directly addresses the to-be-revised information in general world knowledge. When the text directly addresses the to-be-revised information, for example via direct refutation, it elicits the activation of both the correct and the incorrect information. When this occurs, it results in co-activation—the necessary first step in the knowledge revision process.

Kendeou and colleagues (Kendeou et al., 2011; Kendeou & van den Broek, 2007; van den Broek & Kendeou, 2008) first explored the principle of co-activation in the context of refutation texts. Refutation texts directly state a belief incorrectly held by the reader and then directly refute that belief. Several research findings over the past decade have shown that under certain conditions, refutation texts can be an effective means of knowledge revision (for reviews, see Guzzetti, Snyder, Glass, & Gamas, 1993; Sinatra & Broughton, 2011; Tippett, 2010). Kendeou et al. argued that when refutation texts are effective, it is because of the co-activation of the incorrect prior knowledge and the updated "state of affairs." According to the co-activation hypothesis, refutation texts, by design, increase the likelihood that correct and incorrect information will be coactive in readers' working memory; that is, both the updated "state of affairs" and the outdated "state of affairs" coexist in memory. The co-activation is enabled via passive retrieval processes in which the refutation serves to activate the targeted information in general world knowledge (O'Brien et al., 1998, 2010; Rizzella & O'Brien, 2002). When this occurs, readers are likely to detect the discrepancy between information stated in the text and information activated from general world knowledge; this, in turn, can create cognitive conflict (Posner, Strike, Hewson, & Gertzog, 1982), which can trigger additional processing in an attempt to maintain coherence (Graesser & D'Mello, 2012). This additional processing can support knowledge revision.

Kendeou and van den Broek (2007) provided initial evidence for the co-activation hypothesis by directly comparing cognitive processing of college students with or without misconceptions during reading of refutation and non-refutation science texts. The findings showed that readers with misconceptions spent more time reading sentences that explicitly contradicted their prior knowledge, but only when those sentences were embedded in the refutation text; this slowdown in reading is highly indicative of readers' detecting a discrepancy or contradiction during reading (Albrecht & O'Brien, 1993; O'Brien et al., 1998, 2010; Rapp & Kendeou, 2007, 2009). These results were the first to indicate that refutation texts elicit co-activation. Subsequently, van den Broek and Kendeou (2008) provided further evidence using a computational approach. More recently, Kendeou et al. (2011) showed that the disruption in reading caused by the co-activation of conflicting information can lead to additional processing designed to correct the misconception.

Knowledge Revision in the *Real World*

Since at least the late 1970s, many educators (e.g., Clement, 1987, 1988, 1989; Driver & Easley, 1978; McCloskey, 1982; Posner et al., 1982) have been aware of the fact that students bring to the learning task alternative frameworks, preconceptions, commonsense beliefs, or misconceptions that are robust and hinder the acquisition of new knowledge. There is an extensive literature on students' conceptual understanding of various concepts identifying common misconceptions that are pervasive for the understanding and learning of relevant concepts and principles and that need to be taken into consideration for effective educational design (Carey, 2009; Chi, 2005; Clement, 1991; Novak, 1988; Trumper, 2001; Vosniadou & Brewer, 1992, 1994). Thus, learning often requires the revision of previously-acquired-but-incorrect knowledge. Consider, for example, an individual who believes that ostriches bury their heads in the sand to hide from their enemies. One way to assist readers in revising such commonsense beliefs is by presenting them with refutation texts. In the context of the ostrich example, such a text would include a refutation sentence that states that ostriches do not bury their heads. This would be followed by an explanation stating that people often think that ostriches bury their heads because they can regularly be seen positioning their heads near the ground, but the real reason they do this is to listen for enemies.

There is considerable evidence for the potential educational effectiveness of refutation texts (Ariasi & Mason, 2011; Broughton & Sinatra, 2010; Chinn & Brewer, 1993; Diakidoy, Kendeou, & Ioannides, 2003; Diakidoy, Mouskounti, & Ioannides, 2011; Guzzetti et al., 1993; Hynd & Alvermann, 1986; Maria & MacGinitie, 1987; Mason & Gava, 2007; Sinatra & Broughton, 2011; Tippett, 2010). However, other research shows comparable learning from both refutation and non-refutation texts (Alvermann & Hague, 1989; Hynd & Guzzetti, 1998; Mikklä-Erdmann, Penttinen, Anto, & Olkinuora, 2008). The mixed findings reported in the literature may be due, in part, to the different types of refutation texts used, different knowledge domains assessed, different age groups included, and different methodological approaches employed across the experimental database. Another important factor that is often overlooked is the structure or coherence of preexisting knowledge (Braasch, Goldman, & Wiley, 2013; Goldman, Varma, & Coté, 1996). Furthermore, much of the evidence for the effectiveness (or lack thereof) of refutation texts stems from an analysis of learning outcomes (Chi, 2005; Ioannides & Vosniadou, 2002; Murphy & Mason, 2006; Mason, Gava, & Boldrin, 2008; Sinatra, Southerland, McConaughy, & Demastes, 2003). However, the actual cognitive "work" that produces revision takes place during encoding processes, that is, when the refutation text is read and integrated into memory. Thus, in order to gain a deeper understanding of the conditions necessary to produce learning outcomes, it is necessary to understand the associated processes that lead to positive learning outcomes. We turn to the investigation of these processes next.

To better understand the impact of refutation texts in promoting knowledge revision, Kendeou, Walsh, Smith, and O'Brien (2013) systematically examined the online encoding processes that occur while reading. In this set of experiments, participants read a set of short vignettes that followed a standard refutation text structure. Consider the example in table 16.2.

Table 16.2
Sample passage from Kendeou, Walsh, et al. (2013)

Introduction

The Parker family was vacationing at their favorite spot at a scenic New England lake. Every summer they would rent the same cabin right on the water. The two brothers, Danny and Ryan, especially enjoyed the lake for water skiing and tubing. It was an exceptionally hot day so the boys decided to gear up for some water skiing. Danny had trouble adjusting his life jacket because his hands were dripping with sweat. Frustrated, he asked his brother why it was always so hot in the summer and always so cold in the winter. Mrs. Parker overheard her boys talking.

Refutation

Ryan said that he thought it was because the Earth is closer to the Sun in the summer than in the winter. However, Mrs. Parker interrupted and said that this idea was incorrect.

Non-Refutation

She said this was just the sort of thing that the boys should look up on the Internet later. Both of the sons agreed that they would look it up on the computer.

Explanation

She explained that the Earth is actually farther away from the Sun when it is summer in the Northern Hemisphere than when it is winter. Seasons are caused by the Earth being tilted on its axis. As the Earth orbits the Sun, different parts of the world receive different amounts of direct sunlight. Even though the Sun is farther away during summer, the Northern Hemisphere is tilted towards the Sun, causing longer days and more direct sunlight. In the winter, even though the Sun is closer, the Earth is tilted away from the Sun. So Mrs. Parker explained again that

Non-Explanation

Mrs. Parker was always encouraging her boys to find out the answers to questions they had. She thought this was a good way to teach them because if they had to find the answers themselves, they would remember them better. Sometimes Danny and Ryan found this annoying. They would ask their mom what a certain word meant and rather than just tell them, they had to stop what they were doing and go find the dictionary. They knew there was no point in asking her because their mom was not going to give them the answer. The first place they looked indicated that

Correct Outcome

the tilt of the Earth causes the seasons.

Spillover Sentence

The boys were pleased with their answer.

Closing

They finished getting ready and climbed onto the back of the boat. They spent most of the afternoon water skiing until the sun went down and the temperature cooled off.

Each vignette addressed a commonsense, incorrect belief widely held by undergraduate students. The vignettes appeared in one of two elaboration conditions: refutation-plus-explanation and nonrefutation-plus-nonexplanation. Each vignette began with an introduction section that served to introduce the commonsense belief (e.g., "In the Northern Hemisphere seasons are caused because the Earth is closer to the sun in the summer"). The refutation-plus-explanation condition was created by first adding a two-sentence refutation section: The first sentence explicitly stated the commonsense, incorrect belief (e.g., "Ryan said that he thought it was because the Earth is closer to the Sun in the summer than in the winter") and the second sentence served to negate the belief (e.g., "However, Mrs. Parker interrupted and said that this idea was incorrect"). The refutation section was followed by an explanation section in which the refutation was supported by the addition of a causal explanation (e.g., "She explained that the Earth is actually farther away from the Sun when it is summer in the Northern Hemisphere than when it is winter. Seasons are caused by the Earth being tilted on its axis..."). In the nonrefutation-plus-nonexplanation condition, the nonrefutation section neither stated nor negated the commonsense, incorrect belief, and the nonexplanation section continued the story line without including additional information discussing the incorrect belief. Following the elaboration sections, readers were presented with a correct outcome sentence that stated the correct belief (e.g., "The tilt of the Earth causes the seasons"). If the refutation-plus-explanation is sufficient to support the early stages of knowledge revision, then reading times on the correct outcome sentence following the refutation-plus-explanation elaboration should be faster than reading times on the correct outcome sentence following the nonrefutation-plus-nonexplanation elaboration. Faster readings times on the correct outcome sentence would indicate that the reader successfully integrated the correct outcome sentence; the outcome sentence is no longer in conflict with the incorrect belief. The results confirmed this expectation and showed that the refutation-plus-explanation elaboration was sufficient to eliminate the reactivation of commonsense beliefs or misconceptions.

Even though the facilitation in reading times on the correct outcome sentence may reflect knowledge revision, these reading time effects can only be taken as evidence that the correct information has been encoded into an episodic memory trace for the passages read. That is, any observed knowledge revision may be transient. In order to provide evidence as to whether these manipulations produced long-term learning outcomes, Kendeou, Walsh, et al. (2013) administered a posttest of learning to a group of students who read the refutation-plus-explanation texts (both immediately after reading and one month later) and to a group of students who read only filler texts and served as the control group. The findings showed that posttest scores for participants in the refutation-plus-explanation group were higher than were the scores for participants in the control group. Furthermore, participants' posttest scores collected immediately after reading and a month later did not differ. These findings suggest that the observed knowledge revision was not transient. Rather, it was maintained even a month after reading the refutation-plus-explanation texts.

To explore deeper the impact of refutation texts on knowledge revision processes during reading, and to identify with greater precision the content of such processes, Kendeou and colleagues conducted a series of studies using think-aloud protocols (Kendeou & van den Broek, 2005, 2007; Kendeou et al., 2011). This methodology allows for the consideration of a variety of readers' responses (Ericsson & Simon, 1993; Pressley & Afflerbach, 1995; Trabasso & Suh, 1993) and has received extensive validation as a tool to reveal comprehension processes in reading (Afflerbach, Cho, & Kim, 2011; Fox, Ericsson, & Best, 2011; Magliano & Graesser, 1991; Magliano & Millis, 2003). In these studies, readers with identified misconceptions were asked to read and think aloud refutation and nonrefutation texts. Analysis of the think-aloud responses revealed both similarities and differences in the processes that readers with and without misconceptions apply. With regards to similarities, the degree to which readers paraphrased textual information, activated prior knowledge, and connected sentences within the text was unaffected by the accuracy of their prior knowledge or the type of text. Readers' processing differed, however, with respect to engaging in knowledge revision strategies, monitoring their comprehension, and generating correct and incorrect inferences. Specifically, readers with misconceptions engaged in knowledge revision strategies more often than did readers without misconceptions, but only during their reading of refutation text. Readers with misconceptions also monitored their comprehension more often than did readers without misconceptions, but only during their reading of refutation text. In addition, for both refutation and nonrefutation texts, readers with misconceptions generated more correct and fewer incorrect inferences than did readers without misconceptions. These inferences included, among others, attempts to explain information in the text (explanatory inferences) and attempts to make predictions (forward inferences). These findings, taken together, suggest that refutation texts enable co-activation, which, in turn, enables readers to engage in additional processing in an attempt to establish coherence (Graesser & D'Mello, 2012; Graesser, et al., 1994; McNamara & Kintsch, 1996) or to reconcile the inconsistent information (e.g., Kendeou & van den Broek, 2007; Hakala & O'Brien, 1995; Rapp, 2008).

The Knowledge Revision Components Framework

Taken together, our work to date provides insights into a set of core principles that form the basis for knowledge revision in the context of reading comprehension. In this chapter we propose the KReC framework that is formed on the basis of these principles and is supported by a series of studies in our labs utilizing different paradigms and data sources (e.g., Hakala & O'Brien, 1995; Kendeou & van den Broek, 2005, 2007; Kendeou et al., 2011, 2013; Kendeou, Walsh, et al., 2013; O'Brien & Albrecht, 1991, 1992;

O'Brien et al., 1998, 2010; van den Broek & Kendeou, 2008; Rizzella & O'Brien, 2002). These principles are encoding, passive activation, co-activation, integration, and competing activation. We briefly discuss each of these core principles below.

The Encoding Principle

The first principle is that once information has been encoded into long-term memory, it becomes a permanent part of long-term memory and cannot be "deleted." Information is subject to interference and decay, consistent with most models of memory (e.g., Gillund & Shiffrin, 1984; Hintzman, 1986; Kintsch, 1988; Ratcliff, 1978; Ratcliff & McKoon, 1988). However, the main premise is that once information becomes part of memory, it cannot be erased, and there is always the potential that it can be reactivated, even when it interferes with learning and/or comprehension. This interference from previously-acquired-but-no-longer-correct information can occur even if the reader/learner understands that the information is no longer correct (e.g., O'Brien et al., 1998, 2004, 2010). Thus, by definition, we reject any knowledge revision process that assumes an *erase and replace* principle.

The Passive Activation Principle

We adopt the view that inactive information in long-term memory becomes active and available via passive activation processes derived from global models of memory (e.g., Gillund & Shiffrin, 1984; Hintzman, 1986; Kintsch, 1988; Ratcliff, 1978; Ratcliff & McKoon, 1988). One instantiation of a model that captures these assumptions, especially as they relate to memory activation processes during reading, is the resonance model (Myers & O'Brien, 1998; O'Brien & Myers, 1999). The resonance model is consistent with the basic passive memory activation component of several other models relevant to reading comprehension (e.g., Kintsch, 1988; Sanford & Garrod, 1981, 1998, 2005; van den Broek et al., 2005). Because this resonance process is both passive and unrestricted, any information that is related to the current contents of working memory has the potential to become activated, independent of whether it facilitates or interferes with learning and/or comprehension.

The Co-activation Principle

The third principle is that these passive activation processes produce the co-activation of previously-acquired-but-no-longer-correct information and newly encoded information. Co-activation is a necessary condition for knowledge revision because it is the only way that new information can come in contact with, and be integrated with, previously-acquired-but-no-longer-correct information. This principle is best captured by the co-activation hypothesis proposed by Kendeou and colleagues (Kendeou et al., 2011; Kendeou & van den Broek, 2007; van den Broek & Kendeou, 2008).

The Integration Principle

The fourth principle follows directly from the co-activation principle: Knowledge revision can only occur when newly encoded information is integrated with previously acquired information. Any time new information is integrated with previously acquired information (independent of whether the previously acquired information is correct or not), the long-term memory representation of that information is revised to take into account the new information (e.g., Kendeou, Smith, & O'Brien, 2013; Kendeou, Walsh, et al., 2013; O'Brien et al., 1998, 2004, 2010). If newly acquired information does not make contact with, nor become integrated with, previously acquired information, knowledge revision has not occurred.

The Competing Activation Principle

The knowledge revision process involves the integration of newly acquired information with previously-acquired-but-no-longer-correct information. Both pieces of information are tightly bound in one integrated network in memory. Thus, by definition, the activation or accessing of newly acquired correct information has the potential to lead to the activation of the previously-acquired-but-no-longer-correct information. Indeed, as noted throughout this chapter, there is considerable evidence that even after knowledge revision has taken place, the reader/learner is still subject to the activation of, and interference produced by, the outdated, no-longer-correct information (O'Brien et al., 1998, 2010; Kendeou, Smith, & O'Brien, 2013; Kendeou, Walsh, et al., 2013). However, as the amount of newly acquired, correct information is increased, it will begin to dominate the integrated network of information. As this occurs, the newly encoded, correct information will begin to draw increasing amounts of activation to itself and, at the same time, draw activation away from the previously-acquired-but-incorrect information. As activation is drawn away from incorrect information, the amount of interference from that information decreases accordingly. As shown in Kendeou, Smith, and O'Brien, newly acquired information is most effective at eliminating any interference from previously-acquired-but-no-longer-correct information when that newly encoded information provides causal explanations. It is important to note that this is not due to the causal explanations per se but is a function of the interconnections that they provide. As noted earlier, causal information inherently provides a rich set of interconnections (e.g., Albrecht & O'Brien, 1995; Lombrozo, 2006; O'Brien & Myers, 1987; Rizzella & O'Brien, 1996; Trabasso & Suh, 1993; Trabasso & van den Broek, 1985) and therefore provides an efficient and effective means to create a network that will compete for activation and draw sufficient activation so that any interference from previously-acquired-but-incorrect information is reduced and/or eliminated.

To summarize the main principles and their interrelations within the KReC framework, consider the ostriches example we discussed earlier in this chapter. An individual who believes that ostriches bury their heads in the sand to hide from their enemies holds incorrect information that cannot be erased (encoding principle). When he or she comes across a refutation text that states that ostriches do not bury their heads in the sand, the incorrect information will be activated via passive activation processes derived from global models of memory (passive activation principle). These passive activation processes produce the co-activation of previously acquired and newly encoded information, a necessary condition for knowledge revision because it is the only way that new information can come in contact with previously-acquired-but-no-longer-correct information (co-activation principle). The refutation would be followed by a causal explanation stating that people often think that ostriches bury their heads because they can be seen positioning their heads near the ground, but the real reason they do this is to listen for enemies. When this new information is integrated with the previously acquired information, knowledge revision has occurred (integration principle). As the amount of newly acquired, correct information is increased, for example by strengthening the explanation even more, it will begin to dominate the integrated network of information. As this occurs, the newly encoded, correct information that ostriches do not bury their heads will begin to draw increasing amounts of activation to itself and, at the same time, draw activation away from the previously-acquired-but-incorrect information so that any interference from previously-acquired-but-incorrect information is reduced and/or eliminated (competing activation principle).

Concluding Remarks

In this chapter, our goal was to outline a theoretical framework of knowledge revision that aligns itself with findings derived in the context of reading comprehension. In doing so, we restricted our definition of knowledge revision to the modification of the existing knowledge base in memory to accommodate newly acquired information. We conceptualized the knowledge revision process as incremental, conservative, and slow. We built the KReC framework bottom-up by first reviewing basic memory processes that form the central core of most models of reading comprehension and memory in general. Next we reviewed several findings within the reading comprehension literature that constitute a basic form of knowledge revision. Then we extended and generalized those findings to knowledge revision in other domains. Finally, we concluded with the discussion of the core principles of our proposed theoretical account of knowledge revision, the KReC framework.

We acknowledge that there are many ways individuals can be enticed into knowledge revision as reflected by the number of existing models and theories, for example, in the conceptual change literature (e.g., Carey, 2000, 2009; Chi, Slotta, & deLeeuw, 1994; Chi, 2008; Chinn & Brewer, 1993, 1998; Clark, 2006; diSessa, 1988, 2013; Dole & Sinatra, 1998; Hynd & Guzzetti, 1998; Linn, 2008; Nersessian, 2008; Ohlsson, 2009;

Posner et al., 1982; Sinatra & Pintrich, 2003; Thagard, 2008; Vosniadou, 1994, 2008, 2013). What the KReC framework contributes to the existing literature is the fundamental underpinnings of knowledge revision at the level of basic processes and mechanisms. Specifically, KReC outlines basic comprehension processes and text factors that can be accentuated to increase the potential for successful knowledge revision during reading by systematically mitigating the interference from previously-acquired-but-incorrect information. The KReC framework does not include any assumptions regarding grain size or level of coherence of the preexisting knowledge representation. Finally, the KReC framework also has implications for research on persuasion (e.g., Alexander, Sperl, & Buehl, 2001; Petty & Cacioppo, 1986; Murphy & Alexander, 2004, 2008), stereotype formation and updating (e.g., Lassonde & O'Brien, 2013; Uleman, Hon, Roman, & Moskowitz, 1996; Winter & Uleman, 1984), the misinformation effect (e.g., Ecker, Lewandowsky, & Tang, 2010; Johnson & Seifert, 1994, 1998, 1999; Lewandowsky, Ecker, Seifert, Schwarz, & Cook, 2012), and validation (e.g., Rapp, 2008; Richter, Schroeder, & Wöhrmann, 2009; Singer, 2006).

References

Afflerbach, P., Cho, B., & Kim, J. (2011). The assessment of higher order thinking skills in reading. In G. Schraw (Ed.), *Current perspectives on cognition, learning, and instruction: Assessment of higher order thinking skills* (pp. 185–215). Omaha, NE: Information Age Publishing.

Albrecht, J. E., & O'Brien, E. J. (1993). Updating a situation model: Maintaining both local and global coherence. *Journal of Experimental Psychology. Learning, Memory, and Cognition, 19,* 1061–1070.

Albrecht, J. E., & O'Brien, E. J. (1995). Goal processing and the maintenance of global coherence. In R. F. Lorch & E. J. O'Brien (Eds.), *Sources of coherence in reading* (pp. 159–176). Hillsdale, NJ: Lawrence Erlbaum Associates.

Alexander, P. A., Sperl, C. T., & Buehl, M. M. (2001). The persuasiveness of persuasive discourse. *International Journal of Educational Research, 35,* 651–674.

Alvermann, D. E., & Hague, S. A. (1989). Comprehension of counterintuitive science text: Effects of prior knowledge and text structure. *Journal of Educational Research, 82,* 197–202.

Ariasi, N., & Mason, L. (2011). Uncovering the effect of text structure in learning from a science text: An eye-tracking study. *Instructional Science, 39,* 581–601.

Blanc, N., Kendeou, P., van den Broek, P., & Brouillet, D. (2008). Updating situation models: Empirical data and simulations. *Discourse Processes, 45,* 103–121.

Braasch, J. L. G., Goldman, S. R., & Wiley, J. (2013). The influences of text and reader characteristics on learning from refutations in science texts. *Journal of Educational Psychology, 105,* 561–578.

Broughton, S. H., & Sinatra, G. M. (2010). Text in the science classroom: Promoting engagement to facilitate conceptual change. In M. G. McKeown (Ed.), *Bringing reading researchers to life: Essays in honor of Isabelle Beck* (pp. 232–256). New York: Guilford Press.

Carey, S. (2000). Science education as conceptual change. *Journal of Applied Developmental Psychology, 21*, 13–19.

Carey, S. (2009). *The origin of concepts*. Oxford, England: Oxford University Press.

Chi, M. T. H. (2005). Commonsense concepts of emergent processes: Why some misconceptions are robust. *Journal of the Learning Sciences, 14*, 161–199.

Chi, M. T. H. (2008). Three types of conceptual change: Belief revision, mental model transformation, and categorical shift. In S. Vosniadou (Ed.), *International handbook of research on conceptual change* (pp. 61–82). New York: Taylor & Francis.

Chi, M. T. H., Slotta, J. D., & de Leeuw, N. (1994). From things to processes: A theory of conceptual change for learning science concepts. *Learning and Instruction, 4*, 27–43.

Chinn, C. A., & Brewer, W. F. (1993). The role of anomalous data in knowledge acquisition: A theoretical framework and implications for science instruction. *Review of Educational Research, 63*, 1–49.

Chinn, C. A., & Brewer, W. F. (1998). An empirical test of a taxonomy of responses to anomalous data in science. *Journal of Research in Science Teaching, 35*, 623–654.

Clark, D. B. (2006). Longitudinal conceptual change in students' understanding of thermal equilibrium: An examination of the process of conceptual restructuring. *Cognition and Instruction, 24*, 467–563.

Clement, J. (1987). Generation of spontaneous analogies by students solving science problems. In D. Topping, D. Crowell, & V. Kobayashi (Eds.), *Thinking across cultures* (pp. 303–308). Hillsdale, NJ: Lawrence Erlbaum Associates.

Clement, J. (1988). Observed methods for generating analogies in scientific problem solving. *Cognitive Science, 12*, 563–586.

Clement, J. (1989). The concept of variation and misconceptions in Cartesian graphing. *Focus on Learning of Mathematics, 9*(30), 26–30.

Clement, J. (1991). Non-formal reasoning in science: The use of analogies, extreme cases, and physical intuition. In J. Voss, D. Perkins, & J. Segal (Eds.), *Informal reasoning and education*. Hillsdale, NJ: Lawrence Erlbaum Associates.

Cook, A. E., & Guéraud, S. (2005). What have we been missing? The role of general world knowledge in discourse processing. *Discourse Processes, 39*, 265–278.

Cook, A. E., Halleran, J. G., & O'Brien, E. J. (1998). What is readily available during reading? A memory-based view of text processing. *Discourse Processes, 26*, 109–129.

Diakidoy, I. N., Kendeou, P., & Ioannides, C. (2003). Reading about energy: The effects of text structure in science learning and conceptual change. *Contemporary Educational Psychology, 28*, 335–356.

Diakidoy, I. N., Mouskounti, T., & Ioannides, C. (2011). Comprehension and learning from refutation and expository texts. *Reading Research Quarterly, 46*, 22–38.

diSessa, A. A. (1988). Knowledge in pieces. In G. Foreman & P. Pufall (Eds.), *Constructivism in the computer age* (pp. 49–70). Mahwah, NJ: Lawrence Erlbaum Associates.

diSessa, A. A. (2013). A bird's-eye view of the "pieces" vs. "coherence" controversy (from the "pieces" side of the fence). In S. Vosniadou (Ed.), *International handbook of research on conceptual change* (pp. 31–48). New York: Routledge.

Dole, J. A., & Sinatra, G. M. (1998). Reconceptualizing change in cognitive construction of knowledge. *Educational Psychologist, 33*, 109–128.

Driver, R., & Easley, J. (1978). Pupils and paradigms: A review of literature related to conceptual development in adolescent science students. *Studies in Science Education, 5*, 61–84.

Ecker, U. H., Lewandowsky, S., & Tang, D. W. (2010). Explicit warnings reduce but do not eliminate the continued influence of misinformation. *Memory & Cognition, 38*, 1087–1100.

Ericsson, K. A., & Simon, H. A. (1993). *Protocol analysis: Verbal reports as data* (rev. ed.). Cambridge, MA: MIT Press.

Fox, M. C., Ericsson, K. A., & Best, R. (2011). Do procedures for verbal reporting of thinking have to be reactive? A meta-analysis and recommendations for best reporting methods. *Psychological Bulletin, 137*, 316–344.

Garrod, S., & Terras, M. (2000). The contribution of lexical and situational knowledge to resolving discourse roles: Bonding and resolution. *Journal of Memory and Language, 42*, 526–544.

Gernsbacher, M. A. (1990). *Language comprehension as structure building*. Hillsdale, NJ: Lawrence Erlbaum Associates.

Gerrig, R. J., & McKoon, G. (1998). The readiness is all: The functionality of memory-based text processing. *Discourse Processes, 26*, 67–86.

Gerrig, R. J., & O'Brien, E. J. (2005). The scope of memory-based processing. *Discourse Processes, 39*, 225–242.

Gillund, G., & Shiffrin, R. M. (1984). A retrieval model for both recognition and recall. *Psychological Review, 91*, 1–67.

Goldman, S. R., & Varma, S. (1995). CAPping the construction-integration model of discourse comprehension. In C. Weaver, S. Mannes, & C. Fletcher (Eds.), *Discourse comprehension: Essays in honor of Walter Kintsch* (pp. 337–358). Hillsdale, NJ: Lawrence Erlbaum Associates.

Goldman, S. R., Varma, S., & Coté, N. (1996). Extending capacity constrained construction integration: Toward "smarter" and flexible models of text comprehension. In B. K. Britton & A. C.

Graesser (Eds.), *Models of text comprehension* (pp. 73–113). Hillsdale, NJ: Lawrence Erlbaum Associates.

Graesser, A. C., & D'Mello, S. (2012). Emotions during the learning of difficult material. In B. Ross (Ed.), *The psychology of learning and motivation* (Vol. 57, pp. 183–225). Burlington, MA: Elsevier.

Graesser, A. C., Singer, M., & Trabasso, T. (1994). Constructing inferences during narrative text comprehension. *Psychological Review, 101*, 371–395.

Guéraud, S., Harmon, M. E., & Peracchi, K. A. (2005). Updating situation models: The memory-based contribution. *Discourse Processes, 39*, 243–263.

Guéraud, S., & O'Brien, E. J. (Eds.). (2005). Components of comprehension: A convergence between memory-based processes and explanation-based process [Special issue]. *Discourse Processes, 39*(2–3).

Guzzetti, B. J., Snyder, T. E., Glass, G. V., & Gamas, W. S. (1993). Promoting conceptual change in science: A comparative meta-analysis of instructional interventions from reading education and science education. *Reading Research Quarterly, 28*, 117–159.

Hakala, C. M., & O'Brien, E. J. (1995). Strategies for resolving coherence breaks in reading. *Discourse Processes, 20*, 167–185.

Hintzman, D. L. (1986). "Schema abstraction" in a multiple-trace memory model. *Psychological Review, 93*, 411–428.

Hynd, C. R., & Alvermann, D. E. (1986). The role of refutation text in overcoming difficulty with science concepts. *Journal of Reading, 29*, 440–446.

Hynd, C., & Guzzetti, B. J. (1998). When knowledge contradicts intuition: Conceptual change. In C. Hynd (Ed.), *Learning from text across conceptual domains* (pp. 139–163). Mahwah, NJ: Lawrence Erlbaum Associates.

Ioannides, C., & Vosniadou, S. (2002). The changing meanings of force. *Cognitive Science Quarterly, 2*, 5–61.

Johnson, H. M., & Seifert, C. M. (1994). Sources of the continued influence effect: When misinformation in memory affects later inferences. *Journal of Experimental Psychology. Learning, Memory, and Cognition, 20*, 1420–1436.

Johnson, H. M., & Seifert, C. M. (1998). Updating accounts following a correction of misinformation. *Journal of Experimental Psychology. Learning, Memory, and Cognition, 24*, 1483–1494.

Johnson, H. M., & Seifert, C. M. (1999). Modifying mental representations: Comprehending corrections. In H. van Oostendorp, S. R. Goldman, H. van Oostendorp, & S. R. Goldman (Eds.), *The construction of mental representations during reading* (pp. 303–318). Mahwah, NJ: Lawrence Erlbaum Associates.

Kendeou, P., Muis, K., & Fulton, S. (2011). Reader and text factors in reading comprehension. *Journal of Research in Reading, 34*, 365–383. doi:10.1111/j.1467-9817.2010.01436.x.

Kendeou, P., Smith, E. R., & O'Brien, E. J. (2013). Updating during reading comprehension: Why causality matters. *Journal of Experimental Psychology. Learning, Memory, and Cognition, 39*, 854–865.

Kendeou, P., & van den Broek, P. (2005). The effects of readers' misconceptions on comprehension of scientific text. *Journal of Educational Psychology, 97*, 235–245.

Kendeou, P., & van den Broek, P. (2007). Interactions between prior knowledge and text structure during comprehension of scientific texts. *Memory & Cognition, 35*, 1567–1577.

Kendeou, P., Walsh, E., Smith, E. R., & O'Brien, E. J. (2013). *Knowledge revision processes in refutation texts*. Manuscript submitted for publication.

Kintsch, W. (1988). The role of knowledge in discourse comprehension: A construction- integration model. *Psychological Review, 95*, 163–182.

Kintsch, W. (1998). *Comprehension: A paradigm for cognition*. New York: Cambridge University Press.

Kintsch, W., & van Dijk, T. A. (1978). Toward a model of text comprehension and production. *Psychological Review, 85*, 363–394.

Langston, M. C., & Trabasso, T. (1999). Modeling causal integration and availability of information during comprehension of narrative texts. In H. van Oostendorp & S. R. Goldman (Eds.), *The construction of mental representations during reading* (pp. 29–69). Mahwah, NJ: Lawrence Erlbaum Associates.

Lassonde, K. A., & O'Brien, E. J. (2013). Occupational stereotypes: Activation of male bias in a gender neutral world. *Journal of Applied Social Psychology, 43*, 387–396.

Lassonde, K. A., Smith, E. R., & O'Brien, E. J. (2011). Interweaving memory-based processes into a model of relevance instruction. In M. T., McCrudden, J. P., Magliano & G. Schraw (Eds.), *Relevance instructions and goal-focusing in text learning* (pp 75–94). Charlotte, NC: Information Age Publishing.

Lewandowsky, S., Ecker, U. K. H., Seifert, C., Schwarz, N., & Cook, J. (2012). Misinformation and its correction: Continued influence and successful debiasing. *Psychological Science in the Public Interest, 13*, 106–131.

Linn, M. C. (2008). Teaching for conceptual change: Distinguish or extinguish ideas. In S. Vosniadou (Ed.), *International handbook of research on conceptual change* (pp. 694–718). London: Routledge.

Lombrozo, T. (2006). The structure and function of explanations. *Trends in Cognitive Sciences, 10*, 464–470.

Magliano, J. P., & Graesser, A. C. (1991). A three-pronged method for studying inference generation in literary text. *Poetics, 20*, 193–232.

Magliano, J. P., & Millis, K. K. (2003). Assessing reading skill with a think-aloud procedure. *Cognition and Instruction, 21*, 251–283.

Magliano, J. P., Trabasso, T., & Graesser, A. C. (1999). Strategic processing during comprehension. *Journal of Educational Psychology, 91*, 615–629.

Maria, K., & MacGinitie, W. (1987). Learning from texts that refute the reader's prior knowledge. *Reading Research and Instruction, 26*, 222–238.

Mason, L., & Gava, M. (2007). Effects of epistemological beliefs and learning text structure on conceptual change. In S. Vosniadou, A. Baltas, & X. Vamvakoussi (Eds.), *Reframing the conceptual change approach in learning and instruction* (pp. 165–196). New York: Elsevier Science.

Mason, L., Gava, M., & Boldrin, A. (2008). On warm conceptual change: The interplay of text epistemological beliefs, and topic interest. *Journal of Educational Psychology, 100*, 291–309.

McCloskey, M. (1982). *Naïve conceptions of motion*. Baltimore, MD: John Hopkins University, Department of Psychology.

McKoon, G., & Ratcliff, R. (1998). Memory-based language processing: Psycholinguistic research in the 1990s. *Annual Review of Psychology, 49*, 25–42.

McNamara, D. S., & Kintsch, W. (1996). Learning from text: Effects of prior knowledge and text coherence. *Discourse Processes, 22*, 247–288.

McNamara, D. S., & Magliano, J. P. (2009). Towards a comprehensive model of comprehension. In B. Ross (Ed.), *The psychology of learning and motivation* (pp. 297–384). New York: Academic Press.

Mikklä-Erdmann, M., Penttinen, M., Anto, E., & Olkinuora, E. (2008). Constructing mental models during learning from scientific text. In D. Ifenthaler, P. Pirnay-Dummer, & J. M. Spector (Eds.), *Understanding models for learning and instruction: Essays in honor of Norbert M. Seel* (pp. 63–79). New York: Springer.

Murphy, P. K., & Alexander, P. A. (2004). Persuasion as a dynamic, multidimensional process: A viewfinder for individual and intraindividual differences. *American Educational Research Journal, 41*, 337–363.

Murphy, P. K., & Alexander, P. A. (2008). The role of knowledge, beliefs, and interest in the conceptual change process: A meta-analysis and synthesis of the research. In S. Vosniadou (Ed.), *International handbook of research on conceptual change* (pp. 583–616). New York: Routledge.

Murphy, P. K., & Mason, L. (2006). Changing knowledge and changing beliefs. In P. A. Alexander & P. Winne (Eds.), *Handbook of educational psychology* (pp. 305–324). Mahwah, NJ: Lawrence Erlbaum Associates.

Myers, J. L., & O'Brien, E. J. (1998). Accessing the discourse representation during reading. *Discourse Processes, 26*, 131–157.

Nersessian, N. J. (2008). Mental modeling in conceptual change. In S. Vosniadou (Ed.), *International handbook of research on conceptual change* (pp. 391–416). London: Routledge.

Novak, J. D. (1988). Learning science and the science of learning. *Studies in Science Education, 15,* 77–101.

O'Brien, E. J., & Albrecht, J. E. (1991). The role of context in assessing antecedents in text. *Journal of Experimental Psychology. Learning, Memory, and Cognition, 17,* 94–102.

O'Brien, E. J., & Albrecht, J. E. (1992). Comprehension strategies in the development of a mental model. *Journal of Experimental Psychology. Learning, Memory, and Cognition, 18,* 777–784.

O'Brien, E. J., Cook, A. E., & Guéraud, S. (2010). Accessibility of outdated information. *Journal of Experimental Psychology. Learning, Memory, and Cognition, 36,* 979–991.

O'Brien, E. J., Cook, A. E., & Peracchi, K. A. (2004). Updating a situation model: A reply to Zwaan and Madden (2004*). Journal of Experimental Psychology. Learning, Memory, and Cognition, 30,* 289–291.

O'Brien, E. J., & Myers, J. L. (1987). The role of causal connections in the retrieval of text. *Memory & Cognition, 15,* 419–427.

O'Brien, E. J., & Myers, J. L. (1999). Text comprehension: A view from the bottom up. In S. R. Goldman, A. C. Graesser, & P. van den Broek (Eds.), *Narrative comprehension, causality, and coherence: Essays in honor of Tom Trabasso* (pp. 36–53). Mahwah, NJ: Lawrence Erlbaum Associates.

O'Brien, E. J., Rizzella, M. L., Albrecht, J. E., & Halleran, J. G. (1998). Updating a situation model: A memory-based text processing view. *Journal of Experimental Psychology. Learning, Memory, and Cognition, 24,* 1200–1210.

Ohlsson, S. (2009). Resubsumption: A possible mechanism for conceptual change and belief revision. *Educational Psychologist, 44,* 20–40.

Petty, R. E., & Cacioppo, J. T. (1986). *Communication and persuasion: Central and peripheral routes to attitude change.* New York: Springer-Verlag.

Posner, G. J., Strike, K. A., Hewson, P. W., & Gertzog, W. A. (1982). Accommodation of a scientific conception: Toward a theory of conceptual change. *Science Education, 66,* 211–227.

Pressley, M., & Afflerbach, P. (1995). *Verbal protocols of reading: The nature of constructively responsive reading.* Hillsdale, NJ: Lawrence Erlbaum Associates.

Rapp, D. N. (2008). How do readers handle incorrect information during reading? *Memory & Cognition, 36,* 688–701.

Rapp, D. N., & Kendeou, P. (2007). Revising what readers know: Updating text representations during narrative comprehension. *Memory & Cognition, 35,* 2019–2032.

Rapp, D. N., & Kendeou, P. (2009). Noticing and revising discrepancies as text unfolds. *Discourse Processes, 46,* 1–24.

Rapp, D. N., & van den Broek, P. (2005). Dynamic text comprehension: An integrative view of reading. *Current Directions in Psychological Science, 14,* 276–279.

Ratcliff, R. (1978). A theory of memory retrieval. *Psychological Review, 85*, 59–108.

Ratcliff, R., & McKoon, G. (1988). A retrieval theory of priming in memory. *Psychological Review, 95*, 385–408.

Richter, T., Schroeder, S., & Wöhrmann, B. (2009). You don't have to believe everything you read: Background knowledge permits fast and efficient validation of information. *Journal of Personality and Social Psychology, 96*, 538–558.

Rizzella, M. L., & O'Brien, E. J. (1996). Accessing global causes during reading. *Journal of Experimental Psychology. Learning, Memory, and Cognition, 22*, 1208–1218.

Rizzella, M. L., & O'Brien, E. J. (2002). Retrieval of concepts in script-based texts and narratives: The influence of general world knowledge. *Journal of Experimental Psychology. Learning, Memory, and Cognition, 28*, 780–790.

Sanford, A. J., & Garrod, S. C. (1981). *Understanding written language: Explorations of comprehension beyond the sentence.* New York: John Wiley.

Sanford, A. J., & Garrod, S. C. (1998). The role of scenario mapping in text comprehension. *Discourse Processes, 26*, 159–190.

Sanford, A. J., & Garrod, S. C. (2005). Memory-based approaches and beyond. *Discourse Processes, 39*, 205–225.

Sinatra, G. M., & Broughton, S. H. (2011). Bridging comprehension and conceptual change in science education: The promise of refutational text. *Reading Research Quarterly, 46*, 369–388.

Sinatra, G. M., & Pintrich, P. R. (Eds.). (2003). *Intentional conceptual change.* Mahwah, NJ: Lawrence Erlbaum Associates.

Sinatra, G. M., Southerland, S. A., McConaughy, F., & Demastes, J. W. (2003). Intentions and beliefs in students' understanding and acceptance of biological evolution. *Journal of Research in Science Teaching, 405*, 510–528.

Singer, M. (2006). Verification of text ideas during reading. *Journal of Memory and Language, 54*, 574–591.

Thagard, P. (2008). Conceptual change in the history of science: Life, mind, and disease. In S. Vosniadou (Ed.), *International handbook of research on conceptual change* (pp. 374–387). London: Routledge.

Tippett, C. D. (2010). Refutational text in science education: A review of two decades of research. *International Journal of Science and Mathematics Education, 8*, 951–970.

Trabasso, T., & Suh, S. (1993). Understanding text: Achieving explanatory coherence through online inferences and mental operations in working memory. *Discourse Processes, 16*, 3–34.

Trabasso, T., & van den Broek, P. (1985). Causal thinking and the representation of narrative events. *Journal of Memory and Language, 24*, 612–630.

Trumper, R. (2001). A cross-age study of senior high school students' conceptions of basic astronomy concepts. *Research in Science & Technological Education, 19,* 97–109.

Tzeng, Y., van den Broek, P., Kendeou, P., & Lee, C. (2005). The computational implementation of the Landscape Model: Modeling inferential processes and memory representations of text comprehension. *Behavior Research Methods, Instruments, & Computers, 37,* 277–286.

Uleman, J. S., Hon, A., Roman, R. J., & Moskowitz, G. B. (1996). On-line evidence for spontaneous trait inferences at encoding. *Personality and Social Psychology Bulletin, 22,* 377–394.

van den Broek, P., & Kendeou, P. (2008). Cognitive processes in comprehension of science texts: The role of co-activation in confronting misconceptions. *Applied Cognitive Psychology, 22,* 335–351.

van den Broek, P., Rapp, D. N., & Kendeou, P. (2005). Integrating Memory-Based and Constructionist Processes in Accounts of Reading Comprehension. *Discourse Processes, 39,* 299–316.

van den Broek, P., Young, M., Tzeng, Y., & Linderholm, T. (1999). The landscape model of reading: Inferences and the on-line construction of a memory representation. In H. van Oostendorp & S. R. Goldman (Eds.), *The construction of mental representations during reading* (pp. 71–98). Mahwah, NJ: Lawrence Erlbaum Associates.

Vosniadou, S. (1994). Capturing and modeling the process of conceptual change. *Learning and Instruction, 4,* 45–69.

Vosniadou, S. (Ed.). (2008). *International handbook of research on conceptual change.* Hillsdale, NJ: Lawrence Erlbaum Associates.

Vosniadou, S. (2013). Conceptual change in learning and instruction: The framework theory approach. In S. Vosniadou (Ed.), *International handbook of research on conceptual change* (pp. 11–30). New York: Routledge.

Vosniadou, S., & Brewer, W. F. (1992). Mental models of the earth: A study of conceptual change in childhood. *Cognitive Psychology, 24,* 535–585.

Vosniadou, S., & Brewer, W. F. (1994). Mental models of the day/night cycle. *Cognitive Science, 18,* 123–183.

Winter, L., & Uleman, J. S. (1984). When are social judgments made? Evidence for the spontaneousness of trait inferences. *Journal of Personality and Social Psychology, 47,* 237–252.

Zwaan, R. A., Magliano, J. P., & Graesser, A. C. (1995). Dimensions of situation model construction in narrative comprehension. *Journal of Experimental Psychology. Learning, Memory, and Cognition, 21,* 386–397.

17 The Content–Source Integration Model: A Taxonomic Description of How Readers Comprehend Conflicting Scientific Information

Marc Stadtler and Rainer Bromme

When readers approach multiple documents to learn about a scientific debate, it is most likely that they will encounter conflicting views. Knowledge claims published on the Internet, for example, may be based on all sorts of information including accurate insights derived from cutting-edge research as well as idiosyncratic speculations that experts could easily prove wrong (Andreassen et al., 2007). A common concern is that individuals often miss conflicts, overestimate their epistemic capabilities, and acquire information that is deemed inaccurate when evaluated against scientific standards (Brossard & Scheufele, 2013; Scharrer, Bromme, Britt, & Stadtler, 2012; Stadtler, Scharrer, Brummernhenrich, & Bromme, 2013). Indeed, individuals differ regarding what they "take home" from reading conflicting scientific information. Whereas some readers are able to accurately report embedded conflicts after reading, others simply overlook them. Still other readers notice inconsistent statements but then reconcile them by drawing unwarranted inferences. If readers are to construct an optimal understanding of multiple texts, they need to notice a conflict, add it to their mental representation, and develop a personal stance toward it.

Given the possible variation in reactions to conflicting information, a comprehensive theoretical model of how readers comprehend conflicting scientific information from multiple texts would represent an important theoretical and applied contribution to both research and practice. In this chapter, we take a preliminary step in this direction by proposing our content–source integration (CSI) model. The model draws on existing models (Kintsch, 1998; Perfetti, Rouet, & Britt, 1999) and extends them by specifically dissecting the cognitive processes and resources involved when readers access conflicting information. To this end, we synthesize rich empirical research from a variety of disciplines including text comprehension, science communication, and developmental psychology. As depicted in figure 17.1, the CSI model assumes three stages of processing conflicting information. These consist of (1) detecting a conflict on a moment-by-moment level, plus the subsequent stages of (2) conflict regulation and (3) conflict resolution. While describing the logic of each stage, we shall identify

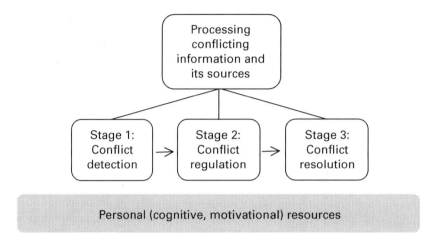

Figure 17.1
The content–source integration model of comprehending conflicting scientific information from multiple documents.

the variables linked to the reader, the text, and the context that determine how readers deal with the affordances of the respective reading tasks.

The Content–Source Integration Model of Comprehending Conflicting Scientific Information

Stage 1: Conflict Detection

Detecting that two or more propositions do not cohere is the first step in comprehending conflicting information. Whether or not readers detect a conflict can be explained with memory-based models of text comprehension such as the resonance model (Myers & O'Brien, 1998) or the construction-integration model (Kintsch, 1998). One necessary precondition for conflict detection is the coactivation of conflicting propositions in working memory. This is accomplished through a passive resonance process in which the information held currently in working memory triggers conceptually related information from long-term memory. The ensuing integration process leads to an inhibitory connection between any conflicting propositions (Kintsch, 1998). As a result, the reader notices a breakdown of coherence, and this is reflected in longer reading times for conflicting compared to nonconflicting control phrases. Recently, neural correlates of conflict detection have also been identified in studies of brain electrical activity using functional magnetic resonance imaging (Ferstl & von Cramon, 2001; Ferstl, Rinck, & von Cramon, 2005; Kiehl, Laurens, & Liddle, 2002). In particular, the N400, a negative deflection in the event-related potential that peaks 400 ms after stimulus presentation, has been used successfully as an indicator of problems associated with word-to-text integration.

Empirical evidence suggests that among attentive adult readers, conflict detection is the rule rather than the exception. This has been established for both expository texts (e.g., Grabe, Antes, Kahn, & Kristjanson, 1991; Zabrucky, Moore, & Schultz, 1987) and narratives (e.g., Albrecht & Myers, 1995; Ferstl et al., 2005; Myers, O'Brien, Albrecht, & Mason, 1994; Rapp & Kendeou, 2007, 2009). Yet, readers sometimes fail to detect propositions that contradict one another. Several memory-based models of text comprehension can explain this sometimes surprising phenomenon. Put briefly, any conditions that reduce the likelihood of coactivation also reduce the likelihood of conflict detection (Epstein, Glenberg, & Bradley, 1984; Kintsch, 1998; van den Broek & Kendeou, 2008). Hence, failure to detect conflicts becomes more likely when the integration of contradictory statements requires inferences to be drawn, when different lexical encodings are used to refer to the same concept, and when the distance between conflicting sentences increases (Epstein et al., 1984; Wiley & Myers, 2003).

However, passive memory processes alone do not determine conflict detection. Reading goals and corresponding strategic behaviors also influence a reader's ability to detect conflicts in text. These may gain in importance the more conflicts are buried in a myriad of textual information, as is the case, for instance, when reading online. Readers would then have to actively check for information consistency, a strategy Wineburg (1991) called "corroboration." Wineburg observed, though, that only expert readers apply this strategy spontaneously when reading multiple documents. The average high school reader, in contrast, often neglects to check for information consistency and thereby runs the risk of missing conflicts.

The goals that readers pursue influence conflict detection in mainly two ways: by setting a standard of coherence and by determining which information is relevant. A standard of coherence refers to the level of comprehension that a reader seeks to attain (e.g., van den Broek, Lorch, Linderholm, & Gustafson, 2001). As such, it is a part of the task model that a reader develops (Rouet & Britt, 2011). Proficient readers then adapt their processing of texts in line with their task-related standard of coherence (e.g., Cerdán & Vidal-Abarca, 2008; Cerdán, Vidal-Abarca, Martínez, Gilabert, & Gil, 2009; Linderholm, Cong, & Zhao, 2008; Pieschl, Stahl, Murray, & Bromme, 2012), and this, in turn, influences the mental representation they develop (Cerdán & Vidal-Abarca, 2008; Cerdán et al., 2009; Linderholm et al., 2008; Linderholm & van den Broek, 2002; Pieschl et al., 2012). Particularly when conflict detection requires activating distant information, a standard may be needed that involves coherence formation across documents. In contrast, a standard that involves coherence formation within local portions of text should be less helpful. In line with this assumption, Stadtler, Scharrer, and Bromme (2011) found that participants who pursued goals requiring global coherence formation (reading to write a summary or an argument) detected the most conflicts between distant sources. Fewer conflicts were detected when participants read to compose a list of keywords representing a more local concern.

A second important function of reading goals is that they constrain what information is relevant and what is irrelevant (Rapp & Mensink, 2011). This, in turn, influences conflict detection because readers usually elaborate relevant concepts more intensively than irrelevant concepts (Kaakinen, Hyönä, & Keenan, 2002). Elaboration then results in a buildup of activation on concepts and thus ensures a swift recall of relevant information from long-term memory. As a result, readers should have no problems detecting conflicts between items of highly relevant information. With regard to irrelevant information, however, the situation is less clear. It may be that readers do not encode irrelevant information sufficiently to ensure its activation by conceptually related information. On the other hand, research on memory-based text processing reveals that if a concept is represented in long-term memory, it will resonate, regardless of relevance due to a "passive, dumb, and unrestricted" activation process (Lassonde, Smith, & O'Brien, 2011, p. 80; Tapiero, 2007). In this way, even irrelevant information can continue to influence the reading process and lead to conflict detection. Stadtler, Scharrer, and Bromme (2012) provided evidence for this assumption in a study presenting readers with multiple documents on a controversial medical topic. The materials contained three straightforward conflicts. The two groups of participants were given different reading goals, such that these conflicts were manipulated to be topically relevant for the experimental group and irrelevant for the control group. The experimental group readers recalled about twice as many conflicts and were better able to apply their knowledge about conflicts in a social knowledge–building task. Analyses of readers' eye-fixation patterns, however, revealed that originally, readers in both groups had noticed the conflicts. Hence, recall differences on the conflicting issues could not be explained by low-relevance readers' simply missing the embedded conflicts. Instead, the authors observed different regulatory behaviors in each group. This pattern of results underlines the preliminary status of moment-by-moment conflict detection and supports the idea that separate stages are involved in the processing of conflicting information.

In sum, there is evidence that proficient readers are able to evaluate the quality of coherence of their evolving text representation. This means that they notice when incoming information is in conflict with previously read information. Textual variables, reading strategies, and reading goals moderate readers' conflict detection performance. However, the fact that readers notice a disruption of coherence formation ensures neither that they interpret this as being due to an objective conflict nor that they integrate the conflict into their situation model (Baker & Anderson, 1982; Otero & Kintsch, 1992; Rapp & Kendeou, 2007, 2009). Thus, moment-by-moment conflict detection as described here can be characterized as preliminary in nature. Any further processing and interpretation of conflicting information is subject to the ensuing stages of conflict regulation and conflict resolution.

Stage 2: Conflict Regulation

There is ample evidence that contradictory knowledge claims cause readers to engage in rich regulatory behavior (e.g., Baker, 1989; Braasch, Rouet, Vibert, & Britt, 2012; Chinn & Brewer, 1993; Otero, 2002; Otero & Graesser, 2001; Rapp & Kendeou, 2009; Stadtler et al., 2012). Although readers' precise reactions may differ, they share the important goal of restoring coherence (Chinn & Brewer, 1993). The pivotal role of coherence in functional reading may be easier to understand if one conceives of texts as readers' windows to the world. During reading, we see the world through another person's, that is, the author's eyes. Hence, establishing coherence is key to reconstructing how the author perceives the world. Note, however, that usually a reader's goal is not to learn about texts or their authors as such. Hence, establishing a coherent representation of texts is not a goal in itself; it is rather a way to attain knowledge that may help to explain and predict the world in an unambiguous way. This may explain why many readers engage in intense regulatory behavior once coherence formation has broken down.

However, an important question remains: How can readers accomplish coherence when the world they read about is inconsistent? Based on a review of pertinent research, we shall identify three prototypical ways of restoring a coherent text representation: (a) ignoring a conflict, (b) reconciling a conflict, and (c) accepting a conflict as due to different sources. We shall also depict factors that determine which route readers may take.

Stage 2a: Restoring Coherence by Ignoring a Conflict   The first and simplest way to restore coherence after having noticed discrepant information is to ignore the conflict: Readers notice a discrepancy but do not engage in regulatory behavior that could help them to interpret the conflict. Because forming coherence among portions of a text is a fundamental goal during reading, ignoring a conflict is usually restricted to settings in which information is irrelevant to a reader's goals. In Stadtler et al. (2012), for instance, readers for whom conflicts were topically irrelevant did not exhibit any marked attempts to restore coherence. This distinguished them from readers for whom the conflicts were topically relevant. The latter group reacted to conflicting information by processing explanatory passages with great care during both first-pass and second-pass reading. They also made slightly longer look backs to the conflicting claims than low-relevance readers did. Low-relevance readers, in contrast, usually reduced their attention immediately after noticing the discrepancy and read explanatory passages as superficially as they read control information. As a result, low-relevance readers remembered fewer conflicts as indicated by their performance on a conflict verification task. They also failed to report an average of about two thirds of the conflicts in their written accounts of the topic. This pattern of results suggests a direct link between readers' decisions to skip regulatory activities and their resulting text representations.

This link was also confirmed in a study by Tapiero and Otero (1999), in which readers were presented with short expository texts containing straightforward conflicts. Different durations of sentence presentations were implemented so that one group had enough time to explore the conflict whereas another group had insufficient time to elaborate it. This manipulation did not influence readers' ability to remember the conflicting information. However, readers who were hindered from elaborating the conflict ignored it when they had to draw inferences based on the situation model they had formed. Tapiero and Otero concluded that readers tag information during initial reading when it contradicts the expectations formed from previous portions of the text. However, in order to integrate a conflict into one's situation model, a deeper level of elaboration may be necessary than is invested by readers who ignore the conflict.

To sum up, if readers ignore conflicting information during reading, this influences their mental text representation. One may conceive of the resulting mental model as impoverished because straightforward conflicts contained in a text are represented only at the level of the text base, if at all (Stadtler et al., 2012; Tapiero & Otero, 1999). A more positive interpretation, however, would acknowledge that readers who ignore a conflict successfully accomplish coherence and thus keep their representation of the world free from unexplained conflicts. Moreover, ignoring conflicting information is a rather parsimonious method of conflict regulation because relevance judgments occur early during reading and without an excessive amount of mental effort (Kaakinen et al., 2002). Under a limited number of circumstances, ignoring conflicting information may thus be conceived as a reasonable way to handle conflicts in texts.

Stage 2b: Restoring Coherence by Reconciling Conflicting Propositions   If a conflict is topically relevant to a reader's goals, ignoring it is hardly a satisfying strategy. In this case, coherence might be accomplished only if the text provides a satisfactory explanation for the occurrence of a conflict or if this can be inferred from prior knowledge (Rapp & Kendeou, 2007; Stadtler et al., 2012). Support for this notion comes from research on the questions that readers ask during text comprehension. In their model of question asking called PREG, Otero and Graesser (2001) reviewed empirical evidence showing that discrepant information stimulates readers to search for explanations and is very much the essence of questions asking during reading. However, sometimes individuals have to handle competing knowledge claims that are not accompanied by any explanation for the discrepancies or do not easily indicate how they might be integrated into a coherent whole. There is mounting evidence from research at the crossroads of developmental psychology, science understanding, and reading comprehension that this leads people to generate their own explanations with which to reconcile opposing claims (e.g., Astuti & Harris, 2008; Baker, 1989; Chinn & Brewer, 1993; Evans, Legare, & Rosengren, 2011; Legare, Evans, Rosengren, & Harris, 2012; Legare & Gelman, 2008; Otero & Kintsch, 1992; Stadtler, Scharrer, Brummernhenrich, et al.,

2013). Reconciling conflicts enables readers to restore coherence and keep their world knowledge free of unexplained conflicts. Legare et al. (2012), for instance, report that individuals across age levels and cultures frequently integrate fragments of natural and supernatural theories from different sources into a seemingly coherent whole. Objectively inconsistent data and theoretical approaches are linked together by, for instance, interpreting unexpected phenomena as exceptions from a general rule or considering phenomena as subtypes of a more general category (for similar observations, see Chinn & Brewer, 1993). As a result, although incommensurate from a scientific viewpoint, a mixture of natural and supernatural theories coexists in both children's and adults' understandings and is used to explain and predict everyday experiences (Keil, 2012; Legare et al., 2012).

A similar principle has been observed in research examining how readers comprehend conflicting text. Otero and Kintsch (1992), for example, asked tenth and twelfth graders to read short passages about scientific issues with straightforward but unexplained conflicts. In post hoc interviews, readers who did not report a conflict were invited to say why. Content analyses of participants' answers revealed that drawing unwarranted inferences accounted for 19% of the cases in which readers failed to report a conflict. In a conflict dealing with methods of attaining superconductivity, for example, some readers inferred that, in earlier times, superconductivity had been achieved by cooling materials down to low temperatures whereas the opposite is the case today. Note that in the original text materials, no time information was included that could have warranted this inference. Similarly, in a study by Baker (1979), undergraduate readers failed to report about half of the internal inconsistencies embedded in an expository text about the Incan culture. Analyses of probed recall data revealed that many readers modified the information to make it more consistent.

Because research on how readers reconcile conflicts often followed a descriptive approach, relatively little is known about what factors encourage readers to reconcile conflicting information. An exception is Baker (1989), who proposes that readers' coherence expectations should matter. She argues that anomalous texts without any explanations for conflicts violate readers' expectations for a consistent text. As a result, readers go to great lengths to restore coherence and generate inferences with which they explain the conflict away. In line with this assumption, studies in which coherence expectations were lowered by warning readers about the existence of conflicts revealed fewer cases of unwarranted inferencing (Baker & Anderson, 1982; Grabe, Antes, Thorson, & Kahn, 1987).

Garcia-Arista, Campanario, and Otero (1996) have suggested a similar explanation for the observation of invalid inferences. They reported a study in which two groups of readers processed the same information that was framed either as an excerpt from a science textbook in a science class or as appearing in a newspaper in a language class. The authors observed a larger number of unwarranted inferences by readers in the science textbook condition. They assumed that individuals expect a more consistent situation when reading science information as compared to reading media materials about everyday events. As a result, they make the situation more consistent to better match their expectations. Similarly, Stadtler, Scharrer, Brummernhenrich, et al. (2013) found that the frequency with which readers reconciled conflicting statements varied as a function of purported source expertise. More unwarranted inferencing was found when readers perceived conflicts as stemming from expert sources as compared to lay sources. The authors proposed that readers might have expected expert sources to provide consistent information and sought to restore coherence by additional inferences when they did not.

To summarize, one way in which readers restore coherence is to generate explanations that reconcile opposing claims. The resulting text representation is below par from a normative stance because readers' explanations might not be warranted by the specific text or by any other authoritative source. However, it should be kept in mind that integrating loosely connected propositions with inferences is a highly functional strategy in most reading situations. This may explain its pervasive use even when readers lack the necessary background knowledge. Hence, the great challenge for readers is to keep the fine line between functional and dysfunctional uses of this strategy when comprehending scientific issues (Keil, 2006). The research we reviewed suggests that high coherence expectations are an important factor encouraging readers to generate invalid inferences. Apart from this, we speculate that generating invalid inferences as a way to resolve conflicts becomes more likely during less constrained situations, thus leaving room for a reader's personal interpretation. Of course, factors associated with the reader, such as their epistemic beliefs, should also exert an influence (Bråten, Britt, Strømsø, & Rouet, 2011; Stahl & Bromme, 2007). Individuals who strongly believe that scientific knowledge is certain and unambiguous, for example, might interpret a disruption of coherence formation as a personal failure of comprehension instead of accepting it as being caused by an objective logical conflict. These individuals might then consider it a reasonable approach to rectify the problem by generating inferences. Certainly, further research is needed to substantiate the assumed link between the factors we identified and a reader's tendency to resolve conflicts by reconciling conflicting propositions.

Stage 2c: Restoring Coherence by Accepting a Conflict as due to Different Sources If it is impossible to reconcile or ignore a conflict, restoring coherence requires readers to connect the conflicting propositions with their sources. Readers may then interpret the momentary disruption of coherence as being due to different perspectives rather than as a genuine break in a text's consistency (Strømsø, Bråten, Britt, & Ferguson, 2013). Perfetti et al. (1999) devised their documents model framework (DMF) in order to move beyond traditional models of text comprehension that are unable to account for the representation of multiple, partly conflicting situations (e.g., Kintsch, 1998). They assumed that readers form an integrated representation of multiple situations (dubbed a situations model) in which central propositions are tagged for their source. Sources are represented in document nodes that make up the intertext model. When the intertext and situations model are interconnected by rich content–source links, the result is a full-fledged documents model.

Researchers have used a variety of methods to gather evidence for the central role of sources for coherence formation in light of conflicting information. The most compelling evidence comes from Braasch et al. (2012). They used eye-tracking technology to study readers' allocation of attention to source information as a function of story consistency. The authors observed that readers' attention to sources was rather low when they processed consistent stories. However, as soon as they noticed a discrepancy in inconsistent texts, they turned their attention to the source information provided in the text. In this way, readers established more content–source links for inconsistent stories as suggested by source memory data obtained after reading. From a different think-aloud study, Strømsø et al. (2013) reported that readers exhibited increased attention to sources when processing information that contradicted what other sources claimed to be true. Interestingly, a great deal of the readers' interactions with source information were confined to mere attention to sources whereas explicit source evaluations were infrequent. The authors interpreted this as reflecting the readers' attempts to connect text information to its respective source. This supposition was supported by a positive correlation between attention to sources during reading and the number of references to source information made in postreading essays. Finally, Bromme, Thomm, and Wolf (2013) have reported an interview study in which they gathered spontaneous explanations for conflicts in medical knowledge generated by laypersons and medical students. Both groups indicated that they considered conflicts of interest and a lack of qualification to be central reasons for contradictions in medical knowledge.

The studies reviewed here suggest that sources play an important role when readers encounter conflicts in text. By forming documents models, they are able to restore coherence. However, accepting a conflict and attributing it to different sources does not in and of itself provide a reader with a consistent knowledge representation. This is why, although an ambitious goal in itself, a documents model may have limited value for an individual who reads to solve a practical problem. Whenever textual coherence does not lead to consistent knowledge, readers might want to additionally resolve the conflict.

Stage 3: Conflict Resolution

Resolving a conflict requires readers to develop a personal stance toward a conflicting issue. To this end, they need to make validity judgments and evaluate the truth conditions of competing claims. Bromme, Kienhues, and Porsch (2010) have argued for a distinction between first- and secondhand evaluation of knowledge claims. Whereas firsthand evaluations imply that readers assess the validity of knowledge claims based on their own understanding of the subject matter, secondhand evaluation can be understood as a bypass, in which readers evaluate source parameters instead. In other words, readers can seek to accomplish conflict resolution by trying to answer one of two questions: "What is true?" or "Whom to believe?" What both strategies have in common is that readers can draw on their folk science containing fragmentary content knowledge, criteria for the evaluation of argument quality, and assumptions about the pertinence of experts for specific topics (Keil, 2010, 2012). Note that a similar distinction between different ways of examining the validity of information has been made in dual-channel theories of social persuasion such as the elaboration likelihood model (Petty & Cacioppo, 1986) or the heuristic–systematic model (Chaiken, Liberman, & Eagly, 1989). One central difference between theories of social persuasion and the distinction suggested by Bromme et al. (2010) is that the former often associate content and source evaluations with different levels of cognitive effort. In contrast, Bromme et al. argue against such an a priori association, stating that both firsthand evaluations asking "What is true?" and secondhand evaluations asking "Whom to believe?" can be conducted in either a thoughtful or a superficial manner. In what follows, we shall give a brief overview of studies from the realm of reading comprehension and science understanding that have examined how readers with little prior knowledge make validity judgments about competing scientific claims via these two routes.

Stage 3a: Resolving Conflicts by Asking "What Is True?"   Examining how readers use their prior knowledge in service of validity judgments is a relatively new area of interest in text comprehension research (Maier & Richter, 2013; Rapp, 2008; Rapp & Kendeou, 2009; Richter, Schroeder, & Wöhrmann, 2009; Singer, 1993; Thomm & Bromme, 2012). As Richter (2003) has pointed out, traditional models of text comprehension tend to conceive of the relationship between text information and prior knowledge as being additive: Readers use their prior knowledge to fill in coherence gaps by means of textual elaborations (e.g., causal or bridging inferences) and thus form an idiosyncratic referential representation of a text's content. However, recently researchers have provided empirical evidence that readers also use their prior knowledge to assess the validity of information. Richter et al. (2009), for example, concluded from a series of studies that judging the validity of knowledge claims is an automatic process that readers engage in routinely when they possess claim-relevant knowledge. Moreover, validation resting on prior knowledge occurs early in the comprehension process and—in contrast to more strategic forms of evaluation—requires little effort.

Note that researchers have examined epistemic validation processes by presenting nonspecialized world knowledge (e.g., "Soft soap is edible," "George Washington was the first president of the United States") that they expect the vast majority of participants to know (Rapp, 2008; Richter et al., 2009). This is a crucial restriction because it does not tell us whether readers would use their prior knowledge in a similar way to assess the veracity of *scientific* claims. One might assume that individuals who read about an unfamiliar topic are aware of the limits of their epistemic capabilities and thus refrain from relying on their prior knowledge when it comes to complex causal or mechanistic knowledge. Recent empirical results, however, suggest the opposite. Maier and Richter (2013) reported a study in which undergraduates read controversial texts on vaccination and global warming. These participants possessed little knowledge prior to reading, yet held strong beliefs favoring one side of the controversy over the other. It turned out that participants' situational representations of the texts were largely dominated by belief-consistent information. Thus, readers kept their referential representations of the situation free of conflicts and successfully resolved conflicts. Stadtler, Scharrer, Rouet, and Bromme (2013) reported similar results. They gave vocational school students straightforward conflicts consisting of opposing claim–explanation passages. Conflicts were chosen that were potentially relevant for the target group, yet the involved claims required pertinent expertise to be either validated or debunked as false (e.g., "potentials of wind energy," "health hazards of piercing"). For each conflict, participants were asked to decide which claim they accepted as more plausible and to give reasons for their decision in a short essay. Essay analyses revealed that readers relied strongly on their prior knowledge when deciding about the veracity of competing knowledge claims.

If readers do not possess pertinent prior knowledge with which to assess the validity of a knowledge claim directly, another way of drawing on their folk science may involve evaluating the coherence of the argument that surrounds it. Early competencies with respect to argument evaluation seem to develop without formal instruction during the elementary school years (Keil, 2012). Second graders, for instance, already start to show some proficiency in debunking circular reasoning as a flawed way of supporting an argument (Baum, Danovitch, & Keil, 2008). Later on, however, progress in critical thinking seems to come to a halt as adolescent and adult readers often fail to evaluate arguments adequately. For example, explanations supporting a claim have such a high appeal that readers give considerable weight to them even when supporting evidence is lacking or has been discredited (e.g., Anderson, Lepper, & Ross, 1980; Ross, Lepper, Strack, & Steinmetz, 1977). Furthermore, the presence of explanations seduces individuals into ignoring alternative explanations (Koehler, 1994; Koriat, Lichtenstein, & Fischhoff, 1980). Other fallacies entail showing an inability to distinguish between hypotheses (claims) and supporting evidence (Kuhn, 1991) or giving weight to irrelevant argumentation (Weinstock, Neuman, & Glassner, 2006).

In summary, evidence exists that readers spontaneously use their knowledge to assess the validity of scientific claims or the surrounding argument. This provides them with a fast and frugal method of resolving conflicts and harnessing scientific knowledge.

However, the general optimism with which readers endorse this strategy stands in sharp contrast to the often fragmentary knowledge base on which they ground their decisions (Keil, 2010). Borrowing a metaphor introduced by Keil (2012), one might conclude that readers are all too often "running on empty" when they use their folk science to answer "what is true" questions.

Stage 3b: Resolving Conflicts by Asking "*Whom to Believe?*"   If direct evaluations of knowledge claims based on one's own understanding tax a reader's capabilities, the reader may prefer to engage in secondhand evaluations. This entails scrutinizing source information to determine which sources to believe and decide which of the conflicting knowledge claims to adopt. In their source evaluations, readers may concentrate on two features; an author's benevolence, that is, intention to provide the best possible information, and an author's expertise, that is, competence to provide accurate and relevant information (Mascaro & Sperber, 2009).

When reading authentic texts, however, source information can be hard to retrieve and interpret: It may be encrypted in document descriptors (e.g., URLs), presented detached from the content (e.g., in an imprint), or not given at all (Britt, Rouet, & Braasch, 2013). Using source information in the service of conflict resolution would then require readers to infer an author's benevolence and expertise from scarce information and then use this to further infer the epistemic status of a message (Mascaro & Sperber, 2009). The complexity of this regulatory cycle may explain the stunning discrepancy between early proficiency in prompted source evaluation (e.g., Danovitch & Keil, 2004; Jaswal, 2010; Keil, Stein, Webb, Billings, & Rozenblit, 2008; Mascaro & Sperber, 2009; Mills, Legare, Grant, & Landrum, 2011) and older individuals' reduced use of source information during reading (e.g., Braasch et al., 2009; Brand-Gruwel, Wopereis, & Walraven, 2009; Brem, Russell, & Weems, 2001; Britt & Aglinskas, 2002; Eveland & Dunwoody, 2000; Gerjets, Kammerer, & Werner, 2011; Stadtler & Bromme, 2008; Wineburg, 1991).

When evaluating the expertise of sources, readers can draw on their folk science that also includes intuitions about the uneven distribution of knowledge in societies (Keil, 2010). In fact, from early childhood on, individuals hold assumptions regarding which academic disciplines provide pertinent knowledge for a particular scientific issue (Keil, 2010; Porsch & Bromme, 2010). For example, 11-year-olds who learn that a source possesses expertise on a given subject are able to infer what other phenomena this source will be knowledgeable about and will then prefer this source over others (Keil et al., 2008). Moreover, Porsch and Bromme (2010) have reported that secondary students could accurately rate the pertinence of different academic disciplines for scientific phenomena. Despite their lack of prior topic knowledge, students' pertinence judgments correlated significantly with an objective measure of pertinence. Moreover, recent training studies have provided promising results in terms of improving readers' skills to apply pertinence assumptions to source evaluation. Macedo-Rouet, Braasch, Britt, and Rouet (2013), for instance, devised a training program for fourth and fifth graders that especially helped poor readers to identify and remember knowledgeable sources in texts. Building on this, Stadtler, Scharrer, Rouet, et al. (2013) developed a similar intervention to help vocational students resolve conflicts between sources from high- and low-pertinent academic backgrounds. As a result of the intervention, trained readers included an increased number of references to the expertise of sources in written justifications of claim agreement whereas no such improvement was found in an untrained control group.

Another important source characteristic influencing readers' evaluations is the benevolence of a source (e.g., Rieh, 2002; Rouet, Britt, Mason, & Perfetti, 1996; Rouet, Favart, Britt, & Perfetti, 1997; Strømsø et al., 2013; Wiley et al., 2009; Wineburg, 1991). Probably due to the high cost of being deceived, people are especially sensitive toward violations of benevolence and display enhanced memory for cheaters (Bell & Buchner, 2009; Bell et al., 2011; Defeldre, 2005). In a recent study, for instance, Kammerer and Gerjets (2012) found that readers of a medical controversy were sensitive toward conflicts of interest. Readers judged Web pages with obvious commercial interests as less trustworthy than others and commented on this in written essays. Interestingly, this difference was more pronounced when the low-trustworthy source presented information that was at variance with other sources. Differences in how experts and novices handle information from potentially malevolent sources have been reported by Rouet et al. (1997). Both expert and novice readers judged historical information from sources with conflicts of interest as less trustworthy than that from other sources. However, whereas novices entirely rejected the documents as biased, experts still used them when arguing about the controversy while taking their potential bias into account. Finally, Porsch and Bromme (2011) reported a study in which they directly pitted the influence of expertise against benevolence when asking readers to interpret a socioscientific controversy. The authors used a case study about whether it was necessary to change the plans for building a tidal power plant that presented conflicting views about the predictability of coastal tides. This conflict was crucial because if the alternative viewpoint was correct, it would be necessary to change the plans and build a different version of the power plant. One source arguing for a change of plans was benevolent but had low expertise (a local resident described with favorable traits); the other had high expertise but was potentially malevolent (an expert working for the power plant company). The results revealed that more readers followed the suggestion for a change of plans if this was presented by the benevolent, low-expertise source. When the refutation was presented by an expert source of low trustworthiness, more readers abstained from a decision. Accordingly, they indicated a higher need for accessing additional documents to develop their own stance and eventually resolve the conflict. From readers' written comments, it emerged that both benevolence and expertise were important source attributes for readers. However, the relation between these attributes is asymmetrical, in that benevolence can suffice to follow an author's opinion whereas expertise alone is not enough.

In sum, readers can accomplish conflict resolution by asking "What is true?" and "Whom to believe?" These routes are not mutually exclusive but tend to complement each other. Past research suggests a strong inclination among readers to resolve conflicts based on their own understanding of the subject matter although their pertinent knowledge base is, at best, sparse. External text features including source information might have less impact on readers' validity assessments unless readers are encouraged explicitly to take them into account (Braasch, Bråten, Strømsø, Anmarkrud, & Ferguson, 2013; Britt & Aglinskas, 2002; Sparks & Rapp, 2011; Stadtler & Bromme, 2008; Wiley et al., 2009).

Brief Conclusion and Future Perspectives

With our CSI model, we have sought to provide a taxonomic model that organizes the cognitive processes and resources involved when readers handle conflicting and possibly inaccurate information. Critical to the model, we identified that readers detect a conflict, restore textual coherence, and eventually resolve a conflict. In this way, readers may possibly develop consistent knowledge, enabling them to make informed decisions (Coulter, 1997). However, our literature review also suggests that readers generally differ in their reactions when encountering conflicting information. Consequently, variations in how readers maneuver through the affordances of comprehending conflicting information are identified at each stage in the CSI model. That said, our stepwise presentation might be interpreted as being only an ideal variant of the comprehension process; other sequences than the one we proposed are certainly possible. Following Richter et al. (2009), for instance, readers may make fast and frugal validity judgments during first-pass reading, that is, even before opposing claims are tagged for their sources and documents models are formed. Moreover, readers who reconcile or ignore conflicts will certainly not engage in any form of conflict resolution because conflicts do not exist in their referential representation of the world.

With respect to the mental representation of conflicting information, we relied on existing models of text comprehension. For example, Perfetti et al.'s (1999) DMF is pivotal to the representation of conflicting information because it can account for the representation of multiple situations without compromising overall coherence. By identifying different routes to conflict resolution, the CSI model may augment the DMF because the latter does not describe the processes by which readers of a controversy eventually resolve a conflict. Given that there is considerable variability with regard to how readers comprehend conflicting information, an important task for future research is to identify factors that determine which route readers may take. We propose that the perceived relevance of information should play a pivotal role because this predicts a reader's willingness to process even complex information in depth (Stadtler et al., 2012). Another perspective for future research follows from the limitation that most of the research reviewed adopted a single-reader, multiple-documents perspective (Goldman, 2004). Different researchers, however, have emphasized that in many authentic reading situations, such as reading on the Web, readers jointly negotiate the meaning of texts in close interactions with friends or other users (Goldman, in press; Jucks & Paus, 2013). Thus, it will be important for future research to improve our understanding of the social aspects of comprehending conflicting scientific information. The discourse with like-minded others may essentially shape the comprehension of scientific information and thus determine to what degree readers pick up and rely on inaccurate information (Brossard & Scheufele, 2013).

Our model also offers some educational implications by pointing out how reader characteristics, contextual scaffolds, and text characteristics support successful comprehension of conflicting scientific information from multiple documents. At the same time, obstacles to successful comprehension are identified within each stage. Educators might find it helpful to use our different stages to dissect the entire process of comprehending conflicting scientific information. This could potentially help to reduce complexity and maintain a high degree of focus when developing and implementing instructional modules in the classroom. In fact, recent years have seen the introduction and empirical testing of several instructional procedures that aim to foster the identification, understanding, and evaluation of scientific information from multiple documents (e.g., Braasch et al., 2013; Britt & Aglinskas, 2002; Graesser et al., 2007; Macedo-Rouet et al., 2013; Stadtler & Bromme, 2008; Walraven, Brand-Gruwel, & Boshuizen, 2013; Wiley et al., 2009). Based on the research reviewed within the present contribution, we would like to highlight some reflections for educational practice. First, although it has often been argued that comprehending multiple (online) documents requires individuals to develop "new literacies" (e.g., Leu et al., 2007), it would certainly be a mistake to neglect the relevance of basic reading skills, such as fast and efficient word decoding, lexical access, and propositional integration on a local level (Hoover & Gough, 1990). In Stadtler et al. (2012), for instance, variance in conflict detection was explained not only by individual differences in deliberate regulatory efforts but also by readers' basic reading skills. On a much larger scale, the strong correlations between online and offline reading reported in PISA (Programme for International Student Assessment) 2009 (Organisation for Economic Co-operation and Development [OECD], 2011) may be taken as another indicator for commonalities between what it takes to comprehend traditional print texts and more complex digital arrangements of multiple documents. Thus, basic reading skills are the foundation for coherence formation, online and offline, and they set the stage for the operation of deliberate regulatory activities such as those relating to the evaluation of competing knowledge claims.

Second, it will be important to motivate learners to acquire and execute strategies associated with information validation. To this end, it might be beneficial to instill an awareness that tentative and conflicting knowledge is normal rather than the exception in science. Empirical support for the link between readers' assumptions about the nature of knowledge and their actual reading behavior comes from research indicating that the spontaneous application of attention to and use of sources while reading depends partly on a reader's epistemic beliefs (e.g., Bråten et al., 2011; Strømsø et al., 2013). Hence, more comprehensive reading interventions should also address the understanding of how knowledge is produced and justified in a given scientific discipline and not just practice reading strategies.

To conclude, there is a clear need for evidence-based instructional methods that can be used to teach students how to approach conflicting and inaccurate scientific information from multiple sources. This is essential if we are to help individuals engage with science without running the risk of their picking up inaccurate information. That said, a pivotal task for both researchers and educators is to examine ways to foster the necessary skills to detect conflicts, connect information with sources, and resolve conflicts on the basis of a proficient evaluation of information and sources. Researchers and practitioners alike might find the CSI model to be helpful when designing and evaluating multiple-document reading interventions.

Acknowledgments

We would like to thank Lisa Scharrer, Eva Thomm, and the editors of this volume, David N. Rapp and Jason L. G. Braasch, for their insightful comments on earlier versions of the manuscript.

References

Albrecht, J. E., & Myers, J. L. (1995). Role of context in accessing distant information during reading. *Journal of Experimental Psychology. Learning, Memory, and Cognition, 21*, 1459–1468. doi:10.1037/0278-7393.21.6.1459.

Anderson, C., Lepper, M. R., & Ross, L. (1980). Perseverance of social theories: The role of explanation in the persistence of discredited information. *Journal of Personality and Social Psychology, 39*, 1037–1049. doi:10.1037/h0077720.

Andreassen, H., Bujnowska-Fedak, M., Chronaki, C., Dumitru, R., Pudule, I., Santana, S., et al. (2007). European citizens' use of E-health services: A study of seven countries. *BMC Public Health, 7*, 53. doi:10.1186/1471-2458-7-53.

Astuti, R., & Harris, P. L. (2008). Understanding mortality and the life of the ancestors in rural Madagascar. *Cognitive Science, 32,* 713–740. doi:10.1080/03640210802066907.

Baker, L. (1979). Comprehension monitoring: Identifying and coping with text confusions. *Journal of Reading Behavior, 11,* 365–374. doi:10.1080/10862967909547342.

Baker, L. (1989). Metacognition, comprehension monitoring, and the adult reader. *Educational Psychology Review, 1,* 3–38. doi:10.1007/BF01326548.

Baker, L., & Anderson, R. I. (1982). Effects of inconsistent information on text processing: Evidence for comprehension monitoring. *Reading Research Quarterly, 17,* 281–294.

Baum, L. A., Danovitch, J. H., & Keil, F. C. (2008). Children's sensitivity to circular explanations. *Journal of Experimental Child Psychology, 100,* 146–155. doi:10.1016/j.jecp.2007.10.007.

Bell, R., & Buchner, A. (2009). Enhanced source memory for names of cheaters. *Evolutionary Psychology, 7,* 317–330.

Bell, R., Buchner, A., Erdfelder, E., Giang, T., Schain, C., & Riether, N. (2011). How specific is source memory for faces of cheaters? Evidence for categorical emotional tagging. *Journal of Experimental Psychology. Learning, Memory, and Cognition, 38,* 457–472. doi:10.1037/a0026017.

Braasch, J. L. G., Bråten, I., Strømsø, H. I., Anmarkrud, Ø., & Ferguson, L. E. (2013). Promoting secondary school students' evaluation of source features of multiple documents. *Contemporary Educational Psychology.* doi:10.1016/j.cedpsych.2013.03.003.

Braasch, J. L. G., Lawless, K. A., Goldman, S. R., Manning, F. H., Gomez, K. W., & MacLeod, S. M. (2009). Evaluating search results: An empirical analysis of middle school students' use of source attributes to select useful sources. *Journal of Educational Computing Research, 41,* 63–82.

Braasch, J., Rouet, J.-F., Vibert, N., & Britt, M. (2012). Readers' use of source information in text comprehension. *Memory & Cognition, 40,* 450–465. doi:10.3758/s13421-011-0160-6.

Brand-Gruwel, S., Wopereis, I., & Walraven, A. (2009). A descriptive model of information problem solving while using Internet. *Computers & Education, 53,* 1207–1217. doi:10.1016/j.compedu.2009.06.004.

Bråten, I., Britt, M. A., Strømsø, H. I., & Rouet, J.-F. (2011). The role of epistemic beliefs in the comprehension of multiple expository texts: Toward an integrated model. *Educational Psychologist, 46,* 48–70. doi:10.1080/00461520.2011.538647.

Brem, S. K., Russell, J., & Weems, L. (2001). Science on the Web: Student evaluations of scientific arguments. *Discourse Processes, 32,* 191–213. doi:10.1080/0163853X.2001.9651598.

Britt, M. A., & Aglinskas, C. (2002). Improving students' ability to identify and use source information. *Cognition and Instruction, 20,* 485–522.

Britt, M. A., Rouet, J. F., & Braasch, J. L. (201). Documents as entities. In M. A. Britt, S. R. Goldman, & J.-F. Rouet (Eds.), *Reading—From words to multiple texts* (pp. 160–179). New York: Routledge.

Bromme, R., Kienhues, D., & Porsch, T. (2010). Who knows what and who can we believe? Epistemological beliefs are beliefs about knowledge (mostly) attained from others. In L. D. Bendixen & F. C. Feucht (Eds.), *Personal epistemology in the classroom: Theory, research, and implications for practice* (pp. 163–193). Cambridge, England: Cambridge University Press.

Bromme, R., Thomm, E., & Wolf, V. (2013). Scientific understanding: From a cognitive disposition to knowledge about science in the real world. *Manuscript submitted for publication.*

Brossard, D., & Scheufele, D. A. (2013). Science, new media, and the public. *Science, 339,* 40–41. doi:10.1126/science.1232329.

Cerdán, R., & Vidal-Abarca, E. (2008). The effects of tasks on integrating information from multiple documents. *Journal of Educational Psychology, 100,* 209–222. doi:10.1037/0022-0663 .100.1.209.

Cerdán, R., Vidal-Abarca, E., Martínez, T., Gilabert, R., & Gil, L. (2009). Impact of question-answering tasks on search processes and reading comprehension. *Learning and Instruction, 19,* 13–27. doi:10.1016/j.learninstruc.2007.12.003.

Chaiken, S., Liberman, A., & Eagly, A. H. (1989). Heuristic and systematic information processing within and beyond the persuasion context. In J. S. Uleman & J. A. Bargh (Eds.), *Unintended thought* (pp. 212–252). New York: Guilford Press.

Chinn, C. A., & Brewer, W. F. (1993). The role of anomalous data in knowledge acquisition: A theoretical framework and implications for science instruction. *Review of Educational Research, 63,* 1–49. doi:10.2307/1170558.

Coulter, A. (1997). Partnerships with patients: The pros and cons of shared clinical decision-making. *Journal of Health Research and Policy, 2,* 112–121.

Danovitch, J. H., & Keil, F. C. (2004). Should you ask a fisherman or a biologist? Developmental shifts in ways of clustering knowledge. *Child Development, 75,* 918–931. doi:10.1111/j.1467-8624 .2004.00714.x.

Defeldre, A.-C. (2005). Inadvertent plagiarism in everyday life. *Applied Cognitive Psychology, 19,* 1033–1040. doi:10.1002/acp.1129.

Epstein, W., Glenberg, A. M., & Bradley, M. M. (1984). Coactivation and comprehension: Contribution of text variables to the illusion of knowing. *Memory & Cognition, 12,* 355–360. doi:10.3758/ BF03198295.

Evans, E. M., Legare, C. H., & Rosengren, K. (2011). Engaging multiple epistemologies: Implications for science education. In M. Ferrari & R. Taylor (Eds.), *Epistemology and science education: Understanding the evolution vs. intelligent design controversy* (pp. 111–139). New York: Routledge.

Eveland, W. P., & Dunwoody, S. (2000). Examining information processing on the World Wide Web using think aloud protocols. *Media Psychology, 2,* 219–244. doi:10.1207/ S1532785XMEP0203_2.

Ferstl, E. C., Rinck, M., & von Cramon, D. Y. (2005). Emotional and temporal aspects of situation model processing during text comprehension: An event-related fMRI study. *Journal of Cognitive Neuroscience, 17,* 724–739. doi:10.1162/0898929053747658.

Ferstl, E. C., & von Cramon, D. Y. (2001). The role of coherence and cohesion in text comprehension: An event-related fMRI study. *Brain Research. Cognitive Brain Research, 11,* 325–340. doi:10.1016/S0926-6410(01)00007-6.

Garcia-Arista, E., Campanario, J. M., & Otero, J. M. (1996). Influence of subject matter setting on comprehension monitoring. *European Journal of Psychology of Education, 11,* 427–441. doi:10.1007/BF03173282.

Gerjets, P., Kammerer, Y., & Werner, B. (2011). Measuring spontaneous and instructed evaluation processes during Web search: Integrating concurrent thinking-aloud protocols and eye-tracking data. *Learning and Instruction, 21,* 220–231. doi:10.1016/j.learninstruc.2010.02.005.

Goldman, S. R. (2004). Cognitive aspects of constructing meaning through and across multiple texts. In N. Shuart-Ferris & D. M. Bloome (Eds.), *Uses of intertextuality in classroom and educational research* (pp. 317–351). Greenwich, CT: Information Age Publishing.

Goldman, S. R. (in press). Reading and the Web: Broadening the need for complex comprehension. In R. J. Spiro, M. DeSchryver, M. S. Hagerman, P. Morsink, & P. Thompson (Eds.), *Reading at a crossroads? Disjunctures and continuities in current conceptions and practices.* New York: Routledge.

Grabe, M., Antes, J., Kahn, H., & Kristjanson, A. (1991). Adult and adolescent readers' comprehension monitoring performance: An investigation of monitoring accuracy and related eye movements. *Contemporary Educational Psychology, 16,* 45–60. doi:10.1016/0361-476X(91)90005-6.

Grabe, M., Antes, J., Thorson, I., & Kahn, H. (1987). Eye fixation patterns during informed and uninformed comprehension monitoring. *Journal of Reading Behavior, 19,* 123–140.

Graesser, A., Wiley, J., Goldman, S., O'Reilly, T., Jeon, M., & McDaniel, B. (2007). SEEK Web Tutor: Fostering a critical stance while exploring the causes of volcanic eruption. *Metacognition and Learning, 2,* 89–105. doi:10.1007/s11409-007-9013-x.

Hoover, W. A., & Gough, P. B. (1990). The simple view of reading. *Reading and Writing, 2,* 127–160.

Jaswal, V. K. (2010). Believing what you're told: Young children's trust in unexpected testimony about the physical world. *Cognitive Psychology, 61,* 248–272. doi:10.1016/j.cogpsych.2010.06.002.

Jucks, R., & Paus, E. (2013). Lexical wordings of technical concepts in multiple documents: Their crucial role for learning in online discourses. *Cognition and Instruction, 31,* 227–254. doi:10.1080/07370008.2013.769993.

Kaakinen, J. K., Hyönä, J., & Keenan, J. (2002). Perspective effects on on-line text processing. *Discourse Processes, 33,* 159–173. doi:10.1207/S15326950DP3302_03.

Kammerer, Y., & Gerjets, P. (2012). The impact of discrepancies across Web pages on high-school students' trustworthiness evaluations. In E. de Vries & K. Scheiter (Eds.), *Proceedings EARLI Special Interest Group Text and Graphics: Staging knowledge and experience: How to take advantage of representational technologies in education and training* (pp. 97–99). Grenoble, France: Université Pierre-Mendès-France.

Keil, F. (2006). Explanation and understanding. *Annual Review of Psychology, 57,* 227–254. doi:10.1146/annurev.psych.57.102904.190100.

Keil, F. (2010). The feasibility of folk science. *Cognitive Science, 34,* 826–862. doi:10.1111/j.1551-6709.2010.01108.x.

Keil, F. (2012). Running on empty? How folk science gets by with less. *Current Directions in Psychological Science, 21,* 329–334. doi:10.1177/0963721412453721.

Keil, F. C., Stein, C., Webb, L., Billings, V. D., & Rozenblit, L. (2008). Discerning the division of cognitive labor: An emerging understanding of how knowledge is clustered in other minds. *Cognitive Science, 32,* 259–300. doi:10.1080/03640210701863339.

Kiehl, K. A., Laurens, K. R., & Liddle, P. F. (2002). Reading anomalous sentences: An event-related fMRI study of semantic processing. *NeuroImage, 17,* 842–850. doi:10.1006/nimg.2002.1244.

Kintsch, W. (1998). *Comprehension: A paradigm for cognition.* Cambridge, England: Cambridge University Press.

Koehler, D. J. (1994). Hypothesis generation and confidence in judgment. *Journal of Experimental Psychology. Learning, Memory, and Cognition, 20,* 461–469. doi:10.1037/0278-7393.20.2.461.

Koriat, A., Lichtenstein, S., & Fischhoff, B. (1980). Reasons for confidence. *Journal of Experimental Psychology. Human Learning and Memory, 6,* 107–118. doi:10.1037/0278-7393.6.2.107.

Kuhn, D. (1991). *Skills of argument.* Cambridge, England: Cambridge University Press.

Lassonde, K. A., Smith, E. R., & O'Brien, E. J. (2011). Interweaving memory-based processes into the goal-focusing model of text relevance. In M. T. McCrudden, J. P. Magliano, & G. Schraw (Eds.), *Text relevance and learning from text* (pp. 75–94). Greenwich, CT: Information Age Publishing.

Legare, C. H., Evans, E. M., Rosengren, K. S., & Harris, P. L. (2012). The coexistence of natural and supernatural explanations across cultures and development. *Child Development, 83,* 779–793. doi:10.1111/j.1467-8624.2012.01743.x.

Legare, C. H., & Gelman, S. A. (2008). Bewitchment, biology, or both: The coexistence of natural and supernatural explanatory frameworks across development. *Cognitive Science, 32,* 607–642. doi:10.1080/03640210802066766

Leu, D. J., Zawilinski, L., Castek, J., Banerjee, M., Housand, B., Liu, Y., et al. (2007). What is new about the new literacies of online reading comprehension? In L. Rush, J. Eakle, & A. Berger (Eds.), *Secondary school literacy: What research reveals for classroom practices* (pp. 37–68). Urbana, IL: National Council of Teachers of English.

Linderholm, T., Cong, X., & Zhao, Q. (2008). Differences in low and high working-memory capacity readers' cognitive and metacognitive processing patterns as a function of reading for different purposes. *Reading Psychology*, *29*, 61–85. doi:10.1080/02702710701568587.

Linderholm, T., & van den Broek, P. (2002). The effects of reading purpose and working memory capacity limitations on the processing of expository texts. *Journal of Educational Psychology*, *94*, 778–784. doi:10.1037/0022-0663.94.4.778.

Macedo-Rouet, M., Braasch, J. L. G., Britt, M. A., & Rouet, J.-F. (2013). Teaching fourth and fifth graders to evaluate information sources during text comprehension. *Cognition and Instruction*, *31*, 204–226. doi:10.1080/07370008.2013.769995.

Maier, J., & Richter, T. (2013). Text–belief consistency effects in the comprehension of multiple texts with conflicting information. *Cognition and Instruction*, *31*, 151–175. doi:10.1080/07370008. 2013.769997.

Mascaro, O., & Sperber, D. (2009). The moral, epistemic, and mindreading components of children's vigilance towards deception. *Cognition*, *112*, 367–380. doi:10.1016/j.cognition.2009.05.012.

Mills, C. M., Legare, C. H., Grant, M. G., & Landrum, A. R. (2011). Determining who to question, what to ask, and how much information to ask for: The development of inquiry in young children. *Journal of Experimental Child Psychology*, *110*, 539–560. doi:10.1016/j.jecp.2011.06.003.

Myers, J. L., & O'Brien, E. J. (1998). Accessing the discourse representation during reading. *Discourse Processes*, *26*, 131–157. doi:10.1080/01638539809545042.

Myers, J. L., O'Brien, E. J., Albrecht, J. E., & Mason, R. A. (1994). Maintaining global coherence during reading. *Journal of Experimental Psychology. Learning, Memory, and Cognition*, *20*, 876–886. doi:10.3758/BF03198406.

OECD. (2011). *PISA 2009 results: Students on line: Digital technologies and performance* (Vol. 6). Paris: OECD.

Otero, J. (2002). Noticing and fixing difficulties while understanding science texts. In J. Otero, J. León, & A. C. Graesser (Eds.), *The psychology of science text comprehension* (pp. 281–307). Mahwah, NJ: Lawrence Erlbaum Associates.

Otero, J. M., & Graesser, A. C. (2001). PREG: Elements of a model of question asking. *Cognition and Instruction*, *19*, 143–175. doi:10.1207/S1532690XCI1902_01.

Otero, J. M., & Kintsch, W. (1992). Failures to detect contradictions in a text: What readers believe versus what they read. *Psychological Science*, *3*, 22–235. doi:10.1111/j.1467-9280.1992.tb00034.x.

Perfetti, C. A., Rouet, J.-F., & Britt, M. A. (1999). Toward a theory of documents representation. In H. von Oostendorp & S. R. Goldman (Eds.), *The construction of mental representations during reading* (pp. 99–122). Mahwah, NJ: Lawrence Erlbaum Associates.

Petty, R. E., & Cacioppo, J. T. (1986). *The elaboration likelihood model of persuasion*. In L. Berkowitz (Ed.), Advances in experimental social psychology (Vol. 19, pp. 123–205). San Diego, CA: Academic Press.

Pieschl, S., Stahl, E., Murray, T., & Bromme, R. (2012). Is adaptation to task complexity really beneficial for performance? *Learning and Instruction, 22,* 281–289. doi:10.1016/j.learninstruc .2011.08.005.

Porsch, T., & Bromme, R. (2010). Which science disciplines are pertinent? Impact of epistemological beliefs on students' choices. In K. Gomez, L. Lyons, & J. Radinsky (Eds.), *Learning in the disciplines: Proceedings of the 9th International Conference of the Learning Sciences* (pp. 636–642). Chicago: International Society of the Learning Sciences.

Porsch, T., & Bromme, R. (2011, August). *Who provides "enough" information? Author attributes and readers' epistemological beliefs in online decision making.* Paper presented at the 14th Biennal Conference for Research on Learning and Instruction (EARLI), Exeter, United Kingdom.

Rapp, D. N. (2008). How do readers handle incorrect information during reading? *Memory & Cognition, 36,* 688–701. doi:10.3758/MC.36.3.688.

Rapp, D. N., & Kendeou, P. (2007). Revising what readers know: Updating text representations during narrative comprehension. *Memory & Cognition, 35,* 2019–2032. doi:10.3758/BF03192934.

Rapp, D. N., & Kendeou, P. (2009). Noticing and revising discrepancies as texts unfold. *Discourse Processes, 46,* 1–24. doi:10.1080/01638530802629141.

Rapp, D. N., & Mensink, M. C. (2011). Focusing effects from online and offline reading tasks. In M. T. McCrudden, J. P. Magliano, & G. Schraw (Eds.), *Text relevance and learning from text* (pp. 141–164). Greenwich, CT: Information Age Publishing.

Richter, T. (2003). *Epistemologische Einschätzungen beim Textverstehen* [Epistemic assessments during text comprehension]. Lengerich, Germany: Pabst.

Richter, T., Schroeder, S., & Wöhrmann, B. (2009). You don't have to believe everything you read: Background knowledge permits fast and efficient validation of information. *Journal of Personality and Social Psychology, 96,* 538–558. doi:10.1037/a0014038.

Rieh, S. Y. (2002). Judgment of information quality and cognitive authority in the Web. *Journal of the American Society for Information Science and Technology, 53,* 145–161. doi:10.1002/asi.10017.

Ross, C., Lepper, M. R., Strack, F., & Steinmetz, J. (1977). Social explanation and social expectation: Effects of real and hypothetical explanations on subjective likelihood. *Journal of Personality and Social Psychology, 35,* 817–829. doi:10.1037/0022-3514.35.11.817.

Rouet, J. F., & Britt, M. A. (2011). Relevance processes in multiple document comprehension. In M. T. McCrudden, J. P. Magliano, & G. Schraw (Eds.), *Text relevance and learning from text* (pp. 19–52). Greenwich, CT: Information Age Publishing.

Rouet, J.-F., Britt, M. A., Mason, R. A., & Perfetti, C. A. (1996). Using multiple sources of evidence to reason about history. *Journal of Educational Psychology, 88,* 478–493. doi:10.1037/0022-0663 .88.3.478.

Rouet, J.-F., Favart, M., Britt, M. A., & Perfetti, C. A. (1997). Studying and using multiple documents in history: Effects of discipline expertise. *Cognition and Instruction, 15,* 85–106. doi:10.1207/ s1532690xci1501_3.

Scharrer, L., Bromme, R., Britt, M. A., & Stadtler, M. (2012). The seduction of easiness: How science depictions influence laypeople's reliance on their own evaluation of scientific information. *Learning and Instruction, 22*, 231–243. doi:10.1016/j.learninstruc.2011.11.004.

Singer, M. (1993). Causal bridging inferences: Validating consistent and inconsistent sequences. *Canadian Journal of Experimental Psychology, 47*, 340–359. doi:10.1037/h0078825.

Sparks, J. R., & Rapp, D. N. (2011). Readers' reliance on source credibility in the service of comprehension. *Journal of Experimental Psychology. Learning, Memory, and Cognition, 37*, 230–247. doi:10.1037/a0021331.

Stadtler, M., & Bromme, R. (2008). Effects of the metacognitive tool met.a.ware on the Web search of laypersons. *Computers in Human Behavior, 24*, 716–737. doi:10.1016/j.chb.2007.01.023.

Stadtler, M., Scharrer, L., & Bromme, R. (2011). How reading goals and rhetorical signals influence recipients' recognition of intertextual conflicts. In L. Carlson, C. Hoelscher, & T.F. Shipley (Eds.), *Proceedings of the 33rd Annual Conference of the Cognitive Science Society* (pp. 1346–1351). Austin, TX: Cognitive Science Society.

Stadtler, M., Scharrer, L., & Bromme, R. (2012). Does relevance matter in comprehending scientific conflicts from multiple documents? Evidence from online and offline data. In E. de Vries & K. Scheiter (Eds.), *Staging knowledge and experience: How to take advantage of representational technologies in education and training? Proceedings of the EARLI SIG 2 Meeting* (pp. 202–204), Grenoble, France: EARLI SIG 2.

Stadtler, M., Scharrer, L., Brummernhenrich, B., & Bromme, R. (2013). Dealing with uncertainty: Readers' memory for and use of conflicting information from science texts as function of presentation format and source expertise. *Cognition and Instruction, 31*, 130–150. doi:10.1080/07370008.2013.769996.

Stadtler, M., Scharrer, L., Rouet, J.-F., & Bromme, R. (2013). *Source information can fuel validity judgments. Empirical investigation of a short training for vocational students.* Paper presented at the 23rd Annual Meeting of the Society of Text and Discourse, Valencia, Spain.

Stahl, E., & Bromme, R. (2007). The CAEB: An instrument for measuring connotative aspects of epistemological beliefs. *Learning and Instruction, 17*, 773–785. doi:10.1016/j.learninstruc.2007.09.016.

Strømsø, H. I., Bråten, I., Britt, M. A., & Ferguson, L. (2013). Spontaneous sourcing among students reading multiple documents. *Cognition and Instruction, 31*, 176–203. doi:10.1080/07370008.2013.769994.

Tapiero, I. (2007). *Situation models and levels of coherence: Toward a definition of comprehension.* Mahwah, NJ: Lawrence Erlbaum Associates.

Tapiero, I., & Otero, J. (1999). Distinguishing between textbase and situation model in the processing of inconsistent information: Elaboration versus tagging. In H. van Oostendorp & S. R. Goldman (Eds.), *The construction of mental representations during reading* (pp. 341–365). Mahwah, NJ: Lawrence Erlbaum Associates.

Thomm, E., & Bromme, R. (2012). "It should at least seem scientific!" Textual features of "scientificness" and their impact on lay assessments of online information. *Science Education*, *96*, 187–211. doi:10.1002/sce.20480.

van den Broek, P., & Kendeou, P. (2008). Cognitive processes in comprehension of science texts: The role of co-activation in confronting misconceptions. *Applied Cognitive Psychology*, *22*, 335–351. doi:10.1002/acp.1418.

van den Broek, P., Lorch, R., Linderholm, T., & Gustafson, M. (2001). The effects of readers' goals on inference generation and memory for texts. *Memory & Cognition*, *29*, 1081–1087. doi:10.3758/BF03206376.

Walraven, A., Brand-Gruwel, S., & Boshuizen, H. A. (2013). Fostering students' evaluation behaviour while searching the internet. *Instructional Science*, *41*, 125–146. doi:10.1007/s11251-012-9221-x.

Weinstock, M. P., Neuman, Y., & Glassner, A. (2006). Identification of informal reasoning fallacies as a function of epistemological level, grade level, and cognitive ability. *Journal of Educational Psychology*, *98*, 327–341. doi:10.1037/0022-0663.89.2.327.

Wiley, J., Goldman, S. R., Graesser, A. C., Sanchez, C. A., Ash, I., & Hemmerich, J. (2009). Source evaluation, comprehension, and learning in Internet science inquiry tasks. *American Educational Research Journal*, *46*, 1060–1160. doi:10.3102/0002831209333183.

Wiley, J., & Myers, J. L. (2003). Availability and accessibility of information and causal inferences from scientific text. *Discourse Processes*, *36*, 109–129. doi:10.1207/S15326950DP3602_2.

Wineburg, S. S. (1991). Historical problem solving: A study of the cognitive processes used in the evaluation of documentary and pictorial evidence. *Journal of Educational Psychology*, *83*, 73–87. doi:10.1037/0022-0663.83.1.73.

Zabrucky, K., Moore, D., & Schultz, N. R. (1987). Evaluation of comprehension in young and old adults. *Developmental Psychology*, *23*, 39–43. doi:10.1037/0012-1649.23.1.39.

18   Inaccuracy and Reading in Multiple Text and Internet/Hypertext Environments

Peter Afflerbach, Byeong-Young Cho, and Jong-Yun Kim

We have several goals for this chapter. We begin with a description of the situated nature of inaccuracy, considering it in relation to models of text comprehension and strategic reading. We propose that the cooperative principle (Grice, 1975) is helpful in accounting for the context-dependent nature of inaccuracy and how the dynamics of reader, text, goal, and situation contribute to the determination that information is inaccurate. We provide three scenarios involving multiple text and Internet reading to illustrate the situated nature of inaccuracy. Then, we synthesize existing research to describe the strategies used by successful readers for determining when text is inaccurate during Internet readings of multiple texts. Next, we use think-aloud protocol data to examine how accomplished high school students, reading in Internet environments, determine accuracy in texts on controversial topics. We conclude with consideration of the importance of the concept of inaccurate information for both reading comprehension theory and reading instruction practice. What is inaccurate information in text? In this chapter, we equate accuracy with truth—an author who strives for accuracy has a goal of providing the reader with truthful information.

The reader who anticipates accuracy in text seeks a trustworthy and reliable account of (a) reality. Inaccuracy in text is a situated phenomenon. There are specific types of inaccurate information, and each is influenced by particular factors in the reader–text interaction. Inaccuracy can result from an intentional manipulation of information, or an unintentional misstatement of fact, that renders text untruthful. Inaccuracy results when there is dissonance between a reader's prior knowledge for a thing and an author's differing account of that thing. Inaccuracy is created when two or more texts describe something in different terms or in a conflicting manner. A determination that one text contains accurate information may earn a related text the label "inaccurate." Inaccuracy is not always absolute—it is contingent on the reading situation in which a reader, a text (representing an author), context, and goals interact in myriad ways.

The concept of inaccurate information has both theoretical and practical importance. When texts are assumed to be considerate (Armbruster, 1984), well-structured (Meyer, 2003), and written to provide readers with accurate information (Grice, 1975), readers' responsibilities are to apply strategies that include importance assignment, prediction, and summarization. The anticipated result of these meaning construction strategies is a representation of the message intended by the author (Kintsch, 1998; van den Broek, Risden, & Husebye-Hartmann, 1995). Accuracy of the text is assumed, and inaccuracy in text is an aberration.

Texts and their purposes are not always transparent, however, and accuracy in text varies. Readers faced with inaccuracy, or the potential for inaccuracy, must apply specific reading strategies that support the evaluation and judgment of text content (Afflerbach, Cho, & Kim, 2011). Readers must also adjust the stances they take toward texts: Deference to the authority of the text is perfectly acceptable in some situations while healthy skepticism is called for in others. For example, a traveler in a strange city seeking guidance on where to eat willingly defers to the assumed expertise of the travel guide author. Back home, the same traveler is incredulous that the local paper could write so disparagingly about a favorite restaurant. A reader's inclination to take appropriate stances toward text and to use effective strategies are developmental in nature (Alexander, 2005); thus, inaccurate information tends to present greater challenges to less experienced readers.

Readers encounter texts that are intended, variously, to convince, cajole, fool, inform, entertain, verify, certify, assert, or mislead. Readers must be able to understand and identify different types of inaccurate information in text, the intentionality of the inaccuracy, and the (un-)intended effects of inaccuracy. Readers must be able to use strategies in relation to inaccuracy, with both traditional print text and Internet-based digital texts (Pressley & Afflerbach, 1995; Afflerbach & Cho, 2009). Particular texts present reading challenges due to their questionable provenance, the low bar for publishing that the Internet sometimes represents, and a possible lack of vetting by an authority in the content of the text (Coiro, 2011).

Inaccuracy Related to Models of Text Comprehension and Strategic Reading

We can infer the processing of inaccurate information, and the strategies readers use in relation to inaccurate text, from models of comprehension. While these models generally assume text accuracy, they can help us anticipate and describe how readers read inaccurate text. According to Kintsch (1998), readers construct meaning at both micro- and macrolevels of text structure to build a textbase model, the accurate representation of text. However, the textbase is a mental representation in which the networked information segments may not be sufficiently coherent. The structure may be fragile, due to lack of cohesion of the pieces of information that comprise the textbase. Successful comprehension of text requires a subsequent stage of processing during which readers build a situation model. Building an accurate situation model is contingent on a complex set of interactions between the reader, text, and context, yielding a representation of "what the text is about." Readers integrate information to build a coherent situation model, eliminating irrelevant information from the textbase model and connecting their relevant prior knowledge to text content (e.g., climate change, the French Revolution) and discourse context (e.g., how the text is created, what message is delivered). The knowledge emanating from diverse sources of text, reader, and context intermingles, and with this strategy-based process readers construct particular meaning from, and with, text.

In this construction-integration model, inaccuracy introduces the possibility that a reader builds a textbase model which accurately represents text but that contains inaccurate information. For example, a history textbook may misstate agreed-upon facts, and a science Web site may provide an incomplete account of the process of photosynthesis. The process of reading at this point is driven by text information at both micro- and macrolevels, and the evaluation of inaccuracies may not be a priority unless the text has serious logical flaws that are evident to readers performing macroprocessing of text information. In addition, readers with limited prior knowledge for the text topic are often not in a position to identify inaccurate information. Kintsch (1998) posits that building a situation model requires readers to screen relevant information from the textbase. This process affords readers the opportunity to use their prior knowledge and contextual clues to critically appraise different aspects of the text information as it is represented in memory. Astute readers may detect inaccuracies, both explicit and hidden, in the text and consider these inaccuracies in the building of a situation model. However, when readers fail to recognize the inaccurate information, or simply receive and accept all text information as true, their situation model is flawed, yielding an inaccurate understanding of the text topic.

Kintsch's (1998) model of text comprehension describes the reader's construction of meaning from a single text. Thus, the model's depiction of the determination of accurate information is similarly limited to cases *within* a single text. Rouet and his colleagues (Britt, Perfetti, Sandak, & Rouet, 1999; Perfetti, Rouet, & Britt, 1999; Rouet, 2006) propose a documents model framework that describes a reader's mental representation constructed *across* multiple texts. The documents model describes both the constructive and integrative strategies needed to build textbase and situation models of individual texts, and the identification and building of possible interrelationships between multiple texts (i.e., intertext model; Britt & Rouet, 2012). It outlines the construction of situation models across texts, as well as the linkages between texts that are created by readers. The conception of situation model is extended to represent both meanings from multiple texts and connections across the texts, deemed the *integrated mental model* (Britt & Rouet, 2012). This global understanding of multiple meanings and textual relationships is the result of readers' integrating their knowledge about contents, topics, genres, and the status of texts, in relation to their reading goals and tasks.

The determination of inaccurate information is a critical task in constructing an integrated mental model of multiple texts. Readers who approach the reading of multiple texts with the understanding that "no single perspective accurately and completely captures the entire situation" (Britt & Rouet, 2012, p. 280) can then apply strategies related to determining accuracy. Strategic readers overview the landscape of meanings presented by different texts, probe details to check for (in)accuracies in individual texts (e.g., comparing and contrasting claims, evidence, assumptions, or purposes that the texts present), and assess reliability of the texts (e.g., identifying the authors, text provenance, and the contexts in which the texts are created). In this recursive process of intertextual reading, the determination of inaccurate information in text requires readers to be responsive to situations in which information from one text contradicts information from another text. If readers fail to perceive and reconcile such conflicts between documents, their integrated document model will lack coherence.

Related, *constructively responsive reading* (Afflerbach & Cho, 2009; Pressley & Afflerbach, 1995) proposes that readers construct meaning by developing a comprehensive understanding of the reading task and task demands, applying appropriate strategies as they read text and continually monitoring and evaluating their reading performance. The model highlights the responsivity of readers situated within particular text and task settings. Accomplished readers use meaning construction processes in relation to the particular characteristics of the text being read, and these readers understand the challenges that inaccurate text presents. Being a strategic, constructively responsive reader involves monitoring the accuracy of text in relation to one's prior knowledge. When reading more than one text, successful readers monitor accuracy between texts, in addition to monitoring the interface of text and prior knowledge. Readers also monitor accuracy and inaccuracy as best suits their reading goals. Pleasure reading and reading for exams may both be monitored, but with different goals and standards for detecting, addressing, and dealing with inaccuracy (Linderholm & van den Broek, 2002). Evaluative strategies also feature in constructively responsive reading: A reader may evaluate suspected inaccurate information by comparing text contents with prior knowledge and other consulted texts.

Inaccurate Information in Reading and the Cooperative Principle

Meaning derived from reading, like all communication, is shaped by context. Understanding of responses to inaccuracy is thus enhanced when models of comprehension account for context. Grice (1975) describes the cooperative principle, involving tacit agreements and understandings that undergird much of human communication. Consider inaccurate information in text from the perspective of Grice's human communication theory. There are three major components of the theory: message, sender, and receiver. Related to this chapter, the message is text, the sender is the author, and the receiver is the reader. The cooperative principle posits that an author who is intent on successful communication will adhere to maxims that include quality (the text must be truthful, reliable, and accurate) and quantity (the information provided by a text should be sufficient to support the goals of the author and the aims of the communication). In turn, the reader expects that the author operate in good faith, not intent on misleading or misinforming.

The cooperative principle helps describe one set of standards for judging accurate and inaccurate information in text. Applied to reading, the expectation of the reader is that the author is generally trustworthy, is intent on clear communication (as opposed to manipulation), will avoid error, and is not prone to deceit. The reader's metacognitive awareness (Veenman, Van Hout-Wolters, & Afflerbach, 2006) that an author or text deviates from the cooperative principle is one important precursor to dealing with inaccuracy. The cooperative principle is also important because it helps us understand the variable nature of, and need for, accuracy in human communication. As with all communication, reading is influenced by varied situational factors—some intended and some unintended, some obvious and some nuanced—that contribute to the accuracy or inaccuracy of text.

Contextual Influences on Inaccurate Information in Text

The prior consideration of models of text processing helps describe the strategies and processes that readers use to identify and deal with inaccurate information in text. As well, theory should describe the parameters and conditions of inaccurate information in text. Inaccuracy necessitates attention to the contexts and situations in which readers must process and reconcile divergent information on the same topic, as with Internet and multiple text reading. Depictions of accomplished readers should describe their strategic work with various types of texts, whether they contain accurate or inaccurate information.

Accurate and inaccurate information can be considered from the perspective of author, reader, and text. How do accuracy and inaccuracy relate to the author of a text? Authors may be complicit with the inaccurate information contained in texts they write, or they may be unaware of it. Those who write propaganda, construct documents with intentional bias, or make claims unsubstantiated by evidence frequently create texts that contain inaccurate information (van Dijk, 1999). Such authors intentionally misrepresent facts or truths. In other cases, authors may inadvertently produce texts that are well-intentioned but inaccurate on their face. When authors write about topics for which they have insufficient knowledge, inaccuracy is a common by-product, and texts contain errors.

Readers are the ultimate arbiters in determining inaccurate information in text. In relation to an author's role in creating inaccuracy, readers need to have relevant prior knowledge of text content, reading strategies, knowledge of discourse, and stances toward reading to detect and deal with inaccuracies that authors intentionally (or unintentionally) include in text. A reader with little or no prior knowledge for a text topic is in a difficult position to determine inaccuracy. That authors are trustworthy and their texts accurate are common default assumptions, but the assumptions themselves may not be accurate. Many school students find themselves in such situations—when the goal is to learn new information, learners often lack the prior knowledge with which they might question a text's accuracy. Likewise, a reader who is uncomfortable or unfamiliar with the notion of challenging a text or author will defer to inaccurate information in text. The reader who has limited knowledge of how and why human beings communicate will be unable to bring related discourse knowledge to bear. Such a reader will not be able to detect irony, identify propaganda, or read a satiric essay with awareness of its potential meanings.

Readers' goals also influence standards for attending to and dealing with inaccuracy. There are situations in which text inaccuracy is beside the point, as when it is irrelevant to the reader's goal or experience. Reading a novel during vacation, when the reader's goal is relaxation, may foster inattention to inaccuracies. Inaccuracies may be present (e.g., the author doesn't provide an accurate description of Oslo in a crime novel), but it doesn't matter. In contrast, reading a (hopefully) factual account of a political candidate's history and qualifications in order to cast a ballot suggests higher stakes for accuracy.

There may be inaccuracies in text that are a result of the text production process. While misspellings, deleted sentences or paragraphs, and the like can create inaccuracy at the orthographic, syntactic, and semantic levels of language, these inaccuracies are typically detected and corrected by proofreading, spell-checking, and good copyediting.

In summary, the reading situation influences the nature of inaccurate information in text and the reader's awareness of it. Authors and their texts interact with readers and their knowledge in a variety of situations, and each situation may have specific standards and requirements for determining the accuracy or inaccuracy of what is read. Just as one reader determines that there is inaccurate information and attends to it, another reader is unaware of the inaccuracy and does not attend to it. Another reader is aware of the inaccuracy, but a lack of developed or applied epistemic knowledge overrides the determination that the information is inaccurate.

Examples of Inaccuracy in Text

The cooperative principle (Grice, 1975), marked by truthful texts, above-board authors, and accomplished readers, does not operate in all communication situations. In this section, we illustrate the absence of the cooperative principle occurring with a corresponding presence of inaccuracy. We use three examples related to Internet reading that demonstrate the willful suspension of accuracy, inaccuracy as a conflict between what is in text and what a reader knows and believes, and an author's unintentionally communicating inaccurate information. Our intent is to demonstrate that the nature of inaccurate information varies, as do the conditions under which the inaccuracy is created, encountered, and rectified. Relatedly, readers' ability and inclination to identify and deal with the inaccuracies that follow will vary.

Example 1: The Willing Suspension of Accuracy

Our first example focuses on inaccurate information related to an author who intentionally misrepresents facts. During the United States presidential campaign of 2012, some news media focused on the nature and relevance of "facts" in speeches given by candidates and in related campaign advertisements. *The Washington Post* established a "Fact Checker" blog and column, in which the claims made by each of the presidential candidates and their campaigns were vetted for accuracy and truth. Misstatements, half-truths, straightforward lies, and other inaccuracies were given "Pinocchio" awards on a scale of 1 to 4, with the most inaccurate (furthest from the truth) statements awarded 4 Pinocchios. Of course, and unfortunately, inaccuracy and misstatement are part of many political campaigns.

Mitt Romney's presidential campaign funded and produced many different print, television, and Internet advertisements. His campaign advisors considered the advertisements that focused on federal welfare policy to be the most effective, in spite of the fact that the content contained in the ads was demonstrated to be grossly distorted, or not true (*Tampa Bay Times*, 2014). When confronted by the media with the idea that the political advertisements deemed most effective were not accurate, Romney employee Neil Newhouse stated, "Fact checkers come to this with their own set of thoughts and beliefs, and we're not going to let our campaign be dictated by fact checkers" (Sargent, 2012). In this example, the production of text containing inaccurate information is intentional. The author of the political advertisements apparently believes that inaccuracy is needed to persuade the reader or listener. This intentional inaccuracy suggests that the astute reader needs to not only be able to detect inaccuracy but also to assume that it might be present in particular genres of text and in venues associated with particular texts. Relatively naive readers are in a difficult position if they expect honesty from campaign communications and if they lack the strategies for identifying author intent and text inaccuracy. Political campaign ads are fertile ground (Pan & Kosicki, 1994) for digging up inaccuracy. In contrast, readers will probably not bring ready skepticism to the reading of operating instructions for heavy machinery.

Example 2: Inaccuracy as a Conflict between What Is in Text and What the Reader Knows and Believes

Inaccuracy also exists in the space between what an individual knows and believes, and text information that challenges that knowledge and belief. Students' scientific misconceptions, a form of prior knowledge, are well documented. They include errant ideas about evolution (Shtulman, 2011), climate change (Leiserowitz, 2006), and astronomy (Diakidoy & Kendeou, 2001). Consider the elementary school student who believes (and, thus "knows") that the moon appears larger when it rises on the horizon because it is closer to Earth and then appears smaller in size as it climbs higher in the night sky because it is then further away. The student, as part of a class assignment, must locate and read three texts on the Internet related to the question, "Why does the moon appear bigger on the horizon?" The accessed texts provide other explanations (some scientific) for the moon's appearance being larger on the horizon. The student is confronted with conflicting accounts of the moon's size—the student's prior knowledge and those contained in the texts—and one must involve inaccurate information.

A possible resolution of this conflict hinges on the student reader's being aware of the inaccuracy—the conflict between old and new information. The reader must be continually metacognitive, noting when text information confirms or challenges something the reader already knows. The reader must address instances of inaccuracy, in the simple case choosing one explanation over the other and in a more complex case achieving a reconciliation among the various explanations. We can also venture that the student must be so invested in the task that the cognitive effort necessary to investigate, reflect on, and solve the problem of inaccurate information is available.

Example 3: An Author's Unintentionally Communicating Inaccurate Information
In some situations, the intent to inform with accurate information is clear, but the attempt fails because the information provided is inaccurate. Consider *Our Virginia: Past and Present* (Masoff, 2010), a history textbook used in many Virginia elementary school classrooms. In a section on the Civil War, the following statement is made: "…[t]housands of Southern blacks fought in the Confederate ranks, including two black battalions under the command of Stonewall Jackson." This statement is considered at best inaccurate by historians (McConnell, 2010). At worst, it is intentionally misleading. The author of *Our Virginia: Past and Present* is not a historian and recounted that she wrote the book using information that she obtained from Internet searches. The assertion that slaves fought for the Confederacy was found on the Web site of the Sons of Confederate Veterans (http://www.scv.org), a group that denies that slavery was the Civil War's main cause. The author of *Our Virginia: Past and Present* did not know enough about history to recognize or query inaccuracies in the "historical" information she gathered from the Internet. She was unable to determine that her source was inaccurate, and this resulted in her constructing an inaccurate historical account—which happens to be part of an elementary school history text.

When a reader has no relevant prior knowledge to compare with that proffered by a text, it is close to impossible to detect inaccurate information. This position was probably shared by many of the students who were required to read the Virginia history textbook. Elementary school students face a particularly challenging task here, as they lack the prior knowledge they need to know that the information is inaccurate. They may also lack the knowledge that they are well within their rights to challenge text when it contains inaccurate information. For some students, questioning the contents and claims in a textbook is an unprecedented activity.

The differences among the preceding three examples illustrate that inaccurate information may be a variable or fixed feature of a particular text. Reader strategies and knowledge, author intent and level of expertise, and the goal for reading all interact to create inaccuracy in text in distinct forms. The need to attend to inaccuracy as well as the means by which readers recognize and deal with inaccuracy in text are situationally determined.

Determining (In)accuracy of Text Information with Multiple Documents

In this section, we build on the previous examples of the situated nature of inaccuracy to describe the process of determining the accuracy of text information and the strategies involved in evaluative reading. We begin with a preliminary theoretical account of accuracy determination, borrowing from existing models of strategic processing of multiple documents. This emerging conceptual work describes the important actions that critical readers use to conduct source evaluation (e.g., assessment of text quality by knowing who created the text and where a text "comes from") and content evaluation (e.g., assessment of information value by knowing how each text contributes or not to consistency between and across the texts). We then describe strategic processes involved in accuracy determination, drawing upon verbal reporting data from accomplished readers situated in Internet contexts. This account of Internet reading illustrates the complexities of accuracy determination as an important evaluative process. Selecting multiple links and texts in a strategic manner is necessary because the Internet presents often-uncertain information spaces, texts of unknown source and purpose, and texts that are not regularly vetted by a reliable authority.

A Conceptual Model of Accuracy Determination

Building a coherent, cross-textual understanding is the desired outcome when reading multiple texts on the same topic, but this goal is not easily achievable for readers who do not apply appropriate strategies. The documents in a reader's hands or on a computer monitor vary in their qualities including readability, information value, reliability, trustworthiness, and accuracy (Goldman, 2004; Rouet, 2006). Failure to note the inaccuracy of text information may contribute to an inaccurate understanding of what is to be learned. Readers may use unfiltered, inaccurate information in learning about a particular topic and may believe that their inaccurate topic understanding is accurate. Thus, successful multiple-text comprehension is marked by the understanding that inaccuracy may be present in the reader and text interaction, and it involves the reconciliation of inaccuracy with a reader's prior knowledge and information in the available texts.

Accuracy determination involves scrutiny, judgments, and decision-making processes related to text. Research on multiple text reading suggests that strategic readers are mindful in investigating individual texts and the document set of which they are part (Britt, Perfetti, Sandak, & Rouet, 1999; Strømsø, Bråten, & Samuelstuen, 2003; Wineburg, 1991). These readers engage in the process of identifying author information, posing questions about the author and text content using relevant prior knowledge and text information, and making hypotheses about the status of each text. Then, readers attempt to locate evidence or information that supports or disconfirms their hypotheses by strategically moving between and across the texts. This allows readers to make decisions as to whether each text in a multiple-text set is deserving of reader attention and whether to continue to read and use it. Accuracy determination is an important consideration in such strategic, often sophisticated interrogations of text sets.

There is a notable body of research on multiple-text comprehension that offers insight into the strategic actions that underlie accuracy determination (Bråten, Strømsø, & Salmerón, 2011; Goldman, 2004; Perfetti, Rouet, & Britt, 1999; Rouet & Britt, 2011; VanSledright, 2002). Based on our understanding of this research, we suggest two important processes of accuracy determination in reading multiple texts: (a) source evaluation and (b) content evaluation. We examine the two processes in an extended reading scenario. In this scenario, our reader is a dedicated coffee drinker who consumes considerable, daily amounts of coffee. The six-cup-a-day habit raises our reader's concerns about the effects of coffee on her overall health. She sets about finding articles to inform her decision on reducing or maintaining her coffee intake. She locates three articles to learn about health effects of coffee. One text is an author's firsthand account of how copious coffee consumption contributes to considerable weight loss. A second text illustrates the problematic influence of coffee on overall health, focusing on caffeine dependence. In contrast, the third text highlights a positive effect of coffee drinking, indicating that caffeine can reduce the risk of Parkinson's disease.

The reader's assessment of the texts involves strategic source evaluation, posing questions that include the following: Who wrote each article? Who can I trust? What is the source of data used for argumentation? She also conducts content evaluation: Does each text contain accurate information? Are there any inconsistencies or inaccuracies among the articles? The reader moves back and forth between source and content evaluation in a recursive manner, intent on making informed decisions about the texts.

The conceptual model of this process, the source evaluation and content evaluation in the coffee drinker and reader scenario, is represented in figure 18.1. We note that before reading, the reader already has prior knowledge and a set of beliefs, goals,

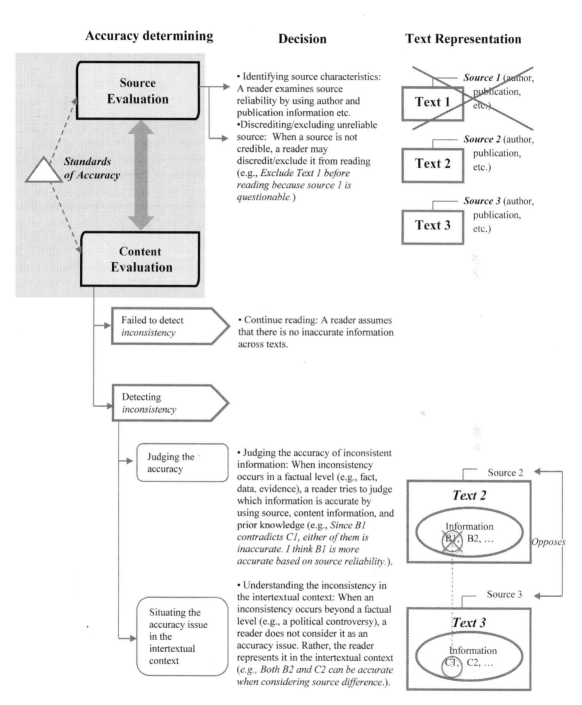

Figure 18.1

A process of determining inaccuracy of text information in reading multiple texts.

attitudes, and motivation related to the topic of coffee. We propose that these cognitive and motivational factors influence her *standards of accuracy*, which figure centrally in the determination of what text information is accurate and inaccurate. In line with the concept of standards of coherence (van den Broek, Risden, & Husebye-Hartmann, 1995), her strategies for determining accuracy may differ from those of another reader who enjoys reading the same text set for leisure.

As figure 18.1 indicates, source evaluation is critical for determining text accuracy. In the source evaluation phase, readers assume that the more trustworthy the source, the less likely it has inaccurate information. Accomplished readers are likely to test and then use this assumption (Britt & Aglinskas, 2002; Wineburg, 1991; Bråten, Strømsø, & Britt, 2009; Goldman, Braasch, Wiley, Graesser, & Brodowinska, 2012). There are at least two related strategies that are relevant to source evaluation. First, readers examine source information in order to judge the reliability of each source before reading (Afflerbach & Cho, 2009). Mindful readers examine available information that may include the author's expertise, credentials, and affiliation. Strategic readers also focus on details of publishing: the specific type of publication (e.g., a blog or an online magazine article), place of publication (e.g., Yahoo! or *The New York Times*), and date. The judgment of text accuracy and reliability informs readers' determinations of whether the text can contribute to an overall comprehension of text sets and to goal attainment (Rouet & Britt, 2011).

For the second stage in figure 18.1, strategic readers may discredit or exclude unreliable sources from reading, based on the source evaluation process (Wiley, Goldman, Graesser, Sanchez, Ash, & Hemmerich, 2009). In the coffee drinker scenario, the reader may exclude one of the texts (text 1: "Coffee for Diet") because it does not meet the source reliability criteria: The accuracy of information in the text is questionable. While the text provides a narrative of the author's experience of weight loss related to drinking five cups of coffee per day, it is an Internet blog posting written by an author who apparently lacks medical expertise. From the reader's perspective, attributing weight loss to coffee drinking seems simplistic. The reliability and accuracy of text information is questioned, and the reader is doubtful that the text can contribute to an accurate and enhanced understanding of coffee and health.

In addition to source evaluation, strategic readers perform content evaluation to ensure that their judgment of text accuracy is legitimate. This process involves complex "linking strategies" that are pivotal for understanding multiple texts and evaluating the quality of texts (Afflerbach & Cho, 2009, p. 80). In regard to accuracy determination, detecting inconsistencies in information that may or may not exist across different texts is a central strategy (Hartman, 1995; Goldman, 2004). When a reader fails to identify inconsistency in the information gathered across texts, this reflects a related failure to determine the accuracy of text contents. The reader assumes that all of the information is accurate. Construction of meaning continues apace, but the product is flawed. In contrast, when a reader determines that different texts contain congruent information and that the texts are accurate, the integration of accurate information across texts yields an accurate construction of meaning.

In many cases, though, multiple texts on the same topic may present the reader with contradictory and disconfirming information (Britt & Rouet, 2012). Moreover, multiple texts about a controversial topic, replete with competing arguments and perspectives, require reader knowledge and expertise to understand the multidimensional problem space. In such conditions, the determination of accurate information in text becomes a more challenging task. In the coffee drinker scenario, consider the reader who has two conflicting sources of information (text 2, "Coffee Dependence," and text 3, "Coffee and Parkinson's Disease"). Both texts appear in the opinion sections of different newspapers and are written by experts in their related disciplines: text 2 by a practicing physician and text 3 by a medical scientist. At first glance, the reader considers both articles to be reliable because of author expertise, believing that the scientist and physician are inscrutable sources of information. Both appear to provide balanced opinions on the health benefits and side effects of coffee drinking.

When reading the two articles, the reader identifies inconsistent information about Americans' coffee drinking habit. Text 2 introduces that 65% of Americans consume more than 14 cups per week (two cups per day) whereas text 3 provides information that two thirds of Americans drink more than one cup every day. In checking source information, the reader determines that text 2 cites a more recent survey about Americans' drinking habits than text 3, and she concludes that information in text 3 is outdated and relatively inaccurate compared with the information in text 2.

The reader understands that the arguments in the two texts are different, based on the examination of the texts' contents. Text 2 focuses on a medical report that surveyed heavy coffee drinkers who have experienced serious caffeine addiction and caffeine withdrawal symptoms (e.g., headache, concentration difficulty, depression) while text 3 highlights a review of studies on coffee and Parkinson's that reports drinking two or three cups of coffee a day can decrease the rate for the disease by 25%. Both texts cite research evidence for their arguments, but the sources are different (i.e., medical studies from different peer-reviewed journals). Given the reader's limited prior knowledge in the areas of nutrition and medical health, she is not able to decide which article is more accurate. The reader is in a difficult position to make accuracy-related decisions. She concludes that the different points made in the two texts are conflicting but that they are not mutually exclusive. Both provide accurate information.

As described thus far, accuracy determination with Internet reading demands active readers who attend to the information about the author and the source of each text while also constructing an understanding of the content of the texts. Readers of multiple texts make informed decisions about text accuracy based on the results of their source evaluation and content evaluation. This process requires readers to generate and use standards for reliability, identify and use textual clues to judge text accuracy, and monitor their reading processes. Determining whether the information is accurate or not is a demanding task for readers, especially when there are many possible texts to choose, and when readers possess little knowledge related to the topic and the domain. In the following section, we investigate a complex, Internet-based task environment in which readers must determine the accuracy of text information. We describe accuracy determination as an important and opportunistic evaluative reading process with which readers negotiate numerous links and texts that may or may not be relevant, reliable, or accurate.

Determining Information Accuracy in Internet Reading Contexts

Throughout both source evaluation and content evaluation processes, successful readers use critical mind-sets in the evaluation of Internet texts that can vary greatly in accuracy, quality, and purpose. These readers access diverse Web sources, knowing that accuracy can be relative to reader, text, author, and task. Readers also perform ongoing evaluation of what is read because they know that the Internet can be an untested information space, occupied by texts created by anonymous authors and organizations that vary in their expertise and credibility (Burbules & Callister, 1996; Fabos, 2008). Based on this awareness of possible risks, successful readers on the Internet use standards when they question, examine, and identify evidence for information accuracy. Sometimes these readers query the information quality to determine the accuracy directly, but they also utilize their assumptions about the accuracy to determine the extent to which the information is useful for their learning.

We use verbal reporting data from a case study (Cho, 2012) to describe the strategic approaches to examining information quality and accuracy taken by accomplished adolescent readers in Internet settings. In this study, adolescent readers performed an Internet reading task, in two 45-minute sessions, with a goal of identifying useful Web sites and working with those Web sites to learn about controversial topics (e.g., alternative energy, human stem-cell research, the death penalty, climate change). These high school readers evaluated text source qualities, including accuracy of information, while navigating and comprehending multiple Web sources. A notable characteristic of the students' evaluative reading is the use of a variety of proxies for text information accuracy and quality, including copyright information, Web addresses, and design features. For example, strategic readers make preliminary accuracy assignments to particular Web sites based on their prior experiences with the Web sites, and the accuracy reputation related to particular types of Web sites, especially open Web sources such as wikis. Consider the following think-aloud excerpt, in which a student describes her plan for finding accurate information:

Now I'm probably going to check out the Wikipedia even though sometimes people say it's not a good source ... some of my teachers tell us not to look at Wikipedia but I find it very useful ... the content might not be accurate here because everybody can create and change it anytime but you gotta check their sources because they are supposed to cite these references at the bottom of the page ... these references might be good to use to gain some good information.

In this excerpt, the reader operates with caution, based on skepticism of Wikipedia as an open source of information, untested in terms of accuracy, reliability, and credibility. However, the reader also brings her own positive experiences in using Wikipedia. She clearly distinguishes between what might be inaccurate (i.e., written information on the site) and what might be accurate and useful for learning and information gathering (i.e., cited references). The reader also differentiates between primary and secondary sources: The information in the secondary source may be distorted, decontextualized from the original meanings and intentions of the primary source. This process of Web source evaluation to a large degree involves readers' prior knowledge and experience related to Internet use, which helps them anticipate the degree of accuracy offered by information from primary and secondary sources.

The source evaluation process, including finding and reading available Web site information (e.g., Web site titles, URLs, author information, source information), helps the reader make determinations about the potential (in)accuracy of Web page content and the overall value of the Web source (Leu et al., 2008). In effect, source information about particular Web sites helps readers determine the caveats and affordances of the Web sites and the related texts. Readers' questions related to source information can include the following: Is information consistently accurate? Is there predictable bias? Is the organization or author trustworthy? Strategic readers are more likely to use such questions, in conjunction with Web site information, before clicking through a particular link and investing time in anticipation of the accuracy and usefulness of the Web site. For example, accomplished readers identify multiple layers of source information in a Web site and make a decision to read the site or not, based on the use of their evaluation standards. As demonstrated in the following think-aloud excerpt, this strategy for source evaluation is not uncommon for highly skilled readers on the Internet:

There is a website here which is a government website ... it's called Obesity Medline Plus and its brief description says obesity means having too much body fat ... it [the website] is "dot gov" and it seems to contain some reliable information about obesity ... but the page itself seems like ... look at the title ... it's almost like a magazine article which might not be reliable ... some of the magazines are very commercial and they are not really based on the facts ... I will check it out but need to be careful.

In this excerpt, the reader is tentative in deciding to further investigate the site. Thus, she attempts to test the link to determine if the Web page is suitably accurate, containing the information that she is seeking. It is notable that the reader not only considers the Web site information but also makes an educated guess about the source of the article. The reader here integrates her knowledge about Internet publishing forms (e.g., magazines, newspapers, blogs) with her general perception of the value of different Web sites, based on their URLs (e.g., .gov, .com, .edu, .org). The perception of the possibility that unreliable articles can be posted on a reliable Web site, and the degree to which such Web sites might allow for inaccuracy, reflects the reader's critical mindset while assessing Web site sources. This anticipatory action is important, reflecting the situated nature of reading and accuracy determination (Afflerbach & Cho, 2010; Coiro & Dobler, 2007). The reader must be conscious about the nature of Internet reading, the different cues that help her determine accuracy, and her goal(s). This attention helps the reader conduct evaluative reading with online sources and creates opportunity for assessing information accuracy.

Readers' prior knowledge related to the content and the author of text plays a critical role in the examination and determination of source accuracy. Strategic readers often pose questions about different aspects of a Web source, including the content (e.g., Does this make sense?), the author (e.g., Who created this Web site?), and the structure and layout (e.g., Is this design effective in communication?). Answering these questions helps readers determine information accuracy and quality. However, examining the content accuracy and author reputation when this information is not available is next to impossible. The knowledge that the reader already possesses related to content knowledge and author reputation plays a critical role in an investigation of these critical questions.

Accomplished readers are often well aware of the bias present in text and on related Web sites. As noted in the model of accuracy determination, expert readers are more adept at developing their perceptions of text bias while performing an evaluation of text content (Goldman et al., 2012; Pressley & Afflerbach, 1995). Likewise, a growing body of research on skilled Internet readers provides think-aloud data that describes the accuracy standards used to determine the usefulness of a Web site (Coiro & Dobler, 2007; Salmerón, Cañas, Kintsch, & Fajardo, 2005). Cho (2012) describes a strategic reader who is interested in learning about mountaintop removal, a divisive coal-mining method. This reader perceives the authors' possible content biases in relation to the Web site and then determines that the biases are healthy because she knows where the biases come from, as described in the following excerpt:

I'm gonna look um look up a website that I already know of called "I love mountains" ... a big thing I am already aware of is mountaintop removal in West Virginia ... and they're [the people in the non-government organization that created the website] really involved with using alternative energy ... of course these people are somewhat biased because they want to end mountaintop removal and of course they're going to support alternative energy ... but ... it's okay that they are partly biased because it's been proven that it [mountaintop removal coal mining methods] is the destruction of the earth and of biodiversity.

The Internet represents a text environment with numerous interconnected sources. In this space, readers may encounter challenges that are threefold: Information is uncertain, information is embedded in a Web site or Web page that is not vetted by a legitimate authority, and the constellation of these uncertain sources is created, posted, and recreated on the Internet. Readers must understand the nature of this Internet information space and be critical in the negotiation of these uncertainties. In regard to the determination of accurate information, readers must be able to perform strategic moves between different texts, between different levels of source evaluation and content evaluation, and between the texts and their knowledge.

We conclude this section noting that accuracy determination is a complex process for the evaluative reading of texts, as both our theoretical model and verbal protocol data demonstrate. Internet reading environments are increasingly complex, as readers navigate and read more texts in a hyperspace with a seemingly infinite number of informational sources. These sources are linked together through the ever-changing architecture of the Web, and readers must make informed decisions about information quality with diverse sources of knowledge (e.g., content-related prior knowledge, knowledge of the author, text, and task, and knowledge that reading requires complex evaluative processes). Together, these sources reflect the situated nature of reading and reflect the complexities of determining inaccuracy in text (Alexander, Kulikowich, & Jetton, 1994; Fabos, 2008; Kuiper, Volman, & Terwel, 2005).

Conclusions

Inaccurate information in text influences comprehension, and the nature of text inaccuracy is best considered in relation to authors' intent and readers' strategies, prior knowledge, goals, epistemic beliefs, and metacognitive awareness. There is a developing literature that describes the situated nature of these complexities and how they impact the work of readers dealing with inaccuracy. As readers encounter texts on the Internet, they process text information, and this processing is situated in a complex environment.

The specifics of Internet reading situations vary greatly, and our attention to this varied situativity is critical as we continue to build an understanding of inaccuracy in text. That the Internet presents readers with a universe of text and text choices, that these texts emanate from sources of varied expertise and legitimacy, and that almost anyone can publish almost anything on the Internet are important details. Not all texts are accurate, and not all adhere to the cooperative principle (Grice, 1975). Combining the above facts helps us anticipate the responsibilities that readers take on when they confront inaccuracy in Internet and hypertext settings and the related challenges they face.

Ongoing research should continue to refine understandings of the nature of inaccurate information in text and of readers' responses to inaccuracy. Related to the notion that texts may contain inaccurate information, or that a difference between a text account and a reader's prior knowledge creates a de facto inaccuracy, is the situated cognition that allows readers to deal with inaccuracy. An important contribution to theory will involve the construction of accounts that articulate readers' developing strategies for identifying and acting upon inaccurate information, from elementary school, when many students first encounter formal instruction related to fact and opinion, through middle and high school, where many students learn the value of claim–evidence structures in written and spoken text. Further, research on developing readers' epistemic beliefs should describe how these readers build the realization that they can challenge the authority of text, and the inaccurate information that texts may contain. Research attention to the development of competency, and growing expertise in determining accuracy, will inform models of evaluative comprehension as well as instruction that helps students meet the demands of text evaluations.

Implications for Instruction

Helping students become adept at identifying inaccurate information and then dealing with it appropriately should be an ongoing goal of instruction. This instruction will be informed by research that describes in detail the developmental trajectory of student readers who are learning to detect and deal with inaccuracy in text. Research should yield information about the types of strategies that student readers need to develop to address inaccuracies when they encounter them. In addition, instruction should focus on the nature of the metacognitive monitoring and evaluation that developing readers must perform to be aware of inaccuracies in text. Finally, instruction should help students understand the relationships between texts and authors, inaccuracy, and the prior knowledge and epistemic beliefs that inform student reading.

In some schools, existing curricula help students focus on distinguishing between facts and opinions and determining whether a text's (or author's) claims are duly supported with evidence. This instructional focus predates Internet reading and helps demonstrate some of the shared characteristics of traditional and Internet reading. Students who are learning to read like historians (VanSledright, 2002; Wineburg, 1991) with traditional text are already searching for evidence to support claims and dealing with texts that present disparate views (or versions of "reality") on the same historical events. These strategies may guide a focus on inaccuracy and transfer readily to Internet reading.

The situated nature of inaccuracy reminds us that readers' epistemic knowledge and beliefs will impact how, when, and whether inaccuracy in text is detected and addressed. When a student reader believes that the contents of text are truthful, the goal for reading is the construction of meaning closest to what the author has written. Students must learn that their world experiences matter when reading particular texts and that challenging the primacy of text when inaccurate information is believed to be present is not only acceptable but preferred. Being a careful and critical reader who detects inaccuracy in Internet texts should relate to students' experiences with popular media. Advertisements, blogs, and other materials where the clear intent is to persuade, argue, or convince are fertile ground for helping students develop the ability to detect inaccuracies. Finding texts and information that are inaccurate, false, or misleading is not difficult, and they can be used as examples of inaccurate text, as well as for understanding the mind-sets and strategies that people utilize for reading them. Finally, students must learn to reconcile their prior knowledge with information in text when the ongoing construction of meaning suggests that one or both sources may contain inaccurate information.

References

Afflerbach, P., & Cho, B. (2009). Identifying and describing constructively responsive comprehension strategies in new and traditional forms of reading. In S. Israel & G. Duffy (Eds.), *Handbook of reading comprehension research* (pp. 69–90). Mahwah, NJ: Lawrence Erlbaum Associates.

Afflerbach, P., & Cho, B. (2010). Determining and describing reading strategies: Internet and traditional forms of reading. In W. Schneider & H. Waters (Eds.), *Metacognition, strategy use, and instruction: A Festschrift for Michael Pressley* (pp. 201–225). New York: Guilford Press.

Afflerbach, P., Cho, B., & Kim, J. (2011). The assessment of higher order thinking skills in reading. In G. Schraw (Ed.), *Current perspectives on cognition, learning, and instruction: Assessment of higher order thinking skills* (pp. 185–215). Omaha, NE: Information Age Publishing.

Alexander, P. (2005). The path to competence: A lifespan developmental perspective on reading. *Journal of Literacy Research, 37,* 413–436.

Alexander, P. A., Kulikowich, J. M., & Jetton, T. L. (1994). The role of subject-matter knowledge and interest in the processing of linear and nonlinear texts [literature review]. *Review of Educational Research, 64,* 201–251.

Armbruster, B. B. (1984). The problem of "inconsiderate texts.". In G. G. Duffy, L. R. Roehler, & J. Mason (Eds.), *Theoretical issues in reading comprehension* (pp. 202–217). White Plains, NY: Longman.

Bråten, I., Strømsø, H. I., & Britt, M. A. (2009). Trust matters: Examining the role of source evaluation in students' construction of meaning within and across multiple text. *Reading Research Quarterly, 44,* 6–28.

Bråten, I., Strømsø, H. I., & Salmerón, L. (2011). Trust and mistrust when students read multiple information sources about climate change. *Learning and Instruction, 21,* 180–192.

Britt, M. A., & Aglinskas, C. (2002). Improving students' ability to identify and use source information. *Cognition and Instruction, 20,* 485–522.

Britt, M. A., Perfetti, C. A., Sandak, R., & Rouet, J. F. (1999). Content integration and source separation in learning from multiple texts. In S. R. Goldman, A. C. Graesser, & P. van den Broek (Eds.), *Narrative comprehension, causality, and coherence: Essays in honor of Tom Trabasso* (pp. 209–233). Mahwah, NJ: Lawrence Erlbaum Associates.

Britt, M. A., & Rouet, J.-F. (2012). Learning with multiple documents: Component skills and their acquisition. In J. R. Kirby & M. J. Lawson (Eds.), *Enhancing the quality of learning: Dispositions, instruction, and learning processes* (pp. 276–314). New York: Cambridge University Press.

Burbules, N., & Callister, T. (1996). Knowledge at the crossroads: Some alternative futures of hypertext learning environments. *Educational Theory, 46*, 23–50.

Cho, B. (2012). *Adolescents' strategy use in an Internet reading task: A verbal protocol analysis.* Manuscript submitted for publication.

Coiro, J. (2011). Predicting reading comprehension on the Internet: Contributions of offline reading skills, online reading skills, and prior knowledge. *Journal of Literacy Research, 43*, 352–392.

Coiro, J., & Dobler, E. (2007). Exploring the online reading comprehension strategies used by sixth-grade skilled readers to search for and locate information on the Internet. *Reading Research Quarterly, 42*, 214–257.

Diakidoy, I. A., & Kendeou, P. (2001). Facilitating conceptual change in astronomy: A comparison of the effectiveness of two instructional approaches. *Learning and Instruction, 11*, 1–20.

Fabos, B. (2008). The price of information. In J. Coiro, M. Knobel, C. Lankshear, & D. J. Leu (Eds.), *Handbook of research on new literacies* (pp. 839–870). New York: Lawrence Erlbaum Associates.

Goldman, S. R. (2004). Cognitive aspects of constructing meaning through and across multiple texts. In N. Shuart-Faris & D. Bloome (Eds.), *Uses of intertextuality in classroom and educational research* (pp. 317–351). Greenwich, CT: Information Age Publishing.

Goldman, S. R., Braasch, J. L. G., Wiley, J., Graesser, A. C., & Brodowinska, K. (2012). Comprehending and learning from Internet sources: Processing patterns of better and poorer learners. *Reading Research Quarterly, 47*, 356–381.

Grice, H. P. (1975). Logic and conversation. In P. Cole & J. Morgan (Eds.), *Studies in syntax and semantics: Vol. 3. Speech acts* (pp. 183–198). New York: Academic Press.

Hartman, D. K. (1995). Eight readers reading: The intertextual links of proficient readers reading multiple passages. *Reading Research Quarterly, 30*, 520–561.

Kintsch, W. (1998). *Comprehension: A paradigm for cognition.* Cambridge, England: Cambridge University Press.

Kuiper, E., Volman, M., & Terwel, J. (2005). The Web as an information resource in K–12 education: Strategies for supporting students in searching and processing information. *Review of Educational Research, 75*, 285–328.

Leiserowitz, A. (2006). Climate change risk perception and policy preferences: The role of affect, imagery, and values. *Climatic Change, 77*, 45–72.

Leu, D., Zawilinski, L., Castek, J., Banerjee, M., Housand, B., Liu, Y., et al. (2008). What is new about the new literacies of online reading comprehension? In L. Rush, A. Eakle, & A. Berger (Eds.), *Secondary school literacy: What research reveals for classroom practice* (pp. 37–68). Chicago: National Council of Teachers of English.

Linderholm, T., & van den Broek, P. (2002). The effects of reading purpose and working memory capacity on the processing of expository text. *Journal of Educational Psychology, 94*, 778–784.

Masoff, J. (2010) *Our Virginia: Past and present.* West Palm Beach, FL: Five Ponds Press.

McConnell, D. (2010). Dozens of errors cited in Virginia textbook. Retrieved from http://www.cnn.com/2010/US/12/30/virginia.textbook.errors.

Meyer, B. J. F. (2003). Text coherence and readability. *Topics in Language Disorders, 23*, 204–221.

Pan, Z., & Kosicki, G. (1994). Voters' reasoning processes and media influences during the Persian Gulf War. *Political Behavior, 16*, 117–156.

Perfetti, C. A., Rouet, J.-F., & Britt, M. A. (1999). Toward a theory of document representation. In H. van Oostendorp & S. R. Goldman (Eds.), *The construction of mental representation during reading* (pp. 99–122). Mahwah, NJ: Lawrence Erlbaum Associates.

Pressley, M., & Afflerbach, P. (1995). *Verbal protocols of reading: The nature of constructively responsive reading.* Hillsdale, NJ: Lawrence Erlbaum Associates.

Rouet, J.-F. (2006). *The skills of document use: From text comprehension to Web-based learning.* Mahwah, NJ: Lawrence Erlbaum Associates.

Rouet, J.-F., & Britt, M. A. (2011). Relevance processes in multiple document comprehension. In M. T. McCrudden, J. P. Magliano, & G. Schraw (Eds.), *Text relevance and learning from text* (pp. 19–52). Greenwich, CT: Information Age Publishing.

Salmerón, L., Cañas, J. J., Kintsch, W., & Fajardo, I. (2005). Reading strategies and hypertext comprehension. *Discourse Processes, 40*, 171–191.

Sargent, G. (2012). Fact checking for thee, but not for me. Retrieved November 22, 2012, from: http://www.washingtonpost.com/blogs/plum-line/post/fact-checking-for-thee-but-not-for-me/2012/08/28/cccd6036-f11d-11e1-892d-bc92fee603a7_blog.html).

Shtulman, A. (2011). Why people do not understand evolution: An analysis of the cognitive barriers to fully grasping the unity of life. *Skeptic, 16*, 41–46.

Strømsø, H. I., Bråten, I., & Samuelstuen, M. S. (2003). Students' strategic use of multiple sources during expository text reading: A longitudinal think-aloud study. *Cognition and Instruction, 21*, 113–147.

Tampa Bay Times (2014). Retrieved January 6, 2014 from: http://www.politifact.com/truth-o-meter/statements/2012/aug/07/mitt-romney/mitt-romney-says-barack-obamas-plan-abandons-tenet/.

van den Broek, P., Risden, K., & Husebye-Hartmann, E. (1995). The role of readers' standards for coherence in the generation of inferences during reading. In R. F. Lorch, Jr., & E. J. O'Brien (Eds.), *Sources of coherence in text comprehension* (pp. 353–373). Mahwah, NJ: Lawrence Erlbaum Associates.

van Dijk, T. (1999). Towards a theory of context and experience models in discourse processing. In H. van Osstendorp & S. Goldman (Eds.), *The construction of mental models during reading* (pp. 123–148). Hillsdale, NJ: Lawrence Erlbaum Associates.

VanSledright, B. A. (2002). Fifth graders investigating history in the classroom: Results from a researcher–practitioner design experiment. *Elementary School Journal, 103*, 131–160.

Veenman, M., Van Hout-Wolters, B., & Afflerbach, P. (2006). Metacognition and learning: Conceptual and methodological considerations. *Metacognition and Learning, 1*, 3–14.

Wiley, J., Goldman, S., Graesser, A., Sanchez, C., Ash, I., & Hemmerich, J. (2009). Source evaluation, comprehension, and learning in internet science inquiry tasks. *American Educational Research Journal, 46*, 1060–1106.

Wineburg, S. (1991). Historical problem solving: A study of the cognitive processes used in the evaluation of documentary and pictorial evidences. *Journal of Educational Psychology, 83*, 73–87.

19   Epistemic Cognition and Evaluating Information: Applying the AIR Model of Epistemic Cognition

Clark A. Chinn, Ronald W. Rinehart, and Luke A. Buckland

In this chapter, we elaborate a model of epistemic cognition and explain how this model can be applied to help account for how people evaluate information, including inaccurate information. *Epistemic cognition* refers to the complex of cognitions that are related to the achievement of epistemic ends; notable epistemic ends include knowledge, understanding, useful models, explanations, and the like. We call our model the AIR model, with the three letters of the acronym referring to the three components of epistemic cognition: *A*ims and value, epistemic *I*deals, and *R*eliable processes for achieving epistemic ends. We will explain each of these components of the model and discuss the role that the cognitions within each component play in people's evaluation of inaccurate (as well as accurate) information. In presenting our model, we will use a variety of examples of people processing inaccurate information, including inaccurate information on the topics of vaccinations, global climate change, and evolution.

The AIR Model

The AIR model has three components, which we briefly introduce below.

Aims and Value

The first component of the model comprises individuals' aims and the value they place on various aims. For example, in investigating Web sites about vaccines, a mother (we'll call her Gisela throughout our examples in this chapter) may be motivated by the goal of finding out the truth about whether vaccines are safe for her children. This goal has practical value for her because she wants her children to be healthy. In contrast, a debate team member debating vaccinations might simply want to find the most rhetorically powerful arguments to persuade people, regardless of the truth of the matter. These are very different aims which can be expected to influence cognitive processing.

Epistemic Ideals

The model's second component consists of a person's *epistemic ideals*, which are the standards that a person uses to evaluate whether epistemic ends have been achieved. For example, philosophers of science have posited that scientists use ideals such as fit with evidence and fit with other theories as core standards for evaluating how good their theories are (e.g., Newton-Smith, 1981). In the vaccine vignette, Gisela may adopt the epistemic ideal that a true explanation will not have any strong counterevidence that threatens it. Gisela may be tacitly committed to this epistemic ideal without being explicitly aware of all of it completely. For example, if asked what her criteria for true scientific explanations are, she might not spontaneously articulate the idea that true explanations are not threatened by counterevidence. Nevertheless, whenever she is presented with an explanation that she knows to be threatened by strong counterevidence, she generally chooses not to believe that explanation; this indicates that the criterion tacitly influences her judgments.

Reliable Processes for Achieving Epistemic Ends

The third component of the model comprises causal schemas specifying the processes by which knowledge and other epistemic products are reliably produced. These schemas may manifest themselves as beliefs (which again may be tacit). For example, Gisela could believe that institutional processes by which scientists replicate results are important for the reliable production of scientific knowledge. Hence, when she reads that a study concluding that vaccines cause autism has not been replicated, she reduces the credence she gives to that study. Thus, Gisela uses beliefs about a reliable process for producing knowledge to discount inaccurate knowledge claims that failed to utilize this reliable process.

Current Literature on Epistemic Cognition

There is a now very large and swiftly growing literature on *epistemic cognition*. The objects of these investigations go by a "bewildering" array of names (Gottlieb & Wineburg, 2012, p. 87), including epistemological beliefs (Schommer, 1990), epistemic beliefs (Schraw, Bendixen, & Dunkle, 2002), the development of epistemic understanding (D. Kuhn, Cheney, & Weinstock, 2000), and personal epistemology (Hofer & Pintrich, 2002). Following R. Kitchener (2002), Greene, Azevedo, and Torney-Purta (2008) suggested that the field adopt *epistemic cognition* as the cover term for all of these targets of investigation. We follow their recommendation. What has unified this work to date is the assumption that epistemic cognition consists broadly of cognitions related to *knowledge* and *processes of knowing* (Hofer & Pintrich, 1997). (In a later section, we will argue that this focus on knowledge and knowing is inappropriately restrictive.)

Contemporary research on epistemic cognition was originally stimulated by the research of developmental psychologists, including Perry (1968/1999) and King and Kitchener (1994), who explored stage theories of development. Stage theorists propose a series of changes in the sophistication of epistemic cognition over time. For example, D. Kuhn and Weinstock (2002) posited four distinct developmental stages of increasing epistemic sophistication: realist, absolutist, multiplist, and evaluatist. According to this theory, young children with a realist perspective believe that ideas are copies of a directly knowable and certain external reality, and "critical thinking" is unnecessary. Children in the absolutist stage view knowledge as a representation of an external reality that can be known with certainty; critical thinking is used to evaluate the accuracy of this representation. The multiplist regards ideas as mere opinions; critical thinking is pointless because there is no way to judge one idea better than another. Finally, the evaluatist regards reality as knowable, but only indirectly, and critical thinking is viewed as a valuable tool for assessing uncertain human judgments about that reality.

Other theorists (e.g., Schommer, 1990) have developed a family of alternative models in which epistemic cognition is treated as a set of potentially independent dimensions of belief rather than as coherent theories. In what is probably the most influential model, Hofer and Pintrich (1997) argued for four dimensions of epistemic beliefs. Two of these dimensions of beliefs are beliefs about the nature of knowledge: (1) beliefs about the certainty of knowledge and (2) beliefs about the simplicity or complexity of knowledge. The other two dimensions of beliefs are beliefs about the process of knowing: (3) beliefs about the source of knowledge (e.g., authority vs. personal experience as sources of knowledge) and (4) beliefs about the justification for knowing (e.g., justifications based on authority vs. personal experience). These four dimensions of beliefs have been the dominant framework guiding research on epistemic cognition during the past 15 years (Chinn, Buckland, & Samarapungavan, 2011; hereinafter CBS).

Belief models of epistemic cognition have been used to explain how people process inaccurate information. For example, Sinatra and Nadelson (2011) used the Hofer and Pintrich (1997) model to explain differences between supporters of evolution and supporters of Christian creationism. They noted, for instance, that creationists are more likely to justify knowledge based on authority (e.g., the authority of the Bible or church authorities) rather than on experience or evidence. Thus, creationists' epistemic belief that knowledge is to be based on biblical authority can explain why they reject evolutionary texts presenting empirical evidence for evolutionary theory and instead accept inaccurate texts compatible with biblical authority.

As another example, Bråten, Strømsø, and Samuelstuen (Bråten, Strømsø, & Samuelstuen, 2008; Strømsø, Bråten, & Samuelstuen, 2008) used the Hofer and Pintrich model to explain students' approaches to processing accurate and inaccurate information about global warming. They used texts that included conflicting information on the topic. They found that students who believed that knowledge about climate change is complex scored better on measures of understanding. They also found that students who believed that knowledge is personally constructed (a belief about the source of knowledge) performed more poorly on comprehension tasks than did students who believed that experts are the source of knowledge. Students' epistemic beliefs were associated with their understanding of texts that included inaccurate information casting doubt on global warming. Thus, research on epistemic cognition indicates that epistemic beliefs influence processing of information.

Elaborating the AIR Model and Applying It to Explain How People Process Accurate and Inaccurate Information

The Hofer and Pintrich (1997) model and other multidimensional belief models (e.g., Schommer, 1990) have stimulated a great deal of productive research. However, CBS (2011) argued for an expanded view of epistemic cognition. This chapter presents a further elaboration of the CBS (2011) model, which we call the AIR model of epistemic cognition. In each of the three sections below, we (1) explicate the epistemic cognition component more fully and (2) explain how the component is involved in successful and unsuccessful processing of inaccurate information.

Component 1: Aims and Value

Explication   Aims are the goals or intended objectives of cognition and action. Epistemic aims are goals to achieve epistemic ends.[1] Epistemologists and philosophers of science have discussed a broad range of epistemic ends, including knowledge, understanding, explanation, justification, true belief, the avoidance of false belief, useful scientific models, and wisdom.

   Our framework differs from previous frameworks in three respects. First, the very inclusion of aims as an explicit component of epistemic cognition is novel. Previous models treated motivation as something distinct from epistemic cognition. However, CBS (2011) argued that, because some aims are clearly epistemic (e.g., achieving knowledge or understanding) whereas others are not (e.g., achieving happiness or preserving one's good self-image), it does not make sense to exclude all aims or goals from the realm of epistemic cognition. CBS (2011) further argued that epistemic aims are critical to understanding epistemic cognition. For example, to understand how a reader will process information presented in a magazine article on global warming, it is critical to know whether she cares anything about epistemic aims such as truth, accuracy, or the like. If she does, she may use epistemic strategies appropriate to attaining truth (such as trying to determine where the weight of the evidence lies); if not, she may fail to process the text at all.

A second difference is that the AIR model includes a broader range of epistemic aims and ends. Most research on epistemic cognition has focused exclusively on cognition pertaining to *knowledge*. This restriction seems, on the surface, to be justified by the fact that that when epistemologists define their own field, they also tend to focus on knowledge. However, as CBS (2011) documented, if one looks more closely at philosophical practices, it becomes clear that epistemologists study a range of (interrelated) epistemic aims—*not* only knowledge. Other epistemic aims that philosophers have considered to be valuable include true beliefs, justified beliefs, understanding, wisdom, explanation, models, evidence, significant (rather than trivial) true beliefs, and the avoidance of false beliefs, among others.

In view of this philosophical work, it would be a conceptual mistake for psychologists to limit their definitions of epistemic cognition solely to cognitions related to *knowledge* and *knowing*. Crucially, these other epistemic ends can differ from knowledge in important ways. For example, whereas scientific *knowledge* claims can potentially be evaluated as true or false, scientific *models* are generally not considered to be straightforwardly evaluable simply as true or false. Instead, models are intended to function as representations which depict some specified aspect of the world in a targeted (usually highly approximated and idealized) way (Giere, 1988). Models are therefore better evaluated in terms of nonbinary criteria of degree of accuracy, degree of similarity, utility, or fruitfulness. This feature of models distinguishes them from traditional accounts of knowledge (e.g., the Platonic), on which the propositional content of a knowledge claim allows it to be evaluated in terms of truth and falsity. Thus, epistemic aims are not limited simply to *knowledge*. What all these aims (including knowledge, understanding, models, true beliefs, etc.) have in common is their representational nature, their providing a particular "take" on how things are, and thus their depiction of the world as one way and not another (K. Z. Elgin, personal communication, February 1, 2013).

The third difference between the AIR model and previous models is its inclusion of the value component, which CBS (2011) argued is crucial for understanding epistemic cognition. For instance, when evaluating vaccination information, a mother may value accurate information about vaccines for the practical goal of enhancing her children's health, whereas she does not particularly value knowledge about kidney disorders, because she thinks that she and her family are unlikely to suffer from kidney disorders. Knowledge about vaccinations is more *significant* for her than knowledge about kidney disorders. The value she assigns to knowledge about various topics will likely affect how she processes and seeks out information on those topics. For example, if she generally values true beliefs about the world (on topics such as global warming), she is more likely to set epistemic aims to acquire them; in contrast, if she places a higher value on camaraderie with her in-group and avoidance of disagreement with her friends (who virulently oppose global warming theory), she may instead set the goal of adopting the beliefs of her in-group (cf. Nussbaum & Bendixen, 2003).

Applications to Processing Inaccurate Information

Individuals' epistemic aims and values can influence how they process texts (both oral and written), including texts that may have inaccurate information. We suggest three influences.

Text Processing Is Influenced by Whether or Not Individuals Set Epistemic Aims on a Topic   In many situations, individuals may adopt nonepistemic aims rather than epistemic aims. Nonepistemic aims are aims not directed at cognitive representational goals such as truth, knowledge, or understanding. Nonepistemic aims thus include experiencing pleasure, avoiding effort and finishing as quickly as possible, outperforming others, garnering social prestige, and protecting one's positive self-image (whether justified or not). In some contexts, nonepistemic aims may effectively supplant or strongly outweigh epistemic aims. In these cases, people are likely to process inaccurate information superficially.

For example, high school students asked to summarize a text on vaccinations in a class may simply want to complete the task as quickly as possible. These students might not care at all whether they acquire any enduring true beliefs about vaccinations or any understanding of the issues but might instead set a nonepistemic aim of just getting done quickly. Because the nonepistemic aim of just finishing has supplanted epistemic aims such as finding out the truth of the matter, these students will likely process the text superficially, without asking themselves whether the text is accurate, and certainly without checking other information sources to corroborate accuracy.

As a second example, Kruglanski's work shows that some people prefer to "seize" quickly on any belief and then "freeze" on that belief, without considering alternatives any further, because they find the sensation of being undecided—of not having a belief on an issue—to be unpleasant (Kruglanski & Webster, 1996). Using the AIR framework, we explain this as the adoption of a nonepistemic aim: People who seize quickly on beliefs have adopted the nonepistemic aim of just attaining any belief at all, regardless of the truth. Thus, these people often seize on the first idea they come across, even if it is grounded in highly inaccurate information. Although people who tend to seize and freeze on the first belief they encounter would probably not describe themselves as indifferent toward the truth, their actual aims—as shown in their behavior—appear to be nonepistemic.

Finally, some research indicates that people have an aversion to engaging in arguments, instead preferring to promote group harmony and avoid any overt disagreement (Chinn & Clark, 2013). Because overt disagreement addressed through argumentative discussion is an important method of advancing knowledge (Goldman, 1999), people who prioritize group harmony over argumentation are, in effect, preferring the aim of group harmony over acquiring the best justified beliefs. Again, nonepistemic aims can harm knowledge acquisition when they are allowed to outweigh epistemic aims.

Thus, a first question to ask about how people process informational text is this: What are their aims as they process the text? When nonepistemic aims trump epistemic aims, people are unlikely to attend much to the accuracy of the information, nor will they invest energy in evaluating accuracy.

When People Do Adopt Epistemic Aims, Text Processing Is Influenced by the Particular Epistemic Aims that They Adopt   If an individual does adopt an epistemic aim when tackling new information, it is psychologically important to know exactly *which* aim (or aims) the individual has adopted. To show why this is important, we discuss three examples below.

First, consider the potential tension between the epistemic aims of acquiring true beliefs and avoiding false beliefs. A person who strongly fears being duped into holding false beliefs will be cautious about adopting new beliefs in the first place; this person may respond to the global warming debate simply by holding belief in abeyance, preferring to avoid the chance of acquiring false beliefs on the topic. There would be little reason for such a person to process information on global warming deeply once a decision to hold belief in abeyance is made. In contrast, a person who values the acquisition of true beliefs more highly may process information more carefully, trying to determine what is accurate and what is inaccurate, willing to take the risk of being wrong. Thus, some people may be more liberal in adopting new beliefs and others more conservative (CBS, 2011). A highly conservative approach may lead people to withhold belief on controversial issues as long as they are controversial.

Second, consider two people with different understandings of scientists' epistemic aims when they conduct research on global warming. A person who regards the aim of science to be the development of imperfect, oversimplified (yet highly useful) models will not be surprised or dismayed to see evidence that a prominent climate model is not perfectly predictive, because this individual understands that successful scientific models represent reality in some respects but not others and are never perfectly predictive (Giere, 1988). In contrast, an individual who views the aim of science as producing knowledge that can be classified straightforwardly as true or false may conclude that modest discrepancies faced by a climate change model prove that the model is false. In this way, people's understanding of the epistemic aims of scientists may strongly shape their evaluations of how well current models fit the evidence.

As a third example, consider the epistemic aims of creationists. Chinn and Buckland (2011) analyzed the epistemic aims of young earth creationists and evolutionary scientists. They argued that the preeminent aim of evolutionary scientists is to account for empirical data, whereas young earth creationists' highest epistemic aims are to know the truth of the Bible and to spread that truth. Thus, a creationist who evaluates inaccurate information asserting that human fossils have been discovered comingled with dinosaur fossils will see this information as fully compatible with their overall aims and will not treat it critically. To understand how creationists evaluate inaccurate texts about creationism or evolution, it is critical to recognize that they are engaging in the evaluation process with epistemic aims that differ from those of noncreationists.

In short, we contend that, to understand how people with epistemic aims evaluate texts that may include inaccurate information, it is critical to know what epistemic aims they have adopted. A productive research strategy for psychologists would therefore be to examine which epistemic aims (if any) people adopt as they seek out or encounter information.

Text Processing Is Influenced by the Interactions between Epistemic and Nonepistemic Aims   The AIR model also posits that interactions between epistemic and nonepistemic aims shape processes of text evaluation. These aims can interact in a variety of different ways to influence text processing. We discuss three examples below.

First, nonepistemic aims can alter epistemic standards that people use. Consider a committed coffee drinker who reads a study showing evidence of harmful effects of caffeine (Kunda, 1990). The coffee drinker harshly evaluates the methodology of the study and concludes that the results are not credible; she thus attains her nonepistemic aim of preserving positive self-beliefs about her health (whether true or not). However, the nonepistemic aim does not completely override the epistemic aim of finding out the truth about whether caffeine is harmful. When she encounters an increasing number of studies reporting similar findings, she does alter her belief and concludes that coffee has some harmful effects (Kunda, 1990). In contrast, when this individual evaluates scientific research that does not challenge her self-beliefs in this way, she is willing to change her beliefs after encountering fewer studies. Thus, her nonepistemic aims lead her to raise her evidentiary standards so that a higher bar is set before she will change her beliefs.

Second, nonepistemic aims may enhance epistemic aims. If the coffee drinker in the previous example had valued the nonepistemic aim of health much higher than the nonepistemic aim of preserving positive self-beliefs about health, then her strong nonepistemic aim to achieve health would enhance the epistemic aim to acquire true beliefs about whether coffee is healthy. A person with this aim would want to be especially careful and evenhanded in evaluating both accurate and inaccurate information about coffee, regardless of which belief was best supported by the evidence.

As a third example of nonepistemic aims' interacting with epistemic aims, a student in a university class learning about vaccines may set as his preeminent aim getting the highest score in the class. Although outperforming others is a nonepistemic aim, if this student also has the belief that he will perform better on exams if he gains a deep understanding of the material, then his nonepistemic goal will spur him to strive hard to achieve the epistemic goal of understanding. If, on the other hand, he has the belief that high scores on exams require rote memorization of terms with little understanding, then his nonepistemic aim will cause him to steer away from the epistemic aim of understanding and instead focus on rote memorization. Thus, interactions of epistemic and nonepistemic aims are complex and may hinge on other beliefs as well as other features of the setting.

These examples are intended to illustrate the possibility that nonepistemic aims may interact in different ways with epistemic aims. An important goal of research should therefore be to uncover the mechanisms by which different interactions have their effects.

Component 2: Epistemic Ideals

Explication   We have adapted the notion of *epistemic ideals* from the work of philosophers of science who have written about scientists' *explanatory ideals* (Toulmin, 1972). An explanatory ideal is a property or attribute of a good, successful explanation; it can thus be viewed as a criterion or standard that must be met for an explanation to be good. Among the explanatory ideals discussed by philosophers are that a good explanation (1) explains a broad scope of evidence, (2) is not contradicted by significant evidence, (3) is fruitful for future research, (4) is internally consistent, (5) coheres with other, accepted scientific explanations, and (6) (in some fields) specifies a causal mechanism (e.g., T. Kuhn, 1977; Newton-Smith, 1981). Laypeople may subscribe to other ideals—for example, that explanations should fit one's personal everyday experiences. In broadening the notion of explanatory ideals to other epistemic ends (knowledge, understanding, models, etc.), we can say that a person's *epistemic ideals* specify the criteria or standards that must be met for them to judge that their epistemic ends have been achieved. Thus, a person might believe that the standards that must be met for a belief to be counted as knowledge are that the beliefs are true and justified. Or she might believe that understanding involves the grasping of connections between ideas; these will be a part of her epistemic ideals for understanding (cf. Kvanvig, 2003).

We propose that people's epistemic ideals fall into five broad categories. First, some ideals specify the *internal structure* of an explanation (e.g., the explanation specifies a causal mechanism; it is internally consistent; it is sufficiently *complex*). Second, other epistemic ideals involve *connections to other knowledge* (e.g., cohering with other explanations). Third, still others involve present and future connections to *empirical evidence* (e.g., explain a broad scope of evidence, are not contradicted by significant evidence, and successfully predict new evidence). Fourth, other ideals involve the standards that one expects to be met when believing testimony from others; for example, testimony is more believable when it is given by someone who is sincere and in a position to know

(Williams, 2002). Fifth, a person can prefer explanations that embody the ideal of being clearly presented and understandable (Staley, 2004); these ideals could be called ideals of good communication (Pluta, Chinn, & Duncan, 2011).

Epistemic ideals are thus the criteria or standards that people use to evaluate whether they have achieved their epistemic ends. For example, one can use the ideal of "explains a broad scope of evidence" as an epistemic criterion or standard for evaluating the acceptability of explanations.

The AIR model differs from previous models in that it merges into a single broad component two components that other models typically keep separate. For example, the Hofer and Pintrich (1997) model separates the structure of knowledge and the justification of knowledge into separate categories. The AIR model posits that these two categories share something crucial: Criteria in both categories are produced as reasons or justifications for claims. For example, when providing reasons (or justifications) for why a scientific theory is good, a person might mention its simplicity and its clear mechanisms (aspects of structure in the Hofer & Pintrich, 1997, model) or its consistency with a broad scope of empirical data or personal experience (aspects of justification in the Hofer and Pintrich framework). *Both* types of reasons are justifications for believing a theory. Indeed, philosophers have mixed these kinds of justifications freely in their lists of epistemic ideals (Newton-Smith, 1981).

In short, all five categories of ideals are criteria that people use to *justify* acceptance of an epistemic product such as an explanation or a theory. For this reason, the AIR model treats them as different subcategories of ideals that are used as standards of justification.

According to the AIR model, there is situational variation in people's use of epistemic ideals. First, a person may apply an epistemic ideal in one situation but not another. For example, students in science classes may apply the ideal of ensuring that their ideas are coherent in one instructional setting but not another (Rosenberg, Hammer, & Phelan, 2006). Second, people may use different ideals on different topics. For example, children expect evidentiary ideals to be relevant to resolving scientific but not aesthetic disagreements (Wainryb, Shaw, Laupa, & Smith, 2001). Third, these ideals may be weighted differently in different situations. For example, scientists generally are thought to treat fit with evidence as their predominant ideal (e.g., Longino, 2002; Solomon, 2001), yet there was a period of many decades when scientists opted for the sun-centered Copernican theory over the earth-centered Ptolemaic theory, even though the Ptolemaic theory's predictions fit the observed positions of the planets more accurately at that time (T. Kuhn, 1962). These scientists evidently judged that the greater simplicity and fruitfulness of the Copernican theory outweighed its slightly poorer fit with the available evidence. Future research should endeavor to map out how the use of epistemic ideals varies across situations and to explain how and why these variations occur.

There is a small but important body of evidence indicating that people, even children, employ epistemic ideals in their reasoning. Samarapungavan (1992) found that children as young as 6 and 7 used explanatory ideals discussed by philosophers. In an explanation-choice task, the children preferred explanations that accounted for a greater range of data, that were not threatened by contradictory data, and that were simpler (other things being equal). Similarly, Pluta et al. (2011) found that seventh graders were able, with minimal instruction, to articulate epistemic criteria for what makes a good model or explanation; in doing so, they collectively generated most of the criteria that philosophers have identified as part of scientific practice.

Applications to Processing Inaccurate Information We propose that people's epistemic ideals influence how they process texts (oral or written) that may contain inaccurate information. We illustrate these influences with the three example below.

First, Chinn and Buckland (2011) analyzed epistemic differences among various groups of creationists and evolutionary scientists. Many of the differences involve *epistemic ideals*. For example, evolutionary scientists evaluate scientific explanations against the epistemic ideals of providing as much explanatory detail as possible, cohering with the rest of science, and invoking only material causes. In contrast, for young earth creationists, good explanations in the domain of speciation should invoke nonmaterial causes (i.e., a divine being), and it is permissible for explanations to be radically incompatible with the rest of science (e.g., belief in an 8,000-year-old cosmos is incompatible with almost all of geology and astronomy and with much of physics). Thus, when creationists read an evolutionary text explaining how evolution works (via material causes), the very content of the explanation violates one of their core epistemic ideals in this domain. Contrarily, inaccurate texts touting God as the origin of species *do* meet their epistemic ideal, and so they evaluate these texts more highly. To understand how supporters of creationism and supporters of evolutionary theory approach and evaluate texts on creationism and evolution, it is critical to appreciate this core difference in their explanatory ideals.

The recent vaccine controversies in the United States and the United Kingdom also illustrate the role of explanatory ideals in shaping the processing of inaccurate information. The antivaccine movement maintains that vaccines should be avoided because they are the cause of serious disorders, particularly autism. Jacobson, Targonski, and Poland (2007) and Kata (2012) have analyzed the reasoning of antivaccine activists. They argued that a prominent feature of the activists' thinking is that, to be counted as a successful causal explanation, every event is required to have an identifiable and determinate cause. This ideal entails that, if a child has autism, there must be an identifiable cause or set of causes, such as a vaccination. In contrast, scientists often do not offer explanations of this type. Instead, scientific explanations are often stochastic, asserting only that a cause brings about a certain effect *on average*. If vaccine opponents' explanatory ideal is that explanations must be able to explain each individual event, stochastic scientific explanations are unsatisfactory from the outset and will be rejected. In contrast, an explanation that straightforwardly attributes individual cases of autism to prior vaccinations will meet their faulty explanatory ideal, and they will likely be much more receptive to this inaccurate information.

As a final example, consider the case of global warming. The claim that human civilization is the cause of rising global temperatures is grounded in complex computer models of planetary ecology, which (for all their complexity) are nonetheless, like all models, oversimplifications. It seems likely, then, that people's explanatory ideals regarding such computer models will be an important influence on their evaluations and the conclusions derived from them. Yearley (1999) studied how the citizens of Sheffield, U.K., understood a computer model used by their city to make projections of air quality. Yearley found that the participating citizens were particularly critical of those aspects of the model that they regarded as oversimplified; for example, including only some (rather than all) pollutants was considered to be suspect. Thus, the participants held epistemic ideals for models that actual models cannot meet, and in fact are not intended to meet, because models deliberately oversimplify. This suggests that public skepticism about explanations and predictions grounded in computer models may arise in part because the public holds models to a higher standard than scientists do. When these individuals read Web sites criticizing computer models for being over-simplifications, they will be inclined to accept these inaccurate claims because their epistemic ideals lead them to be suspicious of any model that does not try to capture all aspects of the real world.

In summary, we conclude that understanding people's epistemic ideals is important for understanding how they respond to inaccurate information. There has been relatively little psychological research, however, on people's epistemic ideals; we think that investigations of these ideals would be very productive.

Component 3: Reliable Processes for Producing Epistemic Products

Explication   The third component of the AIR model consists of schemas specifying the reliable processes by which epistemic products (such as knowledge, understanding, explanations, or models) are produced. This component of epistemic cognition is grounded in the philosophical theory of process reliabilism developed by Alvin Goldman (1976, 1986, 1999). Goldman developed his theory as an account of knowledge and justification, as well as a framework for understanding the individual and social processes that produce knowledge or true beliefs. In the AIR model, the *reliable processes* component of epistemic cognition consists of cognitions related to reliable and unreliable processes for producing epistemic ends.

In explicating the reliable processes component of AIR, we focus on processes for producing one particular type of epistemic end—true beliefs—but the discussion can be straightforwardly extended to other epistemic ends (knowledge, understanding, etc.). We start from the observation that there exist many different causal processes that can be used to try to produce true beliefs; these processes vary in reliability. A reliable process is one that produces a relatively high proportion of true beliefs. An unreliable process, by contrast, produces a relatively low proportion of true beliefs. Here are some examples of various reliable and unreliable processes:

- Under conditions of good lighting, visual observation is a reliable process for producing true beliefs about the prosaic world around us, such as true beliefs about where the furniture is in a room.
- Reasoned argumentation, in which people carefully consider multiple perspectives and share reasons and evidence about which perspective is best, is in general a reliable process for producing true beliefs.
- When scientific research is conducted, true beliefs are more likely to be produced when scientists employ the reliable process of carefully recording data (rather than relying only on memory).
- Asking an expert paleontologist to identify a fossil in her area of expertise is a reliable means of producing true beliefs about the species that was fossilized.
- Reading a horoscope is an unreliable process for producing true beliefs about people's personalities.
- Conducting controlled but unmasked clinical trials is an unreliable process for producing true beliefs about the efficacy of a drug.

One can quickly generate long lists of processes that tend to be reliable or unreliable for producing true beliefs, as well as processes whose degree of reliability is uncertain. Thus, achieving true beliefs about the world requires a vast store of knowledge about the reliability of a wide variety of such processes. This, then, is a core assumption of AIR: A great deal of epistemic cognition consists of networks of knowledge (no doubt largely tacit) of causal processes for producing true beliefs and other epistemic products. We treat these as schemas specifying what these reliable and unreliable processes are.

Conditions under Which Processes Are Reliable The vast network of schemas specifying processes that reliably produce true beliefs includes slots that specify the conditions under which these processes tend to operate successfully, as well as the conditions under which they tend to fail. Consider observation as an example. Although visual observation is typically a good process for producing true beliefs about the everyday world, people are aware of conditions under which observation is degraded and unreliable: Visual observation is not reliable when it is very dark, when the distances are too great, when observers are not paying attention, and so on. People are also aware that visual observation has limits in the kinds of true beliefs it can produce; although visual observation can help produce true beliefs about the number of chairs in the living room, it is not reliable (without aids such as rulers) for determining the precise width of the chairs. Thus, people's knowledge about the process of observation includes knowledge of the conditions under which observation tends to produce true beliefs and conditions under which it does not. People's beliefs about these conditions may be in error. A great deal of research on eyewitness observations and reports shows that people have mistaken beliefs about the conditions under which these observational reports are reliable; for example, most people are unaware that facial recognition of suspects is very poor under conditions in which the suspect wields a weapon (Magnussen, Melinder, Stridbeck, & Raja, 2010; Wise, Pawlenko, Safer, & Meyer, 2009).

Similarly, although reasoned argumentation is in general a good means for producing true beliefs, it is a good means only under certain conditions. If the argumentation degrades into an angry debate that is devoid of reasons, or if some participants are intimidated and do not speak their minds freely, then argumentation is unlikely to be effective. We posit that people who view reasoned argumentation as a reliable belief-producing process have (perhaps tacit) ideas about the conditions that argumentation must meet to produce true beliefs. We posit further that these people have ideas about what kinds of beliefs can be promoted reliably by argumentation and what kinds of beliefs cannot. For example, some people may appreciate that argumentation can help us decide how best to interpret complex data from an experiment that invites alternative interpretations, but if we have a disagreement about whether the clock across a large room reads 3:08 p.m. or 3:03 p.m., it would be more efficient to walk over and take a closer look. Of course, people may also have inaccurate beliefs about argumentation. Bendixen, Zemp, Keller-Johnson, Winsor, and Feucht (2011) reported that a sample of high school students viewed scientific argumentation as an *unreliable* process for producing scientific knowledge. Further, people may believe that heated debate with few reasons and evidence is a reliable way to produce better knowledge, perhaps because they erroneously believe that they will be able to tell from nonverbal signals which debater is correct.

Thus, a crucial component of epistemic cognition is the vast network of causal schemas that specify reliable and unreliable processes for producing epistemic ends, as well as the specification of the conditions under which these processes are (and are not) reliable. People's schemas may be accurate or erroneous. Indeed, many problems in evaluating inaccurate information arise because people's schemas specifying reliable processes are erroneous.

Three Ways to Use Schemas Specifying Causal Processes for Producing True Beliefs

A person's schemas specifying reliable causal processes for achieving epistemic aims can be used in at least three ways. *First, they can be used to guide investigative action.* For example, a person who has a firm grasp of how to carry out a poll of voters' knowledge can develop and execute a plan for conducting the poll and analyzing the data. *Second, the schemas can be used to evaluate processes used by others to produce knowledge claims.* A person with an accurate understanding of polling methodologies can evaluate a polling firm's description of its methodology in order to form judgments about the accuracy of the poll. For example, a knowledgeable person will know that in recent U.S. elections, Internet-based polls proved more accurate than many of the traditional phone polls (Silver, 2013) and will use this information to appraise new polls accordingly. *Third, the schemas can be used to generate the expression of explicit, metacognitive beliefs about how to produce true beliefs.* For example, an experienced pollster would likely have the explicit knowledge needed to provide detailed explanations about how to conduct a poll or what to take into consideration when evaluating a poll.

All three forms of knowledge about the processes discussed above can be useful in developing true beliefs. Consider how all three uses might be involved in a mother's processing of texts about vaccines in the earlier vaccine vignette. Suppose that the mother has a causal schema indicating that one is more likely to acquire true beliefs if one reviews and reflects on diverse information sources. In accordance with this schema, she spends a great deal of time scouring the Internet for information from reputable sites with diverse perspectives; this is an active use of the schema to try to produce true beliefs by seeking and considering diverse information. The mother may also have metacognitive awareness that examining sites with differing perspectives will increase her likelihood of gaining knowledge (a metacognitive use). And she may conclude that a friend who urges her not to vaccinate her child is not credible because her friend has only read antivaccine literature; by failing to consult diverse sources, her friend has used an unreliable process for belief formation, and the mother therefore deems her friend's testimony to be untrustworthy (an evaluative use).

Costs and Benefits of Using Processes   Reliable processes of knowledge development are not cost free. Deploying them requires time, energy, resources, and attention on the part of the inquirer. A process that will reliably produce true beliefs nearly all of the time will not (and should not) be used if it is overly time-consuming and produces beliefs that are not particularly valuable. Conversely, a process that is easy to use but tends to produce false beliefs produces a different kind of cost—the cost of having (and perhaps acting on) false beliefs. A complete theory of how people process accurate and inaccurate information will need to incorporate an account of their conceptions of the reliable processes for producing true beliefs, as well as their conceptions of the costs and benefits of these processes.

Differences from Previous Models of Epistemic Cognition   Our notion of a network of causal schemas specifying reliable processes for producing true beliefs is a notion that is absent from other models of epistemic cognition. As we have noted, the Hofer and Pintrich (1997) model specifies beliefs about the "nature or process of knowing" as one of the two main dimensions of epistemic beliefs, comprising beliefs about the sources and justification of knowledge. However, this dimension has been operationalized in a relatively static manner. Questionnaire measures that assess these dimensions have not asked people about actual processes of the sort we have just described but rather ask whether people think that knowledge is to be justified by (for example) personal experiences or authority (Hofer, 2000, 2004; Muis, 2007); such justifications do not focus on the actual processes by which knowledge is produced. However, we feel that our notion of reliable processes is not a break from the Hofer and Pintrich model but rather an extension that brings to fruition their core notion of processes of knowing.

Applications to Processing Inaccurate Information   A central premise of the AIR model of epistemic cognition is this: To understand how people process accurate and inaccurate information, it is critical to understand their schemas regarding reliable and unreliable processes for producing true beliefs and other epistemic products. We contend that much of what individuals do when evaluating informative texts can be explained in terms of the schemas they use to decide whether the claims in these texts have been generated using processes that reliably produce true claims.

Epistemic claims in texts (e.g., "Evolutionary theory is the best explanation for how species form") are produced using processes that vary in terms of their reliability, and the evaluator's task is to judge whether the processes used in each particular instance were reliable. Individuals will be able to evaluate these processes more accurately if they have (1) a large and rich network of accurate schemas regarding which processes are reliable and which are unreliable and (2) accurate specifications of the conditions under which each process is more or less reliable.

In contrast, individuals with an impoverished array of schemas will be ill equipped to evaluate the knowledge claims they encounter in informational texts. Such individuals may be susceptible to believing whatever they are told in whatever text they read, regardless of its accuracy, and they will judge knowledge claims grounded in unreliable belief-producing processes to be accurate because they mistakenly regard these processes as reliable. Further, such individuals will reject well-founded knowledge claims grounded in reliable processes if they mistakenly judge these processes to be unreliable. The critical point is that evaluating any representative sample of informative text will require evaluators to draw on a very large repertoire of schemas for evaluating the reliability of processes used to produce the particular claims in that text.

Table 19.1 presents an analysis of eight clusters of processes that can be used to produce knowledge claims. It also discusses schemas that are relevant to evaluating the reliability of those processes. While some of the schemas that people apply are accurate, others are inaccurate. The processes discussed in table 19.1 include (1) individual processes such as observation and memory, epistemic virtues and vices, and processes invoking emotion; personal evidence gathering and processes for reasoning about statistical evidence; and (2) social and institutional processes including peer

Table 19.1

Examples of beliefs about reliable processes: How beliefs about eight clusters of reliable and unreliable processes of knowledge formation are relevant to the processing of inaccurate (and accurate) information

Example Processes	Some of What Experts Know about the Processes	People's Schemas about the Processes	Illustration
1. Observation and memory	Much of what we know (or think we know) derives from observations and what we remember of those observations. However, cognitive research has demonstrated that the observation–memory process is highly fallible.	Eyewitnesses, juries, and prosecutors are more confident in human observations and memories than is warranted (Benton et al. 2006; Wise et al., 2009). Inaccurate beliefs about the reliability of these processes contribute to mistaken evaluations of testimony.	If a juror's schemas for evaluating the reliability of eyewitness reports indicate that observation and memory are inaccurate under conditions of dim light, she will be likely to regard the testimony under these conditions as unreliable and any resulting conviction to be dubious. If not, she will likely accept the quite possibly inaccurate information provided by the eyewitness.
2. Epistemic virtues and vices	Epistemologists have written extensively about epistemic virtues (honesty, open-mindedness, etc.) and vices (dishonesty, closed-mindedness, etc.) (e.g., Zagzebski, 1996). The use of virtues tends to produce true beliefs; the use of vices tends to promote false beliefs.	Individuals' intellectual virtues may dispose them to use strategies associated with honesty, open-mindedness, and so on. People disposed to exemplify these virtues are more likely to reason well and achieve true beliefs (Stanovich, 1999).	A woman's neighbor frequently exemplifies the epistemic vice of being gullible; he is far too ready to believe what others say based on flimsy evidence. He tells the woman that he is convinced that vaccines cause autism. If the woman realizes her neighbor is highly gullible, she will discount what he says. If she does not, or if she views her neighbor's credulity as the virtue of open-mindedness rather than the vice of gullibility, she will not discount what he says.

(continued)

Table 19.1
(*continued*)

Example Processes	Some of What Experts Know about the Processes	People's Schemas about the Processes	Illustration
3. Emotion in knowledge-producing processes	Recent philosophical and psychological work shows that emotions impact the processing of knowledge. For example, excessive anger can cloud judgment, or curiosity can spur more intense efforts to find answers to questions (cf. Thagard, 2012)	Teaching of "the scientific method" often presents science as dispassionate and unemotional (cf. Ryan, 1987). People may therefore inaccurately believe that science can produce truths only if scientists are unaffected by emotion.	In 2009, the emails of some U.K. climate scientists were hacked. These emails revealed that some U.K. climate scientists disparaged opponents in sharp terms. If readers of media reports about these emails believe that such displays of emotion are signs that scientists are using unreliable processes, they may discount the findings of global warming scientists. However, if they grasp that scientists' work is imbued with emotion at all times, then they may not be disturbed by these reports.
4. Personal evidence-gathering processes	Considering multiple perspectives while gathering evidence will more reliably produce knowledge (Solomon, 2001).	Researchers have found that people tend to expose themselves only to information that supports their position (Chinn & Brewer, 1993). People who use this approach as a process for achieving beliefs are more likely to develop inaccurate beliefs.	A mother's friend tells her that she opposes vaccines based on reading only antivaccine Web sites. If the mother believes that true beliefs are more likely to be produced by considering multiple perspectives, she will correctly discount her friend's testimony as unreliable.
5. Processes for reasoning about statistical evidence	Gathering evidence will more reliably produce knowledge when one examines statistically analyzed scientific evidence (where relevant) rather than testimonial evidence, under the conditions of properly identifying and ruling out covariates and so on.	Research with adults shows that many believe testimonials are more reliable than larger studies employing statistical methods (Nisbett & Ross, 1980). These inaccurate beliefs will lead people to trust testimonials that are inaccurate over more accurate statistical information.	A mother reads Web sites with testimonials of parents convinced that a vaccine caused their child's autism. If she believes testimonials are reliable, she may choose not to vaccinate her child. If she is aware of the superiority of statistical methods, she will discount these Web sites.

6. Peer review processes	Peer review processes are widely viewed by scientific communities as enhancing the quality of published scientific work, as reviewers spot problems with submitted work.	A theme in antiscience rhetoric is that the scientific review process serves the aims of a minority of ideologically motivated and well-connected scientists who use selective publishing to suppress alternative views. Such beliefs lead to discounting of all scientific evidence.	If people believe that scientific review processes are more likely to produce knowledge than other methods, they will be more likely to believe scientific findings. If not, they may disbelieve published evidence or secondhand reports of this evidence, because they would view the process as untrustworthy.
7. Survey processes	In modern elections, pollsters have developed highly accurate methods for estimating the composition of those who will go to the polls to vote based on estimating the likelihood that those surveyed will actually vote. Aggregates of polls have proven to be even more accurate than individual polls.	In the 2012 U.S. elections, many conservatives did not believe the polls predicting Barack Obama's victory (Noonan, 2012, November 5). They did not appreciate that the methods used by some pollsters to estimate the likelihood that Obama supporters would show up to vote were more reliable than alternatives.	A U.S. citizen reads conservative commentaries discounting polling results prior to the 2012 U.S. election. If the reader has knowledge of accurate methods of political polling, she will discount the commentaries' claims that Romney will win because the polls are inaccurate. If she does not know about accurate polling methods, she may be persuaded by the arguments in the commentary.
8. Media processes	Media commentators have noted that a common rhetorical tactic on controversial topics is to present equal numbers of opposing experts. This "balance" tactic misleadingly suggests there is an equal division of expert opinion, even if 99% of experts support one position over the other (Tannen, 1998).	Media consumers who are aware of these practices should be more critical of these portrayals, and they should seek more information about what experts think and what evidence exists. Those who lack this knowledge may think that issues that are not very controversial among experts are instead highly controversial.	A magazine reader peruses an article giving equal space to global warming supporters and skeptics. If the reader is aware that the mass media regularly employ the balance tactic even when there is little disagreement among experts, she may try to find out what other experts think or what the weight of evidence is. Otherwise, she may become convinced that there is a legitimate controversy and a lack of consensus.

review processes, survey processes, and media processes. We posit that schemas speci-fying social processes of producing knowledge are a very important part of epistemic cognition.

The processes in table 19.1 are by no means exhaustive; they are a small sample of the processes used to produce knowledge. Nevertheless, the wide scope of processes in table 19.1 illustrates the wide range of reliable processes that are involved in generating and evaluating knowledge claims. We will not recapitulate in the text all the points made in the table but will briefly elaborate on four processes involving how people process texts on vaccinations.

We begin with processes involving virtues and vices. A mother, Gisela, hears from her neighbor that his review of Internet sites has convinced him that vaccines are dangerous. However, Gisela also recalls that her neighbor is particularly gullible when it comes to conspiracy theories. She thus attributes to him the epistemic vice of gull-ibility—which is a disposition to accept knowledge claims too readily and uncritically. An epistemic vice is a disposition which leads one to regularly deploy certain unreli-able strategies for achieving epistemic aims. For Gisela's neighbor, the strategy involves believing too readily a claim based on insufficient grounds. In contrast, an epistemic virtue is a disposition that prompts a person to deploy reliable strategies. If Gisela had instead believed that her neighbor tended to very carefully consider information on both sides of a question (i.e., as exemplifying the epistemic virtues of meticulousness, open-mindedness, and impartiality), she would have been more disposed to accept his claims about vaccines. Gisela's judgment that her neighbor frequently exemplifies the vice of gullibility leads her to discount his conclusions.

Distrusting her neighbor, Gisela decides to gather evidence on her own. She applies her schemas specifying reliable processes of searching out and gathering evidence. Gisela thinks that one highly reliable process for reaching a good judgment is to exam-ine sources on multiple sides of an issue. Her own personal searches for information therefore seek out both provaccine and antivaccine Web sites so as to incorporate mul-tiple sides of the issue.

After reading a sample of vaccine-related Web sites, Gisela finds that antivaccine sites frequently rely heavily on personal testimonials, in which parents tell their stories, convinced that their child's autism was caused by a vaccine. Because she believes that determining causes of disorders requires the use of large samples, sophisticated data-gathering processes, and statistical analyses, Gisela judges that personal testimonials are an unreliable means of determining the causes of autism; she deems the accounts to be unreliable and accordingly ignores them.

Delving deeper, Gisela finds that a common assumption of the antivaccine Web sites is that the Centers for Disease Control (CDC) is a corrupt shill for the vaccine indus-try (Jacobson et al., 2007). However, in investigating several family members' diseases over the years, Gisela has personally found the CDC Web site to give good advice; she has also noticed that some of its recommendations diverge from what would be in the commercial interests of the medical industry. Thus, her own experience with the CDC as a source of information indicates that they are a reliable source of knowledge. In addition, she believes that information appears on the CDC Web site only when it commands a high level of consensus in the expert medical community. In sum, from what she believes about the CDC's processes for producing knowledge claims, Gisela considers these processes to be reliable. Accordingly, she discounts the claims made by antivaccine Web sites and instead bestows a high degree of credence on the CDC Web site.

When Gisela reads a newspaper feature placing arguments from a provaccine doctor side by side with the arguments from an antivaccine activist, she is aware that many media outlets try to appear even handed by using the tactic of "presenting both sides equally." But Gisela views this as an unreliable process for generating true beliefs when there is much more evidence on one side than the other. Applying her knowledge of the relative unreliability of this media practice, she does not fall into the trap of thinking that the two sides have equally strong cases to make.

To thoroughly evaluate the full range of claims encountered in inaccurate and accurate sources on the vaccine issue, Gisela needs to deploy a wide variety of quite specific schemas for evaluating the reliability of specific knowledge-generating processes. For example, one argument made by vaccination opponents is "So many people can't all be wrong." To reject this claim based on popular support, Gisela needs to know about the social and interpersonal processes by which consensus can be achieved, as well as the ways in which these can be unreliable. Another claim made by vaccination opponents is "Science was wrong before." To evaluate this claim, she needs knowledge of past errors in the history of science so that she can judge whether the conditions of scientific practice in vaccine research are similar to the conditions of scientific practice at times when errors were made. To evaluate research data reported on Web sites, Gisela also needs to know about the reliability of many different methodologies she reads about (e.g., animal studies, correlational epidemiological studies, double-blind experimental trials, etc.). In short, a large repertoire of schemas for evaluating the reliability of a wide variety of belief-producing processes is needed for effective evaluation of accurate and inaccurate information.

Summary In summary, the AIR model of epistemic cognition makes the following core claims related to reliable processes and evaluating information. First, a very wide array of belief-producing processes are used to produce knowledge claims. Second, the processes used vary in reliability, with some highly reliable at producing true beliefs and others tending instead to promote false beliefs. Third, among reliable processes, certain conditions must be met for those processes to reliably produce true beliefs. Fourth, to evaluate knowledge claims found in the real world, people need a vast store of schemas for evaluating the processes used to produce those claims. These schemas specify the processes used to produce, justify, and verify knowledge, along with the conditions under which they are and are not effective. A great deal of epistemic cognition consists of this store of causal schemas. Fifth, people's schemas vary in their validity. Some people believe in the efficacy of processes that are in fact unreliable for producing true beliefs, as in the case of people who believe that collecting testimonials is a highly reliable method of achieving knowledge.

To understand how people process accurate and inaccurate information, we need to develop a detailed account of the full range of schemas they use to evaluate the processes invoked for knowledge claims they encounter. To date, researchers have extensively investigated only a very few of the relevant schemas. For example, there is a large and swiftly growing literature on people's schemas for processing information about eyewitness testimony, with findings indicating that people believe that the observation and memory processes involved in eyewitness testimony are much more reliable than they actually are (Benton, Ross, Bradshaw, Thomas, & Bradshaw, 2006; Wise et al., 2009). There is also a large literature on how people understand processes of experimentation. However, this research tends to investigate students' understanding of oversimplified forms of experimentation, which poorly represent the messier and more complex practice of real scientists (Chinn & Malhotra, 2002). Much less is known about how people evaluate the more complex research that scientists undertake.

We thus recommend undertaking a great deal more research on a much wider range of people's schemas related to belief-producing processes. This research should also examine the role these schemas play in their evaluation of information and knowledge construction.

Instructional Implications

In this final discussion, we briefly consider instructional implications of our preceding analyses.

Aims and Value   Our discussion of aims and value points to what seems to us to be a seriously neglected instructional issue—promoting a broad disposition to adopt epistemic aims. Instruction designed to promote better reasoning should, for example, encourage students to care about and seek the truth—even if the truth should prove inconvenient. We are not aware of major educational initiatives that have explicitly made this a central instructional focus. Instead, it appears to us that the large body of research aimed at improving students' thinking does so without explicitly considering whether students value knowledge and truth or how these values might be cultivated through well-designed instruction.

Epistemic Ideals   It is possible to work with students explicitly to help them learn and apply epistemic ideals. Our own research project, in collaboration with Ravit Duncan, aims to help students become explicitly aware of epistemic ideals so as to facilitate their use in evaluating epistemic products (Chinn & Buckland, 2012; Chinn, Duncan, Dianovsky, & Rinehart, 2013; Duncan, Freidenreich, Chinn, & Bausch, 2011). Specifically, in the instruction we have designed, middle school students reflect on a variety of scientific models, and then each class of students generates its own list of public criteria which serve as epistemic ideals for their class. Participating students learn to use these epistemic criteria to evaluate the quality of the models and evidence they encounter. For example, students have developed a variety of ideals for high-quality evidence, including that the evidence be free from bias and that its production be methodologically sound. Ideals for good scientific models include "The model should explain all of the good evidence" and "The model is easy to understand." These ideals are public and maintained as class lists that students can easily refer to during the normal course of instruction. The lists are regularly revised and updated as students develop more sophisticated understandings of what counts as good evidence and models. Throughout the year, students refer to the ideals frequently in their written work and in group and class discussions; students particularly appeal to the ideals in their justifications for the models that they have developed. Our work further indicates that students can learn to use epistemic ideals to distinguish inaccurate from accurate methodological information (Dianovsky et al., 2013).

Reliable Processes for Producing True Beliefs   Our analysis has two important implications for instruction related to reliable processes for producing true beliefs. First, we have argued that to properly evaluate knowledge claims, people need a large repertoire of schemas that specify a wide range of belief-producing processes, how reliable these processes are, and the conditions that affect their reliability. It follows that a prime mission of education should be to help students to develop this repertoire of schemas. Accomplishing this will involve much more than teaching students some basics of conducting scientific research. Students need to be aware of a broad range of methods used across many disciplines. For example, they need to learn about the reliability of the processes by which the mass media produce claims. They should examine problems with the prevalent media practice of giving each side equal voice in a controversy, even if one side is supported by only a tiny minority of experts. They should examine questions such as whether reporters may be biased toward writing positive reports of powerful politicians in order to maintain journalistic access to these politicians. They should learn about survey methodologies and about conditions under which experts are more or less trustworthy. Learning a broad range of such schemas would involve a major departure from current educational goals and practice (Allchin, 2011).

Second, students need to learn how to evaluate the reliability of knowledge-generating processes. An instructional method that teaches students a large array of processes and simply tells them which are reliable or unreliable is unlikely to be effective. Students need to see *why* different processes are reliable or unreliable. Otherwise, they may disbelieve what they are told. For example, it may not be sufficient just to tell them that eyewitness testimony is unreliable; they may need to see evidence, or even gather evidence themselves, to be convinced. In short, students need to see and reflect on evidence that bears on the reliability of different processes, so that they develop a deeper appreciation for why they should treat some processes as worthy of trust and others as unworthy.

Conclusion

In this chapter we have articulated a model of epistemic cognition that expands the scope of what has been traditionally investigated by psychologists. We have argued that the AIR model provides a coherent explanatory framework for understanding cognitions about epistemic matters. We have further argued that this model helps account for the processes by which people process accurate and inaccurate information. The aims and value component of the AIR model reveals the epistemic and nonepistemic goals that a person might adopt, as well as the relative value they place on achieving these various goals. The ideals component of the model illuminates the epistemic standards people use to evaluate epistemic products. Ideals for what counts as a good epistemic product will shape how people process texts that involve (potentially inaccurate) knowledge claims. Reliable processes, the third component of the model, encompass people's schemas specifying the processes by which epistemic ends (like explanations and true beliefs) are achieved. We have argued that, to evaluate texts accurately, people need a very large repertoire of schemas related to the multitude of reliable and unreliable processes implicated in knowledge claims. We think that the AIR model is practical in that it helps explain how people process accurate and inaccurate information, as well as being a useful theoretical construct for shaping investigations into people's inquiry, explanatory, and information-processing practices.

Appendix: Relations between the AIR framework and the CBS (2011) framework

The AIR model integrates the categories of the existing 2011 CBS framework into a more coherent and unified framework, one that better models the features of epistemic cognition that are likely to play a role in reasoning and belief formation. For interested readers, this appendix briefly explains how the AIR model relates to the CBS model.

The *aims and value* component of the AIR model is the same as the aims and value component of the 2011 CBS model. There are no differences in this component.

The *epistemic ideals* component of AIR combines two components of the CBS 2011 framework—the structure of knowledge and justification. Like the Hofer and Pintrich (1997) model, the CBS 2011 model distinguished justification and the structure of epistemic ends as separate components of epistemic cognition whereas the AIR model brings them together in the same category. There are three principal reasons for this change. First, when a person makes a claim about and references to structural features of knowledge—for example, "Knowledge is simple"—this can be understood as an ideal that knowledge must meet to be considered adequate. If one believes that knowledge should be complex, then simple knowledge fails to meet this criterion and will be judged inadequate. People often advance structural criteria as justifications for knowledge claims. For example, when giving reasons to support a theory, scientists may provide justifications on the basis of the theory's being parsimonious or elegant (Newton-Smith, 1981). Second, justifications for claims involve implicit or explicit appeals to epistemic ideals. When a student argues for evolution because it's the only way you can explain why some whales have vestigial legs, the student is tacitly applying the ideal that justifications should appeal to evidence. Third, epistemic ideals allows us to bring in additional subcategories of ideals, such as consistency with other knowledge; such ideals are clearly used by people to justify knowledge claims but do not have a clear place in the CBS or other prior frameworks.

The CBS model included a "sources and justification" component as well as a "virtues and vices" component, each of which has been reconceptualized within the *reliable processes* component of the AIR model. The traditional sources of knowledge identified by epistemologists include testimony, memory, observation, and reasoning. Yet each of these sources can be viewed as a label for a reliable process by which we generate and defend our claims to knowledge. For example, observation involves a variety of cognitive processes that have been intensively studied by cognitive scientists. Thus, sources are better viewed as reliable processes. The virtues component of CBS (2011) has also been folded into the AIR model as one very important subtype of reliable processes (as shown in table 19.1 in this chapter). This is in line with reliabilist epistemologists, who treat epistemic virtues as the relatively stable dispositions of character that lead people to deploy reliable processes of belief formation. A virtue (such as open-mindedness) is the disposition to deploy reliable processes of belief formation (such as considering alternative points of view before making up one's mind).

Acknowledgments

This material is based in part upon work supported by the National Science Foundation under Grant No. 0529582. Any opinions, findings, and conclusions or recommendations expressed in this material are those of the author(s) and do not necessarily reflect the views of the National Science Foundation.

Note

1. For readers familiar with the CBS (2011) model of epistemic cognition, the appendix sets out the relationships between that model and the AIR model. In a word, the models contain the same basic categories, but the AIR model reorganizes the categories of the CBS model.

References

Allchin, D. (2011). Evaluating knowledge of the nature of (whole) science. *Science Education, 95*, 1–25.

Bendixen, L. D., Zemp, L. M., Keller-Johnson, J., Winsor, D. L., & Feucht, F. C. (2011). *Epistemic cognition across age groups and domains.* Paper presented at the annual meeting of the American Educational Research Association, New Orleans, LA.

Benton, T. R., Ross, D. F., Bradshaw, E., Thomas, W. N., & Bradshaw, G. S. (2006). Eyewitness memory is still not common sense: Comparing jurors, judges and law enforcement to eyewitness experts. *Applied Cognitive Psychology, 20*, 115–129.

Bråten, I., Strømsø, H. I., & Samuelstuen, M. S. (2008). Are sophisticated students always better? The role of topic-specific personal epistemology in the understanding of multiple expository texts. *Contemporary Educational Psychology, 33*, 814–840.

Chinn, C. A., & Brewer, W. F. (1993). The role of anomalous data in knowledge acquisition: A theoretical framework and implications for science instruction. *Review of Educational Research, 63*, 1–49.

Chinn, C. A., & Buckland, L. A. (2011). Differences in epistemic practices among scientists, young earth creationists, intelligent design creationists, and the scientist creationists of Darwin's era. In R. Taylor & M. Ferrari (Eds.), *Epistemology and science education: Understanding the evolution vs. intelligent design controversy* (pp. 38–76). New York: Taylor & Francis.

Chinn, C. A., & Buckland, L. A. (2012). Model-based instruction: Fostering change in evolutionary conceptions and in epistemic practices. In K. S. Rosengren, S. K. Brem, E. M. Evans, & G. M. Sinatra (Eds.), *Evolution challenges: Integrating research and practice in teaching and learning about evolution* (pp. 211–232). Oxford, England: Oxford University Press.

Chinn, C. A., Buckland, L. A., & Samarapungavan, A. (2011). Expanding the dimensions of epistemic cognition: Arguments from philosophy and psychology. *Educational Psychologist, 46*, 141–167.

Chinn, C. A., & Clark, D. B. (2013). Learning through collaborative argumentation. In C. E. Hmelo-Silver, C. A. Chinn, C. K. K. Chan, & A. M. O'Donnell (Eds.), *International handbook of collaborative learning* (pp. 314–332). New York: Routledge.

Chinn, C. A., Duncan, R. G., Dianovsky, M., & Rinehart, R. (2013). Promoting conceptual change through inquiry. In S. Vosniadou (Ed.), *International handbook of conceptual change* (2nd ed., pp. 539–559). New York: Taylor & Francis.

Chinn, C. A., & Malhotra, B. A. (2002). Epistemologically authentic reasoning in schools: A theoretical framework for evaluating inquiry tasks. *Science Education, 86*, 175–218.

Dianovsky, M., Chinn, C. A., Duncan, R. G., Drescher, C., Goff, A., & Rinehart, R. (2013). *Exploring and leveraging relational thinking for academic performance.* Paper presented at the Relational Thinking Conference, Pittsburgh, PA.

Duncan, R. G., Freidenreich, H. B., Chinn, C. A., & Bausch, A. (2011). Promoting middle-school students' understanding of molecular genetics. *Research in Science Education, 41*, 147–167.

Giere, R. N. (1988). *Explaining science: A cognitive approach.* Chicago: University of Chicago Press.

Goldman, A. I. (1976). What is justified belief? In G. S. Pappas (Ed.), *Justification and knowledge* (pp. 1–23). Dordrecht, the Netherlands: Reidel.

Goldman, A. I. (1986). *Epistemology and cognition.* Cambridge, MA: Harvard University Press.

Goldman, A. I. (1999). *Knowledge in a social world.* Oxford, England: Oxford University Press.

Gottlieb, E., & Wineburg, S. (2012). Between *veritas* and *communitas*: Epistemic switching in the reading of academic and sacred history. *Journal of the Learning Sciences, 21*, 84–129.

Greene, J., Azevedo, R., & Torney-Purta, J. (2008). Modeling epistemic and ontological cognition: Philosophical perspectives and methodological directions. *Educational Psychologist, 43*, 142–160.

Hofer, B. (2004). Exploring the dimensions of personal epistemology in differing classroom contexts: Student interpretations during the first year of college. *Contemporary Educational Psychology, 29*, 129–163.

Hofer, B. K. (2000). Dimensionality and disciplinary differences in personal epistemology. *Contemporary Educational Psychology, 25*, 378–405.

Hofer, B. K., & Pintrich, P. R. (1997). The development of epistemological theories: Beliefs about knowledge and knowing and their relation to learning. *Review of Educational Research, 67*, 88–140.

Hofer, B. K., & Pintrich, P. R. (Eds.). (2002). *Personal epistemology: The psychology of beliefs about knowledge and knowing.* Mahwah, NJ: Lawrence Erlbaum Associates.

Jacobson, R. M., Targonski, P. V., & Poland, G. A. (2007). A taxonomy of reasoning flaws in the anti-vaccine movement. *Vaccine, 25*, 3146–3152.

Kata, A. (2012). Anti-vaccine activists, Web 2.0, and the postmodern paradigm—An overview of tactics and tropes used online by the anti-vaccination movement. *Vaccine, 30*, 3778–3789.

King, P. M., & Kitchener, K. S. (1994). *Developing reflective judgment: Understanding and promoting intellectual growth and critical thinking in adolescents and adults.* San Francisco: Jossey-Bass.

Kitchener, R. (2002). Folk epistemology: An introduction. *New Ideas in Psychology, 20*, 89–105.

Kruglanski, A. W., & Webster, D. M. (1996). Motivated closing of the mind: "Seizing" and "freezing." *Psychological Review, 103*, 263–283.

Kuhn, D., Cheney, R., & Weinstock, M. (2000). The development of epistemological understanding. *Cognitive Development, 15,* 309–328.

Kuhn, D., & Weinstock, M. (2002). What is epistemological thinking and why does it matter? In B. K. Hofer & P. R. Pintrich (Eds.), *Personal epistemology: The psychology of beliefs about knowledge and knowing* (pp. 121–144). Mahwah, NJ: Lawrence Erlbaum Associates.

Kuhn, T. S. (1962). *The structure of scientific revolutions.* Chicago: University of Chicago Press.

Kuhn, T. S. (1977). *The essential tension: Selected studies in scientific tradition and change.* Chicago: University of Chicago Press.

Kunda, Z. (1990). The case for motivated reasoning. *Psychological Bulletin, 108,* 480–498.

Kvanvig, J. L. (2003). *The value of knowledge and the pursuit of understanding.* Cambridge, England: Cambridge University Press.

Longino, H. E. (2002). *The fate of knowledge.* Princeton, NJ: Princeton University Press.

Magnussen, S., Melinder, A., Stridbeck, U., & Raja, A. Q. (2010). Beliefs about factors affecting the reliability of eyewitness testimony: A comparison of judges, jurors, and the general public. *Applied Cognitive Psychology, 24,* 122–133.

Muis, K. R. (2007). The role of epistemic beliefs in self-regulated learning. *Educational Psychologist, 42,* 173–190.

Newton-Smith, W. H. (1981). *The rationality of science.* Boston: Routledge & Kegan Paul.

Nisbett, R., & Ross, L. (1980). *Human inference: Strategies and shortcomings of social judgment.* Englewood Cliffs, NJ: Prentice-Hall.

Noonan, P. (2012, November 5). Monday Morning. Peggy Noonan's Blog, *The Wall Street Journal.* Retrieved May 22, 2013, from http://blogs.wsj.com/peggynoonan/2012/11/05/monday-morning/

Nussbaum, E. M., & Bendixen, L. D. (2003). Approaching and avoiding arguments: The role of epistemological beliefs, need for cognition, and extraverted personality traits. *Contemporary Educational Psychology, 28,* 573–595.

Perry, W. G., Jr. (1968/1999). Forms of intellectual and ethical development in the college years: A scheme. San Francisco: Jossey-Bass.

Pluta, W. J., Chinn, C. A., & Duncan, R. G. (2011). Learners' epistemic criteria for good scientific models. *Journal of Research in Science Teaching, 48,* 486–511.

Rosenberg, S., Hammer, D., & Phelan, J. (2006). Multiple epistemological coherences in an eighth-grade discussion of the rock cycle. *Journal of the Learning Sciences, 15,* 261–292.

Ryan, A. G. (1987). High-school graduates' beliefs about science–technology–society: IV. The characteristics of scientists. *Science Education, 71,* 489–510.

Samarapungavan, A. (1992). Children's judgments in theory choice tasks: Scientific rationality in childhood. *Cognition, 45,* 1–32.

Schommer, M. (1990). Effects of beliefs about the nature of knowledge on comprehension. *Journal of Educational Psychology, 82*, 498–504.

Schraw, G. J., Bendixen, L. D., & Dunkle, M. E. (2002). Development and validation of the Epistemic Belief Inventory (EBI). In B. K. Hofer & P. R. Pintrich (Eds.), *Personal epistemology: The psychology of beliefs about knowledge and knowing* (pp. 261–275). Mahwah, NJ: Lawrence Erlbaum Associates.

Silver, N. (2013). Which polls fared best (and worst) in the 2012 Presidential race? Retrieved June 11, 2013, from http://fivethirtyeight.blogs.nytimes.com/2012/11/10/which-polls-fared-best-and -worst-in-the-2012-presidential-race/?_r=0/

Sinatra, G. M., & Nadelson, L. S. (2011). Science and religion: Opposite ends of core epistemological continua? In R. Taylor & M. Ferrari (Eds.), *Epistemology and science education: Understanding the evolution vs. intelligent design controversy* (pp. 173–194). New York: Routledge.

Solomon, M. (2001). *Social empiricism.* Cambridge, MA: MIT Press.

Staley, K. W. (2004). *The evidence for the top quark: Objectivity and bias in collaborative experimentation.* Cambridge, England: Cambridge University Press.

Stanovich, K. E. (1999). *Who is rational? Studies of individual differences in reasoning.* Mahwah, NJ: Lawrence Erlbaum Associates.

Strømsø, H. I., Bråten, I., & Samuelstuen, M. S. (2008). Dimensions of topic-specific epistemological beliefs as predictors of multiple text understanding. *Learning and Instruction, 18*, 513–527.

Tannen, D. (1998). *The argument culture: Stopping America's war of words.* New York: Ballantine Books.

Thagard, P. (2012). *The cognitive science of science: Explanation, discovery, and conceptual change.* Cambridge, MA: MIT Press.

Toulmin, S. E. (1972). *Human understanding: The collective use and evolution of concepts.* Princeton, NJ: Princeton University Press.

Wainryb, C., Shaw, L. A., Laupa, M., & Smith, K. R. (2001). Children's adolescents', and young adults' thinking about different types of disagreements. *Developmental Psychology, 37*, 373–386.

Williams, B. (2002). *Truth and truthfulness.* Princeton, NJ: Princeton University Press.

Wise, R. A., Pawlenko, N. B., Safer, M. A., & Meyer, D. (2009). What US prosecutors and defence attorneys know and believe about eyewitness testimony. *Applied Cognitive Psychology, 23*, 1266–1281.

Yearley, S. (1999). Computer models and the public's understanding of science: A case-study analysis. *Social Studies of Science, 29*, 845–866.

Zagzebski, L. T. (1996). *Virtues of the mind: An inquiry into the nature of virtue and the ethical foundations of knowledge.* Cambridge, England: Cambridge University Press.

Index

Printed in the United States
by Baker & Taylor Publisher Services